UNITED NATIONS CONFERENCE ON TRADE AND DEVELOPMENT

UNCTAD

TRADE AND ENVIRONMENT REVIEW 2013

WAKE UP BEFORE IT IS TOO LATE

MAKE AGRICULTURE TRULY SUSTAINABLE NOW FOR FOOD SECURITY IN A CHANGING CLIMATE

D1599672

UNITED NATIONS
New York and Geneva, 2013

Note

The views expressed in the articles contained in this Review are the personal views of the authors and do not necessarily reflect the positions of their respective organizations or institutions. Therefore, the views expressed in this Review should be attributed to the authors and not to any institution or to UNCTAD or its member States.

Any reference to a company and its activities should not be construed as an endorsement by UNCTAD, or by the authors or their institutions, of the company or its activities.

Material in this publication may be freely quoted or reprinted, but acknowledgement is requested, together with a reference to the document number. A copy of the publication containing the quotation or reprint should be sent to the Office of the Director, Division on International Trade in Goods and Services, and Commodities, Palais des Nations, 1211 Geneva 10, Switzerland.

For comments on this review, please contact trade.environment@unctad.org. This review is also available at: http://unctad.org/en/Pages/DITC/Trade-and-Environment-Review-Series.aspx.

Foreword

Not long after the 2008-2009 food price crisis, high and volatile food prices are back in the international agenda creating renewed concerns for world food security. Once again, discussions are mostly focused on suggesting quick-fixes linked to some specific contributing factors, such as food price speculation or the increasing use of bio-energy. Insufficient attention is being paid to the fact that the increasing energy intensity of agricultural production and the direct and indirect link between agricultural and fuel prices was among the underlying factors that triggered the 2008 crisis and now contributes again to the current round of food price escalation. Furthermore, the recent drought affecting the main US grain production zones, putting upward pressure on international grain prices, is an incident now increasingly frequent and widespread with global warming. As this Review highlights, agriculture is not only chiefly affected by global warming but also one of its driving forces. Quick fixes will not be able to effectively deal with the complex interplay between energy intensity, greenhouse gas emissions, global warming and food security needs. Rather, what is called for is a better understanding of the multi-functionality of agriculture, its pivotal importance for pro-poor rural development and the significant role it can play in dealing with resource scarcities and in mitigating and adapting to climate change.

Despite significant increases in agricultural productivity and the fact that the world currently already produces sufficient calories per head to feed a global population of 12-14 billion, hunger has remained a key challenge. Around one billion people chronically suffer from starvation and another billion are mal-nourished. Some 70 per cent of these people are themselves small farmers or agricultural laborers. Therefore, hunger and mal-nutrition are not phenomena of insufficient physical supply, but results of prevailing poverty, and above all problems of access to food. Enabling these people to become food self-sufficient or earn an appropriate income through agriculture to buy food needs to take center stage in future agricultural transformation. Millennium Development Goal number one is bound to be missed, mainly because agriculture has not received the attention it deserves for achieving food security and as an engine of sustainable economic, social and environmental development in developing countries.

No doubt, the 2008 food-price crisis led to a reversal of the long-term neglect of agriculture as a vital economic sector in developing countries. Also, the declining trend of public funding for agriculture was arrested and some new funding has recently been committed. However, the implementation of these commitments lacks way behind requirements. One does neither see the necessary level of urgency nor the political willingness, from the international community, for drastic changes. Priority remains heavily focused on increasing production (mostly under the slogan "more with less"). The currently pursued approach is still very much biased towards expansion of "somewhat-less-polluting" industrial agriculture, rather than more sustainable and affordable production methods. It is still not recognized that a paradigm shift is required, in particular accentuated by the increasing pressures coming from climate change mitigation and adaptation. As correctly highlighted in the Review, global warming is a threat multiplier - it compounds, supplements or reinforces other threats so that the bio-physical vulnerability of agriculture increases impacting the most vulnerable people in the world.

Slowing agricultural productivity growth in the future, high population growth in the most resource-constrained and climate-change-exposed regions and a burgeoning environmental crises in agriculture are the seeds for mounting pressures on food security and the related access to land and water. This is bound to increase the severity and frequency of riots, originated by food price increases, with concomitant political instability, and international tension, caused by resource conflicts and migratory movements of starving populations. Thus, the fundamental transformation of agriculture may well turn out to be one of the biggest challenges, including for international security, of the 21st century.

In paragraph 108 of the Rio+20 Declaration, adopted in June 2012, Heads of State reaffirm their "commitments regarding the right of everyone to have access to safe, sufficient and nutritious food, consistent with the right to adequate food and the fundamental right of everyone to be free from hunger. (They) acknowledge that food security and nutrition has become a pressing global challenge and, in this regard, (they) further reaffirm (their) commitment to enhancing food security and access to adequate, safe and nutritious food for present and future generations." It is high time for these commitments to come to reality before the MDGs' deadline of 2015.

In this Trade and Environment Review, more than 50 international experts have contributed their views to a comprehensive analysis of the above-outlined challenges and the most suitable strategic approaches for dealing holistically with the inter-related problems of hunger and poverty, climate change, economic, social and gender inequity, poor health and nutrition, and environmental sustainability. The authors and the UNCTAD secretariat are looking forward to an inspiring dialogue with readers of this Review on one of the most interesting and challenging subjects of present development discourse.

Geneva, March 2013.   Carlos Pérez del Castillo,
                                                             Chairman Consortium Board,
                                                             Global Research Partnership for
                                                             a Food Secure Future (CGIAR).

Contents

Tables

Boxes

Figures

Acknowledgements

This Trade and Environment Review was edited and compiled by Ulrich Hoffmann, Senior Trade Policy Advisor, Office of the Director, Division on International Trade in Goods and Services, and Commodities. Frank Grothaus assisted in proof-reading the manuscript. It was prepared for publishing by Rafe Dent, with assistance on graphics by Sophie Combette and Nadege Hadjemian. The manuscript was language edited by Praveen Bhalla.

Acronyms and abbreviations

AAAS	American Association for the Advancement of Science
AATF	African Agricultural Technology Foundation
AbL	Association for sustainable, i.e. more socially and environmentally beneficial agriculture (Arbeitsgemeinschaft bäuerliche Landwirtschaft/ Germany)
ABSP	Agricultural Biotechnology Support Project
ACP	African, Caribbean and Pacific countries
AF	agroforestry
AFTPs	agroforestry tree products
AHBFI	A Harvest Biotech Foundation International
AKST	agricultural knowledge, science and technology
AoA	Agreement on Agriculture (of the WTO)
ARI	African Re-greening Initiative
AROS	Asian Regional Organic Standard
ASALs	arid and semi-arid lands
ASARECA	Association for Strengthening Agricultural Research in Eastern and Central Africa
ASEAN	Association of Southeast Asian Nations
ASPO	Association for the Study of Peak Oil & Gas (United States)
AVRDC	The Word Vegetable Center
BAU	business as usual (scenario)
BfR	Federal Institute for Risk Assessment (Germany)
birr	Ethiopian currency
BIS	Bank for International Settlements
BMELF	German Federal Ministry for Food, Agriculture and Forests (since 2001 known as the Federal Ministry for Food, Agriculture and Consumer Protection)
BRIC	grouping that refers to the countries Brazil, the Russian Federation, India and China
BSE	bovine spongiform encephalopathy (mad cow disease)
BSI	British Standards Institution
Bt	bacillus thuringiensis
BTI	Boyce Thompson Institute
BVL	Federal Office of Consumer and Food Safety (Germany)
C	carbon
C_3	photosynthetic pathway
C_4	carbon fixation (photosynthetic pathway)
CAFTA	Central America-Dominican Republic-United States Free Trade Agreement
CAP	Common Agricultural Policy
CARE	Cooperative for Assistance and Relief
CAWMA	comprehensive assessment of water management in agriculture
CBD	Convention on Biological Diversity
CBOT	Chicago Board of Trade
CC	climate change
CCP	Committee on Commodity Problems (FAO)
CCTEC	Cornell University: College of Agriculture and Life Sciences
CDE	Centre for Development and Environment (University of Bern, Switzerland)
CDM	Clean Development Mechanism
CEO	chief executive officer
CETIM	Centre Europe - Tiers Monde
CFAR	Climate Forecasting for Agricultural Resources (project)
CFS	Committee on World Food Security (FAO)
CFS-HLPE	High Level Panel of Experts on Food Security and Nutrition to the FAO Committee on World Food Security
CGC	Chinese construction company owned by SINOPEC
CGIAR	Consultative Group on International Agricultural Research
CH_4	methane
CIF	cost, insurance and freight
CIFOR	Center for International Forestry Research
CIMMYT	International Maize and Wheat Improvement Center

CIP	International Potato Research Center
CIRAD	Agricultural Research for Development Centre (France)
CIS	Commonwealth of Independent States
CIWF	Compassion in World Farming
CLIRUN II	hydrologic model
CNV	conventional system
CO_2	carbon dioxide
CO_2e/ CO_2-eq	carbon dioxide equivalent
CORAF	Western and Central African Council for Agricultural Research and Development
COROS	Common Objectives and Requirements for Organic Systems
Crad-L	Caparo Renewable Agriculture Developments Ltd.
CRC	Chemical Rubber Company Press
CRF	Cornell Research Foundation
CRI	Copenhagen Resource Institute
CRI	Climate Risk Index
CRP	Conservation Reserve Program
CSD	UN Commission on Sustainable Development
CSE	Cooperative of SEKEM Employees
CSIRO	Commonwealth Scientific and Industrial Research Organization
CSP	Conservation Stewardship Program
CUT	Compost Utilization Trial
DAC	Development Assistance Committee (of the OECD)
DAP	diammonium phosphate
DEFRA	Department for Environment, Food and Rural Affairs (United Kingdom)
DITC	Division on International Trade in Goods and Services, and Commodities (UNCTAD)
DOK trials	biodynamic-bioorganic-conventional (comparison)
EACC	World Bank´s Economics of Adaptation to Climate Change analysis
EAOPS	East African Organic Products Standard
EBDA	Egyptian Biodynamic Association
EC	European Commission
EEA	European Environment Agency
EED	Church Development Service (Germany)
EESRC	Ethiopian Energy Study and Research Center
EFRs	environmental flow requirements
EFSA	European Union Food Safety Authority
EHEC	e.coli bacterium
EJ	exajoule
EMBO	European Molecular Biology Organization
ENA	European Nitrogen Assessment
EREDPC	Ethiopia Rural Energy Development Assessment and Promotion Center
EROI	energy return on energy invested
ESMAP	Energy Sector Management Assistance Programme (UNDP/ World Bank)
ETB	Ethiopian birr
ETC Group	Erosion, Technology and Concentration Group
EU	European Union
Eurostat	European Statistical Office
FAO	Food and Agricultural Organization of the United Nations
FAOSTAT	Statistics Division of the FAO
FARA	Forum for Agricultural Research in Africa
FAT	Swiss Research Institute for Agriculture and Agricultural Engineering
FAWC	Farm Animal Welfare Council
FAZ	Frankfurter Allgemeine Zeitung (a nationwide German newspaper)
FDI	foreign direct investment
FFS	farmer field schools
FiBL	Research Institute for Organic Agriculture (Switzerland)
FISP	Farm Input Subsidy Program
FOB	free on board
FPIF	Foreign Policy in Focus

FPUs	food production units
FSC	food supply chain
FST	farm systems trial
ft.	feet
FTA(s)	free trade agreement(s)
FVO	Food and Veterinary Office (EU)
G 8	group of 8 developed countries
GAP	good agricultural practice
GATT	General Agreement on Tariffs and Trade
GCMs	general circulation models
GCMs	global climate models
GDP	gross domestic product
GE	genetically engineered/ genetic engineering
GEA	Greening the Economy with Agriculture
GEF	Global Environment Facility
GEO	Global Environment Outlook (UNEP publication)
GFRAS	Global Forum for Rural Advisory Services
GHG	greenhouse gas (emissions)
GIGA	German Institute for Global and Area Studies
GIZ	German Agency for International Cooperation
GLP	global land project
GM	genetically modified
GMO	genetically modified organisms
GOMA	Global Organic Market Access project (FAO, IFOAM & UNCTAD)
GRI	Global Reporting Initiative
GRO	golden rice online
Gt	gigaton
GTZ	German Agency for Technical Cooperation (now GIZ, see above)
GWP	global warming potential
ha	hectare(s)
Hg	hectograms
HLPE	High-level Panel of Experts on Food Security and Nutrition (FAO)
HRC	Human Rights Council
IAASTD	International Assessment of Agricultural Knowledge, Science and Technology for Development
IAP	International Association for Partnership in Ecology and Trade
IATP	Institute for Agriculture and Trade Policy
ICGEB	International Center for Genetic Engineering and Biotechnology
ICRAF	International Centre for Research in Agroforestry
ICRISAT	International Crops Research Institute for the Semi-Arid Tropics
ICT(s)	information and communication technology (-ies)
ICTSD	International Centre for Trade and Sustainable Development
IEA	International Energy Agency
IECA	International Erosion Control Association
IER	Institut d'Economie Rurale
IFAD	International Fund for Agricultural Development
IfEU	Institute for Energy and Environment (Germany)
IFOAM	International Federation of Organic Agricultural Movements
IFPRI	International Food Policy Research Institute
IGBP	International Geosphere-Biosphere Programme
IIED	International Institute for Environment and Development
IITA	International Institute of Tropical Agriculture
IK	indigenous knowledge
IKS	indigenous knowledge studies/ systems
ILC	International Land Coalition
ILRI	International Livestock Research Institute (Africa-based)
ILUC	indirect land use changes
IMAP	global M&A organization
IMF	International Monetary Fund

INBI	Centre for Integrated Research in Biosafety
INSAH	Institut du Sahel
IP	intellectual property
IPCC	Intergovernmental Panel on Climate Change
IPGRI	International Plant Genetic Resources Institute
IPM	integrated pest management
IPPC	Integrated Pollution and Control (EU directive)
IPRs	intellectual property rights
IRI	International Research Institute for Climate Predictions
IROCB	International Requirements for Conformity Assessment Bodies
IRRI	International Rice Research Institute
ISAAA	International Service for the Acquisition of Agri-Biotech Applications
ISIS	Institute of Science in Society
ISO	International Organization for Standardization
ISOFAR	International Society of Organic Agriculture Research
ITC	International Trade Centre of UNCTAD/ WTO
IWMI	International Water Management Institute
kcal	kilocalorie
KDGCBP	Kenya Dairy Goat and Capacity Building Project
kg(s)	kilogram(s)
km^3	cubic kilometer
kWh	kilowatt hour
LAP	Libya Africa Investment Portfolio
lbs/ac	pounds per acre
LDC/LDCs	least developed country/ -ies
LEAD	Livestock, Environment and Development Initiative
LED	light-emitting diode
LEG	organic legume system
LHS	left hand side
LLC	limited liability company
LTAR	long-term agroecological research
LUCCG	Land Use Climate Change Report (to the Welsh Assembly Government)
M&I	municipal and industrial
MAR	mean annual runoff
MDG(s)	Millennium Development Goal(s)
MEA	Millennium Ecosystem Assessment
MENA	Middle East and North Africa (region)
MJ	megajoules
mm	millimeter
Mt	megatons
N	nitrogen (in soil)
N(r)	reactive nitrogen
N$_2$	nitrogen (molecule of two atoms)
N$_2$O	nitrous oxide
NAFTA	North American Free Trade Agreement
NAIP	National Agricultural Innovation Programme (of the Indian Council of Agricultural Research)
NAS	National Academy of Sciences (US)
NASA	National Aeronautics and Space Administration
NBPE	National Biogas Programme Ethiopia
NCAR	National Center for Atmospheric Research (United States)
NCCR	Swiss National Centre of Competence in Research
NFA	National Food Administration (of Sweden)
NGO	non-governmental organization
NH$_3$	ammonium
NNPC	Nigerian National Petroleum Corporation
NO	nitric oxide
NPP	(global, terrestrial) net primary production
NPV	net present value

NUE	nitrogen use efficiency
ODA	official development assistance
ODI	Overseas Development Institute
OEA	Environmental Assessment of Ogoniland
OECD	Organization for Economic Co-operation and Development
OECD-DAC	OECD Development Assistance Committee
OGSs	organic guarantee systems
OI	Oakland Institute
OTC	over-the-counter (transactions)
OTDS	overall trade-distorting support
PANNA	Pesticide Action Network North America
PAS	Public Available Specification
PBS	Program for Biodiversity
PCF	Product Carbon Footprint
PEP	phosphoenol pyruvate
PGA	phosphoglycerate
PGS	participatory guarantee system
PICTIPAPA	International Potato Late Blight Testing Program
ppm	parts per million
PRAI	Principles for Responsible Agricultural Investment
PSDA	Private Sector Development in Agriculture
PV	photovoltaic
PwC	Pricewaterhouse Coopers
R&D	research and development
RASFF	Rapid Alert System of Food and Feed (EU)
REDD	reduction of emissions from deforestation and forest degradation
REN21	Renewable Energy Policy Network for the 21st Century
RHS	right hand side
RNE	German Council for Sustainable Development
RS	Royal Society
RSB	Roundtable on Sustainable Biofuels
RuBP	ribulose bisphosphate
RVACSC	Regional Value-added Citizen Shareholder Corporation
S/SE	South/ South East
SAN	Sustainable Agriculture Network
SANCO	Directorate General for Health and Consumer Affairs (European Commission)
SAR	Special Administrative Region
SARD	sustainable agriculture and rural development
SCAR	Standing Committee on Agricultural Research (of the European Commission)
SCNT	Somatic Cell Nuclear Transfer (cloning)
SCOPE	Scientific Committee on Problems of the Environment
SCORE	Sustainable Consumption Research Exchange
SDF	SEKEM Development Foundation
SDT	special and differential treatment
SEKEM	ancient Egyptian for "vitality from the sun"
SNNPR	Southern Nations Nationalities and Peoples Region
SNV	Netherlands Development Organization
SOC	soil organic carbon
SOFA	The State of Food and Agriculture (FAO publication)
SOM	soil organic matter
SP	special products
SRES	Special Report on Emissions Scenarios (IPCC)
SSA	sub-Saharan Africa
SSG	special agricultural safeguard
SSM	special safeguard mechanisms
SVC	Scientific Veterinary Committee (EU)
t CO_2-eq	tons of carbon dioxide equivalent
TED	Trade, Environment, Climate Change and Development (Branch of UNCTAD)

TER	Trade and Environment Review
toes	tons of oil equivalents
tonnes C ha-1	tonnes of carbon per hectare
UE	Union européenne
UEMOA	Western African Economic and Monetary Union
UK	United Kingdom
UN	United Nations
UN DESA	UN Department of Economic and Social Affairs
UNCTAD	United Nations Conference on Trade and Development
UNDP	United Nations Development Programme
UNEP	United Nations Environment Programme
UNESCO	United Nations Educational, Scientific and Cultural Organization
UNFCCC	United Nations Framework Convention on Climate Change
UNGC	United Nations Global Compact
UNISIST	United Nations International Scientific Information System
UN-NADAF	United Nations New Agenda for the Development of Africa
UNRISD	United Nations Research Institute for Social Development
UNSO	United Nations Statistical Office
US CRS	United States Congressional Research Services
US/ USA	United States of America
USAID	U.S. Agency for International Development
USDA	United States Department of Agriculture
USFDA	United States Food and Drug Administration
UW	University of Wisconsin
VAM	vesicular arbuscular mycorrhizae (fungi)
VEETC	Volumetric Ethanol Excise Tax Credit (US)
VZBV	Federation of German Consumer Organisations (Verbraucherzentrale Bundesverband)
WARDA	West Africa Rice Development Association
WB	World Bank
WFP	UN World Food Programme
WHO	World Health Organization
WMO	World Meteorological Organization
WOCAT	World Overview of Conservation Approaches and Technologies
WRAP	Waste and Resources Action Programme
WRI	World Resources Institute
WSC	World Shipping Council
WTI	West Texas Intermediate (oil price)
WTO	World Trade Organization
WUE	water use efficiency
yr	year

Explanatory notes

Classification by country or commodity group

The classification of countries in this *Review* has been adopted solely for the purposes of statistical or analytical convenience and does not necessarily imply any judgement concerning the stage of development of a particular country or area.

The major country groupings used in this *Review* follow the classification by the United Nations Statistical Office (UNSO). They are distinguished as:

- Developed or industrial(ized) countries: the countries members of the OECD (other than Mexico, the Republic of Korea and Turkey) plus the new EU member countries and Israel.
- Transition economies refers to South-East Europe and the Commonwealth of Independent States (CIS).
- Developing countries: all countries, territories or areas not specified above.

The terms "country" / "economy" refer, as appropriate, also to territories or areas.
References to "Latin America" in the text or tables include the Caribbean countries unless otherwise indicated.
References to "sub-Saharan Africa" in the text or tables do not include South Africa unless otherwise indicated.

For statistical purposes, regional groupings and classifications by commodity group used in this *Review* follow generally those employed in the UNCTAD Handbook of Statistics (United Nations publication, sales no. E/F.08. II.D.18) unless otherwise stated. The data for China do not include those for Hong Kong Special Administrative Region (Hong Kong SAR), Macao Special Administrative Region (Macao SAR) and Taiwan Province of China.

Other notes

The term "dollar" ($) refers to United States dollars, unless otherwise stated.

The term "billion" signifies 1,000 million.

The term "tons" refers to metric tons.

Annual rates of growth and change refer to compound rates.

Exports are valued FOB and imports CIF, unless otherwise specified.

Use of a dash (–) between dates representing years, e.g. 1988–1990, signifies the full period involved, including the initial and final years.

An oblique stroke (/) between two years, e.g. 2000/01, signifies a fiscal or crop year.

A dot (.) indicates that the item is not applicable.

Two dots (..) indicate that the data are not available, or are not separately reported.

A dash (-) or a zero (0) indicates that the amount is nil or negligible.

Decimals and percentages do not necessarily add up to totals because of rounding.

Chapter 1

Key Development Challenges of a Fundamental Transformation of Agriculture

Lead Article: **AGRICULTURE AT THE CROSSROADS: ASSURING FOOD SECURITY IN DEVELOPING COUNTRIES UNDER THE CHALLENGES OF GLOBAL WARMING**

Ulrich Hoffmann
UNCTAD secretariat

Abstract

The problems of climate change, hunger and poverty, economic, social and gender inequity, poor health and nutrition, and environmental sustainability are inter-related and need to be solved by leveraging agriculture's multi-functionality. Against this background, a fundamental transformation towards climate-friendly agriculture, consisting of a mosaic of agro-ecological production practices, must become the new paradigm, but it should not compromise other very important development objectives:

- Addressing the equity challenge, notably food security and farmer livelihoods.

- Enhancing sustainable productivity, based on a new, systemically different definition that focuses on total farm output instead of productivity per unit of labour, and

- Strengthening resilience to resource and energy scarcity and climate change.

It is therefore important to think in systems, rather than overemphasizing a climate focus.

A. Introduction

Climate change (CC) has the potential to damage irreversibly the natural resource base on which agriculture depends, with grave consequences for food security. CC could also significantly constrain economic development in those developing countries that largely rely on agriculture (for more information, see Lim Li Ching, 2010). Therefore, meeting the dual challenge of achieving food security[1] and other developmental co-benefits, on the one hand, and mitigating and adapting to CC, on the other, requires political commitment at the highest level for a fundamental and urgent transformation of agriculture. In fact, time is getting the most important scarcity factor in dealing with CC (Hoffmann, 2011).

The UNCTAD Trade and Environment Review 2013 gives an opportunity to more than 50 experts to analyze various specific aspects of the fundamental transformation of agricultural production methods and systems required for dealing with the serious challenges emanating from global warming and the trade offs to be made in enhancing the mitigation and adaptation potential of agriculture as part and parcel of a pro-poor development approach in agriculture fully exploiting agriculture's multi-functionality.

B. Agriculture - a key driver and a major victim of global warming

As most of the greenhouse gases (GHG), with the exception of methane, have a half life of over a hundred years, global GHG emissions will have to peak by 2020 and drop by 75-80 per cent in the period to 2050 to limit global warming to 2 degrees (The Climate Group, 2008: 19).[2] Yet, total GHG emissions for 2010 are estimated to have increased by more than 6 per cent, a historical record (The Guardian, 2011; and IEA, 2011a: 7), followed by an estimated increase of 3.2 per cent in 2011.[3] Also, according to estimates of analysts at Pricewaterhouse Coopers (PwC), global carbon intensity (i.e. carbon emissions per unit of GDP) has increased for the first time in many years. "Instead of moving too slowly in the right direction, we are now moving in the wrong direction", said one of the PwC analysts. In principal, we follow the GHG emissions trends under the worst case scenario of the Intergovernmental Panel on Climate Change (IPCC) and the International Energy Agency (IEA) (Financial Times, 2011: 1).[4]

Agricultural emissions of methane (CH_4) and nitrous oxide (N_2O), which account for over 90 per cent of total agricultural GHG emissions, grew by 17 per cent in the period 1990–2005 (IPCC, 2007a: 499), roughly proportionate, for instance, to the increase in global cereals' production volume, but about three times as fast as productivity increased in global cereals' production.[5] These GHG emissions are predicted to rise by 35-60 per cent by 2030 in response to population growth and changing diets in developing countries, in particular towards greater consumption of ruminant meats and dairy products, as well as the further spread of industrial and factory farming, particularly in developing countries (IPCC, 2007a: 63). In other words, instead of cutting agricultural emissions by some 40 per cent by 2030, in reality we follow exactly the opposite trend.

As can be seen from figure 1, the recent and future rise in global agricultural GHG emissions is mainly occurring in developing countries. In 2005, the latter accounted for three quarters of nitrous oxide and methane emissions in the agricultural sector. These emissions are mainly caused by some 15-20 developing countries (see figure 2). The countries in figure 2 cause over 70 per cent of agricultural emissions worldwide. Although the least developed countries (LDCs) are not a significant contributor to global agricultural emissions, the latter account for the bulk of national GHG emissions (as can be seen in figure 3, in LDCs agriculture-related GHG emissions account for about 70 per cent of total GHG emissions).

Global warming is a threat multiplier, i.e. compounding, supplementing or reinforcing other threats so that the bio-physical vulnerability of agriculture increases. The main impact of global warming on agricultural production can be summarized as follows:[6]

- Higher temperatures affect plant, animal and farmers' health,[7] enhance pests and reduce water supply increasing the risk of growing aridity and land degradation.
- Modified precipitation patterns will enhance water scarcity and associated drought stress for crops and alter irrigation water supplies. They also reduce the predictability for farmers' planning.
- The enhanced frequency of weather extremes

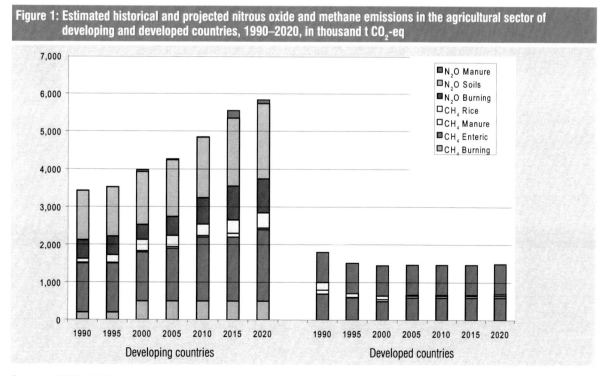

Figure 1: Estimated historical and projected nitrous oxide and methane emissions in the agricultural sector of developing and developed countries, 1990–2020, in thousand t CO_2-eq

Source: IPCC (2007a: 504).

Figure 2: Top 25 GHG emitting countries from agriculture (total and per-capita emissions in CO_2-eq for the year 2000*)

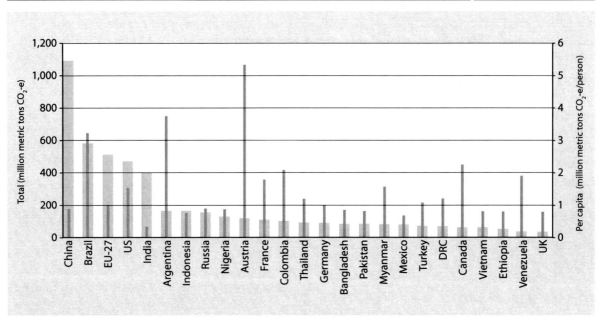

Source: World Resources Institute, quoted in Müller et al. (2011a).
  Note: * CO_2 emissions are confined to fossil fuel combustion only.

Figure 3: LDC GHG emissions by sector, 2005 (per cent of total emissions)

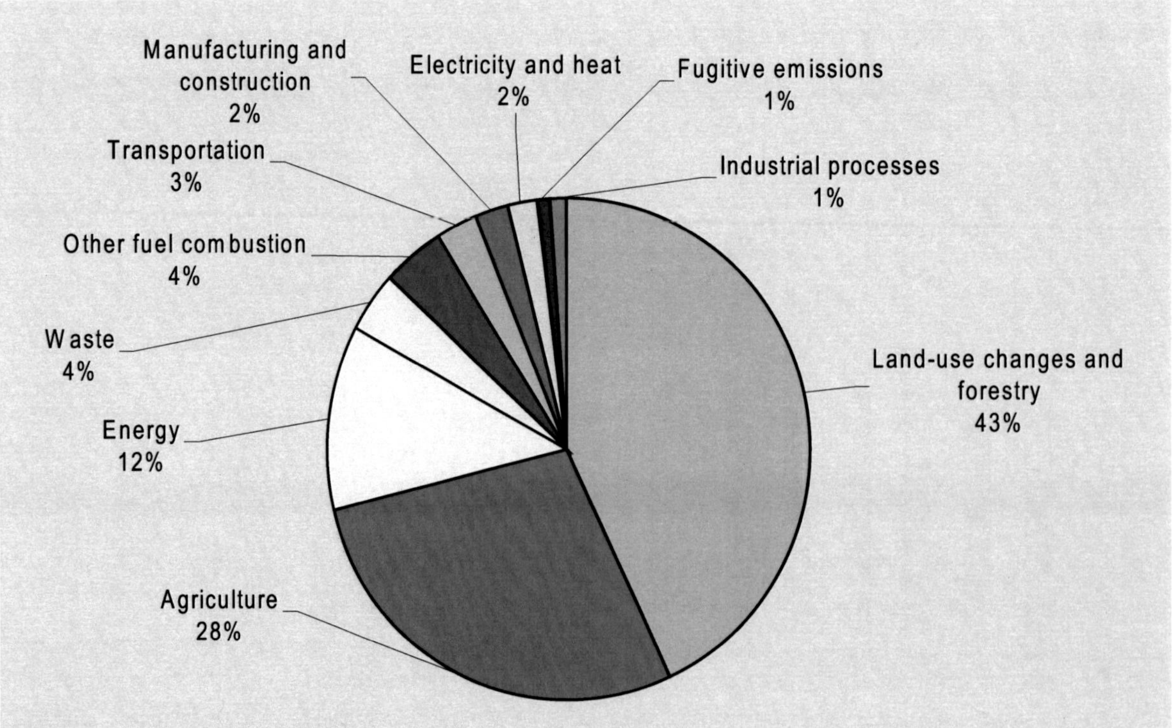

Manufacturing and
construction
2%

Electricity and heat
2%

Fugitive emissions
1%

Transportation
3%

Industrial processes
1%

Other fuel combustion
4%

Waste
4%

Land-use changes and
forestry
43%

Energy
12%

Agriculture
28%

Source: UNCTAD (2010: 127).

Figure 4: Projected climate-change-caused changes in agricultural productivity by 2080, incorporating the effect of carbon fertilisation

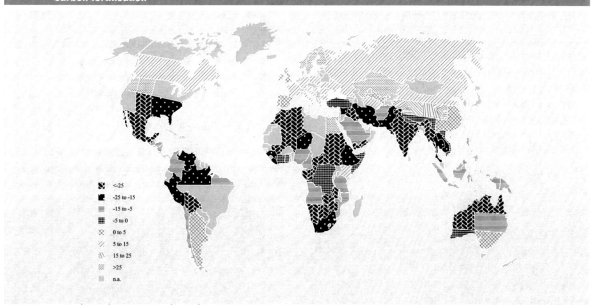

Legend:
- <-25
- -25 to -15
- -15 to -5
- -5 to 0
- 0 to 5
- 5 to 15
- 15 to 25
- >25
- n.a.

Source: Cline (2007) and Yohn et al. (2007).

may significantly influence both crop and livestock production.[8] It may also considerably impact or destroy physical infra-structure for agriculture.[9]

- Enhanced atmospheric concentrations of CO_2 may, for a limited period of time, lead to 'natural' carbon fertilization and thus a stimulus to crop productivity.[10]
- Higher temperatures go hand in hand with higher ozone concentrations. Ozone is harmful to all plants but soybeans, wheat, oats, green beans, peppers, and some types of cotton are particularly vulnerable (FAO, 2012a).
- Global warming will also negatively impact the nutritional quality[11] of some food, in particular the protein and micronutrients' content (for more information, see the comment of Högy and Fangmeier in this Chapter).[12]
- Higher temperatures are likely to increase the exposure of plants and animals to diseases and pests, thus increasing production and handling losses.[13]
- Sea level rise is likely to influence trade infra-structure for agriculture, may inundate producing areas and alter aquaculture production conditions.
- Global warming is not uniformly problematic. It will lead to improved crop productivity in parts of the tropical highlands and extend cropping periods or allow multiple harvests in temperate zones (FAO, 2012a).

The above-mentioned risks and stress factors act individually, but we will also see increasing stress combinations. There is a great deal that is as yet unknown about how such stresses may combine; therefore, more research on the interactions between different abiotic and biotic stresses in key agricultural systems is urgently required (FAO, 2012a). Furthermore, temperature increases are likely to have non-linear effects on yields and food quality.

Climate calamities are likely to hit the poor segments of the population and poor countries particularly hard as their adaptive capacity and resilience[14] is the lowest. Well-off segments of the population can 'buy' food security, at least in the short run (FAO, 2012a: 3).

The impact of global warming has significant consequences for agricultural production and trade of developing countries as well as an increased risk of hunger. Preliminary estimates for the period up to 2080 suggest a decline of some 15-30 per cent of agricultural productivity in the most climate-change-exposed developing-country regions - Africa, South Asia and Central America[15] (see figure 4).[16] For some countries in these regions, total agricultural production could decline by up to 50 per cent. According to FAO (2012a: 43), "in some locations, a combination of temperature and precipitation changes might result in complete loss of agricultural activity; in a few locations, agriculture might become impossible".[17]

The poorest farmers with little safeguards against climate calamities often live in areas prone to natural disasters. More frequent extreme events will create both a humanitarian and a food crisis (FAO, 2009a).

Agriculture provides essential nourishment for people and is the necessary basis for many economic activities. In a large number of developing countries, agriculture accounts for between 20-60% of GDP[18] and provides the livelihoods for approximately 2.6 billion people (i.e. some 40% of global population) (FAO, 2012a). What is more, according to De Janvry and Sadoulet (2009), agriculture-driven growth is three times more likely to reduce poverty than GDP growth in other sectors of the economy.

The current system of industrial agriculture, productive as it has been in recent decades, still leaves about 1 billion people undernourished[19] and poverty stricken, 70% of whom live in rural areas.[20] Millennium Development Goal (MDG) one aims at eradicating extreme hunger and poverty. One of the most effective ways of halving both the number of hungry and poor by 2015 is to take the necessary steps of transition towards more sustainable forms of agriculture that nourish the land and people and provide an opportunity for decent, financially rewarding and gender equal jobs. Meeting health targets from MDG 3 and 6 are also linked to major changes in agriculture, resulting in a more diverse, safe, nutritious and affordable diet. Therefore, the problems of climate change, hunger and poverty, economic, social and gender inequity, poor health and nutrition, and environmental sustainability are inter-related and need to be solved by leveraging agriculture's multi-functionality (Herren et al., 2011).

Against this background, climate-friendly agriculture must become the new paradigm, but it should not compromise other very important developmental objectives:
• Addressing the equity challenge, notably food security and farmer livelihoods.
• Enhancing sustainable productivity, based on a new, systemically different definition that focuses on total farm output instead of productivity per unit of labour.[21]
• Strengthening resilience to resource and energy scarcity and climate change, and
• Reflecting and capitalizing on the multi-functionality of agriculture.

Figure 5: Systemic embedding of climate-friendly agriculture

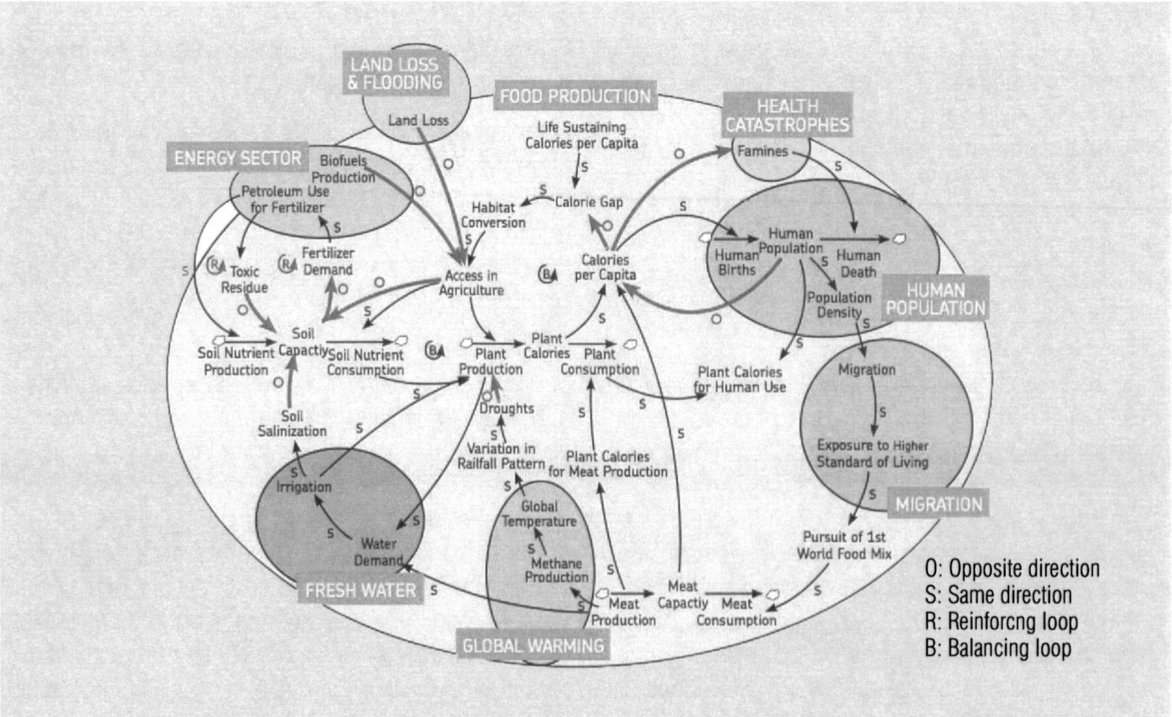

Source: Herren (2012).

It is therefore important to think in systems, rather than overemphasizing a climate focus (see figure 5).

C. Required fundamental transformation of agriculture

To understand the direction and structure of the required fundamental transformation, it is important to appreciate the patterns of the technical climate mitigation potential in agriculture. According to the fourth assessment report of IPCC (2007a: 515), 89 per cent of the technical mitigation potential is related to soil carbon sequestration, about 9 per cent linked to mitigation of methane and only about 2 per cent tied to mitigation of nitrous oxide emissions from soil (correlating with nitrogen fertilizer use). As the world currently follows the worst case scenario of GHG emissions projected by IPCC and IEA (i.e. implying a global warming of 4-6 degrees Celsius), climate resilience and adaptation, in combination with productivity increases, should be prioritized. In general, GHG emissions from agriculture can be reduced by change of production systems and management practices that in many cases also foster productivity and enhance resilience (FAO, 2012a).

Against this very background, the required transformation of agriculture needs to meet the following objectives and approaches, which are further elaborated on by the authors of this Review:[22]

- Increasing the soil carbon content, combined with closed nutrient cycles[23] and an integrated approach to agricultural production.[24]
- Reduction of direct and indirect (i.e. through the feed chain) GHG emissions of livestock production.
- Reduction of indirect (i.e. changes in land-use-induced) emissions through sustainable peatland, forest and grassland management.
- Optimization of organic and inorganic fertilizer use, including through closed nutrient cycles in agriculture.
- Reduction of waste throughout the food chains.
- Changing dietary patterns towards climate-friendly food consumption.
- Reform of the international trade regime for food and agricultural products.

In implementing the above-outlined elements of a fundamental transformation of agriculture, one should not overlook:
1. The interlinkages between the elements.
2. The merits and demerits of single climate-friendly practices versus those of systemic changes

(through agro-ecology, agro-forestry, organic agriculture).
3. The need for a two-track approach:
   (i) reducing environmental impact of conventional agriculture; and
   (ii) broadening scope for and further developing agro-ecological production methods.

D. The paradigm shift has started, but is largely incomplete[25]

The food crisis of 2008 was an important catalyst for realizing the need for fundamental transformation and questioning some of the assumptions that had driven food and agricultural policy in recent decades. The crisis led to a reversal of the long-term neglect of agriculture as a vital economic sector. Also, the declining trend of public funding for agriculture was arrested and some new funding secured, which, however, is still much behind commitments and requirements. Some of the additional funding is now more open to country-led programs with strong state involvement. In this context, some of the additional funding goes to important areas, such as smallholder support, role of women in agriculture, the environmental crisis of agriculture, including climate change, and weakness of international markets.

However, we neither see the necessary level of urgency nor political willingness for drastic change. Priority remains heavily focused on increasing production (mostly under the slogan "more with less"). The currently pursued approach is still very much biased towards expansion of "somewhat-less-polluting" industrial agriculture, rather than more sustainable and affordable production methods. Also, the main problem of hunger is still not appreciated - access to affordable food in rural areas, the lack of means of production and access to resources for smallholders. One does still not recognize that a paradigm shift is required, resulting from (i) deepening integration of food, energy and financial markets; (ii) resource constraints / planetary boundaries; and (iii) the increasing risk caused by climate change. The current demand trends for biofuels, excessively meat-based diets and post-harvest food waste are regarded as given, rather than challenging their rational. There is also little recognition of the prevailing market power asymmetries in food input and output markets. Finally, there is too little and too late progress on restrictions and the development of regulation on land grabs.[26]

The still unresolved reform agenda items are:[27]

- Reduce fuel-intensive, external input-dependent agricultural production methods towards agro-ecological practices, recognizing the multi-functionality of agriculture.
- Discourage industrial livestock production and associated massive use of concentrate feed.
- Discourage expansion of biofuel production: discontinue blending quotas, reduce subsidies, revise trade restrictions.[28]
- Reduce financial speculation (i.e. financialization of food markets) and limit irresponsible land investments (see the commentary of Müller in Chapter 5).

- Reform global agricultural trade rules, giving greater policy space for assuring national food sovereignty, climate-change adaptation/resilience, rethink focus on integrating smallholders into global supply chains (see Chapter 5).
- Reduce food price volatility, without bedding exclusively on hedging options.[29]

In essence, as pointed out by Naerstad (2011: part II, p. 65), "a more radical transformation of agriculture is needed, one guided by the notion that ecological change in agriculture cannot be promoted without comparable changes in the social, political, cultural and economic arenas that also conform agriculture".

Commentary I: Agriculture: A Unique Sector in Economic, Ecological and Social Terms

Jean Feyder
Ambassador, Former Permanent Representative of Luxembourg to the UN and WTO in Geneva

Abstract

More than one billion people are suffering from hunger and malnutrition. Paradoxically, most of them are in rural areas, and only 20 per cent are in city slums, while a small minority are victims of war or civil conflict.

Low prices of food products produced by smallholder farmers can affect their incomes and contribute to poverty and hunger. Only stable and fair prices will give them indispensable buying power.

Adequate regulation of agricultural markets is needed to shield small producers from international competition and dumping of food imports.

Fast deteriorating ecosystems, climate change and water scarcity seriously threaten food security. These challenges can best be met through the adoption of agroecology, organic and other sustainable farming methods.

Agriculture has to be put at the heart of any poverty reduction strategy. It is a multidimensional sector directly linked to the fight against hunger and malnutrition and to food security. At the same time, it is strongly influenced by international trade, finance, development cooperation and, increasingly, it is affected by climate change and environmental degradation. This diversity of functions and activities requires that issues relating to agriculture be treated in a holistic manner, and that the challenge of policy coherence be tackled both at national and international levels (for more detail, see Feyder, 2010).

Hunger and malnutrition are the main causes of mortality in the world today. Each day, they kill about 25,000 people, mostly children. As a result, their right to life and their right to food are most flagrantly violated. The international community agreed to wage war on this scourge of humanity when Heads of State and Government adopted the Millennium Development Goals (MDGs). The first goal committed to halve by 2015 the proportion of the world's population suffering from hunger and malnutrition – some 840 million people.

However, 10 years later more than a billion people – one person in seven – are still suffering from hunger and malnutrition. This is undoubtedly one of the most lethal effects of the world food and financial crises, together with the economic recession of the past few years. These crises have reversed the former trend of a decreasing number of people suffering from hunger and malnutrition. But the FAO also stresses that this trend, observed before the crises, would not in fact have been sufficient to achieve the first of the Millennium Development Goals.

Paradoxically, most of the victims of hunger and malnutrition reside in rural areas. According to the FAO, 50 per cent of them are small peasants, 20 per cent are landless, 10 per cent are nomadic herdsmen or small fishermen and 20 per cent live in city slums. Only a small minority suffer because of war or civil conflict. And whereas in the EU the farming population constitutes only 5 per cent of the total population, it is about 50 per cent in China, 60 per cent in India and between 60 and 80 per cent in sub-Saharan Africa (Feyder, 2010: 16-17).

This rural social class is, above all, often a victim of marginalization and exclusion from its governing classes (political, economic and financial) as well as from the urban milieu where there is a concentration of power and knowledge, and therefore money, including funds for development. Often the urban and rural worlds are separated by a cultural abyss, with the former displaying indifference, incomprehension and contempt.

Hundreds of millions of small peasants, mainly women, cultivate an average of between one and two hectares of land – and often even less – with hoes and machetes, which are the only tools at their disposal. By contrast, a Western European farmer possesses an average holding of 40 hectares, cultivated with increasingly powerful tractors and other machinery, and employs large quantities of pesticides and fertilizers. This also explains the huge productivity gap in agriculture between industrialized countries and a number of emerging countries, such as Brazil, on the one hand, and the great majority of developing countries on the other.

The financialization of agriculture is becoming a major new risk. Land-grabbing often leads to the expulsion of vulnerable rural communities. Financial speculation on food commodities continues to be a major cause of the price surge and volatility witnessed over the past few years (UNCTAD, 2009; UNCTAD and Chamber of Labour, Vienna, 2011). This issue, quite rightly, has been at the top of the international agenda and in G-20 meetings.

The production of agro-fuels takes more and more land away from food production. Yet, even though the use of these fuels contributes little – if at all – to reducing CO_2 emissions, their production continues to soar.

One of the main and more structural causes of the food crisis is disinvestment in agriculture, a sector that has long been neglected. Official development assistance to rural and agricultural development dropped from 18 per cent to 4 per cent between 1980 and 2004 (Feyder, 2010: 55).

Structural adjustment policies have led to massive trade liberalization and the opening up of markets, giving consumers access to cheap, imported food. Meanwhile, peasants have been encouraged to concentrate on producing export crops. However, the 2008 food crisis has radically challenged the relevance of this development model.

In the developing countries, especially the LDC's, imports of chicken, rice, tomato concentrate and milk powder have risen rapidly, ruining local production and the survival conditions of tens of millions of peasant families, not to mention the loss of jobs in the craft and industrial sectors, as they too have been unable to withstand international competition (figure 6 and 7). The trade balance in food products for least developed countries moved from a $1 billion surplus 30 years ago, to a deficit of $7 billion in 2000 and $25 billion in 2008 (Feyder, 2010: 72).

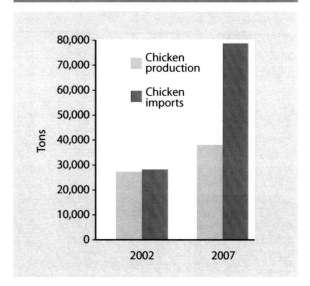

Figure 6: Ghana chicken production and importation, 2002-2007

Source: FAOSTAT.

Thus, the dumping of food onto developing countries has penalized domestic producers who are forced to sell at reduced prices to fewer buyers. According to UNCTAD, the prices of food products and agricultural raw materials fell by 73 per cent and 60 per cent, respectively, between 1980 and 2003. In 2003, the price of coffee was only 17 per cent of what it had been in 1980, and that of cotton was 33 per cent (Nuri, 2005, p.352; see also FAO, 2011d, figure 20). But while producers in developed countries can usually call on their governments for compensation (which, for many, represents up to 60 per cent of their income), farmers in developing countries have no such recourse, and increasingly are unable to cover their costs. This dumping of cheap food onto developing countries has resulted in hunger for peasants and maintains them in poverty (Wise, 2010). As a result of this desperate situation, every year some 50 million people leave the rural areas in search of alternative livelihoods, leading to uncontrolled urbanization.

In the 1970s, Haiti was virtually self-sufficient in rice production, which is one of its main staple crops. However, as a consequence of its structural adjustment programme, the customs tariff, including on rice imported into Haiti, was reduced from 50 per cent to 3 per cent, making it the most "liberalized" country in the world! Today, less than 25 per cent of its rice needs are met by local production (figure 7).

For years, in several United Nations bodies, including

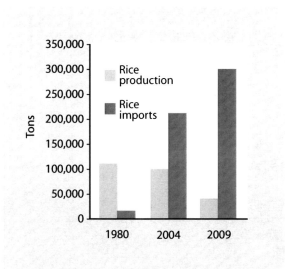

Figure 7: Haïti: Rice production and imports, 1980, 2004, 2009

Source: FAOSTAT.

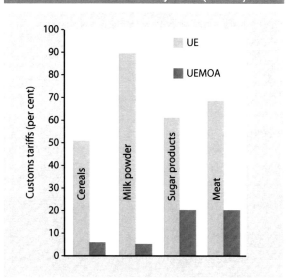

Figure 8: Custom tariffs in the EU and the Western African Economic and Monetary Union (UEMOA)

Source: Berthelot, 2008.

as Chair of UNCTAD's Trade and Development Board, I have been denouncing this negative impact on agricultural and industrial development in countries like Haiti. At the beginning of March 2010, former United States President Bill Clinton, who is currently the United Nations Secretary-General's Special Representative for Haiti, publicly acknowledged before a United States Senate committee that this policy, which he supported as former United States President, had been a mistake. He made a similar statement concerning agriculture in Africa when he said "we blew it". He went on to suggest we draw lessons from these errors and help countries like Haiti to find their way back to self-sufficiency in the food sector.

The solutions for feeding the growing world population and overcoming hunger and malnutrition are complex and must take into account the diversity and multi-functionality of agriculture, the specific conditions of each country, as well as climate change and increasing water scarcity. In developing their agricultural policy, governments should seek the active participation of farmers' associations.

Since 2008, various international conferences have been stressing the need for renewed investment in agriculture in order to relaunch agricultural production. More national and international funds are needed to help improve rural infrastructures and facilitate access to inputs, credit and knowledge. As the

World Bank now argues, this would not only increase agricultural productivity but also reduce poverty three to four times more rapidly than in other sectors of the economy (World Bank, 2008:7). But the commitments made at the L'Aquila Summit of the G-8 in 2009 to reserve more than $20 billion over a three-year period for investment in agriculture are far from being fulfilled.

A policy of fair and stable prices is essential to enable peasants to emerge from poverty and to provide them with sufficient buying power. This also requires adequate regulation of agricultural markets so as to shield vulnerable agricultural producers against dumping and price volatility. In particular, such regulation should protect agricultural markets in developing countries and especially in the LDCs and provide for the setting up of properly managed marketing boards as well as a network of reserve stocks at national and regional levels. It has to be noted that a number of industrialized countries and in particular the EU continue to apply customs tariffs for their most sensitive agricultural products (cereals, milk powder, meat and sugar products) at levels far beyond those applied by many developing countries and in particular LDCs (figure 8).

In order to introduce these changes, the concerned governments need to make maximum use of the flexibility between applied and bound rates offered under WTO rules. This approach has to be understood, accepted and even encouraged by all concerned parties, including the World Bank and the IMF as well as the industrialized countries, mindful of the conditions that led to their own development. Similarly, bilateral trade agreements with these countries should be based on the principle of non-reciprocity.

Many countries need to address the sensitive issue of agrarian reform, including access to land, as a necessary precondition for relaunching agriculture and achieving a substantial reduction in poverty, following the example of a number of East Asian countries. The State might guarantee the peasants access to land, but this does not necessarily involve giving ownership rights to individuals.

Ecosystems are deteriorating at an unprecedented rate, particularly the climate, water, biodiversity and fish resources. Suddenly, peasants worldwide have to realize, with unbelievable brutality, that the conditions in which they live and work are deteriorating fast: erosion is advancing and climate change is affecting cultivation conditions and harvests. As a result, food security, especially for the most vulnerable, is becoming more uncertain. The developing countries, and above all the poorest and the island countries, which are the least responsible for these changes, run the greatest risks. The high-yield model in industrialized countries is now being called into question. There are formidable challenges of adaptation, especially for peasants around the world. And it is becoming clear that small-scale agricultural units are best able to meet this challenge: agroecology, organic farming and some other sustainable production methods that are respectful of nature show the way towards producing more and better quality food, but with less inputs, which are mostly locally available and based on closed nutrient cycles.

Commentary II: Conceptual and Practical Aspects of Climate Change Mitigation Through Agriculture: Reducing Greenhouse Gas Emissions and Increasing Soil Carbon Sequestration

A. Müller and A. Gattinger
Research Institute of Organic Agriculture (FiBL), Switzerland

Abstract

Mitigation in agriculture needs to be based on two pillars:

- Technically, nitrogen inputs should be reduced, organic fertilizers should replace synthetic fertilizers and storage losses should be minimized. Integrated systems with closed, efficient nutrient cycles should be the order of the day in the future.

- Socially, food wastage should be minimized and meat consumption reduced.

In general, reducing GHG emissions and increasing sequestration in agriculture is no easy task, either conceptually or in practice. But there are at least five clear exceptions plus one possible exception at the conceptual level.

First, avoiding open burning of biomass reduces emissions. Given that open biomass burning is the third largest contributor of direct GHG emissions from agriculture – accounting for more than 10 per cent – after nitrous oxide emitted from fertilized soils and methane from enteric fermentation in ruminants, there is a considerable and undoubted mitigation potential linked to this (Smith et al., 2007b; Bellarby et al., 2008). In most industrialized countries, open burning of biomass is prohibited, but in developing countries it is still common practice.

Second, reducing the global numbers of ruminants would directly reduce the corresponding methane emissions that account for about 30 per cent of total direct GHG emissions from agriculture (Smith et al., 2007b; Bellarby et al., 2008). This is mainly an issue for industrialized livestock systems, and not for smallholders. Due to carbon sequestration in pastures, pastoral livestock systems can even be carbon-neutral if stocking rates are adequately low.

Third, 30–40 per cent of food is lost globally, mainly as a result of wastage in industrialized countries and by storage losses in developing countries. Avoiding losses and wastage would therefore reduce the output needed and the corresponding GHG emissions (Godfray et al., 2010). Given the magnitude of losses and wastage, reducing them is essential in any effective climate mitigation policy for agriculture.

Fourth, conversion of pastures and/or forests to agricultural land and of forests to pastures needs to be reduced, as this leads to high CO_2 emissions, of roughly the same order as total direct agricultural GHG emissions (Smith et al., 2007b; Bellarby et al., 2008). Insofar as such land-use change is due to animal husbandry and feedstuff production for ruminants, ideally this reduction should be combined with reduced animal numbers.

Finally, the mitigation potential of carbon sequestration in optimally managed agricultural soils should be exploited. This potential is of the same order of magnitude as total agricultural emissions (Smith et al., 2007a; Bellarby et al., 2008). Soil carbon losses can be reduced and sequestration increased by application of organic fertilizers, minimal soil disturbance and planting legume leys in crop rotations.

Conceptually, these five aspects are uncontested, but, regrettably, they are the only ones of such clarity and importance. Addressing the other most relevant emission sources in agriculture (e.g. nitrous oxide emissions from soils, methane from rice production, manure management) is often highly complex. There are indications that actions and strategies relating to each of the sources may reduce emissions, but the high degree of complexity and context dependency of the underlying processes and their interactions with other processes often hinder clear statements. For example, reduced nitrogen input tends to reduce nitrous oxide emissions, but considerations of other characteristics of a location and cropping system, such as temperature, humidity, soil type, crops and fertilizer types, may dominate; or reduced flooding of rice fields cuts methane emissions but tends to increase nitrous oxide emissions. Nevertheless, indications are strong enough to mention reduced nitrogen applications as a sixth realistic option: the right type, place, rate and timing of nitrogen fertilizer applications are important (for more details, see Müller et al., 2011a; Müller and Aubert, 2013).

Regarding emissions from energy use, agriculture plays a minor role: farm machinery accounts for only 3 per cent of direct agricultural GHG emissions, while efficiency improvements in irrigation would contribute somewhat more, as irrigation accounts for about 7 per cent of emissions (Bellarby et al., 2008). However, reduction of energy use along the agricultural value chain has undoubted mitigation potential. There are significant emissions from transport, processing and storage, all of which are attributed by emission inventories to sectors other than agriculture. Thus, increasing efficiency and reducing the amount of road and air transport would considerably reduce emissions from the food system (for more information on supply-chain-related GHG emissions, see comments by Rundgren, Krain, Linne, and Gaebler in this chapter).

Regarding transport, it is worth pointing out that there is significant misreporting of emissions in national GHG inventories, as imports are not accounted for. National boundaries are the basis for emissions accounting, and "grey" embedded emissions in imported production inputs and consumption goods are added to the balance of the countries of origin. This considerably distorts national emissions from the food systems of countries where imports and exports play a crucial role.

With these remarks, we hope to have offered some options at the conceptual level. At the practical level, there are some difficulties, but differentiating three phases helps. Practical implementation means offering incentives, and establishing monitoring and enforcement mechanisms.

Providing incentives and enforcement are a challenge in many respects, but monitoring is relatively easy for the five proposals outlined above: avoiding burning, reducing animal numbers, avoiding losses and waste, and preventing deforestation and land conversion. Monitoring soil carbon changes can be more demanding, but it is feasible. Given the necessity of fundamental changes in agricultural production in order to increase its sustainability, these five aspects need to play a central role in any mitigation policy for agriculture. In addition, reducing nitrogen inputs should be a key policy target, and changes in how emissions from imports and exports are accounted for are needed to enable unbiased and more accurate assessments of countries' emissions.

We do not touch on enforcement here, but what follows are some remarks on actions that need to be taken to move towards a more sustainable agricultural system as outlined above.

First, open burning of agricultural waste should be prohibited, as has been implemented successfully by industrialized countries. Information and training, and if necessary, even some financial support should accompany such a ban. This will partly influence weed and pest management and alter some nutrient flows, though some additional investment or labour costs may accrue (e.g. in sugarcane without pre-harvest burning). The biomass not burned is a valuable resource, which can be used as source material for compost or mulch (i.e. as organic fertilizer) or for bioenergy production. Clearly, these alternative uses need to be supported by information and training, and perhaps also by investment support. There may be some options for obtaining financial assistance from the carbon markets (e.g. renewable energy or composting projects under the Clean Development Mechanisms).

Second, reduced animal numbers and land-use change can be addressed on the producers' side through optimal stocking rates, efficient grassland management and pastoralism, forest protection and land-use legislation. An optimal combination of crop farming and animal husbandry produces the most efficient nutrient cycles. However, reducing animal numbers is usually not an issue for smallholders in developing countries, and animal husbandry is essential for their food security. Actions on the producers' side would include making inputs more expensive and, correspondingly, increasing output prices, which to some extent would reduce demand. On the demand side, it is primarily an issue on a global scale, and concerns mainly more wealthy consumers, whose increasing demand for meat and dairy products needs to be discouraged. One possible way to reduce demand would be by imposing a "meat tax" (tied to the emissions from animals). It is, however, questionable whether price increases could be high enough to achieve the necessary reductions; there also needs to be a discussion of consumer behaviour, lifestyles and quality of life, and how these are linked to excessive consumption, and meat consumption in particular.

The third issue, closely related to the issue of food wastage, concerns consumer behaviour and perceptions of quality, freshness and needs, which are decisive in this respect. Making food more expensive (through internalization of all external costs) would help, but aspects of justice need to be kept in mind, as significant price increases affect the freedom of choice of less wealthy people much more than that of wealthy people. Thus, again, sustainable lifestyles need to become a major consideration in policy discussions (for a detailed discussion of these aspects, see the commentary of Reisch in this chapter).

The other aspect of wastage is storage losses in many developing countries. In these countries, investment in storage and processing facilities and information and training would greatly help. This should be of primary importance, as it would reduce the needed level and intensity of actions on the other aspects mentioned here. Each unit loss avoided reduces pressure on production. Thus it is less about additional money needed for these measures, than about a shift in focus on where to channel the money that already flows into agriculture and the food system (see the commentary of Parfitt and Barthel in this chapter).

Fourth, reduced nitrogen inputs can be achieved through regulation, following the example of the successful EU Nitrogen Directive. Taxing inputs is another option: a heavy carbon tax would serve a similar goal, due to the use of fossil fuel for synthetic fertilizer production. However, nitrogen regulation should go further than only input reduction. Closed nutrient cycles and increased use of organic fertilizers should be the final goal, as this would also have highly beneficial effects on soil carbon levels and the corresponding mitigation (see the commentary of Leu later in this chapter).

This is linked to efforts for increasing soil carbon sequestration. To achieve this, the necessary steps include abolishing subsidies for synthetic fertilizers and supporting organic fertilizers, reducing soil disturbance in tillage operations and planting legume leys in crop rotations. Support should consist of both investment support and extension services (e.g. for optimal composting and compost use). Additional benefits from higher soil carbon levels include improved soil structure, soil fertility and soil life, which contribute to water holding and retention capacity with corresponding positive effects on climate change adaptation (i.e. increased resistance to drought and extreme weather events).

Finally, embedded emissions need to be made visible. National GHG inventories should be amended to take into account imports and exports in order to obtain a full and more accurate picture of national emissions, and not overlook the responsibilities of consumers abroad.

Commentary III: The Potential of Sustainable Agriculture for Climate Change Adaptation

A. Müller and U. Niggli
Research Institute of Organic Agriculture (FiBL), Switzerland

Abstract

Adaptation in agriculture needs to be based on four pillars:

- Increasing soil fertility: this can be achieved by replacing synthetic fertilizers with organic fertilizers, and monocultures with diverse crop rotations.

- Increasing biodiversity through diverse measures such as crop rotations, use of local varieties, catch crops, hedges and other landscape elements. This applies to field, farm and landscape levels. In addition, the use of sustainable and especially organic crop protection will foster biodiversity of insects, weeds, earthworms and other organisms.

- Providing information and extension services to support sustainable agricultural practices and organic agriculture, agroecology and agroforestry.

- Creating a level playing field for sustainable agriculture at the global level. This involves abolishing distorting subsidies, such as for synthetic fertilizers, and internalization of external costs.

Organic agriculture is an ideal solution as it responds to the first three pillars. In addition, global policies, and trade and competition issues need separate attention.

Adapting agriculture to climate change is unavoidable. For adaptation (on the concept, see box 1) to succeed, it is necessary for farms to take concrete adaptation measures, but also general long-term societal actions are needed. Our comments here focus mainly on adaptation measures for farms.

An aspect often neglected in current discussions on adaptation in agriculture (discussed in detail in Müller, et al., 2012) is that adaptation strategies also need to offer farming families solutions outside agriculture if agricultural production becomes impossible for them. For example, drought resistant varieties and improved efficiency of water use would help adaptation, but in some cases water availability may become too low to continue with agriculture. In such situations, the key question is where agricultural production may be optimally located over the next few decades, where it may be better to abandon it, and which livelihood alternatives will be available.

There are five key impacts and characteristics of climate change in agriculture (e.g. Easterling et al., 2007; Meehl et al., 2007; Rosenzweig and Tubiello, 2007):

- Climate change impacts will vary considerably by region: some regions will be affected positively, and others negatively. However, changes in production conditions will occur everywhere, necessitating adaptation. Regions benefiting from the positive effects of climate change should be able to take full advantage of their changed circumstances.
- Water will become a key issue. In some regions there will be increased water scarcity and drought, while in others extreme precipitation, water logging and flooding will become more frequent.
- Pressure from weeds, pests and diseases will increase.
- Increasing numbers of extreme weather events (e.g. heat waves and heavy precipitation) will pose a further challenge to agricultural production.
- Risks in agricultural production will increase due partly to greater climate variability.

Adaptation in agriculture needs to reduce exposure to these impacts, as well as sensitivity and vulnerability to them. This can be achieved by adopting sustainable agricultural production systems, such as agroecology, agroforestry or organic agriculture (Milestad and

Box 1: The concept of adaptation

We use the three concepts of "exposure", "sensitivity" and "vulnerability" to frame adaptation in agriculture. "Exposure" describes the likelihood that a system will experience certain conditions, such as drought (e.g. Smit and Wandel, 2006). "Sensitivity is the degree to which a system is affected, either adversely or beneficially, by climate variability or change" (IPCC, 2007b). "Vulnerability is the degree to which a system is susceptible to, and unable to cope with, adverse effects of climate change" (IPCC, 2007b).

Darnhofer, 2003; Borron, 2006; Niggli, 2009; El-Hage Scialabba and Müller-Lindenlauf, 2010; Müller et al., 2012).

There are many reasons why sustainable agriculture is a system well suited to adaptation. First, traditionally it uses locally adapted varieties and cropping practices, and it can therefore better adjust to local variability of climate change impacts.

Second, it can respond to increased water stress by maintaining and increasing soil organic matter, as this increases the soil's water holding and retention capacity. Using organic fertilizers, such as compost, and adopting diverse crop sequences, in particular with legume leys, are important means of achieving this. These are core practices of sustainable agriculture, and of organic agriculture in particular, with its strong focus on soil fertility, soil quality and plant health. The higher biodiversity in organic agriculture resulting from an optimal combination of crops with different needs also contributes to optimal water and nutrient use.

Third, high biodiversity also helps reduce the occurrence and severity of weeds and pest outbreaks, and plant and animal diseases (Smith et al., 2011; Niggli, 2009). In addition, complex crop rotations contribute to controlling pests more effectively as they break their life cycles. Improved soil fertility and plant health further reduce vulnerability to pressures from increased pests, weeds and diseases (Altieri, Ponti and Nicholls, 2005).

Fourth, improved soil quality and higher content of organic matter in the soil also reduce vulnerability to extreme events such as drought, flooding and water-logging, and erosion (Siegrist et al., 1998; Fliessbach et al., 2007; Niggli, 2009; El-Hage Scialabba and Müller-Lindenlauf, 2010). In addition, mulching and cover crops are common practices in sustainable agriculture, bare fallows are avoided and erosion is correspondingly reduced. Landscape elements such as hedges or agroforestry provide

shelter and favourable microclimates, improving moisture management and capacity to adapt to high temperatures.

Fifth, the high biodiversity on sustainably managed farms (e.g. organic) also reduces the risk of total production losses due to climate change, and generally increases the resilience of agroecosystems (Altieri and Nicholls, 2006; Campbell et al., 2009). Through the combination of crop and livestock production as well as a larger number of crops grown, total economic failure can be avoided. Additionally, the economic risks are lower for organic farms, as they use fewer off-farm inputs and correspondingly incur lower upfront costs. Price premiums, for instance resulting from certified organic production, offer further potential for improving producers' economic situations. All these aspects combined provide inexpensive but effective risk management strategies, in particular insurance against crop failure (El-Hage Scialabba and Hattam, 2002; Eyhorn, 2007).

Agroecology, agroforestry and, in particular, organic agriculture thus reduce *vulnerability* through risk reduction based on diversification of livelihood strategies, cropping patterns and lower input costs. The focus on soil fertility, soil health and high biodiversity reduces *sensitivity*. This is of particular relevance for optimal water management and for optimal strategies to cope with pests and diseases. Reducing *exposure* is the most difficult, as this means shifting cropping locations or abandoning agriculture altogether in some circumstances.

How such fundamental changes can be supported, where necessary, needs further research. However, there are some readily available strategies that reduce vulnerability and sensitivity, as briefly described below.

First, soil fertility needs to be built up and soil degradation halted. For this, subsidies for synthetic fertilizers should be abandoned, where possible, without compromising food security. Where this is an issue, carefully designed transformation from synthetic to at least partly organic fertilizers, redesigned crop rotations with legumes and plants with different rooting depths, as well as closed nutrient cycles should be implemented. The simultaneous use of synthetic and organic fertilizers may not be advisable for climate change mitigation due to the resulting higher nitrous oxide emissions. However, particularly in a development context, adaptation in agriculture is key, and mitigation must never compromise on this.

Second, biodiversity needs to be enhanced. Local breeding programmes should be established or revitalized and supported, and farmers should be able to produce their own seeds. Practices such as agroforestry, and well-designed crop rotations need to be supported. Landscape elements also contribute to adaptation as they improve the microclimate. Payments for ecosystem services could be one type of financial incentive mechanism to encourage these practices.

This links to the third point: information and training are crucial for successful implementation of these adaptation strategies. Sustainable agricultural practices and organic agriculture, as a holistic agricultural production system, rely on the presence of a considerable body of knowledge.

Fourth, to be successful, adaptation strategies need to be accompanied by policy and trade measures. Massive trade distortions, such as the current subsidies for conventional production (e.g. cotton in the United States) need to be abolished. Similarly, the market power of agribusiness corporations in the seed markets and in plant protection is a hindrance that needs to be removed.

Finally, all external costs of agricultural production should be reflected in the price. Without this, conventional production will always have an unfair competitive advantage due to distorted production costs that do not include all the environmental and social costs of production. If those external costs were to be included in conventional production, it would prove to be more costly than sustainable agriculture.

Commentary IV: Food, Climate Change and Healthy Soils: The Forgotten Link

GRAIN

Abstract

Agriculture is starting to get more attention in international negotiations around climate change. The consensus is that it contributes 10–15 per cent of all global anthropogenic greenhouse gas (GHG) emissions, making it one of the key drivers of climate change. But looking at agriculture alone is not enough; it is also necessary to look at the larger food system. Beyond the emissions that occur on the farm, today's dominant industrial food system generates GHGs by transporting food around the world, by deforestation to make way for plantations and by generating waste. Pulling together the available data on these sources of emissions reveals that the global food system is responsible for around half of all global GHGs. Thus it is the food system as a whole which is at the centre of the problem of climate change.

If measures are taken to restructure agriculture and the larger food system based on food sovereignty, small-scale farming, agroecology and local markets, global GHG emissions could be cut by half within a few decades. There is no need for carbon markets or techno-fixes. What is needed are the right policies and programmes that bring about a shift from the current industrial food system to a sustainable, equitable and truly productive one.

A. Food and climate: piecing the puzzle together

According to most studies, the contribution of agricultural emissions – the emissions produced on the farm – is between 11 and 15 per cent of all global emissions.[29] What often goes unsaid, however, is that most of these emissions are generated by industrial farming practices that rely on chemical (nitrogen) fertilizers, heavy machinery run on petrol, and highly concentrated industrial livestock operations that pump out methane.

The data for agriculture's contribution also often neglect to take into account the contribution of land-use changes and deforestation, which are responsible for nearly a fifth of global GHG emissions (WRI, undated; IPCC, 2004). Worldwide, agriculture is pushing into savannahs, wetlands, cerrados and forests, and is ploughing huge amounts of land. The expansion of the agricultural frontier is the dominant contributor to deforestation, accounting for 70–90 per cent of global deforestation (FAO, 2008; Kanninen et al., 2007). This means that some 15–18 per cent of global GHG emissions are produced by land-use change and deforestation for agriculture. And here too, the global food system and the industrial model of agriculture are the chief culprits. The main driver

of this deforestation is the expansion of industrial plantations for the production of commodities such as soy, sugarcane, oil palm, maize and rapeseed. Since 1990, the area planted with these five commodity crops grew enormously, by 38 per cent (GRAIN, 2010).

These emissions from agriculture account for only a portion of the food system's overall contribution to climate change. Equally important are the emissions caused all along the chain, from when the produce leaves the farm until it is consumed.

Food production is the world's largest economic activity, involving more transactions and employing more people by far than any other sector. Today, food is prepared and distributed using enormous amounts of processing, packaging and transportation, all of which generate GHG emissions, although data on such emissions are hard to find. Studies looking at the EU conclude that about one quarter of overall transportation involves commercial food transport (Eurostat, 2011). Scattered figures on transportation available for other countries, such as Kenya and Zimbabwe, indicate that the percentage is even higher in non-industrialized countries, where "food production and delivery accounts for 60-80% of the total energy – human plus animal plus fuel – used" (Karekezi and Lazarus, 1995). With transportation

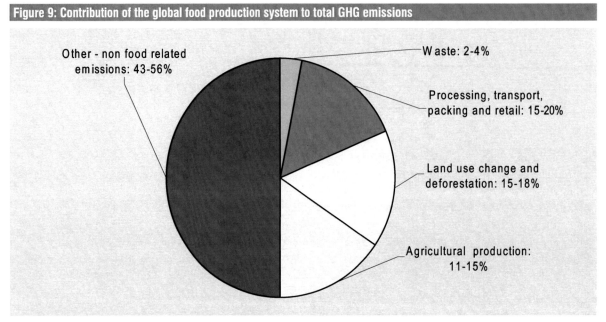

Figure 9: Contribution of the global food production system to total GHG emissions

Other - non food related emissions: 43-56%

Waste: 2-4%

Processing, transport, packing and retail: 15-20%

Land use change and deforestation: 15-18%

Agricultural production: 11-15%

Source: Estimates of GRAIN

accounting for 25 per cent of global GHG emissions, EU data enable an estimate – albeit a conservative one – for the contribution of the transport of food to GHG emissions of at least 6 per cent. Similarly, EU data derived from studies on processing and packaging of food within the EU show that these activities account for 10–11 per cent of GHG emissions (Bolla and Pendolovska, 2011), while refrigeration of food accounts for 3–4 per cent of total emissions (Garnett and Jackson, 2007), and food retail for another 2 per cent (Tassou et al., 2011; Venkat, 2011; Bakas, 2010). Based on the data for the EU, and extrapolating from the scarce figures that exist for other countries, we can estimate, conservatively, that at least 5–6 per cent of emissions result from food transport, 8–10 per cent from food processing and packaging, 1–2 per cent from refrigeration and another 1–2 per cent from retail. This amounts to a total contribution of 15–20 per cent of global emissions from all these activities.

Not all of what the food system produces gets consumed. The industrial food system discards up to *half* of all the food that it produces in its journey from farms to traders, to food processors, to stores and supermarkets. This is enough to feed the world's hungry six times over (Stuart, 2009). Much of this waste rots on garbage heaps and landfills, producing substantial amounts of GHGs. Different studies indicate that between 3.5 and 4.5 per cent of global GHG emissions come from waste, and that over 90

per cent of them come from materials originating in agriculture and its processing (Bogner et al., 2008). This means that the decomposition of organic waste originating in food and agriculture is responsible for 3–4 per cent of global GHG emissions.

Considering all these factors, it would appear that the current global food system, propelled by an increasingly powerful transnational food industry, is responsible for around half of all anthropogenic GHG emissions – between a low of 44 per cent and a high of 57 per cent.

B. Turning the food system upside down

Clearly, we will not resolve the climate crisis if the global food system is not urgently and dramatically transformed. The place to start is with the soil. Food production begins and ends with soil. It grows out of the soil and eventually goes back into it to enable more food to be produced. This is the very cycle of life. But in recent years humans have ignored this vital cycle: we have been taking from the soil without giving back.

The industrialization of agriculture, which started in Europe and North America and was later replicated in the Green Revolution that took place in other parts of the world, was based on the assumption that soil fertility could be maintained and increased through the use of chemical fertilizers. Little attention was paid to the importance of organic matter in the soil.

A wide range of scientific reports indicate that cultivated soils have lost 30 to 75 per cent of their organic matter during the twentieth century, while soils under pastures and prairies have typically lost up to 50 per cent. Without doubt, these losses have provoked a serious deterioration of soil fertility and productivity, as well as a higher risk exposure to droughts and floods.

Taking as a basis some of the most conservative figures provided by the scientific literature, the global accumulated loss of soil organic matter (SOM) over the past century can be estimated to be between 150 and 200 billion tons.[31] Not all this organic matter has ended up in the air as CO_2; significant amounts have been washed away by erosion and deposited at the bottom of rivers and oceans. However, it can be estimated that at least 200 to 300 billion tons of CO_2 have been released to the atmosphere due to the global destruction of soil organic matter. In other words, 25 to 40 per cent of the current excess of CO_2 in the atmosphere results from the destruction of soils and their organic matter.

There is some good news hidden in these devastating figures: the CO_2 that has been emitted into the atmosphere through soil depletion can be put back into the soil through a change in agricultural practices. There has to be a shift away from practices that destroy organic matter to ones that build up the organic matter in the soil. We know this can be done. Farmers around the world have been engaging in these very practices for generations. Research by GRAIN (2009) has shown that if the right policies and incentives were in place worldwide, soil organic matter contents could be restored to pre-industrial agricultural levels within a period of 50 years, which is roughly the same time frame that industrial agriculture took to reduce it. The continuing use of these practices would allow the offset of 24–30 per cent of current global annual GHG emissions.[32]

The new scenario would require a radical change in approach from the current industrial agriculture model. It would focus on the use of techniques such as diversified cropping systems, better integration between crop and animal production, and increased incorporation of trees and wild vegetation. Such an increase in diversity would, in turn, increase the production potential, and the incorporation of organic matter would progressively improve soil fertility,

creating a virtuous cycle of higher productivity and greater availability of organic matter. The capacity of soil to hold water would increase, which would mean that excessive rainfall would lead to fewer, less intense floods and droughts. Soil erosion would become less of a problem, and soil acidity and alkalinity would fall progressively, reducing or eliminating the toxicity that has become a major problem in tropical and arid soils. Additionally, increased soil biological activity would protect plants against pests and diseases. Each one of these effects implies higher productivity and hence more organic matter available to soils, thus making possible higher targets for incorporation of soil organic matter over the years. More food would be produced in the process (see also the commentary of Leu on mitigating climate change with soil organic matter in organic production systems in this chapter).

This shift in agricultural practices would require building on the skills and experience of the world's small farmers, rather than undermining and forcing them off their lands, as is now the case. A global shift towards an agriculture that builds up organic matter in the soil would also contribute to removing some of the other major sources of GHGs from the food system. There are three other mutually reinforcing shifts that need to take place in the food system to support its overall contribution to climate change. The first is a shift to local markets and short circuits of food distribution, which would reduce transportation and the need for packaging, processing and refrigeration. The second is a reintegration of crop and animal production, which would also cut transportation, as well as the use of chemical fertilizers and the production of methane and nitrous oxide emissions generated by intensive meat and dairy operations. And the third is the stopping of land clearing and deforestation, which will require genuine agrarian reform and a reversal of the expansion of monoculture plantations for the production of agrofuels and animal feed. If the world becomes serious about undertaking these four shifts, it is quite possible for global GHG emissions to be cut by half within a few decades, and, in the process, this would go a long way towards resolving the other crises affecting the planet, such as poverty and hunger. There are no technical hurdles standing in the way; the world's farmers already possess the requisite knowledge and skills, and these can be further developed. The only hurdles are political, which is where we need to focus our efforts.

Commentary V: Mitigating Climate Change with Soil Organic Matter in Organic Production Systems

Andre Leu
President, International Federation of Organic Agricultural Movements (IFOAM)

Abstract

Past and present global efforts aimed at reducing carbon dioxide emissions by improving energy-use efficiency and the adoption of renewable energy sources have been unsuccessful. It is therefore critical to look at all readily available options that could significantly mitigate runaway climate change.

Sequestering CO_2 into the soil could bring about a significant reduction in GHG levels. There is scientific evidence that this can be achieved with current good organic agricultural practices and that the best organic farming practices can achieve even higher levels of CO_2 sequestration. Building up soil organic matter is one of the least costly climate change mitigation methods.

Helping farmers adopt these methods on a widespread basis would make a significant difference to the levels of CO_2 in the atmosphere and in the world's oceans. Importantly, this is not based on untested concepts such as carbon capture and storage; it is based on current practices that can be adopted by other land managers.

This could be financed through cap and trade systems that tax emissions. These taxes could then be used to pay farmers for their ecosystem services that fix the atmospheric CO_2 in the soil. Such a system could be either government administered or market-based.

A. Introduction

The world is failing to reduce GHG emissions despite commitments made under the Kyoto Protocol. According to the International Energy Agency (IEA, 2011b), energy-related CO_2 emissions reached a record high of 30.6 gigatonnes (Gt) in 2010 – a 5 per cent jump from the previous record in 2008. Moreover, the reduction in economic activity due to the global economic and financial crisis has not reduced the growth of GHG emissions.

While the first commitment period of the Kyoto Protocol and its Clean Development Mechanism (CDM) led to a small reduction in emissions by the Annex 1 parties to the Protocol, they failed to reduce the overall rate of global GHG emissions. The CDM has had very little impact because its complex rules make it difficult to achieve effective project results. A major issue has been GHG leakage (or rather outsourcing) from the Annex 1 countries to developing countries. Any small gains that have been achieved by the former in reducing GHG emissions have been more than

lost by the polluting industries moving to developing countries and importing GHG-intensive products from there. The non-Annex 1 countries now account for the majority of the world's GHG emissions caused by expanding industries, deforestation, the burning of savannahs and the loss of soil carbon through poor agricultural practices.

The current state of the economies of developed countries, with their massive debts, means that they do not have the funds to shift significantly to the use of renewable energies and improve energy efficiency in the short term. Furthermore, the political climate has changed since the United Nations Climate Change Conference in Copenhagen in 2009, with very few governments willing to accept a slowdown in economic activity to meet emission reduction targets or to introduce major GHG reduction strategies.

The Cancun Climate Change Agreements mean that sequestration has to be part of any strategy mix to stabilize the level of atmospheric CO_2 (UNFCCC, 2011). This gas accounts for around 80 per cent of anthropogenic GHGs (WMO, 2011).

B. Soils as a carbon sink

Soils are the greatest carbon sink after the oceans. According to Professor Rattan Lal of Ohio State University, over 2,700 Gt of carbon is stored in soils worldwide. This is considerably more than the combined total of 780 Gt in the atmosphere and the 575 Gt in biomass (Lal, 2008).

The amount of CO_2 in the oceans is already causing a range of problems, particularly for species with calcium exoskeletons such as coral. Scientists are concerned that the increase in acidity caused by higher levels of CO_2 is damaging these species and threatens the future of marine ecosystems such as the Great Barrier Reef. The world's oceans, like the atmosphere, cannot absorb any more CO_2 without causing potentially serious environmental damage to many aquatic ecosystems (Hoegh-Guldberg et al., 2007).

Despite the fact that soil is the largest repository of carbon after the oceans and has the potential to sequester more CO_2 than biomass, neither soil nor agriculture is incorporated in any formal agreement of the United Nations Framework Convention on Climate Change (UNFCCC) or the CDM.

This needs to be changed because according to the Food and Agriculture Organization of the United Nations, *"Agriculture not only suffers the impacts of climate change, it is also responsible for 14 percent of global greenhouse gas emissions. But agriculture has the potential to be an important part of the solution, through mitigation — reducing and/or removing — a significant amount of global emissions. Some 70 percent of this mitigation potential could be realized in developing countries"* (FAO, 2012b).

C. Soil carbon sequestration through agricultural practices

The ability of soils to absorb enough CO_2 in order to stabilize current atmospheric CO_2 levels is a critical issue, and there is a major debate over whether this can be achieved through farming practices (Lal, 2007; Sanderman et al., 2010).

Two independent global meta reviews have looked at the average amount of CO_2 sequestered by organic farming systems.

A preliminary study by FiBL, published by FAO, collated 45 peer-reviewed comparison trials between organic and conventional systems that used 280 data sets (FAO, 2011b). These studies included data from grasslands, arable crops and permanent crops in several continents. A simple analysis of the data shows that, on average, the organic systems had higher levels of soil carbon sequestration (Gattinger et al., 2011).

Andreas Gattinger and colleagues observed (2011:16): *"In soils under organic management, the SOC [soil organic carbon] stocks averaged 37.4 tonnes C ha-1, in comparison to 26.7 tonnes C ha-1 under non-organic management."* This means that the average difference between the two management systems (organic and conventional) was 10.7 tonnes of carbon. Using the accepted formula that SOC x 3.67 = CO_2 this means an average of more than 39.269 tonnes of CO_2 was sequestered in the organic system compared to the conventional system. The average duration of management of all included studies was 16.7 years (Gattinger et al, 2011). This means that an average of 2,351 kgs of CO_2 was sequestered per hectare every year in the organic system compared to the conventional system.

Another study by the United Kingdom Soil Association found that average organic farming practices removed about 2,200 kg of CO_2 per hectare per year (Azeez, 2009). This is critical information as it clearly shows that organic farmers are currently sequestering significant amounts of carbon. Most importantly, this is not based on untested concepts like "carbon capture and storage" and "clean coal"; it is based on current practices that can be adopted by other farmers.

D. Potential of organic practices

Based on these figures, the widespread adoption of current organic practices globally has the potential to sequester 10 Gt of CO_2, which is around 20 per cent of the world's current GHG emissions.

Grassland	3,356,940,000 ha
Arable crops	1,380,515,000 ha
Permanent crops	146,242,000 ha
Total	4,883,697,000 ha

Source: (FAO, 2010).

Organic @ 2.2 tons per hectare: 10.7 Gt of CO_2 (Azeez, 2009)

Annual GHG emissions: 49 Gt of carbon dioxide equivalent (CO_2e) (IPCC 2007c).

E. Potential exists for higher levels of CO_2 sequestration

All data sets that use averaging have outlying data. These are examples that are significantly higher or significantly lower than the average. They are always worth examining to find out why. Research into them will allow an understanding of which practices significantly increase soil carbon and which decrease or do not increase it.

There are several examples of significantly higher levels of carbon sequestration than the averages quoted in the studies above. The Rodale Institute in Pennsylvania, United States, has been conducting long-running comparisons of organic and conventional cropping systems for over 30 years, which confirm that organic methods are effective at removing CO_2 from the atmosphere and fixing it as organic matter in the soil. La Salle and Hepperly (2008:5) wrote: "*In the FST [farm systems trial] organic plots, carbon was sequestered into the soil at the rate of 875 lbs/ac/year in a crop rotation utilizing raw manure, and at a rate of about 500 lbs/ac/year in a rotation using legume cover crops.*

During the 1990s, results from the Compost Utilization Trial (CUT) at Rodale Institute – a 10-year study comparing the use of composts, manures and synthetic chemical fertilizer – show that the use of composted manure with crop rotations in organic systems can result in carbon sequestration of up to 2,000 lbs/ac/year. By contrast, fields under standard tillage relying on chemical fertilizers lost almost 300 pounds of carbon per acre per year".

Converting these figures into kilograms of CO_2 sequestered per hectare using the accepted conversion rate of 1 pound per acre = 1.12085116 kg/ha and soil organic carbon x 3.67 = CO_2, gives the following results:
- The FST legume based organic plots showed that carbon was sequestered into the soil at the rate of about 500 lbs/ac/year. This is equivalent to a sequestration rate of 2,055.2 kg of CO_2/ha/yr.
- The FST manured organic plots showed that carbon was sequestered into the soil at the rate of 875 lbs/ac/year. This is equivalent to a sequestration rate of 3,596.6 kg of CO_2/ha/yr.
- The Compost Utilization Trial showed that carbon was sequestered into the soil at the rate of 2,000 lbs/ac/year. This is equivalent to a sequestration rate of 8,220.8 kg of CO_2/ha/yr.

Thus there are significant benefits from adding compost.

F. The potential in desert climates

Sekem is the oldest biodynamic farm in Egypt. It was founded in 1977 by Dr Ibrahim Abouleish. The Louis Bolk Institute and Soil&More, two organisations based in the Netherlands, have made a study to calculate soil carbon sequestration at Sekem. Their results show that, on average, Sekem's management practices have resulted in 900 kgs of carbon being stored in the soil per hectare per year in the fields that were 30 years old. Using the accepted formula of SOC x 3.67 = CO_2, this means that Sekem has sequestered 3,303 kg of CO_2 per hectare per year for 30 years (Luske and van der Kamp, 2009; Koopmans et al., 2011). Based on these figures, the widespread adoption of Sekem's practices globally has the potential to sequester 16 Gt of CO_2, which is around 30 per cent of the world's current GHG emissions, into soils (4,883,697,000 ha x 3,303 kgs = 16.1 gt CO_2/yr).

G. The potential in tropical climates

Researchers at the Royal Thai Organic Project near Chiang Mai in Thailand have managed to increase their soil organic matter levels from 1 per cent to 5 per cent over a period of eight years (personal communication). This means that 187.2 tons of CO_2/ha have been sequestered through this project, which equates to 23.4 tons of CO_2/ha/yr. If this was applied globally, it would sequester 114 Gt CO_2/ha/yr – more than double the world's current GHG emissions (4,883,697,000 ha x 23.4 tons of CO_2/ha/yr = 114 Gt CO_2/yr).

H. Deeper carbon systems

There is an emerging body of science which shows that the most stable fractions of soil carbon are stored deeper in the soil than most of the current soil carbon measurements used on farms. Most soil tests tend to work at a depth of around 15 to 20 cm, as this is the usual root zone for many crops. Research is finding that a significant amount of carbon is stored at lower depths and that this tends to be very stable.

Research by Rethemeyer and colleagues using radiocarbon techniques to analyse various soil carbon fractions indicated a progressive enrichment of stable organic compounds with increasing soil depth to 65 cm (Rethemeyer et al., 2005).

Research by Professor Rattan Lal and colleagues from Ohio State University compared carbon levels between no-till and conventional tillage fields and found that, in some cases, carbon storage was greater in conventional tillage fields. The key is soil depth. They compared the carbon storage between no-till and ploughed fields with the plough depth – the first 8 inches (20cm) of the soil – and found that the carbon storage was generally much greater in no-till fields than in plowed fields. When they examined 12 inches (30cm) and deeper, they found more carbon stored in ploughed fields than in the no-till ones. The researchers concluded that farmers should not measure soil carbon based just on surface depth. They recommended going to as much as 3 feet (1 metre) below the soil surface to get a more accurate assessment of soil carbon (Christopher, Lal and Mishra, 2009).

According to Gattinger and colleagues (2011:16), *researchers working on long-term comparison trials between organic and conventional farming systems in Switzerland (the DOK trials), found that, when rotation phases included two years of deep-rooting grass-clover leys, 64 percent of the total SOC stocks were deposited between 20–80 cm soil depths. "In many parts of the world, organic farming systems are relying on the soil fertility build-up of deep-rooting grass-legume mixtures and on the incorporation of plant residues by deep-digging earthworms, making it quite likely that the currently available data sets underestimate the SOC stocks in organically managed soils. This is particularly significant considering that in deeper soil horizons, SOC seems to be more stabilized." (Fliessbach et al., 1999)*

I. Grazing systems

The majority of the world's agricultural lands (68.7 per cent) are used for grazing (FAO, 2010). There is an emerging body of published evidence which shows that pastures and permanent ground cover swards in perennial horticulture build up soil organic carbon faster than any other farming system, and, with correct management, this is stored deeper in the soil (Fliessbach et al., 1999; Sanderman et al., 2010).

One of the significant reasons for this has been the higher proportion of plants that use the C4 pathway of photosynthesis as this makes them more efficient at collecting CO_2 from the atmosphere, especially in warmer and drier climates. According to Osborne and

Beerling (2006:173), "*Plants with the C4 photosynthetic pathway dominate today's tropical savannahs and grasslands, and account for some 30% of global terrestrial carbon fixation. Their success stems from a physiological CO_2-concentrating pump, which leads to high photosynthetic efficiency in warm climates and low atmospheric CO_2 concentrations.*"

This knowledge is now being applied in innovative ways such as holistic stock management, evergreen farming, agroforestry in pastures and pasture cropping.

J. Pasture cropping

Pasture cropping works on the principle that annuals grow naturally through perennial pastures in their normal cycles. It is not the purpose of this paper to explain the technical details of how it is being successfully implemented in a wide variety of climates and soil types around the world. However, a brief overview has been included in Annex 1 to help understand the system. The critical issue for the purpose of this paper is to present the preliminary data on soil carbon sequestration so that the potential of this system can be further investigated.

Research by Jones at Winona, the property of Colin and Nick Seis in New South Wales, Australia, who use a combination of pasture cropping and holistic stock management, shows that 168.5 t/ha of CO_2 was sequestered over 10 years. The sequestration rate for the last two of the 10 years (2009 and 2010) was 33 tons of CO_2/ha/yr (Jones, 2012). This system can be, and is being, successfully used in both arable and pasture systems, including in horticulture. If this was applied around the world, it could potentially sequester 82 Gt of CO_2/yr (4,883,697,000 ha X 16.85 tonnes = 82 Gt).

This is significantly more than the world's GHG emissions of 49 Gt and would help reverse climate change. The increase in soil carbon would also significantly improve the production and adaptation capacities of global grazing systems.

K. The urgent need for more peer-reviewed research

It is not the intention of this paper to use the above types of generic exercises of globally extrapolating data as scientific proof of what can be achieved by scaling up organic systems. These types of very simple analyses are useful for providing a conceptual idea of the considerable potential of organic farming to reduce GHG emissions on a landscape scale. The critical issue here is that urgent peer-reviewed research is needed to understand how and why (and for the sceptics – if) these systems sequester significant levels of CO_2, and then look at how to apply the findings for scaling up on a global level in order to achieve a significant level of GHG mitigation.

The potential of these farming methods is enormous, considering that these data are based on current practices.

L. Permanence

One of the major debates around soil carbon is based on how it can meet the CDM 100-year permanence requirements.

Soil carbon is a complex mix of fractions of various carbon compounds. Two of these, humus and charcoal (char), are very stable: research shows that they can last for thousands of years in the soil. Other fractions are less stable (labile) and can be easily volatilized into CO_2. Soil carbon tends to volatilize into CO_2 in most conventional farming systems. However, correct management systems can continuously increase both the stable and labile fractions through a number of approaches, several of which are discussed later in this paper.

The research conducted by Jones at Winona showed that the majority of the newly increased soil carbon was in the stable fractions. She reported that 78 per cent of the newly sequestered carbon was in the non-labile (humic) fraction of the soil and this rendered it into highly stable long chain forms. Her research found that the carbon levels in the 0-10 cm increment were from the recent decomposition of organic matter and formed short-chain unstable carbon. The carbon below 30 cm was composed of the humic soil fraction and was highly stable (Jones, 2012). Jones's research is consistent with the findings of Christopher, Lal and Mishra, (2009) and Rethemeyer et al. (2005).

Long-term research conducted for more than 100 years at the Rothamsted Research Station in the United Kingdom and the University of Illinois Morrow Plots in the United States showed that the total soil carbon levels could steadily increase and then reach a new stable equilibrium in farming systems that use organic matter inputs. This means that good soil organic matter management systems can increase and maintain the labile fractions as well as the stable fractions over the time periods required by the CDM (Lal, 2007).

M. Adaptation

Even if the world stopped polluting the planet with GHGs, it would take many decades to reverse climate change. This means that farmers have to adapt to the increasing intensity and frequency of adverse and extreme weather events such as droughts and heavy, damaging rainfall. Indeed, many areas of the planet are already experiencing this (Anderson, 2010; Steer, 2011).

N. Greater resilience in adverse conditions

Published studies show that organic farming systems would be more resilient to the predicted weather extremes and could produce higher yields than conventional farming systems in such conditions (Drinkwater, Wagoner and Sarrantonio, 1998; Welsh, 1999; Pimentel et al., 2005; see also the comment of Nemes in this chapter). For instance, the Wisconsin Integrated Cropping Systems Trials found that organic yields were higher in drought years and the same as conventional in normal weather years (Posner, Baldock and Hedtcke, 2008).

Similarly, the Rodale FST showed that the organic systems produced more corn than the conventional system in drought years. The average corn yields during the drought years were 28–34 per cent higher in the two organic systems. The yields were 6,938 and 7,235 kg per ha in the organic animal and the organic legume systems, respectively, compared with 5,333 kg per ha in the conventional system (Pimentel et al., 2005). The researchers attributed the higher yields in the dry years to the ability of the soils on organic farms to better absorb rainfall. This is due to the higher levels of organic carbon in those soils, which makes them more friable and better able to store and capture rainwater, which can then be used for crops (La Salle and Hepperly, 2008).

O. Improved efficiency of water use

Research also shows that organic systems use water more efficiently due to better soil structure and higher levels of humus and other organic matter compounds (Lotter, Seidel and Liebhart, 2003; Pimentel et al., 2005).

Lotter and colleagues collected data for over 10 years during the Rodale FST. Their research showed that the organic manure system and organic legume system (LEG) treatments improve the soils' water-holding capacity, infiltration rate and water capture efficiency. The LEG maize soils averaged a 13 per cent higher water content than conventional system (CNV) soils at the same crop stage, and 7 per cent higher than CNV soils in soybean plots (Lotter, Seidel and Liebhart, 2003).

The more porous structure of organically treated soil allows rainwater to quickly penetrate the soil, resulting in less water loss from run-off and higher levels of water capture. This was particularly evident during the two days of torrential downpours from hurricane Floyd in September 1999, when the organic systems captured around double the amount of water as the conventional systems (Lotter, Seidel and Liebhart, 2003).

P. Critical differences between organic and conventional farming

Organic farming has a range of practices that are regarded as essential for allowing the system to be certified as organic. Most of these practices are easily transferrable to other farming systems, and many of them are now being adopted under the emerging term, "climate smart" agriculture (FAO, 2012c).

Q. The addition of organic matter

The term organic farming is derived from the fact that organic farming systems improve soil health and fertility through the recycling of organic matter. There is a very strong body of evidence which shows that the addition of organic matter improves soil organic carbon (SOC) levels and this is more effective than synthetic, water soluble fertilizers. Lal (2007:822) provides an extensive list from the scientific literature that demonstrates this:

"Application of manures and other organic amendments is another important strategy of SOC sequestration. Several long-term experiments in Europe have shown that the rate of SOC sequestration is greater with application of organic manures than with chemical fertilizers (Jenkinson, 1990; Witter et al., 1993; Christensen, 1996; Korschens & Muller, 1996; Smith et al., 1997). Increase in the SOC pool in the 0–30 cm depth by long-term use of manure compared to chemical fertilizers was 10% over 100

years in Denmark (Christensen, 1996), 22% over 90 years in Germany (Korschens & Muller, 1996), 100% over 144 years at Rothamsted, UK (Jenkinson, 1990) and 44% over 31 years in Sweden (Witter et al., 1993). The data from Morrow plots in Illinois indicated that manured plots contained 44.6Mgha−1 more SOC than unmanured control (Anderson et al., 1990). In Hungary, Arends & Casth (1994) observed an increase in SOC concentration by 1.0–1.7% by manuring. Smith et al. (1997) estimated that application of manure at the rate of 10Mgha−1 to cropland in Europe would increase the SOC pool by 5.5% over 100 years. In Norway, Uhlen (1991) and Uhlen & Tveitnes (1995) reported that manure application would increase SOC sequestration at the rate of 70–227Kgha−1yr−1 over 37-74-year period."

R. Composts' multiple benefits

Composting was pioneered by the organic farming movement through the work of Sir Albert Howard in the 1930s and 1940s, and then strongly promoted by Jerome Rodale in his numerous publications, especially in *Organic Farming and Gardening* that have been widely studied around the world (for more information, see www.rodaleinstitute.org).

There is an increasing body of evidence that composts are superior to raw manures in increasing the level of soil organic matter. The Rodale Institute studies have demonstrated that good organic practices using raw manures and cover crops can sequester 3,596.6 kg of CO_2/ha/yr and that when compost is added this increases to 8,220.8 kg of CO_2/ha/yr (LaSalle and Hepperly, 2008).

S. Avoided emissions

Currently, most of the food and other products from farms are exported from the farm and sent to cities. The disposal of the organic residues in land-fills is responsible for methane emissions. Methane is a significant GHG. Correct composting and bio-digester methods are now recognized as effective ways of avoiding such emissions (for more information on the science of soil methane and soil organic matter, see Annex 2). Research by FiBL shows that more GHGs can be avoided by these methods than by most other farming practices (Gattinger et al., 2011). For example the compost project at Sekem in Egypt has offset methane emissions since January 2007. By using the correct composting methods for organic materials, the project was able to reduce methane emissions by 303,757 tonnes of CO_2e (Helmy Abouleish, personal communication).

Composting the organic wastes in cities and transporting them to the farm brings multiple benefits in closing the nutrient cycle by returning the nutrients that are exported from the farm, avoiding methane emissions and increasing the rate of soil carbon sequestration.

T. Synthetic nitrogen fertilizers degrade soil carbon

One of the main reasons for the differences in soil carbon between organic and conventional systems is that, as research shows, there is a direct link between the application of synthetic nitrogenous fertilizers and a decline in soil carbon.

Scientists at the University of Illinois analysed the results of a 50-year agricultural trial and found that the application of synthetic nitrogen fertilizer had resulted in all the carbon residues from the crop disappearing, as well as an average loss of around 10,000 kg of soil carbon per hectare. This is around 36,700 kg of CO_2 per hectare over and above the many thousands of kilograms of crop residue that is converted into CO_2 every year (Khan et al., 2007; Mulvaney, Khan and Ellsworth, 2009). The researchers found that the higher the application of synthetic nitrogen fertilizer, the greater was the amount of soil carbon lost as CO_2. This is one of the major reasons why there is a decline in soil carbon in conventional agricultural systems and its increase in organic systems.

On the other hand there is a good body of research which shows that using legumes and carbon-based sources such as compost increases the levels of soil organic carbon (LaSalle and Hepperly, 2008).

Researchers from North America and Europe have also shown that organic systems are more efficient in using nitrogen than conventional farming systems. Significantly, because of this efficiency, very little nitrogen leaves the farms as GHGs or as nitrate that pollutes aquatic systems (Drinkwater, Wagoner and Sarrantonio, 1998; Mader et al., 2002).

U. Diverse cropping systems

Another critical aspect of organic production is the use of diverse cropping systems. Certified organic production systems prohibit continuous monocultures in cropping systems. Every certified organic farm needs to have a management plan that outlines its crop (and stock) rotation systems. Lal (2007:822) cites the scientific literature to indicate that this does make a difference:

"Soils under diverse cropping systems generally have a higher SOC pool than those under monoculture (Dick et al. 1986; Buyanoski et al. 1997; Drinkwater et al. 1998; Buyanoski & Wagner 1998). Elimination of summer fallow is another option for minimizing losses of the SOC pool (Delgado et al. 1998; Rasmussen et al. 1998). Growing a winter cover crop enhances soil quality through SOC sequestration. In the UK, Fullen & Auerswald (1998) reported that grass leys set aside increased SOC concentration by 0.02% per year for 12 years. In Australia, Grace & Oades (1994) observed that the SOC pool in the 0–10 cm layer increased linearly with increase in frequency of pasture in the crop rotation cycle. In comparison with continuous cropping, incorporation of cover crops in the rotation cycle enhanced SOC concentration in the surface layer by 15% in Sweden (Nilsson 1986), 23% in The Netherlands (Van Dijk 1982) and 28% in the UK (Johnston 1973) over [a] 12–28-year period. Similar results were reported by Lal et al. (1998) for the US cropland."

V. Erosion and soil loss

The highest percentage of soil carbon is contained in the first 10 cm of soil (Handrek, 1990; Handrek and Black, 2002; Stevenson, 1998). Soil loss and erosion from farming systems is a leading concern around the world (Millennium Ecosystem Assessment, 2005; IAASTD, 2009a). It is a major cause of loss of soil carbon since the highest levels of soil organic matter are in the top layer of the soil.

Comparison studies have shown that organic systems demonstrate less soil loss due to better soil health, and are therefore able to maintain greater soil productivity than conventional farming systems (Reganold, Elliott and Unger, 1987; Reganold et al., 2001; Mader et al., 2002; Pimentel et al., 2005). Reganold, Elliott and Unger compared the effects of organic and conventional farming on particular properties of the same soil over a long period and found, *"...the organically-farmed soil had significantly higher organic matter content, thicker topsoil depth, higher polysaccharide content, lower modulus of rupture and less soil erosion than the conventionally-farmed soil"* (Reganold et al., 1987: 370).

Critics of organic systems point to conventional, no-till production systems as superior to organic systems because the latter use tillage. To our knowledge, there is only one published study comparing conventional, no-till with organic tillage systems. The researchers found that the organic system had better soil quality. According to Teasdale, Coffman and Mangum (2007:1304), "... the OR [organic] system improved soil productivity significantly as measured by corn yields in the uniformity trial ... higher levels of soil C and N were achieved despite the use of tillage (chisel plow and disk) for incorporating manure and of cultivation (low-residue sweep cultivator) for weed control... Our results suggest that systems that incorporate high amounts of organic inputs from manure and cover crops can improve soils more than conventional no-tillage systems despite reliance on a minimum level of tillage."

The latest improvement in organic low/no-till systems developed by the Rodale Institute shows that these systems can deliver high yields as well as excellent environmental outcomes (Rodale, 2006; Moyer, 2011).

W. Soil carbon sequestration can help alleviate poverty

The agreements of the UNFCCC conference in Cancun proposed that hundreds of billions of dollars should be used for funding climate change mitigation activities. FAO believes that 70 per cent of the potential benefits from agricultural mitigation could go to farmers in developing countries (FAO, 2012c).

Schemes that pay farmers for sequestering carbon into the soil, could help alleviate rural poverty and provide a strong financial incentive to adopt good farming practices, if they are done fairly and properly. At an average of 2 tons of CO_2 per hectare at $20 per ton, farmers could earn $40 per hectare per year. While this may not seem like much, for many of the world's farmers working on only a few hectares and earning less than $400 a year, an extra $80 is extremely valuable. On a community scale, it would mean many thousands of dollars going into villages, which would be spent in the local community, creating the multiplier effect of added benefits. Very critically, if this is looked at over the long term, these amounts can become very worthwhile to the farmers. As an example, Sekem has sequestered 3,303 kgs of CO_2 per hectare per year for 30 years. At $20 a ton this is worth a total of $1,980 per hectare for the total time

period (3.3 tons of CO_2 at $20 per ton = $66 /ha/yr).

Based on the results of the Royal Thai Organic Project, Thai farmers could earn $468 per hectare per year for eight years, which amounts to $3,744 per hectare for that time period (23.4 tons of CO_2 at $20 per ton = $468/ha/yr).

If farmers adopted systems similar to the Colin and Nick Seis pasture cropping methods used at Winona, they could earn $337 per hectare per year for 10 years, which totals $3,337 per hectare over that period (6.85 tons of CO_2 at $20 per ton = $337/ha/yr).

The most practical way to ensure smallholder farmers receive funding is for them to be organized into groups. The organic sector already does this with various group certification schemes, such as third-party systems and participatory guarantee systems (PGS). It would be relatively simple to include a soil carbon measurement system in current organic audit systems. Such systems could be grower controlled, and designed to ensure fairness and transparency so that the funds reach the farmers and their communities, rather than benefiting the money market traders.

Implemented properly, these schemes could be seen as social justice systems, where the CO_2-polluting industries would be paying many of the poorest people on the planet for their ecosystem services of sequestering GHGs. For example, 5 billion hectares at $40 per hectare has the potential to redistribute $200 billion from CO_2-polluting industries to rural communities. A significant proportion of this could go to smallholders in developing countries (FAO, 2012c).

Well-designed soil carbon schemes that include soil carbon sequestration have the potential to reduce GHG emissions in the atmosphere as well as alleviate rural poverty in developing countries, and they would provide a substantial financial incentive to adopt good farming practices.

They could be financed through government-administered cap and trade systems. These systems put a cap on the total amount of emissions, and, by taxing emissions that are above the targets, they force the emitters to reach their targets through energy efficiency, the adoption of renewable energy or by other offsets. The cap could be progressively lowered, thereby forcing the industries to continuously find ways to reduce emissions. These taxes could then be used to pay farmers for their ecosystem services of stripping the CO_2 out of the atmosphere and fixing it in the soil. The schemes could be government-administered or market-based.

There have been many concerns expressed about market-based systems, especially those that want to develop complex financial instruments as the trading basis for carbon. The collapse of the price for carbon in market-based systems as well as some schemes where most of the price has gone towards administering the scheme rather than paying the land holders show that there are major problems with these schemes. It is important that most of the funds go to the farmers, rather than to scheme administrators, brokers, carbon traders and other intermediaries. These experiences show the real need for adequate government regulation rather than allowing unregulated carbon markets.

The significant reduction in the price of carbon in 2011-2012 in the government administered European Union scheme shows the need for a realistic government

mandated floor price for carbon to ensure that landholders are adequately compensated for their services of sequestering CO_2 and not subjected to the vagaries of market price fluctuations

One critical issue concerns ownership of the carbon. The carbon should belong to the farmer/landholder, and the payment should be for the service of sequestering it out of the atmosphere and storing it in the soil. The payment is not for the carbon, as this cannot and should not be separated from the soil.

Given the current trends of global GHG emissions and the worst case scenario we seem to follow for global warming it is critical that soil carbon is included in the UNFCCC processes and very importantly that there are mechanisms to financially reward farmers who engage in proven practices such as organic agriculture that sequester CO_2 into the soil.

Annex 1 to Commentary V:

Pasture cropping – annuals in a perennial system

Pasture cropping is where the annual crop is planted in a perennial pasture instead of in a ploghed field. This was first developed by Colin Seis in Australia. The principle is based on a sound ecological fact, namely that annual plants grow in perennial systems. The key is to adapt this principle to the appropriate management system for the specific cash crops and climate.

In Colin's system, the pasture is first grazed using holistic management to ensure that it is very short. This adds organic matter in the form of manure, cut grass and shed roots, and significantly reduces the competition from the pasture when the cash crop is seeded and germinates. The crop is directly planted in the pasture.

According the Colin Seis: "*It was also learnt that sowing a crop in this manner stimulated perennial grass seedlings to grow in numbers and diversity giving considerably more tones/hectare of plant growth. This produces more stock feed after the crop is harvested and totally eliminates the need to re-sow pastures into*

the cropped areas. Cropping methods used in the past require that all vegetation is killed prior to sowing the crop and while the crop is growing."

"*From a farm economic point of view the potential for good profit is excellent because the cost of growing crops in this manner is a fraction of conventional cropping. The added benefit in a mixed farm situation is that up to six months extra grazing is achieved with*

this method compared with the loss of grazing due to ground preparation and weed control required in traditional cropping methods. As a general rule, an underlining principle of the success of this method is 'One hundred percent ground cover one hundred percent of the time'."

"...a 20 Ha crop of Echidna oats that was sown and harvested in 2003 on ..."Winona". This crop's yield was 4.3 tonne/Ha (31 bags/acre). This yield is at least equal to the district average where full ground disturbance cropping methods were used." This profit does not include the value of the extra grazing. On Winona, it is between $50 [and] $60/ha because the pasture is grazed up to the point of sowing. When using traditional cropping practices where ground preparation and weed control methods are utilised for periods of up to four to six months before the crop is sown then no quality grazing can be achieved.

"Other benefits are more difficult to quantify. These are the vast improvement in perennial plant numbers and diversity of the pasture following the crop. This means that there is no need to re-sow pastures, which can cost in excess of $150 per hectare and considerably more should contractors be used for pasture establishment."

Independent studies at Winona on pasture cropping by [the] Department of Land and Water have found that pasture cropping is 27% more profitable than conventional agriculture [and] this is coupled with great environment benefits that will improve the soil and regenerate our landscapes."

Building soil fertility without synthetic fertilizers

Christine Jones has conducted research at Colin Sies's property which shows that in the last 10 years 168.5 t/ha of CO_2 was sequestered:
- The sequestration rate in the last two years (2008–2010) has been 33 tons of CO_2 per hectare per year.

Comparison of soil between
Winona and neighbour

In this paired site comparison, parent material, slope, aspect, rainfall and farming enterprises are the same. Levels of soil carbon in both paddocks were originally the same.
LHS: 0–50 cm soil profile from a paddock in which groundcover has been actively managed (cropped and grazed) to enhance photosynthetic capacity.
RHS: 0–50 cm soil profile from a conventionally managed neighbouring paddock (10 metres through the fence) that has been set-stocked and has a long history of phosphate application.

Notes:
i) The carbon levels in the 0–10 cm increment are very similar. This surface carbon results from the decomposition of organic matter (leaves, roots, manure etc), forming short-chain unstable 'labile' carbon.
ii) The carbon below 30 cm in the LHS profile has rapidly incorporated into the humic (non-labile) soil fraction. Long-chain, non-labile carbon is highly stable.

(Jones, 2012)

- This increase occurred during the worst drought in recorded Australian history.
- The following increases in soil mineral fertility have occurred in 10 years with only the addition of a small amount of phosphorus: calcium 277 per cent, magnesium 138 per cent, potassium 146 per cent, sulphur 157 per cent, phosphorus 151 per cent , zinc 186 per cent, iron 122 per cent, copper

202 per cent, boron 156 per cent, molybdenum 151 per cent, cobalt 179 per cent and selenium 117 per cent (Jones, 2012).

For more information on:
- Pasture cropping, see: http://www.winona.net.au/farming.html.
- Holistic management, see: http://holisticmanagement.org.

Annex 2 to Commentary V:

Methane: Soil management can reduce atmospheric methane

The science on soil methane and soil organic matter is still in its infancy, with many unanswered questions due to the lack of research. However, a recent meta study by van Groenigen, Osenberg and Hungate (2011) has shown that methane output from the soil will increase as the climate warms, which raises concerns that the percentages of GHGs that are sequestered in forestry systems are overestimated.

The methane model used by van Groenigen et al. measured what was volatilized, but not the amount of the methane that was biodegraded in the soil. Methane is produced and degraded as a natural cycle in nature, and most of this degradation takes place in biologically active soils and in the oceans by methanotrophic microbes.

Historically, apart from a few exceptional events during geological time periods, the amount of methane in the atmosphere from the enormous herds of grazing animals on the prairies, savannahs and steppes, and from the decay of organic matter in the vast forests and wetlands of the planet was relatively stable until human activities over the last 200 years disrupted the natural cycles of methane production and degradation (Heimann, 2011; Murat et al., 2011).

Studies by Hellebrand and Herppich (2000) and Levine et al. (2011) showed that a significant amount of methane is biodegraded in soils, and that this has been underestimated due to a lack of research. While the van Groenigen et al. study shows an increase in methane output from soils when the temperature

increases, the Hellebrand and Herppich studies show that the increase in temperature will drive up the rate of biological degradation of methane by methylotropic bacteria and other methanotrophic microorganisms. This explains why historical atmospheric methane levels have been relatively stable, and also why naturally produced methane levels may not increase as the climate gets warmer.

Many studies of methane production only calculate the methane produced by the systems as a one-way output into the atmosphere. This can be correct for some production systems, such as confined animal feed lots and garbage sent to land fill; however, it is not correct for most natural productions systems, such as animal grazing on grasslands, crop production on biologically active soils, orchards and forests, as these systems are based on cycles that also degrade methane. This oversight of the amount of methane that can be biodegraded by the soil or the oceans is a major flaw that needs to be rectified.

Until the decay cycles are properly identified, measured and modelled, the amounts of methane that are emitted by systems are not an accurate measure of methane's contribution to total GHGs. Understanding these cycles and the biological conditions needed to biodegrade methane will give scientists and landholders a major tool to manage one of the most important GHGs.

The need for good soil management practices

A study by Fuu Ming Kai et al. (2011) suggests that the recent reductions in methane output are due to changes in farming practices. This study adds to the data showing that there is good evidence of the potential to reduce the amount of methane in the atmosphere through the following soil management practices as described below:

1. *Avoiding anaerobic soil conditions*. Methane forms in anaerobic conditions such as rice paddies. New methods, such as the system of rice intensification (SRI), use more frequent, shorter watering cycles that avoid anaerobic conditions, thereby significantly reducing methane production.

2. *Open well-aerated soils*. Organic matter can volatilize into CO_2, methane and other gases in farming systems. However, correct management systems can continuously increase the proportion of the non-volatile compounds and form stable fractions of soil organic matter. The research conducted by Jones at Winona showed that the majority of the newly increased soil carbon was in the stable fractions; 78% of the newly sequestered carbon was in the non-labile (humic) fraction of the soil, rendering it highly stable.

3. *Promoting biologically active soils with high levels of methanothropic microbes*. The research by Levine et al. (2011) found that the key to methane degradation is land management practices that achieve high levels of diversity of methanothropic microbes.

Research needs to be conducted into all of these areas to accurately establish the best practices. This must be based on criteria that are measurable, replicable and easily adopted by land managers.

Commentary VI: Agroecology: A Solution to the Crises of Food Systems and Climate Change

Olivier de Schutter
UN Special Rapporteur on the Right to Food

Abstract

The food price hikes of 2008 and 2011–2012 were partly the result of weather-related events linked to climate change, and partly due to the dependence of food production on fossil energies that caused a merger between food and energy markets (on this issue, see also the comment by Rundgren in this chapter) as well as the financialization of food markets. The current efforts to reinvest in agriculture should take into account the need to improve the resilience of food systems so as to reduce their vulnerability to extreme weather events and to the increasingly volatile prices of non-renewable fossil energies. This article explores how agroecology, understood as the application of the science of ecology to agricultural systems, can result in modes of production that are not only more resilient, but also both highly productive and sustainable, enabling them to contribute to the alleviation of rural poverty, and thus, to the realization of the right to food.

A. Reinvesting in agriculture

The food price spikes of 2008 and 2011–2012 prompted governments to start reinvesting in agriculture, a sector that has been neglected in many developing countries for the past 30 years. However, investments that increase food production will not make significant progress in combating hunger and malnutrition if they do not lead to higher incomes and improved livelihoods for the poorest – particularly small-scale farmers in developing countries. And short-term gains will be offset by long-term losses if they cause further degradation of ecosystems, thus threatening the ability to maintain current levels of production in the future. The question, therefore, is not simply *how much*, but also *how* the investments are made. Pouring money into agriculture will not be sufficient; the imperative today is to take steps that facilitate the transition towards a low-carbon, resource-conserving type of agriculture that benefits the poorest farmers.

Agroecology can play a central role in achieving this goal (De Schutter, 2010a; De Schutter and Vanloqueren, 2011). It is possible to significantly improve agricultural productivity where it has been lagging behind, and thus to increase production where it needs most to be increased (i.e. primarily in poor, food-deficient countries), while at the same time improving the livelihoods of smallholder farmers

and conserving ecosystems. This would also slow the trend towards increasing urbanization in the countries concerned, which is placing stress on their public services. Moreover, it would contribute to rural development and preserve the ability of succeeding generations to meet their own needs. In addition, the resulting higher incomes in the rural areas would contribute to the growth of other sectors of the economy by stimulating demand for non-agricultural products (Adelman, 1984).

B. The diagnosis

Since the global food crises, most of the focus has been on increasing overall production using methods consistent with classic Green Revolution approaches. The crises have been attributed to a mismatch between supply and demand, reflecting a gap between slower productivity growth and increasing needs. A widely cited estimate is that, taking into account demographic growth as well as changes in the composition of diets and consumption levels associated with growing urbanization and higher household incomes, the overall increase in agricultural production should reach 70 per cent by 2050 (Burney et al., 2010).

However, apart from the fact that this estimate takes the current demand curves as given and does not consider the leakages and waste in the current food systems (UNEP, 2009), the focus on increasing production may not adequately consider the fact that hunger today is not so much a consequence of stocks being too low or to global supplies being unable to meet demand; rather it is due to poverty. It is their lack of purchasing power that makes it difficult for the poorest segments of the population, including marginal small-scale farmers who are often net-food buyers, to withstand economic shocks such as those that result from sudden increases in the prices of basic food commodities. Increasing the incomes of the poorest is therefore the best way to combat hunger. Investment in agriculture is needed, but it should not only foster production to meet growing needs; it should also reduce rural poverty by boosting the incomes of small-scale farmers. Only by supporting small producers will it be possible to help break the vicious cycle that leads from rural poverty to the expansion of urban slums, in which poverty breeds more poverty.

In addition, agriculture must not compromise on its ability to satisfy future needs. The loss of biodiversity (Esquinas-Alcázar, 2005; Swanson, 2005), the unsustainable use of water, as well as the degradation and pollution of soils and water, undermine the continuing ability of the earth's natural resources to support agriculture. Climate change, which translates into more frequent and extreme weather events, such as droughts and floods, and less predictable rainfall, is already severely affecting the ability of certain regions and communities to feed themselves, and it is destabilizing markets. The change in average temperatures is threatening the ability of entire regions, particularly those where rain-fed agriculture is practiced, to maintain their existing levels of agricultural production (Stern, 2007; IPCC, 2007b). Less fresh water will be available for agricultural production, and the rise in sea levels is already causing the salinization of water in certain coastal areas, rendering that water unsuitable for irrigation purposes.

As is well known, current agricultural practices are exacerbating this situation in a number of ways. For instance, deforestation to enable the expansion of cultivated areas, represents a major source of carbon dioxide (CO_2) emissions (accounting for 17 per cent of total anthropogenic GHG emissions), while methane (CH_4) emissions result from rice paddies and livestock digestion (accounting for 14.3 per cent of emissions). Another GHG emission is nitrous oxide (N_2O), which is produced in particular through the Haber-Bosch process of fabricating nitrogen-based fertilizers (accounting for another 7.2 per cent) (Allen et al., 2009; Meinhausen et al., 2009).

Agroecology is increasingly seen as one way to address these considerable challenges. A wide range of experts within the scientific community and international agencies such as the FAO and Bioversity International (2007), and UNEP (2005) view it as a way to improve the resilience and sustainability of food systems (IAASTD, 2009a; Wezel et al., 2009a). It is also gaining ground in countries as diverse as Brazil, France, Germany and the United States (Wezel et al., 2009).

C. Agroecology: mimicking nature

Agroecology has been defined as the "application of ecological science to the study, design and management of sustainable agroecosystems" (Altieri, 1995; Gliessman, 2007). It seeks to improve agricultural systems by mimicking or augmenting natural processes, thus enhancing beneficial biological interactions and synergies among the components of agrobiodiversity (Altieri, 2002). Common principles of agroecology include recycling nutrients and energy on farms, rather than augmenting nutrients with external inputs; integrating crops and livestock; diversifying species and genetic resources in the agroecosystems over time and space, from the field to landscape levels; and improving interactions and productivity throughout the agricultural system, rather than focusing on individual species. Agroecology is highly knowledge-intensive, based on techniques that are not delivered top-down but developed on the basis of farmers' knowledge and experimentation.[33] Its practices require diversifying the tasks on the farm and linking them to the diversity of species (including animals) that interact at field level.

A variety of techniques have been developed and successfully tested in a range of regions that are based on this approach (Pretty, 2008). *Integrated nutrient management* reconciles the need to fix nitrogen in the soil by importing inorganic and organic sources of nutrients and reducing nutrient losses through erosion control. Thus it also builds up soil organic matter, which enhances soil fertility and can bind significant amounts of carbon in the soil (see commentary of Leu on this issue in this chapter). *Agroforestry* incorporates multifunctional trees into agricultural systems. *Water harvesting* in dryland areas enables the cultivation of formerly abandoned and degraded lands, and improves the water productivity of crops. The *integration of livestock into farming systems*, such as dairy cattle, pigs and poultry, including using zero-grazing cut and carry practices, provides a source of protein to families while also fertilizing soils. The incorporation of fish, shrimps and other aquatic resources into farm systems, such as into irrigated rice fields and fish ponds, provides similar benefits. These approaches involve the maintenance or introduction of agricultural biodiversity as a result of the integration of diverse crops, livestock, agroforestry, fish, pollinators, insects, soil biota and other components.

Such resource-conserving, low-external-input techniques have a huge, yet still largely untapped, potential to address the combined challenges of production, combating rural poverty and contributing to rural development, while also preserving ecosystems and mitigating climate change.

1. Agroecology as a response to supply constraints

Agroecological techniques have a proven potential to significantly improve yields. Pretty et al. (2006) compared the impacts of 286 recent sustainable agriculture projects in 57 developing countries covering 37 million ha (representing 3 per cent of their cultivated area). They found that the interventions increased crop productivity on 12.6 million farms by an average of 79 per cent, while also improving the supply of critical environmental services.[34] A large-scale study by Foresight (2011a) on Global Food and Farming Futures, commissioned by the Government of the United Kingdom, which reviewed 40 projects in 20 African countries where sustainable intensification was developed during the 2000s, reached similar conclusions.[35]

2. The potential of agroecology to increase the incomes of small-scale farmers

One advantage of agroecology is its reliance on locally produced inputs. Many African soils are nutrient-poor and heavily degraded, and therefore need replenishment. Adding nutrients to the soil can be done by applying not only mineral fertilizers, but also livestock manure or by growing green manures. Farmers can also establish what has been called a "fertilizer factory in the fields" by planting trees that take nitrogen out of the air and "fix" it in their leaves, which are subsequently incorporated into the soil (World Agroforestry Centre, 2009). Agroecology

reduces the dependence of farmers on access to external inputs – and thus on subsidies – and on local retailers of fertilizers or pesticides as well as on local moneylenders. Diversified farming systems produce their own fertilizers and pest control systems, thus reducing the need for pesticides (De Schutter, 2004). The local availability of adapted seeds, planting materials and livestock breeds also offers multiple advantages, both for the farmer and for ensuring the supply of the required diversity of such materials for major crops such as maize, rice, millet, sorghum, potato and cassava (De Schutter, 2009a). This is particularly beneficial to small-scale farmers – especially women – who have low or no access to credit, and also lack capital and access to fertilizer distribution systems, particularly since the private sector is unlikely to invest in the most remote areas where communication routes are poor and where few economies of scale can be achieved.

3. Agroecology's contribution to rural development and to other sectors of the economy

Agroecology contributes to rural development because it is relatively labour-intensive and is most effectively practiced on relatively small plots of land. The initial period is particularly labour-intensive because of the complexity of the tasks of managing different plants and animals on the farm and of recycling the waste produced, but this higher labour intensity of agroecology diminishes significantly in the longer term (Ajayi et al., 2009).[36] And although it is seen by many as a liability of sustainable farming, especially where governments give priority to labour-saving measures, the creation of employment in the rural areas in developing countries may in fact constitute an advantage if linked to productivity gains. Indeed, it could present an enormous advantage in the context of massive underemployment and high demographic growth in many developing countries. It would also respond to the urgent need to slow down rural-urban migration, as activities in the services sector in the urban areas appear unable to absorb the excess labour. Growth in agriculture can be especially beneficial to other sectors of the economy if it is broad-based and increases the incomes of a large number of farming households, rather than leading to a further concentration of incomes in the hands of a few relatively large landowners who rely on large-scale, heavily mechanized plantations (Adelman, 1984).

4. Agroecology's contribution to improving nutrition

The approaches espoused by the Green Revolution in the past focused primarily on boosting the production of cereal crops – rice, wheat and maize – in order to prevent famines. However, these crops are mainly a source of carbohydrates and contain relatively few proteins and the other nutrients essential for adequate diets. Yet, of the over 80,000 plant species available to humans, these three crops supply the bulk of our protein and energy needs today (Frison et al., 2006). The shift from diversified cropping systems to simplified cereal-based systems has thus contributed to micronutrient malnutrition in many developing countries (Demment et al., 2003). As a result, nutritionists now increasingly insist on the need for more varied agroecosystems, in order to ensure a more diversified nutrient output from farming systems (Alloway, 2008; DeClerck et al., 2011). The diversity of species on farms managed following agroecological principles, as well as in urban or peri-urban agriculture, is an important asset in this regard.

5. Agroecology and climate change

Agroecology can support the provision of a number of services to ecosystems, including by providing a habitat for wild plants, supporting genetic diversity and pollination, and water supply and regulation. It also strengthens resilience to climate change which is causing more extreme weather-related events. Resilience is strengthened by the use and promotion of agricultural biodiversity at ecosystem, farm system and field levels, made possible by many agroecological approaches (Platform for Agrobiodiversity Research, 2010). Agroecology also puts agriculture on the path of sustainability by delinking food production from a reliance on fossil energy (oil and gas). In addition, it contributes to mitigating climate change, both by increasing carbon sinks in soil organic matter and above-ground biomass, and by reducing CO_2 and other GHG emissions through lower direct and indirect energy use.

D. Scaling up agroecology

There is a clear and urgent need for a reorientation of agricultural development towards systems that use fewer external inputs linked to fossil energies, and instead use plants, trees and animals in combination, mimicking nature instead of industrial processes at the field level. However, the success of such a reorientation will depend on the ability to learn faster from recent innovations and to disseminate what works more widely. Governments have a key role to play in this regard. Encouraging a shift towards sustainable agriculture implies transition costs, since farmers must learn new techniques and revitalize traditional and local knowledge, moving away from the current systems that are both more specialized and less adaptive, and have a lower innovation capacity (Pretty, 2008). In order to succeed in implementing such a transition, the spread of agroecology should be directed at the farmers themselves, who will be its main beneficiaries. Thus farmer-to-farmer learning in farmer field schools or through farmers' movements should be encouraged, as in the Campesino-a-Campesino movement in Central America and Cuba (Degrande et al., 2006; Holt-Giménez, 2006; Rosset et al., 2011).

An improved dissemination of knowledge by horizontal farmer-to-farmer means transforms the nature of knowledge itself, which becomes the product of a network (Warner and Kirschenmann, 2007). It should encourage farmers, particularly small-scale farmers living in the most remote areas and those eking out a living from the most marginal soils, to work with experts towards a co-construction of knowledge, ensuring that advances and innovative solutions will benefit them as a matter of priority, rather than only benefiting the better-off producers (Uphoff, 2002a).

This is key to the realization of the right to food. First, it enables public authorities to benefit from the experiences and insights of the farmers. Rather than treating smallholder farmers as beneficiaries of aid, they should be seen as experts who have knowledge that is complementary to formalized expertise. Second, participation can ensure that policies and programmes are truly responsive to the needs of vulnerable groups, as those groups will question projects that fail to improve their situation. Third, participation empowers the poor – a vital step towards poverty alleviation, because lack of power is a source of poverty, as marginal communities often receive less support than the groups that have better connections with government. Moreover, poverty exacerbates this lack of power, creating a vicious circle of further disempowerment. Fourth, policies that are co-designed with farmers have greater legitimacy, and thus favour better planning of investment and production and better uptake by other farmers (FAO and IIED, 2008). Participation of food-insecure groups in the policies that affect them should become a crucial element of all food security policies, from policy design to the assessment of results to the decision on research priorities. Indeed, improving the situation of millions of food-insecure smallholder farmers cannot be done without them.

Commentary VII: Promoting Resilient Agriculture in Sub-Saharan Africa as a Major Priority in Climate-Change Adaptation

Marcus Kaplan, Chinwe Ifejika-Speranza, and Imme Scholz
German Development Institute

Abstract

- Policies to promote adaptation to climate change in sub-Saharan Africa, while also helping to alleviate poverty, will require multiple investments in rural areas to raise agricultural productivity and improve economic infrastructure and social services as priorities.

- Increased investment in agriculture should take into account its multiple social, economic and environmental functions in order to achieve poverty reduction and food security, and improve the resilience of rural livelihoods to multiple shocks, including climate change.

- Scenarios of the local impacts of climate change should include extreme weather and climate conditions (i.e. with regard to temperature or variability of rainfall) in order to be prepared for the effects of dangerous climate change (i.e. more frequent and intensive droughts and floods) that, in the worst case, could force local populations to permanently move out of affected areas.

A. Challenges facing agriculture in sub-Saharan Africa

Agricultural production in sub-Saharan Africa (SSA), and therefore also livelihoods that depend on agriculture, will be severely affected by the impacts of climate change. Depending on their geographical location, various subregions are likely to experience either less or more rainfall, rising temperatures, and a higher number and intensity of extreme weather events. Generally, yields will decline, although tolerance of different crops to temperature changes and water availability will vary considerably (Lobell et al., 2008; Liu et al., 2008). While the major trends are clear, considerable uncertainties remain (Müller, 2009). For example, for a number of areas in Western Africa some global circulation models expect increases in precipitation, while others project less rainfall for the coming decades. Despite this uncertainty, agriculture throughout Africa faces a serious risk of experiencing negative impacts from climate change (Müller et al., 2011b). Under such circumstances, it will be particularly challenging for poor farmers to prepare for the upcoming changes. It is therefore advisable to focus not only on direct measures to support adaptation of agricultural activities to the impacts of climate change,

but also to take a broader view and aim to increase the overall resilience of rural people and their livelihoods.

Most poor people in developing countries live in rural areas (The World Bank, 2008), many of whom depend on agricultural activities for two purposes: first to ensure food security for their families, and second, for income generation, as agriculture is often their main or even only economic activity. Both aspects also have implications for other, non-farm rural households, either through the degree of availability of food, which can cause fluctuations in local prices, or as an indirect source of employment.

In many rural areas of SSA, agriculture faces various well-known challenges, which constrain the social and economic development of the sector and of the people who depend on it. The fundamental constraints include insecure access of local producers to land, unskilled agricultural manpower for innovative agricultural production systems, limited access to agricultural inputs, as well as limited knowledge of how the local climate (e.g. homogeneous rainfall zones that extend over villages) is changing and is expected to change in the future. These constraints result in lower productivity (Bruinsma, 2009; Rosegrant et al., 2001) and the prevalence of unsustainable agricultural practices, with negative ecological impacts. Water stress and scarcity are increasing, while biodiversity is declining. Soil degradation and declining fertility through, for example, inappropriate soil management and low inputs, create serious problems for current and future agricultural productivity in many parts of SSA (McIntyre et al. 2009a; Vlek, Le and Tamene, 2008). Furthermore, low-output agriculture necessitates the use of more land to maintain its level of production, which is why agriculture is the main driver of deforestation in nearly all developing countries (Scherr and Sthapit, 2009). Such land-use changes for food production cause CO_2 emissions through the release of carbon from above-ground biomass and grazing livestock, reduced carbon sequestration in soils and unsustainable agricultural practices (Scherr and Sthapit, 2009). As a result, land-use changes (including deforestation) account for about 17 per cent of total anthropogenic GHG emissions (Smith et al., 2007b), while biomass burning and the conversion of wetlands contribute to methane (CH_4) emissions, and the application of fertilizers results in nitrous oxide emissions (UNFCCC, 2008).

Today, new global patterns create additional challenges that further aggravate these known constraints on a productive and sustainable agricultural sector in SSA. In addition to economic trends, such as greater international competition for land for various uses, fluctuating food prices, higher energy prices, and international trade policies, climate change seriously threatens the productivity of the agricultural sector and its contribution to economic and social development. The poorer people who depend directly on ecosystem services for their livelihoods are the most vulnerable to permanent changes in temperature and water availability, as well as to an overall higher variability in climatic patterns. They not only have less access to various types of resources, but they also have fewer opportunities for diversifying their livelihoods to include other income-generating activities in order to reduce their dependence on agriculture and other ecosystem services.

One of the main reasons for the poor situation and the high vulnerability of farmers and agriculture in SSA is the long-term neglect of this sector by both national governments and the international donor community starting in the 1980s. Public spending on farming accounts for only 4 per cent of total government spending in SSA (World Bank, 2008), and the agricultural sector is taxed at a relatively high

level. In addition, the share of the agricultural sector in official development assistance (ODA) declined from 18 per cent in 1979 to 3.5 per cent in 2004 (World Bank, 2008). Today, the importance of agriculture for economic growth has generally been recognized, and national, regional and international organizations are making greater efforts to support its development (Challinor et al., 2007; Hazell et al., 2007). In their Maputo Declaration of 2003, member countries of the African Union called upon African governments to increase investment in the agricultural sector to at least 10 per cent of their national budgets. However, most African countries are still far from reaching this target. Moreover, even though the sector is now receiving more attention, owing to the long period of neglect, the many challenges ahead will be difficult to overcome.

Furthermore, most public transfers are largely aimed at mitigating climate change rather than supporting adaptation to its impacts: 79 per cent of dedicated multi- and bilateral funds were approved for mitigation projects (84 per cent if activities for reducing emissions from deforestation and forest degradation (REDD) are included), and only 14 per cent for adaptation projects.[37] Bilateral ODA shows a slightly different pattern, with 70 per cent approved for mitigation and 30 per cent for adaptation (UNEP, 2010). Moreover, most activities and funds focus on reducing emissions and increasing efficiency in the energy and transport sectors, while adaptation and mitigation in agriculture are still underfunded. Looking at bilateral ODA again, agriculture received only 1 per cent of all funds dedicated to mitigation, compared with 10 per cent for adaptation activities in 2009 (UNEP, 2010).

B. Options for multifunctional agriculture and resilient livelihoods

The various constraints on African agriculture as outlined above call for multifunctional approaches that increase the resilience of agricultural systems and livelihoods to the impacts of external disturbances, including climate change. Such agricultural management should aim to contribute to food security and to support economic and social development for all stakeholders, while at the same time minimizing negative impacts on ecosystems. Taking into account the large contribution of the agricultural sector to global greenhouse gas (GHG) emissions, a comprehensive approach should also strive to avoid management practices that increase emissions. Indeed, there are various approaches that may even contribute to reducing agricultural GHG emissions if implemented properly.

Due to the currently low productivity of agriculture in SSA, there is a large potential for improvements towards resilient and multifunctional practices. Most of these sustainable management practices were already well known before the impacts of climate change increased the urgency of their implementation. In their most comprehensive form, integrated approaches also take into account impacts of agricultural and land-use management on local livelihoods, social equity and inclusion, and are part of wider integrated natural resources management (IAASTD, 2009b). Integrated systems do not require a single, strictly defined technology; rather they require a set of varying practices adapted to local biophysical and socio-economic conditions. All these approaches have one feature in common: they seek to depend less on external inputs. Instead, they rather manage the complex dynamics and interactions between different components of agroecosystems and adjoining ecosystems by mimicking nature and by relying on technologies and inputs that are available within the system (De Schutter, 2011; Buck and Scherr, 2011). Integrated systems support adaptation to climate change by strengthening the resilience of the agroecosystem to any disturbances, by increasing the degree of diversification and improving the provision of environmental services. At the same time, their low use of fertilizers and other external inputs can reduce adverse impacts on ecosystem components and result in lower emissions from the production and transport process. Instead of relying on large quantities of external material inputs, farmers' knowledge is the major resource, and key to the appropriate application of inputs and to the successful implementation of new management practices.

It is still uncertain whether multifunctional and integrated management practices can ensure food security and whether they are competitive with conventional, high-input agricultural systems with regard to productivity. While these aspects are still the subject of ongoing discussions (Badgley et al., 2007; Connor, 2008, Gianessi, 2009; Pimentel et al., 2005), there is some evidence that, compared with high-yielding systems in developed countries, organic agriculture and other types of integrated approaches result in lower yields (Badgley et al., 2007; Connor,

2008). However, in many regions in SSA, low-input systems prevail, some of which can be regarded as organic systems, as they use few, if any, external inputs that are either not accessible or are too expensive. In such systems, a complete shift to integrated and adequately managed systems may increase yields (Badgley et al., 2007; Pretty, 2008; UNEP-UNCTAD, 2008). (For a more detailed discussion of the productivity and profitability of organic agriculture, see the commentary of Nemes in this chapter.)

The African continent still faces the highest population growth rates in the world (FAO, 2006; Binswanger-Mkhize, 2009). This, along with current deficiencies in food security and possible future changes in diets, reinforces the urgency to increase agricultural production. Whether this objective should be mainly pursued by either intensifying production on existing agricultural land or by expanding agricultural land to previously unused areas, is currently an issue of debate. Even in a land-rich continent such as Africa, the amount of land suitable for agricultural purposes is declining rapidly (figure 10), and the conversion of other land uses (particularly forests) for agricultural purposes produces additional CO_2 emissions (figure 11). Moreover, land conversion may jeopardize the livelihoods of people who generate ecosystem services from the former land uses (for a more elaborate discussion, see the comments of Pimentel and GRAIN in this chapter).

Intensification, on the other hand, may either be implemented through integrated agroecological approaches, as outlined above, or through larger scale conventional agriculture, which may increase pressure on natural resources and which also runs the risk of leaving smallholders behind. The process of intensifying production on existing agricultural land needs improvements in agricultural management and/or additional inputs, particularly either mineral or organic fertilizers. However, intensifying production requires access to these inputs (which currently remain unaffordable to local farmers) and to knowledge and information in order to implement new management practices in an appropriate way. Otherwise, additional inputs may result in higher emissions of nitrous oxide and carbon dioxide.

However, even if governments and the international community were to pay greater attention to the agricultural sector, it is likely that in some areas agriculture will become extremely difficult or will no longer be viable due to climate change and

Figure 10: Land for agricultural use, 1960–2010 (ha per capita)

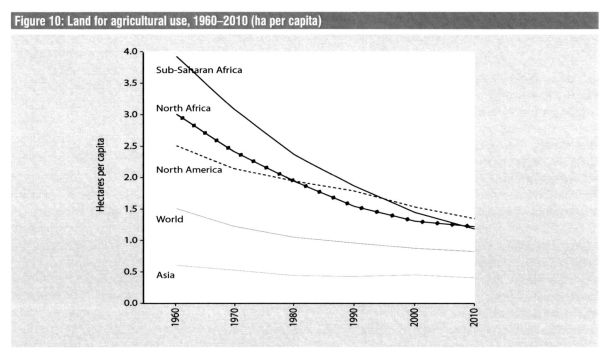

Source: Based on FAOSTAT.

Figure 11: CO$_2$ emissions from land-use change in selected developing regions, 1850–2009

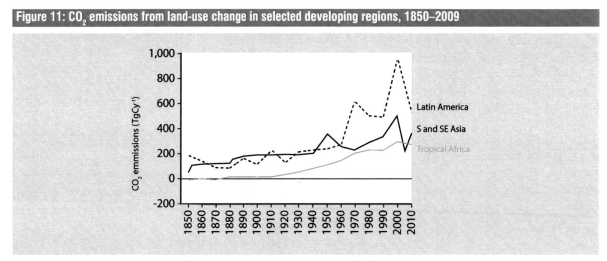

Source: Global Carbon Project, 2010.

environmental degradation (e.g., Fischer et al., 2005). In those instances, adaptation strategies should be adopted that aim to diversify the livelihoods of rural households. Diversification in farming relates to risk spreading through various agricultural practices (such as agroforestry) or mixed crop-livestock systems (that rely on a larger number of different crops and/ or livestock products) to reduce the threat of crop failure in case of unfavourable climatic conditions. Income diversification into non-farm activities reduces the direct dependence on ecosystem services, and

can often generate higher incomes than agricultural activities. This supplementary income can again be used for additional investments in agricultural activities, which in turn could increase income generation from farming (Ellis and Freeman, 2004). Other aspects, such as improvement of education in rural areas (Jayne, Mather and Mghenyi, 2010) or better infrastructure, may also contribute to increasing the resilience of rural livelihoods without being directly related to agriculture.

C. Increasing the resilience of agricultural systems

Domestic and external interventions to develop and strengthen agriculture will have to overcome the fundamental constraints on agricultural development in SSA, such as lack of access to land, agricultural inputs as well as knowledge and information, noted above. If these constraints are not addressed, adaptation to climate change will only be dealing with the symptoms of low adaptive capacity, high vulnerability and low resilience. The constraints are jeopardizing agricultural production at a time when the impacts of climate change can already be observed. Thus there is no time left to allow a sequence of first addressing the fundamental issues before responding to climate change. Rather, all current challenges have to be tackled through an integrated effort, together with appropriate measures to support adaptation and increase the overall resilience of agricultural systems and rural livelihoods.

Specific options for domestic action and external support for those actions are discussed below.

1. Providing access to land

Proper land reform, land registration and secure land-tenure rights for women and men need to be guaranteed to enable investment in sustainable farming practices, the benefits of which often accrue only in the long term. Recently, increased foreign direct investment in land has received much attention in Africa as it contributes – at least in some countries – to compromising traditional land use rights (for a more elaborate analysis, see the comment of Mittal in chapter 4). For these reasons, international guidelines for managing the impacts on local land tenure of large (foreign) investments in land are needed. The recent successful conclusion of intergovernmental negotiations on *Voluntary Guidelines on the Responsible Governance of Tenure of Land, Fisheries and Forests* (FAO, 2011) led by the Committee on World Food Security (CFS) and the report of the High Level Panel of Experts of the CFS (FAO, 2011c) marks a starting point. It is vital that national governments follow these guidelines, review their land laws and incorporate checks and balances to ensure that the investments improve rural development, are pro-poor and do not jeopardize adaptive capacities.

Investment impact assessments are another helpful instrument. They should be carried out prior to a land investment, and need to analyse: (i) whether and how much an investment in land hinders local people's access to resources that they already use or are likely to use in the future as an adaptation option, and (ii) how much the investment is contributing to employment and human capacity-building. Investment impact assessments should be carried out by an agricultural sector coordination unit that includes the finance and justice ministries, and the activities of these units should be informed by information gathered by domestic and international non-governmental organizations (NGOs) when monitoring such investments. While foreign investment is not the only factor hindering access to land, such investment should nevertheless be assessed urgently, as it might further hamper access to land for smallholder farmers and other vulnerable actors. This is because the competition for land is between actors of unequal power. Countries such as Kenya are already focusing on how to improve access to land through a new constitution that ensures equal access to land by men and women. In addition, population pressure and the ensuing land fragmentation could be addressed by strategically developing the skills of populations to allow them to move out of agriculture.

2. Ensuring skilled agricultural manpower for innovative agricultural production systems

Currently low productivity levels of agriculture in SSA already indicate that skill deficits and changes in natural parameters will render age-long indigenous knowledge built from one generation to another inadequate. Farmers need knowledge and information on new climatic parameters in order to implement innovative production systems that are more resilient and at the same time more productive. The dissemination of existing indigenous practices from other climatic regions could also facilitate adaptation to new climatic parameters. Adaptation will need to be oriented towards making more effective use of the natural endowments of farms. This includes, for example, enhancing soil fertility by building up soil organic matter through recycling of biomass and composting, which will significantly improve soil resilience and its water retention capacity. It also includes the use of biomass and organic waste for (off-grid) energy generation.

The need for innovation offers opportunities for public-private partnerships in adaptation to climate change, as the following two examples show. First, innovative information and communication technologies (ICTs), such as short message services on mobile phones (SMS) are currently being used in SSA to disseminate market information and transfer money (Aker and Mbiti, 2010; Jack and Suri, 2011). Communication enterprises, in collaboration with universities, extension services, NGOs and other partners, could develop information services to which farmers could subscribe. Most households in rural areas in developing countries have mobile telephones, and, by improving coverage of the network, information could be disseminated to local producers at little cost; or existing information services could be extended to include innovation-related issues.

Second, successful innovation will increasingly depend on facilitating on-farm learning among farmers. This can be supported by farmer field schools and new forms of hands-on collaboration between farmers, extension workers and researchers (see also the comments of Klerkx as well as Mbuku and Kosgey in Chapter 3 of this Review). In the case of cash crops, private corporations are also promoting the development and dissemination of sustainable agricultural practices in order to respond to consumer demand and to stabilize the supply of agricultural inputs. One example is Unilever which aims at sustainable sourcing for all products by 2020, and chose tea farming in Kenya as a pioneering activity. Smallholders and the Kenyan extension service are major participants in this programme, and local production and dissemination of new knowledge is a key mechanism.

Extension services are crucial for improving agricultural productivity and for increasing the resilience of this sector to climate change. In countries such as Kenya and Malawi, enterprising farmers are now acquiring the information and knowledge they need to maintain and sustain their production themselves (Ifejika Speranza, 2010). However, in addition, local producers could be trained as extension officers recognized by the government in order to offer extension services to other farmers who lack this capacity. This could help to address many shortcomings of current government extension services, such as the limited funding and the frequent transfers of extension officers from one location to another which prevent the development of an ecological and socio-economic memory that might underpin the consolidation of development interventions. Formally trained extension officers could then focus on more specialized services such

as crop-specific services (for more information, see the comment of Klerkx in chapter 3 of this Review). Finally, studies on the adoption of conservation agricultural practices show that partnerships between research, government extension services and private companies are crucial for increasing farmers' productivity.

3. Improving access to inputs

Various crop research institutions have already developed improved crop varieties that would respond to most of the impacts of climate change in Africa (e.g. tolerance to drought and higher temperatures, early maturity, higher yields, higher protein content and pest resistance) in the short term (ICRISAT, 2009). However, improved crop varieties are of no use if the farmers cannot access them due to lack of information and required additional inputs, or because they cannot afford them. Access to information about these new varieties can be improved by using communication and extension services as discussed above. Further opportunities lie in developing indigenous seed enterprises and partnerships with national agencies for rapid farmer participatory varietal testing and release, and through the provision of information to farmers, extension officers and NGO groups about new varieties. These learning experiences are also important for testing new varieties in the field and for analysing practical reasons why there might be reduced acceptance. Improving the policy environment for disseminating seeds across borders is also a strategy followed by research institutions to ensure that improved seeds reach the farmers. Harmonization of regional seed regulations in Africa is expected to improve the rates of release of new varieties, lower the costs in dealing with regulatory authorities, increase trade in improved seed varieties and, ultimately, their adoption by farmers (Minot et al., 2007).

Farmers also have limited knowledge of and access to these new crop technologies (Kijima, 2008; WARDA, 2008; ICRISAT, 2009; CIMMYT/IITA, 2011). To address these shortcomings, governments can financially support local seed breeding companies and distribute free trials to farmers on a promotional basis, after which they would have to pay for subsequent supplies. Microcredit for innovative farming will also be necessary to help overcome the high upfront costs of new management practices required for conservation farming and other integrated approaches. For an initial transition period, government subsidies may also be warranted, as in Malawi, where a Farm Input Subsidy Program (FISP) has been shown to increase maize and legume production (Chibwana et al., 2011), and has been described as a smart subsidy. However, Chibwana et al. (2011:4) also highlight the difficulty of such interventions reaching the poor as "the most vulnerable people in the Malawian communities were not the main recipients of FISP coupons", even when intended as the target groups. The input subsidies initially led to a greater specialization in maize, and to reduced crop diversification and allocation of land to legume crops, due to a lack of legume seeds in the market. The FISP later led to increased maize and legume crop production, when farmers were provided with both improved maize and legume seeds. Chibwana et al. (2011) thus argue that while the FISP contributed to Malawian food security, it needs to be adapted to make it less prone to the unintended effects of concentrating production on one crop relative to the others, in particular, with regard to high input prices.

4. Improving knowledge about local climate changes

Knowing how the local climate is changing and is expected to change in the future as well as the associated risks is crucial for prioritizing adaptation strategies and a shift towards greater resilience. For example, Safaricom from Kenya (who revolutionized money transfer in Kenya) promoted access to information in rural Kenya through Safaricom Foundation Lifeline radio sets, which serve as a platform for radio service broadcasts by the Kenya Meteorological Department (Safaricom Foundation, 2005). Development cooperation should be aware of such innovative projects and programmes, and approach private companies to explore partnerships for their adaptation and further development. Another step is to systematically integrate climate-relevant information into existing national agricultural programmes in order to raise the awareness of decision-makers about the risks their development interventions might encounter. This will already help to integrate climate change adaptation into policies and programmes before their implementation at the local level.

5. Adopting a sectoral approach to adaptation

Agriculture is still the major driver of rural economies in developing countries; increasing resilience to climate change requires a sectoral approach rather than a narrow focus on the productivity of crops, livestock and fisheries. Such an approach would account for the inter-linkages between various land uses, with the goal of achieving multiple goals, including the protection of local livelihoods, conservation of water, forests and biodiversity, improving food security as well as contributing to renewable energy production. Integrated water resource management will be pivotal for ensuring water availability for economic, social and environmental uses under conditions of climate change. This is even more urgent as the shift towards renewable energy technologies will increase competition for water resources (hydropower versus irrigation) and for land (for food crops, biofuels, livestock, forests and biodiversity protection), and it may also exacerbate existing local conflicts over land tenure rights.

Many approaches that generate adaptation benefits and increase resilience also reduce GHG emissions, and therefore present an opportunity for an even more comprehensive mainstreaming effort that includes mitigation aspects. Therefore, new policy coordination mechanisms need to be established or improved at local, national, regional and global levels. Integrating climate-relevant information into existing national agricultural programmes may contribute to raising the awareness of decision-makers to the risks confronting their development interventions. At the local level, a landscape approach could be adopted, taking into account the interlinkages between water, forests and agricultural lands, and the fact that in most cases the same local producers who produce food also manage and use water resources and the forests.

One important objective of coordinated and integrated sectoral policies at national and local levels is to increase the incentives for more sustainable agricultural production systems at the farm level. Such production systems would reduce pressure on natural resources, such as soils and water, and would contribute to improving the provision of ecosystem services, which are essential for agricultural production and productivity. In this regard, supporting the accumulation of soil organic matter and thus increasing soil fertility is one of the most important examples of what is needed and a major challenge in SSA (for a more elaborate analysis on this issue, see the commentary of Leu in this chapter).

Commentary VIII: Yield and Yield Quality of Major Cereals Under Climate Change

Petra Högy and Andreas Fangmeier
University of Hohenheim, Institute for Landscape and Plant Ecology

Abstract

Atmospheric CO_2 enrichment may provide the benefits of higher yields, but, concomitantly, it could worsen cereal quality in terms of protein, amino acid and mineral content. Currently, almost half of the world's human population already suffers from micronutrient deficiencies, and this global health problem will further deteriorate as a result of CO_2 enrichment. On the other hand, an increase in temperature and changing precipitation patterns may reduce yield, while having a positive effect on nutritive value and processing.

Although several developments in agriculture, such as breeding and management practices, have increased yield productivity and availability of cereal-based foods over the past 50 years, more than one billion people worldwide are at risk of food insecurity today (FAO, 2009b). Food insecurity arises when people do not have access to sufficient and nutritious food to meet their dietary needs. An adequate intake of calories does not automatically ensure that the need for micronutrients has been met. In the future, climate change may represent an additionally unprecedented threat to global food security, especially for people in developing countries who depend heavily on agriculture for their livelihoods.

The main driving force behind climate change is the release of greenhouse gases (GHGs) such as carbon dioxide (CO_2) due to human activities. And this is likely to increase over the next few decades (IPCC, 2007d). By conservative estimates, the current concentration of atmospheric CO_2 of about 387 parts per million (ppm) will increase to nearly 550 ppm by 2100;[38] indeed, it is increasing faster than expected. Amid rapidly rising food demand, global atmospheric CO_2 enrichment will affect agroecosystems both directly and indirectly, resulting in changes in yield of major cereals, but potentially affecting yield quality traits as well. As cereals supply the bulk of calories for many populations in the developing world, while also constituting the primary source of both protein and micronutrients, climate change is set to exacerbate many of the problems which developing countries already have to deal with. Currently, there has been surprisingly little research specifically geared to maintaining or enhancing the productivity of agricultural ecosystems under climate change. Neither has there been much research that addresses the issue of vulnerability to climate change of other aspects of food systems such as yield quality (Richardson et al., 2009).

A. Direct effects of atmospheric CO_2 enrichment

Atmospheric CO_2 is the primary source of carbon for cereals, which is taken up by the leaf through stomata. Cereals must absorb light to enable photosynthesis to convert CO_2 into organic compounds such as carbohydrates and amino acids. Water and nutrients are usually acquired from the soil and, together with photosynthate, are used to create new plant tissues. CO_2 effects differ according to the photosynthetic pathway. Elevated CO_2 affects C_3[39] cereals by improving nitrogen use efficiency (NUE) and water use efficiency (WUE), while C_4[40] cereals are affected exclusively via impacts on WUE. Major cereals that have the C_3 photosythetic pathway include wheat, barley and rice, while maize, sorghum and sugarcane are C_4 species. In C_3 cereals, elevated CO_2 is expected to have positive physiological effects by stimulating photosynthesis, mainly by enhancing CO_2 fixation of the chloroplast enzyme RubisCO and inducing stomatal closure. As a consequence, elevated CO_2 results in shifts in biomass allocation and higher yield production (the so-called "CO_2 fertilization effect" referred to by Pritchard and Amthor, 2005). Given adequate water, the effect of CO_2 enrichment on yield performance is higher for C_3 cereals (10.2–15.7 per cent/100 ppm CO_2, Hartfield et al., 2011) than for C_4 crops (1.7 per cent/100 ppm CO_2, Hartfield et al., 2011), because C_3 photosynthesis is not saturated under ambient CO_2 levels.

On the other hand, both C_3 and C_4 cereals might benefit from elevated CO_2 under drought stress due to improvements in water use efficiency. However, the positive yield response to elevated CO_2 has often been due to more grains rather than larger grains. In addition to these effects on the quantity, it appears that CO_2 enrichment also affects the nutritional quality of C_3 cereals (Kimball, Kobayashi and Bindi, 2002). In many instances, the extra carbon is converted into carbohydrates such as starch. Consistently, the amylose content of rice grains, which is a major determinant of cooking quality, has been observed to increase under CO_2 enrichment (Conroy et al., 1994), resulting in more firmness of cooked rice grains.

A negative interaction between nitrogen status in plants and grain quality has been observed in C_3 cereals, made worse by CO_2 enrichment due to changes in leaf nitrogen metabolism. Such changes are largely the result of smaller partitioning of nitrogen in photosynthetic processes (Kimball et al., 2001). As small-grained cereals, such as barley, wheat and rice, may remobilize up to 90 per cent of the nitrogen from the vegetative plant parts during grain filling, less nitrogen investment in the plant under elevated CO_2 could be the primary cause of reduction in grain protein concentration. Although it is known that nitrogen is a key regulator of plant responses to CO_2, the changes in nitrogen metabolism are not well understood at a biochemical level. However, the nutritional value of these three cereals may deteriorate due to CO_2-induced decreases in grain protein concentration by 9.8–15.3 per cent (Taub, Miller and Allen, 2008), with serious consequences for most applications in terms of processing such as bread-making. As elevated CO_2 inhibits nitrate assimilation in C_3 cereals, it will be critical for farmers to carefully manage nitrogen fertilization in order to prevent loss of grain protein (Bloom et al., 2010).

Idso and Idso (2001), on the other hand, have argued that any effects of CO_2 enrichment on protein content in cereals could be ameliorated by increased use of nitrogen fertilizer. It is apparent that greater attention will have to be given to nitrogen management in cereals under CO_2 enrichment in order to increase production efficiency and to maintain both yields and protein concentrations in grains. However, it should be kept in mind that, especially in developing countries, the availability of nitrogen in agriculture is often insufficient to achieve adequate crop yields, and this is one of the causes of malnutrition. Moreover, CO_2-induced alterations in the composition of proteins and amino acids may also affect the nutritive value of grains and processing quality such as bread-making (Högy and Fangmeier, 2008; Högy et al., 2009). In addition, subtle imbalances in macro- and micro-element properties may occur under CO_2 enrichment, resulting in higher risk of "hidden hunger" and malnutrition (Loladze, 2002).

In rice, concentrations of iron and zinc – important for human nutrition – were seen to be lower under elevated CO_2 (Seneweera and Conroy, 1997). Similarly, Högy et al. (2009) reported a decrease in iron in wheat grains under CO_2 enrichment. These findings are vital for the important task of tackling micronutrient deficiencies of iron, zinc, copper, iodine and selenium, as the major grain crops are a critical source of these nutrients for many populations around the world (Caulfield and Black, 2004; Stoltzfus et al., 2004). Currently, almost half of the human population already suffers from micronutrient deficiencies, and this global health problem will worsen under CO_2 enrichment.

Recently, it has been reported that the nitrogen nutritional status of cereals appears to be critical, as the transporting of iron from the rhizophere into grains is dependent on various proteins and other nitrogenous components (Cakmak et al., 2010). CO_2 enrichment can have the effect of reducing the grain iron concentration by worsening the grain protein concentration, and thereby the sink strength of the grain for iron.

CO_2-induced impacts on yield quality of cereals are currently not well understood, and the available information is still inconsistent (DaMatta et al., 2010; Moretti et al., 2010). Nevertheless, it seems that macro- and micronutrient management is necessary for maintaining grain quality under CO_2 enrichment. In addition, innovations in the processing of staple crops and changes in people's diets will be needed in a high-CO_2 world. The effects of CO_2 in terms of reducing the nutritional value of cereals would primarily impact on populations in poorer countries who are less able to compensate by eating more food and more varied diets, or possibly taking nutritional supplements. To meet the increasing demand for healthy food, and with the world's population predicted to increase to 10.1 billion by 2100 (United Nations, 2011), it will be necessary to increase crop production. The use of cereals that can respond effectively to CO_2 enrichment while maintaining high-quality traits may be a powerful option to respond to these increased requirements.

In conclusion, elevated atmospheric CO_2 concentration will have a direct effect on major C_3 cereals, resulting in higher grain yields. However, at the same time, many qualitative compounds associated with cereals as food crops will be adversely affected in the future, notably, declines in proteins, amino acids and minerals such as iron and zinc. As mentioned earlier, these effects have been observed in grains under CO_2 enrichment, resulting in a higher risk of "hidden hunger" and malnutrition, especially in developing countries.

B. Indirect effects of rising temperatures and changes in precipitation patterns

Indirect impacts of atmospheric CO_2 enrichment on agricultural ecosystems may occur due to global warming. Global temperatures are likely to increase by at least 2°C before the end of this century. Moreover, global warming is likely to increase the frequency of heat-stress episodes. It is well known that agricultural productivity is sensitive to temperature during the growing season. As many crops are near their maximum temperature tolerance in Africa, Asia and Latin America, yields are likely to fall sharply with even small increases in temperature. Thus developing countries which face rapid population growth are at a particularly high risk of food shortages caused by temperature increases. Severall studies confirm that a 1°C rise in temperature corresponds to a roughly 10 per cent reduction in yield of major cereals such as wheat, rice and maize due to a shortening of the grain-fill duration (Battisti and Naylor, 2009; Lobell et al., 2008).

The response of cereals to temperature change has been observed to be non-linear, because of the interaction of water and heat stress (Lobell, 2007). Moreover, cereals respond differently to temperature during their life cycle, with a higher temperature optimum during their vegetative development compared with the period of reproductive development. The pollination phase of development, in particular, is one of the most sensitive to episodic temperature increase, and temperature extremes during the reproductive stage can produce some of the greatest impacts

on cereal production. Floral sterility caused by elevated temperature may lower sink demands for carbohydrates and thus hinder the translocation of photosynthates from shoot (source) to grain (sink), resulting in an accumulation of dry matter in the shoot even after flowering. On the other hand, the grain size of cereals remains relatively constant and declines only slowly with increasing temperatures, until the pollination failure point.

Besides yield parameters, grain quality traits of the crops produced are also highly vulnerable to temperature. Temperatures up to the species-dependent optimum accelerate the rate of maturation, causing increases in protein content accompanied by changes in grain protein composition and dough quality characteristics, such as dough strength (Corbellini et al., 1998). Accelerated senescence leads to nitrogen remobilization from vegetative plant parts, and amino acids derived from protein degradation compensate for the temperature-induced decrease in grain filling time and the nitrogen shortage due to reduction of nitrogen uptake from soil by cereal roots. Again, the timing of stress occurrence is an important factor in determining the effect on grain protein concentration. In rice, high temperatures during grain filling were observed to increase the accumulation of all classes of storage proteins at the early filling stage, whereas they reduced the accumulation of prolamins at maturation (Lin et al., 2010). In contrast, carbohydrate synthesis in grains depends primarily on concurrent carbon fixation during grain filling; thus grain starch declined due to shortened duration of starch accumulation or due to the inhibition of key enzymes involved in starch synthesis.

Changes in precipitation (both amount and frequency) can also have devastating impacts on agriculture, with grave consequences for human nutrition and global health. Since water status is important for mineral mobilization, water deficiency may reduce the uptake of iron, zinc and copper from the soil, resulting in decreased concentrations of these minerals in cereal grains such as maize (Oktem, 2008). Micronutrient malnutrition has enormous socio-economic impacts, such as increased mortality and morbidity, impaired growth, development and learning capacity in infants and children as well as loss of working capabilities of adults. This in turn undermines economic growth and perpetuates poverty (World Bank, 2006; WHO, 2002). Climate change is expected to alter the timing and quantity of water available for agriculture while increasing the needs of crops for water as temperatures rise.

Today, many farmers around the world are already experiencing less predictable rainfall and temperatures as well as extreme weather events. As different cultivars respond differently to climatic factors and uncertainties exist about future conditions for cereal production, new varieties of cultivars need to be developed with traits such as heat and drought resistance.

Overall, it can be concluded that indirect impacts due to atmospheric CO_2 enrichment, such as temperature increases and changes in precipitation patterns, may reduce the grain yield of major cereals. On the other hand, protein concentration may increase under rising temperatures, resulting in a higher nutritive value of grains. However, decreases in accumulation of starch and minerals such as iron, zinc and copper in major cereals may affect the nutritional quality of the end-product and food security, as well as the use of those cereals for processing in the future.

C. Outlook

CO_2-induced effects on grain yield and crop quality will likely differ substantially among individual cultivars and species under varying regional climatic conditions. As high CO_2 concentrations cause alterations in evapotranspiration, this may also result in feedback on water magagement and droughts. Water conservation may allow extension of the growth period when water is limited. Less information is available on the interactive effects of climate variability and CO_2 enrichment on the efficiency of resource use (e.g. water, nutrients) and its consequences for yield quantity and quality of major cereals. Higher temperatures and variations in precipitation might reduce the positive CO_2-induced impacts on cereal performance.

With regard to the availability of adequate food supply in the future, a major task is therefore to identify the impacts of climate change on yield quality in terms of nutritive value and end-use processing. Adaptation of cereal production and processing to an increasingly variable climate is thus of the utmost importance, particularly in developing countries, to ensure not only sufficient supplies of cereals, but also their nutritive quality. In order to assure food security in the future, it is vitally important to understand the complex relationships between global environmental changes, farming practices, diet and human health.

Commentary IX: Comparative Analysis of Organic and Non-Organic Farming Systems: A Critical Assessment of Farm Profitability

Noémi Nemes
FAO

Abstract

An analysis of over 50 economic studies demonstrates that, in the majority of cases, organic systems are more profitable than non-organic systems. Higher market prices and premiums, or lower production costs, or a combination of the two generally result in higher relative profits from organic agriculture in developed countries. The same conclusion can be drawn from studies in developing countries, but there, higher yields combined with high premiums are the underlying causes of their relatively greater profitability.

Organic agriculture has triggered a controversial debate over the past few decades, largely because it exposes the true costs and darker sides of chemical-intensive industrial farming systems. There is now a strong body of evidence to prove that organic farming is more environmentally friendly: potential benefits arise from, for example, improved soil fertility, organic matter content and biological activity, better soil structure and less susceptibility to erosion, reduced pollution from nutrient leaching and pesticides, and improved plant and animal biodiversity (Kasperczyk and Knickel, 2006). However, it is not clear whether organic agriculture could be economically attractive enough to trigger its widespread adoption. If organic farming offers better environmental quality and healthier foods but not sufficient economic returns to the majority of farmers, it will obviously remain a luxury form of food production viable for only a very small fraction of farmers. However, the continued growth of organically managed lands worldwide, especially in developing countries, does not support this hypothesis.

A. Comparing the economics of organic versus non-organic farming

There are well over 100 studies that compare the relative profitability of organic versus non-organic agriculture. However, there are fewer long-term comparative studies that analyse the development of profits from each of these systems. Regrettably, the geographical distribution of these studies tends to concentrate on developed countries (mainly the United States) and on certain cash crops (e.g. corn, soy, wheat). For the purpose of this analysis, only studies using data from certified organic farms were considered, covering a minimum period of three years (for developed countries) after conversion and undertaken after 1980. Due to the lack of long-term economic studies in developing countries, studies covering one and two years were included from these countries. Studies that evaluated yields and certain production costs but not profits were not considered.

Several factors complicate the task of comparing economic studies across space and time, such as different costs of living and purchasing power, different interpretations of labour costs, and the changing economic and political environment. Moreover, methodological choice, the time period analysed and the selection procedure for comparable conventional farms have a considerable bearing on profitability. Similarly, the extent of the economic assessment can vary across studies, with some studies focusing merely on the farm level, while others broaden the picture to the level of society, and this can lead to different outcomes. Depending on this choice, opportunity costs and externalities are either included (society level), or, as in most cases, excluded (farm level). When looking at profitability studies, a correct interpretation of the data is crucial: overall comparisons cannot be made, for example between case studies and field experiments, between developed- and developing-country results, and between studies with a very good data base and studies based on farmers' opinions.

B. Yields

Evidence from the more than 50 studies analysed showed that yields in well-established organic farms in developed countries are usually lower than those from conventional farms, to varying degrees. Most European studies including those of organic cereal, vegetable and mixed farming systems showed that they produced somewhat lower yields (BMELF, 1991–1998; FAT, 1997; Offermann and Nieberg, 2000), whereas milk yields most often showed similar results when measured in litres per cow (Younie et al., 1990; FAT, 1993; Offermann and Nieberg, 2000). On the other hand, the majority of long-term studies involving soy-corn rotation in the United States showed that organic yields, on average, were not significantly different (Chase and Duffy, 1991; Hanson, Lichtenberg and Peters, 1997; Drinkwater, Wagoner and Sarrantonio, 1998; Delate et al., 2003; Pimentel et al., 2005). Despite lower soy yields from organic farms in some other United States studies (Mahoney et al., 2004; Chase, 2008; McBride and Greene, 2009), high premiums (McBride and Greene, 2009) or lower production costs (Mahoney et al., 2004; Chase, 2008)

rendered all organic systems more profitable.

Several of the United States studies investigated drier areas as well and found higher yields in the organic systems (Stanhill, 1990; Diebel, Williams and Llewelyn, 1995; Dobbs and Smolik, 1996; Hanson, Lichtenberg and Peters, 1997; Pimentel et al., 2005), suggesting that those systems are more resistant to drought. Similarly, studies in developing countries showed that organic yields were generally higher under normal or favourable conditions (IFAD, 2003; Raj et al., 2005; Gibbon and Bolwig, 2007; Setboonsarng, Yeung and Cai, 2006), and significantly higher under less favorable conditions (Mendoza, 2002). Overall, the majority of economic studies in developing countries showed higher yields from organic production, whereas not one study on developed countries showed higher yields from organic compared with conventional.

When converting to organic agriculture, a paradigm shift must take place, from the high external input packages for treating problems to the use of preventive management and intensive knowledge inputs. Yields are not a characteristic of a production system per se; they depend very much on farm management. Although organic produce generally yields less, yield losses can be mitigated to a certain

---

Box 2: Difficulties in analysing yields from comparative studies

- **Object of comparison (commodity or whole farm-based).** Some authors only look at yields of one or two cash crops separately (Chase and Duffy, 1991; Dobbs and Smolik, 1996: studies from developing countries), whereas others also evaluate average yields of the whole rotation (Hanson et al., 1997; Chase, 2008) and of intercrops (Eyhorn, Ramakrishnan and Mäder, 2007). The latter is more relevant, although more complex for obtaining meaningful results.

- **Unit of comparison (per ha or product).** Some studies evaluate cow yield per hectare (which is usually lower in organic, due to lower stocking densities), whereas others evaluate cow yield per animal (which often provides similar results), and this makes comparisons difficult.

- **Different varieties.** Varieties bred for intensive external input conditions are seldom suitable for low external input systems. Organic systems, especially in developing countries, often use local breeds and varieties which have lower yields, but which are more adapted to low external input conditions in that they require less nutrients and water inputs or have higher pest/disease resistance. However, authors generally do not specify that differences in yields may be due to different varieties.

- **Different growth periods.** Using different varieties also influences the economics of the whole rotation system; for example, many organic farmers in India use desi cotton, which is a whole-season crop, thus after harvest farmers cannot grow anything else in the rotation. Most conventional farmers grow hybrid varieties under irrigation (in the studies analysed), which enables the cultivation of two or three crops per year (Jackson, 2008).

- **Managerial background.** The intensity of previously managed conventional farms is a significant factor contributing to the yield decreases during and after conversion to organic. Yet often the background of organic farms is not clear from the studies, even though it influences the comparative baseline.

extent by proper soil management, shade trees (such as in coffee cultivation), timely removal of diseased plants, and a healthy balance between pests and natural enemies as biological controls (Van der Vossen, 2005). Nevertheless, although an important element of profitability, yields alone do not necessarily indicate profitability.

C. Production costs

In farm economics, there is no absolute definition of what has to be considered as variable costs or as fixed costs; it depends on the aim of the research. Some studies consider only variable costs to calculate gross margins (Younie, Hamilton and Nevison, 1990), whereas others include fixed costs (Wynen, 2001; Gibbon and Bolwig, 2007), and yet others do not differentiate between the two types of costs (Olson and Mahoney, 1999; Delate et al., 2003). By definition, fixed costs are part of the total farm costs that do not vary significantly with the volume of output and can only be changed in the long run, whereas variable costs are those that vary directly with the volume of output. The differentiation between variable and fixed costs is only important when gross margins are calculated, as fixed costs are not accounted for in those margins. However, fixed costs are crucial for farm profitability. During conversion, for instance, several substantial investments have to be made (e.g. new animal-friendly housing system, new orchard varieties that can better withstand bio-physical stress) that are often counted as fixed costs, and for many farmers these costs are the determining factor as to whether converting to organic may be profitable or not. Even though most studies make the distinction between the two types of costs, they may not specify which costs are covered by each of them. Mentioning merely variable and fixed costs does not allow for the appreciation of the variables used, and thus for proper comparisons.

An even more complicated issue is the inclusion of labour costs: some comparisons omit labour costs from the total calculation of net revenues (e.g. Hanson, Lichtenberg and Peters, 1997; Delate et al., 2003), while most include hired labour in the variable costs (Wynen, 2001; Eyhorn, Ramakrishnan and Mäder, 2007; Gibbon and Bolwig, 2007; Chase, 2008); some count (hired) labour costs as fixed costs thus omitting them from gross margin results (FAT, 1993; BMELF, 1994); and yet others count family labour as an opportunity cost or leave this out completely (as

in most studies of developing countries). Another approach, used by Wynen (2001), for instance, counts hired labour as a variable cost and family labour as a fixed cost. Very often in developing countries, only cash costs are included and non-cash costs (e.g. own labour and seeds) are excluded. Regardless of whether labour costs are treated under fixed and/or variable costs, the most important aspect is that they are treated consistently within the case study and are not overlooked.

From the analysis of studies, it follows that even if the different cost elements were standardized, variations among production costs would occur due to the unique character of the operations and factors beyond the control of the farmers: for example, machinery costs depend also on age, size and use, irrigation costs are subject to variations in rainfall, temperature and efficiency of irrigation systems, and labour costs depend on wage rates, working conditions and efficiency of the workers. This being said, production costs tend to be lower in established organic systems (e.g. Helmers, Langemeier and Atwood, 1986; Hanson, Lichtenberg and Peters, 1997; Olson and Mahoney, 1999; Delate et al., 2003; Mendoza, 2002; Eyhorn, Ramakrishnan and Mäder, 2007). In most of the European studies analysed by Offermann and Nieberg in 2000, total costs incurred by organic farms were, on average, slightly lower than those incurred by comparable conventional farms. While variable costs were generally significantly lower (60–70 per cent) in the organic systems, their fixed costs were up to 45 per cent higher than those of the conventional reference group in several countries. The few cases with significantly higher production costs in organic farms were the ones focusing on vegetable production or those in developing countries.

All analysed studies relied on relatively cheap input costs (based on cheap fossil fuel) that have been varying tremendously over the past few years. Input costs are bound to increase in the long run: global nitrogen fertilizer prices surged by 160 per cent during the first quarter of 2008, and fossil-fuel-based agricultural inputs (a substantial proportion of production costs) will sooner or later substantially affect farming systems that rely on the intensive use of synthetic fertilizers and pesticides. In the case of organic agriculture, oil-based inputs negatively affect production costs where plastic mulch is used, and more generally when the system is mechanized.

D. Overall profitability

Over 50 studies were analysed in terms of their research on farm profitability, and although methodological differences prevented us from comparing them systematically, the similarities between the studies from many countries and contexts allowed us to draw some general conclusions. Profitability certainly depends on the choice of crop, which of course is determined partly by environmental conditions and partly by the demand for products and by the availability of government programmes that support the cultivation of particular crops. A comparison of relative profitability depends largely on the kind of comparison group selected. Thus, farm size, farm type and location are important factors in selecting the suitable candidate farms for comparison. Price premiums also seem to be a crucial factor contributing to the good economic performance of organic systems, and in most cases they make organic farms more profitable. However, at least a dozen studies showed that price premiums are not always necessary for organic systems to be more profitable than conventional systems. If higher prices are not available to compensate for possible losses of organic yields, financial profitability will depend entirely on achieving cost reductions.

Overall, the compiled data suggest that organic agriculture is economically more profitable: net returns, taking total costs into account, most often proved to be higher in organic systems. There were wide variations among yields and production costs, but either higher market prices and premiums, or lower production costs, or a combination of these two generally resulted in higher relative profits from organic agriculture in developed countries. The same

conclusion can be drawn from studies in developing countries, but there, higher yields combined with high premiums seemed to be the underlying reasons for higher relative profitability.

Establishing organic markets for staple crops (e.g. organic soybeans, wheat, chillies) that are part of a rotation offers considerable potential to further improve the profitability of organic farms in developing countries. If these crops could be sold at a premium price, the revenues of organic farms would further increase. In developed countries, a further reduction in production costs (energy, fuel, feed) and the use of better varieties (e.g. in terms of resistance and yield) could result in an increase in the relative profitability of organic farms.

E. The need for fair economic comparisons

Organic systems are generally more profitable despite unfair competition in the marketplace due to current government subsidy schemes for conventional production, unequal availability of research and extension services, and the failure of market prices of conventional foods to capture the real environmental, social and health externalities. Existing economic comparisons are therefore heavily biased in favour of conventional farming. There is an urgent need to direct much more research and investments into extension services to support organic agriculture, and shift the bulk of public support from polluting activities to sustainable practices to give an equal footing to organic farming systems. In addition, comparative studies need to take into account the differences in external costs and benefits so as to capture the

Box 3: Profitability of organic cotton production

An Indo-Swiss research team compared agronomic data of 60 organic and 60 conventional farms over two years (Eyhorn, Ramakrishnan and Mäder, 2007) and came to the conclusion that organic farming of cotton was more profitable: variable production costs were 13–20 per cent lower and costs of inputs were 40 per cent lower, yet yields were 4–6 per cent higher in the two years, and, as a result, gross margins for cotton were 30-43 per cent higher. Although there was no price premium for the crops grown in rotation with cotton, organic farms earned 10–20 per cent higher incomes than conventional farms.

In an Indian survey of 125 organic cotton farmers, 95 per cent of respondents saw their agricultural income increase by 17 per cent, on average, after adopting organic agricultural practices, which most of them attributed mainly to reduced costs of production and higher sales prices (MacDonald, 2008). Similarly, in the Indian state of Andhra Pradesh, Raj et al. (2005) found that growing organic cotton was much more profitable than growing conventional cotton (income was + $13 per acre on organic compared with -$30 per acre on conventional farms). In conclusion, all studies found organic cotton farming to be more profitable than conventional.

Box 4: Examples of environmental costs

A study by Pretty et al. (2000) estimated the annual external costs of agriculture in the United Kingdom in 1996 at £2.34 billion ($3.65 billion), equivalent to £208/ha ($324/ha) of arable and permanent pasture. This was 89 per cent of the average net farm income for 1996. Significant costs arose from the contamination of drinking water with pesticides, nitrate and phosphate, from damage to wildlife, habitats, hedgerows, from GHG emissions from soil erosion and organic carbon losses, from food poisoning and from BSE. Another study, which calculated the external costs of agriculture in the United States, including damage to water sources, to soil and air, to wildlife and ecosystem biodiversity and to human health, estimated the costs to range between $5.7 billion and $16.9 billion annually, or $29–$96/ha of cropland (Tegtmeier and Duffy, 2004). These studies only estimated externalities that gave rise to financial costs, thus they are likely to have underestimated the total negative impacts arising from the intensive use of agrochemicals.

real and multiple profits of the respective systems of agriculture.

1. Government support

National or regional agricultural programmes and subsidies are mostly geared towards supporting large-scale agriculture that makes intensive use of chemical inputs, which artificially lowers the price of conventional products. Painter (1991) compared net returns of organic and conventional farms at the end of the 1980s and found that the average governmental subsidy per hectare was 38 per cent higher for conventional production. Researchers in the 1990s also found that conventional systems benefited more from government subsidies than organic ones (Diebel, Williams and Llewelyn, 1995; Smolik, Dobbs and Rickerl, 1995). If subsidies were expanded to support long-term aspects of agricultural productivity, such as soil-building grass and legume crops, the profitability of organic farming would be even higher.

While organic farms in Europe receive considerable support from the EU's agri-environmental programmes, the design of the first pillar of the Common Agricultural Policy (CAP) put organic farming at a disadvantage in the past. The 2003 CAP reform changed this situation, particularly by decoupling direct payments. However, the results of a survey showed that only 11 per cent of organic farmers thought that decoupling had had a positive impact on their profits (Sanders, Offermann and Nieberg, 2008). There is much debate on whether the current levels of organic support are appropriate. Nevertheless, it is clear that a sharp redirection of public support from polluting activities to sustainable practices is necessary, both in developed and developing countries. Subsidies should encourage positive externalities, while advisory and institutional mechanisms, legal measures and economic instruments should correct negative externalities.

2. Research and extension

The achievements of conventional farming systems are based on several decades of intensive research and support, whereas organic research is still in its infancy. Conventional farmers often have better access to information from extension services and university researchers. Organic farmers, on the other hand, need more time and greater managerial efforts and skills to acquire the necessary knowledge on such matters as organic practices, prices and marketing opportunities. Both yield levels and gross margins of rotation crops would probably increase if extension services also provided training and advice on managing these crops organically (Eyhorn, Ramakrishnan and Mäder, 2007). Thus, comparisons of yield and farm economics between conventional and organic can be considered unfair as long as the latter do not benefit from similar research and extension service support that are directed to conventional agriculture.

3. Externalities

The profitability of a farming system must balance economic costs against environmental, social and health costs, as these costs have delayed impacts and indirect effects on farm economics. At present, comparative economic studies of the two farming systems only consider direct economic inputs and outputs in the equation, and broadly overlook the environmental, social and health costs. Accounting for externalities, such as costs associated with run-off, spills, depletion of natural resources and health costs to farmers exposed to pesticides, are lacking. Yet, generally, organic delivers more public goods such as environmental and health benefits. Taking the differences in external costs and benefits into account would give a more accurate profitability picture of the different systems.

In these completely distorted markets that fail

to pro-vide a level playing field between organic and conventional agriculture, subsidies are one way of helping organic farmers to continue with environmentally friendly farming practices. Price supports could take the form of compensation that rewards farmers for the ecosystem and societal services (e.g. landscape) they are performing for the common good. Both external costs and benefits could be quantified in economic terms (e.g. pollution abatement costs), and thus could be taken into account in comparative studies. This would mean a redirection of economic thinking, which would better reflect the true cost of farming practices and, hopefully, lead to the reformulation of policies so that they no longer support polluting activities, but instead correct negative externalities as far as possible.

Commentary X: Strengthening Resilience of Farming Systems: A Prerequisite for Sustainable Agricultural Production

Miguel A Altieri, University of California, Berkeley, and
Parviz Koohafkan, FAO

Abstract

Traditional farming systems have enabled farmers to generate sustained yields to meet their subsistence needs in the context of climatic variability. Part of this performance is linked to the high levels of agrobiodiversity exhibited by traditional agroecosystems. Strategies to enhance diversity in agroecosystems include support to family agriculture and to smallholders, and dynamic conservation of globally important agricultural heritage systems. Diversification is therefore an important farm strategy for managing production risk in farming systems. Strategies to restore diversity in modern farming systems include promoting seed diversity, crop rotations, cover crops, intercropping and crop/livestock mixing. Diversified farming systems managed with modern equipment allow complementary interactions that boost yields with low inputs, thus increasing profits, and, given the diversity of crops, minimizing production risks.

Today, a major challenge facing humanity is how to achieve a sustainable agriculture that provides sufficient food and ecosystem services for present and future generations in an era of climate change, rising fuel costs, social tensions caused by food price hikes, financial instability and accelerating environmental degradation. The challenge is compounded by the fact that the majority of the world's arable land is under "modern" monoculture systems of maize, soybean, rice, cotton and others, which, due to their ecological homogeneity, are particularly vulnerable to climate change as well as biotic stresses. Little has been done to enhance the adaptability of industrial agroecosystems to changing patterns of precipitation, temperatures and extreme weather events (Rosenzweig and Hillel, 2008). This realization has led many experts to suggest that the use of ecologically based management strategies may represent a robust means of increasing the productivity, sustainability and resilience of agricultural production while reducing its undesirable socio-environmental impacts (Altieri, 2002; de Schutter, 2010b).

Observations of agricultural performance after extreme climatic events during the past two decades have revealed that resilience to those events is closely linked to the level of on-farm biodiversity (Lin,

2011). Most scientists agree that a basic attribute of agricultural sustainability is the maintenance of agroecosystem diversity in the form of spatial and temporal arrangements of crops, trees, animals and associated biota. Increasingly, research suggests that agroecosystem performance and stability is largely dependent on the level of plant and animal biodiversity present in the system and its surrounding environment (Altieri and Nicholls, 2004). Biodiversity performs a variety of ecological services beyond the production of food, including recycling of nutrients, regulation of microclimate and of local hydrological processes, suppression of undesirable organisms and detoxification of noxious chemicals. Because biodiversity-mediated renewal processes and ecological services are largely biological, their continued functioning depends upon the maintenance of biological integrity and diversity in agroecosystems. In general, natural ecosystems appear to be more stable and less subject to fluctuations in yield and in the populations of organisms making up the community. Ecosystems with higher diversity are more stable because they exhibit greater resistance, or the ability to avoid or withstand disturbances, and greater resilience, or the ability to recover following disturbances.

Biodiversity enhances ecosystem functions because

those components that appear redundant at one point in time may become important when some environmental change occurs. What is important is that when environmental change occurs, the redundancies of the system enable continued ecosystem functioning and provisioning of services (Vandermeer et al., 1998).

Traditional farming systems, which still persist in many developing countries, offer a wide array of management options and designs that enhance functional biodiversity in crop fields, and consequently support the resilience of agroecosystems (Uphoff, 2002b; Toledo and Barrera-Bassals, 2009). The myriad of traditional systems are a globally important, ingenious agricultural heritage which reflects the value of the diversity of agricultural systems that are adapted to different environments. They tell a fascinating story of the ability and ingenuity of humans to adjust and adapt to the vagaries of a changing physical and material environment from generation to generation. Whether recognized or not by the scientific community, this ancestral knowledge constitutes the foundation for actual and future agricultural innovations and technologies. The new models of agriculture that humanity will need in the immediate future should include forms of farming that are more ecological, biodiverse, local, sustainable and socially just. Therefore, they will necessarily have to be rooted in the ecological rationale of traditional small-scale agriculture, which represents long-established, successful and adaptive forms of agriculture (Koohafkan and Altieri, 2010).

A. Small farms as models of resilience

In continuously coping with extreme weather events and climatic variability through centuries, farmers living in harsh environments in Africa, Asia and Latin America have developed and/or inherited complex farming systems managed in ingenious ways. These have allowed small farming families to meet their subsistence needs in the midst of environmental variability without depending much on modern agricultural technologies (Denevan, 1995). The continued existence of millions of hectares under traditional farming is living proof of a successful indigenous agricultural strategy, which is a tribute to the "creativity" of small farmers throughout the developing world (Wilken, 1987). Today, well into the first decade of the twenty-first century, millions of smallholders, family farmers and indigenous people

are continuing to practice resource-conserving farming. Such traditional systems are testament to the remarkable resilience of agroecosystems to continuous environmental and economic change, which, despite changes, continue to contribute substantially to agrobiodiversity conservation and food security at local, regional and national levels (Netting, 1993).

However, climate change can pose serious problems for the majority of the 370 million of the world's poorest, who live in areas often located in arid or semi-arid zones, and in ecologically vulnerable mountains and hills (Conway, 1997). In many countries, more and more people, particularly those at lower income levels, are now forced to live in marginal areas (i.e. floodplains, exposed hillsides, arid or semi-arid lands), where they are at risk from the negative impacts of climate variability. Even minor changes in climate can have disastrous impacts on the lives and livelihoods of these vulnerable groups. The implications for food security could be very profound, especially for subsistence farmers living in remote and fragile environments that are likely to produce very low yields. These farmers depend on crops that could be badly affected, such as maize, beans, potatoes and rice. Despite the serious implications of predictions, data represent only a broad brush approximation of the effects of climate change on small-scale agriculture. In many cases those data ignore the adaptive capacity of small farmers who use several agroecological strategies and socially mediated solidarity networks to cope with and even prepare for extreme climatic variability (Altieri and Koohafkan, 2008).

Three studies assessing agricultural performance after extreme climatic events reveal the close link between enhanced agro-biodiversity and resilience to extreme weather events. A survey conducted in Central American hillsides after Hurricane Mitch showed that farmers engaged in diversification practices, such as cover crops, intercropping and agroforestry, suffered less damage than their neighbours who practiced conventional monoculture. The survey, spearheaded by the Campesino a Campesino movement, mobilized 100 farmer-technician teams to carry out paired observations of specific agroecological indicators on 1,804 neighbouring sustainable and conventional farms. The study spanned 360 communities and 24 departments in Guatemala, Honduras and Nicaragua. It found that plots where farmers adopted sustainable farming practices had

20 to 40 per cent more topsoil, greater soil moisture and less erosion, and experienced smaller economic losses than their conventional neighbours (Holt-Giménez, 2002). Similarly in Sotonusco, Chiapas, coffee systems exhibiting high levels of vegetation complexity and plant diversity suffered less damage from Hurricane Stan than more simplified coffee systems (Philpott et al., 2008). And in Cuba, 40 days after Hurricane Ike hit the country in 2008, researchers conducting a farm survey in the provinces of Holguin and Las Tunas found that diversified farms exhibited losses of 50 per cent compared to 90 or 100 per cent in neighbouring monoculture farms. Likewise, agroecologically managed farms showed a faster recovery of productivity (80–90 per cent 40 days after the hurricane) than monoculture farms (Rosset et al., 2011). All three studies emphasize the importance of enhancing plant diversity and complexity in farming systems to reduce vulnerability to extreme climatic events. Since many peasants commonly manage polycultures and/or agroforestry systems, their knowledge and practices could provide a key source of information on adaptive capacity centred on the selective, experimental and resilient capabilities of those farmers in dealing with climatic change.

Given the resilience of diversified small farming systems, understanding the agroecological features of traditional agroecosystems is an urgent matter, as this can serve as the foundation for the design of agricultural systems that are resilient to climate change (Altieri and Koohafkan, 2008).

B. Restoring agrobiodiversity in modern agroecosystems

Since the modernization of agriculture, farmers and researchers have been faced with a major ecological dilemma arising from the homogenization of agricultural systems, namely the increased vulnerability of crops to pests and diseases, and now to climatic variability. Both these phenomena can be devastating in genetically uniform, large-scale, monoculture conditions. Monocultures may offer short-term economic advantages to farmers, but in the long term they do not represent an ecological optimum. Rather, the drastic narrowing of cultivated plant diversity has put the world's food production in greater peril (Perfecto, Vandermeer and Wright, 2009).

Given the new climate change scenarios predicted over the next two decades or so by some scientists

(e.g. Rosenzweig and Hillel, 2008), the search for practical steps to break the monoculture nature of modern agroecosystems, and thus reduce their ecological vulnerability, is imperative. As traditional farmers have demonstrated with farming systems that stood the test of time, restoring agricultural biodiversity at the field and landscape level is key to enhancing resilience. Greater diversity of species is probably needed to reduce temporal variability of ecosystem processes in changing environments. The most obvious advantage of diversification is reduced risk of total crop failure due to invasions of unwanted species and/or climatic variability, as larger numbers of species reduce temporal variability in ecosystem processes in changing environments (Loreau et al., 2011). Studies conducted in grassland systems suggest that there are no simple links between species diversity and ecosystem stability. Experiments conducted in grassland plots conclude that functionally different roles represented by plants are at least as important as the total number of species in determining processes and services in ecosystems (Tilman et al., 2001a). This latest finding has practical implications for agroecosystem management. If it is easier to mimic specific ecosystem processes rather than attempting to duplicate all the complexity of nature, then the focus should be placed on incorporating a particular biodiversity component that plays a specific role, such as plants that fix nitrogen, provide cover for soil protection or harbour resources for natural enemies of insect pests.

Contemporary notions of modern mechanized farming emphasize the necessity of monocultures. There is little question, however, that given sufficient motivation, appropriate technology could be developed to mechanize multiple cropping systems (Horwith, 1985). Simpler diversification schemes based on 2 or 3 plant species may be more amenable to large-scale farmers and can be managed using modern equipment. One such scheme is strip intercropping, which involves the production of more than one crop in strips that are narrow enough for the crops to interact, yet wide enough to permit independent cultivation. Agronomically beneficial strip intercropping systems have usually included corn or sorghum, which readily respond to higher light intensities (Francis et al., 1986). Studies with corn and soybean strips 4 to 12 rows wide demonstrated increased corn yields (5 to 26 per cent higher) and decreased soybean yields (8.5 to 33 per cent lower) as strips got narrower. Alternating corn and alfalfa strips provided greater gross returns than single crops. Strips of 20 ft. (approximately 6.1 meters) width were the most advantageous, with substantially higher economic returns than the single crops (West and Griffith, 1992). This advantage is critical for farmers who have debt-to-asset ratios of 40 per cent or higher ($40 of debt for every $100 of assets). Such a level has already been reached by more than 11–16 per cent of farmers in the mid-western United States who desperately need to cut costs of production by adopting diversification strategies.

Legumes intercropped with cereals is a key diversification strategy, not only because of their provision of nitrogen, but also because the mixtures enhance soil cover, smother weeds and increase nutrients (e.g. potassium, calcium and magnesium) in the soil through the addition of biomass and residues to the soil. Such intercropping systems also increase soil microbial diversity such as vesicular arbuscular mycorrhizae (VAM) fungi which facilitate phosphorous transfer to the crops (Machado, 2009). In the case of adverse weather conditions, such as a delay in the onset of rains and/or failure of rains for a few days, weeks or during the cropping period, an intercropping system provides the advantage that at least one crop will survive to give economic yields, thereby serving as the necessary insurance against unpredictable weather. Polycultures exhibit greater yield stability and lower productivity declines during a drought than monocultures. This was well demonstrated by Natarajan and Willey (1986) who examined the effects of drought on polycultures by manipulating water stress on intercrops of sorghum (*Sorghum bicolor*) and peanut (*Arachis* spp.), millet (*Panicum* spp.) and peanut, and sorghum and millet. All the intercrops consistently provided greater yields at five levels of moisture availability, ranging from 297 to 584 mm of water applied over the cropping season. Interestingly, the rate of over-yielding actually increased with water stress, such that the relative differences in productivity between monocultures and polycultures became more accentuated as stress increased.

No-till row crop production is also promising, given its soil conservation and improvement potential, but it is highly dependent on herbicides. However, there are some organic farmers who practice it without synthetic herbicides. A breakthrough occurred with the discovery that certain winter annual cover crops, notably cereal rye and hairy vetch, can be killed by mowing at a sufficiently late stage in their development and cutting close to the ground. These plants generally do not re-grow significantly, and the clippings form an *in situ* mulch through which vegetables can be transplanted with no or minimal tillage. The mulch hinders weed seed germination and seedling emergence, often for several weeks. As they decompose, many cover crop residues can release allelopathic compounds that may suppress weed growth (Moyer, 2010) by means of phytotoxic substances that are passively liberated through decomposition of plant residues. There are several green manure species that have a phytotoxic effect which is usually sufficient to delay the onset of weed growth until after the crop's minimum weed-free period. This makes post-plant cultivation, herbicides or hand weeding unnecessary, yet exhibits acceptable crop yields. Tomatoes and some late-spring brassica plantings perform especially well, and some large-seeded crops such as maize and beans can be successfully direct-sown into cover crop residues. Not only can cover crops planted in no-till fields fix nitrogen in the short term; they can also reduce soil erosion and mitigate the effects of drought in the long term, as the mulch conserves soil moisture. Cover crops build vertical soil structure as they promote deep macropores in the soil, which allow more water to penetrate during the winter months and thus improve soil water storage.

C. Conclusions

There is general agreement at the international level on the urgent need to promote a new agricultural production paradigm in order to ensure the production of abundant, healthy and affordable food for an increasing human population. This challenge will need to be met with a shrinking arable land base, with less and more expensive petroleum, increasingly limited supplies of water and nitrogen, and at a time of rapidly changing climate, social tensions and economic uncertainty (IAASTD, 2009a). The only agricultural system that will be able to cope with future challenges is one that will exhibit high levels of diversity and resilience while delivering reasonable yields and ecosystem services. Many traditional farming systems still prevalent in developing countries can serve as models of sustainability and resilience.

Resilience in agricultural systems is a function of the level of diversity within the agricultural ecosystem. It is therefore essential that strategies for an adaptive response to climate change focus on breaking away from the monoculture nature of modern agroecosystems. Small changes in the management of industrial systems, such as intercropping and/or use of rotational cover cropping in no-till systems, can substantially enhance the adaptive capacity of cropping systems. Weather extremes, including local drought and flooding, are predicted to become more common as a result of rapid climate change.

Environmentally responsible water management will therefore have to be a critical part of sustainable agriculture in the future. Agroecological strategies for conserving water include choosing water-efficient crops, resource-conserving crop rotations, enhancing soil organic matter and intercropping systems.

Commentary XI: Democratizing Control of Agriculture to Meet the Needs of the Twenty-first Century

Marcia Ishii-Eiteman
Pesticide Action Network North America

Abstract

Powerful commercial interests and lack of political resolve hamper the establishment and implementation of policies to advance sustainable and equitable development. To accomplish the deep-seated change required to overcome these impediments, decisive and coordinated action among public and private sector actors and civil society is needed. Priorities for action should include:

- Curtailing corporate concentration in the food system, and increasing market access and competitiveness of small and medium-scale farmers to improve food and livelihood security;

- Reducing the undue influence of large transnational corporations over public policy, research and trade agendas; and

- Strengthening the role of civil society – including farmers' organizations – in designing and implementing policies and in guiding partnerships dedicated to public interest outcomes.

Policies and practices that meet global food needs sustainably and equitably and support a shift towards ecological farming systems can conserve biodiversity, water and energy and reduce greenhouse gas (GHG) emissions (IAASTD, 2009a and b; De Schutter, 2011; UNEP, 2011). Policy options to drive this transformation of agriculture have been described by the United Nations-sponsored International Assessment of Agricultural Knowledge, Science and Technology for Development (IAASTD, 2009a and b; box A). Likewise, the economic viability, environmental urgency and human rights imperative of implementing such a transformation have been well established (De Schutter, 2008; UNCTAD/UNEP, 2008; FAO 2012c; UNEP 2011).

Despite the availability of robust policy options, powerful commercial interests, weak or captured public sector actors and lack of political will continue to hamper the establishment and meaningful implementation of these progressive options. The constraints – outlined below – are systemic; a few superficial changes will not make a significant enough difference to achieve concrete outcomes. Rather, highly targeted and strategic interventions are needed that tackle the core of the problem and democratize control over agriculture.

A. Constraints on the transformation of agriculture

1. Market failures and the need for full cost accounting

A fundamental failure of global markets today is the lack of price signals that incorporate the full array of health, energy and environmental costs associated with agriculture. Consequently, policymakers base their decisions on inaccurate forecasts of the potential and actual costs. Full cost accounting measures, such as national "green accounts" or "total material flow estimates" are good economic practices that more accurately reflect the true costs of food and agricultural industries, and can consequently better inform policy decisions. Sweden, for example, established a national policy to transition towards organic farming based largely on the findings of a full cost analysis of the climate-related, energy, water, environmental and other ecosystem service costs embedded in its "foodshed" (Johansson, 2008).

2. Corporate concentration in food and agriculture

In North America, growing market concentration in multiple agricultural activities, coupled with successive rounds of deregulation, have led to

---

Box 5: Policy options to support a transition to sustainable agriculture

As identified by the IAASTD (2009a and b), promising policy options to advance sustainable and equitable development goals include:
- Strengthening the small-scale farm sector, in particular farmers', women's, indigenous and other community-based organizations, and increasing public investment in rural areas;
- Building local and national capacity in biodiverse, ecologically resilient farming to cope with increasing environmental stresses;
- Increasing local participation and leadership in agricultural research, direction-setting, policy-formation and decision-making processes;
- Revitalizing local and regional rural economies and food systems, and more closely regulating globalized food systems to ensure good public outcomes;
- Mobilizing public and private sector investments and providing market-based incentives to advance equitable and sustainable development goals;
- Establishing equitable regional and global trade arrangements to support developing countries' food and livelihood security goals, and revising ownership laws to ensure poor and/or vulnerable communities' equitable use, access to and control over land, water, seeds and germplasm; and
- Establishing new, transparent, democratically governed institutional arrangements to accomplish these goals.

Source: IAASTD, 2009a and b (see also Ishii-Eiteman, 2009; and Hoffmann, 2011).

---

unprecedented levels of corporate control of the region's food and agricultural system (Hendrickson et al., 2009). As these corporations have extended their operations into Latin America, Asia and Eastern Europe, their global influence has expanded, with adverse consequences for small-scale farmers around the world (McIntyre et al., 2009a; 2009b). The result has been a dramatic reduction in competition and fair access to markets for small and medium-scale producers, labour, independent retailers and consumers. As consolidation has increased, a handful

of transnational agribusinesses have gained growing influence over the production and distribution of food, both domestically and internationally (Hendrickson et al., 2009; Hubbard, 2009; De Schutter, 2010c; see also figure 12 below). This in turn has enabled them to exert significant political influence over public policy and research.

3. Corporate influence over public policy

Agribusinesses spend billions of dollars lobbying

Box 6: Corporate influence over public policy

Transnational corporations exercise significant influence over the formation of national and international public policy. Below are some illustrative examples.
- Soon after forest fires in the Russian Federation devastated its wheat crops in 2010, the multinational grain trader, Glencore, speculating on a profitable spike in wheat prices, urged the Russian Federation to ban wheat exports, thereby provoking the desired price surge that had global repercussions (Patel, 2011).
- In Brazil, a 2010 Congressional bill, co-authored by a lawyer for the Council for Biotechnology Information, linked to Monsanto, BASF, Bayer, Cargill, Dupont and others, proposed repeal of a Biosafety Law prohibition on "genetic use restriction technologies" also known as "terminator technologies" (Camargo, 2010).
- Monsanto and its affiliates lobbied Indonesian legislators in the 1990s to support genetically engineered (GE) crops. In 2005, the firm was fined $1.5 million by the United States Department of Justice for violating the Foreign Corrupt Practices Act by bribing a senior Indonesian Environment Ministry official (Birchall, 2005).
- Chemical companies commonly sit on panels and committees that advise regulators. For example, a representative from Dow Chemical is serving on the Endocrine Disruptor Screening and Testing Advisory Committee of the United States Environmental Protection Agency.
- In 2002, Malaysia banned the highly toxic chemical herbicide, Paraquat. Its manufacturer, Syngenta, joined Malaysia's influential palm oil industry in pressuring the Government to reverse the ban, which it did in 2006. Malaysia's Pesticide Board subsequently ruled that Paraquat use could continue pending results from a study on alternatives. The study has not been released and Paraquat continues to be used (Watts, 2010).

Figure 12: Structure of the global seed industry over the period 1996–2008

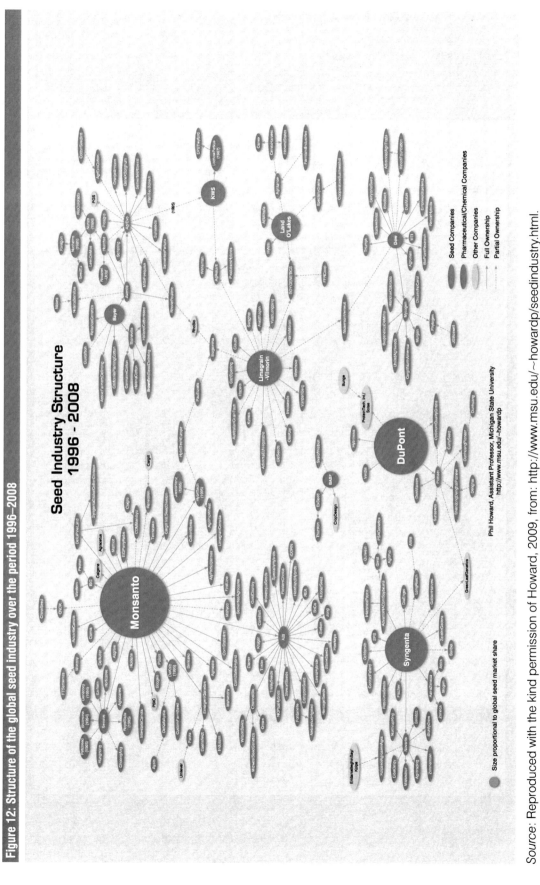

Source: Reproduced with the kind permission of Howard, 2009, from: http://www.msu.edu/~howardp/seedindustry.html.

Note: Consolidation has increased in the international seed industry in recent decades. The chart depicts relationships between major seed companies and their subsidiaries in 2008, after 12 years of consolidation. The largest firms are represented as circles, with the size proportional to their share in the global commercial seed market.

Box 7: Revolving door

Corporate executives from major agribusinesses appointed to public agencies have frequently participated in the drafting of regulatory rules that are favourable to their industry's interests.[a] Below are some examples from various reports.

- A Brazilian attorney represented Monsanto and its Brazilian subsidiary, Monsoy, in various court cases between 1998 and 2002. Moving to government service in 2005, he coordinated the high-level inter-ministerial working group that established the decree to implement Brazil's pro-GE Biosafety Law. The law –applauded by Monsanto[b]– established a National Biosafety Council on which the former Monsanto attorney served as executive secretary from 2005 to 2010.

- A Syngenta lobbyist that represented the biotech company at an EU hearing in 2008 had previously worked for the European Union Food Safety Authority (EFSA) where she had developed GE guidance documents. Her move violated the EFSA's required two-year waiting period. The lobbyist is currently Syngenta's Head of Biotech Regulatory Affairs for Europe, Africa and the Middle East (Testbiotech, 2009 and 2010; SP International, 2010).

- A lawyer for Monsanto moved to the United States Food and Drug Administration (FDA) and the United States Department of Agriculture (USDA) in the 1990s, during which time he approved Monsanto's controversial GE bovine growth hormone and developed pro-agricultural biotechnology policies based on the concept of "substantial equivalence." He returned to Monsanto as vice president for public policy in 1998, before rejoining the FDA in 2010 (Nestle, 2002; USFDA, 2010).

- A former corporate counsel for the pesticide and biotechnology company, DuPont, was appointed in January 2011 to serve as general counsel for the USDA. Soon after, the USDA proposed a dramatic reduction in agency responsibility for regulating GE crops. A two-year pilot program launched in April 2011 now allows biotechnology firms to conduct environmental reviews of their own GE products as part of the United States' regulatory process.[c] In November 2011, USDA announced additional plans to streamline its GE regulatory approval process in order to "reduce the length of the petition process." [d]

Note: a See also Center for Responsive Politics, 2011, Agribusiness lobbying, at: www.opensecrets.org/lobby/indus.php?id=A&year=2010, and Revolving door, at: www.opensecrets.org/revolving/index.php.

b See Monsanto, Monsanto encouraged by enactment of Brazilian biosafety law. News release, 24 March 2005, at: http://monsanto.mediaroom.com/index.php?s=43&item=62.

c USDA (2011). Solicitation of Letters of Interest to Participate in National Environmental Policy Act Pilot Project. Animal and Plant Health Inspection Service [Docket No. APHIS–2010–0117], Federal Register, Vol. 76, No. 67, Thursday, April 7, 2011/Notices: 19309–19310. Washington, DC. USDA's pilot programme is described at: www.aphis.usda.gov/biotechnology/nepa_pilot.shtml.

d USDA's November 2011 plans to speed up the GE approval process are described at: www.aphis.usda.gov/newsroom/2011/11/ge_petition_process.shtml. The collaboration between Monsanto and USDA in preparation of environmental reviews of Monsanto's GE products is analysed at: www.truth-out.org/under-industry-pressure-usda-works-speed-approval-monsantos-genetically-engineered-crops/1323453319. Government documents obtained under a Freedom of Information Act request are available at: www.truth-out.org/why-monsanto-always-wins67976.

public agencies and officials, in both national and international policy-making arenas, and have, in many instances, influenced policy decisions to their benefit (boxes 6 and 7). This influence weakens government commitment to more strictly regulate commercial actors, remove perverse incentives that favour corporate profit over public interest, revise ownership laws and restore public access to and control over productive resources that have been privatized.

4. Legal impediments to sustainable agricultural research and practice

Security of tenure and access to land are vital to enable

farmers to invest in longer term resource-conserving strategies and meet livelihood and food security goals at household and national levels. The lack of national laws to secure small-scale farmers' tenure and access to productive resources (e.g. seeds, germplasm, land, water) undermines efforts to promote a conversion to sustainable practices. Instead, intellectual property (IP) laws have privatized those resources, transferring ownership to commercial interests (IAASTD, 2009a).

IP laws are also driving agricultural research in support of private sector goals, associated with product development rather than ecological resilience or poverty reduction. The Bayh-Dole Act of 1980, for

Figure 13: USAID-funded Agricultural Biotechnology Support Project (ABSP-Phase II): target countries, GE crops in development and project partners

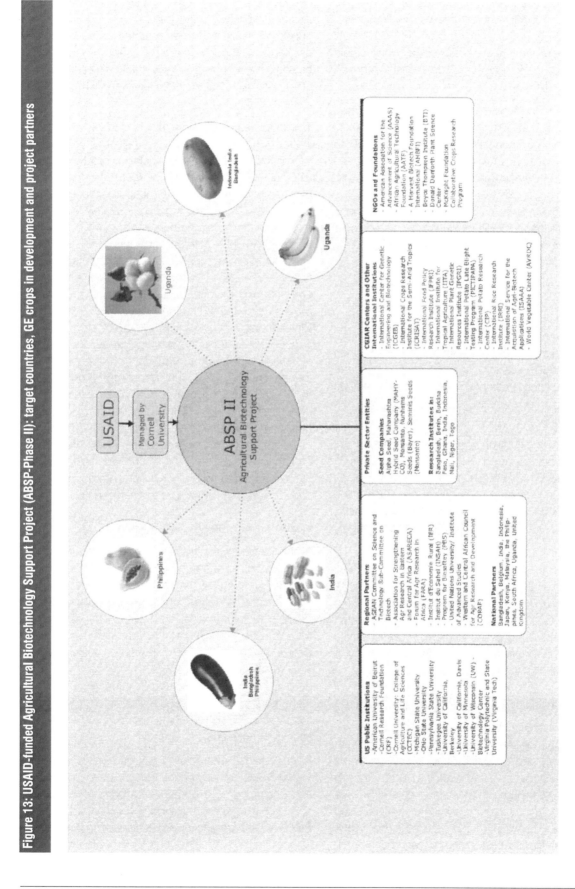

Source: Pesticide Action Network North America (2010). Graphic developed by A. Munimus from project information provided at: http://www.absp2.cornell.edu/.

example, radically altered the political and economic landscape of public sector research in the United States, mandating patents on research outcomes. When universities assign exclusive licensing rights to corporations, core research benefits are removed from the public domain.

Scientists in developing countries are encouraged by incentives and technical support from university patent offices to undertake research that is likely to earn royalty revenues for the university, as observed in Uganda (Louwaars et al., 2005). Increasingly, universities are redirecting their research to meet the short-term financial goals of sponsoring corporations rather than broader public interest goals, as reflected in the emergence of a "university-industrial complex" (Press and Washburn, 2000; Washburn, 2005).

Scientists' ability to conduct independent assessments of patented GE seeds is also impeded by IP rules that require them to first secure approval for their research plan from the patent-holder (Hubbard, 2009). Indeed, in 2009, in a letter to the United States Environmental Protection Agency, over two dozen university scientists complained of the stifling effects of IP laws on independent research and innovation (Pollack, 2009).

Corporate ownership of both productive resources and IP has constrained agricultural transformation in other ways as well (Brennan et al., 2005; Pray, Oehmke and Naseem, 2005). These ownership rules have contributed to the erosion of genetic diversity, local knowledge, social equity and food sovereignty (Dreyfus et al., 2009).

Finally, the lack of adequate anti-trust and competition laws at national and international levels, and weak judicial systems that are unable to properly enforce existing laws have supported the unprecedented pace of corporate consolidation and adverse effects on family farming over the past two decades (De Schutter, 2009b; Hendrickson et al., 2009).

5. Institutional biases

Bias within institutional arrangements – shaped by pre-analytic assumptions, professional inertia and "path dependency," and upheld by geopolitical concerns and the influence of vested interests – can strongly privilege one development model over others (Dreyfus et al., 2009). In the case of agriculture, politically and economically dominant actors, such as the World Bank, international research centres, and developed-

country aid and trade agencies, all played a formative role in establishing the "Green Revolution" model as one to be replicated and emulated, at the expense of alternative models that emphasized more holistic, ecological and farmer-led approaches (Brooks et al., 2009; Dreyfus et al., 2009; Cullather, 2010; Brooks, 2010 and 2011).

The persistence of these biases today is reflected in the number of strategic initiatives of major international donors that seek to promote high-external-input, commercial or industrial agriculture, even among small-scale farmers, despite evidence that reveals the damaging effects of this approach and the need to strengthen site-specific ecological approaches that provide multi-functional benefits. For example, emphasis on increasing productivity through the research, development and export of new products and biotechnologies underpins the United States Feed the Future Initiative,[42] the Agricultural Biotechnology Support Program of the United States Agency for International Development, [43] the agriculture programme of the world's largest private foundation (Bill and Melinda Gates Foundation, 2010) and the Consultative Group on International Agricultural Research (Edwards, 2008; Brooks, 2010 and 2011; Feed the Future, 2010; Tuckey, 2010). Many of these development initiatives are closely interwoven and share the same corporate partners (figure 13). In such cases, bilateral and multilateral development aid provides an effective vehicle for market entry.

6. Global trade: driver or constraint?

Global trade has significant potential to support robust national and regional economies and drive a transition towards ecological agriculture. However, trade liberalization that has opened developing-country markets to international competition too quickly or too extensively has undermined the rural sector and degraded the environment (IAASTD, 2009a and b). As a result, developing countries have been left with diminished capacity for food production, making them more vulnerable to international food price and supply volatility, and reducing their food and livelihood security (Khor, 2008).

A fundamental reform of global trade rules towards fair and ecological agriculture has been proposed and described by a number of experts (e.g. Izac et al., 2009; also see Khor and Lim in chapter 5 of this Review). Yet progress towards establishing a new and fair trade regime remains constrained by the influence of a few powerful countries and commercial interests operating in global policy arenas such as the World Trade Organization (WTO). Anti-democratic processes and asymmetrical power relationships within the WTO prevent civil society and governments of developing countries from securing reform of the global trade regime recommended by, for example, the IAASTD and UNCTAD (Khor, 2008 and 2009; South Centre, 2011).

B. Curtailing concentration of power and excess of influence in the globalized system

The democratizing of institutions that shape global food and agriculture requires both courage and sustained engagement by visionary political leaders, researchers, private sector actors and all sectors of civil society. The participation of all stakeholders, particularly historically marginalized rural communities in developing countries, as equal partners – and not simply as stepping stones in a "consultative" process – is an essential ingredient for revitalizing local and regional food systems, driving innovation that meets global food and livelihood needs, and building robust local economies.

A progressive approach to overcoming the institutional and market-power constraints identified above should include commitment to:

- Undertake a full cost analysis of national and global food and agricultural systems;
- Provide institutional support for small-scale farmers, and women's and workers' organizations that strengthens their negotiating power in markets dominated by transnational buyers;
- Strengthen and broaden the scope of national and international competition policies to reverse trends in farm and agribusiness concentration, end

unfair business practices across the global food production and supply chain, and curtail dominant buyer power which threatens small-scale farmers' food and livelihood security (see De Schutter, 2010c);

- Establish and enforce strong codes of conduct to govern private-public partnerships and public policy-making processes in order to minimize potential conflicts of interest which unfairly or inappropriately benefit private sector actors;
- Establish an international review mechanism to investigate agrifood sector concentration, anti-competitive practices and impacts across national borders, develop standards of corporate behaviour and recommend policy options;
- Revise IP and other ownership rules and incentives in order to reorient public policy and research towards equitable and sustainable development goals;
- Establish means of preventing conflict of interest in partnerships, investments and policy-making processes;
- Build developing countries' capacities for trade analysis and negotiation leading to more equitable trade rules. Strategic impact assessments could provide useful empirical evidence of the social, environmental and economic trade-offs of various trade instruments;
- Restrain financial speculation over food commodities that distorts markets and price signals; and
- Establish and strengthen democratic decision-making processes and increase civil society participation in policy-making processes. The success of the Tamil Nadu Women's Collective in transforming regional food and agricultural systems by supporting rural women as co-decision-makers in the community and in political office is instructive in this respect (IATP, 2010).

Commentary XII: Agriculture, Food and Energy

Gunnar Rundgren
Grolink AB Consultancy, Sweden

Abstract

In a world with a rapidly increasing human population and the simultaneous depletion of natural resources, the industrial logic of replacing human labour with oil and other natural resources makes less and less sense. Increasing energy prices will reverse some of the developments that were made possible by cheap fossil fuel. This poses a challenge for society, but also an opportunity to steer towards a path of true sustainability, including the adoption of more sustainable agricultural methods (such as organic farming) and more localized food production networks. That those changes will also serve to mitigate climate change is another strong argument in favour of such a shift.

A. Introduction

A combination of cheap fossil fuel and market orientation led to the industrialization of farming. While labour productivity in agriculture has skyrocketed, energy productivity has plummeted. The winners have been agribusinesses and the losers have been small farms, especially in developing countries. With increasing shortages of fossil-fuel-based energy and natural resources and the rapid growth of the world's population, we need to fundamentally transform agriculture into a net energy producer, as it was throughout history. The simple equation has always been that it is necessary to get substantially more energy out of the food than is put into its production. As long as energy input is human labour it is an iron law that can only be skipped for shorter periods. Agricultural workers should not only be able to feed themselves, but also other family members who are too young, too old or too sick to work, as well as a few others that supply services. Finally, in almost all societies there have been rulers who have appropriated a large proportion of the production.

B. 250 billion energy slaves

To have an idea of how important the deployment of external energy sources has been for our modern societies, one can contrast the energy embedded in human labour with the external energy sources that are exploited. A rough calculation shows that the 7.71 tons of oil equivalents (toes)[44] of energy used annually by the average American (compared with 0.25 toes used by the average Senegalese), corresponds to the food consumption of 400 people. That represent the "energy slaves" (in the form of fossil fuel) working for him or her. Another way of looking at it, from an economic perspective, is that a barrel of oil represents the energy of 25,000 hours of human toil (i.e. 14 persons working for a year under normal labour standards). Even with an oil price of several hundred dollars per barrel, this is very cheap compared with human labour (Rundgren, 2012).

According to the FAO (2000), 6,000 megajoules (MJ) of fossil energy (corresponding to one barrel of oil) is used to produce one ton of maize in industrial farming, while for the production of maize using traditional methods in Mexico, for example, only 180 MJ (corresponding to 4.8 litres of oil) is used. This calculation includes energy for synthetic fertilizers, irrigation and machinery, but not the energy used for making machinery, transporting products to and from the farm, and for construction of farm buildings. In modern rice farming, the energy return on energy invested (EROI) is less than 1 (i.e. there is more energy consumed than produced) and in modern maize farming it is slightly more than 1, while traditional production of rice and maize gives a return of 60 to 70 times on energy used (FAO, 2000).

The total energy harvested *per hectare* can increase substantially with increased use of ancillary energy, which can take the form of better (and timelier) soil preparation, irrigation[45] and the application of (chemical) fertilizers that are very energy demanding, to name a few. The ratio between energy return and energy input (i.e. efficiency in use of energy) seems to be fairly constant up to a certain level, after which it deteriorates rapidly. Industrial farming systems have long passed this level. Harvested energy *per labour unit* increases dramatically with increased input of energy by a factor of between 10 and 100, allowing the most advanced agricultural systems to have one farmer for more than 100 persons (Bayliss-Smith, 1982).

C. Why oil and grain prices move in tandem

Farming uses energy in many different forms: diesel for tractors and pumps, and electricity for pumps, fans and indoor machinery such as milking machines. Fertilizers account for a large proportion of energy use. Energy represents 90 per cent of the production costs of nitrogen fertilizers, 30 per cent of those of phosphorus fertilizers and 15 per cent of those of potassium fertilizers. According to the United States Congressional Research Services (US CRS, 2004), energy costs in the United States represent between 22 per cent and 27 per cent of the production costs of wheat, maize and cotton and 14 per cent of those of soybeans.[46] These figures do not include embedded energy costs in items such as buildings and machinery, which means that the actual share of energy costs is substantially higher. In Argentina, energy costs were calculated as accounting for 43 per cent of the production costs of grain in 2006 (Baltzer, Hansen and Lind, 2008). When energy prices rise, agricultural commodity prices follow suit, as was seen in the food and oil price hikes in 2007–2008.[47] Higher energy prices influence food prices in four different ways:

i) By making food production more expensive;

ii) By making the production of crops for biofuel more remunerative and therefore reducing the production of food, thereby leading to higher food prices;

iii) Increasing transportation costs, which have a direct impact on food prices;

iv) Reducing competition in the food sector (i.e. increased transportation costs alleviate the pressure of global competition) (Rundgren, 2012).

D. It takes more energy to eat than to farm

The increase of energy use in agriculture was particularly rapid during the period between the Second World War and the first oil price shock in 1973. For example, in the United Kingdom, while the agricultural labour force was reduced to half between 1952 and 1972, energy use tripled (Bayliss-Smith, 1982). In the United States, energy use fell from the mid-1970s to the mid-1980s as a response to higher oil prices, but it stabilized thereafter (Hendrickson, 1994). However, looking at the entire food chain, energy use has constantly increased. Use of energy along the food chain for food purchases by or for households in the United States increased between 1997 and 2002 at more than six times the rate of increase in total domestic energy use. As a share of the national energy budget, food-related energy use grew from 12.2 per cent in 1997 to 14.4 per cent in 2002 (US CRS, 2004) (see also the comment of GRAIN in this chapter). In pre-industrial and semi-industrial agricultural systems, most of the food is sold, eaten and prepared close to where it is produced, but modern food chains are highly centralized and globalized. In industrialized countries, between 10 and 15 times more energy is used in the food system than is contained in the food we eat (Hendrickson, 1994).

A large proportion of the energy in the food system is used by consumers for buying, storing and preparing food. For example, in Sweden in 1997, of the total energy use in the food chain, agricultural production accounted for 15–19 per cent, processing for 17–20 per cent, distribution and retail for 20–29 per cent and consumption for 38–45 per cent. Another 7–11 per cent of the total energy is consumed by much-discussed transport, particularly in the final stretch to the point of purchase by the consumer. For instance, a person driving a car a distance of five kilometres for shopping uses a lot more energy per food unit than a ship transporting meat or soy from another continent. Also, in some developing countries, consumption takes the lion's share of energy use for food, in this case, mainly from cooking over an open fire. The energy used by this traditional method of cooking is equivalent to about 1,500 kWh per capita (corresponding to slightly more than a cubic metre of firewood), which is somewhere between half and one third of what is used per capita for cooking in Sweden or the United States (Uhlin, 1997). Cooking represents more than a fifth of the total energy consumption in Africa and Asia,[48] and in some countries, it represents up to or over 90 per cent of household energy consumption (IEA, 2006). Cooking consumes more energy than the food contains. Thus, while farming in developing countries and traditional systems is energy efficient, cooking is not.

Table 1: Agricultural labour productivity ($ per person/year)

	1990–1992	2001–2003	Agriculture as a share of GDP (%)
Low-income countries	315	363	20
Middle-income countries	530	708	9
High-income countries	14,997	24,438	2
France	22,234	39,220	2
United Kingdom	22,506	25,876	1
United States	20,797	36,216	1
Brazil	1,507	2,790	5
India	332	381	4
China	254	368	12
Malawi	72	130	36

Source: World Bank, 2008.

In a world with a rapidly increasing human population and the simultaneous depletion of natural resources, the industrial logic of replacing human labour with oil and other natural resources makes less and less sense. Increasing energy prices will reverse some of the developments that were made possible by cheap fossil fuel. This poses a challenge for society, but also an opportunity to steer towards a path of true sustainability, including the adoption of more sustainable agricultural methods (such as organic farming) and more localized food production networks. That those changes will also serve to mitigate climate change is another strong argument in favour of such a shift (in this regard, also see the lead article of chapter 1 and the comment of Leu).

The desired objective should not be to abolish the use of external energy and rely solely on manual labour; rather, it should be about finding a new balance that works on a global scale and is sustainable. Renewable energy, such as bio-energy, windmills and water mills have been used in farming for thousands of years. These could be improved and more widely adopted, and solar energy and biogas could also be added to the mix. It is not likely that renewable energy will allow such wasteful systems as exist today. For example, very cheap energy makes it profitable to use that energy to bind atmospheric nitrogen instead of using natural nitrogen fixation.

E. Unequal energy access and unequal terms of trade

Commercialization is promoted as the recipe for development for the almost half a billion smallholder

farmers in the world. Their traditional modes of farming are built on a rather high degree of autonomy, and these regenerate most of the needed resources, such as labour, capital, soil fertility and pest control, within the farming system. By nature, peasants resist commercialization because they wish to minimize risk and dependence (Van der Ploeg, 2009). If they were to be coerced into commercializing their production, most of them would simply not survive in the struggle for "modernization", and if they survived, there would be enormous overproduction. European farms experienced difficulties coping with competition from North America, especially after the introduction of steamship transport. The response was to introduce protectionist measures, even though they faced much less competitive pressure than today's poor farmers in developing countries. In addition, because of productivity gains in developed countries, global agricultural commodity prices fell by about 60 per cent during the period 1960–2000 (Dorward et al., 2002). Over the past few decades, as productivity and energy use by the poorest farmers have remained much the same, the productivity gap has widened, both relatively and in absolute numbers (table 1). As a result, it is clear that smallholder farmers in developing countries have been losing out. At current prices, it would require one lifetime of labour[49] by a farmer on a non-mechanized farm to acquire a pair of oxen and small animal-drawn equipment, and ten generations of labour to buy a small tractor (Mazoyer and Roudart, 2006).

It is entirely unrealistic to believe that smallholder farmers in developing countries, with their limited resources, would be able to compete in world markets for staple foods, where energy access is the main factor of competitive advantage. In reality, an increasing number of developing countries are becoming net food importers. Cheap energy may have been considered a way out of this situation, but this has not been the case. Indeed, it is cheap energy that has kept down the prices of agricultural products, and thereby the market value of smallholder farmers' labour to a dollar per day. And it is cheap energy that has allowed income gaps to widen to unprecedented levels because the rich producers have always been able to use more cheap energy than the poor. Thus the gap between those relying on their own labour and those relying on the use of fossil fuel has increased.

Energy scarcity and rising energy prices will result in less global competition and higher food prices. Such a development, while painful for many societies and for net food importers in the short run, will, nevertheless, be better for the smallholder farmers in developing countries in the long run, because it will encourage energy-efficient, low-external-input-dependent, closed loop, regenerative forms of agriculture with a greater focus on regional markets. Policymakers should seize this opportunity to promote a paradigm shift towards this form of agriculture, instead of promoting continued or increased dependence of agriculture on external inputs (e.g. fertilizers, genetically modified organisms and credits) and continued global competition in a market where the big players have unlimited access to cheap energy.

Commentary XIII: Sustainable Agriculture and Off-Grid Renewable Energy

Mae-Wan Ho
Institute of Science in Society, London

Abstract

Small integrated farms with off-grid renewable energy may be the perfect solution to the food and financial crises while mitigating and adapting to climate change.

A. Food crisis, global economic instability and political unrest

Soaring food prices were a major trigger for the riots that destabilized North Africa and West Asia, and have since spread to many other African countries (Harvey, 2011; Ho, 2011d). The FAO Food Price Index hit an all-time high in February 2011,[50] and reached 211 points in November 2011, some 30 points lower than at its peak, but 10 points higher than the average for 2008. This has been happening as the global economy is still staggering from the 2008 financial (and food) crisis, with public debt expanding and unemployment sky high (Filger, 2011).

Lester Brown (2011), veteran world-watcher, notes that food has quickly become the hidden driver of world politics, and food crises are going to become increasingly common. He says, "Scarcity is the new norm." The world is facing growing demand for food as population increases, yet food crops and land are being diverted to produce biofuels. In 2010, the United States alone turned 126 million tons of its 400 million tons of corn harvest into ethanol. At the same time, the world's ability to produce food is diminishing. Aquifers are running dry in the major food-producing countries where half of the world's population lives. There is widespread soil erosion and desertification, and global warming and weather extremes are already reducing crop yields (Peng et al., 2004; Lobell, Schlenker and Cost-Roberts, 2011; Jones, 2011; *Science Daily*, 2011), hitting the most vulnerable people in sub-Saharan Africa and South Asia the hardest.

Brown (2011) warns, "We are now so close to the edge that a breakdown in the food system could come at any time." He adds: "At issue now is whether the world can go beyond focusing on the symptoms of the deteriorating food situation and instead attack the underlying causes. If we cannot produce higher crop yields with less water and conserve fertile soils, many agricultural areas will cease to be viable... If we cannot move at wartime speed to stabilize the climate, we may not be able to avoid runaway food prices... The time to act is now – before the food crisis of 2011 becomes the new normal."

B. The importance of small family farms

There is an emerging scientific consensus that a shift to small-scale sustainable agriculture and localized food systems will address most, if not all, of the underlying causes of deteriorating agricultural productivity as well as the conservation of natural soil and water resources while saving the climate (Ho et al., 2008; IAASTD (undated); Hoffmann, 2011; De Schutter, 2011).

Small family farming is the dominant form of agriculture in the world, especially in the developing countries of Africa and Asia. Approximately 3 billion people live in rural areas in developing countries, which also include 80 per cent of the poor. Around 2.5 billion people are involved in agriculture as farmers or workers, and at least 75 per cent of farms in the majority of Asian and African countries are 2 ha or smaller (Quan, 2011). As Hoffmann (2011) points out, Millennium Development Goal (MDG) 1 aims at eradicating extreme hunger and poverty, and one of the most effective ways of halving both the number of hungry and poor by 2015 is to make the transition towards more sustainable forms of agriculture "that nourish the land and people and provide an opportunity for decent, financially rewarding and gender equal jobs." At the same time, this would *help* meet the health targets of MDGs 3 and 6 in providing a more diverse, safe, nutritious and affordable diet (see also Ho et al., 2008).

Small farms generally produce more per hectare than large ones, so much so that economists have long observed and debated this apparently paradoxical inverse relationship between farm size and productivity (Quan, 2011). Small farms are 2 to 10 times as productive and much more profitable, and not just in developing countries (Rosset, 2006). The United States Agricultural Census of 1992 found a sharp decline in net income, from $1,400/acre to $12/acre as farm size increased from 4 acres to 6,709 acres (Rosset, 1999). Small farms are also associated with "intensive use of household and community labour, high levels of motivation and much lower supervision and transaction costs" (Quan, 2011), which may well explain their economic advantages, but not their actual productivity. These farms are highly productive because they are typically biodiverse systems that integrate multiple crops and livestock, which enables them to maximize synergetic relationships while minimizing wastes, as they turn wastes such as farmyard manure into fertilizer. In effect, they embody the circular economy of nature (Ho et al., 2008) wherein energy and nutrients are recycled within the ecosystem for maximum productivity and carbon sequestration, both above and below ground (see, for example, Ho, 2008 for a detailed description of this "thermodynamics of organisms and sustainable systems").

C. The importance of renewable energy

To substantially improve living standards, sustainable farming is not enough; access to modern energy is also crucial. Indeed, lack of access to modern energy is generally recognized as the biggest obstacle to sustainable development. According to the International Energy Agency (IEA, 2010), "Lack of access to modern energy services is a serious hindrance to economic and social development and must be overcome if the UN Millennium Development Goals (MDGs) are to be achieved." This view is echoed by the Academy of Science of South Africa (2010), which states: "Access to modern energy services, defined as electricity and clean cooking fuels, is central to a country's development."

Worldwide, 1.4 billion people lack access to electricity, 85 per cent of whom live in rural areas, and 2.7 billion people still rely on traditional biomass fuels for cooking and heating (IEA, 2010). The greatest challenge is in sub-Saharan Africa, where only 31 per cent of the population has access to electricity, the lowest level in

the world, and if South Africa is excluded, only 28 per cent have such access.

There is a close correlation between income levels and access to modern energy. Countries with a large proportion of the population living on an income of less than $2 per day tend to have low electrification rates and a high percentage of the population that relies on traditional biomass. The World Health Organization (WHO, 2011) estimates that 1.45 million people die prematurely each year from household air pollution due to inefficient biomass combustion, a significant proportion being young children. This is greater than premature deaths from malaria or tuberculosis.

Small agroecological farms are ideally served by new renewable energies that can be generated and used on-site and in off-grid situations most often found in developing countries (Ho et al., 2009; Ho, 2010a). The renewable energies generated can also serve local businesses, stimulate local economies and create numerous employment opportunities.

D. Off-grid renewable power systems are entering the mainstream worldwide

Within the past few years, off-grid power systems have entered the mainstream, driven by the ready availability of renewable energy options that can cost less than grid connections.

A United Kingdom company, Energy Solutions, advertises on its website[51] that homes in Europe, including the United Kingdom, "are looking at the potential benefits of supplying some, if not all their domestic power requirement from off-grid sources." This could be for a variety of reasons, such as connection to the grid being too expensive, and the desire to reduce energy bills, protection from power cuts and reduction of GHG emissions. Solar panels, wind turbines and small generators are suitable for most homes, and a system with a battery connected to a battery charger/inverter is the most convenient.

Examples of small-scale off-grid energy provision based on renewables can be found across Scotland (Community Energy Scotland, 2011), such as in remote ferry waiting rooms on the Western Iles and the Charles Inglis Clark Memorial hut on Ben Nevis that uses small wind turbines. Photovoltaic (PV) installations integrated with batteries are often used where only a small amount of power is required, as for lighting, maintaining power for monitoring equipment or maintaining water treatment facilities. However, it is in developing countries, that off-grid renewable energy is rapidly gaining ground. In these countries, power requirements are generally low and electronic lighting and telecommunication equipment are improving rapidly, with low power requirements and reliable performance, and requiring little or no maintenance (Ho, 2010a). Three examples of large-scale off-grid renewable energy use with varying degrees of success are the Grameen Shakti in Bangladesh (Ho, 2011a), Lighting Africa (Ho, 2011b) and Biogas for China's Socialist Countryside (Ho, 2011c).

Grameen Shakti is a non-profit organization founded in 1996 to promote, develop and supply renewable energy to the rural poor of Bangladesh. It started by training "barefoot women engineers" for installing, maintaining and repairing solar panels, lights, telephone charging, batteries and other accessories. It has now become one of the world's largest and fastest

growing renewable energy organizations through a system of microfinancing, training of technicians (mainly women) for installation, maintenance and repair and provision of services, including buy-back. It runs technology centres for training throughout the country (see Ho, 2011a for details). At the end of May 2011, Grameen Shakti had installed 636,322 solar home systems, 18,046 biogas plants and 304,414 improved cooking stoves. It had also trained a total of 28,932 technicians in 46 technology centres nationwide, covering all the districts. Its beneficiaries are 40,000 villages with a total of about 4 million people (Grameen Shakti, 2011). What began as a grassroots endeavour to provide solar light for the rural population has now attracted the backing of the World Bank.

Lighting Africa is now a joint World Bank and International Finance Corporation programme that aims to help develop commercial off-grid lighting

Figure 14: Dream Farm 2: an integrated food and energy system

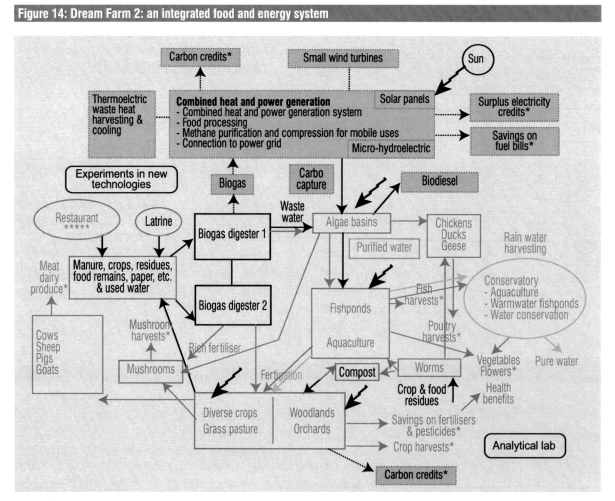

Source: Ho et al., 2008.

Table 2: Green potential of organic agriculture and anaerobic digestion in China

	CO_2e savings (Mt)	(% national)	Energy savings (EJ)	(% national)
Organic agriculture				
N fertilizers saving	179.5	2.38	2.608	3.61
N_2O prevented	92.7	1.23		
Carbon sequestration	682.9	9.07		
Total for organic agriculture	**955.1**	**12.69**	**2.608**	**3.61**
Anaerobic digestion				
Livestock manure GHG saving	70.3	0.09		
Methane produced	215.5	2.86	3.124	4.33
Humus manure methane	7.7	0.10	0.112	0.16
Straw methane	292.5	3.93	4.234	5.86
Total for anaerobic digestion	**586.0**	**7.79**	**7.470**	**10.35**
Total overall	**1,491.1**	**20.48**	**10.078**	**13.96**

Source: Ho, 2010b.
Note: Mt=megatons; EJ= Exajoule

Table 3: Green potential of Dream Farm 2

	CO_2e savings (Mt)	(% national)	Energy savings (EJ)	(% national)
Organic agriculture	955.1	-12.69	2.608	-3.61
Anaerobic digestion	586.0	-7.79	7.470	-10.35
Enery savings local gen.	1,287.1	-17.10	21.660	-30.00
Total	**2,828.2**	**-37.58**	**31.738**	**-43.96**

Source: Ho, 2010b.

markets in sub-Saharan Africa as part of the World Bank Group's wider efforts to improve access to energy.[52] It aims to provide safe, affordable, and modern off-grid lighting to 2.5 million people in Africa by 2012 and to 250 million by 2030. The market for off-grid lighting products is projected to grow at 40 to 50 per cent annually. In 2010 alone, sales of solar portable lanterns that had passed Lighting Africa's quality control tests grew by 70 per cent in Africa, resulting in more than 672,000 people having access to cleaner, safer, reliable lighting and improved energy (see Ho, 2011b for details).

In China, provision of biogas is an important part of the country's New Socialist Countryside programme launched in 2006 to improve the welfare of those living outside booming cities, which include the country's 130 million migrant workers and rural poor. China is one of the first countries in the world to use biogas technology, and it has been revived in successive campaigns by the present government to provide

domestic sanitation and off-grid energy, and to modernize agriculture (for details, see Ho, 2011c; Li and Ho, 2006). An anaerobic digester producing biogas is typically combined with a greenhouse for growing vegetables and other crops, along with a pigsty so that pig and human manure can be digested, while CO_2 generated by the pigs boosts plant growth in the greenhouse. The biogas produced (typically 60 per cent of methane and 40 per cent of CO_2, along with traces of other gases) can be used as cooking fuel and to generate electricity, while the residue provides a rich fertilizer for crops. It is an example of the circular economy that has served Chinese peasants well in traditional Chinese agriculture (Ho, 2006). More elaborate models include orchards and solar panels. According to a recent survey from China's Ministry of Agriculture (Wang, 2011), 35 million household biogas tanks had been installed by the end of 2009 through 56,500 biogas projects. This exponential growth phase that started around 2001 is set to continue, along with medium and big digesters for community and industrial use. Anaerobic digestion of organic wastes is a key off-grid renewable energy technology for a truly green circular economy that could make a real difference for improving the lives of the rural poor.

E. Integrating sustainable farming and renewable energies in a circular economy

A model that explicitly integrates sustainable farming and renewable energies is Dream Farm 2, which optimizes the sustainable use of resources and minimizes waste in accordance with the circular economy principles (figure 14; see also Ho et al., 2008). It is patterned on a design developed by environmental engineer George Chan and the dyke-pond system of the Pearl River Delta that Chinese peasants have perfected over thousands of years – a system so productive that it supported 17 people per hectare in its heyday (Ho, 2006).

In the diagram, a grey background with dotted borders is for energy, green for agricultural produce, grey text for water conservation and flood control, and black is for waste in the ordinary sense of the word, which soon gets converted into food and energy resources. A rounded rectangle is for education and research into new science and technologies.

This ideal Dream Farm is complete with laboratory facilities for education, as well as a restaurant to take advantage of all the fresh produce. It is a perfect setting for developing cottage industries such as food preservation, processing, wine and cheese-making and bread-making, not to mention electronic workshops, battery charging, and retailing of renewable energy components and electronic devices. The synergies between agriculture and industries are obvious, especially in the case of food industries, as they are close to the source of production. Moreover, the organic wastes from these industries can go right back into anaerobic digestion to be converted into

energy and nutrients for agriculture.

Some preliminary estimates, based on data and statistics made available by the Chinese Government and academics on the energy and carbon savings involved are presented in tables 2 and 3.

As can be seen from table 2, the combination of organic agriculture and anaerobic digestion has the potential to mitigate at least 20 per cent of national GHG emissions and save 14 per cent of energy consumption in China. If Dream Farm 2 were to be applied throughout the country, China would mitigate 38 per cent of its GHG emissions, and save 44 per cent of energy consumption, only counting anaerobic digestion, basically as a result of efficiency savings from using "waste" heat in combined heat and power generation, and avoiding loss from long distance transmission of electricity. A conservative allowance of 30 per cent efficiency saving (out of a maximum of about 60 per cent) gives the net carbon and energy savings shown in table 3. Again, this is from anaerobic digestion only. The savings could be far greater if low power consuming LED lighting and other electronic devices were to replace conventional high power consuming models.

With the addition of solar, wind or micro-hydroelectric, as appropriate, and batteries to store and maintain a steady power supply, such farms could compensate, in the best case scenario, for the carbon emissions and energy consumption of the entire country. Surplus energy from the farm could be used to supply homes and businesses in the vicinity through a mini-grid that could eventually link up to the national grid, if necessary or desirable. This could be a model for the natural evolution of connectivity and power-sharing. At the very least, such integrated food and energy farms would contribute to food security while playing their part, along with other sectors of the circular economy, in cutting their own carbon footprint. Furthermore, such small-scale agroecological farming and local renewable power generation are much more resistant and resilient to weather extremes, and indeed to earthquakes and sabotage.

Commentary XIV: Soil Erosion: A Threat to Food Security and Climate Change

David Pimentel and Michael Burgess
College of Agriculture and Life Sciences, Cornell University, Ithaca, New York

Abstract

Soil is the most valuable resource for world food production. Humans worldwide obtain more than 99.7 per cent of their food (calories) from land and less than 0.3 per cent from the oceans and other aquatic ecosystems. Each year about 10 million hectares (ha) (or about 0.7 per cent) of cropland are lost due to soil erosion, thus reducing the cropland available for world food production. This loss is a serious problem because, as the World Health Organization and the Food and Agriculture Organization of the United Nations report, at present 66 per cent of the world population (i.e. 4.7 billion people) is malnourished. Meanwhile, global warming is worsening and can be traced back to a not insignificant extent to increased soil erosion, fossil fuel use and the clearing of forests worldwide.

A. Introduction

The loss of soil from land surfaces by erosion is widespread and reduces the productivity of all natural ecosystems as well as that of agricultural, forest and pasture ecosystems (Lal and Stewart, 1990; Pimentel et al., 1995; Troeh, Hobbs and Donahue, 2004). Concurrently with the escalating human population, soil erosion, water availability, fossil energy use and climate change are emerging as the prime environmental problems throughout the world.

Currently, 66 per cent of the world population (i.e. 4.7 billion people) is malnourished (WHO, 2000; FAO, 2009b). This is the largest number of malnourished people ever in history. With the world population now at 7 billion, and expected to reach 9 billion by 2050, more food supplies will be needed. Considering that, at present, more than 99.7 per cent of human food (calories) comes from the land (FAO, 2011c), while less than 0.3 per cent derives from the oceans and other aquatic ecosystems, maintaining and augmenting the world's food supply basically depends on the productivity and quality of all soils.

Human-induced soil erosion and the associated deterioration in soil quality over many years have resulted in the loss of valuable soils and reduced productivity of the land, with some cropland being abandoned each year (Pimentel et al., 1995; Young, 1998; Pimentel, 2006). Clearly, when soil erosion diminishes soil quality it reduces the productivity of natural, agricultural and forest ecosystems. In addition, the important diversity of plants, animals and microbes is reduced.

In this paper, the diverse factors that cause soil erosion are assessed and the extent of damage associated with such erosion is analysed, with emphasis on the impact this may have on future human food security and climate change.

B. Causes of erosion

Erosion occurs when soil is left exposed to rain or wind energy. For example, about 1,000 mm of rain falling on one hectare (ha) of land in New York State provides the energy equivalent of 60,000 kcal per year. This is about the equivalent of the energy in 8 litres of gasoline. Raindrops hitting soil loosen it, and even if there is a gradient of only 1 per cent, it will cause the soil to flow downhill. This so-called, sheet erosion is the dominant type of erosion (Troeh, Hobbs and Donohue, 2004). The impact of soil erosion is intensified on all sloping land, where more than half of the surface soil is carried away as the water splashes downhill into valleys and streams.

Wind energy also has considerable power to dislodge surface soil particles and transport them over long distances. A dramatic example of this was the wind erosion in Kansas during the relatively dry and windy winter of 1995–1996. During just this one winter period, approximately 65 tons/ha of soil were eroded from this valuable cropland. Wind energy is sufficiently strong to propel soil particles thousands of kilometres, as illustrated by NASA's report of a cloud of soil being blown from the African continent to the South and North American continents.[53]

1. The role of vegetative cover

Land areas covered by plant biomass, living or dead, are more resistant and experience relatively little soil erosion, because raindrop and wind energy are dissipated by the biomass layer and the topsoil is held together by the biomass. For example, in Utah and Montana, it was found that as the amount of ground cover decreased from 100 per cent to less than 1 per cent, erosion rates increased approximately 200-fold (Trimbel and Mendel, 1995). In forested areas, a minimum of 60 per cent of forest cover is necessary to prevent serious soil erosion and landslides (United States Forest Conservation Act, 2002). Therefore, the extensive removal of forests for crops and pasture is followed by intensive soil erosion.

Loss of vegetation that provides soil cover is especially widespread in developing countries where populations are large and agricultural practices are often inadequate to protect topsoils. In addition, cooking and heating in these countries frequently depend on the use of crop residues for fuel (Pimentel and Pimentel, 2008). For example, about 60 per cent of crop residues in China and 90 per cent in Bangladesh are removed routinely from the land and burned as fuel (Wen, 1993). In areas where fuelwood and other biomass are scarce, even the roots of grasses and shrubs are collected and burned (Juo and Thurow, 1998). All these practices leave the soil barren and fully exposed to the forces of rain and wind erosion.

2. Other soil disturbances

While agriculture accounts for about 75 per cent of soil erosion worldwide, such erosion occurs whenever humans remove vegetative cover (Lal and Stewart, 1990). Construction of roads, parking lots and buildings is an example of this problem. However, although the rate of erosion from construction sites may be exceedingly high, it lasts for a relatively brief period, after which, once the land surface is seeded to grass or covered with other vegetation, the erosion declines (IECA, 1991).

Natural ecosystems also suffer losses from erosion. This is especially evident along stream banks, where erosion takes place naturally from the powerful action of adjacent moving water. Increased soil loss occurs on steep slopes (with gradients of 30 per cent or more) when a stream cuts through adjacent land, but even on relatively flat land, with only a 2 per cent gradient, stream banks are eroded during heavy rains and flooding.

C. Assessing soil erosion

It is estimated that approximately 75 billion tons of fertile soils worldwide are lost from agricultural systems each year (Myers, 1993), whereas relatively little erosion occurs in natural ecosystems. Soil scientists Lal and Stewart (1990) and Wen (1997) report that, annually, 6.6 billion tons of soil are lost in India and 5.5 billion tons in China. Considering these two countries together occupy only 13 per cent of the world's total land area, the estimated 75 billion tons of soil lost each year worldwide is conservative. The amount of soil lost annually in the United States is estimated to be about 3 billion tons (NAS, 2003).

1. Soil erosion on cropland worldwide

Currently, about 80 per cent of the world's agricultural land suffers moderate to severe erosion, while 10 per cent experiences slight erosion (Speth, 1994). Worldwide, erosion on cropland averages about 30 t/ha/yr, and ranges from 0.5 to 400 t/ha/yr (Pimentel et al., 1995). As a result of soil erosion over the past 40 years, about 30 per cent of the world's cropland has become unproductive, and much of that has been abandoned for crop use (Kendall and Pimentel, 1994; WRI, 1997).

Worldwide, the nearly 1.5 billion ha of land now under cultivation for crop production are almost equal in area to the amount of cropland (2 billion ha) that has been abandoned by humans since farming began. Such abandoned land, once biologically and economically productive, now produces little biomass, but also it has lost the considerable diversity of plants, animals and microbes it once supported (Heywood, 1995; Pimentel et al., 2006). Moreover, because of the decline in biomass in some agricultural production, less carbon is taken up and sequestered (see the commentary of GRAIN in this chapter).

Each year an estimated 10 million ha of cropland worldwide are abandoned due to their lack of productivity caused by soil erosion (Faeth and Crosson, 1994). Losses from soil erosion are highest in the agroecosystems of Asia, Africa and South

America, averaging 30 to 40 t/ha/yr (Pimentel, 2006). In developing countries, soil erosion is particularly severe on small farms that are often located on marginal lands where the soil quality is poor and the topography frequently steep. In addition, the poor farmers tend to raise row crops, such as corn and beans, which are highly susceptible to erosion because the crop vegetation does not cover the entire tilled soil surface (Stone and Moore, 1997). For example, in the Sierra region of Ecuador, about 60 per cent of the cropland has been abandoned because of the devastation caused by rainfall and wind erosion and inappropriate agricultural practices (Southgate and Whitaker, 1992). Similar problems are evident in the Amazonian region of South America, where vast forested areas have been cleared for cultivation of sugarcane and other crops, as well as for livestock production.

2. Erosion rates on pastures and rangelands

In the United States, in contrast to the average soil loss of 13 t/ha/yr from cropland, pastures lose soil at the rate of about 6 t/ha/yr (NAS, 2003). However, erosion rates on pastures intensify wherever overgrazing is allowed to occur. Even in the United States, about 75 per cent of non-Federal lands require conservation treatments to reduce grazing pressure (Johnson, 1995). More than half of all rangelands in the country – both non-Federal and Federal – are overgrazed and have become subject to high erosion rates (Bailey, 1996).

Although erosion rates on cropland in the United States have decreased during the past two decades, those on pastures and rangelands remain high (6 t/ha/yr) (NAS, 2003). Indeed, high erosion rates are typical on most of the world's pastures and rangelands (WRI, 1997). In many developing countries, heavy grazing by cattle, sheep and goats has removed most of the vegetative cover, exposing the soil to severe soil erosion. In Africa, about 80 per cent of the pasture and rangeland is seriously eroded and degraded (UN-NADAF, 1996). The prime causes of this exposed soil are overgrazing and the removal of crop residues for use as cooking fuel.

3. Soil erosion in forest land

In stable forest ecosystems, where soil is protected by vegetation, erosion rates are relatively low, ranging from only 0.004 to 0.05 t/ha/yr (Roose, 1998). Tree leaves and branches not only intercept and diminish raindrop and wind energy, but also cover the soil under the trees, which further protects it. However, the situation changes dramatically when forests are cleared for crop production or when pastures are developed for livestock production (Southgate and Whitaker, 1992).

D. Effects of soil erosion

1. Water availability

Water is a major limiting factor of crop productivity in all terrestrial ecosystems, because all vegetation requires enormous quantities of water for its growth and for the production of fruit. For example, 1 ha of corn will transpire about 7 million litres of water during the growing season of about three months (Pimentel et al., 2004), and lose an additional 2 million litres of water by evaporation from the soil. During erosion by rainfall, the amount of water runoff significantly increases, with less water entering the soil and therefore less water available to support the growing vegetation. On average, a corn crop of 1 kg requires about 1,000 litres of water for production while rice requires about 2,000 litres.

2. Nutrient loss

Eroded soil carries away vital plant nutrients such as nitrogen, phosphorus, potassium and calcium. Typically, eroded soil contains about three times more nutrients than those left in the remaining soil (Langdale et al., 1992). One ton of fertile topsoil or eroded fertile soil contains an average of 1 to 6 kg of nitrogen, 1 to 3 kg of phosphorus, and 2 to 30 kg of potassium, whereas the topsoil on eroded land has an average nitrogen content of only 0.1 to 0.5 kg per ton (Langdale et al., 1992).

To compensate for the nutrient losses inflicted on crop production, large quantities of fertilizers are often applied. Troeh et al. (2004) point out that the lost soil nutrients cost agriculture in the United States several billions of dollars annually. If the soil base is relatively deep (about 300 mm), and if only 10–20 tons of soil is lost per hectare per year, the lost nutrients can be replaced with the application of commercial fertilizers and/or livestock manure. However, such a replacement strategy is expensive for farmers and the country, and usually is not affordable by the poorer farmers. Not only are the fertilizer inputs dependent on fossil energy, but also the chemicals can harm human health and pollute the environment (NAS, 2003).

3. Soil organic matter

Soil organic matter is a valuable resource because it facilitates the formation of soil aggregates and thereby increases soil porosity. The improved soil structure in turn facilitates water infiltration and ultimately the overall productivity of the soil (Langdale et al., 1992). In addition, organic matter aids cation exchange, enhances plant root growth, and stimulates an increase in important soil microbes (Wardle et al., 2004). When the layer of organic matter is depleted, the productivity of the ecosystem, as measured by plant biomass, declines both because of the degraded soil structure and the depletion of nutrients contained in the organic matter. In addition to low yields, the total biomass of the biota and the overall biodiversity of those ecosystems are substantially reduced (Lazaroff, 2001; Walsh and Rowe, 2001).

Fertile soils typically contain 100 tons/ha of organic matter (i.e. 4–5 per cent of their total soil weight) (Pimentel et al., 2005), which has about 95 per cent of nitrogen and 25–50 per cent of phosphorus. Because most of the soil organic matter is found close to the soil surface as decaying leaves and stems, it is significantly reduced by erosion. Both wind and water erosion selectively remove the fine organic particles in the soil, leaving behind large soil particles and stones. Several studies have demonstrated that the soil removed by either water or wind erosion is 1.3 to 5 times richer in organic matter than the remaining soils, resulting in lower crop yield. For example, the reduction of soil organic matter ranging from 0.9 to 1.4 per cent was found to lower the crop yield potential for grain by 50 per cent (Libert, 1995).

Collectively and independently, the diverse impacts of erosion reduce crop biomass, both because of degraded soil structure and nutrient depletion.

4. Soil depth

Growing plants require soils of adequate depth in which to extend their roots. Various soil biota, such as earthworms, also require a suitable soil depth (Pimentel et al., 1995; Wardle et al., 2004). Thus, when erosion reduces soil depth substantially, from 30 cm to less than 1 cm, there is minimal space for plant roots so that plant growth will be stunted and yield reduced.

5. Biomass and biodiversity

The biological diversity existing in any ecosystem is related directly to the amount of living and non-living organic matter present in that ecosystem (Wright, 1990; Heywood, 1995; Lazaroff, 2001; Walsh and Rowe, 2001; Wardle et al., 2004). Therefore, by diminishing soil organic matter and soil quality, erosion reduces the overall biomass and productivity, which ultimately has a profoundly adverse effect on the diversity of plants, animals and microbes present in the ecosystem. Numerous positive associations have been established between biomass abundance and species diversity (Elton, 1927; Odum, 1978; Sugden and Rands, 1990). Vegetation is the main component of ecosystem biomass and provides the vital resources required both by animals and microbes for their survival.

Along with plants and animals, microbes are a vital component of the soil, and constitute a large percentage of the soil biomass. One cubic metre of soil may support about 200,000 arthropods, 10,000 earthworms plus billions of microbes (Lee and Foster, 1991; Pimentel et al., 2006). A hectare of productive soil may have a biomass of invertebrates and microbes weighing up to 10,000 kg/ha. In addition, soil bacteria and fungi add 4,000 to 6,000 species, thereby contributing significantly to biodiversity, especially in moist, organic soils (Heywood, 1995; Pimentel et al., 2006).

Erosion rates that are 10 to 20 times above the sustainability rate or soil formation rates of 0.5–1 ton/ha/yr reduce the diversity and abundance of soil organisms (Pimentel et al., 2006). In contrast, agricultural practices that control erosion and maintain adequate soil organic matter favour the proliferation of soil biota (Reid, 1985; Pimentel et al., 2006). The application of organic matter or manure also enhances biodiversity in the soil (Pimentel et al., 2006). Species diversity of macrofauna (mostly arthropods) increased 16 per cent when organic matter or manure was applied to experimental wheat plots in the former Soviet Union (Bohac and Pokarzhevsky, 1987). Similarly, species diversity of macrofauna (mostly arthropods) more than doubled when organic manure was added to grassland plots in Japan, and increased 10-fold in Hungarian farmland (Olah-Zsupos and Helmeczi, 1987).

The relationship between biomass and biodiversity was confirmed in field experiments with collards in which arthropod species diversity rose fourfold in experimental plots with the highest collard biomass compared with that in control collard plots. Reports suggest that when the biomass increased threefold, the number of species increased 16-fold. In a study of bird populations, a strong correlation between plant biomass productivity and bird species diversity was reported when a 100-fold increase in plant biomass yielded a 10-fold increase in bird diversity (Wright, 1990).

Soil biota perform many beneficial activities that improve soil quality and ultimately its productivity (Witt, 1997; Sugden, Stone and Ash, 2004; Pimentel et al., 2006). For example, soil biota recycle basic nutrients required by plants for their growth (Pimentel et al., 2006). In addition, the tunneling and burrowing activities of earthworms and other soil biota enhance crop productivity by increasing water infiltration (Witt, 1997). Earthworms, for instance, may construct up to 220 tunnel openings per square metre, which enable the water to infiltrate rapidly into the soil. Other soil biota also contribute to soil formation and productivity by mixing the soil components, enhancing aggregate stability and preventing soil crusting. This churning and mixing of the upper soil redistributes nutrients, aerates the soil, exposes it to the climate for soil formation and increases infiltration rates, thus making soil conditions favourable for increased soil formation and plant productivity. Earthworms bring from 10 to 500 t/ha/yr of soil from underground to the soil surface, while some insects, such as ants, may bring as much as 34 t/ha/yr of soil to the surface (Lockaby and Adams, 1985). Snails are reported to help the formation of 1t/ha/yr of soil.

6. Soil sediments

The long-range transport of dust by wind has implications for human health worldwide. Griffin, Kellogg and Shinn (2001) report that about 20 human infectious disease-carrying organisms, such as anthrax and tuberculosis, are easily transported by the wind in soil particles.

Soil erosion also contributes to global warming, because carbon dioxide (CO_2) is added to the atmosphere when enormous amounts of biomass are exposed and oxidized (Phillips and Helmeczi, 1987; Lal, 2002; Walsh and Rowe, 2001). One hectare of soil may contain about 100 tons of organic matter or biomass, which, if eroded, would contribute about

45 tons of carbon to the atmosphere. A feedback mechanism exists wherein increased global warming intensifies rainfall, which in turn increases erosion and continues the cycle (Lal, 2002).

7. Global climate change

Extensive burning of fossil fuels and forests appears to be increasing the level of CO_2 and other greenhouse gases (GHGs) in the atmosphere, which raises several ethical issues and choices. Clearly there is an urgent need to reduce fossil fuel consumption and deforestation to slow down the rate of global climate change. Reducing fossil fuel consumption will also conserve forests, and controlling deforestation has other benefits, including conserving biological diversity.

A large number of meteorologists and physical scientists estimate that the continued increase in CO_2 and other GHGs will warm the earth from 1.5 degrees Celsius to 4.5 degrees Celsius by the end of this century. The precise rate, extent and regional variations are difficult to predict, but negative impacts are generally projected, especially on crop production. Additional negative impacts on some crops could result from alterations in the ozone layer. Thus the overall changes in temperature, moisture, CO_2, insect pests, plant pathogens and weeds associated with global climate change are projected to reduce food production worldwide (Pimentel, 2011). The extent of alterations of crop yields will depend on specific crops and their particular environmental requirements. Hopefully, implementation of improved agricultural technologies could partially offset some of this decrease in yields. In addition, productive agriculture and an increase in soil carbon could help mitigate climate change (also see the commentary of Leu in this chapter).

In Africa, the projected rise in rainfall associated with global climate change could help improve crop yields to some extent, but it will not entirely solve Africa's food shortages, given the rapid rate of increase of its population. Water shortages are projected to persist and pests are expected to continue to result in serious crop losses (Pimentel, 2011). These factors, as well as serious economic and political problems, imply that food production in Africa is likely to remain slow.

Commentary XV: Competition for Water for Agriculture through 2050[53]

Brent Boehlert, Industrial Economics, Inc., and
Kenneth Strzepek, Massachusetts Institute of Technology

Abstract

Owing to rising populations, increasing per capita water use, environmental flow requirements, and climate change, our results suggest that by 2050 there will be significant threats to water availability for agriculture in many regions of the world. If rising agricultural demands and the full spectrum of climate change effects are taken into account, threats to water availability will be considerably more pronounced. It is therefore likely that, unless broad changes are made to the way environmental and water resources are governed, conflicts over water for agriculture will increase markedly by the middle of the twenty-first century. Changes in governance may include reforming the policies and institutions that manage and allocate water, improving access to water in the poorest regions of the world, enhancing ecosystem services, recognizing water as an economic good in order to promote efficiency of use, improving rain-fed and irrigation infrastructure to increase "crop per drop", and making agriculture more resilient to changes in climate.[54] In the light of these threats to water for agriculture, and therefore to global food availability, it is important – and urgent – that water planning efforts be coordinated and integrated across sectors, particularly in the most vulnerable regions.

Globally, 2,600 km³ of water are withdrawn each year to irrigate crops, representing over two thirds of all withdrawals by people. As water scarcity intensifies and many of the world's river basins approach closure (i.e. all water supplies have been put to use for at least part of the year), water is increasingly transferred out of agriculture to provide for other demands, such as energy generation or growing urban populations. Given that, at current population levels, the food system is already water-stressed and global water resources are under considerable pressure, this will only intensify as populations increase further.[56] Additionally, and perhaps even more problematically, rising incomes in developing countries are causing diets to shift to more water-intensive agricultural products that require greater levels of water service, for example from community standpipes to plumbing systems. Together, these shifts are rapidly increasing per capita water demand in developing countries. Figure 15 presents these projected water use trends for OECD and non-OECD countries through 2050. Importantly, water use is projected to more than double in the municipal sector within non-OECD countries, where agriculture tends to be the most vulnerable to climate change.

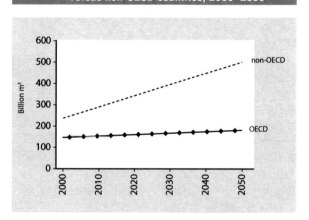

Figure 15: Total projected municipal water use in OECD versus non-OECD countries, 2005–2050

Source: Hughes, Chinowsky and Strzepek, 2010.
Note: Squares with solid lines, non-OECD; diamonds with solid lines, OECD.

Simultaneously, to meet higher food demands for growing populations, agriculture is expanding to new regions and becoming more productive, which rapidly increases the demand for water. As a result, groundwater supplies, on which much of agriculture relies, are declining globally (Konikow and Kendy, 2005). At the same time, energy consumption and other industrial activities in many countries are continuing to increase, causing industrial water consumption to rise. Perhaps most importantly – and most overlooked – environmental flow requirements (EFRs) are increasingly being recognized as a crucial element of a functioning riparian ecosystem and, accordingly, are progressively being instated as part of environmental management (Falkenmark and Rockström, 2006; Smakhtin, 2008). As EFRs are established, remaining water for agriculture will be further diminished. In addition to the growing demand on water resources, climate change will significantly affect the timing, distribution and magnitude of water availability (Arnell, 1998; Milly, Dunne and Vecchia, 2005; IPCC, 2008). Where shifts in water availability reduce regional water supplies, agriculture will be further threatened.

In this paper, we consider the fraction of current withdrawals from surface water systems for agriculture that may be threatened due to increasing water demands in other sectors, limits imposed on withdrawals to meet EFRs, and a range of potential climate change effects.[57] We comment on the relative importance of each competing pressure, and identify geographic "hotspots" where water for agriculture could be substantially reduced.

A. Methods: modelled threats to water for agriculture

Considering the demand- and supply-side factors that

will affect the amount of water available for agriculture, we model the possible implications for agricultural water availability through 2050 under climate change. Specifically, for a number of geopolitical regions/countries, and under three climate change scenarios, we estimate the fraction of current agricultural withdrawals that would be threatened assuming that EFRs and increased municipal and industrial (M&I) demands cause total basin withdrawals to exceed mean annual runoff (MAR) in the basin.[58,59]

We consider a total of three climate change and three demand scenarios. On the demand side, we consider the effects of 2050 M&I demands alone, EFRs alone, and 2050 M&I and EFR demands together. M&I demand projections to 2050 are taken from World Bank projections for 214 countries (Hughes, Chinowsky and Strzepek, 2010). EFRs are assumed to be the basin flows necessary to maintain riparian ecosystems in "fair" condition (for details, see Smakhtin, Revenga and Döll, 2004). For the climate change analysis, we evaluate a baseline (i.e. no climate change) scenario, and two climate change scenarios based on the range of available general circulation models (GCMs). We follow the World Bank's Economics of Adaptation to Climate Change (EACC) analysis (World Bank, 2009), and model the climate change scenarios under the A2 SRES emissions scenario (see IPCC, 2009) using the global climate models (GCMs) of the United States' National Center for Atmospheric Research (NCAR) and of the Commonwealth Scientific and Industrial

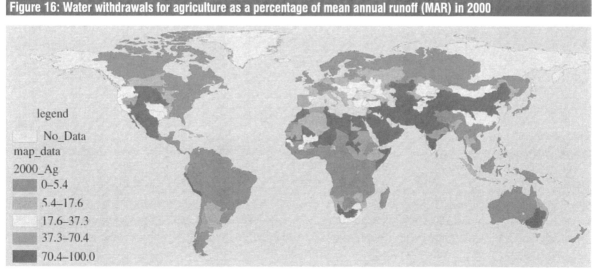

Figure 16: Water withdrawals for agriculture as a percentage of mean annual runoff (MAR) in 2000

legend

No_Data
map_data
2000_Ag
0–5.4
5.4–17.6
17.6–37.3
37.3–70.4
70.4–100.0

Source: Authors' calculations

Research Organisation (of Australia), which the World Bank considers to represent generally wetter and drier climate models, respectively. In total, we consider nine scenarios, each with a different climate-demand combination, and then compare each to the year 2000 baseline.

To model changes in MAR, we use the CLIRUN II hydrologic model (Strzepek et al., forthcoming), which is the latest model in the "Kaczmarek school" of hydrologic models (Yates, 1996) developed specifically for analysing the impact of climate change on runoff and extreme events on an annual basis. CLIRUN II models runoff in 126 world river basins with climate inputs and soil characteristics averaged over each river basin. Because data on 2000 agricultural and M&I withdrawals are available

for 116 economic regions of the world, we intersect the 126 river basins with these economic regions to form 281 food production units (FPUs) (see Strzepek and McCluskey, 2007, and Rosegrant et al., 2009a and 2009b), which form the geographic unit of our analysis. For each FPU, our baseline data include current MAR values, 2000 agricultural withdrawals and 2000 M&I withdrawals. In 2000, roughly 10 per cent of worldwide MAR was withdrawn for agriculture, and 4.3 per cent was withdrawn for M&I use (figure 16).

B. Findings: threats to water for agriculture

We find that EFRs and increased M&I water demands together will cause an 18 per cent reduction in the

Table 4: Percentage of agricultural water threatened in the geopolitical regions, nine scenarios[a]

Region/country	Agricultural withdrawals, 2000 (billion m³)	No climate change			NCAR (wet) climate change			CSIRO (dry) climate change		
		M&I 2050 (%)	EFRs (%)	M&I 2050 and EFRs (%)	M&I 2050 (%)	EFRs (%)	M&I 2050 and EFRs (%)	M&I 2050 (%)	EFRs (%)	M&I 2050 and EFRs (%)
World	**2,946**	**7.3**	**9.4**	**17.7**	**7.1**	**9.1**	**16.5**	**7.0**	**9.1**	**16.9**
Europe	263	2.5	7.7	14.4	2.5	9.6	12.9	2.8	16.5	20.4
European Union	95	0.7	12.8	18.7	0.7	21.2	19.0	1.6	39.0	37.0
North-Western Europe	16	4.5	11.7	8.2	4.5	14.6	10.2	3.2	10.4	8.2
United Kingdom	0.6	0.0	0.0	0.0	0.0	0.0	0.0	0.0	0.0	0.0
Former Soviet Union	186	3.2	10.0	19.7	3.2	11.7	17.4	3.7	12.3	18.9
Africa	246	9.8	5.8	15.8	10.4	6.8	16.9	10.4	6.6	16.9
Sub-Saharan Africa	50	11.9	7.2	16.4	11.9	7.7	17.6	12.1	7.3	16.6
Nile River Basin	146	9.1	0.2	9.2	9.1	0.2	9.2	9.1	0.2	9.6
North America	255	-0.1	15.2	14.9	-0.1	13.8	13.6	-0.1	12.0	12.0
Asia	2,060	8.8	8.9	18.6	8.6	7.8	16.7	8.3	7.4	16.8
China	558	2.7	7.3	10.1	2.3	4.5	6.9	2.3	4.5	6.9
India	866	13.5	12.1	27.7	13.1	11.7	25.5	12.5	10.7	25.7
Latin America and the Caribbean	182	3.8	12.3	16.1	4.4	15.7	19.9	3.8	12.3	16.8
Brazil	21	0.0	0.0	0.0	0.0	0.0	0.0	0.0	0.0	0.0
Oceania	50	0.2	14.3	14.5	0.2	14.3	14.5	0.2	14.3	14.5

Note: [a] Agricultural water availability in North America increases by 0.1 per cent under the 2050 M&I scenarios. This occurs because 2000 M&I and agricultural withdrawals in North America exceed MAR in the Colorado and Rio Grande basins, but M&I declines in 2050. As a result, additional water is made available to these constrained basins.
EFRs ... environmental flow requirements
M&I   ... municipal and industrial demand

availability of worldwide water for agriculture by 2050. Meeting EFRs, which can necessitate more than 50 per cent of the mean annual runoff in a basin, depending on its hydrograph, presents the single biggest threat to the availability of water for agriculture. Next are increases in M&I demands, which are projected to grow upwards of 200 per cent by 2050 in developing countries with rapidly increasing populations and incomes. The combined effect of these higher demands could be dramatic in several hotspots, which include northern Africa, China, India, parts of Europe, the western United States and eastern Australia, among others. These areas tend to be already water-stressed due to low water supplies, current large-scale agricultural or M&I demands, or both.

Table 4 displays the fraction of 2000 agricultural water withdrawals that may be threatened by increasing M&I demands and EFRs under the two climate change scenarios. Under the no climate change scenario, our models indicate that increases in M&I demands, EFRs, and combined M&I demands and EFRs will require 7.3 per cent, 9.4 per cent, and 18 per cent, respectively, of worldwide agricultural water in 2000. By volume, agricultural water in Asia accounts for over two thirds of the global total of threatened agricultural

water by volume. Modelling results indicate that increases in EFRs and M&I demand together will threaten nearly 20 per cent of agricultural water in countries of the European Union and the former Soviet Union. In sub-Saharan Africa, rapidly rising M&I demands also threaten water for agriculture.

Climate change will affect the spatial and temporal distribution of runoff, and thus change availability from the supply side. Based on wet and dry climate scenarios, we find that water availability for agriculture will increase in North America and Asia, and decrease in Africa and Latin America and the Caribbean. In Europe, water availability will increase under the wet model and decrease under the dry model. Overall, these results suggest that by 2050, although the effects of climate change on annual agricultural water availability will be significant, the effects of growing M&I demands and EFRs may be even more pronounced. Importantly, these climate change results consider changes in MAR only, and thus do not account for potential changes in seasonal water availability, increases in crop water demand caused by higher temperatures, changes in the frequency and severity of extreme events, changes in yield from storage reservoirs, and a variety of other important climate change effects.

Commentary XVI: The Impact of Agrifood Supply Chains on Greenhouse Gas Emissions: The Case of a Coffee Value Chain between Tanzania and Germany

E. Krain, K. Linne and M. Gaebler
GIZ, Germany

Abstract

Agriculture is a major source of greenhouse gas (GHG) emissions, and thus contributes significantly to climate change. At the same time it has huge potential to reduce emissions, and could even contribute to capturing (sequestering) carbon dioxide (CO_2) from the atmosphere through the cultivation of tree crops. It is difficult to assess where to make effective changes without knowing facts on emission sources and quantities – you can only manage what you can measure. Therefore, methods to estimate sequestration and emissions are currently being developed and their results indicated in "product carbon footprints" (i.e. GHG emissions per unit of product). While methods vary widely, they seem to converge around the emerging ISO 14067 standard.

There are only a few practical examples of carbon footprint estimates along entire agrifood chains, but they serve as valuable case studies from which to draw some conclusions. Firstly, CO_2 sequestration estimations have generally been excluded from the equation, which discriminates against tree crop agricultural production systems. Secondly, emissions from primary production have usually been well reflected. Thirdly, results from processing and transport have tended to be smaller than was assumed prior to the analyses. Finally, GHG emissions in connection with food preparation, especially for lifestyle and convenience foods, tend to be much higher than was assumed before the studies were undertaken.

Current GHG accounting systems differ considerably in important aspects, such as in terms of whether they include or omit sequestration. If appropriate mitigation strategies are to be developed, harmonized methods are needed that should more accurately portray the overall picture, and, apart from the main sources of emissions, also report adequately on sequestration.

A. Introduction

The question of how to cope with climate change and reduce GHG emissions is currently high on the international agenda. Since agriculture is considered one of the key sectors contributing to such emissions, it is necessary to consider ways and means by which agricultural practices could lower emissions or even capture them (e.g. through sequestration). Lowering emissions is possible by reducing various agricultural inputs while maintaining output at the same level. This is generally understood as increasing the efficiency of a process. A second intervention is to remove GHGs from the atmosphere by, for example "sequestration", which captures CO_2 in biomass from the atmosphere. This is an option particularly suited to the cultivation of perennials (i.e. tree crops). These plants store a large proportion of the captured CO_2 as carbon in their standing and root biomass and even in their leaves and fruit, but the latter are usually quickly consumed or disposed of, thereby returning the CO_2 to the atmosphere. However, the overall balance of CO_2 stored in biomass, and over several years, may be quite substantial and worth considering in terms of climate change mitigation.

1. The generic GHG footprint of a tree crop value chain

When looking generically at a tree-crop-based value chain – from input supply to primary production, transport, processing, trade, retail and consumption – there are many stages involving GHG emissions

Figure 17: Overview of CO_2 sequestration and GHG emissions in a crop-based value chain

Figure 17: Overview of CO_2 sequestration and GHG emissions in a crop-based value chain

Input Supply   Production   Transport & Processing   Trade   Consumption

Eating

Cooking

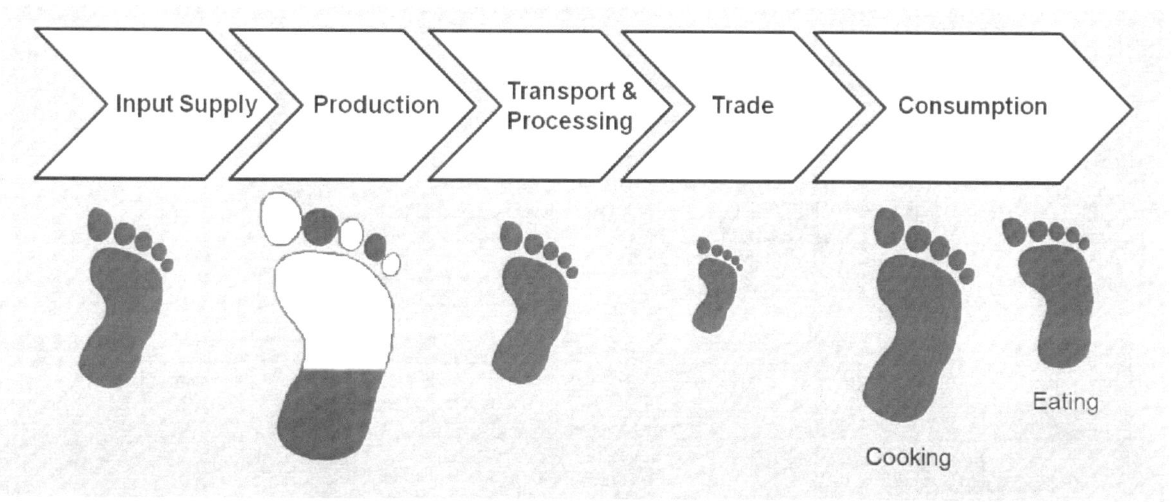

Source: Adapted from Krain et al., 2010.

(usually calculated in CO_2 equivalents – CO_2e) and one location where sequestration takes place (figure 17).

The light parts of the footprints in the above figure denote that CO_2 is sequestered, while the red/dark parts represent emissions. The size of the footprint indicates the volume of emitted or captured CO_2e, usually expressed in tons of CO_2e per output unit. In the above example, it is assumed that more CO_2e is captured than emitted during the primary production process, whereas high amounts of emissions occur when the product is prepared for consumption and consumed. In between, there are emissions connected with the other stages of the value chain.

In the following, the various stages from input supply to consumption are discussed briefly.

Main emission hotspots:
- Land-use change (especially when primary forest is converted into land for annual crop production).
- Application of agrochemicals (especially nitrogen fertilizer produced through an intensive energy-consuming industrial process and nitrogen field emissions in the form of nitrous oxide).
- Fossil fuel and energy-consuming processes during land preparation, crop maintenance, harvesting and conserving of harvests.
- Emissions from waste water (methane).
- Fossil fuel and energy-consuming processes such as industrial processing, and internal, domestic and transnational transportation.

- Finally, emissions resulting from energy consumption in food preparation at the household level.

In order to be able to decide where to reduce emissions within a value chain, it is necessary to determine how much GHG is being emitted (or sequestered) at each stage of the value chain as a basis for identifying the hotspots – you can only manage what you can measure. For this, currently there are more than 50 initiatives working on various footprinting methods and standards, such as ISO 14067, the Greenhouse Gas Protocol Product Accounting and Reporting Standard, and PAS 2050. However, so far there is no single, common calculation method, although there seems to be convergence around the emerging ISO 14067 standard, which appeared as draft in 2012. But none of the standards are product-specific and will still need to be broken down to sector/product group specific rules. Another major task still to be tackled is to develop a method that reflects the actual situation on the farm sufficiently accurately while remaining reasonable with respect to efforts and costs.

B. Some experiences with carbon footprinting in agricultural value chains

So far, for agriculture, there are only very few cases published that span an entire value chain. One such example is examined below in more detail.

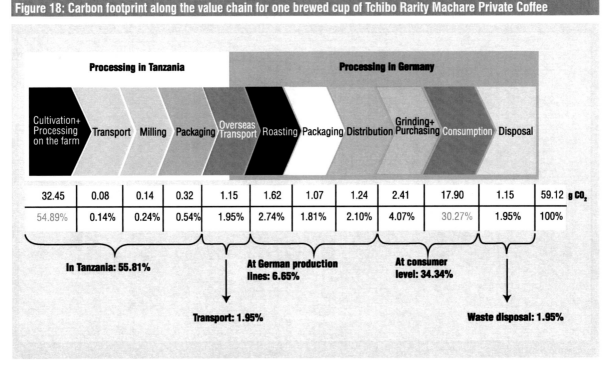

Figure 18: Carbon footprint along the value chain for one brewed cup of Tchibo Rarity Machare Private Coffee

Processing in Tanzania				Processing in Germany							
Cultivation+ Processing on the farm	Transport	Milling	Packaging	Overseas Transport	Roasting	Packaging	Distribution	Grinding+ Purchasing	Consumption	Disposal	
32.45	0.08	0.14	0.32	1.15	1.62	1.07	1.24	2.41	17.90	1.15	59.12 g CO₂
54.89%	0.14%	0.24%	0.54%	1.95%	2.74%	1.81%	2.10%	4.07%	30.27%	1.95%	100%

In Tanzania: 55.81%   At German production lines: 6.65%   At consumer level: 34.34%

Transport: 1.95%   Waste disposal: 1.95%

Source: Adapted from Tchibo GmbH, PCF Pilot Project Germany, 2009.

Under the Product Carbon Footprint (PCF) project Germany, various commodities were examined with respect to their GHG emissions, one of them being a rarity coffee from Machare farm in the United Republic of Tanzania. The assessments were based on ISO 14040/14044 and PAS 2050, a pioneering method developed by the British Standards Institution (BSI) to assess GHG emissions in the life cycles of goods and services.

All emissions measured in figure 18 were calculated with reference to one brewed cup of coffee containing 125 ml of water and 7 g of coffee. It shows that the major emissions occur during primary production (54.89 per cent), followed by consumption (30.27 per cent). Surprisingly, emissions from roasting (2.74 per cent) and even from international transport (1.95 per cent) were rather low. The study mentions that Machare farm is an old coffee farm and that changes in land use were not considered. Normally, emissions from land-use changes are taken into account if they have taken place within the last 20 years (i.e. after 1990). Most of the emissions were related to the application of agrochemicals. However, one important factor, namely the sequestration of CO_2 through the coffee plants, shade trees or other trees in the coffee field, was omitted. If that had been taken into account,

the figures for emissions during primary production would have been significantly lower. For example, the emission balance for the Kenyan Baragwi Farmers' Cooperative Society in figure 20 shows that total GHG emissions at production stage were even negative.

The identification of consumption as a hotspot (apart from primary production) becomes even more interesting when looking at the various ways of preparing coffee.

Coffee is usually prepared for consumption in different ways, and these can have very different carbon footprints, as figure 19 shows. The study assumed a mix of preparation methods with an average of 17.90 g of CO_2e per cup. The normal filter drip method has a footprint of only 10.04 g of CO_2, while a modern automatic coffee machine – which needs a lot of energy to press the water vapour through the coffee powder – emits an enormous quantity of 60.27 g of CO_2e. If all the Machare coffee would have been prepared using only automatic coffee machines, this would have changed the total carbon footprint of the value chain to 101.49 g of CO_2e (59.12–17.90 + 60.27), with the coffee machine accounting for close to 60 per cent of all GHG emissions of the value chain! Looking beyond these figures it must be

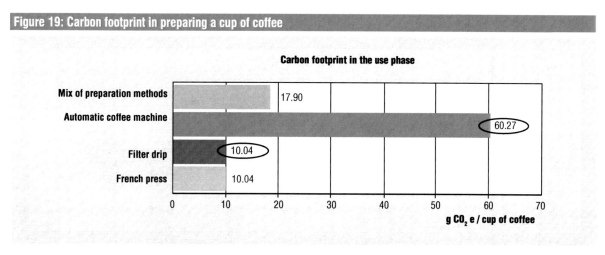

Figure 19: Carbon footprint in preparing a cup of coffee

Carbon footprint in the use phase

Source: Adapted from Tchibo, GmbH, PCF Pilot Project Germany, 2009.

recognized that because these emissions arise from energy consumption, the assumed electricity mix is another important factor in the calculations. If carbon-neutral electricity were to be used, it would reduce, or even neutralize, the carbon emissions from such processes.

This demonstrates very impressively how our modern lifestyle has become a primary source of GHG emissions. It shows that changes are needed not only in primary production, but also in consumption. It also shows where we as consumers can make a difference: do we really need to drink coffee prepared by an automatic coffee machine? And can inventive companies not produce coffee machines that require far less energy? At the same time, governments and policymakers could direct the energy sector into providing more carbon-neutral electricity. The point is that the facts need to be established so that better alternatives can be identified and effective changes made.

C. Reducing the carbon footprint by increasing tree crop biomass and changing cropping systems

It is unfortunate that most of the carbon footprint assessment methods omit, or do not consider, biomass creation, and thus sequestration, through tree crop systems. The underlying argument goes that, on the one hand, the amount of trees in such systems is usually small, and that, on the other hand, they will sooner or later be cut and return their stored GHG to the atmosphere.

First of all, how much CO_2 can be captured in agricultural tree crops? There are very different situations and thus data vary a lot. A mango tree can be grown with a huge canopy – as is often the case in smallholder farms – and can therefore be very similar to a forest tree, or it can be kept short and pruned, as in intensive orchard systems. Following a review of a number of reports, a general conclusion is that the amount of CO_2 captured in biomass is roughly in the order of a factor of 10 from annual crops (5–20 tons of CO_2/ha) to orchard trees (30–70 tons of CO_2/ha) and forests (550–900 tons of CO_2/ha). Thus, if tree crops in the existing farming systems were increased as much as possible over millions of hectares, this would surely considerably increase biomass and thus sequestered CO_2 accumulation. The FAO Ex-Act tool for assessing CO_2e emissions along the life cycle of a commodity takes account of sequestered carbon by trees, and has been employed successfully by GIZ in cashew tree crop systems in Burkina Faso (Tinlot, 2010). Land-use planning and agricultural strategies should make use of such a tool, as it helps determine the right strategies and incentives.

It should also be noted that once a tree dies and decays, this does not automatically mean that all the carbon goes back into the atmosphere. The soil usually harbours significant amounts of carbon, and, apart from emitting GHG, it is also able to bind and store carbon. From our own experience in Kenya (Krain et al., 2011) soils with a depth of 0 cm–60 cm contain around 180 tons of CO_2/ha – often up to 10 times more than the tree biomass.[60] Thus, farming and cropping systems, as well as their ways and methods of cultivation, differ widely with respect to their ability to sequester and store or emit CO_2. For example,

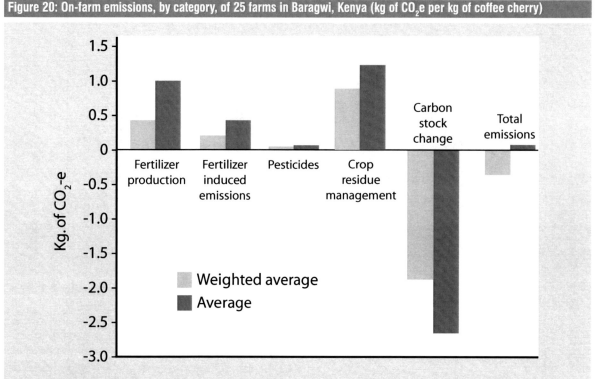

Figure 20: On-farm emissions, by category, of 25 farms in Baragwi, Kenya (kg of CO_2e per kg of coffee cherry)

Source: Linne et al., 2011.

systems involving zero or minimum tillage emit much less CO_2 than ploughing by tractor or hoe.

A recent study (Rikxoort, 2010) conducted within the framework of a GIZ public-private-partnership project on Climate Change Adaptation and Mitigation[61] showed that a coffee cultivation system adhering to a sustainability standard such as the Sustainable Agriculture Network (SAN) standard emits less CO_2e than one that uses conventional methods. In another study within this framework, conducted through the development partnership between GIZ and Sangana Commodities Ltd. in Kenya, 25 coffee farms at Baragwi Farmers' Cooperative Society were sampled in December 2010 to determine emissions and sequestered amounts of CO_2e with the help of the Cool Farm Tool (Linne et al., 2011).[62] It found that on-farm net emissions were, on average, 0.08 kg of CO_2e per kg of coffee cherries (figure 20). The weighted average, according to each farm's production

volume, was -0.3608 kg of CO_2e/kg of coffee cherries. Emissions from fertilizer production and induced emissions from fertilizer use, along with crop residue management, were the primary emission sources – emission hotspots. Carbon sequestration from above ground biomass and management practices, such as incorporation of residues, compost and manure, accounted for the most significant carbon stock changes in the system, which largely offset the emissions.

D. Conclusions

Current GHG accounting systems differ considerably in important aspects, such as in terms of whether they include or omit sequestration. If appropriate mitigation strategies are to be developed, harmonized methods are needed that should more accurately portray the overall picture, and, apart from the main sources of emissions, also report adequately on sequestration.

Commentary XVII: Food Waste Reduction: A Global Imperative

Julian Parfitt, Principal Resource Analyst, Oakdene Hollins, Aylesbury, United Kingdom, and
Mark Barthel, Special Advisor, Waste and Resources Action Programme, Banbury, United Kingdom

Abstract

- Food waste is an issue of importance to global food security and good environmental governance. Yet there is insufficient reliable data from which to estimate the proportion of global food production that is wasted.

- Avoidable losses are regarded as globally significant and therefore constitute a major social and environmental burden. However, less than 5 per cent of all funding for agricultural research is allocated to post-harvest systems (Kader, 2003).

There are three particular reasons why this issue needs to be addressed with urgency:

- Some estimates suggest that waste could account for between a third (FAO, 2011e) and one half (Lundqvist, de Fraiture and Molden, 2008) of all current food production. Reduction of post-harvest waste in developing countries and consumer waste in high-income countries appear to offer the greatest potential social and environmental gains.

- The absolute quantity of food waste, although largely unquantified, will inevitably grow over the coming decades, as production increases to meet future demand and as incomes rise amongst growing populations in new megacities, notably in the BRIC countries (i.e. Brazil, the Russian Federation, India and China), and as diets become more diversified away from starchy staple foods towards fresh fruit and vegetables, dairy, meat and fish.

- Reduction of food waste would contribute to wider policy agendas that are critical to the future, namely increasing production, reducing food insecurity and food price increases, improving sustainability of the global food supply chain (FSC), reducing pressures on land use and freshwater resources and reducing greenhouse gases.

A recent review of global food waste and potential for waste reduction, carried out by the authors of this article for the Government of the United Kingdom's Foresight Programme, The Future of Food and Farming (Foresight, 2011a), provides an overview of the challenges and possible solutions for developing countries.

A. What counts as food waste?

Different ways of defining food waste reflect different research objectives. From a human food supply perspective, it can be defined as edible material intended for human consumption that is discarded, lost, degraded or consumed by pests, from harvest to consumer (FAO, 1981). From a global resource efficiency perspective, the definition might be extended to include food fit for human consumption but intentionally used as animal feed (Stuart, 2009).

Currently, 40 per cent of global grain is fed to cattle (UNEP, 2009).

The term "post-harvest loss" is often used to describe losses between harvest and the onward supply of produce to markets, and equates broadly with waste in the FSC. The latter term is generally applied to post-harvest processing, distribution and retailing in high- income countries and, increasingly, in emerging economies. The FSC therefore encompasses a wide range of activities that include processing, storage, transport and distribution, manufacturing, wholesale and retail. Further upstream, there are factors at the initial, "pre-harvest" stages that also contribute to losses. For example, the capture and discarding of fish stocks before they are landed (usually resulting in their demise). Such fish by-catch represents a significant proportion of fish caught in global fisheries

(FAO, 2005). The parallel situation in agricultural systems involves losses that occur when crops are not harvested but are ploughed back into the soil. Such front-end losses are, by their very nature, difficult to measure accurately.

Losses at the consumer stage involve a complexity of human activities and processes, and encompass food wasted in the home (as a result of purchasing behaviour, food storage, meal planning and preparation, over-portioning and not using leftovers) and out of home within the food hospitality sector, such as plate-scrapings and kitchen waste.

The best environmental and socio-economic outcomes concerning food waste lie in its prevention, but failing that, options for recovering value from food waste need to be considered. These options may include supply of feedstock to lower grade markets for human consumption, or diversion into animal feed or into nutrient and energy recovery options (anaerobic digestion and composting). These routes are still considered "food waste", as the resulting benefits are small compared with the value of the original food product, and the environmental savings are generally modest vis-à-vis the cumulative environmental impacts associated with the agricultural and FSC stages of the food product life cycles.

B. Post-harvest losses in the food supply chain

In many developing countries, agriculture remains the dominant economic sector (FAO, 2009c), yet most of the rural poor rely on short food supply chains with limited post-harvest infrastructure and technologies, which contribute to substantial post-harvest losses. Cereals, the most studied food commodity group in relation to post-harvest losses (Parfitt, Barthel and Macnaughton, 2010), typically incur 40 per cent losses between post-harvest and processing stages in developing countries. The comparable data for industrialized countries suggest similar proportionate losses, but these are associated with the consumer stage (FAO, 2011e). Post-harvest losses result from spillage, poor separation and drying, contamination and consumption by rodents and insects, and fungal and bacterial diseases. At a more fundamental level, poor choice of crop in relation to climatic conditions and inadequate inputs in agriculture are often underlying factors contributing to loss (Foresight, 2011b). The losses of perishable crops, by their very nature, are higher than those of cereals, and vary considerably by region and by commodity type. Data available from low-income countries for a limited range of fresh fruit and vegetables suggest losses of over 50 per cent (FAO, 2011e). Although it has been suggested that post-harvest losses are sometimes overestimated (Parfitt, Barthel and Macnaughton, 2010), this partly relates to the difficulty of deriving "typical" loss estimates for a crop and region when the limited data from field measurements may relate to specific local research objectives, and extreme values may mistakenly be extrapolated to estimate losses from an entire country or region (Tyler, 1982; Hodges, Buzby and Bennett, 2010). Extended food supply chains in developing countries that provide food for growing urban populations are likely to involve many intermediaries between growers and consumers, which may limit the potential for growers to receive higher prices for quality produce, or even to understand what sorts of produce the market requires. The lack of price differentials and agreed quality criteria between different players in the market reduces the incentive for small producers to grade produce or to invest in suitable storage infrastructure and transit packaging. Interventions within these systems tend to focus on improving technical capacity to reduce losses, increase efficiency and reduce the labour intensity of the technologies that are used (Foresight, 2011c; Hodges, Buzby and Bennett, 2010). Attempts to reduce post-harvest losses need to take into account cultural and financial implications of any innovations in post-harvest technologies. In years with food surpluses the prices received for goods tend to be low. One option, therefore, is to store grain surpluses for lean years, but suitable storage facilities may be lacking or expensive. Investment and engineering skills are needed to provide solutions. Indeed, there are many examples of relatively simple technologies which can provide effective solutions and dramatically reduce losses (United Nations, 2007).

Looking to the future, the predicted increase in the global urban population from 50 per cent in the past few years to 75 per cent in 2050, which is expected to be concentrated in low-income and emerging economies, is likely to lead to an extension of FSCs, and consequently increase post-harvest food losses significantly (United Nations, 2008). However, infrastructural improvements, particularly dry- and cold-storage facilities, pack houses, roads, ports, telecommunications and power supplies, have the potential to counteract such developments. In some

BRIC countries, public sector investment is being considered for accelerating this process. For example, in India the Government is discussing an "evergreen revolution", which will involve the development of food processing units (Foresight, 2011c).

C. Emerging economies and high income countries

In emerging economies and high-income countries, FSCs involve closer links between growers, suppliers, processors, distribution systems and markets, thereby ensuring greater economies of scale, competitiveness and efficiency. Development of more industrialized FSCs could also foster growth in the food processing sector. In medium- and high-income countries, it has often been argued that the centralized processing of food leads to better resource efficiency and less waste overall. However, research on consumer food waste suggests that this is not the case (WRAP, 2009): consumers waste significant quantities of food, thus potentially negating the benefits of centralized food processing. Further losses are associated with cosmetic quality standards applied by retailers to fresh fruit and vegetables, which can reduce the volume of marketable and edible food reaching consumers. This trend is increasingly being counterbalanced by the growing influence of retailers and manufacturers in agricultural development groups, crop sustainability groups and sustainable agriculture initiatives, all of which are bringing about improvements in growing practices and further reductions in post-harvest losses.

In emerging economies, supermarkets are the main vehicle for providing diversified diets for the expanding middle classes and the urban poor. These developments are almost entirely dependent on foreign direct investment, and show high growth rates in Eastern Europe, parts of Asia and Latin America (Reardon, Timmer and Berdegué, 2007). The nature and pace of these developments are influenced by the extent to which retailers bypass existing markets and traditional wholesalers to secure produce of the required standard and volume. Many of the factors that may increase waste identified in the FSCs of emerging economies are similar to those in high-income countries, such as payment terms that discourage small growers, and systems for demand forecasting, order planning and replenishment that sometimes lead to overproduction.[63] However, there are lessons that might be learnt from industrialized

countries. For instance, the combined effects of contractual penalties for non-delivery of order volumes, residual shelf-life product take-back clauses and poor demand forecasting were estimated to drive up overproduction and higher levels of wastage by 10 per cent in the United Kingdom FSC (Defra, 2007).

D. Food waste by consumers in low-income countries

To date, there are little published robust data on the scale of consumer food waste in low-income countries and emerging economies. However, a conclusion from a recent workshop on global food waste prevention (Foresight, 2011c) was that, overall, the scale of consumer waste appears to be lower in these countries, but in some of the emerging economies, particularly Brazil and urban China, it seems to be approaching that of the OECD countries. In much poorer communities, there is typically a wider range of outlets for discarded food, and these cultures commonly arrange for the most hungry and destitute people to obtain leftover food scraps. The net loss to human consumption can therefore be lower, albeit with higher safety risks, particularly if the water used for food preparation is insanitary.

E. Conclusions: low-income countries show the greatest potential for food waste reduction

A significant reduction in global food waste is an important step towards securing food for the growing global population, which is estimated to exceed nine billion people by 2050. The potential to meet the resulting increase in demand cannot be met through further productivity gains alone, or by extending the area of land for agricultural production. It is therefore essential to obtain more from global food production by wasting less. This will require action on many fronts, across high-income and lower income countries alike. The *Foresight Review* (Foresight 2011d) identified the main actions needed in order to bring the maximum benefit to developing countries. These are briefly discussed below.

Greater investment in storage, packaging and transport infrastructure in low-income countries by national governments and the donor community. Relatively low-cost interventions that could achieve sizeable food waste reduction include: basic packaging for transport of fresh produce, innovation in low-technology storage to reduce grain losses on small farms, and simple cool chain options that are not fuel-intensive. These investments could potentially increase the income of participants in the food chain, including growers, particularly if they enable access to more remunerative markets. In addition, the evidence shows that domestic or international markets and effective local policies aimed at upgrading activities and food standards are crucial to achieving success (FAO, 2003; Kader, 2005).

Connecting smallholder growers in low-income countries to urban/regional and international food chains through better infrastructure, and possibly linked also with various forms of ethical trading. Substantial investment in infrastructure is needed to reduce post-harvest losses and to provide smallholder farmers with better access to markets, with lower transaction costs and better returns. The use of communication technologies (mobile phones in particular) for improving market information and access to other important services (e.g. weather forecasts, locally appropriate crop varieties, good agricultural practices) would enable producers to make better planting, harvesting and supply decisions, meet market requirements and avoid, or at least reduce, seasonal gluts and higher wastage rates (Foresight, 2011c).

Targeting of aid budgets to encourage small growers to produce improved quality produce for local and regional markets in a similar way to the United Nations World Food Programme's Purchase for Progress initiative,[64] which includes the provision of guaranteed contracts, agricultural extension services and crop insurance for local communities, and a social safety net, as well as food aid from local rather than international sources. Such measures help to reduce post-harvest losses as they encourage investment in post-harvest infrastructure and reduce price fluctuations.

Encourage training in the sciences relevant to food storage and distribution in low-income countries through dedicated programmes and bursary schemes. This should include the training of people to support the planning and maintenance of the more advanced post-harvest and FSC technologies needed to feed growing urban populations.

Development of a global benchmarking network to estimate food losses, with priority given to emerging economies. Much of the data available on losses have not been collected systematically, and there are few up-to-date direct field measurements. If progress is to be made towards a global benchmark for food waste, more empirically based loss estimates are necessary. Such an undertaking would require strong leadership in international agencies with an interest in food security and development issues. Given the wide variability of FSCs, it would be unrealistic to gather data from a representative sample of the global FSCs. A more targeted approach has greater chance of success, with priority assigned to those systems likely to experience higher wastage rates, and focusing on the most critical FSC stages, such as from farms to distribution centres for fresh produce in emerging economies. Selected supply chain segments should be monitored to establish how changes in technology and infrastructure have influenced losses.

Commentary XVIII: The Role of Sustainable Consumption in Fostering a Fundamental Transformation of Agriculture

Lucia Reisch
Copenhagen Business School, Denmark

Abstract

- Major changes in food behaviour towards more sustainable consumption systems must happen, in particular in the industrialized countries.

- Key issues of concern are excessive meat and dairy, sugar and fat consumption in "modern diets", overconsumption in some parts of the world and underconsumption in others as well as food waste.

- In order to foster sustainable food consumption, it is necessary to coordinate policies relating to food, the environment, health and social cohesion.

A. Definition of sustainable food consumption

The Oslo Roundtable on Sustainable Production and Consumption has defined sustainable consumption in general as: "the use of goods and services that respond to basic needs and bring a better quality of life, while minimizing the use of natural resources, toxic materials and emissions of waste and pollutants over the life cycle, so as not to jeopardize the needs of future generations" (Norwegian Ministry of the Environment, 1994). As regards consumption in the food domain, there is no broadly accepted definition to date, but several attempts to clarify and sharpen the concept have been made. Definitions differ depending on the thematic focus – environment and climate, public health and life opportunities, malnutrition and critical access to food. Still, a core set of criteria can be distilled. Perhaps the most encompassing approach has been introduced by the Sustainable Development Commission (2005) of the United Kingdom. The commission considers food and drinks sustainable if they:

- Are safe, healthy and nutritious, for consumers in places such as shops, restaurants, schools and hospitals;
- Can meet the needs of less well-off people;
- Provide a viable livelihood for farmers, processors and retailers, whose employees enjoy a safe and hygienic working environment, whether nationally or abroad;
- Respect biophysical and environmental limits in their production and processing, while reducing energy consumption and improving the wider environment;
- Meet the highest standards of animal health and welfare, compatible with the production of affordable food for all sectors of society; and
- Support rural economies and the diversity of rural cultures, in particular through an emphasis on local products that keep food miles to a minimum.

Definitions from a social science perspective highlight the importance of the socio-cultural dimension – the necessary "fit" of food patterns with people's everyday lives – for developing effective policies (e.g. Hayn et al., 2006). Here, food consumption is considered sustainable only if it:

- Is environmentally sound (with regard to water, soil, climate, biodiversity, avoidance of unnecessary risks);
- Is health promoting;
- Allows for socio-cultural diversity; and
- Is applicable in everyday life styles.

From a worldwide perspective, the question of fair distribution and access to healthy and safe food – discussed under the key term "food security" – comes to the fore. Achieving sustainable consumption of food requires confronting problems of both underconsumption and overconsumption. As regards the former, 1.3 billion people exist on incomes of $1 a day or less, and over 800 million people are hungry or starving. Yet the problem of food security goes beyond

Figure 21: Growth rate of meat consumption over the past 40 years (kg/person/yr)

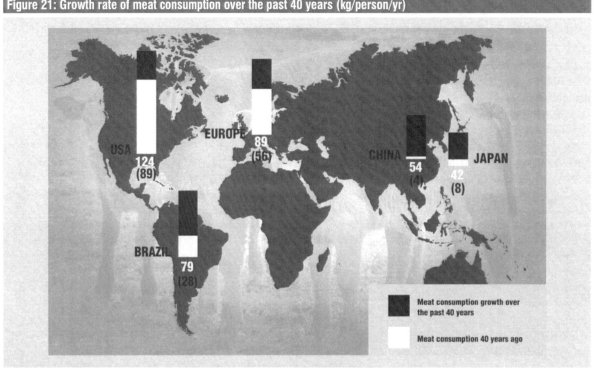

Source: Compassion in World Farming Trust, 2004: 3, based on data from FAOstat.

that of hunger and access; it also covers the problem of "hidden hunger" (i.e. deficits in vital micronutrients), which, according to a WHO estimate, affects about 1.2 billion people worldwide. At the same time, there is a worldwide increase in the number of people who are overweight or obese, both in developing and affluent industrial countries.

While the environmental impacts of food consumption and production have been debated since the 1990s – with a focus on greenhouse gas (GHG) emissions – the connections between climate/environment and health have only recently become a concern in political documents (e.g. Health Council of the Netherlands, 2011). According to this approach, a systems perspective of sustainable food consumption seems to replace the traditional "silo perspective" of separate sustainability dimensions prominent in many national policies. In 2010, the European Commission listed the following criteria for diets to be considered as having a "health value":
• Nutrient and energy content (nutritional value),
• Natural food properties ("aesthetic/gustatory" and "digestive"),
• Ecological nature of food production (sustainable agriculture),
• Health and toxicological criteria (food safety).

As regards the latter, consumers' perception of food safety is clouded by unhealthy food additives, toxic residues and other by-products, as well as potential risks from genetically modified and nano-technologically enhanced foods. This provides a major impetus for the growth of organic food sales.

Based on a broad understanding of sustainable consumption, as reflected in the definitions cited above, we define sustainable food consumption as a choice of food which is beneficial and life-enhancing for individuals, society and the planet. However, sustainable food consumption in such a comprehensive sense is seldom considered in policy-making. The following section illustrates why major changes in food behaviour towards more sustainable consumption systems must take place, particularly in industrialized countries.

B. Main problematic trends and needed changes

Given the growing world population and demographic change, problems are predicted to become more serious in the future; for example, agricultural production must face the impacts of climate change, conflicts over land use are predicted to increase, and health and social costs – both at the individual and social level – will rise because of food-related health threats. A key ethical issue is ensuring food security for the worlds' growing population – a goal that will not easily be achieved. In many developing countries, shortage of drinking water will also be a major problem. To meet the needs of a growing world population and the increasing demand for meat in developing countries, particularly in China and India (figure 21), there would have to be an exponential growth in land use for agriculture, while at the same time the most productive cereal producing areas in China, India and North America will be approaching their biophysical limits (Tempelman, 2006).

The reasons for this unsustainable development pattern include the industrialization and globalization of agriculture and food processing, consumption patterns that are shifting towards more meat and dairy in diets, modern food styles, an abundance of food on the one hand and a lack of food security on the other, and the continuously growing gap between rich and poor on both a worldwide scale and within individual societies. These factors are the result of national and international policies and regulations, business practices and particular values. The main problematic trends and needed changes are discussed below.

In industrialized countries, there is a wide range of available food products. Because most food products are available at affordable prices year round, food seasonality has lost its meaning. Besides an abundant choice of healthy fruit and vegetables throughout the year, consumers in most EU countries benefit from comparatively low prices and considerable convenience, which have accompanied changes in food production and globalization. A major drawback in this progress, however, is that consumers have become increasingly estranged from the production of their foodstuffs, and, despite the recent recurrence of interest in regional foods and new trends such as slow food and organic produce, consumer knowledge of seasonality or regional supply has been lost (see, for example, Tischner and Kjaernes, 2007; Blay-Palmer, 2008).

At the level of the individual, food habits and preferences are shaped by cultural traditions, norms, fashion and physiological needs, as well as by personal experience with and exposure to specific foods and their supply (i.e. availability and accessibility of foodstuffs). Such preferences and tastes, together with finances, time and other constraints (e.g. work

patterns, household decision-making), influence food consumption. Price, in particular, is a major determinant. Food preferences also differ significantly by household-specific characteristics such as age, income, education, family type and status in the labour force, as well as nationality (European Commission, 2006). Researchers have therefore made an effort to cluster consumers into groups that represent different "nutrition styles" or "food styles" so that they can be targeted with messages about "proper food" (Michaelis and Lorek, 2004; Friedl et al., 2007; Schultz and Stieß, 2008).

The following observable developments and trends in food consumption in many OECD and most EU countries are problematic with regard to sustainable food consumption (Reisch, Scholl and Eberle, 2010):

- *Changes in diet.* Particularly in OECD and EU countries, there is a trend towards higher consumption of meat (especially pork and poultry), cheese and bottled drinks, and a declining consumption of milk and potatoes (OECD, 2001; European Environment Agency, 2005).

- *Weakening of nutritional competencies despite increasing knowledge of healthy nutrition.* Competencies in nutrition and home economics (i.e. cooking and food storing, and financial competencies) have declined. At the same time, knowledge of healthy foods and healthy nutrition has increased.

- *A decline in time spent on nutrition.* Time spent on food purchasing and cooking, as well as on eating, has decreased significantly over the past few years. In general, however, women still spend more time than men on food purchasing and cooking (Hamermesh, 2007).

- *A decline in relative consumer spending on food.* Although absolute household expenditures on food increased during the 1990s in many EU countries,[65] the average share of expenditure on food in total household expenditure in European households has declined steadily with rising incomes (Michaelis and Lorek, 2004; European Environment Agency, 2005). For many consumers, price is the dominant criterion in food purchase, followed by quality, freshness, (long) shelf life and taste.

- *An increase in convenience, readymade and fast foods and out-of-home consumption.*[66] In addition to a tendency towards consuming highly processed foods (fast and convenience food), consumption of readymade meals is continuing to rise within the EU (RTS, 2006). Out-of-home consumption also accounts for a significant and growing proportion of European food intake; for example, in 2002 one fourth of meals and snacks were eaten out (Michaelis and Lorek, 2004).

- *Increasing diet-related uncertainty on the part of consumers.* A decade of food scares, together with differing expert evaluations of risk, contradictory and short-lived nutrition-related information in the media, a greater variety of available foodstuffs, and the globalization and distancing of food production have produced growing consumer uncertainty about food (Bergmann, 2002). Indeed, rather than helping consumers navigate the vast array of information about food, the multitude of food labels has led to consumer confusion and information overload that prevents them from quickly finding relevant key information (Derby and Levy, 2001; Hawkes, 2004). As a result, (re-)building consumer trust in the information about food provided by both the State and the market is a major challenge (Kjaernes, Harvey and Warde, 2007).

- *Problems of overweight and obesity in spite of increasing health awareness.* In most industrialized countries, the wealth of available food, combined with increasingly sedentary lifestyles and modern diets, is leading to rising obesity levels. In these countries, the rise in adiposity (i.e. fat-storing body tissue) is occurring particularly among children and teenagers, but is also evident among lower socio-economic groups (WHO, 2005; Reisch and Gwozdz, 2010). In developing countries, obesity is mostly a problem among the well-off (Witkowski, 2007).

- *Complexity of food choices.* The above developments in food supply have greatly increased the complexity of food choice: the more options and novelties on offer, the more complicated it becomes to find the right information and the more complex the decision-making process. Although information brokers – from testing organizations to food magazines to Web 2.0 Slow Food communities – may be able to reduce such complexity for a few people, many consumers remain overwhelmed and prefer to stick to their habitual choices (Mick, Broniarczyk and Haidt, 2004). The success of food discounters such as Trader Joe's in the United States, which offers a very narrow food assortment, is due to an attractive mix of few choices (and hence, low search costs) and their provision of standard quality organic products sold at fair and low prices. This is in contrast with what established

super- and hypermarkets offer.

- *Increasing food waste.* Today, large quantities of food are wasted, particularly by food retail firms and consumers. For instance, according to one recent study, households in the United Kingdom waste one third of the food they buy, 61 per cent of which could have been eaten if it had been better managed.

Much hope is pinned on the increasing consumer interest in organic and fair trade foods. The markets for organically grown products and for fair traded food products have grown steadily (Krier, 2005; Willer, Yussefi-Menzler and Sorenssen, 2008). Nevertheless, the market share remains low, with organic food accounting for 0.5–5 per cent (Willer, Yussefi-Menzler and Sorensen, 2008) and fair traded food for less than 1 per cent of the total food market (Krier, 2005). Also, turnover is stagnating in many markets because of a fall in the prices of non-organic foods and an increase in price competition.

C. Towards a policy of sustainable food consumption

On the demand side, national governments generally play a relatively weak role. To date, the main driver behind regulatory command and control instruments relating to food consumption and production is the need to respond to acute threats to the life and health of citizens. It is only for the past few years that government concerns about food intake have broadened to consider everyday diet and health issues. These concerns (especially as they relate to obesity and its health impacts) are slowly resulting in policy actions, but most of these measures are only designed to provide information, and rarely take the form of regulation. Command and control is usually applied in cases that can be left neither to voluntary agreements nor to the market because of the high risks involved, or because of time pressure and doubts about the effectiveness of voluntary agreements. Thus, regulation concentrates on food safety issues, and aims to protect consumers' health, their lives (e.g. standards of hygiene) and their economic interests (e.g. competition policies).

With regard to sustainability in the food sector, governments and their administrations generally become involved only as organizers of (public) certification, standardization and inspection schemes. One example of this role is evident in the State-run labelling of organic and regional foods observable in about half of all EU countries (Organic Europe, 2010). Such labels constitute an important tool for raising consumer awareness about the health and environmental aspects of their food and for facilitating informed decision-making.

Another relatively recent approach to promoting sustainable food consumption is self-regulation in the form of public procurement of sustainable food (or guidelines for procurement) for public insitutions, such as kindergartens and schools, staff canteens in the public sector, prisons and hospitals. However, examples from various EU member States – especially the United Kingdom and Sweden – demonstrate that such self-regulation requires time and effort, and seems to be effective and improve the quality of the food served only when the initiatives are closely monitored by the governments (Sustain, 2010). A recent report concludes unambigiously that "the only way to achieve a radical improvement in public sector food – for example in our schools, hospitals and care homes – is for government to introduce a new law which sets high, and rising standards for the food served" (Sustain, 2010: 2).

Market-based instruments targeting households and individuals seem to be less prevalent in the food domain, though they are applied upstream in the food supply chain (e.g. subsidies to organic farmers). Very recently, initiatives have been launched to tax certain food types, such as "junk food" in Hungary, or their ingredients, such as a tax on specific types of fat in Denmark.

The dominant policy instrument in the food domain is an information-based and educative focus on raising awareness. This is often accompanied by voluntary instruments of self-commitment, cooperation and networking. While efforts to educate consumers, especially young consumers, in growing, processing, cooking and storing food are declining in most societies – due to the increase in out-of-home and readymade food consumption, and in other priorities in formal school curricula – there are some ongoing efforts to develop "food literacy" among young consumers with regard to choosing and preparing healthy (e.g. more fruit and vegetables) and sustainable (i.e. organic, regional, fair-trade) food. As one element of a national food strategy, France has recently started to systematically train the sensory and taste competences of schoolchildren.

The achievement of behavioural change in favour of more sustainable food consumption is a long-term goal that requires constant and continuing efforts of all the actors involved. Barriers are evident at the institutional, informational, infrastructural (i.e. the availability, affordability and accessibility of a sustainable supply) and personal levels. Government support for sustainable food entrepreneurs and community-based food initiatives could help make the sustainable choice easier (and more affordable).

A substantial barrier to effective consumer information and education is the disturbing fact that scientific evidence is not conclusive, and that some recommendations to consumers, such as the recommendation that organic or local products should always be preferred to conventional or imported products, might not be well-founded. "Organic" and "local" are two pillars of sustainable food consumption that have recently been challenged by scientific reports (e.g. Reinhardt et al., 2009).

Available research generally agrees on the issues giving rise to the lack of sustainability of the current food domain (Reisch, Scholl and Eberle, 2010): the distance between food consumers and producers (in miles as well as minds), the significant loss of biomass from the field to the table (including generated waste), and the high level of consumption of animal products in the form of meat and dairy products. Consequently, these are the critical aspects of non-sustainability that governments need to address as a priority.

Despite the growing attention paid to food issues at the policy level, approaches that integrate the different sustainability issues into coherent policy approaches or action plans – or at least into policy tools that do not contradict each other – are hard to find. The same is true for explicit strategies for sustainable consumption. Policies relating to nutrition and food, the environment, health and social cohesion are seldom coordinated. Furthermore, explicit policies for sustainable consumption, in general, and for food consumption, in particular, are rare. Policy tools are usually designed one-dimensionally for specific policy domains, and adopted policy tools primarily target individual consumers.

As a result of the current power structure in the European food domain, which is characterized by a dominant, highly concentrated, powerful retail industry, governments tend to limit themselves to a marginal role and to non-invasive instruments, such as consumer information and education. Another reason for the reluctance to implement strict national food policies is that sustainability goals and policies risk conflicting with European laws. For instance, the EU has recently requested that Sweden withdraws its National Food Administration's (NFA) proposal to the EU on guidelines for climate-friendly food choices because they may conflict with European trade goals. The EU Commission found that the recommendation to eat more locally produced food contravenes the EU's principles of free movement of goods.

Governments also struggle to understand the definition of sustainable food and sustainable diets, and they often have no real vision about the possible forms that sustainable food systems might take. As a starting point, an understanding of the difference between sustainable *food* and sustainable *diet* seems to be crucial. For instance, one can eat very healthy, sustainably produced food, but simply eat too much or too little of it. Alternatively, food could come from sustainable farming, but it could still be highly processed and over- packaged. Hence, a priority for governments should be to develop *integrated, cross-sectoral, population-wide food policies* on such issues as agriculture and food supply, availability and access to food, physical activity, welfare and social benefits, fiscal policies, animal welfare, and information and social marketing (Robertson, Lobstein and Knai, 2007).

A review of current European sustainable development strategies and action plans highlights the following major goals regarding sustainable food consumption (in order of priority):
• Lowering obesity levels and increasing health,
• Increasing organic food consumption and production,
• Reducing GHG emissions, and
• Reducing food waste.

As sustainable development strategies are a result of societal debates in the various countries, they reflect mainstream thinking about the areas in which policy instruments are appropriate and necessary. However, these explicit goals neglect other relevant aspects of food and drink sustainability: the social and economic dimensions in both the global and local sense. The United Kingdom's Sustainable Development Commission (2008) emphasizes the need to move beyond reflections on "safe, healthy and nutritious food" to include consideration of "the needs of the less well off". That is, it is necessary to consider decent

economic, living and working conditions of those working along the food chain, respect for animals, support for rural economies and cultural aspects.

Another issue is reflected in recent discussions in academic circles that has not yet received sufficient attention from policymakers: self-sufficiency of countries in terms of food supplies, and the uneven impacts of food production on the soil. This is a rather complex issue which is made all the more challenging by WTO rules and EU policies that promote international trade above all else. However, it is an area that needs to be carefully analysed (for a more elaborate discussion, see the lead article and the commentary of Chemnitz and Santarius in chapter 5 of this Review).

The above-outlined requirements appear to be relevant for building a framework for sustainable food consumption and production: short-term action on the agreed problems and medium-term specification of how to redesign food systems (Reisch, Lorek and Bietz, 2011). A parallel debate on a "European food model" and its common values (for example, as regards genetically modified organisms and nanotechnologies) is also necessary. Such a debate should include the possibility of a "green economy" strategy for the food sector.

However, developing such integrative strategies and identifying the most sustainable way to ensure the nutrition of the world's current and future populations requires further research. More research is also needed on ways to achieve sustainable food consumption patterns. The overwhelming view in the scientific literature is that the most effective ways for affluent societies to reduce the environmental impact of their diets are to cut down on the amount of meat and dairy products consumed, especially beef, buy organic, seasonal and locally available food products, and avoid products transported by aeroplane.

Over and above these concerns, governments should develop cross-sectoral, population-wide policies on a variety of issues, including those relating to agriculture and food supply, availability of and access to food, physical activity, welfare and social benefits, sound environmental production and consumption, fiscal policies, the role of individual consumer decision-making, public procurement and public provision of food. Based on these policies, governments should develop action plans on sustainable food consumption.

Current food consumption patterns not only threaten the quality of life of individuals; they also have negative environmental, social and economic impacts. Policies and programmes to counteract these impacts are complicated because of the multiple interdependencies between the actors and issues involved in the food system. While useful and useable consumer information on the consequences of food consumption, early consumer education and case-based consumer advice can empower consumers, better knowledge will not automatically change preferences and behaviour. Rather, availability, affordability and social attraction of sustainable food choices, as well as easy access to them, seem to be the key levers to foster sustainable food consumption by individual consumers. "Making the sustainable choice the easy choice", promoting healthy foods, rethinking menus in canteens and simplifying food labelling are worthwhile policy initiatives to explore, keeping in mind the diversity of social settings and welcoming cultural diversity in food consumption.

Commentary XIX: Food Safety and Systemic Change: Limitations of Food Controls for Safeguarding Food Safety

Jutta Jaksche, Policy Officer Food
Federation of German Consumer Organisations (Verbraucherzentrale Bundesverband, VZBV)

Abstract

Increasing globalization has accelerated the industrialization of agricultural practices and cost pressures among producers. This has led to larger scales of production of a very limited number of commercially lucrative agricultural goods in a decreasing number of production units, with several unresolved food-safety risks that are difficult to manage.

In the absence of effective regulation, production standards in globalized markets will follow a "race to the bottom" with the result that in terms of environmental, social and ethical criteria the cheapest and lowest standards might be applied.

Although there are comprehensive control mechanisms to ensure food safety, they are insufficient to guarantee food safety for all internationally traded products. What is lacking is a proactive, preventive approach.

The current approaches to assuring food safety are complicated and expensive, especially for small-scale producers, and in the end producers and consumers pay the additional costs. The notion that more controls are sufficient to guarantee adequate food safety has proved wrong: additional controls have not been able to halt or reverse the trend of increasing contaminants in food products and greater environmental pollution. A systemic change towards low-risk, sustainable production techniques will ease the problems of food safety and may also improve the level of trust of consumers in agricultural products.

A. Changes in consumption habits in a globalized world

Consumers in the European Union (EU) are able to consume foods from all over the world during virtually any season of the year. This is possible because of world trade which has become more and more interconnected in the globalization process of the past few decades. But globalization is partly blind to many social and environmental impacts of production, because of cost pressures and resulting scale requirements.

Race to the bottom takes place because good social and environmental conditions lead to higher costs. If there is no transparency for consumers or no other limitation "a race to the bottom" is going to be the overwhelming model for investment.

For example, Western demand for imported animal feed drives the production of soybeans, corn and wheat overseas and leads to non-site-specific production schemes. The European agricultural and food sector is highly dependent on feed imports, which enable it to be the world's biggest exporter of food products.

According to estimates of a German group of associations, coordinated by the Arbeitsgemeinschaft bäuerliche Landwirtschaft (AbL) and the EuroNatur Stiftung (2011: 8), "the EU's need for agricultural lands outside of the Community (including some 19 million hectares for the production of imported soy and protein feeds) is estimated to be in the order of 35 million hectares – this is twice the utilized agricultural area of Germany."[67] The relationship between feed, livestock and animal manure has been neglected, with negative effects on the environment, ground water, oceans, biodiversity, animal welfare and public health. Livestock production now needs to be re-linked to locally available agricultural land and de-linked from being a direct competitor of human food supply.

Another trend concerns the de-globalization of food

chains. In a survey of consumers, which asked them to what extent they were concerned about food safety in global supply chains, 37 per cent replied that they were very concerned, while 42 per cent responded that they were somewhat worried (European Commission, 2010).

There is growing consumer preference for regional products over products from very distant countries of origin. According to a survey by Nestlé (2011) the attractiveness of regional products has exceeded that of organic farming: 81 per cent of respondents claimed they bought regional food, and of these, 37 per cent reported buying regional food on a regular basis, whereas 44 per cent reported buying it from time to time. The motivations for such consumer preference are their belief that these products are of better quality, they feel more secure when knowing about the origin of the products, and their desire to promote sustainability and the local economy. This is also why consumers like to see the place of origin marked clearly on food products.

The past few decades have witnessed a massive change in production as well as in processing and consumption habits. Knowledge on how to prepare food has been lost, and convenience foods and eating out as a result of time pressure have become increasingly popular. Costs of food packaging often exceed the costs of the foods themselves.

B. Sustainable agriculture

Often food safety measures, such as inspection of food and recalls of tainted food, take place at the end of the food chain. While these measures are indispensable, more important should be prevention, both for reducing related transaction costs and for gaining the trust of consumers. Prevention in the context of food safety means starting at the initial stages of production: looking into the use of resources and the mode of agricultural production. It is now well known that intensive use of fossil fuels in agriculture will not be sustainable in the future; neither will the use of other resources, such as phosphate and phosphorous. But systematic change is necessary not only because of the eventual scarcity of these external inputs, but also because of problems with assuring food safety in highly intensive conventional agricultural production systems.

It is clear that while efforts are being made to combat animal diseases and product contamination

in agricultural production systems, not enough is being done to prevent them. This leads to negative and unsustainable interdependencies between agricultural production and public health, as illustrated by the example of antibiotic resistance. The European Food Safety Authority (EFSA) evaluated the public health risk of bacterial strains resistant to certain antimicrobials in food and food-producing animals. It drew the conclusion that the use of antimicrobials in food-producing animals was a risk factor for the spread of those bacterial strains and for public health. As a result of this study experts recommended imposing restrictions and banning certain antibiotics (EFSA, 2011).[68] The experts also concluded that the extensive intra-EU trade in animals was an additional risk factor for antibiotic resistance.

There needs to be greater attention to combating and avoiding global epidemics – so-called pandemics, many of which are zoonoses (i.e. diseases which can be transmitted from animals to humans). A paper by the European Commission's Directorate General for Health and Consumer Affairs (SANCO, 2011) defines prevention as consisting of measures to decrease occurrence and transmission of animal diseases by farming and food chain practices and animal transport, in order to ensure a high level of animal health, public health and food safety. This includes limiting the incidence of zoonoses in humans and other biological risks. SANCO estimates that the cost for a vaccination bank at EU level, maintaining only the vaccines for foot and mouth disease, is about €1.4 million per year. The total value of the antigen stored in a vaccine bank is estimated at €10.6 million from 2012 onwards, and the stock has to be renewed every five years.[69] According to the SANCO study, the main tools and instruments of prevention are monitoring and surveillance in member States and biosafety measures such as disinfection, segregation and cleaning. (For a critical discussion of biosafety, see Idel and Reichert in chapter 2 of this Review.) In the event of an animal disease breaking out, prevention and control strategies include import restrictions, such as legislation and control of animal movements across national borders. However, what is missing is a discussion of the limits of animal transport and the density of animal production to avoid outbreaks and to maintain production at a level commensurate with regional market requirements and environmental carrying capacity.

First of all, we need a concept for sustainable agricultural production, and not only for Europe.

This has to be defined according to site-specific conditions. Researchers have defined critical "planetary boundaries" to ensure human safety, the transgressing of which could be catastrophic. (Rockström et al., 2009) Nine of the boundaries identified are climate change, stratospheric ozone, land-use change, freshwater use, biological diversity, ocean acidification, nitrogen and phosphorus emissions into to the biosphere and oceans, aerosol loading and chemical pollution. According to a report by Rockström et al. (2009) three of the nine boundaries have already been transgressed, all of them connected with agricultural production.[70]

The German Council for Sustainable Development (2011) recommends that the organic farming concept be made the gold standard for agricultural production, to be used as a guideline, though it needs to be continuously developed. Dusseldorp and Sauter (2011) also note that low-external-input agricultural practices in developing countries have resulted in higher yields (on average 80 % higher) relative to conventional production systems. They assume that external inputs often are not available to farmers in developing countries, that the use of mineral fertilizers on grounds with low retention of nutrients reduces yields, and that high-yielding varieties are not appropriate for sites with suboptimal conditions.

Organic farming is regarded as site-specific and sustainable because of its circular flow of inputs. As demand for organic products is higher than supply in Germany, there is upward pressure on prices and more and more organic products are being imported. Thus growing organic foods for export could well be an option for small-scale producers, as noted by an evaluation of Church Development Service (Evangelischer Entwicklungsdienst) and Bread for the World (Brot für die Welt) (2011). However, markets in this segment are developing nearly along the same lines as conventional markets, resulting in unfair competition between producers within the EU and those abroad.

Many well-informed consumers are appalled at the way German farming systems operate. Some agriculture in Europe may never be economical without subsidies. Public money should not be spent for preserving this kind of agriculture. Subsidies should be spent for a system of agricultural production that is fit and viable for the future, in a manner that is adapted to the soils and living conditions of animals and people. There is an urgent need for change to protect public goods.

C. Food control

The outbreak of the BSE crisis some 10 years ago created a massive crisis of confidence, which prompted the Commission of the European Communities (2000) to undertake a study that resulted in the so-called White Paper on Food Safety.[71] It was and still is the crucial strategic document for food safety in the EU. We at the Federation of German Consumer Organisations wondered whether that strategy has been successful. Is the principle of traceability fully operational so that we become aware of existing risks as early as possible? Do only safe globally traded goods reach our plates? Is the precautionary principle of the EU regulation on food safety being implemented?[72] And why do consumers still have distrust in the precautionary principle as applied?

According to a Eurobarometer survey on risk perception in the EU (European Commission, 2010), 11 per cent of those surveyed believed that the probability of eating foods which have negative effects on health was very high, and 37 per cent believed that it was fairly probable. There were similar data for Germany. Furthermore, many consumers are still asking for a systemic change in agricultural production methods. The Eurobarometer survey also reveals that people are increasingly worried about chemical residues from pesticides in fruit, vegetable and cereals, with an average of 31 per cent of respondents in the EU expressing such concerns, 91 per cent in Greece, 80 per cent in France and 75 per cent in Germany. Concerning the use of antibiotics or hormones in meat, an average of 30 per cent of respondents throughout Europe reported being very worried, 99 per cent in Cyprus and 63 per cent in the Netherlands. The EU average for respondents expressing concern about the cloning of animals for food products was 30 per cent, and 29 per cent were concerned about pollutants such as mercury in fish and dioxins in pork. Forty-two per cent of those surveyed did not believe that the public authorities in the EU viewed the health of citizens as more important than the profits of producers, and more than 81 per cent felt that public authorities should do more to ensure that food is healthy and inform people about healthy diets and lifestyles.

The White Paper on Food Safety makes manufacturers, importers, carriers and retailers responsible for the food safety of products. They have to ensure and document the safety of their goods. Additionally, a system of food controls is being implemented through official monitoring of food and veterinary matters. The competent authorities try to detect problems with food safety as early as possible and take appropriate measures. The Federal Office of Consumer and Food Safety (BVL) in Germany tried to develop emerging risk identification systems. But it is not clear how effective these can be. One of the obligations of businesses is to trace the origin of products when they are observed to pose a health hazard and help remove those products from the market as quickly as possible. The idea is to trace the complete food and feed production chain, from the source of production to the retailer.

D. Limits of food safety

Food safety is closely linked to questions of animal and plant health and animal welfare. In the EU, the Food and Veterinary Office (FVO) is responsible for verifying compliance with EU standards concerning these three areas. According to SANCO (2010), it carries out 250 inspections annually, of which one third are undertaken in developing countries. The FVO looks at the legal framework and whether regulatory measures are in place to ensure that producers apply the standards stipulated and enforce them. It also checks the work of the competent authorities and their surveillance and control measures (e.g. whether they have adequate facilities, such as laboratories, independence of work, information policy, certification practices, control systems and records). It also looks at production establishments, handling and storage sites and laboratories.

According to SANCO we know from the work of FVO, that the main food safety problems concern the following areas: the legal and administrative infrastructure, a lack of understanding of control system requirements (especially of EU requirements), inadequate control and enforcement mechanisms, and lack of, or inadequate, facilities for control and certification purposes (SANCO, 2010). Although there is no doubt that there is greater cooperation between the competent authorities in the different countries in technical assistance and capacity-building with regard to European food safety, there are problems, such as inadequate infrastructure in exporting countries. In addition to that, some official food and feed authorities reflect more the interests of the business community than consumer interests. Food safety is also in danger because of a growing amount of unsafe products (such as dietary supplements) offered via the Internet.

The growing market for enriched food (e.g. containing vitamins and minerals) presents food safety risks because of the risk of overconsumption of those additives. Another problem arises from pharmaceutically active substances not approved in Europe and sold as food on the Internet.

Imported products are still largely a "black box" in the sense that laboratories in Europe are only able to find residues they are looking for. Without information about the agricultural production methods and related inputs (for instance the use of veterinary drugs in animal husbandry) those laboratories are unlikely to find the residues. The control system in the EU needs to be continuously improved. In contrast with the industry, the authorities are not sufficiently interconnected and are always one step behind new technologies, new active pharmaceutical ingredients and new products that pose new risks. From notifications about unsafe foods in the EU's Rapid Alert System of Food and Feed (RASFF), it is evident that food and feed products imported into the EU are not automatically safe. Pathogenic micro-organisms, allergens, genetically modified organisms (GMOs), mycotoxins and residues in food released from packaging are the principal causes of unsafe foods. Food safety and food quality require global efforts by the industry and the official regulatory and controlling authorities. Five per cent of foodstuff consumed in the EU originates from third countries (SANCO, 2010). The question therefore arises as to how a global alert system could be organized and whether the European system is suitable for other countries, particularly developing countries.

John Dalli, the former Commissioner for Health and Consumer Policy (2010: 3), noted that "more than sixty countries outside the EU were connected to the RASFF Window, a new online platform, which allow[s] them to download RASFF notifications that might concern them. The Commission would continue its efforts to support those countries in setting up their alert systems, through the *Better Training for Safer Food* programme, to enable them to tackle food safety incidents that gradually become more global in nature." Cooperation between countries and between public health and food safety authorities is essential to manage hazards in food. This has been starkly illustrated by the case of EHEC O104: H4, a deadly E.coli bacterium strain caused by contaminated sprouts that killed at least 45 people and caused a major food crisis in Germany in 2011.

E. International food standards

Collective standards, such as GlobalGAP, Safe Quality Food, Quality and Safety or Label Rouge (for more information, see Guenther and Will, 2007), are increasingly serving as quality assurance schemes for corporations involved in the global food chain. They serve as a guarantee for stable food quality in a world of horizontally and vertically integrated producers.

As consumer organizations show in recent market surveys, processed food is considerably more expensive and very often enriched with unnecessary food additives that pose the risk of overdosage. Many of these processed food products also contain aromas, additives for conservation and/or taste-enhancing substances aimed at keeping them fresh, appealing and non-perishable while being shipped worldwide. In this respect, products of big companies everywhere in the world adhere to the same standards. However, the way food standards are set and who sets them is not transparent to consumers. Indeed, many consumers realize that their understanding of food safety and their ethical concerns are not automatically being considered in the international market, and that standards often work against consumer interests (Mühleib, 2010). For instance, there are conflicts between consumers in the EU and exporting business in the United States over GMOs, chlorinated poultry and hormones in meat and dairy production. The majority of European consumers are wary of products of cloned animals or genetically modified fish, but commercial pressure groups often try to influence public debate and sentiment on this issue.

According to Tanzmann (2011), the Church Development Service and Bread for the World want food standards to be negotiated at the multinational level. But the solution is not that standards should be lowered to a level that would enable compliance by all producers. Consumers' desire for food safety varies depending on the cultural background of the country where products are consumed. If the Federal Institute for Risk Assessment (BfR) in Germany, for instance, defines the limit values for residues, these refer to the minimal quality producers have to comply with. This is why there will always be a conflict between the interests of consumers in developed countries and producers in developing countries. Horton and Wright (2008) have shown that developing countries would stand to benefit if the United States and Europe adopted the same standards. But from the perspective of European consumers, harmonization of United States and European standards would, in most instances, have negative effects, as illustrated by the example of chlorinated poultry.

F. Equivalence of production and of quality management instruments

Consumers may discriminate against products from developing countries if the standards of those countries are not accepted as equivalent to European standards. Equivalence in this context does not mean that products should be produced using the same processes, but in a comparable way. Products, processing techniques and ways of conforming with food safety requirements may differ.

Although there is a comprehensive set of control instruments for food safety, it will not be sufficient to safeguard food safety for all internationally traded products. In sum, a systematic approach towards the control system is missing. Instead of harmonizing the elements of standards, their number is still growing. Many requirements and standards of food safety have been introduced by multinational agribusiness to their advantage, but rarely in cooperation with the farmers who have to manage the requirements. Equivalence of production and of quality management instruments should be judged by bodies that are independent of industry and in accordance with consumer demand.

G. Conclusions

Increasing globalization has accelerated the industrialization of agricultural practices and cost pressures among producers. This has led to larger scales of production of homogeneous agricultural goods in a decreasing number of production units, with several unresolved food-safety risks that are difficult to manage.

Many food safety issues are related to diseases of plants and animals and to the use of external inputs such as agrochemicals and antibiotics. Intensified agricultural production has a negative impact on public health and well-being, and that process seems to have reached its limits. Because of the pressures of competition, producers are constantly seeking to reduce their production costs. This means that in the absence of effective regulation, production standards will follow a "race to the bottom" with the result that in terms of environmental, social and ethical criteria the cheapest and lowest standards might be applied.

Although there are comprehensive control mechanisms to ensure food safety,[73] they are insufficient to guarantee food safety for all internationally traded products. What is lacking is a proactive, preventive approach. Instead of different safety standards and requirements being harmonized, the number of divergent requirements is still growing. Many standards and requirements have been introduced to the advantage of multinational agribusinesses, but often not in cooperation with the farmers who have to conform with those requirements.

Controls to safeguard European food safety have certain limitations. The current approaches to assuring food safety are complicated and expensive, especially for small-scale producers, and in the end producers and consumers pay the additional costs. The notion that more controls are sufficient to guarantee adequate food safety has proved wrong: additional controls have not been able to halt or reverse the trend of increasing contaminants in food products and greater environmental pollution. A systemic change towards low-risk, sustainable production techniques will ease the problems of food safety related to the production and processing of food. It may also improve the level of trust of consumers in agricultural products.

The food industry, should help improve the basis for healthy nutrition by ensuring the quality of raw materials and inputs in processed food. The industry should also ensure that production is environmentally friendly and applied to the locations where production takes place.

Governments need to cooperate nationally and internationally to incorporate the prevention of risk factors into other policy-making areas. Measures relating to areas such as food security and food safety, food production, agriculture, health, environment, trade, taxation, education and urban development need to be coherent and should adhere to the precautionary principle.

References

Academy of Science of South Africa (2010). Turning science on: Improving access to energy in sub-Saharan African. Sixth annual meeting of the African Science Academy Development Initiative, 7–10 November. Available at: http://www.nationalacademies.org/asadi/2010_Conference/PDFs/TurningScienceOn.pdf.

Adelman I (1984). Beyond export-led growth. *World Development*, 12(9): 937–949.

Ajayi CO, Akinnifesi FK, Sileshi G and Kanjipite W (2009). Labour inputs and financial profitability of conventional and agroforestry-based soil fertility management practices in Zambia. *Agrekon*, 48(3), September: 246–292.

Aker J.C and Mbiti IM (2010): Mobile phones and economic development in Africa. CGD Working Paper 211, Center for Global Development, Washington, DC. Available at: http://www.mempowerment.org/wp-content/uploads/2010/12/Mobile-Phones-and-Economic-Development-in-Africa.pdf.

Allen M, Frame DJ, Huntingford C, Jones CD, Jason A, Lowe JA, Meinshausen M and Meinshausen N (2009). Warming caused by cumulative carbon emissions towards the trillionth tonne. *Nature*, 458: 1163–1166.

Alloway BJ, ed. (2008). *Micronutrient Deficiencies in Global Crop Production*. New York and Heidelberg, Springer Verlag.

Altieri MA and Nicholls C (2006). Agroecology and the search for a truly sustainable agriculture. Berkeley, CA, University of California.

Altieri MA, Ponti L and Nicholls C (2005). Enhanced pest management through soil health: toward a belowground habitat management strategy. *Biodynamics* (Summer): 33–40.

Altieri MA (1995). *Agroecology: The Science of Sustainable Agriculture*. Second edition. Boulder, CO, Westview Press.

Altieri MA (2002). Agroecology: the science of natural resource management for poor farmers in marginal environments. *Agriculture, Ecosystems and Environment,* 93: 1–24.

Altieri MA and Koohafkan P (2008). Enduring farms: Climate change, smallholders and traditional farming communities. *Environment and Development Series* 6. Penang, Third World Network.

Altieri MA and Nicholls C (2004). *Biodiversity and Pest Management in Agroecosystems*. Second edition. Boca Raton, FL, CRC Press.

Anderson I (2008). Foot and Mouth Disease 2007: A Review and Lessons Learned. London.

Anderson SH, Gantzer CJ and Brown JRC (1990). Soil physical properties after 100 years of continuous cultivation. Joint Soil Water Conservation 45, 117-121.

Anderson I (2010). Agricultural development, food security and climate change: Intersecting at a global crossroads. Available at: http://web.worldbank.org/WBSITE/EXTERNAL/TOPICS/EXTSDNET/0,,contentMDK:22782615~pagePK:64885161~piPK:64884432~theSitePK:5929282,00.html.

Arbeitsgemeinschaft bäuerliche Landwirtschaft (AbL), EuroNatur Stiftung (2011). Consistent Reform of the EU Agricultural Policy Now. Paper jointly produced by associations engaged in environmental protection, nature conservation, agriculture, development policy, consumer affairs and animal welfare. Rheinbach/Hamm, June. Available at: http://www.die-bessere-agrarpolitik.de/uploads/tx_gapdoc/German_Platform-Paper_EU-GAP-2013-engl_01.pdf.

Arends T and Casth P (1994). The comparative effect of equivalent amounts of NPK applied in farmyard manure or in fertilizers, as a function of soil properties. Agrok mas Talajtan 43. 398-407.

Arnell N (1998). Climate change and water resources in Britain. *Climate Change,* 39, 83–110.

Azeez G (2009). Soil carbon and organic farming. Bristol, Soil Association. http://www.soilassociation.org/Whyorganic/Climatefriendlyfoodandfarming/Soilcarbon/tabid/574/Default.aspx.

Badgley C, Moghtader, J, Quintero, E, Zakem, E, Chappell, MJ, Avilés-Vázquez, K, Samulon, A, Perfecto, I (2007): Organic agriculture and the global food supply. *Renewable Agriculture and Food Systems,* 22: 86–108.

Bailey AW (1996). Managing Canadian rangelands as a sustainable resource: Policy Issues; rangelands in a sustainable biosphere. In: *Proceedings of the Fifth International Rangeland Congress*, volume 2: 5–7.

Bakas I (2010). Food and greenhouse gas (GHG) emissions. Copenhagen Resource Institute (CRI). Available at: http://www.scp-knowledge.eu/sites/default/files/KU_Food_GHG_emissions.pdf.

Baltzer K, Hansen H, Lind KM (2008). A note on the causes and consequences of the rapidly increasing international food prices. Copenhagen, Institute of Food and Resource Economics, University of Copenhagen.

Battisti DS and Naylor RL (2009). Historical warnings of future food insecurity with unprecedented seasonal heat. *Science*, 323: 240–244.

Bayliss-Smith TP (1982). *The Ecology of Agricultural Systems*. Cambridge, Cambridge University Press.

Bellarby J, Foereid B, Hastings A and Smith P (2008). Cool Farming: Climate impacts of agriculture and mitigation potential. Amsterdam, Greenpeace International. Available at: http://www.greenpeace.org/international/Global/international/planet-2/report/2008/1/cool-farming-full-report.pdf.

Bergmann K (2002). *Dealing with Consumer Uncertainty: Public Relations in the Food Sector*. Heidelberg, Springer.

Berthelot J (2008). Pour un modèle agricole dans les pays du Sud. *Monde Diplomatique*, November.

Bill & Melinda Gates Foundation (2010). Agricultural development: strategy overview. Seattle. Available at : http:www.gatesfoundation.org.

Binswanger-Mkhize HP (2009): Challenges and Opportunities for African Agriculture and Food Security: High Food Prices, Climate Change, Population Growth, and HIV/ AIDS. Paper presented at the FAO. *Expert Meeting on How to feed the World in 2050*. Rome.

Birchall J (2005). Monsanto agrees to $1.5m crop bribe penalty. *Financial Times,* 6 January. Available at: http://www.ft.com/intl/cms/s/0/42d799ac-6019-11d9-bd2f-00000e2511c8.html#axzz1TzUIJrfL.

Blay-Palmer A (2008). *Food Fears: From Industrial to Sustainable Food Systems*. Aldershot, Ashgate.

Bloom AJ, Burger M, Asensio JSR and Cousins AB (2010). Carbon dioxide enrichment inhibits nitrate assimilation in Arabidopsis and wheat. *Science*, 328: 899–903.

BMELF (1991–1998). *Agrarbericht*. Bundesministerium für Ernährung, Land - und Forstwirtschaft, Bonn.

BMELF (1994). Agrarberichte der Bundesregierung. Bonn, Bundesministerium für Ernährung, Landwirtschaft und Forsten. (Cited by Padel S and Zerger U, Economics of organic farming in Germany. In: Lampkin N and Padel S, eds. *The Economics of Organic Farming: An International Perspective*. Wallingford, CAB International, 1994).

Bogner J, Pipatti R, Hashimoto S, Diaz C, Mareckova K, Diaz L, Kjeldsen P, Monni S, Faaij A, Gao Q, Zhang T, Ahmed MA, Sutamihardja RTM and Gregory R. (2008). Mitigation of global greenhouse gas emissions from waste: Conclusions and strategies from the Intergovernmental Panel on Climate Change. Fourth Assessment Report of Working Group III (Mitigation). Available at: http://wmr.sagepub.com/content/26/1/11.short?rss=1&ssource=mfc.

Bohac J and Pokarzhevsky A (1987). Effect of manure and NPK on soil macrofauna in chernozem soil. In: Szegi J, ed. *Soil Biology and Conservation of Biosphere. Proceedings of the 9th International Symposium*: 15–19. Budapest, Akademiai Kiado.

Bolla V and Pendolovska V (2011). Driving forces behind EU-27 greenhouse gas emissions over the decade 1999-2008: Statistics in focus 10/2011. Available at: http://tinyurl.com/6bhesog.

Borron S (2006). Building resilience for an unpredictable future: How organic agriculture can help farmers adapt to climate change. Rome, FAO.

Brennan M, Pray C, Naseem A and Oehmke J (2005). An innovation market approach to analyzing impacts of mergers and acquisitions in the plant biotechnology industry. *AgBioForum,* 8: 89–99.

Brooks S (2010). *Rice Biofortification: Lessons for Global Science and Development*. London, Earthscan.

Brooks S (2011). Is international agricultural research a global public good? The case of rice biofortification. *Journal of Peasant Studies*, 38(1): 67–80. Available at: http://dx.doi.org/10.1080/03066150.2010.538581.

Brooks S, Leach M, Lucas H and Millstone E (2009). Silver bullets, grand challenges and the new philanthropy. STEPS Working Paper 24, STEPS Centre, Brighton.

Brown L (2011). The new geopolitics of food. *Foreign Policy*, 8 June. Available at: http://www.foreignpolicy.com/articles/2011/04/25/the_new_geopolitics_of_food?page=0,0.

Bruinsma J (2009): The Resource Outlook to 2050: By how much do Land, Water and Crop Yields Need to Increase by 2050? Paper presented at the FAO *Expert Meeting on How to Feed the World in 2050, Rome.*

Buck LE and Scherr SJ (2011): Moving ecoagriculture into the mainstream. In: Worldwatch Institute, *State of the World*

2011: Innovations that Nourish the Planet. Washington, DC, W.W.Norton & Company: 15–24.

Burney JA, Davis SJ and Lobell DB (2010). Greenhouse gas mitigation by agricultural intensification. *Proceedings of the National Academy of Sciences*, 107(26):12052–12057.

Buyanoski HA and Wagner GH (1998). Carbon cycling in cultivated land and its global significance. Global Change Biol. 4, 131-141.

Buyanoski HA, Brown JR, Wagner GH (1997). Sanhorn field: Effects of 100 years of cropping on soil parameters influencing crop productivity. In: Soil organic matter in temperate ecosystems in North America (eds. Paul EA, Paustian E, Elliot T, Cole CVJ), pp.205-225. Boca Raton, FL, CRC Press.

Cakmak I, Pfeiffer WH and McClafferty B (2010). Biofortification of durum wheat with zinc and iron. *Cereal Chemistry*, 87: 10–20.

Camargo R (2010). Projeto de líder do governo é redigido por lobby. Congresso em Foco, 12 December. Available at: http://congressoemfoco.uol.com.br/noticias/manchetes-anteriores/projeto-de-lider-do-governo-e-redigido-por-lobby/.

Campbell A, Kapos V, Scharlemann JPW, Bubb P, Chenery A, Coad L, Dickson B, Doswald N, Khan MSI, Kershaw F and Rashid M (2009). Review of the literature on the links between biodiversity and climate change: Impacts, adaptation and mitigation. Technical Series No. 42. Montreal, Secretariat of the Convention on Biological Diversity.

Caulfield LE and Black RE (2004). Zinc deficiency. In: M Ezzati et al. eds. *Comparative Quantification of Health Risks: Global and Regional Burden of Disease Attributable to Selected Major Risk Factors.* Geneva, World Health Organization: 257–279.

Challinor A, Wheeler, T, Garforth, C, Craufurd, P, Kassam, A (2007): Assessing the vulnerability of food crop systems in Africa to climate change. *Climatic Change,* 83: 381–399.

Chase C (2008). Pricing for profit. Ames, IA, Iowa State University. Available at: http://www.extension.iastate.edu/agdm/wholefarm/html/c1-55.html.

Chase CA and Duffy MD (1991). An economic analysis of the Nashua tillage study: 1978–1987. *Journal of Production Agriculture,* 4: 91–98.

Chibwana C., Fisher M. and Shively G. (2011): Cropland Allocation Effects of Agricultural Input Subsidies in Malawi. World Development, 40 (1): 124-133.

Christensen BT (1996). The Askov long-term experiments on animal manure and mineral fertilizers. In: Evaluation of soil organic matters: models using existing datasets (eds. Powlson DS, Smith P and Smith JU). NATO, ASI 138, 301-312. Heidelberg, Germany. Springer.

Christopher, S. F., Lal, R., Mishra, U. 2009. Long-term no-till effects on carbon sequestration in the Midwestern U.S. *Soil Science Society of America Journal,* 73: 207-216.

Church Development Service (Evangelischer Entwicklungsdienst - EED) and Bread for the World (Brot für die Welt) (2011) Lobby brief 5: Lebensmittelstandards und die Reform der EU-Agrarpolitik. Available at: http://www.eed.de//fix/files/doc/110517_Aktuell_09-13_GAP_LobbyBriefe.pdf.

CIMMYT / IITA 2011: DTMA Project platform. January - April 2011. Available at: http://dtma.cimmyt.org/index.php/component/docman/doc_download/139-dtma-project-platform-january-april-2011.

Cline W (2007). Global warming and agriculture: Impact estimates by country. Centre for Global Development. Washington, D.C. Available at: www.cgdev.org/content/publications/detail/14090.

Community Energy Scotland (2011). Community Renewable Energy Toolkit. Available at: http://www.communityenergyscotland.org.uk/community-renewable-energy-toolkit.asp.

Compassion in World Farming Trust (2004). Reducing meat consumption – the case for urgent reform. Petersfield, United Kingdom. Available at: www.ciwf.org.uk/includes/documents/cm_docs/2008/g/global_benefits_summary.pdf.

Connor DJ (2008): Organic agriculture cannot feed the world. *Field Crops Research,* 106: 187–190.

Conroy JP, Seneweera S, Basra AS, Rogers G and Nissen-Wooller B (1994). Influence of rising atmospheric CO_2 concentrations and temperature on growth, yield and grain quality of cereal crops. *Australian Journal of Plant Physiology*, 21(6): 741–758.

Conway GR (1997). *The Doubly Green Revolution*. London, Penguin.

Corbellini M, Mazza L, Ciaffi M, Lafiandra D and Borghi B (1998). Effect of heat shock during grain filling on protein composition and technological quality of wheats. *Euphytica*, 100: 147.

Cullather N (2010). The Hungry World: America's Cold War Battle against Poverty in Asia. *Cambridge, MA, and London, Harvard University Press.*

Dalli J (2010). Foreword. In: *Annual Report 2009, Rapid Alert System for Food and Feed (RASFF)*. Brussels, European Union. Available at: http://ec.europa.eu/food/food/rapidalert/docs/report2009_en.pdf.

DaMatta FM, Grandis A, Arenque BC and Buckeridge MS. (2010). Impacts of climate changes on crop physiology and food quality. *Food Research International*, 43: 1814–1823.

De Schutter O (2008). *Building Resilience: A Human Rights Framework for World Food and Nutrition Security*. Report of the Special Rapporteur on the Right to Food to the United Nations Human Rights Council, A/HRC/9/23, Geneva, 18 September. Available at: http://www.srfood.org/images/stories/pdf/officialreports/or1-a-1-hrc-9-23final-eng.pdf.

De Schutter O (2009a). *Seed Policies and the Right to Food: Enhancing Agrobiodiversity, Rewarding Innovation*. Report of the UN Special Rapporteur on the right to food to the General Assembly, document no. A/64/170, October. New York, United Nations.

De Schutter O (2009b). *Agribusiness and the Right to Food*. Report of the Special Rapporteur on the Right to Food to the United Nations Human Rights Council, A/HRC/13/33, Geneva, 22 December. Available at: http://www.srfood.org/.

De Schutter O (2010a). *Agroecology and the Right to Food*. Report of the United Nations Special Rapporteur on the Right to Food to the Human Rights Council. Document no. A/HRC/16/49, December. New York, United Nations.

De Schutter O (2010b). Report submitted by the Special Rapporteur on the right to food. United Nations General Assembly. Human Rights Council, Sixteenth session, Agenda item 3 (A/HRC/16/49).

De Schutter O (2010c). Addressing concentration in food supply chains. Briefing note 03. United Nations Human Rights Council, Geneva, 1 December. Available at: http://www.srfood.org/images/stories/pdf/otherdocuments/20101201_briefing-note-03_en.pdf.

De Schutter O (2011). *Agroecology and the Right to Food*. Report presented at the Sixteenth Session of the United Nations Human Rights Council, Agenda item 3A//HRC/16/49, Geneva, 20 December. Available at: http://www.srfood.org/images/stories/pdf/officialreports/20110308_a-hrc-16-49_agroecology_en.pdf.

De Schutter O and Vanloqueren G (2011). The new Green Revolution: How twenty-first century science can feed the world. The Solutions Journal, Vol. 2, Issue 4: 33-44. Available at: www.thesolutionsjournal.org

DeClerck FAJ, Fanzo J, Palm C and Remans R (2011). Ecological approaches to human nutrition. *Food and Nutrition Bulletin*, 32 (suppl. 1): 41S–50S.

Defra (2007). Report of the Food Industry Sustainability Strategy's Champions' Group on Waste. London, Department for Environment, Food and Rural Affairs. Available at: http://archive.defra.gov.uk/foodfarm/policy/foodindustry/documents/report-waste-may2007.pdf.

Degrande A, Kanmegne J, Tchoundjeu Z, Mpeck M-L, Sado T and Tsobeng A (2006). Mechanisms for scaling-up tree domestication: How grassroots organisations become agents of change. Nairobi, International Centre for Research in Agroforestry (ICRAF).

De Janvry A and Sadoulet E (2009). Agricultural growth and poverty reduction: Additional evidence. World Bank Research Observer, Vol. 25, No. 1. Washington, D.C. Available at: http://econpapers.repec.org/article/oupwbrobs/v_3a25_3ay_3a2010_3ai_3a1_3ap_3a1-20.htm.

Delate K, Duffy M, Chase C, Holste A, Friedrich H and Wantate N (2003). An economic comparison of organic and conventional grain crops in a long-term agroecological research (LTAR) site in Iowa. *American Journal of Alternative Agriculture* 18: 59–69.

Delgado JA, Sparks RT, Follet RF, Sharkoff JL, Riggenbach RR (1998). Use of winter cover crops to conserve soil and water quality in the San Lois Valley of South Central Colorado. In: Erosion impact on soil quality (ed Lal R), pp125-142. Boca Raton, FL, CRC.

Demment MW, Young MM and Sensenig RL (2003). Providing micronutrients through food based solutions: A key to human and national development. *Journal of Nutrition*, 133: 3879–3885.

Denevan WM (1995). Prehistoric agricultural methods as models for sustainability. *Advanced Plant Pathology*, 11: 21–43.

Derby BM and Levy AS (2001). Do food labels work? In: Blum PN and Gundlach GT, eds. *Handbook of Marketing and Society*. Thousand Oaks, Sage: 372–398.

Dick WA, Van Doren Jr DM, Triplett Jr CB, Henry JE (1996). Influence of long-term tillage and rotation combinations on crop yields and selected soil parameters: Results obtained for a Mollic Ochraqualf soil. OARDC Res. Bull. 1180, Wooster, OH.

Diebel PL, Williams JR and Llewelyn RV (1995). An economic comparison of conventional and alternative cropping systems for a representative northeast Kansas farm. *Review of Agricultural Economics,* 17(3): 120–127.

Dobbs TL and Smolik JD (1996). Productivity and profitability of conventional and alternative farming systems: A long-term, on-farm paired comparison. *Journal of Sustainable Agriculture*, 9(1): 63–79.

Dorward A, Kydd J, Morrison J and Urey I (2002). A policy agenda for pro-poor agricultural growth. Imperial College at Wye. Available at: http://www.sarpn.org.za/wssd/agriculture/policy_agenda/Policy_Agenda_long.pdf.

Dreyfus F, Plencovich C, Petit M, Akca H, Dogheim S, Ishii-Eiteman M, Jiggins J, Kiers T and Kingamkono R (2009). Historical analysis of the effectiveness of AKST systems in promoting innovation. In: McIntyre B et al., eds. *Global Report*. Washington, DC, IAASTD. Available at: http://www.agassessment.org/index.cfm?Page=IAASTD Reports&ItemID=2713.

Drinkwater LE, Wagoner P and Sarrantonio M (1998). Legume-based cropping systems have reduced carbon and nitrogen losses. *Nature,* 396: 262–265.

Drinkwater LE, Wagoner P and Sarrantonio M (1998). Legume-based cropping systems have reduced carbon and nitrogen losses. *Nature*, 396: 262–265.

Dusseldorp M and Sauter A (2011). Forschung zur Lösung des Welternährungsproblems – Ansatzpunkte, Strategien, Umsetzung, Büro für Technikfolgen-Abschätzung beim Deutschen Bundestag, Endbericht zum TA-Projekt, Arbeitsbericht, Nr. 142, February.

Easterling WE, Aggarwal PK, Batima P, Brander KM, Erda L, Howden SM, Kirilenko A, Morton J, Soussana J-F, Schmidhuber J and Tubiello FN (2007). Food, fibre and forest products. In: IPCC, Parry ML et al. eds., *Climate Change 2007: Impacts, Adaptation and Vulnerability*. Contribution of Working Group II to the Fourth Assessment Report of the Intergovernmental Panel on Climate Change. Cambridge, Cambridge University Press: 273–313.

Edwards M (2008). Just another emperor? The myths and realities of philanthrocapitalism. New York, Demos and The Young Foundation.

EFSA (2011). EFSA evaluates the public health risk of bacterial strains resistant to certain antimicrobials in food and food-producing animals. Press release, 2 August 2011. Available at: http://www.efsa.europa.eu/en/press/news/110802a.htm.

El-Hage Scialabba N, Hattam C, eds. (2002). *Organic Agriculture, Environment and Food Security*. Rome, FAO. Available at: www.fao.org/docrep/005/y4137e/y4137e00.htm.

El-Hage Scialabba N, Müller-Lindenlauf M (2010). Organic agriculture and climate change. *Renewable Agriculture and Food Systems,* 25(2): 158–169.

Ellis F and Freeman HA (2004): Rural Livelihoods and Poverty Reduction Strategies in Four African Countries. *Journal of Development Studies,* 40: 1–30.

Elton CS (1927). *Animal Ecology.* London, Sidgwick and Jackson.

Esquinas-Alcázar J (2005). Protection of crop genetic diversity for food security: Political, ethical and technical challenges. *Nature*, 6 December: 946–953.

European Commission (2000). White Paper on Food Safety. Brussels, 12 January. Document COM (1999) 719 final. Available at: http://ec.europa.eu/dgs/health_consumer/library/pub/pub06_en.pdf.

European Commission (2006). *Special Eurobarometer: Health and Food.* Brussels.

European Commission (2010). Eurobarometer Survey Report on Risk Perception in the EU. *Eurobarometer Special* 354. Brussels.

European Environment Agency (2005). Household consumption and the environment. EEA Report No. 11/2005. Copenhagen. Available at: http://www.eea.europa.eu/publications/eea_report_2005_11/at_download/file.

Eurostat (2011). From farm to fork: a statistical journey along the EU's food chain. Issue number 27/2011. Available at: http://tinyurl.com/656tchm and http://tinyurl.com/6k9jsc3.

Eyhorn F (2007). *Organic Farming for Sustainable Livelihoods in Developing Countries? The Case of Cotton in India.* Zürich, vdf-Hochschulverlag. Available at: http://www.vdf.ethz.ch/loadAllFrames.asp?showArtDetail=3111 (See also: Eyhorn, Assessing the potential of organic farming for sustainable livelihoods in developing countries: the case of cotton in India. Available at: http://www.zb.unibe.ch/download/eldiss/06eyhorn_f.pdf).

Eyhorn F, Ramakrishnan M and Mäder P (2007). The viability of cotton-based organic farming systems in India. *International Journal of Agricultural Sustainability,* 5(1): 25–38.

Faeth P and Crosson P (1994). Building the case for sustainable agriculture. *Environment,* 36(1): 16–20.

Falkenmark M and Rockström J (2006). The new blue and green water paradigm: Breaking new ground for water resources planning and management. *Journal of Water Resources Planning and Management,* May/June: 129–132.

FAO (1981). Food loss prevention in perishable crops. *FAO Agricultural Service Bulletin,* FAO Statistics Division, Rome.

FAO (1995). Chapters 2, 3 and 4. In: FAO, *Future Energy Requirements for Africa's Agriculture.* Prepared for the African Energy Programme of the African Development Bank. Rome, FAO. Available at: http://www.fao.org/docrep/V9766E/v9766e00.htm#Contents.

FAO (2000). *The Energy and Agriculture Nexus.* Rome.

FAO (2003). Ministerial Round Table on the Role of Water and Infrastructure in Ensuring Sustainable Food Security, Rome, 29 November–10 December 2003. Available at: www.fao.org/DOCREP/MEETING/007/J0690E.HTM.

FAO (2005). Discards in the world's marine fisheries – an update. FAO Fisheries technical paper 470, Rome. Available at: www.fao.org/docrep/008/y5936e/y5936e00.htm.

FAO (2006): *World Agriculture: Towards 2030/2050.* Interim report. Rome.

FAO (2007). *The State of Food and Agriculture.* Rome.

FAO (2008). Advisory Committee on Paper and Wood Products, Forty-Ninth Session, Bakubung, South Africa, 10 June.

FAO (2009a). Enabling agriculture to contribute to climate change mitigation. Submission by FAO to UNFCCC. Rome. Available at: http://unfccc.int/resource/docs/2008/smsn/igo/036.pdf.

FAO (2009b). *The State of Food Insecurity in the World.* Economic Crisis: Impacts and Lessons Learned. Rome. Available at: http://www.fao.org/docrep/012/i0876e/i0876e00.htm.

FAO (2009c). *Statistical Yearbook 2009.* Rome. Available at: www.fao.org/economic/the-statistics-division-ess/publications-studies/statistical-yearbook/fao-statistical-yearbook-2009/en/.

FAO (2010). *Yearbook 2010.* Rome. Available at: http://www.fao.org/economic/ess/ess-publications/ess-yearbook/ess-yearbook2010/yearbook2010-reources/en/.

FAO (2011a). High-level Panel of Experts on Food Security and Nutrition to the Committee on World Food Security. Price Volatility and Food Security. Rome. Available at: www.fao.org/fileadmin/user_upload/hlpe/hlpe_documents/HLPE-price-volatility-and-food-security-report-July-2011.pdf.

FAO (2011b). Organic agriculture and climate change mitigation. A report of the Round Table on Organic Agriculture and Climate Change. December 2011, Rome, Italy.

FAO (2011c). *Land tenure and International Investments in Agriculture.* A report by the High Level Panel of Experts on Food Security and Nutrition of the Committee on World Food Security, Rome. FAOStat. Rome. http://faostat.fao.org/.

FAO (2011d). The State of Food and Agriculture 2010-2011. Rome. Available at: www.fao.org/docrep/013/i2050e/i2050e.pdf.

FAO (2011e). *Global Food Losses and Food Waste.* Rome. Available at: www.fao.org/fileadmin/user_upload/ags/publications/GFL_web.pdf.

FAO (2012a). Food security and climate change. Report of the High-level Panel of Experts on Food Security and Nutrition to the Committee on World Food Security. Report No. 3. Rome, June. Available at: www.fao.org.

FAO (2012b). Climate smart agriculture for development. Available at: http://www.fao.org/climatechange/climatesmart/en/.

FAO (2012c). Climate-Smart Agriculture. Rome. Available at: http://www.fao.org/climatechange/climatesmart/en/.

FAO and Bioversity International (2007). Sustainable agriculture and rural development (SARD). Policy Brief 11. Rome.

FAO and IIED (International Institute for Environment and Development) (2008). The right to food and access to natural resources: Using human rights arguments and mechanisms to improve resource access for the rural poor. Right to Food Study, FAO, Rome.

FAT (1993). Bericht über biologisch bewirtschaftete Betriebe 1991. Eidg. Forschungsanstalt für Betriebswirtschaft und Landtechnik, Tänikon, Switzerland. (Cited by Mühlebach I and Mühlebach J, Economics of organic farming in Switzerland. In: Lampkin NH and Padel S, eds. *The Economics of Organic Farming: An International Perspective.* Wallingford, CAB International, 1994).

FAT (1997). Bericht über biologisch bewirtschaftete Betriebe 1990-96, Ergebnisse der Zentralen Auswertung von Buchhaltungsdaten. Tänikon, Eidgenössische Forschungsanstalt für Agrarwirtschaft und Landtechnik.

Feed the Future (2010). Guide. Available at: www.feedthefuture.gov.

Feyder J (2010). *Mordshunger – Wer profitiert vom Elend der armen Länder?* (Hunger kills: Who profits from the misery of poor countries?) Frankfurt, Westend. (Also in French: *La Faim tue,* l'Harmattan, 2011).

Filger S (2011). Global financial crisis 2008 versus 2011: Is history about to repeat itself? 3 June. Available at: http://www.globaleconomiccrisis.com/blog/archives/tag/financial-crisis-2011.

Financial Times (2011). Special report on managing climate change. London, 28 November. Available at: www.ft.com/climate-change-2011.

Fischer G, Shah, M, Tubiello, FN, van Velhuizen, H(2005): Socio-economic and climate change impacts on agriculture: An integrated assessment, 1990–2080. *Philosophical Transactions of the Royal Society B ,* 360: 2067–2083.

Fliessbach A, Imhof D, Brunner T and Wüthrich C (1999). Tiefenverteilung und zeitliche Dynamik der mikrobiellen Biomasse in biologisch und konventionell bewirtschafteten Böden. *Regio Basiliensis* 3: 253–263.

Fliessbach A, Oberholzer HR, Gunst L and Mäder P (2007). Soil organic matter and biological soil quality indicators after 21 years of organic and conventional farming. *Agriculture, Ecosystems & Environment,* 118: 273–284.

Foresight (2011a). *The Future of Food and Farming.* Final project report. London, Government Office for Science. Available at: www.bis.gov.uk/assets/bispartners/foresight/docs/food-and-farming/11-546-future-of-food-and-farming-report.pdf.

Foresight (2011b). *Science Review: SR56 Global Food Waste Reduction: Priorities for a World in Transition.* Available at: www.bis.gov.uk/foresight/our-work/projects/published-projects/global-food-and-farming-futures/~/media/BISPartners/Foresight/docs/food-and-farming/science/11-588-sr56-global-food-waste-reduction-priorities.ashx.

Foresight (2011c). Expert Forum on the Reduction of Food Waste, UK Science and Innovation Network and Foresight, London, 23–24 February 2010. Available at: www.bis.gov.uk/assets/bispartners/foresight/docs/food-and-farming/workshops/11-608-w4-expert-forum-reduction-of-food-waste.pdf.

Foresight (2011d). *The Future of Food and Farming*, Synthesis Report C7: Reducing waste. Available at: www.bis.gov.uk/assets/bispartners/foresight/docs/food-and-farming/synthesis/11-627-c7-reducing-waste.pdf.

Francis CA, Jones A, Crookston K, Wittler K and Goodman S (1986). Strip cropping corn and grain legumes: A review. *American Journal of Alternative Agriculture,* 1: 159–164.

Friedl B, Hammer M, Jäger J, Lorek S, Omann I and Pack A (2007). *SUFO: TROP. Sustainable Food Consumption: Trends and Opportunities.* Final report year 2. Vienna, Austrian Academy of Sciences Press.

Frison EA, Smith IF, Johns T, Cherfas J, Eyzaguirre PB (2006). Agricultural biodiversity, nutrition and health: Making a difference to hunger and nutrition in the developing world. *Food and Nutrition Bulletin,* 27(2): 167–179.

Fullen MA and Av. K (1998). Effects of grass ley set aside on runoff, erosion and organic matter levels in sandy soil in East Shropshire, UK. Soil Till. Res. 46, 41-49.

Fuu Ming Kai, Tyler SC, Randerson JT and Blake DR (2011). Reduced methane growth rate explained by decreased Northern Hemisphere microbial sources. *Nature,* 476: 194–197.

Garnett T and Jackson T (2007). Frost Bitten: An exploration of refrigeration dependence in the UK food chain and its implications for climate policy. Paper presented at the 11th European Round Table on Sustainable Consumption and Production, Basel, June 2007. Food Climate Research Network, Centre for Environmental Strategy, University of

Surrey. Available at: www.fcrn.org.uk/research-library/refrigeration/general/frost-bitten-refrigeration-dependence-uk-food-chain .

Gattinger A, Müller A, Häni M, Oehen B, Stolze M and Niggli U (2011). Soil carbon sequestration of organic crop and livestock systems and potential for accreditation by carbon markets. In: FAO, *Organic Agriculture and Climate Change Mitigation*. A report of the Round Table on Organic Agriculture and Climate Change, Rome, December: 10–32.

German Academy of Sciences Leopoldina (2012). Statement: Bioenergy - Chances and Limits. Berlin. Available at: www.leopoldina.org/uploads/tx_leopublication/201207_Stellungnahme_Bioenergie_LAY_en_final.pdf.

German Council for Sustainable Development, (2011). Rat für Nachhaltige Entwicklung (RNE): Gold-Standard Ökolandbau: Für eine nachhaltige Gestaltung der Agrarwende: Empfehlungen des Rates für Nachhaltige Entwicklung vom 11. Juli, Texte Nr. 40.

Gianessi L (2009): The potential for organic agriculture to feed the world is being oversold. *Outlooks on Pest Management,* 20(2): 4–5.

Gibbon P and Bolwig S (2007). The economics of certified organic farming in tropical Africa: A preliminary assessment. DIIS Working Paper no. 2007/3, Danish Institute for International Studies, Copenhagen.

Giovannucci D, Scherr S, Nierenberg D, Hedebrand C, Shapiro J, Milder J, and Wheeler K (2012). Food and agriculture: The future of sustainability. Study for the UN Department of Economic and Social Affairs (UN DESA) under the project Sustainable Development in the 21st Century. New York. Available at: www.un.org/esa/dsd/dsd_sd21st/21_pdf/agriculture_and_food_the_future_of_sustainability_web.pdf.

Gleick PH (1996). Basic water requirements for human activities: Meeting basic needs. *Water International,* 21: 83–92.

Gliessman S (2007). *Agroecology: The Ecology of Sustainable Food Systems.* Boca Raton, FL, CRC Press.

Global Carbon Project (2010): *Carbon Budget 2009.* Available at: http://www.globalcarbonproject.org/carbonbudget/.

Godfray H, Beddington J, Crute I, Haddad L, Lawrence D, Muir J, Pretty J, Robinson S, Thomas S and Toulmin C (2010). Food security: The challenge of feeding 9 billion people. *Science,* 327: 6.

Grace P and Oades JM (1994). Long-term field trials in Australia. In: Long-term experiments in agricultural and ecological sciences (eds. Leigh RA and Johnston AE), pp. 53-81. Wallingford, UK: CAB International.

GRAIN (2009). Earth matters: Tackling the climate crisis from the ground up. *Seedling,* October. Available at: http://www.grain.org/e/735.

GRAIN (2010). Global agribusiness: Two decades of plunder. *Seedling*, July. Available at: http://www.grain.org/article/entries/4055-global-agribusiness-two-decades-of-plunder.

Grameen Shakti (2011). Programs at a glance, May. Available at: http://gshakti.org/index.php?option=com_content&view=category&layout=blog&id=54&Itemid=78.

Griffin DW, Kellogg CA and Shinn EA (2001). Dust in the wind: Long range transport of dust in the atmosphere and its implications for global public and ecosystem health. *Global Change & Human Health,* 2(1): 20–33.

Guenther D and Will M (2007*). Food Quality and Safety Standards as Required by EU Law and the Private Industry: A Practitioners' Reference Book.* Second edition. Eschborn, GTZ. Available at: www2.gtz.de/dokumente/bib/07-0800.pdf.

Hamermesh DS (2007). Time to eat: Household production under increasing income inequality. *American Journal of Agricultural Economics,* 89(4): 852–863. American Agricultural Economics Association.

Handrek K (1990). *Organic Matter and Soils.* Melbourne, CSIRO Publishing (reprinted).

Handrek K and Black N (2002). *Growing Media for Ornamental Plants and Turf.* Sydney, UNSW Press.

Hanson J, Lichtenberg E and Peters SE (1997). Organic versus conventional grain production in the mid-Atlantic: An economic and farming system overview. *American Journal of Alternative Agriculture,* 12(1): 2–9.

Hartfield JL, Boote KJ, Kimball BA, Ziska LA, Izaurralde RC, Ort D, Thomson AM and Wolfe DW (2011). Climate impacts on agriculture: Implications for crop production. *Agronomy Journal,* 103(2): 351–370.

Harvey F (2011). Failure to act on crop shortages fuelling political instability, experts warn. *The Guardian,* 7 February. Available at: http://www.guardian.co.uk/environment/2011/feb/07/crop-shortages-political-instability.

Hawkes C (2004). *Nutrition Labels and Health Claims: The Global Regulatory Environment*. Geneva, World Health Organization.

Hayn D, Eberle U, Stieß I and Hünecke K (2006). Ernährung im Alltag. In: Eberle U et al., eds. *Ernährungswende. Eine Herausforderung für Politik, Unternehmen und Gesellschaft*. Munich, Oekom: 73–84.

Hazell P, Poulton, C, Wiggins, S, Dorward, A (2007): The future of small farms for poverty reduction and growth. 2020 Discussion Paper No.. 42, International Food Policy Research Institute, Washington, DC.

Health Council of the Netherlands (2011). *Guidelines for a Healthy Diet: The Ecological Perspective*. Publication no. 2011/08E, The Hague.

Heimann M (2011). Atmospheric science: Enigma of the recent methane budget. Nature 476, 157-158.

Hellebrand HJ and Herppich W (2000). Methane degradation in soils: Influence of plants and fertilisation. Jahrestagung der Gesellschaft für Ökologie (Annual Session of the Ecological Society), Kiel 11-15 September, Poster, Potsdam, Institute of Agricultural Engineering.

Helmers GA, Langemeier MR and Atwood J (1986). An economic analysis of alternative cropping systems for east-central Nebraska. American Journal of Alternative Agriculture, 1: 153.

Hendrickson J (1994). Energy use in the U.S. food system: A summary of existing research and analysis. Madison, WI, Center for Integrated Agricultural Systems, University of Wisconsin.

Hendrickson M , Miele M, Burt R, Chataway J, Cotter J, Darcy-Vrillon B, Debailleul G, Grundy A, Hinga K, Johnson BR, Kahiluoto H, Lutman P, Madden U and Navrátilová M (2009). Changes in agriculture and food production in NAE since 1945. In: McIntyre et al. eds. *North America and Europe Regional Report*. Washington, DC, IAASTD.

Herren H R (2012). Rio+20: What are the options when "business as usual" is not an option? Presentation at the BioFach workshop on Rio+20 and the Green Economy – Putting Organic Food & Farming Centre Stage, Nuremberg, 15 February.

Herren, H R, Binns, P, Najam, A, Khan, s, Halberg, N, Cim Li Ching, Treyer, S, Lal, R, Atapattu, S, Kodituwakku, D, Tamo, M, Neuenschwander, P, Fernandez, M, Bassi, A, Kassam, A, De Fraiture, C. Kingamkono, R, Perfecto, Y, Khan, Z.R., (2011). UNEP Green Economy Report: Agriculture, Nairobi. Available at: www.unep.org/greeneconomy.

Heywood VH (1995). *Global Biodiversity Assessment*. Cambridge, Cambridge University Press.

Ho MW (2006). Circular economy of the dyke-pond system. *Science in Society*, 32: 38–41.

Ho MW (2008). *The Rainbow and the Worm, the Physics of Organisms*. Third edition. Singapore and London, World Scientific. Available at: http://www.i-sis.org.uk/rnbwwrm.php.

Ho MW (2010a). Green growth for developing nations. *Science in Society*, 46:18–20.

Ho MW (2010b). Sustainable agriculture essential for green circular economy. ISIS lecture at the Ten+One Conference, Bradford University, 29 November–1 December 2010. Available at: http://www.i-sis.org.uk/sustainableAgricultureEssentialGreenCircularEconomy.php.

Ho MW (2011a). Grameen Shakti for renewable energies. Science in Society, 49: 14–16.

Ho MW (2011b). Lighting Africa. *Science in Society,* 50: 38–40.

Ho MW (2011c). Biogas for China's New Socialist countryside. *Science in Society,* 49: 20–23.

Ho MW (2011d). The new politics of food scarcity. *Science in Society*, 51. Available at: www.i-sis.org.uk/The_New_Politics_of_Food_Scarcity.php.

Ho MW, Burcher S and Lim LC et al. (2008). Food futures now: *organic*sustainable*fossil fuel free. ISIS/TWN Report. London and Penang. Available at: www.i-sis.org.uk/foodFutures.php.

Ho MW, Cherry B, Burcher S and Saunders PT (2009). Green energies, 100% renewables by 2010. London and Penang, ISIS/TWN. Available at: http://www.i-sis.org.uk/GreenEnergies.php.

Hodges RJ, Buzby JC and Bennett B (2010). Postharvest losses and waste in developed and less developed countries: Opportunities to improve resource use. *Journal of Agricultural Science*, 149(S1): 37-45. Available at: www.bis.gov.uk/assets/bispartners/foresight/docs/food-and-farming/science/11-561-sr15-postharvest-losses-and-waste.pdf.

Hoegh-Guldberg O, Mumby PJ, Hooten AJ, Steneck RS, Greenfield P, Gomez E., Harvell ED, Sale PF, Edwards AJ, Caldeira K, Knowlton N, Eakin CM, Iglesias-Prieto R, Muthiga N, Bradbury RH, Dubi A and Hatziolos ME (2007).

Coral reefs under rapid climate change and ocean acidification. *Science*, 318: 1737–1742.

Hoffmann U (2011). Assuring food security in developing countries under the challenges of climate change: Key trade and development issues of a fundamental transformation of agriculture. UNCTAD Discussion Paper No. 201, Geneva, 15 March. Available at: www.unctad.org/en/Docs/osgdp20111_en.pdf.

Högy P and Fangmeier A (2008). Effects of elevated atmospheric CO_2 on grain quality of wheat. *Journal of Cereal Science*, 48: 580–591.

Högy P, Wieser H, Köhler P, Schwadorf K, Breuer J, Franzaring J, Muntifering R and Fangmeier A (2009). Effects of elevated CO_2 on grain yield and quality of wheat: Results from a three-year FACE experiment. *Plant Biology*, 11: 60–69.

Holt-Giménez E (2002). Measuring farmers' agroecological resistance after Hurricane Mitch in Nicaragua: A case study in participatory, sustainable land management impact monitoring. *Agriculture, Ecosystems and Environment,* 93: 87–105.

Holt-Giménez E (2006). *Campesino a Campesino: Voices from Latin America's Farmer to Farmer Movement for Sustainable Agriculture*. Oakland, Food First Books.

Horton LR and Wright E (2008). Reconciling food safety with import facilitation objectives: Helping developing country producers meet U.S. and EU Food requirements through transatlantic cooperation. Position paper of the International Food and Agricultural Trade Policy Council, Standard Series, June. Washington, DC. Available at: http://www.agritrade.org/Publications/documents/IPCStandardsPositionPaper.pdf.

Horwith B (1985). A role for intercropping in modern agriculture. *BioScience*, 35: 286–291.

Howard PH (2009). Visualizing consolidation in the global seed industry, 1996–2008. *Sustainability*, 1(4), 8 December: 1266-1287. Available at: http://www.mdpi.com/2071-1050/1/4/1266.

Hubbard K (2009). Out of hand: Farmers face the consequences of a consolidated seed industry. Farmer to Farmer Campaign. Available at: http://farmertofarmercampaign.com/.

Hughes G, Chinowsky P and Strzepek K (2010). The costs of adaptation to climate change for water infrastructure in OECD countries. *Utilities Policy,* 18(3): 142–153.

IAASTD (2009a). International assessment of agricultural knowledge, science and technology for development,. Washington, D.C. Island Press. Accessible at: www.agassessment.org.

IAASTD (2009b). Summary for decision makers. Washington, DC. Available at: www.agassessment.org.

IAASTD (undated). What is the International Assessment of Agricultural Knowledge, Science & Technology? A compilation from its plenary decisions and official documents. Available at: http://www.agassessment-watch.org/docs/IAASTD_on_three_pages.pdf.

IATP (Institute for Agriculture and Trade Policy) (2010). Women at the center of climate-friendly approaches to agriculture and water. Minneapolis. Available at: http://www.iatp.org/documents/women-at-the-center-of-climate-friendly-approaches-to-agriculture-and-water-use.

ICRISAT (International Crops Research Institute for the Semi-Arid Tropics) (2009): Climate change adaptation: Moving forward with hope for the "poorest of the poor" in the semi-arid tropics; Available at: http://unfccc.int/files/adaptation/sbsta_agenda_item_adaptation/application/pdf/icrisat_may09.pdf.

Idso SB and Idso KE (2001). Effects of atmospheric CO_2 enrichment on plant constituents related to animal and human health. *Environmental and Experimental Botany*, 45: 179–199.

IEA (2006). *World Energy Outlook*. Paris, OECD/IEA.

IEA (2010). *Energy Poverty: How to make Modern Energy Access Universal*. Special early excerpt of the *World Energy Outlook 2010* for the United Nations General Assembly on the Millennium Development Goals. Paris.

IEA (2011a). International Energy Agency, CO_2 emissions from fuel combustion: Highlights, 2011 Edition. Paris. Available at: www.iea.org/co2highlights.

IEA (2011b). Prospect of limiting the global increase in temperature to 2°C getting bleaker. Press release, 30 May. Available at: www.iea.org/newsroomandevents/news/2011/may/name,19839,en.html.

IECA (1991). *Erosion Control – A Global Perspective*. Proceedings of Conference XXII. International Erosion Control Association, Steamboat Springs, CO. 20–22 February 1991.

IFAD (2003). The adoption of organic agriculture among small farmers in Latin America and the Carribbean. Report no. 1337. Rome.

Ifejika Speranza C. (2010): Resilient Adaptation to Climate Change in African Agriculture. DIE Studies 54. Deutsches Institut für Entwicklungspolitik, Bonn.

IPCC (2004). Consequences of land-use change. In: *Climate Change 2001*. Working Group I: 3.4.2. Available at: http://tinyurl.com/6lduxqy.

IPCC (2007a). Intergovernmental Panel on Climate Change, Report of Working Group III to the 4th Assessment Report (Climate Change 2007: Mitigation of Climate Change), Cambridge, United Kingdom. Available at: www.ipcc.ch/ipccreports/ar4-wg3.htm.

IPCC (2007b). Glossary. In: IPCC, Parry ML et al., eds. *Climate Change 2007: Impacts, Adaptation and Vulnerability*. Contribution of Working Group II to the Fourth Assessment Report of the Intergovernmental Panel on Climate Change. Cambridge, Cambridge University Press.

IPCC (2007c). *Climate Change 2007: Synthesis Report*. Contribution of Working Groups I, II and III to the Fourth Assessment Report of the Intergovernmental Panel on Climate Change (Pachauri RK and Reisinger A, eds). Available at: http://www.ipcc.ch/publications_and_data/ar4/syr/en/contents.html.

IPCC (2007d). *Climate Change 2007: The Physical Science Basis*. Contribution of Working Group I to the Fourth Assessment Report of the Intergovernmental Panel on Climate Change. Cambridge, Cambridge University Press.

IPCC (2008). Climate change and water. Technical paper (Bates BC et al., eds.). Geneva, IPCC Secretariat.

IPCC (2009). IPCC special report on emissions scenarios 4.6. A roadmap to the SRES scenarios. Available at: http://www.ipcc.ch/ipccreports/sres/emission/112.htm.

Ishii-Eiteman M (2009). Food Sovereignty and the International Assessment of Agricultural Knowledge, Science and Technology for Development. In: Patel R, ed. Grassroots Voices Special Section: Food sovereignty, *Journal of Peasant Studies*, 36(3), July: 689–700.

IWMI (International Water Management Institute) (2007). *Water for Food, Water for Life*. Available at: http://www.iwmi.cgiar.org/assessment/Publications/books.htm.

Izac AM , Egelyng H, Ferreira G, Duthie D, Hubert B and Louwaars N (2009). Options for enabling policies and regulatory environments. In: McIntyre et al., eds. *Agriculture at a Crossroads: Global Report*. Washington, DC, IAASTD. Available at: www.agassessment.org.

Jack W. and Suri T. (2011): Mobile Money: The Economics of M-PESA. Available at: http://www9.georgetown.edu/faculty/wgj/papers/Jack_Suri-Economics-of-M-PESA.pdf.

Jackson GJ (2008). Organic Cotton Farming in Kutch, Gujarat, India. *Outlooks on Pest Management*, February: 4-6.

Jayne TS, Mather D and Mghenyi E (2010): Principal challenges confronting smallholder agriculture in sub-Saharan Africa. *World Development,* 38: 1384–1398.

Jenkinson DS (1990). The turnover of organic carbon and nitrogen in soil. Philosophical Transactions of the Royal Society, B-Biological Sciences 329,361-368.

Johansson S (2008). The Swedish foodshed: Re-imagining our support area. In: Farnworth C, Jiggins J and Thomas EV, eds. *Creating Food Futures: Trade, Ethics and the Environment*. Aldershot, Gower: 55–66.

Johnson PW (1995). *Agriculture*. Food and Drug Administration, Rural Development. Washington, DC, Government Printing Office.

Johnston AE (1973). The effects of ley and arable cropping systems on the amount of organic matter in the Rothamstead and Woburn ley-arable experiments. Rothamstead Report for 1972, Part 2, pp. 131-159.

Jones CE (2012). Carbon that counts. Soil Carbon Coalition. Available at http://soilcarboncoalition.org/files/JONES-Carbon-that-counts-20Mar11.pdf.

Jones N (2011). Climate change curbs crops. *Nature News*, 5 May. Available at: http://www.nature.com/news/2011/110505/full/news.2011.268.html.

Juo ASR and Thurow TL (1998). Sustainable technologies for use and conservation of Steeplands. Bulletin 448. Food & Fertilizer Technology Center for the Asian and Pacific Region, Taipei. Available at: www.fftc.agnet.org/library.php?func=view&id=20110804181442&type_id=4.

Kader AA (2003). A perspective on post-harvest horticulture. *Horticultural Science,* 38: 1004–1008.

Kader AA (2005). Increasing food availability by reducing post-harvest losses of fresh produce. *Acta Horticulturae,* 682: 2169–2175.

Kanninen M et al. (2007). Do trees grow on money? *Forest Perspective,* 4. Jakarta, Center for International Forestry Research (CIFOR).

Karekezi S and Lazarus M (1995). *Future Energy Requirements for Africa's Agriculture* (Chapters 2, 3 and 4). Available at: http://www.fao.org/docrep/V9766E/v9766e00.htm#Contents.

Kasperczyk N and Knickel K (2006). Environmental impacts of organic farming. In: Kristiansen P, Reganold J and Taji A, eds. *Organic Agriculture: A Global Perspective.* Collingwood, CSIRO: 259–282. Available at: http://www.publish.csiro.au/pid/5325.htm.

Keane J, Page S, Kergna A and Kennan J (2009). Climate change and developing country agriculture: an overview of expected impacts, adaptation and mitigation challenges, and funding requirements, ICTSD/International Food & Agricultural Trade Policy Council, Issue Brief No. 2. Available at: www.ictsd.org.

Kendall HW and Pimentel D (1994). Constraints on the expansion of the global food supply. *Ambio,* 23: 198–205.

Khan SA, Mulvaney RL, Ellsworth TR and Boast CW (2007). The myth of nitrogen fertilization for soil carbon sequestration. *Journal of Environmental Quality,* 36(6), 24 October: 1821–1832.

Khor M (2008). The impact of trade liberalization on agriculture in developing countries: The experience of Ghana. Penang, Third World Network.

Khor M (2009). The food crisis, climate change and the importance of sustainable agriculture. *Environment & Development Series* 8. Penang, Third World Network. Paper presented at the High-Level Conference on World Food Security: The Challenges of Climate Change and Bioenergy, Rome, 3–5 June.

Kijima, Y (2008): New technology and emergence of markets: Evidence from NERICA rice in Uganda; Available at: http://www.csae.ox.ac.uk/conferences/2008-EDiA/papers/025-Kijima.pdf.

Kimball BA, Kobayashi K and Bindi M (2002). Responses of agricultural crops to free-air CO_2 enrichment. *Advances in Agronomy,* 77: 293–368.

Kimball BA, Morris CF, Pinter Jr PJ, Wall GW, Hunsaker DJ, Adamsen FJ, LaMorte RL, Leavitt SW, Thompson TL, Matthias AD and Brooks T J (2001). Elevated CO_2, drought and soil nitrogen effects on wheat grain quality. *New Phytologist,* 150: 295–303.

Kjærnes U Harvey M and Warde A (2007). *Trust in Food: A Comparative and Institutional Analysis.* New York, Palgrave.

Konikow LF and Kendy E (2005). Groundwater depletion: A global problem. *Hydrogeology Journal,* 13: 317–320.

Koohafkan P and Altieri MA (2010). Globally important agricultural heritage systems: A legacy for the future. Rome, FAO.

Koopmans CJ, Bos M M and Luske B (2011). Resilience to a changing climate: Carbon stocks in two organic farming systems in Africa. In: Neuhoff D, Halberg N, Rasmussen I, Hermansen L, Ssekyewa C and Mok Sohn S, eds. *Organic is Life – Knowledge for Tomorrow.* Proceedings of the Third Scientific Conference of the International Society of Organic Agriculture Research (ISOFAR), 28 September–1 October. Vol. 2 Socio-Economy, Livestock, Food Quality, Agro-ecology and Knowledge Dissemination, Namyangju, Rep. of Korea: 273–276.

Korchens M and Müller A (1996). The static experiment Bad Lauchst, Germany. In: Evaluation of soil organic matter: models using existing datasets (eds. Powlson DS, Smith P and Smith JU). NATO, ASI138, 369-378. Heidelberg, Germany. Springer.

Krain E, Mavrakis E, Mohamud M, Wanjohi P and Ingwe A (2011). Climate Change and diversification of coffee production: Prospects of cultivating passion fruit as an alternative to coffee in Kenya. Nairobi, Promotion of Private Sector Development in Agriculture (PSDA), Deutsche Gesellschaft für Internationale Zusammenarbeit (GIZ).

Krain E, Ng'endo M, Dietz J, Ndegwa DN, Njeru J and Chege P (2010). Climate change in value chain development: Conceptual ideas based on experiences with the tea, passion fruit and energy saving stoves value chains in Kenya. Nairobi, Promotion of Private Sector Development in Agriculture (PSDA), German Technical Cooperation Agency (GTZ).

Krier JM (2005). *Fair Trade in Europe 2005.* Brussels, European Parliament. Available at: http://fairtrade.net/sites/news/FairTradeinEurope2005.pdf.

Lal R (2002). One answer for cleaner air, water: Better agricultural practices. *Ohio State Research News*. Available at:http://researchnews.osu.edu/archive/sequest.htm.

Lal R (2007). Carbon sequestration. *Philosophical Transcriptions of the Royal Society B – Biological Sciences,* 363(1492), 27 February: 815–830.

Lal R (2008). Sequestration of atmospheric CO_2 in global carbon pools. *Energy and Environmental Science*, 1: 86–100.

Lal R, Kimble JM, Follett RF, Cole CV (1998). The potential of US cropland to sequester carbon and mitigate the greenhouse effect. Chelsea, MI: Ann Arbor Press.

Lal R and Stewart BA (1990). *Soil Degradation*. New York, Springer.

Langdale GW, West LT, Bruce RR, Miller WP and Thomas, AW (1992). Restoration of eroded soil with conservation tillage. *Soil Technology*, 5: 81–90.

LaSalle TJ and Hepperly P (2008). Regenerative organic farming: A solution to global warming. Kutztown, PA, The Rodale Institute: 5.

Lazaroff C (2001). Biodiversity gives carbon sinks a boost. *Environment News Service,* 13 April.

Lee KE and Foster RC (1991). Soil fauna and soil structure. *Australian Journal of Soil Research*, 29: 745–776.

Legg W and Huang H (2010). Climate change and agriculture. *OECD Observer* no. 278, March. Trade and Agriculture Directorate, OECD, Paris. Available at: http://tinyurl.com/5u2hf8k.

Levine UY, Teal TK, Robertson GP and Schmidt TM. (2011). Agriculture's impact on microbial diversity and associated fluxes of carbon dioxide and methane. *ISME Journal*, 5(10): 1683–1691.

Li KM and Ho MW (2006). Biogas China. Science in Society, 32: 34–37.

Libert B (1995). *The Environmental Heritage of Soviet Agriculture*. Oxford, CAB International.

Lim Li Ching (2010). Climate change implications for agriculture in Sub-Saharan Africa. FAO/Institute for Sustainable Development/Third World Network research paper. Rome. Available at: www.fao.org.

Lin BB (2011). Resilience in agriculture through crop diversification: adaptive management for environmental change. *BioScience*, 61: 183–193.

Lin CJ, Li CY, Lin SK, Yang FH, Huang JJ, Liu YH, Lur HS (2010). Influence of high temperature during grain filling on the accumulation of storage proteins and grain quality in rice (*Oryza sativa* L.). *Journal of Agricultural and Food Chemistry*, 58: 10545–10552. Available at: http://pubs.acs.org/doi/abs/10.1021/jf101575j.

Linne K, Archer J, Schmidt G and Kuhrt C (2011). *Climate Change Adaptation and Mitigation in the Kenyan Coffee Sector*. Guide book. Climate Module, Sangana PPP. Deutsche Gesellschaft für Internationale Zusammenarbeit (GIZ), Ecom Agroindustrial Group. Available at: http://www.4c-coffeeassociation.org/index.php?id=6.

Liu J, Fritz, S, van Wesenbeek, CFA, Fuchs, M, You, L, Obersteiner, M, Yang, H (2008): A spatially explicit assessment of current and future hotspots of hunger in sub-Saharan Africa in the context of global change. *Global and Planetary Change,* 64: 222–235.

Lobell DB (2007). Changes in diurnal temperature and national cereal yields. *Agricultural and Forest Meteorology*, 145: 229–238.

Lobell DB, Lobell B., Burke MB, Tebaldi C, Mastrandrea MD, Falcon WP and Naylor RL (2008). Prioritizing climate change adaptation needs for food security in 2030. *Science*, 319: 607–610.

Lobell DB, Schlenker W and Cost-Roberts J (2011). Climate trends and global crop production since 1980. *Science,* 333(6042): 616–620. Available at: http://www.sciencemag.org/content/333/6042/616.

Lockaby BG and Adams JC (1985). Pedoturbation of a forest soil by fire ants. *Journal of Soil Science Society of America*, 49: 220–223.

Loladze I (2002). Rising atmospheric CO_2 and human nutrition: Toward globally imbalanced plant stoichiometry? *Trends in Ecology & Evolution*, 17: 457–461.

Loreau M, Naeem S, Inchausti P, Bengtsson J, Grime JP, Hector A, Hooper DU, Huston MA, Raffaelli D, Schmid B, Tilman D and Wardle DA (2011). Biodiversity and ecosystem functioning: Current knowledge and future challenges. *Science*, 294: 804–808.

Lotter DW, Seidel R and Liebhart W (2003). The performance of organic and conventional cropping systems in an extreme climate year. *American Journal of Alternative Agriculture*, 18(3):146–154.

Louwaars N , Tripp R, Eaton D, Henson-Apollonio V, Hu R, Mendoza M, Muhhuku F, Pal S and Wekundah J (2005). Impacts of strengthened intellectual property rights regimes on the plant breeding industry in developing countries: A synthesis of five case studies. Wageningen, Centre for Genetic Resources.

Lundqvist J, de Fraiture C and Molden D (2008). Saving water: From field to fork – Curbing losses and wastage in the food chain. SIWI Policy Brief. Stockholm, Stockholm International Water Institute. Available at: www.siwi.org/documents/Resources/Policy_Briefs/PB_From_Filed_to_Fork_2008.pdf.

Luske B and van der Kamp J (2009). Carbon sequestration potential of reclaimed desert soils in Egypt. Driebergen, The Netherlands, Soil and More International and the Heliopolis Academy and the Louis Bolk Institute, Department of Agriculture.

MacDonald M (2008). Agri-impact assessment – II: More from the cotton fields. Agrocel Industries Ltd, January. Available at: http://www.traidcraft.co.uk/OneStopCMS/Core/CrawlerResourceServer.aspx?resource=E6A72D61-958F-4D17-B902-8FAC3C0C57ED&mode=link&guid=6ae1f5d397fb4ee5bf3574b7e90cf83d.

Machado S (2009). Does intercropping have a role in modern agriculture? *Journal of Soil and Water Conservation,* 64: 55AA–57A.

Mader P, Fließbach A, Dubois D, Gunst L, Fried P and Niggli U (2002). Soil fertility and biodiversity in organic farming. *Science,* 296(5573): 1694-1697.

Mahoney P, Olson KD, Porter M, Huggins DR, Perillo CA and Crookston RK (2004). Profitability of organic cropping systems in southwestern Minnesota. *Journal of Renewable Agriculture and Food Syst*ems, 19(1): 35–46.

Mazoyer M and Roudart L (2006). *A History of World Agriculture: From the Neolithic Age to the Current Crisis.* (Translation by James H. Membrez). London, Earthscan.

McBride WD and Greene CR (2009). The profitability of organic soybean production. *Renewable Agriculture and Food Systems,* 24(4): 276–284.

McIntyre B, Herren, HR, Wakhungu, J, Watson, RT (2009a): *Agriculture at a Crossroads: Sub-Saharan Africa.* Vol. V Washington, DC, International Assessment of Agricultural Knowledge, Science and Technology for Development.

McIntyre B, Herren HR, Wakhungu J and Watson RT (2009b). *North America and Europe Regional Report.* Vol. IV of Agriculture at a Crossroads. IAASTD. Island Press, Washington, DC. Available at: www.agassessment.org.

Meehl GA, Stocker TF, Collins WD, Friedlingstein P, Gaye AT, Gregory JM, Kitoh A, Knutti R, Murphy JM, Noda A, Raper SCB, Watterson IG, Weaver AJ and Zhao Z-C (2007). Global climate projections. In: IPCC, Solomon S et al., eds. *Climate Change 2007: The Physical Science Basis.* Contribution of Working Group I to the Fourth Assessment Report of the Intergovernmental Panel on Climate Change. Cambridge and New York, Cambridge University Press.

Meinhausen M, Meinshausen N, Hare W, Raper SCB, Frieler K, Knutti K, Frame DJ and Allen MR (2009). Greenhouse-gas emission targets for limiting global warming to 2°C. *Nature,* 458: 1158–1162.

Mendoza TC (2002). Comparative productivity, profitability and energy use in organic: LEISA and conventional rice production in the Philippines. Paper presented at the 14th World Congress, IFOAM, Victoria, Canada, 21–28 August.

Michaelis L and Lorek S (2004). *Consumption and the Environment in Europe: Trends and Futures.* Copenhagen, Danish EPA.

Mick DG, Broniarczyk M and Haidt J (2004). Choose, choose, choose, choose, choose, choose, choose: Emerging and prospective research on the deleterious effects of living in consumer hyperchoice. *Journal of Business Ethics,* 52: 207–211.

Milestad R and Darnhofer I (2003). Building farm resilience: the prospects and challenges of organic farming. *Journal of Sustainable Agriculture,* 22(3): 81–97.

Millennium Ecosystem Assessment (2005). *Ecosystems and Human Well-being: Synthesis.* Washington, DC, Island Press: 6–9.

Milly PCD, Dunne KA and Vecchia AV (2005). Global pattern of trends in streamflow and water availability in a changing climate. *Nature,* 438: 347–350.

Minot N., Smale M., Eicher C., Jayne T., Kling J., Horna D. and Myers R. (2007). Seed development programs in sub-Saharan Africa: A review of experiences. Available at: http://www.aec.msu.edu/fs2/responses/jayne_myers_

african_seed_review.pdf.

Moretti CL, Mattos LM, Calbo AG and Sargent SA (2010). Climate changes and potential impacts on postharvest quality of fruit and vegetable crops: A review. *Food Research International*, 43(7): 1824–1832.

Moyer J (2010). *Organic No-Till Farming*. Emmaus, PA, Rodale Press.

Moyer J (2011). *Organic No-till Farming*. Acres USA, Austin TX.

Mühleib F (2010). Lebensmittelsicherheit und Prozessqualität von Lebensmitteln in Europa - Was sind unsere Ansprüche? Wie können sie gesichert werden? Available at: http://www.vzbv.de/mediapics/lebensmittelsicherheit_ europa_dossier_igw_2010.pdf.

Müller A and Aubert C (2013). The potential of organic agriculture to mitigate the impact of agriculture on global warming: A review. In: Penvern S, ed. *Organic Farming: Prototype for Sustainable Agricultures?* Berlin, Springer (forthcoming).

Müller A, Jawtusch J and Gattinger A (2011a). Mitigating greenhouse gases in agriculture - A challenge and opportunity for agricultural policies. Study of FiBL for ActAlliance, Bread for All, Chruch of Sweden and DanChurchAid. Stuttgart. Available at: www.brot-fuer-die-welt.de/downloads/fachinformationen/greenhouse-gases.pdf.

Müller A, Osman-Elasha B and Andreasen L (2012). The potential of organic agriculture for contributing to climate change adaptation. In: Halberg N and Müller A, eds. *Organic Agriculture for Sustainable Livelihoods*. London, Routledge.

Müller C (2009): Climate change impact on sub-Saharan Africa: An overview and analysis of scenarios and models. Discussion paper, Deutsches Institut für Entwicklungspolitik, Bonn.

Müller C, Cramer, W, Hare, WL, Lotze-Campen, H (2011b): Climate change risks for African agriculture. *PNAS*, 108: 4313–4315.

Mulvaney RL, Khan SA and Ellsworth TR (2009). Synthetic nitrogen fertilizers deplete soil nitrogen: A global dilemma for sustainable cereal production. *Journal of Environmental Quality*, 38: 2295–2314.

Murat A, Verhulst KR, Saltzman ES, Battle MO, Montzka SA, Blake DR, Tang Q and Prather MJ (2011). Recent decreases in fossil-fuel emissions of ethane and methane derived from firn air. *Nature*, 476: 198–120.

Murphy S and Wise T A (2012). Resolving the food crisis. Assessing global policy reforms since 2007. Global Development and Environment Institute at Tufts University and Institute for Agriculture and Trade Policy. Available at: http://iatp.org/files/2012_01_17_ResolvingFoodCrisis_SM_TW.pdf.

Myers N (1993). *Gaia: An Atlas of Planet Management*. Garden City, NY, Anchor/Doubleday.

Naerstad A (2011). A viable food future, part I and II. The Development Fund, Norway. Oslo. Available at: http:// www.utviklingsfondet.no/files/uf/documents/A_Viable_Food_Future_updated_web.pdf and http://www. utviklingsfondet.no/files/uf/documents/Rapporter/A-Viable_Food_Future_part2_en_web.pdf.

NAS (National Academy of Sciences) (2003). *Frontiers in Agricultural Research: Food, Health, Environment, and Communities*. Washington, DC.

Natarajan M and Willey RW (1986). The effects of water stress on yield advantages of intercropping systems. *Field Crops Research*, 13: 117–131.

Nestlé (2011). Die Nestlé Studie 2011 – So is(s)t Deutschland, Wandel des Alltags, Wandel der Ernährung. Available at: http://www.nestle.de/Unternehmen/Nestle-Studie/Nestle-Studie-2011/Pages/default.aspx.

Nestle M (2002). *Food Politics: How the Food Industry Influences Nutrition and Health*. Berkeley, Los Angeles and London, University of California Press.

Netting R McC (1993). *Smallholders, Householders: Farm Families and the Ecology of Intensive, Sustainable Agriculture*. Palo Alto, CA, Stanford University Press.

Niggli U (2009). Organic agriculture: A productive means of low-carbon and high biodiversity food production. In: UNCTAD, *Trade and Environment Review 2009/2010*. Geneva, UNCTAD: 112–142.

Nilsson LG (1986). Data of yield and soil analysis in the long-term soil fertility experiments. J.R. Swed. Acad. Agr. Forestry, suppl. 18, 32-70.

Norwegian Ministry of the Environment (1994). Oslo Roundtable on Sustainable Production and Consumption. Available at: http://www.iisd.ca/consume/oslo000.html.

Nuri A (2005). ONU: Droits pour tous ou loi du plus fort? Geneva, Centre Europe – Tiers Monde (CETIM): 352.

Odum EP (1978). *Fundamentals of Ecology*. New York, Saunders.

OECD (2001). Household food consumption: Trends, environmental impacts and policy responses. Paris, OECD. Available at: www.oecd.org/officialdocuments/displaydocumentpdf/?cote=ENV/EPOC/WPNEP%282001%2913/FINAL&doclanguage=en.

Oerke, EC (2006). Crop losses to pests. Journal of Agricultural Science, Vol. 144, Issue 01 (February), pp. 31-43. Available at: http://journals.cambridge.org/action/displayAbstract?fromPage=online&aid=431724.

Offermann F and Nieberg H (2000). Economic performance of organic farms in Europe. In: *Organic Farming in Europe: Economics and Policy*, Vol. 5. Stuttgart, University of Hohenheim.

Oktem A (2008). Effect of water shortage on yield, and protein and mineral compositions of drip-irrigated sweet corn in sustainable agricultural systems. *Agricultural Water Management*, 95: 1003–1010.

Olah-Zsupos A and Helmeczi B (1987). The effect of soil conditioners on soil microorganisms. In: Szegi J, ed. *Soil Biology and Conservation of the Biosphere: Proceedings of the 9th International Symposium*. Budapest, Akademiai Kiado: 829–837.

Olson KD and Mahoney PR (1999). Long-term cropping studies at the University of Minnesota: The variable input cropping management system study. Washington, DC, United States Dept. of Agriculture, Economic Research Service.

Organic Europe (2010). Country reports. Available at: http://www.organic-europe.net/country_reports/default.asp.

Osborne CP, Beerling DJ (2006). Nature's green revolution: the remarkable evolutionary rise of C4 plants. *Philosophical Transactions of the Royal Society B: Biological Sciences,* 361(1465): 173–194.

Painter K (1991). Does sustainable farming pay? A case study. *Journal of Sustainable Agriculture,* 1(3): 37–48.

Parfitt J Barthel M and Macnaughton S (2010). Food waste within food supply chains: Quantification and potential for change to 2050. *Philosophical Transactions of the Royal Society B,* 365: 3065–3081. Available at: www.bis.gov.uk/assets/bispartners/foresight/docs/food-and-farming/drivers/dr20-food-waste-within-supply-chains.pdf.

Patel R (2011). At Glencore's pinnacle of capitalism, even hunger is a commodity. *The Guardian*, 5 May. Available at: http://www.guardian.co.uk/commentisfree/2011/may/05/glencore-hunge-commodity-food-prices.

Peng S, Huang J, Sheehy JE, LazAa RC, Visperas RM, Zhong X, Centeno GS, Khush GS and Cassman KG (2004). Rice yields decline with higher night temperatures from global warming. *Proceedings of the National Academy of Sciences*, 101: 9971–9975.

Perfecto I, Vandermeer J and Wright A (2009). *Nature's Matrix: Linking Agriculture, Conservation and Food Sovereignty*. London, Earthscan.

Phillips A and Helmeczi B (1987). The effect of soil conditioners on soil microorganisms. In: Szegi J, ed. *Soil Biology and Conservation of the Biosphere, Proceedings of the 9th International Symposium*. Budapest, Akademiai Kiado: 829–837.

Philpott SM, Lin BB, Jha S and Brines SJ (2008). A multi-scale assessment of hurricane impacts on agricultural landscapes based on land use and topographic features. *Agriculture, Ecosystems and Environment*, 128: 12–20.

Pimentel D (2006). Soil erosion: a food and environmental threat. *Environment, Development and Sustainability.* 8: 119–137.

Pimentel D (2011). *Global Climate Change: Its Implications on Food and the Environment.* Rachel Carson Council, Inc. Silver Spring, MD.

Pimentel D and Pimentel M (2008). Food, Energy and Society. Boca Raton, FL, Taylor and Francis.

Pimentel D, Berger B, Filiberto D, Newton M, Wolfc B, Karabinakis B, Clark S, Poon E, Abbett E and Nandagopal S (2004). Water resources: Agricultural and environmental issues. *Bioscience,* 54(10): 909–918.

Pimentel D, Harvey C, Resosudarmo P, Sinclair K, Kurtz D, McNair M, Crist S, Spritz L, Fitton L, Saffouri R and Blair R (1995). Environmental and economic costs of soil erosion and conservation benefits. *Science,* 267: 1117–1123.

Pimentel D, Hepperly P, Hanson J, Douds D and Seidel R (2005). Environmental, energetic, and economic comparisons of organic and conventional farming systems. *Bioscience,* 55(7): 573–582.

Pimentel D, Huang X, Cordova A and Pimentel M (1997). Impact of population growth on food supplies and environment. *Population and Environment*, 19(1): 9–14.

Pimentel D, Petrova T, Riley M, Jacquet J, Ng V, Honigman J and Valero E (2006). Conservation of biological diversity in agricultural, forestry, and marine systems. In: Burk AR, ed. *Focus on Ecology Research*. New York, Nova Science Publishers: 151–173. (Also in: Schwartz J, ed. (2007), *Focus on Biodiversity Research*. New York, Nova Science Publishers: 1–25.)

Pimentel D, Tort M, D'Anna L, Krawic A, Berger J, Rossman J, Mugo F, Doon N,Shriberg M, Howard E, Lee S and Talbot J(1998). Ecology of increasing disease. *Bioscience*, 48(10) October: Available at: http://dieoff.org/page165.htm.

Platform for Agrobiodiversity Research (2010). The use of agrobiodiversity by indigenous and traditional agricultural communities in adapting to climate change. Synthesis paper. Climate Change project, Bioversity International and the Christensen Fund.

Pollack A (2009). Crop scientists say biotechnology seed companies are thwarting research. *New York Times*, 20 February. Available at: http://www.nytimes.com/2009/02/20/business/20crop.html?_r=1.

Posner JL, Baldock JO and Hedtcke JL (2008). Organic and conventional production systems in the Wisconsin integrated cropping systems Trials: 1.1990–2002. *Agronomy Journal*, Volume 100 issue 2, pp. 253-260.

Postel SL (1998). Water for food production: Will there be enough in 2025? *BioScience,* 48(8): 629–637.

Pray C, Oehmke J and Naseem A (2005). Innovation and dynamic efficiency in plant biotechnology: An introduction to the researchable issues. *AgBioForum*, 8: 52–63.

Press E and Washburn J (2000). The kept university. *The Atlantic Monthly*, March. Available at: http://www.theatlantic.com/doc/200003/university-for-profit.

Pretty J (2008). Agricultural sustainability: Concepts, principles and evidence. *Philosophical Transactions of the Royal Society B: Biological Sciences,* 363(1491): 447–465.

Pretty J, Brett C, Gee D, Hine RE, Mason CF, Morison JIL, Raven H, Rayment MD and van der Bijl G (2000). An assessment of the total external costs of UK agriculture. *Agricultural Systems*, 65(2): 113–136.

Pretty JN, Noble AD, Bossio D, Dixon J, Hine RE, Penning de Vries FWT and Morison JIL (2006). Resource-conserving agriculture increases yields in developing countries. *Environmental Science and Technology*, 40(4): 1114–1119.

Pritchard SG and Amthor JS (2005). *Crops and Environmental Change*. New York, Food Production Press.

Quan J (2011). A future for small-scale farming. *Science Review*: SR25. Foresight Project on Global Food and Farming Futures, Government Office for Science Foresight.

Raj DA, Sridhar K, Ambatipudi A, Lanting H and Brenchandran S (2005). Case study on organic versus conventional cotton in Karimnagar, Andhra Pradesh, India. Second International Symposium on Biological Control of Arthropods, available at: http://www.bugwood.org/arthropod2005/vol1/6c.pdf.

Rasmussen PE, Albrechet SL, Smiley RW, (1998). Soil C and N changes under tillage and cropping systems in semiarid Pacific Northwest agriculture. Soil Till. Res. 47, 197-205.

ReardonT,Timmer C and Berdegué J (2007). Supermarket expansion in Latin America and Asia. Washington, DC, United States Department of Agriculture.

Reganold JP, Elliott L and Unger Y (1987). Long-term effects of organic and conventional farming on soil erosion. *Nature*, 330, 26 November: 370–372.

Reganold JP, Glover JD, Andrews PK and Hinman HR (2001). Sustainability of three apple production systems. *Nature,* 410: 926–930.

Reid WS (1985). Regional effects of soil erosion on crop productivity-northeast. In: Follett RF and Stewart BA, eds. *Soil Erosion and Crop Productivity*. Madison, WI, American Society of Agronomy: 235–250.

Reinhardt G, Gärtner S, Münch J and Häfele S (2009). Ökologische Optimierung regional erzeugter Lebensmittel: Energie- und Klimabilanzen. Heidelberg, Institut für Energie und Umwelt (IfEU).

Reisch LA and Gwozdz W (2010). Chubby cheeks and climate change: Childhood obesity as a sustainable development issue. *International Journal of Consumer Studies,* 35(1): 3–9.

Reisch LA, Lorek S and Bietz S (2011). Policy instruments for sustainable food consumption. CORPUS Discussion Paper 2. Funded by the European Commission, FP 7 | Project No. 244103. Available at: http://www.scp-knowledge.eu/sites/default/files/Food_Policy_Paper.pdf.

Reisch LA, Scholl G and Eberle U (2010). Sustainable food consumption. CORPUS Discussion Paper 1. Funded by the European Commission, FP 7 | Project No. 244103. Available at: http://www.scp-knowledge.eu/sites/default/files/Food_Discussion_Paper_1.pdf.

Rethemeyer J, Kramer C, Gleixner G, John B, Yamashita T, Flessa H, Andersen N, Nadeau M and Grootes P (2005). Transformation of organic matter in agricultural soils: Radiocarbon concentration versus soil depth. *Geoderma*, 128: 94–105.

Richardson K, Steffen W, Schellnhuber HJ, Alcamo J, Barker T, Kammen DM, Leemans R Liverman D, Munasinghe M, Osman-Elasha B, Stern N and Waever O (2009). Synthesis Report – Climate Change: Global Risks, Challenges and Decisions. International Scientific Congress on Climate Change, Copenhagen, 10–12 March.

Rikxoort v.H (2010). Carbon footprinting. In: GIZ, ed. Climate Module, Sangana PPP, Kompetenzfeld Agrarhandel und Standards, Deutsche Gesellschaft für Technische Zusammenarbeit (GIZ), June.

Robertson A, Lobstein T and Knai C (2007). Obesity and socio-economic groups in Europe: Evidence review and implications for action. SANCO/2005/C4-NUTRITION-03. Funded by the European Commission, Brussels. European Commission. Available at: http://ec.europa.eu/health/ph_determinants/life_style/nutrition/documents/ev20081028_rep_en.pdf.

Rockström J, Steffen W, Noone K, Persson Å, Stuart III Chapin F, Lambin E, LentonT, SchefferM, Folke C, Schellnhuber HJ, Nykvist B, de Wit C, Hughes T, van der Leeuw S, Rodhe H, Sörlin S, Snyder P, Costanza R, Svedin U, Falkenmark M, Karlberg L, Corell RW, Fabry VJ, Hansen J, Walker B, Liverman D, Richardson K, Crutzen P, and Foley J. (2009). Planetary boundaries: Exploring the safe operating space for humanity. *Ecology and Society,* 14(2): 32. Available at: http://www.ecologyandsociety.org/vol14/iss2/art32/.

Rodale Institute (2003). Farm Systems Trial. Kutztown, PA.

Rodale Institute (2006) No-till revolution. Kutztown, PA. Available at: http://www.rodaleinstitute.org/no-till_revolution.

Roose E (1998). Soil and water conservation lessons from steep-slope farming in French speaking countries of Africa. In: Moldenhauer WC and Hudson N, eds. *Conservation Farming on Steep Lands.* Schertz, Ankeny, Iowa, Soil and Water Conservation Society and World Association of Soil and Water Conservation: 130–131.

Rosegrant MW, Paisner, MS, Meijer, S, Witcover, J (2001): *2020 Global Food Outlook: Trends,Alternatives, and Choices.* Washington, DC, International Food Policy Research Institute.

Rosegrant MW, Ringler C, Msangi S, Sulser T, Zhu T and Cline S (2009a). International model for policy analysis of agricultural commodities and trade (IMPACT): Model description. In: IFPRI (2008), *International Food Policy Research Institute Report.* Washington, DC: 42.

Rosegrant MW, Ringler C and Zhu T (2009b). Water for agriculture: Maintaining food security under growing scarcity. *Annual Review of Environment and Resources,* 34: 205–222.

Rosenzweig C and Hillel D (2008). *Climate Change and the Global Harvest: Impacts of El Nino and Other Oscillations on Agroecosystems.* New York, Oxford University Press.

Rosenzweig C and Tubiello F (2007). Adaptation and mitigation strategies in agriculture: An analysis of potential synergies. *Mitigation and Adaptation Strategies to Global Change*, 12: 855–873.

Rosset PM (1999). *The Multiple Functions and Benefits of Small Farm Agriculture in the Context of Global Trade Negotiations.* Policy Brief 4, FoodFirst, September.

Rosset PM (2006). *The Multiple Functions and Benefits of Small Farm Agriculture in the Context of Global Trade Negotiations.* London, Thousand Oaks, CA and New Delhi, World Food Programme, The Society for International Development and SAGE Publications, 1001-6370 (2006) 43:2; 77-82.

Rosset PM, Sosa BM, Jaime AMR and Ávila Lozano DR (2011). The Campesino-to-Campesino agroecology movement of ANAP in Cuba: Social process methodology in the construction of sustainable peasant agriculture and food sovereignty. *Journal of Peasant Studies*, 38(1): 161–191.

RTS Resource Ltd. (2006). *Western Europe ready meals 2010. Wolverhampton: RTS Resource Ltd. The Creative Industries Centre.* Available at: http://www.readymealsinfo.com/reports/WesternEuropeReadyMeals2010.pdf.

Rundgren G (2012). Garden Earth: From hunter and gatherer to capitalism - and thereafter, Regeneration, Uppsala, Sweden.

Safaricom Foundation (2005): Safaricom Foundation Lifeline radio project unveiled. Available at: http://www.lifelineenergy.org/documents/Safaricom_Foundation_160505.pdf.

SANCO (2010). Food and veterinary office controls in developing countries, November. Available at: http://www.bvl. bund.de/SharedDocs/Downloads/07_Bundesamt/Veranstaltungen/symposium_2011_vortrag_FrankAndriessen_ FVO.pdf?__blob=publicationFile&v=2.

SANCO (2011). Policy impact in the Common Agriculture Policy: Case study of animal health, SANCO Working paper presented at the meeting of the Working Group on the Assessment of SANCO Policy Impact on the Common Agriculture Policy of the Advisory Group on the Food Chain, Animal and Plant Health, 11 February.

Sanderman J, Farquharson R and Baldock JA (2010). Soil carbon sequestration potential: A review for Australian agriculture. A report prepared for the Department of Climate Change and Energy Efficiency CSIRO. Available at: http://www.csiro.au/files/files/pwiv.pdf.

Sanders J, Offermann F and Nieberg H (2008). Impact of the CAP reform on organic farming in Germany. Paper prepared for the 109th EAAE Seminar on the CAP after the Fischler Reform: National Implementations, Impact Assessment and the Agenda for Future Reforms, in Viterbo, Italy, 20–21 November.

Scherr SJ and Sthapit S (2009): Mitigating climate change through food and land use. *Worldwatch Report* 179. Washington DC, Worldwatch Institute.

Schultz I and Stieß I (2008). Linking sustainable consumption to everyday life: a socio-ecological approach to consumption research. In: Tukker A, Charter M and Vezzoli C, eds. *System Innovation for Sustainability, Vol. 1: Perspectives on Radical Changes to Sustainable Consumption and Production.* Sheffield, Greenleaf Publishing: 288–300.

Science Daily (2011). Study maps global 'hotspots' of climate-induced food insecurity. 3 June. Available at: http://www. sciencedaily.com/releases/2011/06/110602204807.htm.

Seneweera S and Conroy JP (1997). Growth, grain yield and quality of rice (*Oryza sativa* L.) in response to elevated CO_2 and phosphorus nutrition. *Soil Science and Plant Nutrition*, 43: 1131–1136.

Setboonsarng S, Leung PS and Cai J (2006). Contract farming and poverty reduction: The case of organic rice contract farming in Thailand. ADB Institute discussion paper no. 49. Tokyo, Asian Development Bank Institute.

Siegrist S, Staub D, Pfiffner L and Mäder P (1998). Does organic agriculture reduce soil erodibility? The results of a long-term field study on loess in Switzerland. *Agriculture, Ecosystems and Environment,* 69: 253–264.

Smakhtin V (2008). Basin closure and environmental flow requirements. *Water Resources Development,* 24(2): 227–233.

Smakhtin V, Revenga C and Döll P (2004). A Pilot Global Assessment of Environmental Water Requirements and Scarcity. *Water International,* 29(3), 307–317.

Smit B and Wandel J (2006). Adaptation, adaptive capacity and vulnerability. *Global Environmental Change,* 16: 282–292.

Smith D, Powlson SDS, Glendining MJ, Smith JU (1997), Potential for carbon sequestration in European soils: preliminary estimates for five scenarios using results from long-term experiments. Global Change Biology 3, 67-79.

Smith J, Wolfe M, Woodward L, Pearce B and Lampkin N (2011). Organic farming and biodiversity: A review of the literature. Aberystwyth, Organic Centre Wales.

Smith P, Martino D, Cai Z, Gwary D, Janzen H, Kumar P, McCarl B, Ogle S, O'Mara F, Rice C, Scholes B, Sirotenko O, Howden M, McAllister T, Pan G, Romanenkov V, Schneider U and Towprayoon S (2007a). Policy and Technological Constraints to Implementation of Greenhouse Gas Mitigation Options in Agriculture. Agriculture, Ecosystems and Environment (118): 6–28. Available at: www.elsevier.com/ loacate/agree.

Smith P, Martino D, Cai Z, Gwary D, Janzen H, Kumar P, McCarl B, Ogle S, O'Mara F, Rice C, Scholes B and Sirotenko O (2007b). Agriculture. In: IPCC, *Climate Change 2007: Mitigation.* Contribution of Working Group III to the Fourth Assessment Report of the Intergovernmental Panel on Climate Change. Cambridge, Cambridge University Press.

Smolik JD, DobbsTL and Rickerl DH (1995). The relative sustainability of alternative, conventional, and reduced-till farming systems. *American Journal of Alternative Agriculture*, 10(1): 25–35.

South Centre (2011). A trade framework supportive of a transition towards a green economy in the food and agriculture sector of developing countries. Paper prepared for the FAO (forthcoming). Geneva.

Southgate D and Whitaker M (1992). Promoting resource degradation in Latin America: Tropical deforestation, soil erosion, and coastal ecosystem disturbance in Ecuador. *Economic Development and Cultural Change*, 40(4):

787–807.

SP International (2010). Explanation demanded over lobbying by biotech firm. SP International, Rotterdam, 25 January. Available at: http://international.sp.nl/bericht/40536/100125-explanation_demanded_over_lobbying_by_biotech_firm.html.

Speth JG (1994). *Towards an Effective and Operational International Convention on Desertification*. Paper prepared for the International Convention on Desertification, International Negotiating Committee, United Nations, New York.

Stanhill G (1990). The comparative productivity of organic agriculture. *Agriculture Ecosystems and Environment*, 30: 1–26.

Staver C, Guharay F, Monterroso D and Muschler RG (2001). Designing pest-suppressive multistrata perennial crop systems: Shade-grown coffee in Central America. *Agroforestry Systems*, 53: 151–170.

Steer A (2011). Agriculture, food security and climate change: A triple win? Available at: http://web.worldbank.org/WBSITE/EXTERNAL/NEWS/0,,contentMDK:22750055~pagePK:34370~piPK:34424~theSitePK:4607,00.html.

Stern N (2007). *The Economics of Climate Change. The Stern Review*. Cambridge, Cambridge University Press.

Stevenson J (1998). Humus chemistry. In: *Soil Chemistry*. New York, John Wiley & Sons Inc.: 148.

Stoltzfus RJ, Mullany L and Black RE (2004). Iron deficiency anemia. In: M Ezzati et al., eds. *Comparative Quantification of Health Risks: Global and Regional Burden of Disease Attributable to Selected Major Risk Factors*. Geneva, World Health Organization: 163-209.

Stone RP and Moore N (1997). *Control of Soil Erosion*. Factsheet, Ontario Ministry of Agriculture, Food and Rural Affairs.

Strzepek K and McCluskey A (2007). The impact of climate change on regional water resources and agriculture in Africa. Washington, DC, World Bank Development Research Group.

Strzepek K, Balaji R, Rajaram H and Strzepek J (2013). A water balance model for climate impact analysis of runoff with emphasis on extreme events (forthcoming).

Stuart T (2009). *Waste: Uncovering the Global Food Scandal*. New York, WW Norton and Co. Inc. Available at: http://tinyurl.com/m3dxc9.

Sugden AM and Rands GF (1990). The ecology of temperate and cereal fields. *Trends in Ecology and Evolution*, 5: 205–206.

Sugden AM, Stone R and Ash C (2004). Ecology in the underworld. *Science*, 304:1613.

Sustain (2010). Yet more hospital food failure. Good Food for Our Money campaign. Available at: http://www.sustainweb.org/pdf/GFFOM_Hospital_Food_Second_Report.pdf.

Sustainable Development Commission (2005). Sustainability implications of the Little Red Tractor Scheme. Report. London.

Sustainable Development Commission (2008). Green, healthy and fair. Report. London.

Swanson T (2005). *Global Action for Biodiversity*. London, James & James Science Publishers. (Originally published in Earthscan Publications, London, 1997).

Tanzmann S (2011). Lebensmittelstandards diskriminieren Kleinbauern in: *Die Agrarpolitik endet nicht an Europas Grenzen, Die EU Agrarreform und ihre internationale Verantwortung*. Ein Dossier vom Evangelischen Entwicklungsdienst und "Brot für die Welt". In: *Zusammenarbeit mit der Redaktion Welt-Sichten*, 2/2011: 16–18.

Tassou SA, Ge Y, Hadawey A, Marriott D, (2011). Energy consumption and conservation in food retailing. *Applied Thermal Engineering*, 31: 147–156.

Taub DR, Miller B and Allen H (2008). Effects of elevated CO_2 on the protein concentration of food crops: A meta-analysis. *Global Change Biology*, 14: 565–575.

Tchibo GmbH (2009). PCF pilot project Germany: Case study of Tchibo Privat Kaffee Rarity Machare. Hamburg, November.

Teasdale JR, Coffman CB and Mangum RW (2007). Potential long-term benefits of no-tillage and organic cropping systems for grain production and soil improvement. *Agronomy Journal, Sept–Oct, 99 (5): 1297-1305*.

Tegtmeier EM and Duffy M (2004). External costs of agricultural production in the United States. *International Journal of Agricultural Sustainability*, 2(1): 1–20.

Tempelman E (2006). Product service systems for need area food: An overview, in New Business for Old Europe, Tischner U and Tukker A (editors), Greenleaf Publishing Ltd., Sheffield, United Kingdom.

Testbiotech-Institute for Independent Impact Assessment in Biotechnology (2009). Leading European Food Safety Authority staff member moves into industry. Munich, 10 November. Available at: http://www.testbiotech.org/en/node/260.

Testbiotech-Institute for Independent Impact Assessment in Biotechnology (2010). EFSA's revolving door to biotech industry unacceptable. Munich, 24 March. Available at: http://www.testbiotech.org/en/node/354/.

The Climate Group (2008). Breaking the climate deadlock. A global deal for our low-carbon future. Report submitted to the G-8 Hokkaido Toyako Summit. London. Avaialable at www. http://www.theclimategroup.org/what-we-do/programs/Breaking-the-Climate-Deadlock/.

The Guardian (2011). London, 30 May. Available at: www.guardian.co.uk/.

Tilman D, Fargione J, Wolff B, D'Antonio C, Dobson A, Howarth R, Schindler D, Schlesinger WH, Simberloff D and Swackhamer D (2001). Forecasting agriculturally driven global environmental change. *Science,* 292: 281–284.

Tilman D, Reich PB, Knops J, Wedin D, Mielke T and Lehman C (2003). Diversity and productivity in a long-term grassland experiment. *Science*, 5543: 843–845.

Tinlot M (2010). Intégration de filières à la mitigation au changement climatique: Cas de la filière anacarde au Burkina Faso. Mission report, GIZ / FAO, Rome.

Tirado R and Cotter J (2010). Ecological farming: drought-resistant agriculture, Greenpeace Research Laboratories, University of Exeter, United Kingdom. Available at: www.greenpeace.org/international/en/publications/reports/Ecological-farming-Drought-resistant-agriculture.

Tischner U and Kjaernes U (2007). Sustainable consumption and production in the agriculture and food domain. In: Lahlou S and Emmert S, eds. *SCORE Proceedings: SCP Cases in the Field of Food, Mobility, and Housing.* Workshop of the Sustainable Consumption Research Exchange (SCORE!) Network, Paris, June 2007: 201–237. Available at: http://www.score-network.org/files/9594_Proceedings_worshop.07.pdf.

Toledo VM and Barrera-Bassals N (2009). *La Memoria Biocultural: La Importancia Ecologia de las Sabidurias Tradicionales*. Barcelona, ICARIA Editorial.

Trimbel, SW and Mendel, AC (1995). The cow as a geomorphic agent. A critical article. *Geomorphology*, 13: 233-253.

Troeh FR, Hobbs AH and Donahue RL (2004). *Soil and Water Conservation*. Upper Saddle River, NJ, Prentice Hall.

Tscharntke T, Clough Y, Wanger TC, Jackson L, Motzke I, Perfecto, I, Vandermeer J, and Whitbread A (2012). Global food security, biodiversity conservation and the future of agricultural intensification, Biological Conservation, Vol. 151, Issue 1 (July), pp. 53–59. Available at: www.sciencedirect.com/science/article/pii/S0006320712000821.

Tuckey B (2010). Starving Africa's future? *Foreign Policy in Focus*, 11 August. Washington, DC, Institute for Policy Studies. Available at: http://www.fpif.org/articles/starving_africas_future.

Tyler PS (1982). *Misconception of Food Losses*. Tokyo, United Nations University Press.

Uhlin HE (1997). Energiflöden i livsmedelskedjan (Energy flow in the food chain). Stockholm, Naturvårdsverket.

Uhlen G (1991). Long-term effects of long-term crop rotation, fertilizers, manures, straw and crop rotation on total C in soil. Acta Agr. Scand. 41, 119-127.

Uhlen G and Treitnes S (1995). Effects of long-term crop rotation, fertilizers, farm manure and straw on soil productivity. Nor. J. Agr. Sci, 9, 143-161.

UN/DESA (2010). World Population Prospects, 2010 Revision. Available at: http://esa.un.org/unpd/wpp/unpp/panel_population.htm.

UNCTAD (2009). *Trade and Development Report 2009: Responding to the Global Crisis: Climate Change Mitigation and Development*. New York and Geneva. Available at: www.unctad.org/Templates/WebFlyer.asp?intItemID=5003&lang=1.

UNCTAD (2010). Least Developed Countries Report 2010: Towards a New International Development Architecture for LDCs. Geneva. Available at: www.unctad.org/Templates/Page.asp?intItemID= 3073&lang=1.

UNCTAD and Chamber of Labour, Vienna (2011). Price formation in financialized commodity markets: The role of information. Geneva. Available at: www.unctad.org/en/docs/gds20111_en.pdf.

UNEP (2005). *Agroecology and the Search for a Truly Sustainable Agriculture*. Mexico.

UNEP (2009). *The Environmental Food Crisis: The Environment's Role in Averting Future Food Crises*. Nairobi. Available at: www.unep.org/pdf/FoodCrisis_lores.pdf.

UNEP (2010). Bilateral Finance Institutions and Climate Change. A Mapping of 2009 Climate Financial Flows to Developing Countries. Available at: http://www.unep.org/pdf/dtie/BilateralFinanceInstitutionsCC.pdf.

UNEP (2011). *Towards a Green Economy: Pathways to Sustainable Development and Poverty Eradication – A Synthesis for Policy Makers*. Available at: www.unep.org/greeneconomy.

UNEP-UNCTAD (2008): *Organic Agriculture and Food Security in Africa*. UNEP-UNCTAD Capacity-building Task Force on Trade, Environment and Development. Geneva. Available at: www.uncatd.org/trade_env.

UNFCCC (2008): Challenges and opportunities for mitigation in the agricultural sector. Bonn.

UNFCCC (2011). *The Cancun Agreements: An Assessment by the Executive Secretary of the United Nations Framework Convention on Climate Change*. Available at: http://cancun.unfccc.int/.

United Nations (2007). Reducing post-harvest losses to improve food security: Timor Leste. Projects funded by the United Nations Trust Fund for Human Security. United Nations. Available at: ochaonline.un.org/TrustFund/ProjectProfiles/Reducingpostharvestlosses/tabid/2125/language/en-US/Default.aspx.

United Nations (2008). *World Urbanization Prospects. The 2007 Revision Population Database*. New York, United Nations Population Division.

United Nations (2011). *World Population Prospects: The 2010 Revision*. Department of Economic and Social Affairs, Population Division. Available at: http://esa.un.org/unpd/wpp/index.htm.

United States Forest Conservation Act (2002). Riparian forest buffer panel (Bay Area regulatory programs). Available at: http://www.riparianbuffers.umd.edu/manuals/regulatory.html.

UN-NADAF (United Nations New Agenda for the Development of Africa) (1996). UN-NADAF mid-term review: Focus on key sectors – Environment. *Africa Recovery,* 10(2): 23.

Uphoff N (2002a). Institutional change and policy reforms. In: Uphoff N. ed. *Agroecological Innovations: Increasing Food Production with Participatory Development*. London, Earthscan Publications.

Uphoff N (2002b). *Agroecological Innovations: Increasing Food Production with Participatory Development*. London, Earthscan.

US CRS (2004). Energy use in agriculture: Background and issues. Washington, DC, United States Congressional Research Services, 19 November.

USFDA (2010). Meet Michael R. Taylor, J.D., Deputy Commissioner for Foods. U.S. Food and Drug Administration, Washington, DC. Available at: www.fda.gov/AboutFDA/CentersOffices/OfficeofFoods/ucm196721.htm.

Van der Ploeg JD (2009). *The New Peasantries: Struggles for Autonomy and Sustainability in the Era of Empire and Globalization*. London and Sterling, VA, Earthscan.

Van der Vossen HAM (2005). State-of-the-art of developing durable resistance to biotrophic pathogens in crop plants, such as coffee leaf rust. In: Zambolim L, Zambolim EM and Várzea VMP, eds. *Durable Resistance to Coffee Leaf Rust*. Visconde do Rio Branco, Brazil, Suprema Gráfica e Editora: 1–29.

Van Dijk (1982). Survey of Dutch soil organic research with regard to humification and degradation rates in arable land. In: Use seminar on land degradation (eds. Boels DD, Davis B, Johnston AE), pp. 133-143. Rotterdam, The Netherlands: Balkema.

Van Groenigen K, Osenberg C and Hungate B (2011). Increased soil emissions of potent greenhouse gases under increased atmospheric CO_2. *Nature*, 475: 214–216.

Vandermeer J, van Noordwijk M, Anderson J, Ong C and Perfecto I (1998). Global change and multi-species agroecosystems: Concepts and issues. *Agriculture, Ecosystems and Environment*, 67: 1–22.

Venkat K (2011). The climate change impact of US food waste (updated). CleanMetrics Technical Brief, CleanMetrics Corp. Available at: www.cleanmetrics.com/pages/ClimateChangeImpactofUSFoodWaste.pdf.

Vlek PLG, Le QB and Tamene L (2008): Land Decline in Land-rich Africa: A Creeping Disaster in the Making. Rome, CGIAR Science Council Secretariat.

Vörösmarty CJ, Green P, Salisbury J and Lammers RB (2000). Global water resources: Vulnerability from climate change and population growth. *Science*, 289: 284–288.

Walsh KN and Rowe MS (2001). Biodiversity increases ecosystems' ability to absorb CO_2 and nitrogen. Brookhaven National Laboratory. Available at: http://www.bnl.gov/bnlweb/pubaf/pr/2001/bnlpr041101.htm.

Wang F (2011). Present status of rural biogas development in China. Center for Energy and Environmental Protection, Ministry of Agriculture, China. Available at: http://www.enp.wur.nl/NR/rdonlyres/B1F76376-2F00-4278-84F1-8D9C 14A7D822/140754/052207WangExperiencesofHouseholdBiogasUseinChina.pd.

WARDA (Africa Rice Center) (2008): NERICA: the new rice for Africa: A compendium. Cotonou, Africa Rice Center (WARDA), Rome, FAO, Tokyo, Sasakawa Africa Association. Available at: http://www.warda.org/publications/ nerica-comp/Nerica%20Compedium.pdf.

Wardle DA, Bardgett RD, Klironomos JN, Setala H, van der Putten WH and Wall DH (2004). Ecological linkages between aboveground and belowground biota. *Science*, 304: 1629–1633.

Warner KD and Kirschenmann F (2007). *Agroecology in Action: Extending Alternative Agriculture through Social Networks*. Cambridge, MA, MIT Press.

Washburn J (2005). *University, Inc.: The Corporate Corruption of American Higher Education*. New York, Basic Books.

Watts M (2010). Paraquat monograph. Penang, Pesticide Action Network Asia and the Pacific. Available at: http://www. panap.net/sites/default/files/monograph_paraquat.pdf.

Welsh R (1999). The economics of organic grain and soybean production in the midwestern United States. Policy Studies Report No. 13, Henry A. Wallace Institute for Alternative Agriculture, Greenbelt, MA.

Wen D (1993). Soil erosion and conservation in China. In: Pimentel D, ed. *Soil Erosion and Conservation*. New York, Cambridge University Press: 63–86.

Wen D (1997). Agriculture in China: Water and energy resources. In: Tso T, Tuan F and Faust M, eds. *Agriculture in China: 1949-2030*. Beltsville, MD, IDEALS: 479–497. Available at: http://conservancy.umn.edu/handle/58873.

West TD and Griffith DR (1992). Effect of strip-intercropping corn and soybean on yield and profit. *Journal of Production Agriculture*, 5: 107–110.

Wezel A and Soldat V (2009). A quantitative and qualitative historical analysis of the scientific discipline of agroecology. *International Journal of Agricultural Sustainability*, 7(1): 3–18.

Wezel A, Bellon S, Doré T, Francis C, Vallod D and David C (2009). Agroecology as a science, a movement and a practice: A review. *Agronomy for Sustainable Development*, 29: 503–515.

WHO (2000). *Nutrition for Health and Development: A Global Agenda for Combating Malnutrition*. Progress report. Geneva.

WHO (2002). *The World Health Report 2002: Reducing Risks, Promoting Healthy Life*. Geneva.

WHO (2006). *Fuel for Life: Household Energy and Health*. Geneva, World Health Organization.

WHO (2011). Indoor air pollution and health. Fact sheet N°292, September. Available at: www.who.int/mediacentre/ factsheets/fs292/en/.

Wilken GC (1987). *Good Farmers: Traditional Agricultural Resource Management in Mexico and Guatemala*. Berkeley, CA, University of California Press.

Willer H, Yussefi-Menzler M and Sorensen N, eds. (2008). *The World of Organic Agriculture: Statistics and Emerging Trends 2008*. Bonn, International Federation of Organic Agriculture Movements (IFOAM) e.V.

Winter TC, Harvey J., Franke OL and Alley WM (1998). Ground water and surface water: A single resource. *USGS Circular 1139*. United States Geological Survey.

Wise TA (2010). The true cost of cheap food: The globalisation of the food market has made food cheap, but who is benefiting? *Resurgence*, No. 259, March/April.

Witkowski TH (2007). Food marketing and obesity in developing countries: Analysis, ethics, and public policy. *Journal of Macromarketing*, 27: 126–137.

Witt B (1997). Using soil fauna to improve soil health. University of Minnesota digital Conservancy. Available at: http://conservancy.umn.edu/bitstream/58873/1/2.8.Witt.pdf.

Witter E, Mortensson AM, Garcia FV (1993). Size of the microbial mass in a long-term field experimment as effected by different N fertilizers. Soil Biology Biochemistry 28, 659-669.

WMO (2010). World Meteorological Organization press release No. 904 on the global climate in 2010. Cancun/Geneva, 2 December. Available at: www.wmo.int/pages/mediacentre/press_releases/pr_904_en.html.

WMO (2011). The state of greenhouse gases in the atmosphere based on global observations through 2010, *WMO Greenhouse Gas Bulletin*, No. 7, 21 November. Geneva, World Meteorological Organization. Available at: http://www.wmo.int/pages/prog/arep/gaw/ghg/documents/GHGbulletin_7_en.pdf.

World Agroforestry Centre (2009). Creating an evergreen agriculture in Africa for food security and environmental resilience. Nairobi.

World Bank (2006). Reposititioning nutrition as central to development: A strategy for large-scale action. Washington, DC.

World Bank (2008). World Development Report 2008: Agriculture for Development. Washington, DC. Available at: http://web.worldbank.org/WBSITE/EXTERNAL/EXTDEC/EXTRESEARCH/EXTWDRS/0,,contentMDK:23062293~pagePK:478093~piPK:477627~theSitePK:477624,00.html.

World Bank (2009). Economics of adaptation to climate change (EACC). Available at: http://beta.worldbank.org/content/economics-adaptation-climate-change-study-homepage.

WHO (2005). *The European Health Report 2005*. Available at: http://www.euro.who.int/__data/assets/pdf_file/0004/82435/E87325.pdf.

WRAP (2009). Household food and drink waste in the UK. Banbury, Waste and Resources Action Programme. Available at: www.wrap.org.uk/retail_supply_chain/research_tools/research/report_household.html.

WRI (undated). World GHG emissions flow chart, at: http://tinyurl.com/2fmebe.

WRI (World Resources Institute) (1997). *World Resources 1996-1997*. New York, Oxford University Press.

Wright DH (1990). Human impacts on energy flow through natural ecosystems, and replications for species endangerment. *Ambio*, 19: 189–194.

Wynen E (2001). The economics of organic cereal-livestock farming in Australia revisited. In: *Proceedings of the RIRDC Inaugural Conference on Organic Agriculture*, Sydney, 27–28 August.

Yates D (1996). WatBal: An integrated water balance model for climate impact assessment of river basin runoff. *International Journal of Water Resources Development,* 12(2): 121–139.

Yohe GW, Lasco RD, Ahmad QK, Arnell NW, Cohen SJ, Hope C, Janetos AC, Perez RT (2007). Perspectives on climate change and sustainability. Climate change 2007: Impacts, Adaptation and Vulnerability. Contribution of Working Group II to the Fourth Assessment Report of the Intergovernmental Panel on Climate Change. Cambridge University Press. Cambridge, United Kingdom, 811-841. Available at: www.ipcc.ch/pdf/assessment-report/ar4/wg2/ar4-wg2-chapter20.pdf.

Young A (1998). *Land Resources: Now and for the Future.* Cambridge, Cambridge

Younie D, Hamilton M and Nevison I (1990). Sensory attributes of organic and conventional beef. *Animal Production*, 50: 565–566.

Notes

1   Food security is generally defined as consisting of four pillars: (i) availability (i.e. the supply side of food security, resulting from production, stocks and trade); (ii) access (influenced by income, markets and prices); (iii) utilization (related to diets, food preparation and conservation practices); and (iv) stability (i.e. periodic shortfalls, fluctuation of supply). For more information, see *inter alia* FAO (2012a).

2   On the basis of current trends, carbon emissions will keep growing by about 3 per cent per annum and at this rate will reach the remaining emission limit of 565 gigatons to keep global warming below 2 degrees within no more than 16 years. www.rollingstone.com/politics/news/global-warmings-terrifying-new-math-20120719.

3   For more information, see ibid.

4   According to Fatih Birol, the IEA's chief economist, the current trends are perfectly in line with a temperature increase of about 6 degrees later this century. Ibid.

5   Global cereal production volume grew by 17 per cent and cereal yields increased by 6 per cent in the period 1990/1991 to 2005/2006 (author's calculation, based on FAOSTAT).

6   For more information, see Keane et al. (2009).

7   It is often overlooked that productivity of outdoor workers is bound to considerably decline because of global warming. In India, for instance, it is estimated that productivity of outdoor workers has already dropped by 10 per cent since the early 1980s and that another 2 degrees temperature increase might result in an additional reduction of 20 per cent (Rundgren, 2012).

8   For an overview of recent significant climate anomalies, see Tirado and Cotter (2010: 4–5).

9   The recent catastrophic floods in Pakistan and the massive forest and peat-soil fires in Russia are but two illustrative examples of the impact that can be expected. As the case of Pakistan demonstrates, both the country and the international community are poorly prepared to effectively cope with such extremes. Apart from the dire consequences for future agricultural production, there is also the risk of serious destabilization of society and the political system. Estimates of the flood-caused economic damage are as high as 20 per cent of Pakistan's GDP.

10 It is estimated that elevated atmospheric CO_2 concentration alone may increase crop yields by some 10–15 per cent. Crops that tend to benefit from the effect of carbon fertilization include rice, wheat, soybeans, fine grains, legumes, and most trees. Benefits for other crops, including maize, millet, sorghum and sugarcane are more limited. However, these estimates need to be considered with utmost care, as other changes such as distribution of precipitation, elevation of atmospheric O_3 concentration, enhanced demand for nitrogen, and increases in temperature can make the yield increases highly uncertain (Smith et al., 2007a: 25). See also the comment of Högy and Fangmeier in this Chapter.

11 The quality of food is determined by three elements: (i) calories (i.e. the energy content); (ii) proteins; and (iii) micro-nutrients.

12 Fruit and vegetables are very valuable for dealing with micronutrient deficiencies (the value of global trade in vegetables, for instance, exceeds that of cereals). Yet, there is insufficient knowledge and research on the effects of climate change on fruit and vegetable yields and quality (FAO, 2012a).

13 It is estimated that currently about 30-40 per cent of the potential global crop yield is destroyed by pathogens and pests (Oerke, 2006).

14 Resilience is the capacity to absorb or cope with shocks and stresses. Adaptive capacity is defined by overlapping resources and abilities that can be employed to respond to and create changes (Naerstad, 2011: part ii, p. 33).

15 What makes the situation in Africa, South Asia and Central America particularly precarious is the fact that the population of Africa is projected to double in the period 2010-2050; that of South Asia and Central America to increase by more or somewhat less than 40 per cent (UN/DESA, 2010).

16 Climate change is already clearly visible. According to the World Meteorological Organization, the decade from 2001 to 2010 had a global temperature that was 0.46°C above the 1961-1990 average; the highest value ever recorded for a 10-year period. Warming was especially strong in Africa, parts of Asia and the Arctic, Central Asia and Greenland/Arctic Canada (WMO, 2010). According to the global Climate Risk Index (CRI), developed by Germanwatch and Munich Re NatCatSERVICE, the 10 most climate-risk-exposed countries in the period 1990-2009 were: Bangladesh, Myanmar, Honduras, Nicaragua, Viet Nam, Haiti, Philippines, Dominican Republic, Mongolia, and Tajikistan (the CRI reflects both relative and absolute climate impact per country: for more info see www.germanwatch.org/klima/cri.htm).

17   It is estimated that already by 2025 continuing population growth and current agricultural practices will jack up the number of countries that suffer from an acute scarcity of either good cropland or fresh water from 21 at the moment to some 57, with a total population of 2 billion. Water scarcity may be one of the most powerful crop yield reducers in the coming decades. (Giovannucci et al., 2012: 22).

18   The economic significance of agriculture in developing countries is usually under-estimated when limiting it to agriculture's contribution to GDP, because large parts of agricultural production are informal and not part of the monetary economy.

19   It is also worth noting that, for the first time in history, there are as many overweight people as undernourished. The consequences of the emerging dietary habits are on a disastrous trajectory for human and ecosystem health. Therefore, one also needs to target the quality of nutrition rather than simply "more production" (Giovannucci et al., 2012: iv and vi).

20   According to FAO, Sub-Saharan Africa has the highest share of undernourished people, some 30 per cent in 2010, whereas the Asia Pacific region has the most undernourished people (about 578 million). Two-thirds of the world's undernourished live in just 7 countries: Bangladesh, China, the Democratic Republic of Congo, Ethiopia, India, Indonesia and Pakistan (cited in Giovannucci et al., 2012: 6).

21   As highlighted by De Schutter and Vanloqueren (2011:38), "large, mechanized, mono-cropping operations are more competitive than small farms ..., but competitiveness and productivity are different things. Big farms outperform small farms according to only one measure of economic efficiency: productivity per unit of labour". According to Tscharntke et al. (2012: 54), "it is well established that small and diversified farms rather than large monocultures show greater productivity per area; a phenomenon referred to as the 'paradox of the scale' or the 'inverse farm size-productivity relationship'."

22   See also IAASTD (2009a).

23   As emphasized by Naerstad (2011: part II, p. 37), "soil organic matter as humus can only be produced by the diversity of life that exists in soils - it cannot be human-made. When the soil organic matter recycling and fertility service is impaired, all life on earth is threatened, as all life is either directly or indirectly reliant on plants and their products, including the supply of food, energy, nutrients, construction materials and genetic resources".

24   Increasing soil organic matter by good management practices is generally synergistic because it captures atmospheric CO_2, increases soil fertility and improves the soil structure for more resilience and better adaptation to climate change (FAO, 2012a).

25   This section draws on findings of Murphy and Wise (2012).

26   One response was the (voluntary) Principles for Responsible Agricultural Investment (PRAI), developed by the secretariats (not the member countries) of the World Bank, FAO and UNCTAD, which have been widely criticized as far too weak (Murphy and Wise, 2011: 31). In May 2012, the FAO's Committee on World Food Security (CFS) endorsed The Voluntary Guidelines on the Responsible Governance of Tenure of Land, Fisheries and Forests in the Context of National Food Security, which outline principles and practices that governments can refer to when making laws and administering land, fisheries and forests rights. The guidelines are based on an inclusive consultation process started by FAO in 2009 and then finalized through CFS-led intergovernmental negotiations that included participation of government officials, civil society organizations, private sector representatives, international organizations and academics. The aim of the guidelines is to promote food security and sustainable development by improving secure access to land, fisheries and forests and protecting the rights of millions of often very poor people. While the guidelines acknowledge that responsible investments by the public and private sectors are essential for improving food security, they also recommend that safeguards be put in place to protect tenure rights of local people from risks that could arise from large-scale land acquisitions, and also to protect human rights, livelihoods, food security and the environment (for more information, see http://www.fao.org/news/story/en/item/142587/icode). As the guidelines were only adopted in mid-2012, it is as yet too early to judge whether they will have a real impact on effectively governing existing and new foreign land acquisitions.

27   For an elaborate discussion, see Naerstad (2011).

28   For a recent in-depth review, see: German National Academy of Sciences Leopoldina (2012).

29   For an elaborate discussion, see: FAO (2011a).

30   The IPCC (2007a) suggests 10–12 per cent, the OECD suggests 14 per cent (Legg and Huang, 2010), and the World Resources Institute (WRI, undated) suggests 14.9 per cent.

31   Figures used for the calculations were: (a) an average loss of 4.5--6 kg of SOM/m^2 of arable land and 2–3 kg of

SOM/m^2 of agricultural land under prairies and not cultivated; (b) an average soil depth of 30 cm, with an average soil density of 1 gr/cm^3; (c) 5,000 million ha of agricultural land worldwide and 1,800 million ha of arable land (FAOSTAT, 2002-2004); and (d) a ratio of 1.46 kg of CO_2 for each kg of destroyed SOM .

32   This conclusion is based on the assumption that organic matter would be incorporated at a global annual average rate of 3.5 to 5 tons per hectare of agricultural land. For more detailed calculations, see GRAIN, 2009, table 2.

33   Agroecological research combines modern science with local knowledge. In Central America, for instance, the coffee groves that grow under high canopy trees were improved by identifying the optimal shade conditions for minimizing the entire pest complex and maximizing the beneficial microflora and fauna, which improved yield and coffee quality. Such good practices are developed through a trial-and-error process by coffee-growers, but identifying conditions for success in order to promote their dissemination may benefit from the knowledge of experts (Staver et al., 2001).

34   The 79 per cent figure relates to the 360 reliable-yield comparisons from 198 projects, but the results were wide ranging, with 25 per cent of the projects reporting a 100 per cent increase or more.

35   However, it should be pointed out that not all these projects comply fully with the principles of agroecology.

36   Research on agroforestry in Zambia does not support "the popular notion that agroforestry practices are more labour intensive" (Ajayi et al., 2009: 279).

37   See: www.climatefundsupdate.org.

38   According to the IPCC, an atmospheric CO_2 concentration of 550 ppm will lead to a 3°C rise in global average temperatures.

39   C_3 is a metabolic pathway for carbon fixation in photosynthesis, converting CO_2 and ribulose bisphosphate (RuBP) into two 3-carbon molecules of 3-phosphoglycerate (3-PGA).

40   C_4 is a metabolic pathway for carbon fixation in photosynthesis, which fixes CO_2 to phosphoenol pyruvate (PEP) and converts it into the 4-carbon intermediate malate.

41   The whole paper can be downloaded at ftp://ftp.fao.org/docrep/fao/011/ak355e/ak355e00.pdf.

42   Statements by Feed the Future officials are revealing: they refer to the "discovery and delivery" of "breakthrough" technologies, frequently mentioning biotechnology rather than agroecological approaches. See statements by USDA Secretary Tom Vilsack at:http://www.america.gov/st/develop-english/2010/May/20100521164320 akllennoccm1.705134e-02.html; USAID Director Rajiv Shah at: http://www.usaid.gov/press/releases/2010/pr100616.html; and Monsanto Corporation at: http://www.america.gov/st/develop-english/2010/July/2010072 2113758cpataruk0.2630579.html&distid=ucs. See also Gates Foundation at: http://www.gatesfoundation.org/agriculturaldevelopment/Pages/why-we-fund-research-in-crop-biotechnology.aspx.

43   This USAID programme partners with biotechnology industry leaders such as Monsanto, Mayco and Bayer. For details, see: http://www.absp2.cornell.edu/.

44   A toe is a common unit of energy, which expresses the amount of energy released when a ton of oil is burnt (1 toe = 42 GJ = 11 MWh = 10 Gcal).

45   Water pumping consumes considerable energy.

46   Soybeans can be grown without nitrogen fertilizers as they have natural nitrogen fixation properties, which is the main reason for their lower energy demand.

47   While there were also other factors driving the increase in food prices, such as the diversion of some crops for the production of biofuels, increased meat consumption and speculation, the higher oil price was doubtless a major driver.

48   The introduction of energy-saving stoves or the use of other fuels that are easier to regulate should be a priority, not only for the conservation of forests and saving of energy, but also because the traditional stoves emit considerable indoor soot and smoke, which are a health hazard and one of the biggest killers. Between 1.5 million (WHO, 2006) and 4 million (Pimentel et al., 1998) people die from these emissions every year.

49   Assuming that the farmers can save their entire surplus, which is highly unlikely.

50   See: http://www.fao.org/worldfoodsituation/wfs-home/foodpricesindex/en/.

51   See: Off-grid systems, at: www.energy-solutions.co.uk/off-grid/.

52 See Lighting Africa, Catalyzing markets for modern lighting, at: www.lightingafrica.org/.

53 See: http://earthobservatory.nasa.gov/Features/Dust/.

54 This paper draws heavily from a 2010 article by the authors entitled, Competition for Water for the Food System, published in *Philosophical Transactions of the Royal Society: Biological Sciences*, 365(1554): 2765-3097.

55 A thorough discussion of these and other solutions is provided in several comprehensive reports (e.g. IWMI, 2007).

56 The relationship between population, water and food production has been explored in depth by a number of authors (see, for example, Gleick, 1996; Pimentel et al., 1997; Postel, 1998; Vörösmarty et al., 2000; Tilman et al., 2001; and IWMI, 2007).

57 Note that this paper does not consider threats to agricultural withdrawals from groundwater resources that are not directly linked to surface water systems, as these resources are unlikely to serve as a viable substitute for surface water in future years. In many regions of the world, groundwater reserves have declined to the point where well yields have fallen dramatically, land has subsided, and aquifer salinization has occurred (Konikow and Kendy, 2005). As the global demand for groundwater continues to increase, groundwater tables and well yields will decline more rapidly, reducing surface water runoff and forcing those that rely on groundwater resources to seek new sources. Both will have negative effects on the availability of water for agriculture.

58 In this paper, our focal "geopolitical regions" are Europe, Africa, North America, Asia, Latin America and the Caribbean, and Oceania. Within Europe, we also focus on the European Union, north-western Europe, the United Kingdom, and the former Soviet Union. Sub-Saharan Africa and the Nile River basin are reported for Africa, and in Asia, we report findings for China and India. Finally, we identify impacts on Brazil.

59 Following Winter et al. (1998), we assume that regional groundwater withdrawals deplete river basin runoff and therefore implicitly consider subsurface water in our modelling exercise. It must be noted that this analysis may underestimate threats to agriculture, for two reasons: (i) we make these comparisons relative to current agricultural demands rather than the expected higher demands of 2050; and (ii) we do not consider the effects of drought or increased extreme events. On the other hand, the analysis may overestimate threats because we model withdrawals rather than consumptive use and thus do not account for reuse of return flows.

60 Measurements were taken in 10 plots of passion fruit in mixed cropping systems in each of two different areas of the Central and Western Provinces of Kenya.

61 For further information, see: www.4c-coffeeassociation.org/our-services/work-on-climate-change.html.

62 See: www.growingforthefuture.com/content/Cool+Farm+Tool.

63 For a more detailed discussion of the development of food supply chains in low-income countries and emerging economies, see Parfitt, Barthel and Macnaughton, 2010.

64 See: www.wfp.org/purchase-progress.

65 In some EU countries (e.g. Germany), absolute expenditure on food has remained constant since the 1960s.

66 See, for example: www.neweconomics.org/publications/inconvenient-sandwich.

67 Further information about the Platform's views in English, see: www.die-bessere-agrarpolitik.de/English-documents.1024.0.html.

68 See also: www.efsa.europa.eu/en/topics/topic/amr.htm?wtrl=01.

69 The SANCO study cited Anderson (2008).

70 See also, Stockholm Resilience Centre, Stockholm University, Tipping towards the unknown, at: www.stockholmresilience.org/planetary-boundaries.

71 Regulation (EC) No 178/2002, laying down the general principles and requirements of food law, establishing the European Food Safety Authority and laying down procedures in matters of food safety, http://ec.europa.eu/dgs/health_consumer/library/pub/pub06_en.pdf.

72 Article 7 of Regulation EC 178/2002 "formally establishes the precautionary Principle as an option open to risk managers when decisions have to be made to protect health but scientific information concerning the risk is inconclusive or incomplete in some way.". See: http://ec.europa.eu/food/food/foodlaw/precautionary/index_en.htm, http://eur-lex.europa.eu/LexUriServ/LexUriServ.do?uri=COM:2000:0001:FIN:EN:PDF.

73 For more details, see: Guenther and Will, 2007.

Chapter 2

Livestock Production: A Climate Change and Food Security Hot Spot

Lead Article: LIVESTOCK PRODUCTION AND FOOD SECURITY IN A CONTEXT OF CLIMATE CHANGE, AND ENVIRONMENTAL AND HEALTH CHALLENGES

Anita Idel, Federation of German Scientists and Tobias Reichert, Germanwatch

Abstract

To optimize the interrelationship between the global climate and cattle and maximize the latter's contribution to global food security, the following steps need to be taken:

- More research on grassland management aimed at optimizing its capacity to serve as a carbon sink.

- More support for grazing.

- Land-use change should be brought under strict control, including that related to imported animal feed.

- Livestock production should have a stronger link to the regional feed base.

Prevailing trends towards further industrialization of agriculture, along with landless, large-scale livestock production, are likely to contribute to an increase in greenhouse gas (GHG) emissions by more than a third till 2030. According to the 4th IPCC Assessment Report, "Without additional policies, agricultural N_2O [nitrous oxide] and CH_4 [methane] emissions are projected to increase by 35-60% and 60%, respectively, to 2030, thus increasing more rapidly than the 14% increase of non-CO_2 GHG observed from 1990 to 2005" (IPCC, 2007: 63).

There is a tendency to ignore the need to reduce meat consumption as well as to implement a legal framework for sustainable production methods to address their medium and long-term effects on climate, environment and animal welfare.[1] Industrial livestock production should be curbed so that the total stock of raised animals such as cattle, pigs, chickens and sheep is reduced and the consumption of animal feed should be commensurate with sustainable local production potential. Reduced consumption of animal products is a particular challenge for those countries where animal protein consumption is high – representing a false model of imaginary prosperity. The fact that an increasing number of people are becoming vegans may help (in terms of the reduced demand for animal protein and energy-rich food),

but "to conclude that a vegan agricultural and food system would be the preferable solution, is far too simplistic" (Garnet, 2010; Fairlie, 2010, D'Silva and Webster, 2010).

Over the past few decades, feeding systems have turned more and more from being local/regional to global; the basic source of fodder is less and less the farm itself. The resulting problem of expansion and intensification of livestock production is associated with the shift from a feed system based on grass and plant remains to one based mainly on crops, even for ruminants. However, the major issue is not whether livestock is the world's largest user of land, but rather how the land and livestock are managed. While sustainable and animal-friendly systems are characterized by areas/space for outdoor keeping and grazing, industrial animal rearing is characterized as landless. Thus the data indicating livestock as the world's largest user of land are average values that also include a relevant part of sustainably used grasslands.

The intensification of livestock systems, and especially feeding systems, has gone hand in hand with more specialization and rationalization, thereby creating livestock systems that are increasingly dependent on energy input and foreign fodder sources. The growing demand for such feed has led to a huge demand for land, which is a crucial factor - leading to land-grabbing and land conversion, including the deforestation of rainforests. Only little by little is a wider public realizing in the context of land-grabbing that there is a huge demand for land in the South resulting mainly from demand for animal feed in the North. In a recent study, von Witzke and Noleppa (2011) estimate that in order to produce those agricultural products that were imported by the European Union (EU) in 2007-2008, 53 million hectares (ha) of arable land were used in other parts of the world. The EU, on the other hand, used only 18 million ha for products it exported during that period. As a result, the EU imports "virtual land" in the order of 35 million ha. This represents a third of the 105 million ha used in the EU as arable land. The single biggest factor that contributes to this imbalance is the import of soy, which uses 18 million ha outside the EU, mainly in Latin America (see below). This spatial separation of industrial livestock systems from feed crop production is clearly linked with less rigid environmental regulations (Naylor et al., 2005).

Greater standardization and specialization in industrial agriculture is closely related to the de-linking of crop and livestock production. This separation causes higher energy and fertilizer consumption, which while increasing the scale of production and yields, both of crops and livestock, gives rise to enormous risks such as pest infestation and diseases. The prevailing system of industrial livestock production with its specific breeding, feeding and general husbandry practices leads to ever larger numbers of animals being subjected to enormous and irresponsible performance and rearing stress.

Irrespective of the animal protection aspect, the concept of "biosecurity" in livestock production can be considered a failure. This is because the attempt to treat low immunity and the increasing threat of infection by an ever increasing use of drugs and disinfectants gives rise to resistance problems, the inevitable selection of dangerous microbes and alarming levels of residues in water, soil, food and animal feed.[2]

A sustainable approach requires a drastic reduction of industrial animal feed production and a concomitant decline in the production of animal products. Instead of replacing the production of human food by animal feed, animal and crop production should be reintegrated in order to:
• Use the nutrients contained in grass and harvesting

residues as animal feed that cannot be directly used for human consumption; and
• Use manure as fertilizer on grasslands and croplands.

This requires a move from the existing one-sided orientation and selection aimed at maximum performance of both crops and livestock, towards a more holistic view that promotes interactions and the productivity of the system as a whole. Furthermore, it is imperative to reduce the environmental, health and climate-related impacts from the massive use of synthetic nitrogen fertilizers, and promote the use of animal excrement as natural fertilizer. Discarding the latter and defining it as waste constitutes a huge loss of nutrients and minerals (similar to post-harvest losses of food).[3]

The sustainable production of food of animal origin requires the development of cooperation on a regional level, as well as cooperation between small and medium-sized farms and pastoralists. There is a significant untapped potential for sustainable grassland and ruminant management, including their use by pastoralists. The importance of working animals has also been underestimated. Yet they are particularly useful in the context of peak oil, which leads to higher costs of mechanization. However, their effective utilization needs to be optimized at the local level, in particular as regards feed selection, right of passage[4] and the functionality of mostly inadequate equipment.

A. Effects of inexpensive energy and nitrogen fertilizers

The availability of cheap fossil fuel has driven the expansion of animal food production (i.e. the mast of cattle, pigs and chickens as well as the production of milk and eggs) (see the comments of Rundgren in chapter 1 and Heinberg in chapter 5 of this Review). This concerns the production, processing and transportation of animal products as well as plant and equipment. The ecological, climatic and socio-economic problems resulting from intensive animal husbandry and the related animal welfare violations analysed in this article are largely the result of the ample availability of inexpensive energy.[5]

Energy for the production of cheap synthetic nitrogen fertilizer is the main contributing factor in the expansion and intensification of animal production. Higher nitrogen fertilizer use becomes the leading driver of the increases in agricultural production in general. Its use has increased eightfold in the past 40 years (figure 1), while global cereal production has scarcely doubled. The still increasing amount of synthetic N fertilizer use is not only out of scale but is compensable by organic methods as animal fertilizer and compost as well as legumes in crop rotation. The increase in synthetic N fertilizer use, through its direct and indirect effects, is responsible for the biggest contribution of agriculture to climate change. In the production of synthetic nitrogen fertilizer (through the Haber-Bosch process)[6] some 5 tons of carbon dioxide (CO_2) are released per ton of ammonia, (Hellebrand and Scholz, 2005) and 2–5 per cent of the nitrogen fertilizer applied to the soil is released as nitrous oxide (N_2O), which has a global warming potential 296 times higher than that of CO_2. Some ammonia (NH_3) is also released (Sutton et al., 2011, see below).[7]

Over the past few years, livestock systems, have been identified as the main contributor to agricultural GHG emissions. One critical aspect is the increase in the total number of livestock. However, the extent of GHGs emitted depends on the given agricultural system. The system boundaries are key determinants of the resulting data concerning the GHG balance. Therefore, transparency regarding these system boundaries is a necessary condition for comparing the results of different studies. Since these boundaries are often either not clearly defined or set inadequately,

most of the available studies are of limited analytical value and are hardly comparable.

As monocultures for animal feed cover almost 40 per cent of the global cropland, and animal feed absorbs virtually half of global cereal production, livestock is the main driver of climate change from agriculture.[8] In other words, the sustainability or intensity of feeding systems is key to the GHG balance of given agricultural systems (Schulze et al., 2009). Schulze et al. believe that the damage caused by N_2O as calculated by the Intergovernmental Panel on Climate Change (IPCC) is an underestimation, and suggest doubling the damage factor at the very least.

The high energy and fertilizer inputs in intensive livestock production have the following impacts, apart from the direct and indirect impacts on climate:

• The economies of scale associated with the non-internalization of ecological, social, health and climate costs allow cheap mass production of animal feed based on monocropping without crop rotation.

• The worldwide availability of inexpensive concentrate feed allows the rampant expansion of the number of animals, independent from the locally available animal feed supply.

• Synthetic fertilizers and pesticides substitute for crop rotation, including the green fertilizers and legumes required for nitrogen enrichment of the

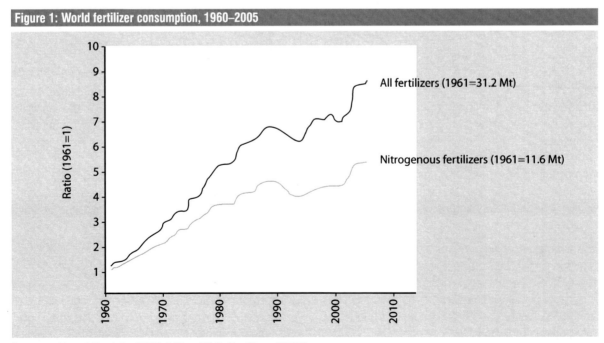

Figure 1: World fertilizer consumption, 1960–2005

All fertilizers (1961=31.2 Mt)

Nitrogenous fertilizers (1961=11.6 Mt)

Source: Royal Society, 2009 (citing FAO, Fertilizer, 2009).

soil. As a result, the farm's internal supply of animal feed is drastically reduced.

With mounting numbers of livestock, the volume of animal excrements (faeces and urine) drastically soars. Most of the proteins fed to livestock in the EU originate from countries in South America, but the excrements are produced in European countries. At the same time, however, excrements lose their importance as natural fertilizers because of the high use of mineral fertilizers on the fields. For decades, research has

been focusing on how to use synthetic nitrogen fertilizers more efficiently. Due to the contamination of the excrements with animal-administered drugs and disinfectants, they pose a huge disposal problem. As excrements are used less and less as natural fertilizers, related skills diminish and research on this subject is no longer done. A common way of getting rid of slurry is to dump it on pasture lands – often as a kind of waste disposal – which greatly reduces pasture quality.[9]

Box 1: Key findings of the European Nitrogen Assessment

The European Nitrogen Assessment (ENA), implemented in the 6th EU Research Framework Programme, focuses on the implications of the mounting use of nitrogen fertilizers in agriculture (Sutton et al., 2011). The authors of the Assessment reviewed the direct connection between inexpensive energy and the production of synthetic nitrogen fertilizer. The Assessment recommends more research on the interplay between the carbon and nitrogen cycles and their impact on soil fertility, climate and the ecosystem.

In the technical summary of the Assessment, Sutton and Billen (2011:XXXV), emphasize that "the deliberate production and release of N(r) [reactive nitrogen] in the Haber-Bosch process can be considered as perhaps the greatest single experiment in global geo-engineering that humans have ever made. (…) What was not anticipated was that this experiment would lead to a 'nitrogen inheritance' of unintended consequences with N(r) leaking into the environment in multiple forms, causing an even larger number of environmental effects."

The Assessment focuses on "five key societal threats" from excess nitrogen use, in terms of its impact on water quality, air quality, greenhouse balance, ecosystems and biodiversity. The authors state that "the understanding of N cycling has undergone a paradigm shift since 1990. Until then, the perception was that: (1) N(r) mineralization is the limiting step in N cycling; (2) plants only take up inorganic N(r); and (3) plants compete poorly for N(r) against microbes and use only the N(r) which is 'left over' by microbes. Since then studies have shown that plants compete effectively for N(r) with micro-organisms and take up organic N in a broad range of ecosystems" (Sutton and Billen, 2011: XXXVII). The authors also point out that till 1990 the impression that plants only take up inorganic N(r) demonstrates how industrialization of agriculture has influenced research and extension services in a one-sided way, and has eroded the importance of related local farming knowledge.

The authors highlight how little that "paradigm shift" has been taken into account in advisory and counselling services. They note, "In cereal farming, the use of only mineral N(r) fertilizers, instead of animal manures or composts, as well as the simplification of the crop rotation scheme that this had made possible, has in some cases resulted in a decline of soil organic matter. In the long-term this practice of using only mineral fertilizer has decreased the buffer capacity of the soil towards inorganic N inputs, thus increasing its propensity to N leaching." They add that "nitrogen-enriched terrestial ecosystems lose significant amounts of N via nitrate leaching and gaseous emissions (N_2, N_2O, NO, NH_3) to the environment. Estimates of denitrification to N_2 remain highly uncertain, due to difficulties in measurement and a high degree of temporal and spatial variability. There remain substantial uncertainties in the average fraction of N(r) applied to fields that is emitted as N_2O, ranging from 1% to 3,5-4,5% of fertilizer N applied, using bottom-up and top-down estimates, respectively." And regarding ammoniac, the authors conclude: "Further research is needed to better understand the relative contribution of direct and indirect N_2O emissions." (Sutton and Billen, 2011:XXXVIII).

How ineffective enforcement and implementation of existing nitrogen and related EU directives[a] have been becomes apparent in the authors' summary: "Europe (EU-27) is a hot spot in this sense, producing 10% of global anthropogenic N(r) even though its surface covers less than 3% of the total world continental area." (Sutton and Billen, 2011: XXXV). The authors also criticize the low procurement costs: "(…) the low price of N(r) fertiliser, combined with its clear benefits to agricultural production, does not provide a strong incentive for farmers to use less than the (private) economic optimum" (Sutton and Billen, 2011: XXXVI).

Source: (Sutton et al., 2011).

Note: [a] For instance, Nitrates Directive, Water Framework Directive, Groundwater Directive, Ambient Air Quality Directive, National Emissions Ceilings Directive, Urban Waste Water Treatment Directive, Marine Strategy Framework Directive, Integrated Pollution and Control (IPPC) and Habitats Directive.

Through economies of scale, farms where livestock production is still based on farm-generated feed come under increasing economic pressure. Industrial mega-farms or farms that are much larger than the regional average drive this trend (see also the commentary of Ostendorff in this chapter).

B. Sustainability requires a new definition of the terms productivity and growth

The conventional approach to agricultural growth aims at increasing crop yields per hectare, taking into account the costs of procured inputs such as energy, fertilizer, pesticides and labour. This calculation fails to consider not only the externalized costs (damage to soil, water bodies and air pollution through residues and contamination, as well as the social implications), but also the decline in soil fertility through soil erosion, compaction and nitrification – a development that has not yet been fully appreciated because of the ample availability of cheap synthetic fertilizers (Troeh, Hobbs and Donahue, 1991). For example, farmers in the United States apply fertilizers worth about $20 billion annually to offset the effects of soil nutrient loss due to soil erosion (Troeh et al., 1991).

There is a deplorable problem of perception, because efforts to strengthen intensive agricultural production and increase yields through enhanced use of synthetic fertilizers give the wrong impression that the production of animal feed is not in competition with food production. The negative impacts of the enhanced use of synthetic nitrogen fertilizers are

not taken into account, and related costs remain externalized. According to the European Nitrogen Assessment (Sutton et al., 2011), the total costs of nitrogen pollution of water, the atmosphere, and other impacts on ecosystems and climate change are estimated to be between €70 billion and €320 billion per annum (i.e. €150–€736 per person per year), which is more than twice the monetary benefits derived from nitrogen in agriculture.

Between 1961 and 2009 the number of animals reared for meat and dairy production increased rapidly. According to the FAO (FAOSTAT, 2011), in 2009 a total amount of 1.38 billion heads of cattle and buffalo were reared globally – the number doubled during the last 50 years. During the same period, the number of pigs more than doubled, from 406 million to 941 million. The number of chickens grew the most dramatically: almost fivefold, from 3.8 billion to 18.6 billion. Since not only the number of animals increased, but also the average weight per animal, meat production rose at an even faster rate: beef production more than doubled, to 62.8 billion tons in 2009, pork production quadrupled, to 106.3 billion tons, and chicken meat production increased tenfold, to 80.3 billion tons. This rapid expansion of global meat production was only possible because the feed supply for the animals increased at a similarly dramatic rate. The EU is a prime example in this respect. Its imports of soybean cake – a crucial source of protein in intensive and industrial animal production – rose tenfold between 1961 and 2009, and now stands at almost 44 billion tons per year (figure 2). The focus on cake is because

Figure 2: EU imports of soybean cake and soybeans 1961–1965 to 2006–2008 (millions of tons)

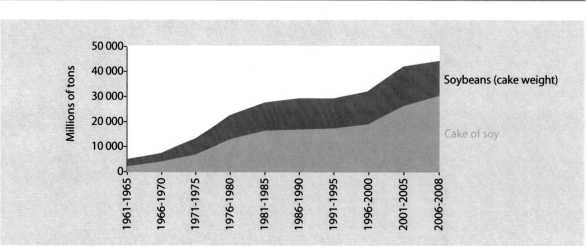

Source: Authors' calculations based on FAOSTAT, 2010.

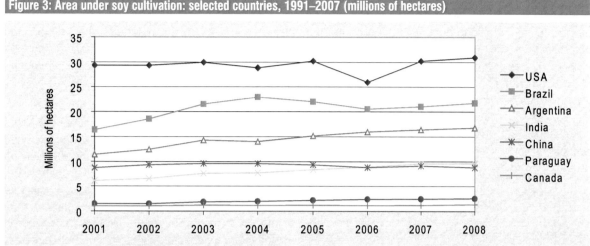

Figure 3: Area under soy cultivation: selected countries, 1991–2007 (millions of hectares)

Source: Authors' calculations based on FAOSTAT.

only this is used as animal feed, while soybean oil is used for human consumption, industrial and energy use.

C. The role of agricultural and trade policy in the industrialization of animal production

An important driver of this development has been the EU's Common Agricultural Policy (CAP) and its link to trade policy. Until the early 1990s, the EU guaranteed prices for livestock products – especially beef and dairy products – that were significantly higher than world market prices. This provided an effective incentive for European farmers to increase production. At the same time, the CAP intervened in the markets for feedstock. While high prices for cereals in the EU were also guaranteed, there was no support for oilseeds and their products – oils and cakes. This situation is also reflected in the EU's agricultural trade policy: while livestock products and cereals were, and generally still are, protected by high tariffs, oilseeds and their products have experienced no, or only very low, tariffs. These tariffs were fixed multilaterally in the General Agreement on Tariffs and Trade (GATT), the predecessor of the World Trade Organization (WTO).

In the 1980s, the EU attempted, relatively successfully, to support oilseed production with other policy instruments, such as production premiums. However, these were found to run counter to its GATT commitments. With the shift from price support to

payments based on the area planted with certain crops, some support for oilseed production could be provided. However, the Blair House Agreement, a bilateral agreement between the European Community and the United States, which paved the way for the WTO Agreement on Agriculture, placed a limit on the area planted with oilseeds in the EU that could benefit from payments. As a result, the EU's imports of soybeans and soybean cake, which had remained at roughly a constant level in the 1980s, started to increase in the 1990s. The BSE crisis in 2000–2001 gave an additional boost to EU soy imports. In these years alone, the EU's soy imports jumped from 33.7 million tons to 40.2 million tons (FAOSTAT and authors'calculations).

The EU's rising import demand was mainly met by South America, especially Argentina and Brazil, where the area planted with soy rose from just over 10 million ha (in both countries combined) in 1980 to over 48 million ha in 2009 (figure 3). This triggered the massive deforestation of the tropical rainforests in Brazil and the conversion of grasslands (*cerrado* in Brazil and *pampas* in Argentina) to cropland.

It is estimated that the land-use changes directly related to the expanded soy production in Argentina, Brazil and Paraguay were responsible for, on average, over 420 million tons of CO_2-equivalent (CO_2e) emissions annually between 2000 and 2009 (Reichert and Reichardt, 2011). This amounts to about 18 per cent of the total GHG emissions of these countries.[10]

The rapid expansion of feed, in particular, enabled the EU not only to meet its rising demand for meat and dairy products, but also to become a net exporter of beef, dairy products and pork. Since the guaranteed domestic prices were usually significantly higher than world market prices, exports were only possible through "refunds" for exporters, which covered the difference between the internal and external prices. These "export subsidies" turned out to be a major issue of conflict in international trade. The significant European exports of animal products (as well as wheat and sugar) gave the wrong impression that the EU was producing overall agricultural surpluses. The fact that this was only possible because of the ever-increasing imports of animal feed was largely neglected in the public debate.

Consequently, the reforms of the CAP in the early 1990s focused on cutting down surplus production by reducing guaranteed prices for cereals and beef, and (initially) to a much lesser extent, for milk. The income losses were partly compensated by specific area payments to farmers. One condition for receiving those payments was that a certain proportion of arable land would have to be kept idle – the most direct instrument for addressing the "overproduction" problem. The amount of land to be "set aside" was fixed by the EU on an annual basis, depending on market conditions. On average, it was around 10 per cent of the cropland. As a result, exports of cereals and beef fell significantly, and while the EU remains a net exporter of wheat, it is now a net importer of beef and sugar. At the same time, net exports of pork more than doubled, from around 400,000 tons annually in the late 1980s to around one million tons annually in recent years. The figure for 2008 was as high as 1.4 million tons (FAOSTAT). The expansion of pork production and exports was less directly linked to agricultural policy instruments, and more a result of the increasing industrialization of animal production discussed earlier.

Since the animals are separated from their natural environment, and feed can be sourced globally, the suitability of a certain area for animal and feed production is less important than the infrastructure for transporting and processing feed and animals. The animal breeds and the barns for industrial animal production have also become globally standardized. As a result, northern France, northern Germany, Denmark and the Netherlands, with their proximity to Rotterdam as the largest port for receiving imports of soybeans and soybean cake, along with a well-developed infrastructure and a mature food industry, have become the main pork (and chicken) producing regions in the EU. This has been partly supported by CAP-related investment assistance through subsidized interest rates.

In sum, the intensity of livestock production is decisively determined by the intensity of animal feed, which in turn is correlated with the enhanced use of energy and synthetic fertilizers for the production of that feed. This is why a comparative analysis of the ecological and climate balance of livestock production requires data on where and how the animal feed was produced. In this regard, the land-use changes required for intensive and monoculture-based feed production are a particular source of concern with regard to their social, ecological and climate impacts.

The dependence on foreign fodder sources is only one outcome of the fundamental change in agricultural livestock systems. Another main driver of industrial agriculture is that food retailers are demanding increasingly standardized products in terms of quantities, sizes and fattening periods. Since the 1960s, standardization by and for industrialized meat and dairy production systems has resulted in the replacement of wild and cultured, biodiversity-rich land by monotonous landscapes. As a result, wild biodiversity suffers, as reflected in the decrease in wild bees (in many areas sufficient pollinators are lacking), butterflies and hedges, for example. The loss of breeds and the low, regular utilization of the remaining ones lead to the loss of traditional knowledge.

The many years of State support for performance testing and estimation of breeding values, aimed uniquely at achieving more (financial) yield per unit, ran contrary to the goals relating to "genetic diversity" as embodied in the Convention on Biological Diversity (CBD) (IOeW et al., 2004). The CBD is based upon three pillars that represent the aims of international policy in future development: (i) conservation of biological diversity, (ii) fair and equitable access and benefit sharing of biological diversity, and (iii) the sustainable use of animal and plant genetic resources and their habitats. As wildlife and wild plants need their specific environments/habitats, plants and livestock breeds need a "cultured habitat" of which they are a part, and thus influence and are influenced by that habitat. If the genetic resources of animals and plants are not used, they disappear as part of the whole system and can no longer play their part in their system. Agro-biodiversity should be used in a way that develops it further, rather than being "underutilized" as at present, and therefore risking disappearance.

D. Risks associated with selective breeding for higher productivity

Although selection is aimed at high performance in both animal and crop breeding, there is a major distinction between the two. A certain and increasing proportion of crops, such as vegetables, are grown in greenhouses or under plastic foil for commercial purposes. However, the vast majority of crops are still planted in the open and are exposed to the vagaries of the weather (unlike animals). Since the 1950s, animal production, by increasingly relying on animal feed (and their imports), synthetic growth hormones, vitamins, amino acids and mineral supplements, has become less dependent on location (Idel and Petschow, 2004). A growing number of chickens, pigs and, increasingly, cattle are raised in a way that completely shields them from the effects of the sun and the weather.[11]

Breeding increasingly overburdens animals that have been selected to maximize their production. For example, hens that are bred to maximize egg production generate about 300 eggs per annum; chickens selected for meat production reach their slaughter weight after less than five weeks of intensive raising; young pigs, less than six months old, are slaughtered when they reach about 100 kg; and some cows are bred to maximize milk production, delivering over 10,000 litres during one lactation period alone (most of them do not get older than five years, because of these excessive performance requirements). Many of these animals suffer from "occupational" diseases, such as inflammation of the fallopian tubes in hens, udder inflammation of cows, or problems with joints in pigs, hens and cattle caused by excessively rapid weight gain (see also the commentary on animal welfare issues of D'Silva in this chapter).

The tenet that "performance is an expression of good health" is no longer valid. Indeed, forcing their enhanced performance causes animal stress and "burnout" (in poultry, pigs and cattle for mast) resulting in a short life span (dairy) and requiring the frequent administering of drugs such as antibiotics and analgesics. In addition, hormones are being widely used to overcome fertility problems of cows that are

bred for maximizing milk production. Generally, high external input systems aim at minimizing the energy losses of animal bodies caused by physical movement and adaptation to changes in temperature and feed. This ostensibly reduces the energy consumption of body functions and maximizes the production of animal products. These consistently restrictive conditions are a major factor that contributes to the breeding of uniform animals and their selection for high performance.

As a result, the flexible adaptive capacity of animals to changing and divergent production conditions has been replaced by inflexible, static and location-specific behaviour. An extreme example is the use of standardized cages for hybrid hens, whether in California, Hong Kong, Norway or Oman. The light and temperature in the sheds where the cages are kept, along with the concentrated feed and limited physical movement, are all designed to ensure maximum and standardized egg production. Generally, the adaptation is achieved at the cost of adaptive capacity: the animals have few reserves to respond to changing environmental conditions such as variations in temperature, feed or stress from transport. Despite this being common knowledge, this stress from breeding is dealt with not by changes in breeding practices, including breeding goals, but only by changing the raising methods: chickens' beaks and pigs' tails are trimmed and the animals are often held in stress-reducing dimmed light in order to reduce the extent and consequences of cannibalism among the animals that results from enhanced stress (Compassion in World Farming, 2009a). In addition, antibiotics are increasingly used to treat the greater incidence of illness among animals resulting from high-performance breeding.

The development of a solid immune system in animals, which is so important for open-air rearing of animals, receives little attention under such conditions. Besides the greater susceptibility to illness in animals, the targeted selection for maximum performance raises other animal protection and welfare issues. As the performance of female animals directly correlates with the targeted selection in breeding, fattening performance declines and with it the performance of male animals. For example, the fattening of brothers of egg-producing hens is considered uneconomical. As a result, in the EU more than 300 million male chickens are killed each year as soon as they hatch. Similarly, in the United Kingdom, for instance, male calves of breeds that are selected for maximizing milk performance are killed – some 150,000 each year (Weeks, 2007).

Ignoring the animal health and welfare issues associated with this development, genetic engineering has been used for decades to maximize animal performance. And in spite of extensive public and private research on genetic manipulation over the past 30 years, until today no transgenic animals are used for commercial agriculture purposes owing to significant biological and technical problems (Then 2011, and 2012). As early as the mid-1980s, some researchers envisaged the technology-linked failure of transgenic manipulation. This failure became the engine for cloning research. The objective was to clone transgenic individuals in those exceptional cases where they had desirable properties and no or few unintended problems. Yet cloning too has been relatively unsuccessful in the past 25 years, with the rare successes due mainly to coincidence.

Only a few viable animals have been produced using the "Dolly method".[12] According to the European Food Safety Authority (EFSA, 2007: 9), "(T)he overall success rate of the cloning procedure is still low and differs greatly between species. The overall success rate, expressed as the percentage of viable offspring born from transferred embryo clones, ranges approximately from 0.5 to 5 %, depending on the species." Of the surviving cloned animals, "Dolly" remained a unique specimen. The hope that whole stables could be filled with animals cloned from one individual in order to achieve an identical fattening result with a standard and economical feeding and treatment regime – a hope of unlimited mass industrial production – has remained a distant dream. In any case, sameness in terms of desirable fattening and other performances would lead to greater vulnerability to sickness and contagion.

Already, the current practice of the use of only a few commercial animal races and hybrids for industrial livestock production is leading to a loss of genetic diversity, and carries the risk that animals are more vulnerable to infectious diseases and pests. This interrelationship has been analysed at length by an international team of researchers (Muir, Gane and Zhang, 2008). With regard to chickens, for example, the findings confirm that almost all animals raised for poultry meat (some 19 billion worldwide) are based on only three races, and hens raised for maximum egg production stem from only one race.

E. The push for biosecurity poses a threat to animal and consumer protection

Over the past few decades, the immune system has increasingly been perceived as a mere protection system, primarily against bacteria, rather than as an interface between the worlds of micro- and macroorganisms. As a result, two facts have been overlooked: bacteria are an indispensable component of our immune system; and bacteria have existed much longer on our planet than humans, so that our development over millions of years has been more with rather than against bacteria.[13]

Since the immune system links us to our environment, reacting to each pathogenic problem by enhancing sterility (by attempting to eradicate all microorganisms) poses a risk to our future development. Thus the belief that this strategy enhances security – also called biosecurity – is a fallacy. It *may* work in some individual cases, but it increases the inherent risks and may compound future problems. In particular, the regular and extensive use of antibiotics and disinfectants for human and animal health unavoidably leads to the emergence of pathogens with higher resistance and infection potential.

By way of illustration, the bacterium *Pseudomonas aeruginosa*, which is resistant to many antibiotics, can survive disinfectants and even thrives on hygiene products. Such extremes have been known for decades as "hospital germs", because they have mushroomed in hospitals. The principle is the same: the unintentional selection of more and more dangerous germs. The more resistant a germ already is to treatment with antibiotics, the greater the likelihood that it will survive the next wave of treatment with antibiotics and disinfectants.

Against this background, "biosecurity", through repeated use of new antibiotics and disinfectants, is not only no solution, but in the long term it is also highly risky. Humans and animals need the contact with microorganisms for strengthening their immune system, in particular at the juvenile stage. Thus ostensible "biosecurity" in intensive livestock production is a problem in that it hampers the development of a healthy immune system and it strengthens the resistance of germs and pathogens, making it increasingly difficult for the chemical and pharmaceutical industry to contain those germs and pathogens. The evolutionary dynamics of germs allows them to (quickly) adjust to new antibiotics or

- The destruction, waste and contamination of resources associated with the industrialization of agriculture have created a misconception that agriculture always and generally poses a problem. Thus it proves to be extremely difficult to perceive the potential for sustainable agricultural development in grassland, livestock and cropland management.

- For decades, more and more intensified agricultural practices have damaged the environment. Thus, one of the main objectives of nature protection has been seen as taking land away from any kind of agricultural production. This has indirectly and unwittingly led to more "collateral damage" by creating greater pressure for further intensifying production on the remaining agricultural land. It has been based on the perception that the more intensively existing land is used, the greater will be the available area for nature conservation. It overlooks the fact that it is industrial agriculture that has exerted pressure on resources and land use, and led to widespread contamination of land in general.

- The availability of ample, relatively inexpensive energy and synthetic fertilizers has distracted attention from the importance of soil fertility, as the most basic and precious resource of agriculture, and its loss through erosion. Related to that, the potential of sustainable grassland management and pastoralism for global food security, soil and climate protection has been, and still is, underestimated, and therefore the long-term dangers of converting permanent grassland to other uses are overlooked.

- The inherent growth and productivity pressure of industrial agriculture has devastating impacts on our environment and well-being, and thus violates the third pillar of the CBD (i.e. the sustainable use of animal and plant genetic resources and their habitats).

- Any attempt at maximizing single crop yields is irreconcilable with the optimization of ecological services. Yet public and private support to seeds, cultivation, plant protection and fertilization focus entirely on such a yield maximizing strategy. Conversely, the means for exploring and studying the ecosystemic potential of agriculture and specific production systems or methods in different landscapes have been woefully inadequate.

- The economic interests of different economic actors that derive significant profits from the industrialization of agriculture, including the use of chemical inputs, are one of the main reasons for the lack of implementation of the key recommendations of the International Assessment of Agricultural Knowledge, Science and Technology (IAASTD), namely the prevention of social, environmental and climate damage; internalization of environmental externalities; and analysis and further development of the multi-functionality of ecosystems (McIntyre et al., 2009).

antiviral drugs. This often happens much faster than the time required by research teams to develop new and effective medicines.

There should never have been a competitive race between chemical treatments and microorganisms, as the latter have evolved over a period of about 2.5 billion years. Only exceptionally aggressive and resistant cases are perceived by the general public as a real danger, but even those cases have become more frequent over time. Even so, the general tendency and the fatally latent danger are being ignored.

F. Deforestation and animal feed production

Box 2 lists some explanatory factors for the lack of awareness of the potential of sustainable grassland management with ruminants for achieving food security and sustainable development. There is a widespread belief, that rainforests are being destroyed only to be

converted to land for pasture. In reality, however, the cutting of forests is often triggered by a sequence of income-generating cycles, of which pasture for cattle is one. Contrary to prairies and pampas, the soils of tropical rainforests have a lower content of grass seeds and are less fertile because of the washing out of nutrients. This is why deforested areas tend to be used sometimes only temporarily as pasture, and thereafter for growing crops for fodder production and, increasingly, for biofuel production.[14] The expansion of agrofuel production and related land-grabbing offer the opportunity to raise the public's awareness of the ecological and social consequences of animal feed production on former forest and pasture land.

Through the pressing of soy, about 20 per cent of oil can be generated in volume terms and 80 per cent is left over as cake (bruised grain). Future discussions on soy cultivation should include an understanding of this commercially attractive dual character of soybeans relative to other leguminous crops such as rape seeds. Apart from attractive prices in different markets, it is also likely that demand in the three market segments – soy cake for animal feed, and soy oil for vegetable oil and biodiesel – will increase further, and thus provide producers and milling companies with greater flexibility. Moreover, soy cake for animal feed provides approximately the same income as the 20 per cent share of the soy oil used as vegetable oil and biodiesel.[15]

As is the case for permanent grassland, in (mostly non-rain-)forests too the largest share of the stored carbon can be found in the soil. Because of the visible above-ground biomass, it is generally perceived that forests are more important for carbon storage than grasslands, when in fact grasslands are globally as important. In addition, there are two distinctions between grasslands and forests: unlike permanent grasslands, the storage of carbon in forests is subject to saturation; and, in contrast to permanent grasslands, commercially used forests will, in the long term, always be harvested and large parts of the carbon stored in the biomass of the soils will end up being released into the atmosphere. Instead soils under grazed pastures are always covered.

G. Grasslands and ruminants: an example of misconceptions and opportunities[16]

Cattle rearing is an illustrative example of how non-transparent and illogical system boundaries can lead to wrong conclusions, including the misconception of the cow being a major contributor to climate change.

First, there is the issue of an excessively generic analysis of animal husbandry, which does not distinguish between different production systems. Instead of a comparative analysis of data of resource-efficient sustainable production, on the one hand, and energy-intensive industrial production, on the other, very often average values are used. Second, the analysis is mostly confined to only one GHG – methane – and excludes N_2O emissions mainly caused by the use of synthetic nitrogen fertilizers for intensive production of animal feed. Third, a sound assessment of the effects of agricultural production on climate requires taking into account not only emissions, but also cycles, as sustainable agriculture and forestry are the only economic activities with the potential to provide natural sink functions (carbon sequestration).

However, regarding the relevance for climate, in the relatively common emission comparisons

between cattle raising and vehicular traffic, cattle tend to fare badly. As an apparently logical result of such comparisons, even more intensive livestock production is being advocated, in particular that of chickens and pigs (Würger, 2010). But this neglects to take account of carbon and nitrogen cycles, and, in particular, the positive effects of sustainable grassland management for the climate as a whole. The related importance of grassland is based on the vast area it covers, accounting for 40 per cent of the global land surface. Sustainable pasture management enhances soil fertility linked to carbon-rich humus, and thereby 1,0 ton of humus removes 1,8 tons of CO_2 from the atmosphere, as each ton of humus contains more than 500 kg of carbon.[17] A prominent example in this regard is grazing, which allowed prairie soils over millennia to reach a depth of several metres.

Why do cows generate methane, which has a global warming potential 25 times higher than CO_2?

Cows can only digest grass through the symbiosis of billions of microorganisms in their rumen (paunch). Part of these microorganisms can decompose cellulose and lignin in grass and thus make the nutrients contained therein available to the cows. In the course of this digestion process methane is generated by microorganisms. And just as humans exhale CO_2, cows exhale both CO_2 and methane. Through this symbiosis, ruminants such as cows do not compete with human beings for food – an ability inevitably linked to methane production.

The exclusive focus on methane from cows is short-sighted, if the analysis is confined to emissions and their potential negative effects. Some data from Europe illustrates this crucial point. It is N_2O, and not methane, that constitutes the largest threat to climate in the context of livestock production. Livestock production is responsible for 75 per cent of all N_2O emissions and 90 per cent of all ammonia emissions, in particular due to intensive fertilizer use for the production of animal feed. Whereas methane has a global warming potential 25 times higher than CO_2, the global warming potential of N_2O is 296 times higher than that of CO_2. It is assumed that, on average, 2–5 per cent of consumed nitrogen fertilizers are converted into N_2O (Sutton and Billen, 2011; Schulze et al., 2009).

Against this background, besides its adverse ecological impacts, intensive feeding of livestock in the context of global hunger and warming has three

Box 3: Erroneous conclusions on extensive and intensive livestock production systems due to ill-defined system boundaries

In order to give a stronger impetus to sustainable production in agricultural policy, research and extension in the future, it is imperative to objectively evaluate the different agrarian systems. To date, sufficient comparative studies are lacking. In addition, there are significant deficiencies in terms of the comparability of data and the lack of transparency concerning the specific system boundaries. This often leads to data not being correctly assigned, which risks leading to erroneous conclusions. A prominent example in this regard is the study by Steinfeld et al. (2010), which does not distinguish between extensive and intensive production systems. In that study, only one table on major fluxes of carbon associated with intensive and extensive livestock production systems (Asner and Archer, 2010: 73, table 5.1) attempts to provide a separate account of carbon fluxes for each system. But that table has numerous analytical problems and goes so far as to suggest that extensive livestock systems would have significantly higher negative climate effects than intensive systems.

Important carbon streams under intensive and extensive livestock production systems

Category	Extensive	Intensive
CO_2 emissions from production	(Gt)	(Gt)
Nitrogen fertilizers for animal feed crop production		0.04
Fuel for transport of feed to production facility		0.06
Fuel for transport of animals in the production facility	0.03	0.03
Plouged cropland		0.02
Unploughed cropland		0.01
Processing of animals		0.03
Fuel for transport outside the production facility	0.001	0.001
Ecologically-related CO_2 emissions		
Desertification	0.2	
Deforestation in the tropics	1.2 (1.7)	
Spreading of bushy areas	- 0.3	
Methane emissions of livestock		
Digestion of ruminants	1.5	0.2
Liquid and solid manure	0.2	0.2
Total CO_2 emissions	1.1	0.2
Total methane emissions	1.7	0.4
Total GHG emissions in CO_2 equivalent	3.2	

Source: Asner and Archer, 2010: 73, table 5.1.

First and foremost, it is surprising that the sum of emissions from extensive livestock production systems is estimated to be 3.2 gigatonnes (Gt) and thus is higher than the sum of emissions of the individual items. An explanation for this is not provided. Estimates for total emissions from intensive production are not provided at all.

Our criticism regarding this accounting approach concerns, in particular, the assignment methodology:

- Emissions caused by deforestation are entirely accorded to grassland management (i.e. to extensive management methods). However, in reality, pasture usage is often only an interim use of the conversion of land that is eventually changed to cropland (nutrient-poor soils of tropical forests are converted to cropland relying on external fertilizer inputs). The fact that soy cultivation is responsible for some 17 per cent of deforestation is mentioned in the study's text, but the table accords these emissions entirely to extensive production systems, even though soy meal as animal feed is a central component of intensive production systems.

- Although a figure for CO_2 emissions related to fertilizer production for animal feed production is provided and is related to intensive livestock production, N_2O emissions are not accounted for. A footnote explains that those emissions are excluded because they are dealt with in another chapter. Although the importance of N_2O emissions in intensive systems is indeed highlighted in that other chapter, its impact on climate is not quantified.

Box 3: (continued)

- Emissions caused by land degradation are only calculated for extensive systems, whereas land degradation resulting from intensive animal feed production remains unaccounted for.

- Methane emissions linked to faeces generation are considered to be of the same magnitude in extensive and intensive systems, although methane is not generated in manure under the aerobic conditions of extensive pasturing.

As a result, even this analysis, which purports to provide an overview of the available scientific knowledge regarding intensive versus extensive production systems, contains some serious methodological shortcomings. It is apparent that the comparative analysis underestimates the negative environmental and climate impacts of intensive production systems and overestimates those of extensive production systems. This renders the results and the policy recommendations scientifically questionable.[a]

Note: [a] For a more elaborate critique, see Idel, 2010 and 2012.

additional adverse effects:

- Livestock are competing with humans for food. Normally, livestock, particularly cattle, should derive their feed from agricultural land or soils that cannot be used for direct food production for humans. On the contrary, cattle can generate milk and meat from grass and they can also provide productive power.
- The intensive production of animal feed has direct and indirect impacts on climate through
  - Nitrous oxide, ammonia and CO_2 emissions caused by synthetic nitrogen fertilizers;
  - Increased methane emissions linked to the huge scale of industrial livestock production and the excessive use of (unnatural) concentrate feed;
  - Excessive generation of animal excrements related to large-scale production and unnatural feeding;
  - Higher gas emissions through the mixing of urine and faeces caused by a lack of pasturing that would allow natural segregation.
- The increased use of concentrate feed displaces the consumption of grass, and thereby removes the following positive effects of pasture on climate:
  - The permanent and dense grass cover protects soils and prevents their erosion.
  - Sustainable pasture and grassland management promotes the biological activity (photosynthesis) of grass and its roots. In addition, microorganisms, particularly worms, convert biomass into humus, which contains over 50 per cent of carbon.[18]

H. Grasslands of the world[19]

In 2005, the Food and Agriculture Organization of the United Nations (FAO) published a survey of worldwide

grasslands (Sutti, Reynolds and Batello, 2005). Grasslands in semi-arid zones contain *green* grass only for a short period after the rainy season, which is otherwise characteristic of the rain-intensive regions of the world. Climate experts of the Grassland Carbon Working Group studied the importance of grasslands as carbon sinks and published country-specific information on grassland ecosystems. Grassland covers a total area of 52.5 million km², i.e. about 40 per cent of the total land surface of our planet.[20] (White, Murray, and Rohweder, 2000). According to the FAO, grassland accounts for about three quarters of the 4.9 billion ha of agriculturally used land. Even so, knowledge about its specific properties for each climatic zone is surprisingly limited. As a result, the potentials of grasslands[21] are grossly underestimated and are not part of the debate on the future of our planet. This could and should change.

The giant grasslands of the world store in their soil more than a third of the global carbon stock. In savannah soils, it is estimated that more than 80 per cent of the biomass can be found in the roots (Reichholf, 2004; Grace et al., 2006). However, as grasslands receive little attention, it is highly likely that their ecological, agricultural and climate potentials are not fully perceived. The ploughing of grassland causes huge losses of carbon and biomass contained in the soil – in many regions up to a third of the stored amount (Guo and Gifford, 2002; Poeplau et al., 2011). So far, the increasing demand for protein- and energy-rich animal feed for industrial livestock production has been one of the main factors behind the removal of tropical rainforests and the conversion of grassland to cropland (Don et al., 2011). Additionally, the rising consumption of biofuels is taking its toll. Many monocultures not only destroy ecosystems, but are also questionable from an energy point of view, if one deducts the energy input for their production from the energy output (particularly due to the expanding production of both concentrate feed and biofuels). Sustainably used grassland can generate a higher volume of usable energy per unit of land than ethanol from maize. At the same time, it can make a higher contribution to the reduction of GHG emissions and increase soil fertility. Trials in the United States have shown that yields from permanent grasslands over a decade surpassed those of monocultures by 238 per cent (Tilman, Hill and Lehman, 2006).

I. Global landscape gardeners

In grasslands, roots play a crucial role in humus generation. Simply put: the roots of today are the humus of tomorrow. Whereas crops only grow during their vegetation period until they are harvested, grass in permanent grassland forms more and more root biomass virtually on a permanent basis as long as daylight and a minimum of humidity are available and temperatures are still slightly above zero. The formation of roots directly depends on the rhythm of the pasturing. Very important in this regard is that grassland should have constructive pauses during pasturing so that grass plants can recover and obtain, besides water and CO_2, sufficient organic nitrogen and other nutrients from the excrements of grazing animals. Thereafter, solar energy through photosynthesis drives the growth of new grass and additional root biomass.

An illustrative example for such a natural process – including regenerative periods – can be found in the biggest annual migration of animals on our planet: the migration of the huge herds of gnus in Africa. Safaris there offer a retrospective view of nature's history: as all other grasslands, savannahs emerged from the co-evolution of grass plants and grazing animals. Huge herds of bison and aurochs (ancestors of today's domestic cattle) contributed to the development of soils in Eurasia, although they have disappeared from the collective memory of human settlers. In contrast, many Americans today still recall stories of their ancestors about the huge herds of bison. The number of bison that populated the prairies of North America in the early decades of the nineteenth century is estimated to have been about 30 million animals. Today, North American soils suffer from an average humus loss of more than 25 per cent. This also applies to prairie soils several metres thick on which

monocultures such as soy, maize or cereals have been cultivated for decades. However, the better the situation in some preferential locations, the lower is the perception of existing problems. In order to show that soil quality and fertility are suffering from industrial soil management systems, the humus content of soils needs to be regularly monitored and documented.

J. Cattle as ideal users of feed

Taking account of carbon and nitrogen cycles not only leads to a different assessment of the impacts of agriculture on climate; it also provides a different perspective of animal husbandry, particularly that of ruminants. Ignorance with regard to the potential of grasslands arises from the misconception that cattle are poor feed users, which, since the end of the 1970s, has also been taught to students. In this regard, cattle and other ruminants are not contextualized as animals that developed in co-evolution with grasslands over thousand of years, using grass and hay as fodder that, without additional labour, was turned into meat and milk. Instead these ruminants are assessed in terms of their efficiency in digesting cereals, maize and soy.

The fact that cattle consume, on average, 7 kg or more of cereals per kilogram of beef (a figure which exceeds the intake of pigs and chickens[22]) is a result of a faulty system, not faulty animals. It does not take into consideration their negative impact on resource consumption because of inappropriate system boundaries. The widespread assumption that one cow, which produces some 10,000 litres of milk annually, would be better for the ecosystem and the climate than two animals providing 5,000 litres each is questionable because:

1. The higher the production performance of cows per day or per year, the more intensive the required feeding practices. It is only possible to achieve a production of more than 6,000 liters of milk per cow per annum through greater intensity of feeding based on concentrate feed. Such feed in turn is produced as a result of very high inputs of biological and fossil resources, involving higher emissions of CO_2 and N_2O.
2. Non-high-performance cattle can satisfy their entire demand for feed by consuming roughage without any external fodder supply.
3. Sustainably used pastures can contribute to humus accumulation and thus help to reduce atmospheric CO_2 through carbon fixation.

4. Nearly all cows with an annual milk production of 5,000 liters have a longer than average life span. Conversely, most cows with an annual milk performance of 10,000 liters have a shorter than average life span. The higher the milk production of the animal per day or per year, the higher the risk of its vulnerability to diseases and burnout. This is the reason why the average life span of a cow in Germany, for instance, has fallen to less than five years. Burnout, infertility and mastitis have become "occupational diseases" of dairy cows, resulting in their being slaughtered prematurely, and statistically they produce only 2.3 calves.

Figure 4: The importance of cow longevity to protect the environment, the climate and the economy

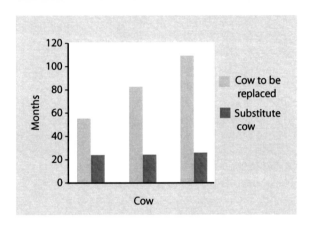

5. In addition to the life span of the cow to be replaced, fodder and additional labour as well as GHG emissions by the substitute cow need to be taken into account. Figure 4 shows that irrespective of the age of the cow destined for slaughter, the age of the substitute cow is always the same. The latter is about 28 months old: 19 months at the time of insemination plus nine months gestation. The replacement rate of a production unit indicates the percentage of cows that will have to be replaced annually to keep the dairy production rate unchanged. In production units with a very high dairy performance, the replacement rate often exceeds 50 per cent. That is why longevity leads to lower replacement rates. High replacement rates thus imply that, in addition to the direct ecological effects of dairy cows, the ecological and climate impacts of the substitute cows have to be taken into consideration in evaluating their dairy performance. The earlier a dairy cow has to be slaughtered, the longer is the period that a substitute animal needs

feeding and emits GHGs. For a dairy cow younger than 5 years, a substitute animal will have to be reared during half of the lifetime of the cow to be replaced. Thus, any productivity calculation of a dairy cow should not be confined to its annual milk, but should also take into account its performance over its lifetime (Idel, 2008).

6. In the performance balance, all too often only data for produced milk are provided, which do not represent the volume of marketable milk. Pressures for increasing dairy production result in a certain share of milk originating from diseased cows, which cannot be sold because the cows are being treated with antibiotics.

7. To arrive at a correct calculation of the productivity and the impact on climate of a dairy cow, its own beef production and that of its progeny also have to be taken into account. Dairy and beef performance are normally negatively correlated – the higher the dairy production of a cow breed, the lower its meat output, in particular that of the sons and brothers.[23] Comparing a production system with an average milk production of 5,500 litres relative to one producing 9,000 litres per year, Rosenberger and Rutzmoser (2002) note that the latter shows significantly higher emissions of methane (15.7 per cent higher), nitrogen (32 per cent higher), and phosphorous (31.7 per cent higher).[24]

The industrialized agricultural production system excludes livestock from grasslands and increases the input of protein-rich concentrate feed derived from maize, soy and cereals, resulting in a situation where cows and humans compete for food. In the context of such intensive feeding systems, ruminants, confusingly, are considered inefficient fodder consumers relative to pigs and chickens. In terms of feed consumption and output, one cow does therefore not equal another.

Cattle, sheep and buffaloes have the wonderful capacity to digest pasture forage in symbiosis with microorganisms in the rumen and turn it into milk and meat. In this sense, cattle are ideal fodder consumers and are therefore predestined for grazing in those areas that are suitable as pastures or grasslands. In addition they can use grass resulting from green fertilization through sustainable crop rotation in order to produce milk, meat and labour. Accordingly, it is only at first glance that milk and meat from intensive production appear to be cheap. The true costs of intensive animal feed production are reflected in terms of: (i) damage to the ecosystem and the climate; (ii) reduction of biological diversity; (iii) the conversion of permanent grassland and converted rainforests (including the CO_2 thus released from their carbon-rich soils); (iv) oil consumption for the production of synthetic nitrogen fertilizers and agrochemicals; (v) N_2O emissions caused by excessive use of synthetic fertilizers; (vi) the nitrification of soils and water courses; and (vii) enhanced ammonia load in the atmosphere.

It is true that cattle emit methane, but they and other ruminants are indispensable for global food security. Under sustainable pasture conditions, cattle produce milk and meat from grass and forage, and thereby make a significant contribution to the preservation of soil fertility and to climate change mitigation. This is why not only do cows have to be rehabilitated, but the correct agricultural system needs to be adopted. The decision whether we will protect or destroy the climate through the way we choose to rear cattle is up to us.

Commentary I: Excessive Industrialization of Livestock Production: The Need for a New Agricultural Paradigm

Friedrich Ostendorff
Deputy Chairman, Agricultural Committee of the German Parliament

Abstract

The excessive industrialization of chicken and pork production is a glaring example of the industrial model of agriculture, which has turned agriculture into a major climate, environmental, social and animal welfare hazard. In order to redress this situation, policies should adopt a post-industrial paradigm for agriculture, which supports multi-functional farms instead of agricultural factories. This should include the application of the forerunner and the polluter pays principle to financial incentives schemes, the tightening of regulatory laws, better market stewardship and preference for transparency, and farmer and consumer participation in policy-making.

Treating a farm as a factory that uses inputs such as pesticides, feed, fertilizers and fuel to produce outputs such as corn, chicken and pork has become the dominating principle of today's agriculture, which is exposed to the drivers and pressures of globalization. Although this model of industrialized agriculture produces impressive economies of scale, it is highly problematic owing to its detrimental impact on climate, the environment, human health and animal welfare, particularly as the associated costs remain externalized.

The vertically integrated and geographically concentrated chicken industry has been the iconic example of industrialized agriculture for decades. Between 1961 and 2009, chicken production worldwide grew from 7.5 to 80.3 million tons and pork production increased from 24.7 to 106.3 million tons (FAOStat, 2011).

This increase in production occurred in parallel with the massive industrialization and concentration of production structures. At the beginning of this century, around 74 per cent of poultry production was controlled by industrial companies (FAO, 2002). In the major poultry producing countries, a few players dominate the markets, such as Tyson in the United States, which holds 23 per cent of the national market share and processes 41 million chickens per week (Rohstoffe kompakt, 2010); or the PHW Group in Germany, which

holds around 40 per cent of the national market share in chicken production and accounts for 70 per cent of chicken breeding (FAZ, 2011; Fichtel, 2009), as well as 80 per cent of the world market in poultry vaccine production (Winters, 2008).

The problem with industrialized agriculture is that it creates massive environmental and social collateral damage. Industrial chicken and pork production is part of globally integrated production chains. They largely depend on imported feedstuff, mainly soybeans from South America, often grown on land formerly occupied by rainforests and planted as monocultures with high fertilizer and pesticide inputs. The soybeans are then shipped over thousands of miles before they reach the chicken and pork factories, which are concentrated around harbours and along highways. In these factories, chickens of very few breeds are fattened within four to six weeks, often under inhumane living conditions.

The worldwide distribution of frozen chicken parts (whose production benefits to a large extent from significant direct and indirect subsidies) can have devastating impacts on many local markets in developing countries, as illustrated by the example of European chicken parts exported to West Africa.

Industrialization has turned agriculture upside down: the source of food has become a reason for hunger in many regions of the world and the main source of biodiversity has become one of its greatest threats. At the same time, what used to be a GHG sink has become a major polluter. According to the FAO (2006a), the major sources of GHG emissions related mainly to pork and chicken production are the production of nitrogen fertilizer for feed crops (41 million tons of CO_2 for the main producing countries), on-farm fossil fuel consumption (90 million tons of CO_2 per year), livestock-related land-use changes (2.4 billion tons of CO_2 per year) and methane emissions (more than 10 million tons per year).

The question then is how can agricultural production be reorganized so that it becomes a solution rather than a problem? Five basic principles to reform agricultural policies are proposed here.

A. A new agricultural paradigm

Although industrial agriculture is still widely promoted by current agricultural policies, there are growing calls for change. Jacques Diouf, former Director-General of the FAO, stated: "The present paradigm of intensive crop production cannot meet the challenges of the new millennium" (FAO, 2011). If this is true for agriculture as a whole, what we need is a new, post-industrial paradigm for agriculture.

The problem with factory farming lies first of all in its fundamental misconception of agriculture. Farms should not be factories – they should not be places of large-scale production halls; instead they should be highly integrated, living systems where every part of the system plays a crucial role in the functioning of the system as a whole. A traditional farm is based on its internal resources rather than on external inputs. Its main source of energy is solar, and not fossil. The animals of the farm produce – besides organic fertilizers – food (milk, eggs, meat) based on products that humans cannot consume and digest (e.g. grass, fibre and organic waste).

By ignoring the integrated nature of the farm, industrialization has turned agriculture into a major environmental, social, health and animal welfare hazard. Agricultural policies should therefore no longer follow the industrial model of agriculture. Rather, the farm model should become the new paradigm for agricultural policies. This concept of a farm is not a blueprint, but it can teach us how to tackle the great challenges to agriculture of our time, such as climate change, biodiversity, energy, water and food security.

B. Financial incentives: reversing rules and exceptions

Rules and exceptions relating to current public support schemes for agriculture should be reversed. Sustainable farming practices should become the rule, and industrial farming treated and regulated as the exception to this rule. Agricultural policies should apply the forerunner and the polluter-pays principles. The forerunner principle, which sets the best sustainable practices available in a region or production sector as a reference for farming systems, should be mainstreamed. Public farm payments should move from a "logic of compensation" to a "logic of investment in best practices". "Public money for public goods" should become the driving principle for financial support to agriculture.

The polluter pays principle, on the other hand, obliges farm industries that use unsustainable practices to compensate society for their negative impacts on the environment and on public health. This principle needs to replace the practice of compensating farmers for not polluting the environment.

C. Tightening regulatory law

Normally, industrial farming is undertaken within the rule of law, even though it may be threatening to health, the environment and animal welfare. Therefore, regulatory laws should be tightened in order to prevent negative externalities and the ability of industrial agriculture to gain comparative advantages by imposing external costs on society. Tightened regulatory laws should be internationalized so as to allow better law enforcement and prevent the transfer of agricultural factories to countries with weaker legislation. Also, health, environmental, social and animal welfare standards for agricultural products should be more effectively harmonized internationally than is currently the case.

D. Better market stewardship

Agricultural policies should establish new forms of market organization, which support farmers and consumers in regaining ownership of their regional and local markets. Farmers should be supported in establishing producer organizations that strengthen their bargaining power and enable them to gear food products to more regionalized and local markets. Such an approach should also involve a change of regulations relating to competition in order to stop the abuse of buyer power by oligopolistic processing and retailing companies and reverse the current concentration in the food chain.

E. Transparency and participation

Transparency should become a key principle of agricultural policy. Information about the reality of agricultural production, the social situation of farmers and farm workers, the environmental implications of production processes, and the living conditions of animals should not be hidden any more behind factory doors and lobby brochures; it must be made public. The first big agriculture-related crises of the twenty-first century in Europe – BSE and the foot-and-mouth outbreak in 2001 – resulted in calls for a fundamental change in agriculture. As a consequence, Germany implemented an "agricultural turnaround", at the core of which was consumer involvement and greater transparency in agriculture.

The development of a new agricultural model should no longer emerge from top-down policies implemented in closed-door factories. Instead, farmers and consumers should play an active part in policy-making. Examples from the current reform of the EU Common Agricultural Policy show the demand for and success of participatory policy approaches.

Agricultural research should also become more participative and inclusive, as stressed by the International Assessment of Agricultural Science and Technology for Development (IAASTD). After a period of almost exclusive financing of biotechnology and genetic engineering, public support should be redirected towards integrated research that embraces farmers' local knowledge of best practices as well as the knowledge of scientists from the various disciplines concerned. Investments in participatory research schemes should specifically focus on the new challenges, supporting modern low-input, organic and solar-based production, small-scale farming, enhancement of on-farm biodiversity, improved grassland management and crop diversification to reduce vulnerability.

Commentary II: Why Industrial Livestock Farming Is Unsustainable

Joyce D'Silva
Compassion in World Farming

But for the sake of some little mouthful of flesh we deprive a soul of the sun and light, and of that proportion of life and time it had been born into the world to enjoy. Plutarch

Abstract

- Farm animals are sentient beings whose well-being needs to be protected.

- Industrial farming keeps animals in isolation or crowded together in totally unnatural conditions.

- Animals have been selectively bred for their meat or high milk yield, with devastating impacts on their health and welfare.

- Industrial livestock farming uses huge amounts of grain and soy to feed the animals in a world where many go hungry.

Over millennia, we humans have developed sophisticated forms of shelter for ourselves, from rudimentary huts to air-conditioned houses. We may well have become less hardy in the process, but a lot more comfortable and weather-proofed.

Non-human creatures have used the natural shelter of woodlands and earth burrows or built their own more sophisticated housing, such as bird and pig nests or beehives, but they have always remained in contact with the land, with trees, vegetation and water and enjoyed the freedom of the skies. (Perhaps the human substitute for this is the garden or yard attached to the house, or our attempts to "go for a walk" in the countryside or swim in the sea.)

While a huge proportion of the earth's population make their living from farming the land, often including breeding or tending to some farm animals, the confinement of vast numbers of animals in industrial farms is a relatively new experience for both farmers and animals. This experiment in the industrialization of livestock farming has proved a disaster for the well-being of the animals, provided short-lived gains for agribusiness interests, led to the devastation of precious ecosystems and generated huge amounts of toxic gases and other harmful wastes. It may also be a contributory factor to the growing epidemic of obesity and the scandalous growth in numbers of malnourished people.

Removing animals from the land has led to unnatural systems of indoor animal confinement, either individually or in huge numbers, in vast sheds. This has broken up the social bonds which are so vital to animal well-being. Isolated animals, such as calves in narrow veal crates, or pregnant sows in even narrower sow stalls (gestation crates), suffer not only from physical discomfort but from psychological deprivation. This can be observed in their tendency to develop stereotypic behaviour, similar to the lion in a zoo cage. Sows kept in these narrow crates may spend up to 22 per cent of their active time with such stereotypic behaviour (Jensen, 1980). Larger numbers of animals crowded together can become aggressive, finding nothing to do all day and no escape from their pen-mates, often resulting in injury.

Science today confirms what most of us know through common sense, that animals are intelligent, sentient beings, capable of a range of emotional states and capacities. We no longer hark back to Descartes who believed that a screaming dog being dissected alive was exhibiting a purely mechanical reaction. Darwin himself recognized that animals were capable of many emotions similar to humans, when he stated: "We have seen that the senses and intuitions, the various emotions and faculties, such as love, memory, attention and curiosity, imitation, reason etc, of which man boasts, may be found in an incipient, or even sometimes a well developed condition, in the lower animals" (Darwin, 1871). Sadly, Darwin's wisdom in this respect lay forgotten for decades.

Pigs can operate computer challenges with more ability than dogs – but that only proves that some element of pigs' intelligence is not unlike our own. Pigs are, of course, uniquely intelligent at being pigs. The concrete and slatted floor of the average pig factory farm frustrates the natural exploratory or rooting behaviour of pigs, who like to spend 73 per cent of their daylight hours in such behaviour (Stolba and Wood-Gush, 1989). The metal bars surrounding and immobilizing the pregnant sow can reduce her to desperate despondency (SVC, 1997) or frantic stereotypic, repetitive behaviour, such as chewing on the bars (Broom et al., 1995).

Laying hens kept from puberty in a crowded cage, with often less floor space than a sheet of typing paper, can produce eggs for around a year and could carry on for longer. But by the time these "spent" hens reach the slaughter house, one survey showed that 36 per cent have broken bones (Gregory et al., 1990). Producing enough calcium to provide the shells for the 300+ eggs she lays each year, coupled with lack of exercise from being caged, render the hen's bones fragile and brittle. In addition, the cage prevents the hen from carrying out the regular sequence of activities she would do in a natural environment – pecking at the ground for food, stretching and flapping her wings, dust-bathing to clean her feathers, flying up to a perch at night (away from predators) and laying her eggs in a secluded nest. Thus the cages constitute a combination of physiological and mental deprivation.

More and more animals, particularly pigs and poultry, but also cattle, are being kept in industrial farms throughout the world. The FAO reports that industrial animal production systems are increasing at six times the rate of traditional mixed farming systems (FAO, 2006b). Around 70 per cent of farm animals are now kept in these systems, permanently housed, out of sight and, sadly, out of mind. And the global burden of farm animal suffering is only likely to increase.

This is not a conflict between scientific progress and human empathy with animals. The scientific dossier on the suffering caused to animals in industrial farming systems is constantly growing. New research shows the capacity of chickens – and fish – to feel pain (Danbury et al., 2000; Sneddon, Braithwaite and Gentle, 2003). Other research shows states of

neuroticism in crated sows (SVC, 1997; Athene Trust, 1986) or distressed behaviour in cows deprived of their calves.

Apart from keeping these animals throughout their lives in totally unnatural social groupings and conditions of deprivation, industrial farming has inflicted another scandalous technology upon these creatures. It has taken selective breeding to a whole new level of sophistication, with disastrous impacts on the day-to-day lives of the animals. For example, there are three global companies now responsible for the breeds of chickens bred for meat (broiler chickens) sold widely worldwide. Those chickens now grow so fast that they reach slaughter weight in five or six weeks – half the time it took 40 years ago. Bred for more breast muscle (meat), they tend to tip forward and, unable to support their heavy bodies, have become prone to appallingly painful leg problems. A research team sponsored by the Government of the United Kingdom found that 27 per cent of chickens were painfully lame for days before they went to slaughter (Knowles et al., 2008). John Webster (Emeritus Professor at Bristol University and former head of the Veterinary School) observed that "approximately one quarter of heavy strains of broiler chicken and turkeys are in chronic pain for approximately one third of their lives" (Webster, 1994).

Dairy cows such as the ubiquitous black-and-white Holsteins have been bred to produce so much milk that they are metabolically being pushed to the limit, now producing up to or even more than 20,000 litres a year, many times more than calves would have drunk from their mothers. They are prone to suffering from high rates of painful conditions like mastitis and lameness, associated with their breeding, feeding and housing conditions. Cows that are kept in zero-grazing indoor systems are at higher risk of mastitis, lameness, metritis, ketosis, teat tramp, difficult births and some bacterial infections (EFSA, 2009). Again, the combination of breeding for productivity and the totally unnatural environments has proved highly injurious to the animals' welfare. Yet some go so far as to advocate keeping dairy cows in sealed units (LUCCG, 2010) so that their methane emissions can be "scrubbed" and put to good use. Such a myopic recommendation, which directly affects the lives of the animals themselves, should surely be subject to an assessment of its effects on animal health and welfare.

So where do the best solutions lie? Perhaps the answers to these problems of toxic emissions from factory farms, overexploitation of the earth's resources, rural poverty, urban obesity and poor animal welfare can be found in applying a mixture of good science, common sense and compassion to produce genuine win-win situations.

It is now well known that permanent pasture can act as a carbon sink. Recent research comparing the environmental impacts of four different kinds of dairy farms found that a well-managed dairy herd kept outdoors year-round left a carbon footprint 6 per cent smaller than that of a high-production dairy herd kept in permanent housing. In addition, average net farm greenhouse gas emissions declined by about 10 per cent by keeping the herd outdoors year-round and cut ammonia emissions by around 30 per cent (Rotz et al., 2009). As ruminant animals, these cows could pursue their natural grazing behaviour, and although their productivity was lower in terms of litres produced, their milk was higher in protein and fat content. Thus the nutritional output from indoor and outdoor cows was similar.

To achieve high welfare standards the needs of the animals themselves should be considered. If poultry such as chickens, turkeys and ducks have wings with which to fly, they should not be bred to become so heavy that they are no longer able to fly, and, in the case of turkeys, no longer able to mate naturally due to their weight. Animals should not be bred in ways that their own physiology becomes their worst enemy, as is the case with broiler chickens. If hens stretch their wings and flap them, they should have space to do so. If pigs spend most of their time rooting with their highly sensitive snouts, they should never be kept on fully slatted floors, where such behaviour is impossible. If the animals are kept indoors, they must be provided with a deeply enriched environment, which provides comfortable bedding material, plenty of space and opportunities for natural behaviour to flourish.

Animals' bodies should not be mutilated through practices, such as docking pigs' tails, in order to keep them in factory farm conditions. Animals should be fed with as near a natural diet as possible, and not be deprived of normal quantities of food as is the case with the breeder birds of the broiler variety. They should not be deprived of necessary nutrients as happens with calves that are fed a low-iron, liquid diet to produce "white" veal; nor should they be force-fed for gourmet purposes, such as for the production of *foie gras*. Moreover, animals should be provided with the company of their own kind, in numbers as close as possible to natural conditions. Isolation and overcrowding should not be allowed.

Box 4: Twelve Farm Animal Welfare Criteria

Society is progressively recognizing animals' capacities and needs. The Lisbon Treaty of the European Union (EU) includes an article which recognizes that animals are "sentient beings" and requires member States to protect their welfare (EU, 2008). From the EU to some states in the United States to New Zealand and Australia, there are moves to phase out and ban some of the more extreme confinement systems associated with industrial farming.

The European Commission-sponsored Welfare Quality research project established a list of twelve farm animal welfare criteria. These are:

- Animals should not suffer from prolonged hunger,
- Animals should not suffer from prolonged thirst,
- Animals should have comfort around resting,
- Animals should have thermal comfort,
- Animals should have enough space to move around freely,
- Animals should be free of physical injuries,
- Animals should be free of disease,
- Animals should not suffer pain from inappropriate management or handling,
- Animals should be able to express normal, non-harmful behaviours,
- Animals should be able to express other species-specific normal behaviours,
- Animals should be handled well in all situations,
- Positive emotions should be promoted and negative emotions, such as fear, distress, frustration and apathy should be avoided.

Source: www.animalwelfareplatform.eu/.

Box 5: The Five Freedoms

1. Freedom from hunger and thirst – by ready access to fresh water and a diet to maintain full health and vigour.
2. Freedom from discomfort – by providing an appropriate environment including shelter and a comfortable resting area.
3. Freedom from pain, injury or disease – by prevention or rapid diagnosis and treatment.
4. Freedom to express normal behaviour – by providing sufficient space, proper facilities and company of the animal's own kind.
5. Freedom from fear and distress – by ensuring conditions and treatment which avoid mental suffering.

Source: www.fawc.org.uk/freedoms.htm.

It is vital that those in charge of the animals are not only trained but are also compassionate. However, good management is never an excuse for keeping animals in a poor environment in the first place. Well-managed industrial pig farms are still detrimental to animal well-being, even if their managers do their best to mitigate the harmful impacts.

Various methods to ensure good animal welfare standards have been developed, such as the much admired Five Freedoms and the Twelve Farm Animal Welfare Criteria, developed for the European Commission's Welfare Quality project (see boxes 4 and 5).

It is not just farmers or agribusiness companies that need to act to achieve animal-friendly farming. If consumers continue to call for "cheap meat", the factory farms will continue. The irony is that such farms are in fact costly to the environment, to the animals and to small-scale farmers who cannot compete. The message to consumers who can afford meat every day is to reduce their consumption, and, when they buy meat, to spend a little more – but less frequently – on purchasing only animal-friendly, environmentally friendly products. A report commissioned by Compassion in World Farming and Friends of the Earth (United Kingdom) shows that it will be possible to feed the world population in 2050 using a combination of mixed farming and organic methods, along with good animal welfare systems, but only if, globally, consumers of large quantities of animal products cut back on their consumption (Compassion in World Farming and Friends of the Earth, 2009b).

Genuine win-wins are possible. It is up to individuals, governments, lending banks and global agricultural and food institutions to make ethical choices and drive policies and practices in the right direction. The earth, the animals and our fellow humans need such a commitment.

Commentary III: Integrated Crop, Livestock and Energy Management: The Case of Biogas in Rural Ethiopia

Stanley Gwavuya
Knowledge Management Coordinator, Partnership for Development Initiative Trust, Zimbabwe

Abstract

• Biogas technology enhances synergies in crop, livestock and energy systems because the by-product of fermentation (slurry) from saved dung is used as fertilizer and the saved crop residues are used as animal feed.

• Labour otherwise used for collecting firewood and dung can be directed towards economically productive activities such as agriculture.

• Increased agricultural productivity and/or overall income improve the attractiveness of biogas as a labour-saving technology so that a positive synergy effect (limited to households collecting their own energy sources and in the absence of a subsidy) between economic development and improved energy utilization can be realized.

A. Introduction and background

Biomass, consisting of firewood, charcoal, dung and crop residues, remains the main source of energy in sub-Saharan Africa (Davidson and Sokona, 2001). In Ethiopia, for instance, biomass supplies over 90 per cent of the total national energy demand, and rural households are almost entirely dependent on this source for their energy needs. The main sources of energy are woody biomass (78 per cent), dung (8 per cent), crop residues (7 per cent) and petroleum (5 per cent). Households account for 90 per cent of national energy consumption, while rural households account for 82 per cent of the national energy consumption derived mainly from biomass energy sources (Esthete, Sonder and Heedge, 2006).

The widespread use of biomass energy sources has been found to be largely inefficient, adversely affecting the environment, human health and food security (Dewees, 1989; Dang, 1993; IEA, 2006). Environmental problems arise from deforestation, land degradation and air pollution that lead to greenhouse gas (GHG) emissions. Annual deaths from indoor air pollution resulting from the use of biomass-sourced energy have been estimated at around 1.3 million

worldwide, which is higher than deaths from malaria, and almost half of all HIV/AIDS deaths, the majority of which occur in sub-Saharan Africa (IEA, 2006). Although firewood remains the main biomass energy source, it is becoming scarce in the rural areas of Ethiopia, and households are increasingly using dung and crop residues instead. The growing scarcity of firewood is leading to reduced agricultural production as households allocate labour away from agriculture, as more agricultural land is allocated to firewood production, and as households use more dung and crop residues for fuel rather than for fertilizer and animal feed respectively (Cooke, Köhlin and Hyde, 2008). Scarcity of firewood also places an increasing burden on women and children who are its main collectors.

Biogas, which offers one technically possible energy alternative for rural areas, can help mitigate some of the consequences of an overreliance on biomass energy and is gaining popularity in Africa (UNESCO and Tata Energy Research Institute, 1982). With the potential to serve up to 2 million family units, biogas technology has been promoted since 1979 in order to help overcome the increasing energy crisis in Ethiopia (ESMAP, 1996). However, studies indicate that community digesters are prone to failure compared with individual family units. A feasibility study carried out by Esthete, Sonder and Heedge (2006) revealed that of the 600 to 700 domestic plants in Ethiopia, about 60 per cent had stopped functioning due to a range of problems, including water shortage, dung shortage, technical problems, abandonment and loss of interest. Despite past failures, there is renewed interest in biogas energy in Ethiopia. In 2007, the National Biogas Programme Ethiopia (NBPE) initiated a multi-stakeholder-driven programme to develop a viable and sustainable commercial biogas sector (Ethiopia Rural Energy Development and Promotion Center and SNV Ethiopia, 2008). Initially, family size biogas plants ranging from 4 m³ to 10 m³ are being constructed in selected regions of Tigray, Amhara, Oromia and Southern Nations Nationalities and Peoples Region (SNNPR).

A survey of 80 randomly selected households in the Dale and Arsi Negele districts of Ethiopia was conducted between April and May 2010 to assess the economics of firewood and dung use in rural Ethiopia, to improve understanding of household energy use patterns and analyse the potential of biogas technology as a possible alternative, so as to increase the chances of success in promoting cleaner energy sources (Schlag and Zuzarte, 2008). The findings of the study are presented briefly in the next section, followed by some of its conclusions and recommendations.

B. Research findings from household surveys and cost benefit analysis

Agricultural production systems in the surveyed areas are mainly small-scale and subsistence-oriented, geared to livestock and crop production. The mainly rain-fed crop production has two seasons, the main season (*Meher*) beginning in April/May with harvests in November/December, and a shorter season (*Belg*) from February to June. The livestock and crop production systems are highly integrated: crop residues are stored as animal feed while dung is an important source of fertilizer. Households in the surveyed areas use a combination of energy sources throughout the year. Firewood is the largest source of energy with the highest amount being used in the third quarter of each year. Other cooking fuels consist mainly of dung and crop residues, but also kerosene, charcoal and electricity. Use of crop residue is high at harvest time, which runs from October to January,

when more crop residues are available. Dung collection is more prominent during the dry season when it is easier to process. It is then stored for use during the wet season.

C. Analysis of the potential of biogas energy

A cost-benefit analysis of 4 m³ and 6 m³ biogas plants promoted by the NBPE was conducted. While the 6 m³ plant is the most common, the 4 m³ plant is appropriate under conditions where livestock numbers are low. For qualifying households, NBPE recommends a livestock holding of at least four cattle for the 4 m³ biogas plant and six cattle for the 6 m³ biogas plant. Among the surveyed households, about 38 per cent qualified for the 4 m³ biogas plant and about 19 per cent for the 6 m³ plant. Investment costs used in this study were based on data provided by the NBPE, based on prices prevailing in March 2010. The total costs of investing in a biogas plant amounted to 11,109 Ethiopian birr (ETB) ($855) for a 4 m³ plant and 11,906 ETB ($916) for a 6 m³ plant. The NBPE pays a subsidy of 4,000 ETB ($308) per plant regardless of size. The remaining costs for each of those plants are borne by the farmers. The costs of operating the plant also included the opportunity costs of time used in collecting dung and the costs of water needed to feed the biogas plant.

The 4 m³ and 6 m³ biogas plants have the potential to replace up to 2,208 kg and 3,319 kg, respectively, of firewood per year when operating at full capacity, and they can save up to 6,015 kg and 9,021 kg of dung, respectively, per year. However, the potential to replace firewood with biogas was assumed to be only 60 per cent, as the current set-up does not support *Injera* 25 baking which accounts for up to 60 per cent of rural households' total energy use (EESRC, 1995). Obtained biogas was valued in terms of replaced firewood and dung.

To capture the benefits for different household types in terms of energy management, a cost-benefit analysis was performed using three scenarios: (i) for households that invest in biogas to replace purchased firewood or (ii) to replace collected firewood; and (iii) for households that use dung as an energy source in addition to collected firewood. All three scenarios assumed that dung and slurry would be used as fertilizer. For collected energy sources with no market value, the marginal productivity of female labour in farm production was used. Dung carries additional value for its fertilizer content. According to laboratory tests conducted on dung samples taken, 1 kg of diammonium phosphate (DAP) is equivalent to approximately 16 kg of dry manure. According to the survey findings, DAP has an average farm gate price (purchase price plus transport costs) of 7.50 ETB ($0.59) per kilogram. This translates into 0.47 ETB per kilogram of dung. Combining collection costs and fertilizer opportunity costs, dung has a shadow price of 0.72 ETB ($0.04) per kilogram and 65.45 ETB ($5) per gigajoule when used as an energy source.

The survey found rates of return on capital invested in biogas plants to be above 10 per cent (table 1), which showed that adopting biogas technology is more beneficial for households that purchase all of their firewood. This factor also makes biogas attractive to this segment of rural households, as benefits are financially recovered through savings on firewood purchase. Households that use dung for combustion stand to benefit more (higher net present value (NPV)) than those collecting firewood by adopting biogas technology. Under all three scenarios, dung and slurry used as fertilizer accounted for over 65

per cent of costs and benefits respectively. These results are highly sensitive to changes in time savings, expenditure levels and price of replaced fuel in all three household scenarios. These factors are crucial, as they are likely to determine anticipated benefits and perceived opportunity costs of capital, which influence households' decision on whether to invest in biogas. Without the subsidy given to farmers by the NBPE, investing in the biogas plant is very risky for households that collect their own firewood.

D. Conclusions and recommendations

Biogas technology presents an opportunity to enhance synergies in crop, livestock and energy systems in rural Ethiopia. The by-product of the fermentation – slurry – retains the nutrient content that is otherwise lost through direct combustion of dung for energy. Crop residues that might otherwise be used for energy are saved for animal feed. However, low shadow prices of energy sources collected by households mean that biogas is unable to compete unless heavily subsidized. The present subsidy scheme makes biogas an attractive option, but this

Table 1: Cost-benefit analysis of biogas plants compared with different traditional sources of household energy in Ethiopia (Ethiopian birr*)

| | Purchasing firewood | | Collecting firewood | | Collecting dung | |
	4 m³	6 m³	4 m³	6 m³	4 m³	6 m³
Costs						
Investment costs	7 109	7 906	7 109	7906	7 109	7 906
Maintenance costs	680	680	680	680	680	680
Water costs	1 860	2 790	1 860	2 790	1 860	2 790
Dung value	41 965	62 948	41965	62 948	41 965	62 948
Total costs	51 614	74 324	51 614	74 324	51 614	74 324
Benefits						
Biogas value	17 101	25 651	1 650	2 475	4 650	5 475
Lighting energy saved	4 572	4 572	4 572	4 572	4 572	4 572
Time saved	3 720	3 720	3 720	3 720	3 720	3 720
Slurry value	46 628	69 943	46 628	69 943	46 628	69 943
Total benefits	72 021	103 886	56 570	80 710	59 570	83 710
Net present value	20 407	29 561	4 957	6 386	7 957	9 386
Internal rate of return (per cent)	28.29	34.78	10.52	11.90	14.57	15.13

Source: Survey data and SNV, 2010.
Note: * € 1 = 18 ETB, $1 = 13 ETB, a weighted average (April 2010).
　　　　Discount rate 4%; period of use of biogas plant 20 years.

would not be the case if subsidies were removed.

From the cost-benefit assessment of biogas plants, investing households stand to benefit mainly through the use of slurry as a fertilizer, as well as through cost savings on energy use for traditional cooking and lighting and the associated labour savings. Consequently, profitability depends largely on the use of slurry as a fertilizer and on the price of replaced energy sources. Thus, promotion of dung and slurry is vital for the success of the biogas programme in Ethiopia and for improving agricultural production for food security. A synergy to be further exploited is the labour-saving effect of biogas compared with wood or dung collection. Thus, the more incentives there are to switch to sustainable energy sources such as biogas, the greater will be the profitability and improvement of labour productivity in agriculture and other sectors.

The economic attractiveness of biogas plants would be considerably improved if suitable biogas *injera* stoves were developed for use by investing households. These stoves have the potential to enhance the use of biogas plants, thereby increasing the benefits accruing to households. Cheaper alternatives to biogas plants and improvements in the technology remain an option in catering to poor households.

References

Asner G and Archer S (2010). Livestock and the global carbon cycle. In: Livestock in a changing landscape, London , Steinfeld H et al., eds.: 69–82.

Athene Trust (1986). Does close confinement cause distress in sows? A review of the scientific evidence. Prepared by the Scottish Farm Buildings Investigation Unit, Aberdeen, Scotland.

Blasbalg TL (2011). Changes in consumption of omega-3 and omega-6 fatty acids in the United States during the 20th century. *American Journal of Clinical Nutrition,* 93: 950–962.

Broom DM, Mendl MT and Zanella AJ (1995). A comparison of the welfare of sows in different housing conditions. *Animal Science,* 61: 369-385.

Compassion in World Farming and Friends of the Earth (2009a). Compassion in World Farming (2009). Welfare of pigs in the European Union: The urgent need for reform of existing legislation and effective enforcement. Available at: www.ciwf.org.uk/includes/documents/cm_docs/2009/w/welfare_of_pigs_in_the_european_union_2009.pdf.

Compassion in World Farming and Friends of the Earth (2009b). Eating the Planet: Feeding and fuelling the world sustainably, fairly and humanely. Available at: ciwf.org/eatingtheplanet.

Cooke P, Köhlin G and Hyde WF (2008). Fuelwood, forests and community management: Evidence from household studies, 5. *Environment and Development Economics,* 13: 103–135.

D'Silva, J and Webster J (2010). *The Meat Crisis.* London and Washington, Earthscan.

Danbury TC, Weeks CA, Waterman-Pearson AE, Kestin SC and Chambers JP (2000). Self-selection of the analgesic drug carprofen by lame broiler chickens. *Veterinary Record,* 146: 307–311.

Dang H (1993). Fuel substitution in sub-Saharan Africa. *Environmental Management,* 17(3): 283–288.

Darwin C (1871). *The Descent of Man, and Selection in Relation to Sex.* Princeton, NJ, Princeton University Press.

Davidson O and Sokona Y (2001). Energy and sustainable development: Key issues for Africa. In: UNEP, *Proceedings of the High-Level Regional Meeting on Energy and Sustainable Development for the Ninth Session of the Commission on Sustainable Development, Nairobi, 10–13 January*: 1-19.

Dewees PA (1989). The woodfuel crisis reconsidered: Observations on the dynamics of abundance and scarcity. *World Development,* 17(8): 1159–1172.

Don A, Osborne B et al. (2011): Land use change to bioenergy production in Europe: Implications for the greenhouse gas balance and soil carbon. Global Change Biology, doi: 10.1111/j.1757-1707.2011.01116.x. Available at http://onlinelibrary.wiley.com/doi/10.1111/j.1757-1707.2011.01116.x/abstract (last call 13 march 2012).

Don A, Schumacher J and A Freibauer (2011): Impact of tropical land use chance on soil organic carbon stocks – a meta-analysis. Global Change Biology Vol 17, issue 7, pp 658-670.

EESRC (1995). Tigrai energy resources and household energy consumption. Paper presented at the Energy Symposium, Mekelle University, Ethiopia, 6 –8 April 1995.

EFSA (2009). Scientific opinion of the Panel on Animal Health and Welfare on a request from European Commission on welfare of dairy cows. *The EFSA Journal,* 1143:1–38.

Esthete G, Sonder K and Heedge R (2006). Report on the feasibility study of a national programme for domestic biogas in Ethiopia. Netherlands Development Organisation (SNV) Ethiopia.

ESMAP (1996). Ethiopia energy assessment. Report No. 179/96. Joint UNDP/World Bank Energy Sector Management Assistance Programme, Washington, DC.

Ethiopia Rural Energy Development and Promotion Center (EREDPC) and SNV Ethiopia (2008). National Biogas Programme Ethiopia. Programme implementation document.

EU (2008). Consolidated Version of the Treaty on the Functioning of the European Union. *Official Journal of the European Union,* C 115/47. Available at: http://eur-lex.europa.eu/LexUriServ/LexUriServ.do?uri=OJ:C:2008:115:0047:0199:en:PDF.

European Food Safety Authority (EFSA) (2007): DRAFT Scientific Opinion on Food Safety Animal Health and Welfare and Environmental Impact of Animals derived from Cloning by Somatic Cell Nuclear Transfer (SCNT) and their Offspring and Products Obtained from those Animals. Brussels, p:9.

Fairlie S (2010). Meat. A Benign Extravagance. Hampshire, Permanent Publications.

FAO (2002). *World Agriculture: Towards 2015/2030.* Rome.

FAO (2006a). *Livestock's Long Shadow: Environmental Issues and Options.* Rome.

FAO (2006b). Protecting Animal Genetic Diversity for Food and Agriculture: Time for Action. Animal Genetic Resources Group, FAO, Rome. Available at: www.fao.org/ag/magazine/pdf/angr.pdf.

FAO (2009): Grasslands: Enabling their potential to contribute to greenhouse gas mitigation. Rome.

FAO (2011). Foreword. In: FAO, *Save and Grow: A Policy Makers Guide to the Sustainable Intensification of Smallholder Crop Production.* Rome.

FAOStat (2011). Rome, FAO.

FAZ (*Frankfurter Allgemeine Zeitung*)(2011). Lebensmittelpreise: Geflügel von Wiesenhof soll teurer werden. Frankfurt am Main, 11th February.

Fichtel K (2009). *Wo die Frühstückseier ihren Ursprung haben. Hamburger Abendblatt,* Hamburg, 21st November.

Garnet T (2010). Livestock and climate change. In: D'Silva J and Webster J eds. *The Meat Crisis.* London and Washington, DC, Earthscan: 34–56.

Grace J, San Jose J, Meir P, Miranda H and Montes R (2006). Productivity and carbon fluxes of tropical savannas. *Journal of Biogeography,* 33: 387–400.

Gregory NG, Wilkins LJ, Eleperuma SD, Ballantyne AJ and Overfield ND (1990). Broken bones in domestic fowls: Effect of husbandry system and stunning method in end-of-lay hens. *British Poultry Science,* 31: 59–69.

Guo L and Gifford R (2002). Soil carbon stocks and land use change: A meta analysis. *Global Change Biology.,* 8 Oxford: 345–360.

Hellebrand. HJ and V Scholz (2005): Lachgasemissionen und Treibhausbilanz nachwachsender Rohstoffe. www.atb-potsdam.de/Hauptseite-deutsch/Institut/Abteilungen/Abt2/Mitarbeiter/jhellebrand/jhellebrand/publikat/N2O-DPG-2005.pdf.

Idel A (2008): Sience oder Fiction? 25 Jahre Klonforschung an Tieren. Landwirtschaft 2009. Der Kritische Agrarbericht. Hamm, Agrarbündnis (Ed.), pp:221-227.

Idel A (2010). Die Kuh ist kein Klima-Killer! Wie die Agrarindustrie die Erde verwüstet und was wir dagegen tun können. Marburg, Metropolis-Verlag. (A revised and enlarged English translation of the book "The cow is not a climate killer! How the agricultural industry destroys the earth and what we can do against it" is in preparation).

Idel A (2012). Klimaschützer auf der Weide: Tierhaltung, Klima, Ernährung und ländliche Entwicklung (climate protectors on pasture: animal husbandry, climate, nutrition and rural development). Study for Germanwatch and Arbeitsgemeinschaft bäuerliche Landwirtschaft commissioned project, "Jetzt handeln: Klima- und entwicklungsfreundliche Agrarpolitik".

Idel A and Petschow U (2004). Das globale Huhn (the global hen). In: *Ressourcenkonflikte,* Vereinigung zur Kritik der politischen Ökonomie e.V., Münster, PROKLA 135, Zeitschrift für kritische Sozialwirtschaft.

IEA (2006). Energy for cooking in developing countries. In: IEA, *World Energy Outlook 2006:* 419–445.

IOeW (2004). Oeko-Institut e.V., Schweisfurth-Stiftung, FU Berlin, Landesanstalt für Großschutzgebiete (Eds.), Petschow U, Agrobiodiversität entwickeln! Handlungsstrategien für eine nachhaltige Tier- und Pflanzenzucht. Endbericht. Berlin.

IPCC (2007) – see Metz et al. (2007). Available at: www.ipcc.ch/publications_and_data/ar4/wg3/en/contents.html.

Jensen P (1980). Fixeringens effect pa sinsuggors beteende – en etologisk studie. Institutionen for husdjurshygien med hovslagarskolan. Report 2. Uppsala, Lantbruksuniversitet.

King FH (1911). Farmers of Forty Centuries; Or, Permanent Agriculture in China, Korea, and Japan. Mineola, NY, Dover Publications Inc. Available at: http://www.gutenberg.org/ebooks/5350.

Knowles TG, Kestin, SC, Haslam SM, Brown SN, Green LE, Butterworth A, Pope SJ, Pfeiffer D and Nicol CJ (2008). Leg disorders in broiler chickens: Prevalence, risk factors and prevention. *Plos One,* 3(2): e1545.

LUCCG (2010). Land Use Climate Change Report to the Welsh Assembly Government. Available at: http://tinyurl. com/5txbbmw.

McIntyre B, Herren H, Wakhungu J and B Watson (Eds.) (2009): International Assessment of Agricultural Knowledge, Science and Technology for Development (IAASTD): Agriculture at a Crossroads. Washington. Available at www. agassessment.org.

Metz B, Davidson OR et al. (eds) (2007): Contribution of Working Group III to the Fourth Assessment Report of the Intergovernmental Panel on Climate Change (IPCC), Cambridge. www.ipcc.ch/publications_and_data/ar4/wg3/ en/contents.html.

Muir W, Gane K-S and Zhang Y (2008). Genome-wide assessment of worldwide chicken SNP genetic diversity indicates significant absence of rare alleles in commercial breeds. *Proceedings of the National Academy of Science*, 105 (45), 11 November: 17312–17317.

Naylor R, Steinfeld H, Falcon W et al. (2005). Losing the Links Between Livestock and Land. Science vol 310 (5754): 1621-1622.

Nkonya E, Gerber N, Baumgartner P, von Braun J, De Pinto A, Graw V, Kato E, Kloos J and Walter T (2011). The economics of desertification, land degradation, and drought: Toward an integrated global assessment. Washington, DC, International Food Policy Research Institute.

Paul H, Ernsting A, Semino S, Gura S and Lorch A (2009). *Agriculture and Climate Change: Real Problems, False Solutions.* Report published for the 15th Conference of the Parties of the UNFCCC in Copenhagen, December 2009. Available at: www.econexus.info/sites/econexus/files/Agriculture_climate_change_copenhagen_2009. pdf.

Poeplau C, Don A et al. (2011): Temporal dynamics of soil organic carbon after land-use change in the temperate zone – carbon response functions as a model approach. Global Change Biology Volume 17, Issue 7, pp 2415–2427, July 2011.

Reichert and Reichardt (2011): Saumagen und Regenwald, Berlin and Bonn, Forum Umwelt und Entwicklung und Germanwatch.

Reichholf JH (2004). Der Tanz um das goldene Kalb. Berlin, Der Ökokolonialismus Europas: 126–127.

Rohstoffe kompakt (2010). *Tyson Foods – Fleisch in großem Stil!* Issue 06/2010. Nürnberg.

Rosenberger E and K Rutzmoser (2002): Ökologische Folgewirkungen der Zucht auf höhere Milchleistungen. Gruber Info 4/02 pp 26-31.

Rotz CA, Soder KJ, Skinner RH, Dell CJ, Kleinman PJ, Schmidt JP and Bryant RB (2009). Grazing can reduce the environmental impact of dairy production systems. Plant Management Network International, St Paul, MN. Available at: www.plantmanagementnetwork.org/sub/fg/research/2009/impact.

Royal Society (2009). Reaping the benefits: Science and sustainable intensification of global agriculture. RS Policy document 11/09, London.

Schlag N and Zuzarte F (2008). Market barriers to clean cooking fuels in sub-Saharan Africa: A review of the literature. Stockholm, Stockholm Environment Institute.

Schulze ED, Luyssaert S, Ciais P, Freibauer A, Janssens I (2009). Importance of methane and nitrous oxide for Europe's terrestrial greenhouse-gas balance. *Nature Geoscience*, 2: 842–850.

Sneddon LU, Braithwaite BA and Gentle, MJ (2003). Do fishes have nociceptors? Evidence for the evolution of a vertebrate sensory system. Proceedings of the Royal Society London, Biological Sciences, 270: 1115–1121. Available at: http://rspb.royalsocietypublishing.org/content/270/1520/1115.full.pdf.

SNV (2010). The Potential of Small-Scale Biogas Digesters to Alleviate Poverty and Improve Long Term Sustainability of Ecosystem Services in Sub-Saharan Africa. Available at: http://www.abdn.ac.uk/sustainable-international-development/uploads/files/Final_Report_-_Potential_of_Small-Scale_Biogas_Digesters_in_Sub-Saharan_ Africa%5B1%5D.pdf.

Steinfeld H, Mooney HA, Schneider F and Neville LE, eds. (2010). *Livestock in a Changing Landscape* Vol 1 and 2. Commissioned by CIRAD, FAO, LEAD, ILRI, SCOPE and the Woods Institute. Washington, DC, Island Press.

Stolba A and Wood-Gush DGM (1989). The behaviour of pigs in a semi-natural environment. *Animal Production,* 48: 419–425.

Sutti JM, Reynolds SG and Batello C, eds.(2005). *Grasslands of the World*. Rome, FAO.

Sutton MA and Billen G (2011). Technical summary. In: Sutton MA, Howard CM, Erisman JW, Billen G, Bleeker A, Grennfewlt P, van Grinsven H and Grizetti B, eds. *The European Nitrogen Assessment: Sources, Effects and Policy Perspectives*. Cambridge, Cambridge University Press: XXXVIII.

Sutton MA, Howard CM, Erisman JW, Billen G, Bleeker A, Grennfewlt P, van Grinsven H and Grizetti B, eds. (2011). *The European Nitrogen Assessment: Sources, Effects and Policy Perspectives*. Cambridge, Cambridge University Press.

SVC (1997). The welfare of intensively kept pigs. Brussels, Scientific Veterinary Committee. Available at: http://ec.europa.eu/food/fs/sc/oldcomm4/out17_en.html.

Then Ch (2011): Joint input of Test biotech and Friends of the Earth Europe input on food derived from genetically engineered animals. Munich and Brussels, Friends of the Earth Europe and Test Biotech. http://www.testbiotech.de/node/540.

Then Ch (2012): Open letter about EU's assessment of GM animals. Brussels and Munich, Eurogroup for animals, Friends of the Earth Europe, IFOAM EU Group, Test Biotech.

Tilman D, Hill J and Lehman C (2006). Carbon-negative biofuels from low-input high biodiversity grassland biomass. *Science,* 314: 1598–1600.

Troeh FR, Hobbs JA and Donahue RL (1991). Tillage practices for conservation. In: Troeh FR, Hobbs JA and Donahue RL, eds. *Soil and Water Conservation*, 2nd edition. Englewood Cliffs, NJ, Prentice-Hall.

UNESCO and Tata Energy Research Institute (1982). Consolidation of information: A review of the literature on promotion of biogas systems. In: *General Information Programme and UNISIST*. Paris.

von Witzke H and Noleppa S (2011). EU agricultural production and trade: Can more efficiency prevent increasing 'land-grabbing' outside of Europe?, Research report, Berlin, Humboldt Universität zu Berlin and agripol.

Webster J (1994). *Animal Welfare: A Cool Eye Towards Eden*. Oxford, Blackwell Science.

Weeks C (2007): UK calf transport and veal rearing. Compassion in world farming, London - http://www.ciwf.org.uk/includes/documents/cm_docs/2008/u/uk_calf_transport_and_veal_rearing.pdf.

White R, Murray S and Rohweder M (2000). Pilot analysis of global ecosystems. Grassland Ecosystems. WRI, Washington; Grace, J., San Jose, J., Meir, P., Miranda, H. and R. Montes. 2006. Productivity and carbon fluxes of tropical savannas. Journal of Biogeography 33: 387-400.

Winters H-C (2008). *PHW in Cuxhaven entwickelt sich positiv*. Article in *Cuxhavener Nachrichten* 23 February, Cuxhaven.

Würger T (2010). Das Rülpsen der Rinder (the belching of cattle). *Der Spiegel*, 42/2010: 68, Hamburg.

Notes

1   Animal suffering and welfare are directly affected by industrial livestock production. For more information, see the comment of Joyce D'Silva in this chapter; see also D'Silva and Webster, 2010.

2   It is beyond the scope of this article to analyse the damaging effects of legal and illegal disposal of dangerous substances in animal feed for industrial livestock production and the use of contaminated sludge as fertilizer on cropland.

3   This article does not discuss the non-recycling of human faeces in soil; for a discussion of this issue, see King, 1911.

4   By way of illustration, after its accession to the EU, Romania restricted the free movement of horse- or cow-drawn transport in favour of motorized transport.

5   "Inexpensive" or "cheap" here means that a considerable proportion of the costs of production remain externalized in prices.

6   This process, used for the industrial production of ammonia, involves the nitrogen fixation reaction of nitrogen gas and hydrogen gas over an enriched iron or ruthenium catalyst.

7   Ammonia is not categorized as a GHG that has a direct impact on the climate, such as CO_2, N_2O and CH_4, but it does have a relevant indirect impact through its effect on the atmosphere.

8   For some years, monocultures for agro-energy production are increasing the amount of N_2O emitted from agriculture (for a more elaborate analysis, see Hurni et al. in chapter 4 of this Review).

9   Besides the general use of animal excrements, this also concerns the separate use of urine and faeces. Normally the separation is done through pasturing: the natural separation for mammals prevents the modification of the nitrogen compounds in the urine through the bacteria contained in the faeces.

10 Calculated using the Climate Analysis Indicators' Tool of the World Resources Institute, at: http://cait.wri.org.

11 The fact that animal breeding is more advanced than crop breeding does not reflect a higher level of technological innovation. By way of illustration, the commercialization of some transgenic crops is far more developed than transgenic animals.

12 In 1996, the cloned sheep "Dolly" was born after thousands of attempts with embryos. Dolly was the first mammal that was created by and survived the technology of somatic cell nucleus transfer (SCNT). Although armed with a patent, the "Dolly" method is (as all other genetic and cloning methods) not a blue print to get identical copies.

13 Indeed the human-microbial relationship is extremely close. A massive amount of 10^{14} bacteria exist on and in humans – a number 10 times higher than the 10 billion cells in a human body.

14 Against this background, biofuel certificates that confirm that the feedstock was not produced on cropland derived from deforestation are only useful if the time span before conversion is well defined.

15 For more information, see, for instance, www.indexmundi.com/commodities/?commodity=soybean-oil, and Fairlie, 2010. Imbalances in the patterns of fatty acids through the rejection or replacement of other oils by cheaper soy oil are not further elaborated here. For more information in this regard, see Blasbalg, 2011.

16 For a more elaborate analysis, see Idel, 2010.

17 0,55 t of C + 1,25 t of O2 = 1,8 t of CO_2.

18 There is a crucial interplay between grassland and ruminant management; as mentioned above, 40 per cent of all land is grassland and perennial grass is very effective for carbon sequestration. Whilst forests expand their biomass volume by only about 10 per cent per year, savannahs can reproduce 150 per cent of their volume (Idel, 2010, 2012; Paul et al., 2009).

19 On the CO_2 assimilation potential of grasslands, see FAO, 2009.

20 Not accounted for are permanent ice-covered surfaces of Greenland and the Antarctic, where there is no grassland yet. In Europe, grassland covers about a quarter of the total land surface.

21 Inter alia carbon sink function, protection for erosion, protein and energy source, source of income for about one tenth of the world population.

22 As hybrid pigs and chickens are fed with concentrates in intensive production systems, grass-fed land races of rare pigs, geese, chickens and others cannot compete against them, so that they end up on the list of species that are threatened with extinction (for more information, see FAO: The State of the world's animal genetic resources for food and agriculture. www.fao.org/docrep/010/a1250e/a1250e00.htm).

23 This effect is a logical consequence of the increase of the sex-specific performance of female animals. The focus on boosting dairy performance is at the expense of the energy being used for meat generation. Based on the same logic, the brothers of hybrid laying hens gain weight very slowly.

24 In the United Kingdom, due to unsatisfactory fattening performance, a large percentage of male calves of high performance dairy cows (i.e. Holstein, Friesian, Jersey) are being killed every year immediately after they are born (Weeks, 2007).

25 Injera is a thin, flat and spongy bread made from teff flour with a diameter of about 60 cm, and is an important part of the traditional diet in Ethiopia. It is traditionally prepared on a flat clay pan of matching diameter.

Chapter **3**

The Role of
Research and Technology and
Extension Services

Lead Article: THE ROLE OF RESEARCH, TECHNOLOGY AND
                  EXTENSION SERVICES IN A FUNDAMENTAL
                  TRANSFORMATION OF AGRICULTURE

Hans R. Herren
President, Millennium Institute

Abstract

The main challenges confronting sustainable agricultural knowledge, science and technology (AKST) development relate to achieving a transition from the conventional industrial agriculture model with its high external inputs and vested interests of the main players in supplying agricultural inputs, output processing and marketing. This requires political will on the part of policymakers to implement the new course of action suggested by several specialized institutions, including the IAASTD, UNCTAD, UNEP, UN-DESA and the High Level Panel of Experts on Food Security and Nutrition as well as by the recent FAO-OECD Expert Meeting on Greening the Economy with Agriculture, held in September 2011. There is ample evidence in these reports to justify new investments in AKST for sustainable agriculture. Pressure at the policy level is growing due to the series of food crises, both with respect to shortages and price increases, experienced over the past few years. The tendency remains strong to continue with business as usual, which aims at quick fixes and quick results.[1] If the repetition of the food crises that are becoming more frequent is any indication, then these quick fixes will run their course fast, with enormous negative social, environmental and economic consequences.

The case for a change in paradigm is well documented. Merely fine-tuning the present systems or redefining the status quo with new terms such as "sustainable crop production intensification" or "climate smart agriculture", among others, will not bring about the paradigm shift needed. To stop the "mining" of natural capital and, in particular, to drastically reduce GHG emissions from agriculture and make it more climate resilient requires a genuine, fundamental transformation backed by additional research. Agroecology has the proper foundations to support the needed transition from where we are today to where we need to be by 2050, with all our agriculture, whether it is small or large-scale, both at the local and global levels. Agriculture and farmers need to be among the key considerations of policymakers, as people may suffer from financial crisis but they cannot survive without food and water.

Agriculture should be top of the agenda in the debate on sustainable development and the green economy following the Rio+20 conference. It is only if agriculture, in its multifunctional role, takes centre stage that the other aspects of sustainable development will fall into place. The challenge for AKST is posed and the solutions for a new agricultural paradigm presented. It is now up to policymakers to swing into action. The time for more reports and debates on the merits of this or that technology has passed; we owe it to future generations to act now, and decisively, to safeguard our climate by building resilience and multifunctionality into our food systems to cope with the inevitable changes. These are the yardsticks against which we will have to measure progress towards sustainable agriculture. The AKST policies of tomorrow will need to address these challenges and develop the needed science, tools and criteria to implement the transition and measure progress.

A. Introduction

There is an imperative need for a fundamental change in the way the world grows, processes and consumes its food. As stated in the Report of the International Assessment of Agricultural Knowledge, Science and Technology for Development (IAASTD, 2009), "Business as usual is not an option". What is meant by this is that in order to transform agriculture and the broader food system, agricultural knowledge, science and technology (AKST) need to be recast to address the past (unsolved), present and future challenges of food and nutrition security, poverty and hunger, and preserve rural livelihoods, health and the environment. The process that led to the IAASTD (also known as the Ag Assessment) and its implementation was unique in the sense that it included all stakeholders, from producers to consumers, as well as input suppliers and processors. The process was decided at the United Nations World Summit on Sustainable Development in Johannesburg in 2002, under a joint initiative of the World Bank and the Food and Agriculture Organization of the United Nations (FAO), and was supported by the United Nations Environment Programme (UNEP), the United Nations Development Programme (UNDP), the United Nations Educational, Scientific and Cultural Organization (UNESCO), the World Health Organization (WHO) and the Global Environment Facility (GEF). This intergovernmental support gave the IAASTD the broad base needed to set the stage for changing the course of agriculture through a recasting of the AKST, or at least it was thought so, given that the report was ultimately also endorsed by 59 countries and welcomed by an additional three.

Since 2009, few AKST policies at the national, regional or international levels have actually changed. More reports have been written, mostly only to dilute the strong key messages of the IAASTD regarding the centrality of smallholder farmers who practice highly diverse forms of cultivation, the inappropriateness of an undue reliance on biotechnology and genetic engineering to solve the main problems of our agricultural and food systems, as well as the need to allow countries to choose their own agricultural trade, research and development (R&D) policies that suit their specific conditions and needs.

In 2008, the IAASTD already observed that what happens with AKST, and agriculture in general, in developed countries strongly affects what happens in developing countries, because of the highly interconnected world in terms of trade and knowledge exchange. It should be noted that while, overall, R&D in agriculture has diminished in importance over the past two decades, foreign aid is now on the rise again as a response to several food crises, although mostly in the form of quick fixes such as the provision of seeds, pesticides and fertilizers. Foreign aid continues to command large investments, mostly controlled and decided by developed countries, which still tend to consider their agriculture as the "role" model for developing countries. Unfortunately, there remains a tendency to increase short-term investments in quick fixes mostly after major catastrophes and food emergencies. Such actions, although needed in order to alleviate short-term humanitarian problems, seldom tackle the root of the perennial hunger problem, and merely provide a bridge to the next emergency. This form of aid is clearly inadequate for solving the causes of the repeated hunger and poverty problems; there is a need to rethink the overall approach to food security.

The IAASTD (2009) and UNCTAD (Hoffmann, 2011) as well as the High Level Panel of Experts on Food Security and Nutrition to the FAO Committee on World Food Security (CFS-HLPE, 2011) give a very good account of the magnitude of past investments in agricultural R&D at national and regional levels, as well as their sources, both public (i.e. by multilateral and member States of the Development Assistance Committee (DAC) of the OECD) and private. There was a slight decline of such investments until 2003, after which they started showing signs of recovery when developing-country governments began increasing their spending on agriculture, and DAC and multilateral aid agencies also increased the amount allocated to agriculture, both in total volume and as a share of official development assistance (ODA) (UN-DESA, 2011).

From the data provided in these reports, it is clear that there is a serious and urgent need to accelerate the modest upward trend in agricultural investments. As stated in the IAASTD report (2009), there is also a need to rectify the imbalance in the sources of funding by substantially increasing public support to AKST, both in developed and developing countries, since the research is supposed to deliver common public goods. This would help counteract the trend in private investments which emphasizes a narrow approach that tends to focus largely on promoting plant breeding, biotechnology and genetic engineering as solutions to the problems of climate change adaptation and mitigation, food security, hunger and poverty, rural livelihoods and the associated health and environmental problems. However, the complexity of the agricultural and wider food systems urgently requires an upgrading and change of course away from the reductionist approach to problem solving. The far more socially, environmentally and, ultimately, economically rewarding route of investing in smallholder and family-run agroecological farming systems does not receive the attention it deserves.

The fundamental issue in agriculture today is not that there is too little food produced; after all we produce an average of 4,600 kcal per person/day – roughly double the amount needed for healthy nutrition. A number of issues linked to this overproduction need to be addressed through new AKST policies:

- Only a few commodities make up the bulk of global food production, which does not satisfy the need for more diverse and localized production of quality and affordable food;
- The excess food is produced mostly in industrialized countries (with some developing-country exceptions such as India) with the help of price- and trade-distorting subsidies and at great social costs;
- The excess food is produced also at great environmental costs, contributing between 47 and 54 per cent of the total greenhouse gas (GHG) emissions that are partly responsible for climate change (see the comment of GRAIN in chapter 1 of this Review).
- Animal feed production, particularly cereals for ruminants, has a negative impact on animal and consumer health (due to meat quality, and antibiotic and hormone residues), and on the environment through carbon cycles when feed is transported around the world. There is also the environmental problem of animal factories which needs to be overcome, along with an emphasis on animal welfare, climate change and human health considerations.
- Consumption of biofuels, in the form of cereals and vegetable oils, should be reassessed and policies revised to reverse the strong growth of such consumption, which is clearly unsustainable. Besides, some observers have found no evidence of added benefits of biofuels in terms of lower GHG emissions, but they do affect food prices negatively (CFS HLPE, 2011; Lagi et al., 2011).

The shift in AKST investments at international, regional and national levels therefore needs urgently to address these fundamental issues, as suggested both by the IAASTD and more recently by UNEP (2011).

In 2003, member States of the African Union committed to spend 10 per cent of their national budgets on agricultural development. So far, only a handful of them are meeting this laudable target. That decision was made based on the recognition that it is in each country's best interest to have a strong agricultural sector, backed by a well-developed research and extension capacity. The latest food crisis in the Horn of Africa may yet give more credence to the need for urgent action, in particular to develop sustainable solutions to the increasing impacts of climate-change-induced phenomena, such as those caused by El Niño and la Niña.

The United Nations Conference on Sustainable Development – Rio+20 – held in June 2012 was another good opportunity to strongly commit to a new agricultural and food system along the lines of a multifunctional agricultural system, as defined in the IAASTD report. As Hoffmann and GRAIN illustrate in chapter 1 of this Review, agriculture is strongly implicated as part of the climate-change problem. It must therefore also be part of the solution. Enormous health problems have arisen from "modern diets" of highly processed and chemical-laced foodstuffs, not to mention the ecological impacts of existing conventional food production systems that overuse water, fertilizers and other fossil-fuel-based inputs, and are therefore, by definition, unsustainable. Furthermore, the so-called conventional/industrial agriculture is supported by perverse subsidies in developed countries that reinforce unsustainable practices, on the one hand, and overconsumption and waste on the other. In developing countries, farmers trying to compete with these subsidized products are forced to cut corners and exploit their natural resources. Due to poor investment in agriculture, these farmers suffer from a lack of knowledge exchange and insufficient or a complete absence of investment capacity to innovate and purchase miscellaneous inputs, including information and equipment. Moreover, they do not benefit from insurance schemes. Agriculture everywhere is a rather risky business which needs to be backed by insurance schemes to assure farmers their survival in bad years, which are becoming more regular events as climate-change impacts increase.

The transition from an energy-intensive form of agriculture, be it by importing the inputs or producing them locally, to a system that builds productive ecosystem services to sustain multifunctional, sustainable, resilient, viable and equitable agriculture requires major new investments in institutions and infrastructure. This inevitably requires the creation of new research centres and initiatives, which should be dedicated to research, education and extension under a fully participatory system that will also favour women and cover ecosystem services, organic farming, agroecology and agroforestry. The ultimate aim of those centres and initiatives should be the transformation of the present agricultural research system at national, regional and international levels to cater to the needs of a new agricultural paradigm (see the comments of Reij in this chapter and of Altieri and Koohafkan in chapter 1 of this Review). Technological and scientific innovations should respond to the needs identified by the end-users to meet the goals of multifunctional agriculture, instead of driving those needs.

Contrary to many preconceptions, agroecology is not the low-productivity system of our ancestors; rather it is a modern, knowledge-based, science- and technology-empowered food, fibre and fodder production system, and it is the only one capable of assuring food security in the medium and long term (see also the comment of Nemes on the productivity and profitability of organic agriculture in chapter 1). The merging of knowledge with technology and science to create innovations that address the broad range of issues in a systemic manner, in contrast to the reductionist approach that promotes biotech and genetic engineering industries, needs to be strongly promoted through public sector investments. Areas that require special and increased attention are soil sciences for the restoration, building and maintenance of soil fertility without the massive input of synthetic fertilizers, the development of mixed cropping and animal husbandry systems within rotation patterns that favour healthy plant growth, first line of defense for pest and disease control, and the production of quality plant and animal products that improve the health of consumers and the environment. AKSTs that fulfil these criteria are holistic in nature, take a landscape or river-basin view and emphasize the sustainable utilization of biodiversity, water, soil and energy within the agroecosystems.

In an effort to evaluate the feasibility of sustainable "green" agriculture to deal with the problems and

challenges that lie ahead, while providing the needed food and nutrition security for the projected 9 billion people by 2050, UNEP (2011) sought to examine how green investments would help achieve greater economic, environmental and social sustainability. Following the *Stern Review*'s (2007) recommendations to invest an extra 1 or 2 per cent of gross domestic product (GDP) in a green economy, two scenarios were identified, using the Millennium Institute's T21 system dynamics model, in which the suggested additional investments in green agriculture would be undertaken globally.[2] In the first scenario (G1), an additional 0.1 per cent of GDP would be invested in green agriculture annually (equal to $118 billion – in constant 2010 dollars) between 2011 and 2050. In the second scenario (G2), 0.16 per cent would be invested in green agriculture annually (equal to $198 billion) during the same period. These additional investments would be undertaken in equal one-fourth measures in the following four activities along the lines suggested by the IAASTD (2009):

- Promoting sustainable agricultural management practices (i.e. environmentally sound practices such as no/low-tillage and organic agriculture);
- Minimizing pre-harvest losses through training and pest control activities;
- Developing or improving food processing for the prevention of post-harvest losses and better storage, especially in rural areas;
- Supporting research and development in agronomy, photosynthesis efficiency, soil biology and fertility (to close the yield gap), adaptation to climate change through biological processes and new crops, and for efficiency improvements in energy and water use.

It should be noted that R&D implies the participation in research and knowledge dissemination of the different stakeholders, in particular farmers – who are often women – in developing countries. UNEP (2011) shows that investments in sustainable agriculture can meet the need for food security in the long term, while reducing agriculture's carbon footprint, thereby making it part of the climate change solution. The modelling results summarized in table 1 are in line with the expectations of a new agricultural paradigm and the findings of many organic and agroecology case studies. They show that not only food security, but also environmental and social goals, can be achieved with a sustainable and resilient agricultural system.

In table 1, the "green scenario" (G2) is compared

Table 1: Green scenario 2: Impact of green investments in agriculture (amounting to 0.16 per cent of GDP)

Year	2011	2030		2050	
Scenario	Base year	Green	BAUᵃ	Green	BAUᵃ
Agricultural production ($ billion/yr)	1,921	2,421	2,268	2,852	2,559
Crops ($ billion/yr)	629	836	795	996	913
Livestock ($ billion/yr)	439	590	588	726	715
Fisheries ($ billion/yr)	106	76	83	91	61
Employment (millions)	1,075	1,393	1,371	1,703	1,656
Soil quality (Dmnl)	0.92	0.97	0.8	1.03	0.73
Agriculture water use (KM3/yr)	3,389	3,526	4,276	3,207	4,878
Harvested land (billions of ha)	1.2	1.25	1.27	1.26	1.31
Deforestation (millions of ha/yr)	16	7	15	7	15
Calories per capita/day (kcal) available for supply	2,787	3,093	3,050	3,382	3,273
Calories per capita/day (kcal) available for household consumption	2,081	2,305	2,315	2,524	2,476

Source: UNEP, 2011.

Note: ᵃ BAU = business as usual (scenario).

with a "business-as-usual" (BAU) scenario, where the same amount of additional investment, equalling 0.16 per cent of GDP/year, is made in conventional and traditional agriculture over a 40-year period. The results are impressive, and although these are compiled on a global scale, the basic principles also apply to the investments made to facilitate the transition towards multifunctional and sustainable agriculture that adopts traditional and low-input techniques as currently practiced in most developing countries by small-scale farmers as well as by some larger scale operations. Overall, these investments will lead to improved soil quality, increased agricultural yield and reduced land and water requirements. They will also increase GDP growth and employment, improve nutrition and reduce energy consumption and carbon dioxide (CO_2) emissions.

B. Agricultural production and value added

In the green scenario, total agricultural production (i.e. agricultural products, livestock, fisheries and forestry) would increase significantly compared with the BAU scenario. This change would be driven by increased crop production that would be capable of meeting the needs of a growing population projected to reach over 9 billion by 2050. Similarly, value added in agricultural production would increase by more than 11 per cent compared with the BAU scenario. It is important to note that despite an increase in agricultural production and

value added, there would be no increase in the area harvested, while deforestation rates would be halved and water-efficiency increased by one third. This suggests positive synergies between investments in ecological agriculture and forest management.

C. Livestock production, nutrition and livelihoods

Additional investments in green agriculture would also lead to increased levels of livestock production and rural livelihoods, and improved nutritional status. Such investments are projected to lead to growth in employment of about 60 per cent compared with current levels, and to an increase of about 3 per cent compared with the BAU scenario. The modelling also suggests that investments in green agriculture could create 47 million additional jobs compared with BAU over the next 40 years. The additional investments in green agriculture could also lead to improved nutrition as a result of enhanced production methods. Meat production would increase by 66 per cent due to additional investments between 2010 and 2050, while fish production would be 15 per cent below 2011 levels and yet 48 per cent higher than the BAU scenario by 2050. Most of these increases would be the result of greater outlays for organic fertilizers instead of chemical fertilizers, and reduced losses because of better pest management and biological control.

D. GHG emissions

Total CO_2 emissions in the agricultural sector are projected to increase by 11 per cent relative to 2011, but will be 2 per cent below BAU. While energy-related emissions (mostly from fossil fuels) are projected to grow, it is worth noting that emissions from (chemical) fertilizer use, deforestation and harvested land would decline relative to BAU. When accounting for carbon sequestration in the soil from ecological practices, and for synergies with interventions in the forestry sector, net GHG emissions would decline considerably. These reductions would not be sufficient, however, and would need to be substantially stepped up to make agriculture GHG-neutral. Depending on how the GHG emissions are calculated, at production or food system level, the reduction would have to be between 30 and 50 per cent of the emissions resulting from present day agricultural practices, just to stay at 450 parts per million (ppm) of CO_2. This, by any measure, is still too high and risks continuing to expose ecosystems to irreversible damages. It is therefore necessary to take a much more bold approach to transitioning towards organic and similar agricultural practices that are able to absorb three to four times as much CO_2 as conventional and industrial practices before saturation occurs within some 50 years (IAASTD, 2009).

Agriculture therefore undoubtedly represents the lowest hanging fruit for climate change mitigation by simply doing what we already know how to do, and at little costs for the transition. In addition, the transition would be accompanied by a number of windfalls, from a substantial reduction in health-care costs due to healthier eating and living habits to a drastic reduction of ecosystem service costs and substantial savings from stopping perverse subsidies. Thus a transition to organic/agroecological farming practices should be the absolute priority when investing in AKST and new agricultural practices.

Overall, combining these results with research from other sources presents the following results:

- Returns on investments in "brown" agriculture will continue to decrease in the long run, mainly due to increasing costs of inputs (especially water and energy) and stagnating/decreasing yields.

- The costs of negative externalities of "brown" agriculture will continue to increase gradually, initially neutralizing and eventually exceeding any economic and development gains.

- Greening agriculture and food distribution will result in more calories per person/day, more jobs and business opportunities – especially in rural areas – and greater market access opportunities, especially for developing countries.

While each of the proposed measures will contribute to the shift towards a greener agricultural sector, the combination of all these interrelated actions will yield additional positive synergies. For instance, investment in more sustainable farming practices will lead to soil conservation, which would increase agricultural yield in the medium to longer term. This would allow more land for reforestation, which in turn would reduce land degradation and improve soil quality.

Looking at the key issue of resilience needed in the years ahead to deal with the challenges of climate change, in particular in developing countries that will be affected much more than developed countries, investment in AKST will need to be well above the level indicated in the *Stern Review*, given that there is the need to allow for a catch-up period of at least 20 years to adapt the research systems (universities, national and regional) to the needs of small-scale farmers who are practicing sustainable agriculture. Also, the enormous diversity in most tropical and sub-tropical agricultural systems adds to the need for decentralization of the research and the accompanying measures, such as knowledge and information dissemination.

E. Enabling conditions

Despite the clear logic and economic rationale for moving more rapidly towards sustainable agriculture, the transition will require a supportive policy environment and enabling conditions that could help level the playing field between conventional and sustainable agricultural practices. In particular, large investments in rural infrastructure, including roads, power, internet access, access to health care and quality schooling, as well as investments in non-farming but agriculture-related jobs, are essential for maintaining the rural areas as lively, interesting and rewarding places so as to keep the youth from migrating to the ever-growing urban slums.

F. The way forward

Implementation of the key findings and options for action of the IAASTD report will make agriculture part of the climate-change solution. It will also assure sustainable quality and quantity of food production to nourish the growing and more demanding population while supporting strong rural development in agriculture-related jobs.

The groundbreaking findings of the IAASTD process need to be internalized and translated into plans that can be implemented by the relevant government agencies responsible for AKST, as well as by national and international development agencies and non-governmental organizations (NGOs). The IAASTD report needs to be seen as the basis for action and for developing a genuine multifunctional agricultural system. New assessments need to be done at the global and regional levels to update the original report, complement gaps and take into account new social, environmental and economic developments. Assessments also need to be conducted at national levels, as recommended by the IAASTD (2009), as agricultural policies are very much a national issue, and also because agriculture is highly local. A review of the reports on agriculture that have been published since the release of the IAASTD report series, *Agriculture at a Crossroads,* in 2009, have added little except confusion to the call for a change in paradigm and to the assertion that business as usual is no longer an option. The funds and valuable expert time spent on rewriting and, more often than not, diluting the strong original message for a transition to multifunctional agriculture along the lines of agroecology, for example, could have been better used to start implementing it instead.

The main expected outputs from implementing the IAASTD options for action at research, development and extension policy level, as in the green scenario which the Millennium Institute developed for UNEP (2011), may be summarized as follows:
• *Green agriculture is capable of nourishing a growing and more demanding world population at higher nutritional levels.* An increase in food energy consumption from today's 2,100 kcal per person/day to around 2,500 kcal by 2050 is possible with the use of knowledge, science and technology in support of agroecology. It is possible to gain significant nutritional improvements from an increase in quantity and diversity of food (especially non-cereal) products. Public, private and civil society initiatives for improving food security and social equity will be needed to enable an efficient transition at the farm level, and to assure a sufficient quality of nutrition for all during this period.
• *Agroecology can significantly reduce poverty and*

the associated negative social and environmental impacts. For every 10 per cent increase in farm yields, there has been a 7 per cent reduction of poverty in Africa, and more than 5 per cent in Asia. An increase in overall GDP derived from an increase in agricultural labour productivity is, on average, 2.5 times more effective in raising the incomes of the poorest quintile in developing countries than an equivalent increase in GDP derived from an increase in non-agricultural labour productivity. Evidence suggests that the application of green farming practices has increased yields by 54–179 per cent, especially on small farms.
• *A transition to agroecology provides significant environmental benefits.* Agroecology-based food production has the potential to rebuild natural capital by restoring and maintaining soil fertility; reducing soil erosion and inorganic agrochemical pollution; increasing water use efficiency; decreasing deforestation, biodiversity loss and other land-use impacts; and significantly reducing agricultural GHG emissions. Importantly, green agriculture has the potential to transform agriculture from being a major emitter of GHGs to one that is net GHG-neutral – and possibly provides even a GHG sink – while reducing deforestation and freshwater use by 55 per cent and 35 per cent respectively.
• *Agroecological food production has the potential to be a net job creator,* and tends to employ more people per unit of agricultural production than conventional agriculture. Additionally, facilities for ensuring food safety and higher quality of food processing in rural areas could create new, high-quality jobs in the food production chain. The two scenarios (G1 and G2) conceived by the Millennium Institute suggest that investments in ecological agriculture could create 12 million and 66 million additional jobs, respectively, compared with the BAU scenario over the next 40 years.
• *A transition to agroecological farming practices will require additional investments.* The aggregate global cost of the investments and policy interventions required for a transition towards green agriculture is estimated to average between $83 and $141 billion per annum over the period 2011 to 2050 for the 1 or 2 per cent GDP scenarios, respectively, and it will provide significant ancillary benefits to other economic sectors and the environment. It should be noted that compared with the present level of (perverse) subsidies to industrial agriculture of more than $300 billion per annum, the investment

suggested by the *Stern Review* is very modest – too modest in fact to achieve the needed levels of GHG mitigation and realize the full potential of environmental services.

Sustainable agriculture requires investments in research and capacity-building in the following key areas: soil fertility management, more efficient and sustainable water use, crop and livestock diversification, and plant and animal health management, as well as pre- and post-harvest loss reduction. It also requires substantial investments in appropriate levels of mechanization, building upstream and downstream supply chains for businesses and trade, reduction of food processing waste, supporting and implementing capacity-building efforts, such as farmer field schools (including expanding and equipping agricultural extension services with modern ICT tools), and facilitating improved market access for smallholder farmers and cooperatives.

Not unlike agricultural modernization, sustainable agriculture requires institutional strengthening, including reform of land rights, good governance and infrastructure development, such as roads, electrification and internet access in rural areas in developing countries (IAASTD, 2009). These can be summed up as enabling conditions.

- *Sustainable agriculture also requires national and international policy innovations, including in international trade policy.* Such policy changes should focus particularly on reforming "environmentally harmful" subsidies that artificially lower costs of agricultural inputs and promote their excessive use. Policy measures are needed that reward farmers for positive externalities such as reducing fossil-fuel-based agricultural inputs and implementing other sustainable/green agricultural practices. Changes in trade policies that increase access of agricultural exports originating in developing countries to markets in high-income countries are also necessary, along with reforms of trade-distorting production and export subsidies. These will facilitate greater participation by smallholder farmers, cooperatives and local food-processing enterprises in food production value chains. Governments will also need to consider supporting their farmers by means of prize stabilization funds. In addition, they should consider setting up strategic reserves to cope with unexpected events, and, more and more likely, extreme weather events such as droughts, floods and storms resulting from climate change (for a more detailed discussion, see chapter 5 of this Review).

Commentary I: Effective Extension Services for Systemic Change: Achievements and Barriers to Implementation

Laurens Klerkx
Communication and Innovation Studies, Wageningen University, Wageningen, The Netherlands.

Abstract

The role of extension services has widened beyond simply dissemination of information, and now includes the brokering and facilitation of multi-stakeholder innovation networks. This expanded role needs to be further developed, in terms of boosting their capacities, and recognized as catalytic to systemic change.

A. Introduction

In the light of the challenges facing the current agricultural sector, innovation is crucial to achieving a systemic shift from conventional, industrial, monoculture-based production systems that are highly dependent on external inputs, towards more sustainable production systems that both improve the productivity of small-scale farmers and facilitate self-sustained local rural development. This requires system-wide adaptations in both production and consumption systems, as well as a reordering of the value chain. Many countries are attempting to reform their agricultural innovation support systems with the aim of developing flexible and responsive capacities to achieve this systemic change. Central to this reform is the shift from a linear approach to innovation, in which public sector agricultural research and extension delivers new technology in a pipeline configuration (i.e. through a linear flow from research, via extension, to farmers), to a systemic approach in which innovation is the result of a process of networking, interactive learning and negotiation among a heterogeneous set of public, private and civil society actors (World Bank, 2006; IAASTD, 2009). Such an approach recognizes that systemic change in agriculture beyond new technical practices requires institutional change involving alternative ways of organizing, for example markets, labour, land tenure and distribution of benefits.

This paper discusses the changing role of extension services in such an innovation system, aimed at contributing to a systemic change in agricultural production systems.

B. Changing definitions and roles of extension

In many countries, advice to farmers is provided not just by a single public extension service, but rather by several extension services (also increasingly called "advisory services") which consist of a plethora of public, private and NGO-based advisers (Rivera and Sulaiman, 2009). This implies that extension systems today can be very broadly defined as "systems that should facilitate the access of farmers, their organizations and other market actors to knowledge, information and technologies; facilitate their interaction with partners in research, education, agri-business, and other relevant institutions; and assist them to develop their own technical, organizational and management skills and practices" (Christoplos, 2010: 3). The role of extension in rural areas has thus expanded to include services that go beyond agriculture, and may include the following (Christoplos, 2010):

- Dissemination of information about technologies, new research, markets, input and financial services, as well as climate and weather.
- Training and advice for individual farmers, groups of farmers, farmer organizations, cooperatives and other agribusinesses along the market chain.
- Testing and practical adaptation of new on-farm technologies and practices.
- Development of business management skills among smallholder farmers and other local entrepreneurs.
- Facilitating linkages among market actors (e.g. for financial and non-financial inputs, processing

The International Potato Centre (CIP) in Peru serves as an innovation broker through the Papa Andina network in the context of value chain innovations (which link farmers to markets) in Bolivia, Ecuador and Peru (for details, see Devaux et al., 2009 and 2010). By applying a so-called participatory market chain approach, relevant market chain actors are brought together to discuss possible innovations, and trust has been built amongst organizations as diverse as agricultural research organizations, NGOs, farmer groups and traders, which in the past had not generally interacted. These actors are brought together on stakeholder platforms, both at the local level amongst potato providers, local authorities and a range of service providers (e.g. inputs), and also at the market chain level, including traders, processors, supermarkets, researchers and extension agents. As a result, new products have been created with greater value added for small farmers. For example, potato chips made from indigenous potato varieties produced by smallholders are marketed in Peru under the Lay's label which is owned by the multinational corporation, Pepsico (Thiele et al., 2009).

and trading), including brokering collaboration and promoting learning among them.

- Linking smallholder farmers, rural entrepreneurs and other members of the agricultural community with institutions that offer training and education in fields relevant to the agricultural sector.
- Facilitating linkages between farmers, their organizations and the public sector.
- Supporting institutional development processes and social, institutional and organizational innovations.
- Supporting the development of informal and formal farmer organizations, and rural youth organizations, and helping them to articulate their demands.
- Support for implementing government policies and programmes through information, awareness and advice on technological options, including land stewardship, food safety and animal welfare.
- Contributing to the development of more appropriate policies and programmes by facilitating feedback from farmers and local entrepreneurs.
- Increasing awareness of new opportunities for certification of "green," fair trade and other production methods.
- Facilitating access to non-extension government support (such as weather-related insurance, phytosanitary and certification services) and subsidy programmes, including payment to farmers for environmental services and other schemes related to carbon credits.
- Facilitating access to credit from rural finance institutions for farmers and local entrepreneurs.
- Providing nutrition education.
- Mediating in conflicts over natural resources.
- Providing legal and fiscal advice.

C. The role of extension as systemic "innovation brokers"

The above description of the expanded role of extension services makes it clear that to enhance multi-stakeholder interaction for systemic change, extension services need to provide more than only one-on-one technical advice and training (although this remains an important and essential function of extension); they also need to serve as *innovation brokers* in innovation systems (Klerkx, Hall and Leeuwis, 2009), enhancing the formation of multi-stakeholder learning and innovation networks and acting as facilitators of those networks. Such innovation brokers perform three core functions:

- Articulating demand: articulating innovation needs and visions as well as corresponding demands in terms of technology, knowledge, funding and policy, achieved through problem diagnosis and foresight exercises.
- Supporting the creation of networks: facilitating linkages amongst relevant actors (i.e. scanning, scoping, filtering and matchmaking of possible cooperation partners).
- Undertaking innovation process management: enhancing convergence of goals and interests and mutual understanding in multi-stakeholder networks comprising actors with different institutional reference frames related to norms, values, and incentive and reward systems.

There are several examples of the usefulness of this innovation broker role in developing countries for achieving the needed (simultaneous) adaptations at several levels in production systems and value chains (see boxes 1 and 2).

Box 2: Innovation brokering for inclusive, demand-driven research and innovation in India: National Agricultural Innovation Programme

To make research more demand-driven and supportive of farmers' innovation processes, the National Agricultural Innovation Programme (NAIP) of the Indian Council of Agricultural Research focuses on establishing consortia of public research organizations in partnership with farmers' groups, the private sector, civil society organizations and other stakeholders around agricultural development themes. Within NAIP's layered and decentralized governance structure, the Project Implementation Unit is responsible for coordinating and facilitating implementation, while consortium implementation committees coordinate the research consortia. In other words, the NAIP aims to connect research more effectively with innovation practices. It performs this task by using technology forecasting to help develop a vision of what can be achieved, bringing actors together and organizing multi-stakeholder priority setting exercises, and operating as an agent of change in the policy and institutional environment to enable innovation. Establishing this kind of enabling environment requires changes in funding systems, incentives, skills and an organizational culture to make research more receptive to demand-driven, participatory approaches that are gender-sensitive and encompass whole sectors (farmers, other rural entrepreneurs, input supply and agri-processing industries, traders and retailers). Additional requirements are the development of business planning skills, support for incubator organizations for transforming innovative research ideas into sound commercial ventures, and the use of ICT systems to manage knowledge, enhance information-sharing and match the demand for information to its supply.

Source: www.naip.icar.org.in.

D. Innovative extension approaches at the farm level

These innovation brokers typically target a variety of stakeholders for achieving systemic change, and often act at regional, national and sectoral levels. They may also target relatively small groups of more innovative and entrepreneurial farmers. In addition, innovative extension modalities and methods have been developed to support systemic change at the farm level and the scaling up of innovations that facilitate such change. Three promising approaches are farmer field schools (FFS), the use of video-mediated learning, and the use of information and communication technologies (ICTs) and mobile phones.

FFS are a participatory method of sustainable technology development based on adult education principles, such as experiential learning (Davis, 2008) and a form of farmer-to-farmer extension. Groups of farmers meet in an informal setting on their farms with a facilitator, such as an extension worker. The FFS is an interactive training method to enable farmers to become technical experts on their farming systems, and farmers are helped to diagnose problems, find solutions, conduct experiments and disseminate what they have learned to other farmers.

Participatory or farmer-led video presentations are a powerful tool that can significantly increase the impact of good practices and research (Van Mele, 2008; Van Mele, Wanvoeke and Zossou, 2010). They offer the advantage of being more cost-effective than farmer-to-farmer extension, and can sometimes have a stronger learning impact, because they offer a better means of explaining underlying biological or physical processes. Furthermore, farmer-led videos can valorize and build on farmers' knowledge and explain innovation in their own language. The Africa Rice Center in Côte d'Ivoire has facilitated the development and translation of 11 rice videos (Van Mele, Wanvoeke and Zossou, 2010) which have been translated into 30 African languages. Open air video shows have enhanced learning, experimentation, confidence, trust and group cohesion among rural people. The farmer-led learning videos (i) enable unsupervised learning, (ii) foster local creativity and experimentation, (iii) facilitate institutional innovations, and (iv) improve social inclusion of the poor, the youth and women.

Following the rapid spread of the Internet and mobile phones in many developing countries, a range of ICTs (such as information kiosks and telecentres) and mobile-phone-based "infomediaries" have emerged (Ballantyne, 2009), which enable smallholder farmers to access, for example, relevant sources of market information, input prices and animal health information. An example of positive change in animal health care systems is FARM-Africa, an NGO working in Kenya which developed a decentralized animal health-care system in its Kenya Dairy Goat and Capacity Building Project (KDGCBP) (Kithuka, Mutemi and Mohamed, 2007). The KDGCBP system works with community animal health workers, who buy drug kits and mobile phones at a subsidized price. The project also installs community phones at veterinary shops, powered by solar panels and batteries in villages that lack electricity. The phone system allows animal health workers to share information and updates and conduct referrals, and it results in lower transaction costs, which enhances the efficiency of animal health-care provision.

E. Barriers to implementation of effective extension services for systemic change

Implementation of an innovation broker role for extension services and the use of extension methods such as FFS and participatory videos, while key to achieving systemic change, are not without challenges and barriers. These relate to capacity and funding.

- *Capacity*: while extension services are urged to develop into facilitating organizations that connect farmers with different sets of service providers, many still adhere to a linear transfer-of-technology paradigm (Rivera and Sulaiman, 2009). Extension organizations either do not see the innovation broker role as central to their core business, or they do not give the freedom to execute the innovation broker role within their mandate. Thus there are still constraints in terms of mind-set and capacity, which need to be overcome by (re-)training extension providers and retooling or reinventing extension in order to play the role of innovation broker. However, this will not be an easy process.

- *Funding*: funding agencies such as donors and governments should recognize the importance of the brokering and facilitating role of extension. These are typically activities with "soft impacts" which are not easy to capture in the hard indicators needed to show effectiveness, and hence there may be a reluctance to fund such activities (Klerkx, Hall and Leeuwis, 2009). Developing adequate measurements of the "intangibles" that matter for stimulating innovation and systemic change is therefore a major concern (GFRAS, 2011). It is worth noting that recent studies (e.g. Davis et al., 2012; Friiss-Hansen and Duveskog, 2012; Yorobe Jr., Rejesus and Hammig, 2011) have found positive impacts of methods such as FFS.

Commentary II: Combining Indigenous African Knowledge with Modern Knowledge Systems for Food Security in Changing Climatic Conditions: Challenges and Prospects

H.O Kaya, and Y. N. Seleti
IKS Centre of Excellence, North-West University, Mmabatho, South Africa

Abstract

Improving the use of indigenous knowledge systems (IKS) through their effective combination with modern knowledge and technology systems is an important issue, in particular for Africa. Modern technology systems often tend to marginalize African IKS and are thus not sustainable. Any interface between the two will only be relevant if indigenous agricultural practices are applied to agriculture in Africa in a way that enables African farmers to become knowledge creators and recognizes IKS as an important source of knowledge. To enable the exchange of information between the two knowledge systems, participatory measures should be taken to capture and conserve African IKS and disseminate it among agricultural researchers and extension workers, ensuring that both systems of knowledge are relevant in local settings.

A. Introduction

African communities living in different ecological conditions have developed their own local or indigenous knowledge and technological systems over the years to ensure food security in changing climatic conditions (Kazinga, 2002). Werner (2000) defines indigenous knowledge systems as bodies of knowledge, skills and beliefs generated locally, and traditionally transmitted orally from one generation to the other. WHO (2001) has defined food security as existing when all people at all times have access to sufficient, safe, nutritious food to maintain a healthy and active life. Sefa (2004) states that, for their survival, more than 60 per cent of the people in Africa, especially in the rural areas, depend on IKS for food security, health, natural resource management, conflict resolution and natural disaster management, including adaptation to and mitigation of the effects of climate change such as drought and floods. These local knowledge systems are affordable, culturally acceptable and hence sustainable. Through an examination of secondary sources, this paper provides examples of IKS in agriculture, and discusses the prospects and challenges of interfacing IKS with modern knowledge and technological systems to enhance food security in changing climatic conditions.

B. Indigenous African agricultural knowledge and technological systems for food security

Archaeological findings in various parts of Africa show that agriculture started several millennia before the Christian era. It has been found that the growing of domestic wheat/barley in the western desert of Egypt dates as far back as around 7,000 B.C., and there is evidence of animal husbandry (sheep/goats) dating back to around 6,000 B.C. African food technologies have not only withstood the test of time but have also spread across the globe, adapting to and mitigating climate change (Sefa, 2004). Some of the indigenous African agricultural knowledge and technological systems are enumerated and discussed below.

(i) Mixed or multiple cropping. This is the growing of two or more crops simultaneously on the same piece of land. The concept behind this system is that planting multiple crops has various advantages for household and community food security, including preventing the loss of soil nutrients, reducing weeds and insect pests, increasing resistance to climate extremes (wet, dry, hot, cold), reducing plant diseases, increasing overall productivity and using scarce resources to the fullest extent. It also provides insurance against crop failure due to abnormal weather conditions. There are different variants of intercropping systems practiced in Africa. These include mixed intercropping, row intercropping and relay intercropping. Mixed intercropping, whereby the component crops are totally mixed in the field, is the basic form used in most African countries. An example of a common practice in the coastal areas of East Africa (Kenya and the United Republic of Tanzania) is mixed growing of perennials such as cashews, coconuts and mangoes. Other combinations include cassava mixed with bananas, maize mixed with legumes, sorghum with pigeon peas, and cotton with cowpeas.

(ii) Shifting/rotational farming. Zarb (2011) defines rotational farming as the cultural and physical integration of forest and agriculture, which stresses the connection between the agricultural system and the ecosystem. When the fields are fallow, they allow the regeneration of the soil and land, and this is followed by another cycle of farming. The fallow period promotes rich nutrients to create a continuing system of agriculture. The cycle aids the regeneration of fauna and flora thereby conserving local biodiversity. Samuel (2000) elaborates the advantages of this system based on his experiences in the Congo and Cameroon. The local communities there were able to cultivate a wide variety of plant species due to a 6- to 10-year period of fallow. According to his observation, the rotational farming system as an indigenous food security strategy, was not a stand-alone system, but was combined with other systems such as kitchen gardens, animal husbandry, hunting and gathering.

However, the current discourse on the challenges of climate change has created prejudice against rotational farming (CARE, 2004). People tend to blame deforestation, forest fires and slash-and-burn practices as some of the causes of carbon emissions. This criticism is refuted by Anderson (2007) using his observations of rotational farming in eastern Nigeria. He indicates that the fallow system offers opportunities for adaptation of farming to climate change. According to his study, the shifting cultivators nurture the forests even during the cultivation phase. If fallow periods are long enough, rotational farming is a stable system that maintains soil fertility, and can therefore be expected to be carbon neutral. The biomass accumulation in rotational farming is lowest after two cycles (each lasting at least six years), highest after one or four cycles, and intermediate after six to ten cycles.

(iii) Selection of specific crops and agricultural practices suited to particular climatic and ecological conditions. In arid and semi-arid areas, nomadic pastoralists practice extensive grazing, and cultivators grow drought resistant crops such as millet and sorghum, short-cycle cowpeas, phaseolus beans and groundnuts (Carpenter, 2006). In humid and sub-humid conditions, farmers grow food crops such as millet, sorghum, maize, groundnuts, cassava, cowpeas, sweet potatoes, rain-fed rice, soybeans, bananas and yams.

(iv) The importance of indigenous African post-harvest technologies for the preservation of perishable food crops, such as root crops (e.g. cassava, yams and sweet potatoes) grown mainly in the humid and sub-humid tropics, cannot be overemphasized, given that much of the food harvest produced in African countries is lost to spoilage and infestations (Kawesa, 2001). Traditional African societies that have been largely dependent on these staples have developed various local storage and processing techniques for them over the years. According to Kawesa, the cultural-historical evolution of these societies in relation to their food plants has, in general, made them strongly eco-centric in their thinking, in contrast to the techno-centric approach prevailing in the Western world. The different staples are adapted to particular ecosystems and the crops harvested need different approaches in the post-harvest technologies. For instance, cassava has highly perishable roots that can be stored for only a few days. To overcome this constraint, some African societies have developed indigenous techniques (that have been substantially improved by recent research) for storing the roots for substantial periods (Bakr, 2000). Most cassava-consuming cultures also process the roots using a variety of soaking, drying or fermentation techniques to produce stable dried products in which the level of the toxic, cyanide, is substantially reduced.

(v) Rearing of drought-resistant animals such as goats, sheep and cows. Phephe (2000) discusses the advantages of keeping savannah goats in the arid and semi-arid climate of Southern Africa. They are hardy and adaptable, with a natural resistance to tick-borne diseases, such as heartwater, and other external parasites, and require minimum handling and care. They are also heat- and drought-resistant, and easily endure cold and rain, while their pigmented skin provides protection from strong ultraviolet rays. They have relatively simple and low nutritional requirements, and can survive and reproduce where other small stock breeds cannot exist. The savannah goats fetch a higher net profit because of lower input costs. They breed year round, exhibit early sexual maturity and have long reproductive lives. In addition, range performance trials have shown that they are resistant to mouth and hoof problems.

(vi) African indigenous communities have rich knowledge of natural disaster management, as illustrated by Pitso (2008). For example, the Batswana, Zulu and other ethnic groups in Southern Africa have used the behaviour of various animals, birds, plants and insects as early warning indicators of natural disasters such as drought, floods and famine.

(vii) In her study of indigenous food security systems in eastern Zambia, Matike (2008) looks at the role played by traditional granaries as a post-harvest strategy to ensure food security. The traditional granary is the poor man's food store, built using local materials, knowledge and skills to store and preserve seeds and food crops, such as maize, millet and sorghum, dried beans and cassava, for future use and planting. The granaries are built on elevations to protect the grains from moisture, insects and rodents.

(viii) Traditional governance has played an important role in food security, according to a study by Disatsagae (2007). For example, the study observed that among the Zulu and Xhosa people in South Africa, local chiefs maintained community granaries to protect their people from starvation during natural disasters such as famines, floods and drought.

(ix) Observing nature to predict weather. Nganyi rainmakers in the Luhya community of western Kenya have been predicting the weather for generations, using changes in nature to guide their advice on how the community should time its farming (Ogallo, 2010). However, the erratic weather patterns caused by climate change mean that these rainmakers can no longer use natural signs, such as observing when trees shed their leaves or the behaviour of ants, to make their predictions. Moreover, they do not have access to the technologies available to meteorologists. A joint project by the United Kingdom and Canada links the rainmakers with government meteorologists. The two groups get together each season and produce a forecast which is disseminated using a variety of methods suited to communities where many people are illiterate.

C. Combining indigenous African knowledge with modern knowledge and technologies: Prospects and challenges

With over 40,000 plant species and over 1,000 ethnic groups, Africa has both the cultural and indigenous plant diversity needed to invigorate its agricultural economy and ensure its food security under changing climatic conditions (UNDP, 1999). People in the region use close to 4,000 indigenous plants for food, including fruit, cereals, legumes, leafy vegetables (about 1,000 different kinds), tubers and roots, and many non-foods such as gums and additives. The high cultural diversity is linked to versatile indigenous knowledge and related practices, including a variety of food processing techniques and recipes. However, in spite of this great potential, indigenous knowledge has not been effectively used to reduce current widespread malnutrition and poverty. The types of indigenous foods consumed by most African communities, especially in the rural areas, and the methods of handling, processing, marketing, distribution and utilization are deeply rooted in tradition and experience, leading to the development of various indigenous food technologies. These technologies are based on local knowledge, experience, art, culture and belief systems, and have been distilled from local experiences over centuries. They affect the economic and social lives of the operators, are simple, labour-intensive, and predominantly home-based and controlled by women. However, they are also time-consuming, with poor or no quality control.

Matike (2008) provides examples of best practices in combining indigenous and modern technologies in eastern Zambia, such as local farmers using modern sprayers to treat their farms with organic fertilizers and pesticides (liquid tea). In the United Republic of Tanzania and in other parts of Africa, increasingly, indigenous seasonal foods are being stored in modern food storage and preservation facilities, including driers and fridges, to prolong their shelf life (Kawesa, 2001). However, Kawesa argues that while the interface between African indigenous knowledge and modern knowledge systems is important to enhance food security and promote climate change adaptation and mitigation, in the context of African indigenous knowledge systems, food production and consumption are much more than just economic or nutritional activities. The processes and practices involved take place within specific social, cultural and political contexts which are not always understood by scholars, researchers and policymakers trained in Western environments and perspectives. This has led to the failure of many development projects that aimed to improve the efficiency of African indigenous food technologies. For example, the Green Revolution demonstrated the consequences of "outsider" knowledge: it generally succeeded in places where the technology was developed, and failed in those places where local farmers' needs, values and constraints differed from those where the technology was developed (Glaeser, 1990).

Increasingly, a growing number of African scientists and policymakers are becoming aware that IKS can make a significant contribution to enhancing food security and sustainable development (Flora, 1992). Such knowledge is relevant to the modern scientific world for a number of reasons, including for the protection of biodiversity and the intellectual property of the indigenous knowledge holders. IKS could be used as the basis for the construction of a truly alternative agriculture for food security and sustainable community livelihoods in Africa, which is

why it is being increasingly included in the agendas of research and development institutions. There needs to be a "deconstructive" process in the "reconstruction" of an alternative science applicable to agriculture. In order to achieve just and sustainable agriculture for food security under changing climatic conditions, it is necessary to recognize that knowledge has multiple sources, including IKS. In a study that mapped and audited indigenous agricultural knowledge in the Uasin Gishu and Keiyo districts in the Rift Valley Province (Kenya), Kiplang' at and Rotich (2008) have suggested measures for improving the capturing, preserving and disseminating of African indigenous knowledge to agricultural researchers, extension workers and farmers. This should facilitate the exchange of information between indigenous knowledge practitioners and agricultural extension services, promote cultural acceptability of development projects and programmes, increase agricultural productivity and food security, promote local agricultural content in modern technological applications, and create community-based income-earning opportunities for local farmers.

Commentary III:

The Symbiosis Between Modern Science and Traditional Knowledge for Enhancing Food Security and Climate Change Adaptation

S.M. Mbuku

Kenya Agricultural Research Institute, National Beef Research Centre, and I.S. Kosgey, Department of Animal Sciences, Egerton University, Njoro, Kenya[3]

Abstract

This comment demonstrates the richness of indigenous knowledge (IK) and the diversity of IK-related indicators for monitoring climate variability and change. Although the indicators were not compared with seasonal forecasts issued by the respective formal institutions, it is evident that this rich knowledge is yet to be fully harnessed and combined with modern science. Knowledge-sharing among scientists and pastoralists, combined with capacity-building, is necessary for improving the quality of climate forecasts, and enabling pastoralists and extension agents to interpret the probabilistic climate information in order to generate "best bet" on-farm practices for the various seasons. This will eventually contribute to increased food and nutrition security in developing countries.

Climate change and variability are issues of great concern globally, and are more pronounced in developing countries that face many development challenges. Current reports indicate that the world's climate is changing at unprecedented rates, affecting ecosystem functions and processes, biodiversity and the human population. Therefore, there is a need to develop all-inclusive robust strategies for climate change mitigation and adaptation to the changing environmental conditions. Modern technologies have played an important role in the sustainable management of natural resources in the past, but with the likelihood of further changes occurring, modern science alone cannot conserve nature or mitigate the effects of, and facilitate adaptation to, climate change to enhance food security. To achieve this, it will be necessary to integrate traditional knowledge and institutions with modern science. This commentary provides examples from Kenya – a country in sub-Saharan Africa that has enormous biodiversity – to show the potential of traditional knowledge for promoting conservation of biological diversity and climate change mitigation. General lessons are also drawn from other areas in Africa on the use of traditional knowledge, practices and institutions in designing responses to climate change.

A. Introduction

Strategies of mitigation and adaptation to changing environmental conditions have been emphasized in numerous discussions at a number of forums, including the United Nations Framework Convention on Climate Change Conferences. For the majority of communities throughout the world that directly utilize natural resources for their livelihoods, the expected changes in climate during this century present significant threats of disturbances (Thomas et al., 2007), especially where changes may be unprecedented and pervasive (Cooper et al., 2008).

The Fourth Assessment Report of the Intergovernmental Panel on Climate Change (IPCC, 2007) indicates that the exact nature of changes in climate remains uncertain, but the likeliest scenario is increased variability, particularly at the extremes. Therefore, approaches for mitigating the accompanying direct and collateral effects need to be discussed by indigenous communities, scientists, development partners and the political class.

There are potential synergies from combining IK with emerging and new patterns in science to produce optimum knowledge. IK usually builds on holistic pictures of the environment by considering a large number of variables qualitatively, while science tends to concentrate on a small number of variables quantitatively. Recent studies by Abedi and Badragheh (2011) indicate that IK is a valuable source of practices and a time-tested tool that would be useful to harness for sustainable development and for improving food security. It is becoming crucially important to recognize the limits of our scientific knowledge (Brown, 2004) and to review our understanding of what uncertainty and variability implies, as well as to examine how indigenous communities live their everyday lives. This commentary provides examples from Kenya and draws general lessons from other areas in Africa about the use of traditional knowledge, practices and institutions in designing responses to climate change and variability.

B. Congruence of indigenous and scientific knowledge systems in climate prediction

The role of climate and weather information in helping the farming community to make critical decisions for adaptation to climate change and variability cannot be overemphasized. Farm-based decision-making in developing countries relies to a large extent on indigenous weather forecasts, partly because of the absence of formal climate information systems in some developing countries. In other countries where meteorological services are developed, there exist several challenges in communicating this information to vulnerable communities. But overall, it has been observed that the accuracy of modern meteorological predictions and IK-based forecasts is fairly comparable (Orlove et al., 2010).

Traditionally, farmers have been using their own knowledge to predict rainfall – knowledge that has evolved through observations and experience over several decades and passed on from one generation to the other. In weather forecasting, they have been using a set of indicators and have developed a reliability factor for each of them. However, it is only when IK is used, challenged and adapted to changing contexts that it will contribute to climate change adaptation. Despite the increasing interest in the use of IK, scepticism towards it persists, which limits its spread to management practice and science (Gilchrist, Mallory and Merkel, 2005; Orlove et al., 2010).

Consequently, it is useful to document and compare these experiences across agro-ecological zones and livelihood groups with a view to drawing some lessons and recommendations on how indigenous forecasting may be strengthened to support adaptation in different settings.

C. Indigenous knowledge and drought monitoring: a case of Kenyan agro-pastoralism

Agro-pastoral production systems have been classified based on a number of criteria (Otte and Chilonda, 2003). Pastoralists and agro-pastoralists usually derive IK-based forecasts just before the beginning of the farming season. In northern Kenya, the Rendille pastoralists utilize a number of indicators from local weather, ranging from temperature, humidity and wind conditions to the presence or absence of certain types of clouds, rainfall patterns and amounts. These weather indicators are also used in formal climate monitoring.

Additionally, when predicting prolonged drought, the Rendille pastoralists observe the flora and fauna for any unusual behaviour, such as noises of certain birds, the appearance of sparrow weavers (green bird), bees migrating, livestock species looking emaciated even when there is plenty of pasture, the invasion of certain ants, the making of noise by crickets at night, and unusual flowering of certain trees (e.g. *Lonchocarpus sp. sterile*). Astrological constellations, like the position of the sun and moon are also observed in great detail by the Rendille and Gabra pastoralists. Interestingly, a number of these indicators have also been used for drought monitoring in other communities such as the Kamba agro-pastoralists of Kenya (Speranza et al., 2009).

There are, however, some dissenting opinions over the effectiveness of indicators used by the communities across countries and the world, and further studies are necessary to better capture the nature of the indicators. Luseno et al. (2003) suggest that indigenous methods for climate forecasting could offer insights to improve the value of modern seasonal forecasts for pastoralists in East Africa. They argue that indigenous forecasting methods are needs-driven, focus on the locality and timing of rains, and are "communicated in local languages and typically by experts' known and trusted by pastoralists". In contrast, in Burkina Faso (Roncoli et al., 2000) and

Lesotho (Ziervogel and Downing, 2004), there is less use of local forecasting knowledge, which is attributed to increased climate variability, leading to less consistency between indicators and outcomes due to the changing social environment. Consequently, farmers in these countries have also been showing interest in how they might be able to use seasonal meteorological forecasts to make critical farming decisions.

Developed countries have tended to reject the IK of local communities as primitive, non-quantitative, employing non-conventional methods and unscientific. However, more recently, IK systems have attracted the attention of many observers in both developed and developing countries. Practitioners are starting to realize the importance of recognizing and working with IK, which builds on generations of experience, to best support the adaptive capacity and strategies of rural communities (Speranza et al., 2009; Orlove et al., 2010).

D. Adaptation strategies

Large proportions of pastoral rangelands in arid and semi-arid lands (ASALs) have been systematically degraded over time, while absolute numbers of livestock have increased and are now threatening the health of ASAL habitat through overgrazing and, subsequently, soil erosion (Mganga et al., 2010). Consequently, most of the ASALs are currently unable to support growth of natural vegetation, besides diminishing the carbon sink. This raises doubts about the sustainability of pastoralism as a means of livelihood. In the ASALs of northern Kenya, the main factor influencing the productivity of livestock, which is the predominant economic activity, is feed availability (Peacock and Sherman, 2010). Yet there are few alternatives to livestock mobility as an efficient adaptive management strategy to overcome feed deficits.

The pastoralist groups in Kenya have developed fairly effective coping strategies in response to drought events aimed at minimizing losses or facilitating recovery after drought. The practice of keeping mixed herds of grazers and browsers not only ensures that the animals make use of the different resources (e.g. grasses and shrubs), but it is also a risk management strategy, as the different groups of animals are unlikely to be affected in the same way during periods of drought. Additionally, many households keep animals elsewhere, with relatives and friends, to guard against losses through disease, raids or drought. Such animals always come in handy after a disaster, as the pastoralist families are able to restock quickly and carry on with their lives. Communal ownership and management of natural resources are central to pastoralism in northern Kenya because they ensure that livestock keepers move freely as they search for water and pastures in different locations at different times of the year.

Nyong, Adesina and Osman Elasha (2007) observed that the people of the African Sahel practice zero tillage, mulching, fallowing, agro-forestry and organic farming – practices that create carbon sinks. They report that IK has been used in weather forecasting and vulnerability assessment, and for implementation of adaptation strategies such as conservation of biodiversity, use of emergency fodder in times of drought, multi-species composition of herds and mobility.

The unpredictable nature of rangelands forces the pastoralists to embark on strategies to take advantage of the good years. For instance, they often stock more productive females in their herds to ensure that animals lost are easily replaced when climatic conditions improve (i.e. when grass and water become abundant). Also, they keep a large number of animals, which is one of the paramount aspects of pastoralism that generally is not well understood and that often leads outsiders to call for de-stocking to levels in line with carrying capacity.

Outside observers also tend to overlook the fact that the way animals are grazed may be more important than the numbers, considering the mobile nature of pastoralists. Unfortunately, many of these strategies that have served drought-affected communities well in the past may become inadequate in the light of the more frequent occurrence of droughts and unprecedented weather extremes in recent years.

With dwindling natural resources, especially pasture and water, there is little the pastoralists can do to access such resources. It is important that external players work with these pastoralists to identify ways of creating access to those resources. For instance, farmers could be encouraged to plant pastures that can be sold to pastoralists at subsidized rates so that the pastoralists would not have to graze their animals in cultivated zones, which often gives rise to conflicts with crop farmers at present.

Commentary IV: Addressing the Causes of Land Degradation, Food and Nutritional Insecurity and Poverty: A New Approach to Agricultural Intensification in the Tropics and Subtropics

Roger RB Leakey

Agroforestry and Novel Crops Unit, School of Marine and Tropical Biology, James Cook University, Cairns, Australia

Abstract

The shortage of new land for agriculture and the poverty of smallholder farmers in the tropics are serious constraints on the expansion of modern intensive agriculture to overcome the food crisis. Consequently, there is an urgent need for both the rehabilitation of degraded farmland and for the realization of new income-generating opportunities.

This commentary presents a tried and tested award-winning (Equator Prize) three-point action plan using biological nitrogen fixation and a "new wave" of crop domestication focusing on marketable and highly nutritious traditional foods. If widely adopted, this package could fill the yield gap of crops such as maize, thereby promoting new livestock enterprises and satisfying global food demand to 2050. It could also create new business and employment opportunities in diversified local rural economies and perhaps help expand agribusinesses.

The Green Revolution enabled a considerable increase in the productivity of conventional high-input agriculture, thereby saving millions of people from starvation. However, this achievement came at a high cost to the environment as a result of land conversion through deforestation, land degradation and the overexploitation of natural resources, especially soil and water. Moreover, such high-input agriculture is now also recognized as being a major contributor to climate change. Furthermore, despite the improved productivity of major food staples, there are still billions of people suffering from poverty, malnutrition and hunger. Consequently, there have been many calls for a new approach to food production, especially in the tropics and subtropics where the problems and issues are the most urgent and prevalent. The key issues to be addressed are land rehabilitation, food and nutritional security, and income generation – all within sustainable land-use practices. The overriding questions are: How can the land be used to feed a growing population without further damage to the local and global environment? How can food and nutritional security be achieved on a declining area of available land? And how can the land be used to enhance the livelihoods and incomes of the rural poor?

Answers to these questions fall into two main camps: there are some who believe that the only way forward is by intensifying the high-energy-input Green Revolution model involving further productivity improvements through research and breakthroughs in crop and livestock genetics; others think that more ecologically based approaches involving low-input agriculture are the way forward. To consider the merits of these two contrasting and highly polarized views, we look at the environmental and socio-economic problems arising from land conversion to agriculture, and offer some solutions.

Current land-use practices in the tropics have led to deforestation, overgrazing and overexploitation of soils and water resources (figure 1), causing a cascade of negative impacts: land degradation, loss of soil fertility, loss of biodiversity, the breakdown of agro-ecosystem functions, declining yields, hunger and malnutrition, and declining livelihoods. Associated with these are reduced access to traditional wild foods, loss of income and the increased need for costly (often unaffordable) agricultural inputs. The response of proponents of intensive, high-input industrial farming is to redouble efforts to increase the yield of staple food crops by enhancing their capacity to

Figure 1. The cycle of land degradation and social deprivation

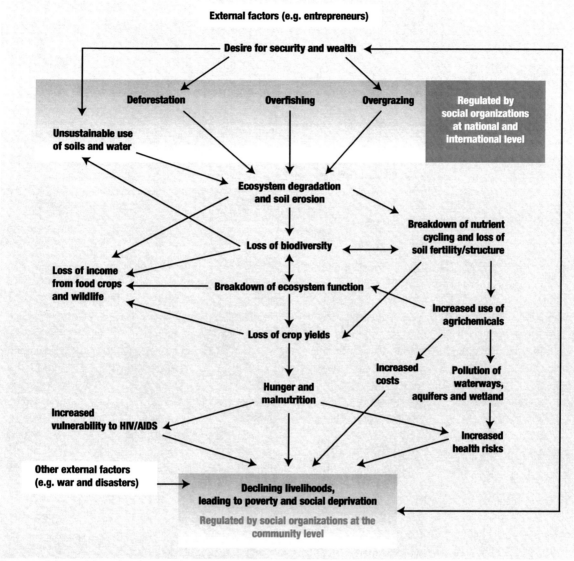

Source: Adapted from Leakey et al., 2005.

withstand biotic and abiotic stress. This approach fails to recognize three important points: (i) since farmers are failing to grow staple foods anywhere near their existing biological potential, resulting in what is called the "yield gap" – the difference between potential yield per hectare and actual yield achieved by farmers (figure 2), increasing the biological potential will not help; (ii) poor, smallholder farmers locked in a poverty trap cannot afford to buy the requisite fertilizers and pesticides (even if they had adequate access to them) that would allow them to practice monoculture agriculture; and (iii) the overriding dominance of starchy food staples in modern agriculture may

provide adequate calories for survival, but they lack the proteins and micronutrients necessary for healthy living, not to mention the sensory pleasures provided by traditional and highly nutritious foods which used to be gathered from the forest. In addition, the widespread clearance of forests from the landscape, especially from hillsides, exposes soils to erosion and increases run-off, resulting in landslides and flooding that destroy property and lead to the death of large numbers of people. Loss of perennial vegetation also contributes to climate change.

Therefore, an alternative approach to agricultural intensification is required. Indeed, several recent

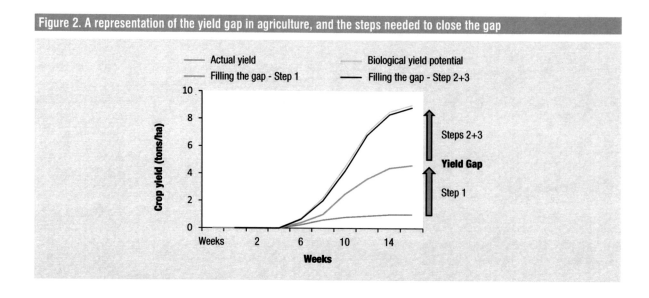

Figure 2. A representation of the yield gap in agriculture, and the steps needed to close the gap

reviews of agriculture (IAASTD, 2009; Royal Society, 2009) and of issues relating to the role of agriculture in the global environment (e.g. Hassan, Scholes and Ash, 2005; UNEP, 2007; CAWMA, 2007) have suggested that "business as usual" is no longer the appropriate option due to the scale of the problems and the constraints facing poor farmers. We need to go back to basics and look at the cycle of land degradation and social deprivation (figure 1). Clearly, a focus on crop yield is important, but, rather than trying to increase yield potential, we need to focus on closing the yield gap. In the worst cases, farmers growing maize are achieving only 0.5–1 ton per hectare when the potential is around 10 tons per hectare. In this situation, closing the gap could increase food production by 15- to 20-fold; but even if it were increased by only 2- to 3-fold, on average, this would be well over the 70 per cent increase that might be required to feed the 9 billion people predicted to populate the world by 2050, according to IFPRI (2011).

The primary cause of the yield gap is poor crop husbandry, which has a number of adverse effects, including loss of soil fertility and agroecosystem functions (such as the cycling of nutrients, carbon and water), impeding the operation of life cycles and food webs that maintain the natural balance between organisms, and reducing pollination and seed dispersal. Typically, reduced soil nitrogen is the major constraint on crop growth in degraded soils. This can be restored by harnessing the capacity of certain legumes to fix atmospheric nitrogen in root nodules colonized by symbiotic bacteria (*Rhizobium* spp.). Numerous techniques have been developed to integrate appropriate legume species within farming systems. Probably the most effective and easiest to adopt are high-density improved fallows with species such as *Sesbania sesban* and *Tephrosia vogelii* or relay cropping with *Gliricidia sepium* (Cooper et al., 1996; Buresh and Cooper, 1999). Cultivating leguminous crops such as beans and peanuts can also contribute to this process. Together the legumes can increase soil nitrogen to a level that will produce maize yields of 4–5 tons per hectare within 2–3 years. This would help narrow the yield gap and greatly increase food security. However, it would not address the problem of the low levels of other soil nutrients, which means that the complete closure of the yield gap would require another approach involving the provision of inorganic nutrients, such as rock phosphate or chemical fertilizers, which have to be purchased. This necessitates income generation.

However, before addressing the need for income, it is necessary to find ways of restoring agroecosystem function. The legumes will start this process. For example, one of the more damaging weeds of cereal crops such as maize, millet and sorghum is *Striga hermonthica*. It is a root parasite on these cereals and its seeds germinate in response to root exudates from the young cereal plants. Interestingly, however, since *Sesbania sesban* and the fodder legumes *Desmonium intortum* and *D. uncinatum* also trigger *Striga* germination, they can be used to promote suicide germination in the absence of the cereal hosts (Khan et al., 2002). *Desmodium* spp. also acts as a repellent to insect pests of cereals, such as the stem borers *Busseola fusca* and *Chilo partellus*. Likewise,

Figure 3. Procedures for closing the yield gap

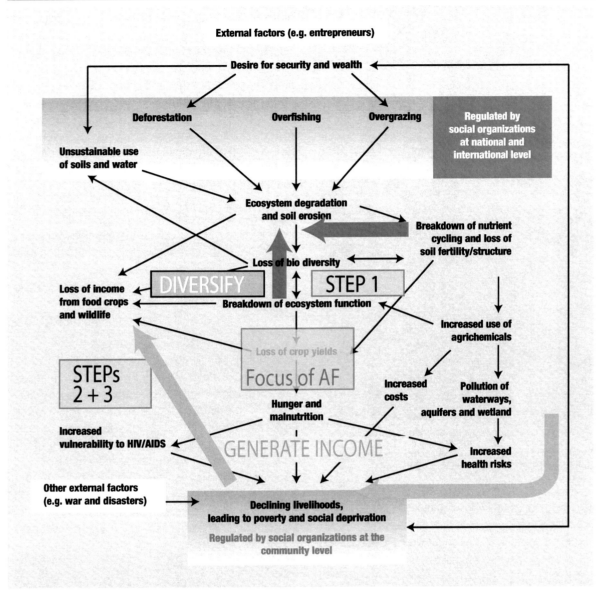

simple agroecological benefits can be attained by planting Napier grass (*Pennisetum purpureum*) as an intercrop or around small fields, as they attract the pests away from the crops (Khan et al., 2006).

The two interventions described above can therefore be used to restore soil fertility and initiate an agroecological succession, thereby rehabilitating farmland and reversing some of the land degradation processes. This may be considered as the first step towards closing the yield gap (figure 3).

The next step to a fully functional and more productive agroecosystem involves the integration of trees within the farming systems. Some trees are of course cash

crops such as coffee, cocoa and rubber, which in the past were either grown as large-scale monocultural plantations or as a two species mix, such as cocoa under the shade of coconuts or *Gliricidium sepium*. Increasingly, however, they are becoming smallholder crops grown in much more diverse species mixing, such as bananas with fruits trees like mango, avocado and local indigenous trees that produce marketable products (Leakey and Tchoundjeu, 2001). This practice is well developed in Latin America and Asia, and is becoming widely recognized as a way to restore the biodiversity normally found in natural forests (Schroth et al., 2004; Clough et al., 2011). Certainly, the replacement of shade trees with trees

Intensive rice cultivation in the valley bottom, with hillsides planted with diverse commercially important trees for income generation and environmental benefits. Indonesia alone has about three million hectares of these "agroforests".

that also produce useful and marketable products is a good strategy for farmers to enable them to maximize output from the land and minimize the risks associated with excessive reliance on a single crop species.

There has also been another silent farmer-led revolution in the tropics, especially in South-East Asia. In Indonesia, in particular, many farmers who used to practice shifting agriculture have replaced the natural fallow with a commercial fallow (agroforest) based on tree crops. They grow rice in the valley floors and plant a wide range of useful and commercially important tree species among the other food crops which they have planted on the valley slopes (Michon and de Foresta, 1999). These trees become productive successively in later years, creating a continuous supply of marketable produce (e.g. cinnamon, tung nut, damar, duku and rubber) for several decades, often ending in a timber crop. This diversification of the farming system with perennial crops therefore

achieves several important outcomes. It protects sloping land from erosion, improves water infiltration into the soil, sequesters carbon and so mitigates climate change, generates income, enhances biodiversity and promotes agroecosystem functions. In other words, it performs all the functions that large-scale monocultures fail to do, and the livelihoods of the farmers are far better than those locked in poverty due to growing a failed maize crop in Africa, for instance. This approach to agriculture achieves high crop yields that are close to the biological potential of the best and most fertile land, and it generates income from tree crops on the more marginal land, creating a land-use mosaic with many environmentally beneficial impacts (photograph from Vietnam). Importantly, there is also some evidence that complex perennial vegetation, such as a natural forest or an agroforest, is better than a herbaceous crop at recycling moisture to the atmosphere that can be advected downwind to fall as rain. Thus agroforests are likely to be beneficial to rain-fed agriculture in dry and drought prone areas of the world.

In a further initiative, over the past 20 years agro-foresters have sought to take this strategy to a higher level by starting to domesticate some of the very wide range of tree species which have been the source of locally important food and non-food products traditionally gathered from the forest (Leakey et al., 2005; Leakey, et al., 2012). The approach has been to apply well-known horticultural techniques of vegetative propagation for cultivar development (Leakey, 2004; Leakey and Akinnifesi, 2008). Unconventionally, this has been implemented at the village level as a

A multifunctional agriculture landscape in Viet Nam with many income-generating tree-based production systems on hillsides surrounding an area of intensive food production on the most fertile soils.

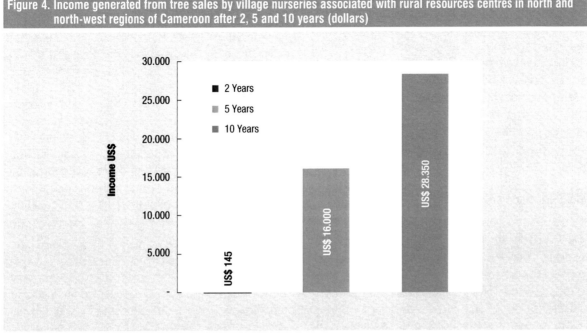

Figure 4. Income generated from tree sales by village nurseries associated with rural resources centres in north and north-west regions of Cameroon after 2, 5 and 10 years (dollars)

Source: Based on Asaah et al., 2011.

participatory process with local communities, rather than on a research station (Leakey, Schreckenberg and Tchoundjeu, 2003; Tchoundjeu et al., 2006; Asaah et al., 2011). This participatory approach has been implemented to ensure that the farmers are the instant beneficiaries of the domestication, and that they are empowered by the development of their indigenous and local knowledge. Because wild populations of tree species contain 3- to 10-fold variations of almost any trait of commercial interest (Leakey et al., 2005), there is considerable potential for substantial improvements in characteristics such as fruit/nut size, quality and chemical content. This means that new, highly productive cultivars yielding good quality produce and the product uniformity required by markets are easily obtainable. Furthermore, because the multiplication process is implemented by vegetative propagation based on mature tissues with the capacity to flower and fruit, the long unproductive period usually associated with tree crops is circumvented, and trees become productive in 2–3 years.

Proof of concept has recently been demonstrated by the implementation of a participatory tree domestication project in Cameroon (Tchoundjeu et al., 2006, 2010; Asaah et al., 2011). In 12 years the project grew from four villages and a small number of farmers to over 450 villages with 7,500 farmers. The flow of benefits, such as income generation, started

within less than five years (figure 4), and the farmers are reporting many other ways in which the project has also improved their lives (Asaah et al., 2011). Perhaps the most significant outcome has been the fact that young men and women in these communities now see a future for themselves by remaining within the community rather than migrating to local towns. In addition, the processing and value addition of produce from domesticated trees and other crops have been found to provide off-farm employment and to stimulate local enterprise and trade.

Historically, crop domestication has been implicated in the rise of civilizations that have become settled, politically centralized, socially stratified, economically complex and technologically innovative societies (Diamond, 1997). As the first wave of crop domestication primarily benefited the industrial countries of the northern latitudes, it seems that the time is now ripe for a second wave of domestication to favour tropical and subtropical countries, which would enhance social equity and environmental rehabilitation worldwide (Leakey, 2011; Leakey and Asaah, forthcoming).

The creation of new cash crops from the domestication of traditionally important, highly nutritious and useful species may be considered the second step towards closing the yield gap, because they can generate the income needed for the purchase of fertilizers and other agricultural inputs (figure 2). The trees can be used to enrich and improve the farming systems, whether by providing shade for commodity crops, or by forming agroforests on hillsides, orchards, field and farm boundaries, fodder banks or woodlots. However, farmers have many other competing demands for their money, including for local ceremonies, health care, children's education, farm infrastructure and market transport. Consequently, the third step to closing the yield gap is to further expand the commercialization of these new tree crops, thus creating business opportunities and employment.

Most of the traditionally important products from tropical forests have been marketed locally for centuries. Over the past decade, an increasing number of these have been processed as new foods, and for use in medicinal, nutraceutical and cosmetic products, based on the fruits, nuts, gums, resins and fibres. Some of these have entered regional and international markets. However, the marketing and trade of commodities from tropical producers have often been exploitative. As a result, with the emergence of this new trade there has been a parallel initiative to ensure that the producers receive a fair price (see, for example, the Fair Trade Foundation at: www.fairtrade.org.uk). In addition, ways have been sought to develop marketing partnerships aimed at the pro-poor commercialization of the traditionally important products derived from indigenous trees (Lombard and Leakey, 2010). These partnerships work to develop the products to a marketable standard and establish strong and viable trade associations that are forward thinking and market oriented. Through these partnerships it is possible to establish long-term relationships and supply agreements which ensure

that the producers remain in the value chain.

Another aspect that deserves attention is the importance of livestock in agriculture. The 2020 projections of the International Food Policy Research Institute (IFPRI) suggest that 40 per cent more grain production will be needed and that more meat will be consumed by the world's population. As mentioned earlier, grain production could be greatly increased by closing the yield gap. Recent developments have also demonstrated that fodder trees can be used to increase the productivity of cattle and goats. The integration of fodder trees and livestock into a farm is one of the elements of diversification that could be part of step 2.

Another recent development has been the establishment of public-private partnerships between multinational companies, national and international research teams and local producer communities to promote and produce new products for international trade. Examples include Daimler AG in Brazil which is manufacturing components for the motor industry based on products from agroforestry systems produced by local communities (Panik, 1998), as well as Unilever plc. that is developing a new oil crop for margarine production with communities in Ghana and the United Republic of Tanzania using kernel oil from *Allanblackia* spp. (Jamnadass et al., 2010).

All of these developments offer a new approach to agriculture delivered by agroforestry practices (Leakey, 2010), which is more sustainable – environmentally, socially and economically – than current conventional approaches. This model conforms to the concepts of multifunctional agriculture promoted by the International Assessment of Agricultural Knowledge, Science and Technology for Development (IAASTD, 2009) which was ratified by over 60 countries in 2009.

Commentary V: Adapting to Climate Change and Improving Household Food Security in Africa Through Agroforestry: Some Lessons From the Sahel

Chris Reij

Facilitator African Re-greening Initiatives, Centre for International Cooperation, Free University, Amsterdam

Abstract

The future of farming in Africa's drylands and sub-humid regions will largely depend on the success of all stakeholders in developing agroforestry systems that are managed by farmers, produce multiple impacts and do not lead to recurrent costs for governments. As aptly put by a farmer from Tigray, "Trees are our backbone" (Waters-Bayer and Gebre-Michael, 2007).

Many small and bigger re-greening successes can be found in Africa's drylands. These can be used as starting points for scaling up. Scaling up can be achieved by building a grassroots organization, but it is vital to develop national policies and legislation concerning land and tree tenure, which would induce millions of small-scale farmers in Africa to invest in natural resources, in general, and in trees in particular. The development of agroforestry systems in Niger, for instance, took off as soon as farmers began perceiving an exclusive right to their on-farm trees. In parts of Mali the process began in 1994, after a change in the forestry law and after farmers were informed about the change.

Different forms of re-greening in Africa require a mix of investments, changes in policies and legislation, the building of social capital and of a movement in support of re-greening, as well as action-oriented research to quantify multiple impacts. This will make it possible to help farmers adapt to climate change, while improving household food security and alleviating rural poverty. However, there is still one major obstacle: very rapid population growth. For instance, the annual demographic growth rates in Niger and Mali are in the order of 3.6 per cent, which means that their populations will double in less than 20 years. Even if it were technically possible to feed a rapidly growing population, it will be hard to create better livelihood opportunities for most of the young people.

A. The macro context

Macro conditions in the Sahel and in other drylands in Africa seem challenging over the next decades. Temperatures are expected to increase and crop yields to remain stable at best, but most likely they will decline due to depletion of soil fertility levels and more erratic rainfall, while the population is set to double. The Sahel has faced similar challenges in the past and has been able to cope with such changes. At the end of the 1960s and the early 1970s, rainfall suddenly declined by about 30 per cent, causing widespread hunger and hardship. And many research reports analysing agriculture and the environment in the Sahel in the 1980s were very pessimistic (e.g. Marchal, 1985; Raynaut, 1987). They used terms such as failure and breakdown to describe trends in agriculture.

B. Developing new agroforestry parklands to intensify agriculture

Farmers and pastoralists in the Sahel needed some years to adapt to the lower rainfall. Recent studies on long-term trends in agriculture and the environment in the region show some surprising trends (Reij, Tappan and Belemvire, 2005; Botoni and Reij, 2009; Reij, Tappan and Smale, 2009). The first is that farmers in several densely populated regions of Niger have been protecting and managing on-farm natural regeneration of trees and bushes. This process, which began around 1985, has led to on-farm re-greening on about 5 million hectares – the largest scale of environmental transformation in the Sahel and possibly in Africa. This on-farm protection and management of useful trees, such as *Faidherbia albida* (a nitrogen-fixing species that improves soil

Young, high-density agroforestry parkland in the southern Zinder region (Niger). The parkland is dominated by *Faidherbia albida.*

fertility and provides fodder for livestock), *Piliostigma reticulatum* (for fodder), *Combretum glutinosum* (for firewood), *Adansonia digitata* (for leaves and fruit that provide high-quality nutrition), *Guiera senegalensis* (for fodder), has enabled the feeding of about 2.5 million people. The annual production value of the new trees is in the order of at least €200 million, all of which goes to farmers, not necessarily in the form of cash but in the form of produce.

The development of new agroforestry systems has had the following impacts:

- Trees reduce wind speed, and farmers in densely populated parts of Niger now plant crops once instead of 3 or 4 times as they did 20 years ago when the crops were covered by sand or destroyed by sand blast.
- The shade of the trees reduces temperature and hence evaporation.
- A number of woody species produce fodder.
- Other species fix nitrogen and contribute to soil fertility. For instance, depending on their age, a good stand of *Faidherbia albida* fixes up to 150 kg of nitrogen per hectare.
- Some trees produce fruit and leaves, with high vitamin content, for human consumption.
- They also contribute to biodiversity.
- Trees mitigate climate change by sequestering carbon.
- They help adapt to climate change by reducing wind speeds and temperatures.
- The trees improve household food security, because they create more complex and productive farming systems that are more resilient to drought. Even if crops fail, trees produce.

- The trees help increase aggregate agricultural production and thus contribute to reducing rural poverty.

This on-farm re-greening has occurred only in regions with high population densities and sandy soils, which is not surprising, as increasing population induces farmers to intensify agriculture. For farmers, protection and management of woody species that spontaneously regenerate on-farm is the least costly form of agricultural intensification as it does not require the procurement of external inputs; the only investment is that of their labour, while village institutions are responsible for the new tree stock (capital assets). It should be emphasized that this re-greening occurs mainly on-farm. In regions with low population densities, the vegetation continues to degrade and the remaining patches of natural vegetation tend to be encroached upon and deteriorate.

Many examples of farmer-managed re-greening can be found in other Sahel countries as well. For instance, it was recently discovered that farmers in Mali's Seno Plains protect and manage natural regeneration on about 450,000 ha,[4] where 90–95 per cent of the trees are younger than 20 years. As elsewhere, this region had a good tree cover in the 1950s and 1960s, but due to droughts in the 1970s and 1980s, much of the vegetation was destroyed for field cultivation. This led to large-scale wind and water erosion and declining crop yields. In the second half of the 1980s and the 1990s, farmers, governments and donors began to react to the crisis by supporting the planting of on-farm trees in a growing number of regions. Consequently, the number of such trees has been increasing in a number of regions, though not everywhere.

Some observers argue that this process of re-greening can be attributed to an increase in rainfall in the Sahel since the mid 1990s. However, a comparison of tree densities in southern Niger and northern Nigeria, which have similar soils and population densities, reveals that on-farm tree densities in northern Nigeria are much lower than in southern Niger despite the fact that the former has higher rainfall.[5] Rainfall is important for re-greening, but it seems that human management is a more important determining factor than rainfall.

C. Water harvesting techniques to rehabilitate degraded land

Farmers in the Sahel have not only developed new agroforestry systems; they have also used simple water harvesting techniques to rehabilitate strongly degraded land. In the early 1980s, the northern part of the central plateau of Burkina Faso was a kind of laboratory for testing different water harvesting techniques, such as improved traditional planting pits (also known as *zaï*) and contour stone bunds, which slow down rainfall runoff and induce it to infiltrate into the soil. As a result, more water becomes available for plant growth and some water helps recharge local groundwater levels. Tree densities and the diversity of woody species on rehabilitated land are usually higher than on adjacent land. This is because, where farmers invest in water harvesting techniques, they almost always also invest in improved soil fertility management. The manure or compost they use contains seeds of trees and bushes on which their livestock browse. If farmers decide to protect and manage the young trees which emerge together with their crops, they create a new agroforestry system in the process. The scale of land rehabilitation in Niger and Burkina Faso since the end of the 1980s is in the order of 500,000 ha. Land that used to be barren and degraded has become productive. Crop yields vary from a few hundred kg/ha in years of poor rainfall to up to 1.5–2 tons/ha in years of normal or good rainfall. The yield levels are not only determined by rainfall, but also by the quantity and quality of organic fertilizers used. Hardly any inorganic fertilizers are used. Land rehabilitation on the central plateau of Burkina Faso feeds an additional 400,000 people.

D. The role of external interventions and the potential for scaling up farmer-managed re-greening

External interventions have helped catalyse processes of re-greening, as in the Maradi Region in Niger in around 1985 by Tony Rinaudo, who worked for an NGO called Serving-In-Mission (Tougiani, Guero and Rinaudo, 2008). Other NGOs as well as an IFAD-funded project have also supported the spreading of farmer-managed re-greening and other best practices in natural resource management by organizing farmer-to-farmer study visits. During these visits, farmers (men and women) with experience in specific re-greening techniques are given an opportunity to discuss these with other farmers working under similar agroecological conditions. For instance, farmers from Burkina Faso have visited the large-scale on-farm re-greening in Mali's Seno Plains, and farmers from the Seno Plains have visited farmers in Burkina's Yatenga

region to learn about soil fertility management practices.

The question is under what conditions can a rapid expansion of farmer-managed re-greening be expected? Based on experiences in Niger and Mali, rapid expansion can be catalysed if the following conditions exist: (i) high population density, because this induces resource users to intensify agriculture; (ii) sandy soils, as these can easily be penetrated by roots; (iii) current low on-farm tree densities; and (iv) enabling policies and legislation. Farmers will be more likely to invest in trees if they are given clear ownership rights to their trees. In 1985, all trees in Niger were owned by the State, but in 2011 the perception of farmers is that they have ownership of their on-farm trees. It is vital that such perceptions are supported by forestry laws.

E. Re-greening in the Horn of Africa

Kenya is the only country in Africa, and possibly in the world, in which the (new) constitution obliges farmers to grow trees on 10 per cent of their land. Relevant ministries are currently discussing how this could be implemented. Many farmers in the fertile highlands already have 10 per cent of their land under trees (*Grevillea robusta*), but this is not the case in Kenya's arid and semi-arid lands. Tree planting in drylands across Africa tends to have a dismal track record, with survival rates usually ranging between only 0 and 20 per cent.[6,7] The protection and management of on-farm natural regeneration in drylands, including in Kenya's drylands, will help increase the number of on-farm trees.

Even casual observers travelling to Tigray (Ethiopia) will be struck by the scale of natural regeneration in parts of this region. It is not easy to find data about the scale of re-greening, but it covers at least one million hectares. Most of the re-greening has occurred in what are usually called enclosures, which are degraded lands set aside for rehabilitation. A number of activities are combined in these enclosures: water harvesting techniques to get more water into the soil, natural regeneration and some enrichment planting, usually with exotic species. For instance, in the valley of Abraha Atsbaha, such activities led to an increase in water levels in the valley, which enabled the digging of several hundred shallow wells. In 2008, even when rainfall was very low and cereal cops failed, many families managed to cope better with drought

An enclosure and natural regeneration in the Tigray region (Ethiopia).

A dense stand of young Combretum glutinosum trees on Mali's Seno Plains annually produces tons of litter per hectare (March 2011).

because they were able to irrigate fruit trees as well as the vegetable gardens around the wells. What has been achieved in parts of Tigray since the early 1990s under adverse conditions is another of those re-greening successes in Africa's drylands that have largely gone unnoticed.

F. A Green Revolution in Africa or another kind of green revolution?

The current thinking about a Green Revolution in Africa involves increasing the use of chemical fertilizers and improved seeds, expansion of irrigation, mechanization and improving market access. However, the costs of chemical fertilizers are high and their use in drylands is not always efficient, as the soil's content of organic matter is low. The challenge is to first increase the organic matter, and the most efficient way of doing so is, in many cases, by increasing the number of on-farm trees. Trees can produce significant quantities of litter which helps maintain or improve soil organic matter content (as illustrated by the picture above). Farmers prune the trees early in the rainy season, which supplies firewood for cooking and reduces competition with crops. Moreover, the trees provide dispersed shade to the crops, which protects them part of the day against the sun. Farmers leave the pruned branches on the land until the leaves are sufficiently dry, after which the branches are collected for firewood, while the leaves are left behind on the land.

Farmers who have managed to increase the soil's content of organic matter would benefit greatly from small doses of inorganic nitrogen (N) fertilizer. Small-scale farmers in Africa (and elsewhere) who have

limited financial resources but want to intensify their agricultural production have one major low-cost option, which is to increase the number of trees. Some drylands in Africa still suffer from the legacy of subsidized mechanization of the 1960s and 1970s, which stimulated the removal of on-farm trees. Even today mechanization and large-scale farms tend to be regarded by many policymakers as the way forward, despite the considerable damage it often does to the soils (as illustrated by the picture below).

A large mechanized commercial farm in Ethiopia's Rift Valley close to the town of Hawass, with a tractor ploughing the land (top right). The land does not have a single tree on it to protect it against the sun and wind. This field loses tons of topsoil every year due to wind and water erosion.

Commentary VI: Genetic Engineering and Biotechnology for Food Security and for Climate Change Mitigation and Adaptation: Potential and Risks

Jack A. Heinemann
Centre for Integrated Research in Biosafety (INBI) and School of Biological Sciences, University of Canterbury, Christchurch, New Zealand[8]

Abstract

World hunger is a multifaceted problem that cannot be solved by technological changes alone.

Industrial agriculture is unsustainable, and technological adjustments based on genetic engineering have not been able to achieve the relevant Millennium Development Goals; instead, they have introduced products that restrict farmer-based innovation, in situ conservation and access to the best locally adapted germplasm.

Alternative agricultural models, such as agroecology, demonstrate potential to reduce poverty, increase food security and reduce agriculture's environmental footprint because they increase agroecosystem resilience, lower external inputs, boost farmers' incomes and are based on technologies that, for the most part, can be understood, implemented and further modified by poor and subsistence farmers.

Global food production is increasing faster than demand (IAASTD, 2009). Aside from price spikes in 2008 and 2010-2012, food prices have been at one hundred year lows (Nellemann et al., 2009). Despite this, billions of people are malnourished and a billion are starving (Hoffmann, 2011; Khan and Hanjra, 2009).

Current agricultural practices, including the harvesting of natural resources such as ocean fisheries, are having enormous and unsustainable environmental impacts (Khan and Hanjra, 2009; Rivera-Ferre, 2008). And increased agricultural production is putting pressure on ever-shrinking ecosystem services (Daily et al., 1998; IAASTD, 2009). These services are needed to maintain the productivity of land as well as fresh and salt water used to produce food (MEA, 2005; Tilman et al., 2002). The unfortunate feedback cycle is that as agriculture expands into ever more marginally productive ecosystems, its impact on climate change grows (Nellemann et al., 2009).

A. Hunger is a choice

The current failures to feed the world are not due to limitations of technology, but to social choices (Heinemann, 2009; IAASTD, 2009; Kiers et al., 2008). Importantly, these choices undermine the availability of balanced diets in areas where hunger and malnutrition are endemic (Nord, 2009).

The cost of food and the environmental cost of food production could be dramatically reduced just by cutting food waste. According to Nellemann et al. (2009: 7), "[D]eveloping alternatives to the use of cereal in animal feed, such as by recycling waste and using fish discards, could sustain the energy demand for the entire projected population growth of over 3 billion people" by 2050. Some of this waste from farm to fork could be reduced by technological advances, as well as by cutting consumer rejection before and after purchase, but mostly it could be overcome by a change in social policy and attitudes, especially among consumers in developed countries who waste up to 10 times the amount of food wasted in developing countries (Gustavsson et al., 2011).

Demand for food alone is not the only cause of agriculture's growing footprint. Many countries, even those experiencing famine, rely on the export of food to generate income (Vandermeer and Pefecto, 2007). In recent decades, large-scale conversions of the agroecosystem in some countries have been correlated with an increase in food insecurity, motivated by the push to produce more export commodities at the expense of foods of higher nutritional value for

Table 2. Changes in food security in Argentina						
Food supply for human consumption (per person/day)	1990– 1992	1995– 1997[a]	2000– 2002[b]	2005– 2007[c]	1990–1992 to 1995–1997 (%)[d]	1995–1997 to 2000–2002 (%)[d]	2000–2002 to 2005–2007 (%)[d]
Dietary energy supply (kcal)	3,010	3,160	3,140	3,000	0.9	-0.1	-0.9
Total protein intake (grams)	95	100	99	94	1	-0.3	-0.9
Animal protein (grams)	61	64	63	62	0.9	-0.5	-0.3
Fat (grams)	106	113	110	108	1.2	-0.4	-0.5

Source: Based on data from FAOSTAT.
Notes: [a] Period of first introduction of commercial GM plants; industry figures report 1.7 million hectares of GM crops were being cultivated in 1996 (ISAAA Brief No. 36).
[b] According to industry figures, during this period, 13.5 million hectares of GM crops were being cultivated (ISAAA Brief No. 36).
[c] According to industry figures, during this period 19.1 million hectares of GM crops were being cultivated (ISAAA Brief No. 37).
[d] Annual rate of change – not total change over the period.

domestic consumption (Pengue, 2005; and table 2 above).

New or improved technologies could help feed the world (Heinemann, 2009; IAASTD, 2009). Before considering which technological approaches are best for reducing the effects of climate change on agriculture and mitigating agriculture's contribution to factors causing climate change (such as greenhouse gases), it will be essential to determine which problems are best solved by technological tools and which can be solved by changes in the socio-economic and socio-political status quo. This will entail considering some painful questions about the causes of the problems. Conspicuously, few are likely to have been caused by a lack of technology (*Nature*, 2010).

B. Choosing among technological paths to pro-poor, climate-resilient agriculture

The right technology delivered in the right way should be able to help reverse agriculture's adverse impact on climate change, and ultimately contribute to food security (Heinemann, 2009; Scialabba, 2007a). Otherwise, proposed technological solutions to these problems will not be sustainable, make their fair contribution to the Millennium Development Goals or help distribute the benefits more equitably among the peoples of the world. As concisely stated by the Director of the International Assessment of Agricultural Knowledge, Science and Technology for Development (IAASTD), "business as usual is not an option".[9] One form of "business as usual" is the highly damaging traditional agricultural practice. Damaging

traditionalist approaches are due more to the neglect of farmers than to farmers preferring to use them. Poor and subsistence farmers are challenged by a lack of adequate extension and community support services that disseminate knowledge, affordable financing and access to markets for the sale of surplus production.

Another form of "business as usual" is the intensive use of external inputs in agriculture, and, especially, support to massive monocultures, both of which are concentrated in developed countries and some rapidly industrializing developing countries. Unlike unsustainable traditional approaches, input-intensive agriculture – loosely referred to as conventional or industrial agriculture – has been promoted by policy decisions. The policies and technologies associated with industrial agriculture involve a shift in innovation resources from public control to the private sector (IAASTD, 2009; Spielman, 2007) as a result of the private sector investing more than the public sector in research and development. Private investment further leverages much of what remains of public investment through government policies that promote co-funding by the private sector, the pursuit of intellectual property (IP) by public sector institutions (e.g. universities and agriculture agencies), and public sector licensing of IP from the private sector (IAASTD, 2009; Vanloqueren and Baret, 2009). Industrial agriculture also receives large public subsidies (direct and indirect) in developed economies, which stifle producers and markets in developing countries and further undermine the ability of poor and subsistence farmers to intensify production and reduce their environmental footprint (Kiers et al., 2008; Spielman,

2007). Furthermore, industrial agriculture has neither produced a sustainable, highly productive agroecosystem nor curbed agriculture's impact on climate change.

Of the many biotechnology options available for testing or implementing, perhaps the one that receives the most attention is genetic engineering (GE) for the production of genetically modified organisms (GMOs) – plants, animals and microbes (IAASTD, 2009). As currently applied, GE has come to symbolize agricultural production systems that make intensive use of external inputs and promote monocultures (Rivera-Ferre, 2008). This is because of the types of commercialized GM products that are the most common (i.e. soybeans, maize, rapeseed and cotton), because of the particularly large agroecosystems that have adopted GM crops, mainly those in Argentina,

Brazil, Canada, Paraguay, the United States and Uruguay (figure 5), and because of the most common commercialized GM traits: herbicide tolerance and insecticide production. Herbicide tolerance, in particular, lends itself to mechanized delivery of an inseparable co-technology, a chemical for weed management. This weed-control strategy requires large tracts of monoculture to avoid herbicide drift onto neighbouring or other agricultural land. Finally, because of the relatively small number of countries that have adopted GM crops and the few companies that have commercialized it, individual country- and company-specific policies and business plans have had an important influence on the adoption of this biotechnology.

That some of the largest agricultural countries in the world have adopted GM versions of a few crops

Figure 5. Degrees of commitment to GM agriculture (estimates for 2007)

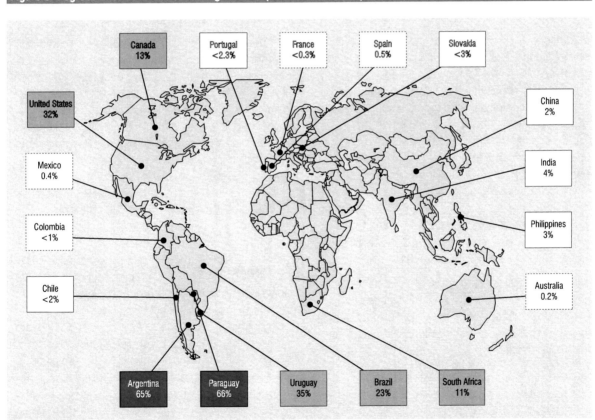

Sources: Reproduced from Heinemann, 2009.

Note: Only two countries in the world have converted the majority of their agricultural systems to GM cropping (black boxes). According to industry figures, Argentina and Paraguay are true "mega countries" of GM crops (James, 2007). The majority of the top 20 GM producing countries commit less than 1–5 per cent of their agricultural production to GM (white boxes with solid lines indicate above 1 per cent). Even the world's largest producer, the United States, commits no more than about a third of its cropping capacity to GM (grey boxes for countries having more than 10 per cent).

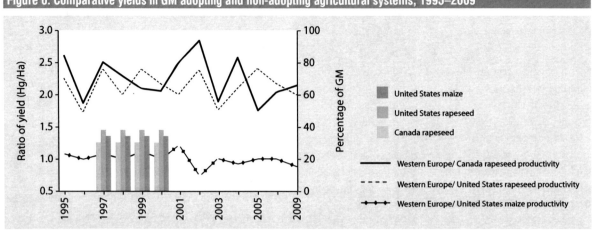

Figure 6. Comparative yields in GM adopting and non-adopting agricultural systems, 1995–2009

Sources: FAOSTAT for ratio of yield; and GMO Compass for percentage of GM maize and rapeseed
(accessed May 2011).

Note: Left axis is the ratio of yield in hectograms (Hg) per hectare (Ha) for two crops, rapeseed (top) and
maize (bottom), and three producers, Western Europe, Canada and the United States. Right axis
represents the proportion of GM by crop type in the North American agricultural systems.

should not be taken as evidence that GE has delivered sustainably and reliably greater yields. Contrasting North American and Western European production of maize and rapeseed is instructive in this regard because they both have high-input, high-production agroecosystems. In Canada, for example, rapeseed (canola), and in the United States, maize, are almost exclusively produced from GM plants. Collectively, Western Europe has shunned the cultivation of GM maize and rapeseed (figure 6). Yet maize yields are very similar in the two agroecosystems, and Western Europe's rapeseed yields are about double those of North America. This trend has not changed since the adoption of GM plants in North America.

Broadly speaking, countries making a substantial shift to GM crops are in a group where food security has either shown no improvement (e.g. United States), or where it is declining (e.g. Argentina). (figure 6; and Heinemann, 2009).

C. How some biotechnologies are failing

Arguably, some GM products have lowered the overall impact of industrial agriculture. For example, the use of glyphosate-based herbicides on GM crops has reduced the need for tilling as a weed control strategy (Pengue, 2005; Service, 2007). Similarly, the use of GM insecticide plants (often called Bt plants), particularly cotton, has reduced the use of external chemical insecticides.

Unfortunately, these benefits are both contested and deterministically unsustainable (Heinemann, 2009). The predictable pattern and quantity of glyphosate herbicide use in GM agriculture has caused the evolution of resistance in weeds on a scale never experienced in the decades of glyphosate use prior to GM crops, leading to a return to tilling and the use of other herbicides for weed control (Gaines et al., 2010; Powles, 2008; Service, 2007). Meanwhile, the unique pattern of use of glyphosate on GM soybeans has reduced *in situ* nitrogen fixation by chelating nickel, a required co-factor for enzymatic activities in the microbial symbionts (Zobiole et al., 2010), and reduced normal iron uptake and storage in soybeans (Bellaloui et al., 2009). Glyphosate on herbicide tolerant plants also reduces root biomass, elongation and lateral root formation (Bott et al., 2008). Systemic distribution of glyphosate throughout the plant is associated with increased susceptibility to colonization by disease-causing fungi (Kremer, Means and Kim, 2005). These effects further reduce the sustainability of GM approaches. Likewise, replacing complementary and diverse pest control practices, such as integrated pest management (Mancini et al., 2008), and the judicious use of natural sources of Bt insecticides, as in organic agriculture, along with the mass planting of GM Bt crops, is causing the appearance of secondary pests (Lu et al., 2010; Zhao, Ho and Azadi, 2011).

Moreover, whatever the comparative benefits of GE may be, they are largely lost when GE/

Figure 7: Food security in GM and non-GM adopting countries in South America compared, 1992–2007 (kcal/person/day)

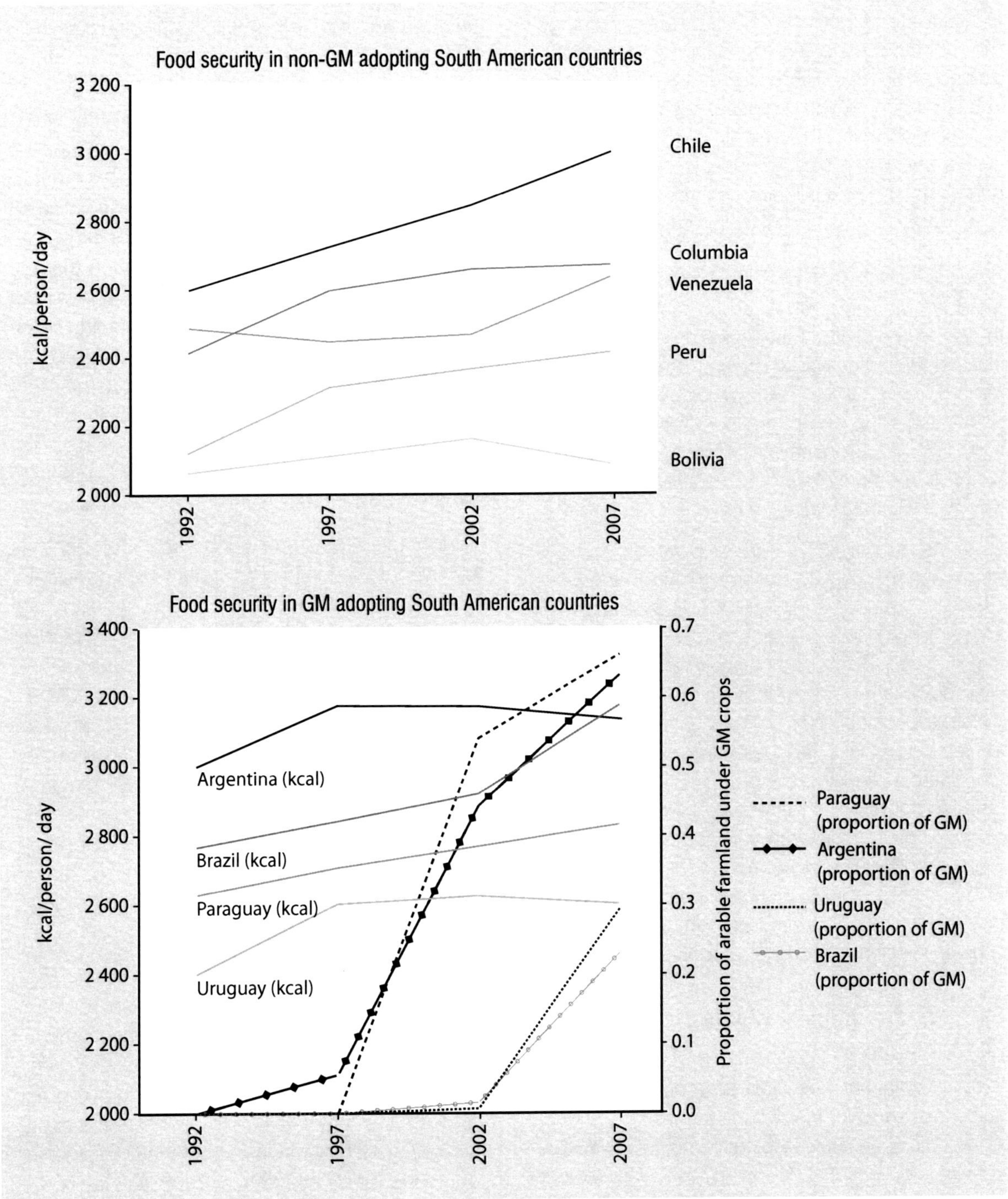

Food security in non-GM adopting South American countries

Chile

Columbia
Venezuela

Peru

Bolivia

Food security in GM adopting South American countries

Argentina (kcal)

Brazil (kcal)

Paraguay (kcal)

Uruguay (kcal)

------ Paraguay
(proportion of GM)

◆ Argentina
(proportion of GM)

.... Uruguay
(proportion of GM)

Brazil
(proportion of GM)

Sources: FAOStat.

Note: A collection of South American countries that have not adopted GM-based agricultural systems show similar improvements in food security (top panel). Countries with varying proportions of GM (right axis, bottom panel) show mixed results. Those with rapid adoption of greater amounts of GM in their agriculture are more prone to increased insecurity levels (measured in kcal, left axis).

industrial agriculture is compared with alternative biotechnologies such as agroecological technologies (Pimentel et al., 2005; Pretty, 2001). Land converted to agriculture from other uses, guided by agroecology, requires time to condition and bring to full potential (Badgley et al., 2007; Pimentel et al., 2005). Once this has been achieved, agroecological approaches have been observed to generate higher yields than industrial agriculture, as shown in several compilations and meta-analyses at country, continental and global levels (Badgley et al., 2007; Uphoff, 2007). Plants grown on agroecological farms are more resilient to stress than those grown by means of industrial agriculture (Lotter, Seidel and Liebhardt, 2003; Pimentel et al., 2005). Agroecological farms require far less fossil-fuel-derived energy and sequester more carbon (Pimentel et al., 2005; Scialabba, 2007b). In addition, the adoption of agroecological approaches contributes to sustainable societies by reducing poverty and improving food security (Scialabba, 2007a; UNEP and UNCTAD, 2008).

After approximately 30 years of commercialization and pre-commercial GE research and development, it has not made a substantial contribution to sustainable agriculture. The IAASTD (2009) was therefore justified in questioning whether GE could deliver on Millennium Development Goals or reduce agriculture's contribution to climate change. However, had the incentives for delivering GM products been different, and the goals of public and private innovation not been so thoroughly intertwined in this biotechnology (Vanloqueren and Baret, 2009), would GE have produced different results? In other words, has GE failed because of policy decisions and its particular history of commercialization, or because the technology itself has been inappropriate?

D. Why some biotechnologies could succeed

Again, comparisons with alternative biotechnologies may be instructive for responding to these questions. The two biotechnologies being contrasted with GE here are conventional breeding, with or without marker-assisted selection, and agroecology. The traits considered are drought tolerance and nutrient enhancement.

1. Drought tolerance

Agriculture makes tremendous demands on groundwater, and water shortages are a global drag on food production. This has driven the search for plants that maintain or improve yield under conditions of water deprivation. Despite many attempts, to date there are no commercially available GM plants with traits that reduce the effects of abiotic stress (Heinemann, 2008). The closest so far is a variety of "drought tolerant" maize, called MON 87460, which is under regulatory consideration in some countries. According to the developer's data, the GM maize had a marginally ($p<0.05$) statistically significant increase in yield in only one of four field tests, which is unconvincing for the general expectation that the variety is higher yielding under stress. The developer claims that "the major component contributing to the improved yield of MON 87460 under water-limited conditions is the increased number of kernels per ear" (Monsanto, 2009: 45), rather than claiming that the variety produces more usable biomass. The developer calls this trait a change in "yield potential", rather than an increase in yield.

Drought tolerance has long been a goal of conventional breeding, and current hybrids already exhibit some tolerance (Monsanto, 2009), with improvements on this baseline expected. According to the World Bank (2007:162), the "International Maize and Wheat Improvement Center (CIMMYT), after more than 30 years of research to produce drought-tolerant maize varieties and hybrids, is now seeing results in eastern and southern Africa. Evaluated against existing hybrids, the new ones yield 20 percent more on average under drought conditions. Similarly, recent evidence points to significant yield gains in breeding wheat for drought and heat-stressed environments."

Agroecological approaches further reduce the need for intensive breeding or GE to produce drought-tolerant varieties. Increasing the organic matter in soil, using cover crops and interspersing fallow years significantly increases latent soil moisture, making agroecological farms far more resilient to drought-related stress (Heinemann, 2008). Water percolating through the soils in agroecological test plots has been reported to be between 15 per cent and more than 30 per cent higher than in conventional plots under drought conditions, and has demonstrated commensurate increases in yields compared with matched conventional management (Lotter, Seidel and Liebhardt, 2003; Pimentel et al., 2005; Scialabba, 2007a).

2. Nutrient enhancement

Micronutrient deficiencies contribute significantly to malnutrition (Scialabba, 2007a), which is why developing plants that are enriched with micronutrients has been a long-term goal. It is therefore particularly unfortunate that the largest group of commercialized GM plants, those tolerant to glyphosate herbicides, are also less able to take up some important micronutrients from the soil (Bellaloui et al., 2009; Bott et al., 2008). Importantly, spray drift at non-lethal concentrations has a similar effect on non-GM crops (Bellaloui et al., 2009). Because glyphosate can be used multiple times during the growing season on herbicide tolerant GM plants, non-GM crops are now routinely exposed to spray drift.

Attention has been drawn to the development of GM rice that produces ß-carotene, which can be converted by humans to vitamin A (Heinemann, 2009; Schubert, 2008). However, high micronutrient varieties are not unique to GE; for instance, maize lines that produce nearly four times the amount of ß-carotene (8.57 μg g^{-1}) of second generation GM rice varieties (2.6 μg g^{-1}) have been developed through conventional breeding (Yan et al., 2010). This is mentioned not to disparage the technical achievement of introducing the biosynthetic pathway for ß-carotene into rice, but to emphasize the importance of protecting crop genetic diversity and its ongoing potential to be tapped for use in balanced diets (Zamir, 2008).

Combined studies have found that balanced diets are more accessible to poor and subsistence farmers using agroecological rather than industrial farming approaches. This is because of the use of multicropping and the integration of livestock rearing, and the higher micronutrient content of the plants they grow, and because these farmers tend to earn more, which allows them to purchase other foods (Scialabba, 2007a; UNEP and UNCTAD, 2008).

Proponents of ß-carotene-enriched GM rice argue that safety regulations have been the primary hindrance to the transfer of this product to poor and subsistence farmers in societies that suffer from significant vitamin A deficiency (Dubock, 2009). However, malnutrition is caused by the lack of a balanced diet rather than the lack of access to GM crops. Moreover, these commentators neglect to take into account the estimated 70 patents and 32 patent holders that had to agree to the use of their intellectual property prior to release of the GM rice (Graff et al., 2003; Spielman,

2007; WHO, 2005). These protracted negotiations were recently resolved with an agreement that exempted specified countries from having to pay royalty fees for growing this variety of GM rice provided that the rice was not exported (GRO, online). Given the difficulties in containing transgenes, including those in rice (Vermij, 2006), this humanitarian licence may transfer liability for gene flow and potential patent infringement to the farmer and the adopting country (Heinemann, 2007). Non-GM varieties and agroecological technologies are usually protected by less restrictive IP instruments, and as process innovations are not prone to accidental and unavoidable escape in the way that seeds and pollen are, this liability would not be incurred through their use.

E. Conclusions

Technological solutions are rarely sustainable if they do not rectify the cause of the problem. Regardless of the ability of industrial agriculture to produce food surpluses in previous decades (Rivera-Ferre, 2008), future technologies must produce sustainable solutions and be useful to those who are now malnourished. As stated by Uphoff (2007: 218), "The most direct way to reduce poverty is to raise the productivity of those factors of production controlled by the poor: first of all, their labor, but also their knowledge and skills, and for many though not all, small areas of land. Increased factor productivity of land, labor, capital and water can have second-order benefits for the poor, urban as well as rural, by lowering the price of food and other things on which the poor spend most of their meager incomes." The export of the industrial model of agriculture and its associated GE-based technologies that are embedded in particularly exclusionary IP instruments, such as patents, to food-poor countries shows little promise of addressing the needs of the hungry poor (IAASTD, 2009; Pray and Naseem, 2007; WHO, 2005; World Bank, 2007).

Fortunately, other technologies show promise, both for increasing yield in yield-limited agroecosystems and for promoting what the present system has not been able to achieve, namely sustainable societies in poor countries (Rivera-Ferre, 2009; UNEP and UNCTAD, 2008). This is obtained when technologies reduce external inputs and on-farm costs of seeds, incorporate multicropping and livestock for balanced diets, promote ongoing farmer innovation under an appropriate IP rights framework, and are produced by a public sector that offers the appropriate incentives (Heinemann, 2009; Vanloqueren and Baret, 2009).

Climate change has been rapid, but not unpredictable; indeed, its occurrence has often been predicted even if the message has been resisted for decades. Likewise, a familiar message for decades has been that agriculture is making unsustainable demands on ecosystem resources worldwide, and is contributing to climate change. One of the most important lessons to be learnt before deciding on a technological pathway to reduce agriculture's appetite for resources and its footprint on the climate is that early warning of deleterious but avoidable outcomes need to be taken seriously, rather than ignored as in the past. If we allow the same voices to be drowned out again, we will fail to protect those who will suffer the most from climate change and its damaging effects on agricultural production.

References

Abedi M and Badragheh A (2011). Importance of indigenous knowledge in rural areas. *Life Science Journal,* 8: 445–450.

Anderson A (2007). Shifting cultivation and deforestation: Experiences from Eastern Nigeria, *World Development,* 24 (11): 1713–1729.

Asaah EK, Tchoundjeu Z, Leakey RRB, Takousting B, Njong J and Edang I (2011). Trees, agroforestry and multifunctional agriculture in Cameroon. *International Journal of Agricultural Sustainability,* 9: 110–119.

Badgley C, Moghtader J, Quintero E, Zakem E, Chappell MJ, Avilés-Vázquez K, Samulon A and Perfecto I (2007). Organic agriculture and the global food supply. Renewable Agriculture and Food Systems, 22: 86–108.

Bakr R (2000). Cassava drying. Ibadan, Cassava Information Centre.

Ballantyne P (2009). Accessing, sharing and communicating agricultural information for development: Emerging trends and issues. *Information Development* , 25(4): 260–271.

Bellaloui N, Reddy KN, Zablotowicz RM, Abbas HK and Abel CA (2009). Effects of glyphosate application on seed iron and root ferric (III) reductase in soybean cultivars. Journal of Agricultural and Food Chemistry, 57: 9569–9574.

Botoni E and Reij C (2009). Silent transformation of environment and production systems in the Sahel: Impacts of public and private investments in natural resource management. Ouagadougou, CILSS and Free University Amsterdam.

Bott S, Tesfamariam T, Candan H, Cakmak I, Römheld V and Neumann G (2008). Glyphosate-induced impairment of plant growth and micronutrient status in glyphosate-resistant soybean (Glycine max L.). Plant and Soil, 312: 185–194.

Brown JD (2004). Knowledge, uncertainty and physical geography: Towards the development of methodologies for questioning belief. *Transactions of the Institute of British Geographers*, 29: 367–381.

Buresh RJ and Cooper PJM (1999). The science and practice of short-term fallows. *Agroforestry Systems,* 47:1–358.

CARE (2004). Review of farmer perspectives and assessment of smallholder forestry systems in relation to reforestation in Central Africa. New York, World Food Programme.

Carpenter PB (2006). *Economic and Ecological Analysis of Environmental Impacts in sub-Saharan Africa.* London, Earthscan Publications Ltd.

CAWMA (2007). *Water for Food: Water for Life*: *A Comprehensive Assessment of Water Management in Agriculture* (Molden D, ed.). London, Earthscan.

CFS-HLPE (2011). *Price Volatility and Food Security*: tables 4, 5 and 6. Available at: http://www.fao.org/fileadmin/user_ upload/hlpe/hlpe_documents/HLPE-price-volatility-and-food-security-report-July-2011.pdf.

Christoplos I (2010). Mobilizing the potential of rural and agricutural extension. Rome and Lindau, FAO and Global Forum for Rural Advisory Services.

Clough Y, Barkmann J, Juhrbandt J, Kessler M, Wanger TC, Anshary A, Buchori D, Cicuzza D, Darras K, Putram DD, Erasmi S, Pitopang R, Schmidt C, Schulze CH, Seidel D, Steffan-Dewenter I, Stenchly K, Vidal S, Weist M, Wielgoss AC and Tscharntke T (2011). Combining high biodiversity with high yields in tropical agroforests. *Proceedings of the National Academy of Sciences,* 108: 8311–8316.

Cooper PJ, Leakey RRB, Rao MR and Reynolds L (1996). Agroforestry and the mitigation of land degradation in the humid and sub-humid tropics of Africa. *Experimental Agriculture*, 32: 235–290.

Cooper PJM, Dimes J, Rao KPC, Shapiro B, Shiferaw B and Twomlo S (2008). Coping better with current climatic variability in the rain-fed farming systems of sub-Saharan Africa: An essential first step in adapting to future climate change? *Agriculture, Ecosystems and Environment*, 126: 24–35.

Daily G, Dasgupta P, Bolin B, Crosson P, du Guerny J, Ehrlich P, Folke C, Jansson AM, Jansson B-O, Kautsky N, Kinzig A, Levin S, Mäler K-G, Pinstrup-Andersen P, Siniscalco D and Walker B (1998). Food production, population growth, and the environment. Science, 281: 1291–1292.

Davis K (2008). Extension in sub-Saharan Africa: Overview and assessment of past and current models and future prospects. *Journal of International Agricultural and Extension Education*, 15(3): 15–28.

Davis K, Nkonya E, Kato E, Mekonnen DA, Odendo M, Miiro R, and Nkuba J (2012). Impact of farmer field schools on agricultural productivity and poverty in East Africa. *World Development*, 40(2): 402-413.

Devaux A, Horton D, Velasco C, Thiele G, Lopez G, Bernet T, Reinoso I and Ordinola M (2009). Collective action for market chain innovation in the Andes. *Food Policy,* 34(1): 31–38.

Devaux A, Andrade-Piedra J, Horton D, Ordinola M, Thiele G, Thomann A and Velasco C (2010). Brokering innovation for sustainable development: The Papa Andina case. ILAC Working Paper 12, Institutional Learning and Change Initiative, Rome.

Diamond J (1997). *Guns, Germs and Steel: The Fates of Human Societies*. London, WW Norton & Co.

Disatsagae S (2007). Traditional food security systems in Southern African rural households. Mafikeng, South Africa, Indigenous Knowledge Systems Programme, North-West University. (Unpublished).

Dubock A (2009). Crop conundrum. Nutrition Reviews, 67: 17–20.

Flora CB (1992). Reconstructing agriculture: The case for local knowledge. *Rural Sociology,* 57(1): 92– 97.

Friis-Hansen E and Duveskog D (2012). The empowerment route to well-being: An analysis of farmer field schools in East Africa. *World Development,* 40(2): 414-427.

Gaines TA, Zhang W, Wang D, Bukun B, Chisholm ST, Shaner DL, Nissen SJ, Patzoldt WL, Tranel PJ, Culpepper AS, Grey TL, Webster TM, Vencill WK, Sammons RD, Jiang J, Preston C, Leach JE and Westra P (2010). Gene amplification confers glyphosate resistance in Amaranthus palmeri. Proceedings of the National Academies of Science, 107: 1029–1034.

GFRAS (Global Forum for Rural Advisory Services) (2011). Guide to extension evaluation. Lindau.

Gilchrist G, Mallory M and Merkel F (2005). Can local ecological knowledge contribute to wildlife management? Case studies of migratory birds. *Ecology and Society,* 20: 1–12.

Glaeser B (1990). *The Green Revolution Revisited: Critique and Alternatives*. London, Allen & Unwin.

Graff GD, Cullen SE, Bradford KJ, Zilberman D and Bennett AB (2003). The public–private structure of intellectual property ownership in agricultural biotechnology. Nature Biotechnology, 21: 989–995.

GRO online (posting date). Intellectual property-related issues. Available at: http://www.goldenrice.org/Content2-How/how9_IP.html.

Gustavsson J, Cederberg C, Sonesson U, van Otterdijk R and Meybeck A (2011). Global Food Losses and Food Waste: Extent, Causes and Prevention. Rome, FAO.

Hassan R, Scholes R and Ash N, eds. (2005). *Ecosystems and Human Well-Being, Vol 1: Current State and Trends*. Washington DC, Island Press, for Millennium Ecosystem Assessment.

Heinemann JA (2007). A typology of the effects of (trans)gene flow on the conservation and sustainable use of genetic resources. Bsp35r1. Rome, FAO.

Heinemann JA (2008). Desert grain. The Ecologist, 38: 22–24.

Heinemann JA (2009). Hope not Hype. The future of agriculture guided by the International Assessment of Agricultural Knowledge, Science and Technology for Development. Penang, Third World Network.

Hoffmann U (2011). *Assuring Food Security in Developing Countries under the Challenges of Climate Change: Key Trade and Development Issues of a Fundamental Transformation of Agriculture*. UNCTAD Discussion paper 201, UNCTAD/OSG/DP/2011/1, Geneva. Available at: http://www.unctad.org/en/Docs/osgdp20111_en.pdf.

IAASTD (2009). Agriculture at a Crossroads. International Assessment of Agricultural Knowledge, Science and Technology for Development. Global report. Washington, DC. Available at: www.agassessment.org/.

IFPRI (2011). Press release on keynote lecture by Dr Mark Rosegrant to Ag Economic Forum, St Louis, MO, 23 May.

IPCC (2007). *Climate Change 2007: The Physical Science Basis. Contribution of Working Group I to the Fourth Assessment Report of the Intergovernmental Panel on Climate Change*. Cambridge, Cambridge University Press.

James C (2007). Executive summary of the global status of commercialized biotech/GM crops. ISAAA Brief No.37. Manila, Nairobi and New York, International Service for the Acquisition of Agri-biotech Applications. Available at: http://www.isaaa.org/.

Jamnadass R, Dawson IK, Anegbeh P, Asaah E, Atangana A, Cordeiro NJ, Hendrickx H, Henneh S, Kadu CAC, Kattah C, Misbah M, Muchugi A, Munjuga M, Mwaura L, Ndangalasi HJ, Sirito Njau C, Nyame SK, Ofori D, Peprah T, Russell J, Rutatina F, Sawe C, Schmidt L, Tchoundjeu Z and Simons AJ (2010). *Allanblackia*, a new tree crop in

Africa for the global food industry: Market development, smallholder cultivation and biodiversity management. *Forests, Trees and Livelihoods,* 19: 251–268.

Kawesa B (2001). *The Status of Postharvest Technologies in Africa.* Dar es Salaam, IDS, University of Dar es Salaam. (Unpublished).

Kazinga AO (2002). African farmers' knowledge and relation to science. In: Lori A, ed. *Farmer First: Farmer Innovation and Agricultural Research.* New York, ITP Publications: 57–86.

Khan S and Hanjra MA (2009). Footprints of water and energy inputs in food production: Global perspectives. Food Policy, 34: 130–140.

Khan ZR, Hassanali A, Overholt W, Khamis TM, Hooper AM, Pickett JA, Wadhams LJ and Woodcock CM (2002). Control of witchweed *Striga hermonthica* by intercropping with Desmodium spp. and the mechanism defined as allelopathic. *Journal of Chemical Ecology,* 28: 1871–1885.

Khan ZR, Midega CAO, Hassanali A, Pickett JA, Wadhams LJ and Wanjoya A (2006). Management of witchweed, *Striga hermonthica*, and stemborers in sorghum, *Sorghum bicolor*, through intercropping with greenleaf desmodium, *Desmodium intortum. International Journal of Pest Management,* 52: 297–302.

Kiers ET, Leakey RRB, Izac A-M, Heinemann JA, Rosenthal E, Nathan D and Jiggins J (2008). Agriculture at a crossroads. Science, 320: 320–321.

Kiplang'at JN and Rotich DC (2008). Mapping and auditing of agricultural indigenous knowledge in Uasin Gishu and Keiyo Districts in Rift Valley Province, Kenya. Paper presented at the World Conference on Agricultural Information, Tokyo University of Agriculture, Tokyo, 24–27 August 2008.

Kithuka J, Mutemi J and Mohamed AH (2007). Keeping up with technology: The use of mobile telephony in delivering community-based decentralised animal health services in Mwingi and Kitui districts, Kenya. FARM-Africa Working Paper 10. London, FARM-Africa.

Klerkx L, Hall A and Leeuwis C (2009). Strengthening agricultural innovation capacity: Are innovation brokers the answer? *International Journal of Agricultural Resources, Governance and Ecology,* 8(5/6): 409–438.

Kremer RJ, Means NE and Kim S (2005). Glyphosate affects soybean root exudation and rhizosphere micro-organisms. International Journal of Environmental Analytical Chemistry, 85: 1165–1174.

Lagi M, Bar-Yam Y, Bertrand KZ and Bar-Yam Y (2011). The food crisis: A quantitative model of food prices, including speculators and ethanol conversion. Cambridge MA, New England Complex Systems Institute. Available at: http://necsi.edu/research/social/food_prices.pdf, September.

Leakey RRB (2004). Physiology of vegetative reproduction. In: Burley J, Evans J and Youngquist JA, eds. *Encyclopaedia of Forest Sciences.* London, Academic Press: 1655–1668.

Leakey RRB (2010). Agroforestry: a delivery mechanism for multi-functional agriculture. In: Kellimore, LR ed. *Handbook on Agroforestry: Management Practices and Environmental Impact.* Environmental Science, Engineering and Technology Series, U461-471. Hauppauge, NY, Nova Science Publishers: 1655–1668.

Leakey RRB (2011). Participatory domestication of indigenous fruit and nut trees: New crops for sustainable agriculture in developing countries. In: *Biodiversity in Agriculture: Domestication, Evolution and Sustainability.* Cambridge, Cambridge University Press.

Leakey RRB and Akinnifesi FK (2008). Towards a domestication strategy for indigenous fruit trees in the tropics. In: Akinnifesi FK, Leakey RRB, Ajayi OC, Sileshi G, Tchoundjeu Z, Matakala P and Kwesiga F, eds. *Indigenous Fruit Trees in the Tropics: Domestication, Utilization and Commercialization.* Wallingford, CAB International: 28–49.

Leakey RRB and Asaah EK (forthcoming). Underutilised species as the backbone of multifunctional agriculture – The next wave of crop domestication. *Acta Horticulturae.*

Leakey RRB and Tchoundjeu Z (2001). Diversification of tree crops: Domestication of companion crops for poverty reduction and environmental services, *Experimental Agriculture,* 37: 279–296.

Leakey RRB, Cornelius JP, Page T, Tchoundjeu Z, Weber JC and Jamnadass R (2012). Tree domestication in agroforestry: Progress in the second decade. In: Nair PK and Garrity D, eds. *Agroforestry – The Way Forward.* Dordrecht, Netherlands, Springer.

Leakey RRB, Schreckenberg K and Tchoundjeu Z (2003). The participatory domestication of West African indigenous fruits. *International Forestry Review,* 5: 338–347.

Leakey RRB, Tchoundjeu Z, Schreckenberg K, Shackleton S and Shackleton C (2005). Agroforestry tree products (AFTPs): Targeting poverty reduction and enhanced livelihoods. *International Journal of Agricultural Sustainability,* 3:1–23.

Lombard C and Leakey RRB (2010). Protecting the rights of farmers and communities while securing long term market access for producers of non-timber forest products: Experience in Southern Africa. *Forests, Trees and Livelihoods,* 19: 235–249.

Lotter DW, Seidel R and Liebhardt W (2003). The performance of organic and conventional cropping systems in an extreme climate year. American Journal of Alternative Agriculture, 18: 1–9.

Lu Y, Wu K, Jiang Y, Xia B, Li P, Feng H, Wyckhuys KAG and Guo Y (2010). Mirid bug outbreaks in multiple crops correlated with wide-scale adoption of Bt cotton in China. Science, 328: 1151–1154.

Luseno WK, McPeak JG, Barrett CB, Little PD and Gebru G (2003). Assessing the value of climate forecast information for pastoralists: Evidence from southern Ethiopia and northern Kenya. *World Development,* 31: 1477–1494.

Mancini F, Termorshuizen AJ, Jiggins JLS and van Bruggen AHC (2008). Increasing the environmental and social sustainability of cotton farming through farmer education in Andhra Pradesh, India. Agricultural Systems, 96: 16–25.

Marchal J-Y (1985). La déroute d'un système vivrier au Burkina: agriculture extensive et baisse de production. *Etudes Rurales,* 99/100: 265–277.

Matike E (2008). *Indigenous cassava postharvest technologies in eastern Zambia.* MA dissertation (unpublished), Department of Sociology, North-West University, Mafikeng, South Africa.

MEA (2005). Ecosystems and human well-being: Synthesis. In: Millennium Ecosystem Assessment. Washington, DC, Island Press: 137.

Mganga KZ, Nyangito MM, Musimba NKR, Nyariki DM, Mwangombe AW, Ekaya WN, Muiru WM, Clavel D, Francis J, Kaufmann R and Verhagen J (2010). The challenges of rehabilitating denuded patches of a semi-arid environment in Kenya. *African Journal of Environmental Science and Technology,* 7: 430–436.

Michon G and de Foresta H (1999). Agro-forests: Incorporating a forest vision in agroforestry. In: Buck LE, Lassoie JP and Fernandez ECM, eds. *Agroforestry in Sustainable Agricultural Systems.* New York, CRC Press and Lewis Publishers: 381–406.

Monsanto (2009). Petition for the determination of non-regulated status for MON 87460 07-CR-191U.

Nature (2010). Editorial: How to feed a hungry world. Nature, 466: 531–532.

Nellemann C, MacDevette M, Manders T, Eickhout B, Svihus B, Prins AG and Kaltenborn BP (2009). The Environmental Food Crisis: The Environmment's Role in Averting Future Food Crises. Nairobi, United Nations Environment Programme.

Nord M (2009). Food insecurity less prevalent in Canada than in the United States. Amber Waves, Washington, DC, United States Department of Agriculture.

Nyong A, Adesina F and Osman Elasha B (2007). The value of indigenous knowledge in climate change mitigation and adaptation strategies in the African Sahel. *Mitigation and Adaptation Strategies to Global Change,* 12: 787–797.

Ogallo L (2010). The marriage of science and rainmakers among the Luhya (Kenya). Agriculture and Environment: Food Security. Available at: www.scidev.net/en/agriculture-and-environment/tropical-cyclones-1/features/the-marriage-of-science-and-rainmakers.html.

Orlove B, Roncoli C, Kabugo M and Majugu A (2010). Indigenous climate knowledge in southern Uganda: The multiple components of a dynamic regional system. *Climate Change,* 100: 243–265.

Otte J and Chilonda P (2003). Classification of cattle and small ruminant production systems in sub-Saharan Africa. *Outlook on Agriculture,* 32: 183–190.

Panik F (1998). The use of biodiversity and implications for industrial production. In: Leihner DE and Mitschein TA, eds. *A Third Millennium for Humanity? The Search for Paths of Sustainable Development.* Frankfurt, Peter Lang: 59–73.

Peacock C and Sherman DM (2010). Sustainable goat production: Some global perspectives. *Small Ruminant Research,* 89: 70–80.

Pengue WA (2005). Transgenic crops in Argentina: the ecological and social debt. Bulletin of Science, Technology & Society, 25: 314–322.

Phephe S (2000). The indigenous goat breeds of Southern Africa. Mafikeng, South Africa. North-West University. (Unpublished).

Pimentel D, Hepperly P, Hanson J, Douds D and Seidel R (2005). Environmental, energetic, and economic comparisons of organic and conventional farming systems. BioScience, 55: 573–582.

Pitso SF (2008). Use of indigenous knowledge in natural disaster management among the Batswana. MA dissertation (unpublished), Department of Sociology, North-West University, Mafikeng, South Africa.

Powles SB (2008). Evolved glyphosate-resistant weeds around the world: Lessons to be learnt. Pest Management Science, 64: 360–365.

Pray CE and Naseem A (2007). Supplying crop biotechnology to the poor: Opportunities and constraints. Journal of Development Studies, 43: 192–217.

Pretty J (2001). The rapid emergence of genetic modification in world agriculture: Contested risks and benefits. Environmental Conservation, 28: 248–262.

Raynaut C (1987). L'agriculture nigérienne et la crise au Sahel. Politique africaine, 27: 97–107.

Reij C, Tappan G and Belemviré A (2005). Changing land management practices and vegetation in the Central Plateau of Burkina Faso (1968–2002). Journal of Arid Environments, 63(3): 642–659.

Reij C, Tappan G and Smale M (2009). Agricultural transformation in the Sahel: Another kind of "Green Revolution". IFPRI Discussion Paper no. 00914. Available at: www.ifpri.org/millionsfed.

Rivera W and Sulaiman RV (2009). Extension: Object of reform, engine for innovation. Outlook on Agriculture, 38(3): 267–273.

Rivera-Ferre MG (2008). The future of agriculture. EMBO Reports, 9: 1061–1066.

Rivera-Ferre MG (2009). Response. EMBO Reports, 10: 105–107.

Roncoli C, Kirshen P, Ingram K and Flitcroft I (2000). Opportunities and constraints to using seasonal precipitation forecasting to improve agricultural production systems and livelihood security in the Sahel-Sudan Region: A case study of Burkina Faso. CFAR—Phase 1, IRI Forum on Climate Predictions, Agriculture and Development, 26 – 28 April 2000, New York.

Royal Society (2009). Reaping the Benefits: Science and the Sustainable Intensification of Global Agriculture. London.

Rundgren G (2012). Garden Earth: From hunter and gatherer to capitalism – and thereafter (forthcoming book, translation from original version published by Gidlunds in Swedish April 2010).

Samuel P (2000). The efficacy of rotational farming in Central Africa: Cases from the Congo and Cameroon. Kinshasa, University of Kinshasa. (Unpublished).

Schroth G, da Fonseca GAB, Harvey CA, Gascon C, Vasconelos HL and Izac A-MN (eds.) (2004). Agroforestry and Biodiversity Conservation in Tropical Landscapes. Washington DC, Island Press.

Schubert D (2008). The problem with nutritionally enhanced plants. Journal of Medicinal Food, 11: 601-605.

Scialabba N E-H (2007a). Organic Agriculture and Food Security. Rome, FAO.

Scialabba N E-H (2007b). Organic agriculture and food security in Africa. In: Nærstad A, ed. Africa Can Feed Itself. Oslo AiT AS e-dit: 214–228.

Sefa P (2004). Indigenous Knowledge in Global Contexts. Toronto, University of Toronto Press.

Service RF (2007). A growing threat down on the farm. Science, 316: 1114–1117.

Speranza CI, Kiteme B, Ambenje P, Wiesmann U and Makali S (2009). Indigenous knowledge related to climate variability and change: Insights from droughts in semi-arid areas of former Makueni District, Kenya. Climate Change, 100: 295–315.

Spielman DJ (2007). Pro-poor agricultural biotechnology: Can the international research system deliver the goods? Food Policy, 32: 189–204.

Stern N (2007). The Economics of Climate Change – The Stern Review. Cambridge, Cambridge University Press. Available at: http://webarchive.nationalarchives.gov.uk/ and http://www.hm-treasury.gov.uk/sternreview_index.htm.

Tchoundjeu Z, Asaah E, Anegbeh PO, Degrande A, Mbile P, Facheux C, Tsobeng A, Atangana AR and Ngo-Mpeck ML (2006). Putting participatory domestication into practice in West and Central Africa. *Forests, Trees and Livelihoods,* 16: 53–70.

Tchoundjeu Z, Degrande A, Leakey RRB, Simons AJ, Nimino G, Kemajou E, Asaah E, Facheux C, Mbile P, Mbosso C, Sado T and Tsobeng A (2010). Impact of participatory tree domestication on farmer livelihoods in West and Central Africa. *Forests, Trees and Livelihoods,* 19: 219–234.

Thiele G, Devaux A, Reinoso I, Pico F, Montesdeoca F, Pumisaco M, Velasco C, Flores P, Esprella R, Thomann A and Manrique K (2009). Multi-stakeholder platforms for innovation and coordination market chains. Quito, International Potato Centre. (Unpublished working paper.)

Thomas DSG, Twyman C, Osbahr H and Hewitson B (2007). Adaptation to climate change and variability: Farmer responses to intra-seasonal precipitation trends in South Africa. *Climatic Change,* 83: 301–322.

Tilman D, Cassman KG, Matson PA, Naylor R and Polasky S (2002). Agricultural sustainability and intensive production practices. Nature, 418: 671–677.

Tougiani A, Guero C and Rinaudo T (2008). Community mobilisation for improved livelihoods through tree crop management in Niger. *GeoJournal* Volume 74, Number 5, 377-389. Available at: www.springerlink.com/content/y2p64655317v14q6/.

UN-DESA (2011). *World Economic and Social Survey 2011: The Great Green Technological Tranformation.* E/2011/50/Rev. 1, ST/ESA/333, United Nations, New York. Available at: http://www.un.org/en/development/desa/policy/wess/wess_current/2011wess.pdf.

UNDP (1999). *Conserving Indigenous Knowledge: Integrating New Systems of Integration.* New York.

UNEP (2007). *Global Environmental Outlook 4: Past, Present and Future Perspectives.* Nairobi.

UNEP (2011). Agriculture. In: UNEP, Towards a Green Economy: Pathways to Sustainable Development and Poverty Eradication - A Synthesis for Policy Makers. Available at: http://www.unep.org/greeneconomy/Portals/88/documents/ger/GER_2_Agriculture.pdf.

UNEP and UNCTAD (2008). Organic Agriculture and Food Security in Africa, UNCTAD/DITC/TED/2007/15. UNEP-UNCTAD Capacity-building Task Force on Trade, Environment and Development, Geneva.

Uphoff N (2007). Agroecological alternatives: Capitalising on existing genetic potentials. Journal of Development Studies, 43: 218–236.

van Mele P (2008). Multiple approaches to enhance communication between rice farmers, rural service providers and scientists. *Outlooks on Pest Management,* 19 (6): 260-263.

van Mele P, Wanvoeke J and Zossou E (2010). Enhancing rural learning, linkages, and institutions: The rice videos in Africa. *Development in Practice,* 20(3): 414–421.

Vandermeer J and Perfecto I (2007). The agricultural matrix and a future paradigm for conservation. Conservation Biology, 21: 274–277.

Vanloqueren G and Baret PV (2009). How agricultural research systems shape a technological regime that develops genetic engineering but locks out agroecological innovations. Research Policy, 38: 971–983.

Vermij P (2006). Liberty Link rice raises specter of tightened regulations. Nature Biotechnology, 24: 1301–1302.

Waters-Bayer A and Gebre-Michael Y (2007). Trees are our backbone: Integrating environment and local development in Tigray Region of Ethiopia. IIED Issues Paper no. 145. London, International Institute for Environment and Development.

Werner P (2000). Indigenous knowledge for development: A framework for action. Maseru, Centre for Resource and Environmental Studies, National University of Lesotho.

WHO (2001). Achieving household food and nutrition security in societies in transition. Geneva.

WHO (2005). Modern food biotechnology, human health and development: An evidence-based study. Geneva.

World Bank (2006). Enhancing agricultural innovation: How to go beyond the strenghthening of research systems. Washington, DC.

World Bank (2007). World Development Report 2008: Agriculture for Development. Washington, DC.

Yan J, Kandianis CB, Harjes CE, Bai L, Kim E-H, Yang X-M, Skinner DJ, Fu Z, Mitchell S, Li Q, Fernandez MGS, Zaharieva M, Babu R, Fu Y, Palacios N, Li J, DellaPenna D, Brutnell T, Buckler ES, Warburton ML and Rocheford T (2010). Rare genetic variation at Zea mays crtRB1 increases [beta]-carotene in maize grain. Nature Genetics, 42: 322–327.

Yorobe Jr, JM, Rejesus RM and Hammig MD (2011). Insecticide use impacts of integrated pest management (IPM) farmer field schools: Evidence from onion farmers in the Philippines. *Agricultural Systems,* 104 (7): 580–587.

Zamir D (2008). Plant breeders go back to nature. Nature Genetics, 40: 269–270.

Zarb J (2011). Small holding up: Sustainable farming industry overview. *Ecologist*, 1(3): 4.

Zhao JH, Ho P and Azadi H (2011). Benefits of Bt cotton counterbalanced by secondary pests? Perceptions of ecological change in China. Environmental monitoring and assessment, 173: 985–994.

Ziervogel G and Downing TE (2004). Stakeholder networks: Improving seasonal climate forecasts. *Climate Change,* 65: 73–101.

Zobiole LHS, Oliveira RS Jr, Kremer RJ, Constantin J, Yamada T, Castro C, Oliveira FA, and Oliveira A Jr. (2010). Effect of glyphosate on symbiotic N2 fixation F. A. and nickel concentration in glyphosate-resistant soybeans. Applied Soil Ecology, 44: 176–180.

Notes

1   As aptly stated by Rundgren (2012), "How we discuss 'efficiency' or 'productivity' and 'technology' has strong biases, clearly visible in agriculture, where the systems that waste most, pollute most and use much external energy are those that are considered 'modern', 'efficient' and 'productive'. The function of technology to put other peoples' resources in the service of the already wealthy, and to constantly increase the gap is obscured by our myths about 'progress'".

2   *Sustainable or green agriculture* refers to the increasing use of farming practices and technologies that simultaneously: (i) restore, maintain and increase farm productivity and profitability while ensuring the provision of food on a sustainable basis, (ii) reduce negative externalities and gradually lead to positive ones, and (iii) rebuild ecological resources, i.e. soil, water, air and biodiversity ("natural capital" assets) by reducing pollution and using resources more efficiently. Green agriculture is exemplified by a diverse, locally adaptable set of agricultural techniques, practices and market branding certifications. Examples of these include organic agriculture and agroecology (referred to preferentially in this article as an approach to agriculture based on the principles and science of ecology, for meeting people's need for food which gives equal attention to the goals of sustainability, resilience and equity – and not only to production – which represents more accurately the transition goals to multifunctional agriculture) (modified from UNEP, 2011). The principles underlying sustainable or "green farming practices and technologies" include: (i) restoring and enhancing soil fertility through the increased use of naturally and sustainably produced nutrient inputs, diversified crop rotations, and livestock and crop integration; (ii) reducing soil erosion and improving the efficiency of water use by applying minimum tillage, and cover crop cultivation techniques; (iii) reducing the use of chemical pesticides and herbicides by implementing integrated biological pest and weed management practices; and (iv) reducing food spoilage and loss by improving post-harvest storage and processing facilities (modified from UNEP, 2011).

3   The authors thank Egerton University (Njoro, Kenya), the Kenya Agricultural Research Institute (Nairobi, Kenya), the Institute of Animal Production in the Tropics and Subtropics (Section of Animal Breeding and Husbandry) and the Food Security Center, Hohenheim University (Stuttgart, Germany) for providing facilities to undertake the study that formed the basis for this commentary. This paper was written when one of the authors was a Visiting Professor at Hohenheim University.

4   For an example of Mali's Seno Plain, see ARI update 2011 no.4 at: www.africa-regreening.blogspot.com.

5   The lower on-farm tree densities in northern Nigeria may be due to differences in tree ownership.

6   Personal communication with foresters across the Sahel.

7   This makes it hard to explain why governments and donor agencies, at least until recently, stubbornly continued to support and promote tree planting. It is more rational to promote natural regeneration and to plant only those tree species that do not regenerate spontaneously, but which resource users would like to have on their fields.

8   The author wishes to thank Jason Tylianakis, Giles-Eric Séralini and Brigitta Kurenbach for comments on earlier drafts of this paper.

9   See: www.agassessment.org/docs/NAE_press_release_final.doc.

Chapter 4

The Role of Changes in Land Use

Lead Article: KEY IMPLICATIONS OF LAND CONVERSIONS IN AGRICULTURE

Hans Hurni, Thomas Breu, Peter Messerli and Brigitte Portner,
Centre for Development and Environment, University of Bern[1]

Abstract

Land conversions in agriculture are important for food security in developing countries at the present time, and are likely to increase even more in the future.

- In relation to overall land use, land conversions take place (a) within agricultural land, from meadows or pastures to cropland and to land for producing animal feed or biofuel feedstock; and (b) to agricultural land from other land use types, such as from forests, drylands and wetland areas. The dynamics of these processes are estimated to be in the range of 0.2 to 0.3 per cent of the global land area, suggesting that 26–39 million hectares of land are converted annually.

- The effects of land conversions on small-scale farming can be both positive and negative. Farmers convert new land for improving their livelihoods, but they are negatively affected by land degradation and the intrusion of built-up areas into agricultural land. Strategies should focus on medium- to low-potential areas in support of small-scale farmers and pastoralists to help them sustainably increase their agricultural production.

- Land conversion to biofuel feedstock production can provide a moderate additional income, although farmers are likely to be negatively affected by associated land losses. On a global level, however, efforts to achieve economies of scale, density and more intensive production of biofuel feedstock, along with other land deals, may threaten food security. Today's policy incentives disproportionately favour large-scale biofuel feedstock production, mostly for export markets. Innovative arrangements are needed to ensure that land conversions to biofuel feedstock production are made in a responsible manner, and that small-scale farming, including mixed-crop livestock and pastoral systems, can be integrated into global agriculture.

- Land prices and speculation are likely to increase once land is converted to more economically integrated modes of production, while subsistence-oriented, small-scale farming will remain unattractive and thus will further lose out against more powerful actors if national and international policies do not implement counter-strategies.

- Overall, the impacts of land conversions on climate are likely to be negative. While small-scale farming and livestock rearing are often climate neutral, deforestation remains extremely harmful, the large-scale rearing of ruminant livestock has negative impacts on greenhouse gases, and so far little is known about the overall impacts of biofuel feedstock production on climate.

A. Introduction

Land cover and land use are constantly changing, *both* within and outside the agricultural sector (table 1). Table 1 shows that only a few of the globally dominant land use and cover systems are stable in terms of their land area. A larger number of systems are expanding (italics) at the expense of others that are decreasing (bold).

Agricultural expansion into forest lands is the most threatening global change process. Deforestation is likely to continue in the near future. All non-protected forest areas are threatened by over-extraction of timber, deforestation, and land-use conversions to forest plantations, grazing land, or cropland. This process is estimated to already contribute about 11 per cent to global greenhouse gas (GHG) emissions – a considerable amount that could be avoided. All agricultural activities, together, account for another 15 per cent of GHG emissions, amounting to an estimated total of 26 per cent of GHGs (IPCC, 2007). More recently, croplands for biofuel production have also started to expand into forest lands and woodlands, while land leases and sales to transnational corporations are a further major cause of this expansion.

Agricultural expansion into dryland areas is a process often driven by the spread of small-scale farming into less suitable cultivation areas. At the same time, biofuel production continues to spread into non-agricultural drylands (e.g. savannah, bush, shrub and scrublands). Here too, transnational land leases and sales are significant, although they represent a recent trend (ILC, 2011).

Land-use changes on agricultural land, however, must also be considered, as their implications may be as great as the expansion of agriculture into areas devoted to other types of land use and land cover. Conversions may take place on agricultural land, for example from intensive pasture land to cropland. Additional cropland is created mainly as a result of population pressure, but also for industrialized farming, such as large-scale farms or tree plantations in recently deforested areas.

Since 2005, about 0.5 per cent of the global land surface has been converted from cropland and dryland for food and feed to cropland for biofuel production (i.e. biodiesel, ethanol). Here again, transnational land leases and sales, although not yet important in quantitative terms, are nevertheless an indicator of current and future trends. However, biofuel production and land leases still account for a relatively small proportion of cultivated land compared with that being used for the production of animal feed (e.g. maize, cereals and soybeans). About 40 per cent of global cereal production is used for animal feed. Together with pasturing, three quarters of all agricultural land is thus being used to generate animal products (e.g. milk, meat and eggs), while only one quarter is used for producing non-meat and non-dairy products, such as cereals, vegetables, tuber crops and other plants.

Table 1: Global land use and cover types, and major spatial changes (percentage and million hectares)

Land use and/or cover	Share (%)	Surface (millions of ha)	Changes in land use
1. Agricultural land	26	3,380	One third of the land is degraded
Cropland	*11*	*1,430*	*Gains from forests and meadows*
Intensive pastures	**7**	**910**	**Loss to cropland and animal feed**
Animal feed production	*4*	*520*	*Gains from cropland and pastures*
Agroforestry	2.5	325	Mostly stable land-use system
Badlands	*1*	*130*	*Slight increase from cropland and pastures*
Biofuel production	*0.5*	*65*	*Gains from forests and pasture land*
2. Forest land	**30**	**3,900**	**Largest spatial area losses observed**
Degraded forests	**14**	**1,820**	**Most converted land use type (partly grazed)**
Dense forests	**12**	**1,560**	**Most threatened land cover type**
Protected forests	4	520	Stable forest areas
3. Dryland	35	4,550	Largest protected areas realized
Deserts and tundra	21	2,730	Stable land cover (partly grazed)
Protected drylands	**10**	**1,300**	**Losses to biofuel and land conversions (partly grazed)**
Shrublands (grazed)	**4**	**520**	**Threatened by climate change and land losses to biofuels and other conversions**
4. Built-up areas	*5*	*650*	*Rapid urban expansion into agricultural lands and drylands*
5. Wet areas	**4**	**520**	**Water surfaces and wetlands**
Global land surface	100	13,000	Global land area (excl. Greenland and Antarctica)

Source: Based on FAOSTAT (2006), with authors' estimates for sub-categories and breakdowns.
Note: Bold fonts indicate general losses of a particular type, normal fonts indicate stable situations, and italics indicate general gains in surface area.

Part of the general gain in cultivated land is converted to grazing land, some of which has turned into badlands due to extreme land degradation and soil depletion. The pressure being exerted on croplands has increased not only for the production of human food and animal feed, but also for the production of fibre (e.g. cotton, sisal) and, more recently, biofuels (feedstock, tree plantations, biodiesel and ethanol).

Last but not least, another extremely important spatial trend is urban expansion into agricultural and dryland areas. On a global level, an estimated 5 per cent of the land surface is currently being used for urban and infrastructure construction. This trend is continuing unabated, as it closely correlates with economic growth (i.e. growth of gross domestic product (GDP)). For example, in Germany the share of built-up areas has reached 10 per cent of the total land area (Hurni et al., 1996).

The main questions that emerge from table 1 in relation to land conversions in agriculture are:

• What is the magnitude of land conversions in relation to overall land use?
• What are the effects on small-scale farming and on food security, both locally and globally?
• What are the implications for land prices resulting from speculation and land grabbing?
• What are the implications for climate change?

In the following sections, this article discusses three important processes in greater detail: the recent emergence of biofuels; the consequences of changing consumption patterns and animal production systems; and the impacts of land conversions on small-scale farming. These activities currently employ over 2.6 billion people, or 40 per cent of the world population, involving women, men and children (von Braun, 2005). No other sector in the global economy employs a comparable number of persons.

B. Land conversions for biofuel production

Importance of biofuel production. There has always been a close link between agriculture and energy, as land that is being worked requires energy inputs, while agriculture can also produce energy as an output. Traditionally, agro-energy is produced in the form of fuelwood, charcoal and animal dung. These forms are still widely used in developing countries and continue to be the most important energy source, not only for the 2.6 billion people engaged in small-scale farming (IEA, 2006), but also for most people living in towns. At the same time, the potential for liquid biofuel production is greatest on cropland in the global South, where land and labour are available at lower costs than in the global North (Hazell and Pachauri, 2007; Fargione et al., 2008; Smeets et al., 2007).

Current production and use of liquid biofuels, which are now competing for land with agricultural commodities such as food, takes place mainly in industrialized and emerging economies, but production is also on the rise in developing countries (SOFA, 2008; HLPE, 2011a). Only about 0.5 per cent of the global land surface is being used to produce liquid biofuels (see table 1). Ethanol is produced mainly in Brazil, Canada, China, France and the United States. Germany leads in biodiesel production, followed by Brazil, Argentina, France and the United States (REN21, 2011: 5). Biodiesel exporters in developing countries are rare, with only Malaysia and Thailand expected to become significant players in the near future, besides Brazil and Argentina. The major feedstock used for ethanol is maize and sugarcane, while for biodiesel it is oil palm and soybean (OECD and FAO, 2011).

Brazil, the European Union (EU) and the United States are the main users of liquid biofuels, while China and India are emerging users (IEA, 2010a). Most biofuel is used for road transport, and a limited amount is used in the marine transport sector and, most recently, in aviation. The share of biofuels contributing to global final energy consumption is still low, at 0.6 per cent in 2009, but production is increasing rapidly. In 2010, about 86 billion litres of ethanol and at least 19 billion litres of biodiesel were produced. Ethanol production grew fivefold between 2000 and 2010, and biodiesel increased more than twentyfold (REN21, 2011).

Today, biofuels provide about 2.7 per cent of the fuel used in global transportation. This share is expected to rise to between 4 and 9.3 per cent in 2030 and up to 20 per cent in 2050 (REN21, 2011; IEA, 2009; IEA, 2010b). Global ethanol and biodiesel production are projected to increase over the next decade to 155 billion litres and 42 billion litres, respectively, and projected use is expected to be greater than projected production in the EU and the United States (OECD and FAO, 2011). At 7 per cent, the volume of biofuels in current international trade is rather small (IEA, 2009), but as projected demand and use will not be at the same locations, this share will also increase, as will pressure on land, biofuel feedstock and other sources of energy from biomass. At the same time, demand for alternative forms of energy production is also expected to increase (Cotula, Finnegan and Macqueen, 2011).

Current trends. A number of policies in both developed and developing countries support the massive increase in biofuel production, based on motivations such as climate change mitigation, increasing energy security and furthering rural development. These policies, which include tax exemptions, blending and consumption mandates, and subsidies, are believed to be the main drivers of the global production of biofuels (FAO-OECD, 2009; DEFRA, 2010; HLPE 2011a). For example, overall government support for biofuels amounted to $13–15 billion in OECD countries in 2007 (Steenblik, 2007). This was more than total aid commitments to agriculture and to sectors related to food security, which amounted to approximately $12 billion in 2007–2008 (OECD-DAC, 2010). In 2009, government support for biofuels in the United States and the EU alone amounted to $8 billion (IEA, 2010a).

At present, direct government support to the biofuel sector is declining, while development and commercial banks, pension funds and private equity funds are investing larger sums (REN21, 2011; OI, 2011; van Gelder and German, 2011). At the same time, alliances between governments and multinational business lobbies have promoted biofuel development in both developed and developing countries (Franco et al., 2010), leading to the emergence of many players seeking to produce and invest in biofuel production.

The investment landscape in agriculture and biofuel production today is very diverse. Direct players such as traditional agricultural companies aiming to produce crops on the land have been complemented by indirect players working on the global stock exchanges who treat land as a speculative commodity (HLPE, 2011b). Investors are foreign, domestic or from the diaspora, but their importance varies globally: in Brazil, for example, sugarcane production is predominantly financed by domestic entrepreneurs and the government, while in the United Republic of Tanzania, domestic banks play an important role (van Gelder and German, 2011).

In 2006, approximately 1 per cent of global arable land (i.e. approximately 14 million hectares) was used for biofuel crops (IEA, 2006). Lambin and Meyfroidt (2011) estimate that in 2007 approximately 25 million hectares were already being used for such crops, and they project an annual increase of 1.5 to 3.9 million hectares based on the current policy environment, with land requirements for such crops in 2030 amounting to 44 to118 million hectares. The IEA (2010b) estimates of 20 per cent of land for those crops in 2050, would translate into between 100 and 650 million hectares (Murphy et al., 2011). If produced on cropland only, this would amount to 7–45 per cent of that land-use category, which would severely threaten food production. The current land conversion level to crop production for biofuels is estimated to be less than 0.5 per cent of the global land area (less than 65 million ha, as indicated in table 1).

Most land conversions for biofuel production are believed to be taking place at the expense of forests and pastures (Melillo et al., 2009; Fischer et al., 2009; Havlik et al., 2010; Lambin and Meyfroidt, 2011). Studies of the palm oil industry in South Asia, for example, show that from 1990 to 2005 close to 60 per cent of oil palm expansion was at the expense of forests, with strong negative impacts on biodiversity and carbon stocks (Koh and Wilcove, 2008; Koh et al., 2011). The magnitude of land acquisitions and conversions for biofuel production is extremely difficult to assess as there is a lack of information on the locations of biofuel crop plantations and biofuel feedstock origins. The fact that many crops used for biofuels, such as maize or oil palm, can have multiple uses, further complicates attempts to estimate the extent of biofuel production. Furthermore, the magnitude of indirect changes adds to the problem, as it is often difficult to establish direct causality, and the initial purpose of land conversions might not always be clear (Chalmers et al., 2011; Gao et al., 2011; Gawel and Ludwig, 2011).[2]

Impacts on carbon. Direct land-use changes seem to have a relatively small impact on carbon emissions, whereas indirect land-use changes could create a large carbon debt (Fargione et al., 2008; Melillo et al., 2009; Lapola et al., 2010; Bowyer, 2010). Nitrous oxide emissions from increased use of fertilizers will contribute more to global warming than such carbon losses (Melillo et al., 2009). Zah et al. (2007) studied environmental costs from field to tank and found that although most biofuel sources reduce GHGs by more than 20 per cent compared with conventional fuel, the major ones, such as United States corn, Brazilian sugarcane and Malaysian palm oil, have greater aggregate environmental costs than fossil fuel.

Negative impacts on natural resources. Biofuels are either competitive or cause additional land degradation. Besides soil and land, among the most contested resources is water, as the cultivation of some biofuel feedstock such as sugarcane leads to increased water withdrawals and to social and environmental problems from field to watershed, particularly where water is already scarce (de Fraiture, Giordano and Yongsong Liao, 2008; UNEP, 2011b). Additionally, fertilizer and pesticide use in cultivation, inappropriate farming practices, and untreated water from processing plants can lead to land degradation and increased risks for local populations (German et al., 2010).

Much of the land promoted for large-scale biofuel production is declared as "marginal" or "unused", but it is frequently used as common land by villagers or pastoralists. Increased investment could provide opportunities for local livelihoods and national economies (Vermeulen and Cotula, 2010), but it may also result in dispossession of land, restricted access to natural resources and conflicts among resource users (see, for example, Sulle and Nelson, 2009; Burgers et al., 2011; Findlater and Kandlikar, 2011).

Impacts on land prices. Initial fears that increased investment may result in higher land prices (FAO, 2008) have been replaced by evidence that much of the land is obtained at prices below its actual value (OI, 2011). Investors acquire vast areas of land in many developing countries because it is given almost for free (Li, 2011). Land deals often lack transparency, and where local people are involved in biofuel production, employment contracts are often vague (OI, 2011; Cotula, 2011).

Impacts on food markets. Recent growth in biofuel production and processing was the major driver of the food price hike in 2008 (SOFA, 2008; HLPE, 2011a). Increased competition for, and restricted access to, natural resources, as well higher and volatile food prices can lead to reductions in calorie intake and to increased levels of malnutrition. Moreover, they disproportionately affect the most vulnerable groups (Rosegrant et al., 2008). To counteract growing food insecurity due to biofuel production, a recent HLPE report (2011a) and the FAO-OECD Expert Meeting on Greening the Economy with Agriculture, held in

September 2011 (FAO-OECD, 2011), among others, called upon the Committee on World Food Security to "demand of governments the abolition of blending targets for biofuels and the removal of subsidies and tariffs on biofuel production and processing."

Policymakers have promoted biofuels as a means to foster rural development based on the expectation that their production will involve the participation of smallholders in outgrower schemes and create employment. This strategy seems to be successful where an already established biofuel industry exists, although much depends on policies, local authorities and smallholder cooperatives (German et al., 2010; Rist, Feintrenie and Levant, 2010). In emerging biofuel industries, however, smallholders do not benefit; rather, they bear much of the risk of an unsettled industry (Vermeulen, Sulle and Fauveaud, 2009; German et al., 2010).

In the current economic context, establishing biofuel production is competitive where economies of scale are realized, and this is usually the case where large-scale plantations are combined with industrial processing. But large-scale production means that small-scale producers may be excluded, so that instead of creating employment opportunities, labour is saved (Li, 2011) and inequities increase. Therefore the question is whether it is feasible to promote innovative business models that would bridge large-scale and small-scale production through policy instruments aimed at steering this development in order to achieve economies of scale, particularly for feedstock processing, and creating market access for smallholders (Dufey, 2007; Arndt et al., 2009; Malik et al., 2009; Vermeulen, Sulle and Fauveaud, 2009; Gmünder and Portner, 2010).

There is a consensus that the provision of energy from agriculture is needed in many places to meet demand, particularly in the rural South. Processed forms of bioenergy such as biofuels can be an opportunity, but this energy should not be produced at the expense of food, the environment or the poor, which is mostly the case when produced on large-scale plantations that produce feedstock for export instead of for local consumption. While many countries have policies in place to steer development, they still lack enforcement (Schoneveld et al., 2011).

There is considerable uncertainty about how present law or voluntary certification schemes, such as the

Roundtable on Sustainable Biofuels (RSB, 2011), could be effectively implemented. Governments urgently need to remove mandatory targets and biofuel subsidies that stimulate large-scale biofuel feedstock production. They should also ensure that much-needed investments in agriculture are made in a responsible way, that smallholders have rights to secure access to land and natural resources, and, where they are involved in large-scale energy-agribusiness, they should be offered decent working conditions.

C. Land conversion for livestock production

Livestock production and animal source food have played a critical role in human development (Randolph et al., 2007) and have regained prominence in the recent debate on the food crisis. According to estimates by the FAO (2006a), the livestock sector accounts for 40 per cent of agricultural GDP and (partially) employs 1.3 billion people. The sector is of particular importance to the economy in developing countries, where it contributes up to 80 per cent of agricultural GDP and serves as a major source of livelihood for about 600 million rural poor (CGIAR, 2005). Besides its economic importance to agriculture in general, livestock are a major asset, particularly in pastoral and agropastoral systems (FAO, 2009a), fulfilling various functions in rural households and communities. In addition to being an important source of food and income, livestock offer considerable

potential for reducing the vulnerability of their owners and expanding livelihood opportunities (Randolph et al., 2007).

It is estimated by CGIAR (2005) that currently two thirds of the world's domestic animals, such as ruminants, are kept in developing countries, where over 90 per cent are owned by rural smallholders. By 2007, the production of meat and eggs in developing countries had surpassed that in developed countries, and the production gap for milk was almost closed (FAO, 2009a). The world's livestock population experienced an unprecedented overall increase of 53.7 per cent between 1980 and 2009 for the four major animal categories of cattle, sheep and goats, pigs, and chicken. In 2009, total stocks in these categories amounted to almost 23 billion animals: 1.38 billion cattle (6 per cent), 1.96 billion sheep and goats (8.6 per cent), 942 million pigs (4.1 per cent), and 18.63 billion chicken (81.3 per cent). As table 2 shows, the increase in livestock has been most pronounced in Africa and Asia, whereas the statistics show declining livestock holdings in Europe and a moderate increase in America and Oceania.

The trend of increasing livestock populations worldwide seems to be continuing, in line with an expected doubling of meat consumption by 2050 compared with the present rate of consumption (Nardone et al., 2010). This will result in annual global meat production of 465 million tons and a milk output of 1,043 million tons (FAO, 2006a). However,

Table 2: Growth of livestock and shares of different livestock, by region, 1980–2009 (per cent)

	America	Asia	Africa	Europe	Oceania	World
Increase in cattle	23.2	24.4	59.6	-49.7	10.5	13.4
Increase in sheep and goats	-15.7	64.8	81.9	-47.8	-47.0	25.2
Increase in pigs	4.9	46.9	170.2	-24.5	20.7	18.0
Increase chickens	138.1	343.7	168.6	-12.2	106.9	158.2
Share of cattle, 2009	36.9	31.3	20.0	9.1	2.8	100.0
Share of sheep and goats, 2009	6.7	49.9	30.3	7.6	5.6	100.0
Share of pigs, 2009	17.0	59.6	2.9	19.9	0.6	100.0
Share of chicken, 2009	27.7	53.3	8.0	10.4	0.6	100.0
Total share of livestock	26.0	51.9	10.4	10.4	1.2	100.0
Total increase	37.6	120.0	120.1	-33.5	22.8	53.7
Increase in human population, 1980–2005	41.5	49.6	88.7	5.5	46.0	46.1

Source: FAOSTAT, 2011.

it is expected that growth rates of meat production will decrease, whereas those of milk will continue to rise rapidly, as increased demand for dairy products in developing countries appears to be continuing unabated (FAO, 2006a).

As a result of increasing demand for livestock products and the rapid growth in livestock production, livestock systems have experienced profound changes (IAASTD, 2008). However, not all livestock systems have been equally affected and challenged by changing conditions and risks from the effects of climate change that can affect the food system (Godfray et al., 2010). Industrial livestock systems are on the rise worldwide and are indispensable for meeting the global demand for livestock products. These intensive systems are, however, being increasingly confronted with environmental restrictions and rising feed prices (Seré et al., 2008). Mixed crop-livestock systems where crops and animals are integrated on the same farm (IAASTD, 2008) will continue to be critical to future food security, as a large proportion of the global population depends on these systems for its livelihood (Thornton et al., 2009). It is expected that farmers in these systems will further diversify and intensify their production in the face of the challenges posed by increasing competition for land and rising costs of inputs as well as access to services (Seré et al., 2008). Pastoral systems are confronted with different developments and resulting adaptation requirements. On the one hand, in suitable areas, improvements in pastures and adapted management systems could increase the economic viability of livestock rearing. However, on the other hand, pastoral systems will also have to cope with the growing encroachment of crop production (Seré et al., 2008), accelerating pasture degradation, and increasingly difficult access to feed and water resources (Thornton, 2010).

Drivers of change in the livestock sector. It is commonly assumed that the major drivers of the observed increase in production and consumption of livestock products are related to the growing global population and to dietary changes as a result of rising incomes among a considerable proportion of the world's population (Nellemann et al., 2009; FAO, 2006a). However, population growth is only one of many factors, and, arguably, not the most prominent (table 2). A study by FAO (2009a) showed a positive correlation between increased incomes and livestock consumption in countries with lower incomes, but

a less positive, or even a negative, correlation for countries with higher GDP per capita. Besides the important role of income levels, urbanization plays a considerable role in boosting consumption of meat and milk products as a result of people adding variety to their diet (Delgado, 2003). Dietary trends can be summarized in terms of decreasing intake of fruit and vegetables and increasing intake of meat, sugar, salt and pre-cooked and convenience foods (Popkin, 1998; WHO/FAO, 2003 cited in IAASTD, 2008). Socio-cultural factors, such as traditions and religious beliefs, also have a major influence on the consumption of livestock products, while natural endowment having a direct impact on production potential. One example of socio-cultural differentiation is South Asia, where meat consumption is lower than expectations based on income levels (FAO, 2009a). Further drivers of livestock production that affect consumption and prices are related to the development of markets and to improvements in transport and trade (Hawkes, 2006).

Between 1980 and 2007, meat production in developed countries increased by only 24.3 per cent, whereas it almost quadrupled in developing countries. It was mainly the East and South Asian countries, China and Brazil that accounted for this increase. China showed the biggest growth in meat production during this period (652 per cent) and today accounts for almost 50 per cent of the meat produced in developing countries, or 31 per cent of the total world production (FAO, 2009a). India, on the other hand, showed impressive growth of milk production, accounting for 15 per cent of the world's milk supply, but it remains a rather small producer of meat in relation to its size and population (FAO, 2009a).

Annual meat consumption per capita worldwide is projected to increase sharply, by 29 per cent from 2000 – from 37.4 kg to over 52 kg in 2050 (FAO, 2006b). According to Bouwman et al. (2005) and Bruinsma (2003), the greatest increase in meat consumption is expected to occur in developing countries (42 per cent) and transition economies (33 per cent). In industrialized countries, a moderate increase of 14 per cent (representing an annual meat consumption of roughly 100 kg per person) is forecast. Given that the conversion rate of plant to animal matter is only about 10 per cent (Godfray et al., 2010), a further increase in meat consumption will necessarily alter the ratio of food and feed production and will have major implications for the prices of staple foods and land conversions.

Livestock production and land conversion. It is estimated that about 26 per cent of the global land area is used for livestock grazing, mainly as pastoral systems and to a much lesser extent as mixed crop-livestock systems (Delgado et al., 1999; FAO, 2006a). Unlike industrial livestock production systems, these systems do not rely on external inputs of fertilizers, pesticides, irrigation and feed. Fodder production is often absent in extensive pastoral systems, or is limited to shorter periods of complementary feeding (e.g. winter fodder) or to feed products derived from decentralized and non-industrialized food processing.

In order to feed the current global livestock population, about 40 per cent of total arable land is used for feed-crop production. FAO (2006a) estimates that "livestock production accounts for 70% of all agricultural land and 30% of the land surface of the planet". Despite the overall strong increase in the livestock population, between 1980 and 2009 the area under pasture worldwide increased by only by 2 per cent, while the area under crops increased by 66 per cent (FAOStat, 2011). The world forest area declined between 1990 and 2010 by 3.3 per cent, or by almost 138 million ha (World Bank, 2011) – larger than the area of Peru. These figures imply that the absolute land area and the share of arable land used for feed production and grazing are still growing at the expense of forest lands. The FAO (2006b) reports that grazing land is a key driver of deforestation, particularly in the Amazon Basin, where 70 per cent of the cleared forests is used as pasture and for feed crops. Although most of the world's feed-crop production still takes place in OECD countries, in the recent past it has been observed that different developing countries in South America (FAO, 2009a), but increasingly in Africa as well, are rapidly expanding their production of feed crops, notably maize and soybean.

Based on the development scenarios in FAO's report, *World Agriculture: Towards 2015/2030*, Bruinsma (2003) and Wirsenius, Azar and Berndes (2010) calculate an increase of 280 million ha in the total agricultural area by 2030, or 5 per cent more than today. Lambin and Meyfroidt (2011) present a high estimate for an increase in the area under permanent pasture of 151 million ha by 2030, which would be in line with most land use models that project an increase

of about 10 per cent for the period 2010–2050. In the event that grazing systems are not expanded but livestock production is intensified to meet the anticipated demand for livestock products, cropland for animal feed production would have to increase by 115 million ha (Lambin and Meyfroidt, 2011).

The observed growth in global livestock demand and how it translates in the future into allocated land area will largely depend on international investments in agricultural land, particularly in developing and transition economies (HLPE, 2011b). According to data for 2011 from the International Land Coalition (ILC), 9 per cent of registered large-scale land acquisitions were related to grazing grounds or animal feed production. The ILC estimates the total arable land and pasture area used or allocated to international land investors for livestock to be 55 million ha. Investments directly related to livestock production are thus a very prominent driver of large-scale land acquisitions, given that about 203 million ha of land worldwide are estimated to have been leased or sold or are under negotiation in the period between 2000 and 2010 (Anseeuw et al., 2012).

Livestock production and environmental implications. Today, more than half of the earth's land surface is used for agriculture, and estimates suggest that 40 per cent of this is moderately degraded, while another 9 per cent is highly degraded, resulting in a global reduction in crop yield of 13 per cent (Breu et al., 2011; Oldeman, 1994; Wood, Sebastian and Scherr, 2000). In addition, it is estimated that about 20 per cent, or 680 million ha of the world's grazing land, and 73 per cent of rangelands located in dryland areas have been degraded as result of overgrazing since 1945 (Delgado et al., 1999). Overgrazing is a function of grazing and recovery time, the number of grazing animals and natural resource buffering capacity. The effects of overgrazing include a reduction in soil cover, compaction leading to reduced water infiltration, and water- and wind-induced soil erosion. At the same time, overgrazing can alter the composition of the vegetation, with palatable perennial species being replaced by less palatable plants due to their reduced ability to compete (Liniger et al., 2010). Drylands and mountain areas are particularly affected by such overgrazing, as in many cases livestock is the main asset of the people living in these often marginal areas (FAO, 2006b; Delgado et al., 1999). Reduction of overgrazing and better pasture productivity can be achieved by institutional and regulatory measures relating to access and use of commonly pooled resources, by better pasture management practices, and by improving livestock quality and productivity. Besides challenges related to overgrazing, the livestock sector and the different segments of the production chain also have a considerable effect on water use, water quality and hydrology, and ecosystems. Estimates by the FAO (2006a) indicate that activities related to the livestock sector account for more than 8 per cent of global water use, while feed production accounts for another 7 per cent.

Besides its direct effects on the natural resource base, the livestock sector is a major factor contributing to climate change. It is estimated that livestock-related activities are responsible for 18 per cent of the world's GHG emissions or about 80 per cent of the overall emissions from agricultural activities (Steinfeld et al., 2010). Greenhouse gases in the livestock sector arise either directly (through enteric fermentation and manure) or indirectly, and along the food chain (land-use change, feed production, processing and transport). Livestock rearing is responsible for 9 per cent of carbon dioxide (CO_2) emissions, which are released when forests and other natural vegetation are replaced by pasture and feed crops. Steinfeld et al. (2010) estimate that 34 per cent of livestock-related carbon emissions are due to deforestation, 25 per cent are from enteric fermentation and 25.9 per cent from manure. A similar amount of CO_2 is released by the on-farm use of fossil fuel, by the manufacturing of chemical fertilizers, by transport and by livestock product processing. The livestock sector is also responsible for emissions of other GHGs, including 37 per cent of human-induced methane (which has 23 times the global warming potential (GWP) of CO_2), 65 per cent of anthropogenic nitrous oxide (with 296 times the GWP of CO_2) and 64 per cent of ammonia, which is a major cause of acid rain (FAO, 2006a; FAO, 2009a; Steinfeld et al., 2010).

Implications for the development of the livestock sector. The livestock sector plays an important role in global economic development and in the livelihoods of about 2.6 billion persons directly involved in the agricultural sector. In particular, the sector, in combination with other agricultural activities, provides opportunities for poverty reduction and greater food security for the growing world population. However, rapid changes in this fast-growing sector also substantially risk

marginalizing smallholders and their multifunctional agricultural systems, thereby affecting the food security of the world's poor, particularly in developing and transition economies. A second area of concern relates to the risk of livestock-induced environmental degradation impeding ecosystem services. Third, uncontrolled further development of livestock poses a major threat to human health, given that zoonotic diseases transmitted between animals and humans account for 60 per cent of all human pathogens.

In order for the livestock sector to address the above challenges and contribute to global development, it must become an integral part of global agriculture, meeting social, ecological and economic requirements simultaneously. To achieve this, all three livestock production systems below will have to be carefully adapted and further developed. The key to such a development is for investments in the livestock sector to be made not only (1) in industrial production systems but also (2) in mixed livestock crop systems and (3) in pastoral systems. Economically viable and socially acceptable investments will need to address increased productivity, environmental concerns, and the competing land resource demands of crop and livestock production systems. To achieve this, enabling institutional and policy frameworks and cooperation at different levels are needed. In order to make livestock systems a part of sustainable agriculture international cooperation will be necessary, as well as coordinated action at the regional and local levels to achieve changes in the way livestock products are produced and consumed. This transformation will demand action from all actors in livestock and agriculture systems, including producers, investors, procurers, decision-makers, researchers and not least of all, from consumers (for more information, see the lead article of Idel and Reichert in chapter 2 of this Review).

D. Conversions due to small-scale farming and rural poverty

In the coming decades, global agriculture faces three major challenges: (i) producing approximately 70 per cent more food for a projected population of 9 billion people by 2050 (FAO, 2009b), (ii) dealing with a variety of increasing risks and shocks, including climate change and commodity price volatility, and (iii) ensuring and enhancing the provision of ecosystem services such as climate change mitigation and water regulation. These challenges most prominently concern small-scale farming, which provides a livelihood for about 2.6 billion people living mostly in low-income countries of the global South (von Braun, 2005). These women, men and children account for about 99 per cent of the global agricultural population and currently cultivate approximately 50 per cent of the world's agricultural land, providing an estimated 25 per cent of global cereal production (table 3) and about half of total food production (IAASTD, 2008).

Changing agricultural practices have enabled world grain harvests to double in the past four decades, largely due to production gains resulting from Green Revolution technologies, including high-yielding cultivars, chemical fertilizers and pesticides, mechanization and irrigation (Foley et al., 2005). Yet the majority of small-scale farming continues to be characterized by low labour productivity, and low to moderate land productivity. Sub-Saharan Africa and Latin America have experienced the least agricultural development, but may have the largest potential for improvement in the coming decades.

Small-scale farming involves growing crops to be used at least in part by individual households. Such farming is a significant source of livelihood, and some of the crops are sold in local or national markets

(Lininger, 2011). Farming systems have evolved through adaptation to various natural conditions. Some systems focus on cropping, others on livestock rearing, and still others on a combination of both. In Africa and Asia, average farm size is 1.7 ha, and grain yields may vary from 0.5 to 1.5 tons per hectare in a low-potential, manual, traditional and small-scale system. Farms in developing countries are tending to become smaller, while farms in middle- to high-income countries are becoming larger (von Braun, 2005).

Of the 1.4 billion people living in extreme poverty (defined as those living on less than $1.25/day) in 2005, approximately 1 billion (i.e. around 70 per cent) lived in rural areas (IFAD, 2011). Significant progress in poverty alleviation has been achieved in East Asia, where today the incidence of rural poverty (based on the $1.25/day line) is around 15 per cent. In South Asia and sub-Saharan Africa, 45–60 per cent of the population still suffers from extreme poverty, while 80–90 per cent of the rural population lives on less than $2/day (IFAD, 2011). Thus, small-scale farming and rural poverty are intrinsically linked.

While there are households that live in persistent poverty, relatively large proportions of people continuously move in and out of poverty, sometimes in

Table 3: Assessment of small-scale versus large-scale farming at the global level			
	Total	**Small-scale (metabolic)**	**Large-scale (mechanized)**
Land under cultivation (million ha)[a]	**1 600**[b]	800	800
Percentage	100	50	50
People in agriculture (million)	**2 600**[b]	2 575	25
Percentage of people in agriculture	100	99	1
Number of farms (million)	608	**600**[a]	8
Percentage of small- and large-scale farms	100	88.7	1.3
Cultivated area per farm (ha)	**2.6**[c]	**1.3**[c]	**100**[c]
Percentage of land under cereal production	50	50	50
Average cereal yields (tons/ha)	**2**[c]	**1**[c]	**3**[c]
Annual cereal production (million tons)	**1 600**[b]	400	1200
Percentage cultivated on small- and large-scale farms	100	25	75

Sources: Estimations (in normal font) by the Centre for Development and Environment, based on available data (in bold) from: [b] public sources (FAO, WB, IAASTD), and [c] Von Braun, 2005.

Notes: [a] Cultivated land is composed of most of the cropland, plus parts of animal feed production land, as well as some agroforestry and biofuel areas (see also table 1).

a matter of years. Households fall into poverty primarily as a result of a lack of resilience to risks and shocks. Apart from important aspects, including political or social conflicts, ill health and unforeseen social expenses, many risks relate to farming practices, loss of access to land and natural resources, market dynamics and price volatility, poor harvests due to environmental risks and climate variability, and weakened institutional environments. Conversely, households can escape from poverty when they have secured access to land, education and ownership of physical assets. Furthermore, opportunities such as markets, infrastructure and enabling institutions play a key role (IFAD, 2011).

In conclusion, the status of small-scale farming is intrinsically linked to a complex interplay of determinants relating to a specific local context, but it is also driven by developments at national and global levels. Among these, the competing demands for food, feed, fibre and fuel are the most prominent factors that intensify pressures on land. These so-called "teleconnections" of land-use change, where production and consumption of land-based products are increasingly distant and range across varying spatial scales, represent a major challenge for devising future strategies for sustainable small-scale farming (GLP, 2005).

Land conversions through small-scale farming. Today, nearly half of the global land surface is devoted to agricultural activities (Oldeman, 1994; Foley et al., 2005). This spread of agricultural land for a growing world population represents, perhaps, the most prominent feature of global change. The coming decades will witness further significant demographic changes, with the rural population expected to peak between 2025 and 2045, followed by a decline, and the developing world's urban population will outnumber the rural population. In South-East Asia, the rural population is already decreasing; in North Africa, West Asia and in South and Central Asia, numbers may start to decline around 2025, and in sub-Saharan Africa, around 2045 (IFAD, 2011). Nevertheless, poverty will remain largely a rural problem. Any strategy for rural development and poverty alleviation will thus have to consider that the majority of the world's poor will live in rural areas for many decades to come.

In trying to understand the significance of small-scale farming for more recent land conversions, demogra-

phic trends alone provide an incomplete basis. We need to draw a more differentiated picture in space and time, and understand how the relationship between population growth and land conversion is mediated by other factors such as environmental conditions, land settlement policies and market forces. Agricultural land has steadily grown by 0.3 per cent per annum during the past two decades. Yet most of this must be attributed to the extension of permanent pasture, while cropland has remained fairly static. There have been important regional differences, with a decrease of cropland in Europe that is offset by large gains in Africa and Latin America. At the same time, irrigated areas have shown a progressive but slowing growth rate during that period (Wood et al., 2000). Therefore, it may be assumed that small-scale farming currently plays a prominent role in land conversions in Africa and to a certain extent in Latin America, although pasture extension related to commercial farming is probably more important. In Asia, the role of small-scale farming in land conversion is less significant.

In regions affected by small-scale land conversions, it appears that rapid agricultural expansion and intensification mainly occurs at the fringes of high-potential areas, where the natural potential is perceived to be underutilized. On the one hand, this concerns forest edges and steep mountain slopes; on the other hand, these areas of rapid agricultural expansion are mainly in semi-arid areas with good soils and the potential for high productivity if water can be provided.

According to Chomitz (2007), approximately 70 million people live in remote tropical forests, and about 800 million rural people live in or near tropical forests and savannahs. The forests provide a livelihood for these people, as they offer land for farming, mainly through shifting cultivation; but they are also an important source of food, income, fuel and medicines. Such land-use practices have caused a 700–1,100 million ha net loss of forests over the past 300 years (UNEP, 2011b). However, much evidence shows that in recent times, commercial agriculture and other activities such as road and urban constructions, rather than shifting cultivators and subsistence farmers, have been the main drivers of deforestation (DeFries et al., 2010; Geist and Lambin, 2002; Mertz et al., 2009; Rudel et al., 2000).

Drylands, a second hotspot of small-scale agricultural

Figure 1: Actual and potential benefits from agricultural activities according to current agricultural potential.

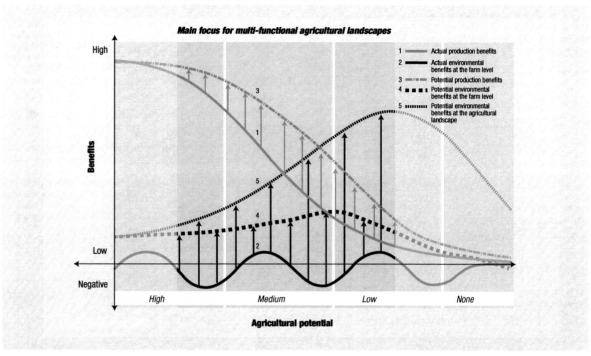

Note: Shaded area shows the main focus on promoting multi-functional agricultural landscapes.
Source: Authors

expansion, cover approximately 41 per cent per cent of the global land surface, and they are home to more than 2 billion people, 90 per cent of whom live in developing countries (UNEP, 2011b). Overall, approximately 2 per cent of global terrestrial net primary production (NPP) is lost each year due to dryland degradation, or between 4 and 10 per cent of the potential NPP in drylands (Zika and Erb, 2009). Among various other triggers such as urbanization, desertification, wildfire and overgrazing, the transformation of grasslands to croplands and inadequate cultivation practices play a key role in such degradation processes. In addition, the expansion of large- and small-scale agriculture is pushing pastoralists into more marginal areas, thereby forcing them into vicious circles of impoverishment and desertification.

Towards future strategies: Small-scale farming in multifunctional agricultural landscapes. Small-scale farming must be at the centre of any strategy that pursues the goal of feeding a growing world population while addressing rural poverty in a context of increasing environmental degradation and climate change. It should build on a thorough understanding of the manifold and changing pressures on small-scale

farming, the conversions related to such pressures, and the resulting economic, social and environmental impacts from the local to the global level.

There is a growing consensus that sustainable agricultural intensification in small-scale farming must address the systemic interactions between agricultural productivity, environmental service provision and the improvement of human well-being. A diversity of agricultural and land-use practices, combined in multifunctional agricultural landscapes is likely to achieve the best set of outcomes. While agricultural intensification will continue to play an important role in future global food production, context-specific approaches are also needed in order to achieve sustainable land use based on biophysical as well as socio-economic considerations (DeFries and Rosenzweig, 2010). Moreover, hot spot areas of agricultural expansion on the fringes of high potential areas should become the main focus for such multifunctional agricultural landscapes. Figure 1 schematically presents the core elements of such an approach.

In Figure 1, total production and environmental

benefits are depicted along a gradient of decreasing agricultural potential. This stipulates that from high potential areas – often dominated by intensified and large-scale agriculture – the production benefits decrease rapidly towards more marginal areas, dominated by small-scale and often subsistence farming (curve 1). Meanwhile, the highest potential for additional production benefits can be located in medium to lower agricultural potential areas (curve 3). Hence these areas might offer the best returns on investments for productivity increase. In terms of actual environmental benefits (curve 2), assessment is more difficult, but generally they would appear to be rather negative both in high- and low-potential areas comprising large- as well as small-scale farming. However, the potential environmental benefits increase slightly from high- to lower-potential areas at the farm level (curve 4), and significant environmental benefits can be expected at the agricultural landscape levels (curve 5). While large-scale enterprises cover whole landscapes, small-scale enterprises allow for multiple use areas in-between, thereby increasing environmental services and offsetting trade-offs of more intensive components.

In summary, strategies for sustainable intensification of small-scale farming should focus on developing agricultural landscapes in areas with medium to low potential for agriculture. There, the highest additional production potentials can be tapped while environmental benefits can be increased significantly. Such strategies, in order to leapfrog agricultural development for improved well-being without compromising environmental health, will require investments on a global scale, as well as an enabling policy and institutional environment. For this purpose, the ongoing revaluation of rural areas for ecosystem service provision beyond the economically productive function of land represents an opportunity that should be harnessed. Under the guidance of strengthened public institutions from the local to the global level, multifunctional small-scale agriculture and pastoralism should feature at the top of rural development agendas. Key domains of intervention relate to legal and institutional security of land and natural resources, agricultural extension and capacity development, innovative mechanisms that reward ecosystem service provisions, improved economic governance and a regulated integration into agricultural markets, as well as political empowerment of largely marginalized segments of rural populations.

E. Implications of land conversions for food security

Implications of global and local change. Global food security is primarily dependent on the production of food in agriculture (including food products from forests and fisheries), but also on the distribution and availability of food for consumers and subsistence farmers, and finally, on the amount of food stored at household, community, enterprise, national and international levels. Food production will depend on how much land is allocated to other uses such as feed, fibre or all forms of fuel, how much increase in production is possible, particularly from small-scale farming, and on the extent of change in consumption patterns to animal protein. Last but not least, food production is dependent on the availability of inputs such as seeds, land, water, natural and industrial fertilizers, and in particular, on the effects of climate change on agricultural production in the near and distant future.

In small-scale farming, food security will depend on the extent of further pressures exerted on farm sizes, the extent of soil degradation that occurs, the degree of pressure on land, the spread of water scarcity, the extent to which small farm productivity can be enhanced with inputs and research, and whether market access can be facilitated. In sum, there are a number of intrinsic drivers of rural poverty that need to be addressed as a priority.

Improvement of food security from local to global levels. The following 10 measures could help small-scale farmers to contribute to food security:

1. *Regulating land conversions:* preventing land conversions on land used by small-scale farmers and pastoralists will secure their livelihoods as long as they have no alternatives.
2. *Ensuring land tenure:* external investments in land quality will become attractive for small-scale farmers when their land is secured, even if these are not directly beneficial for production but rather for maintaining ecosystem services. Tenure needs to be guaranteed by States with the support of the international community.
3. *Improving market access:* market chains should be developed for small-scale farm products, including for the pre-processing and labelling of products for storage and easier transport, thereby making products more competitive.

4. *Developing gender equity:* equal rights for female farmers are seldom guaranteed in small-scale farming, yet women are often the main actors on the farm, and their empowerment, both economically and in decision-making, would contribute to improved livelihoods.

5. *Raising farm productivity:* production per hectare on small-scale farms could be doubled in the coming 40 years with only moderate inputs, improved seeds and breeds, better farm implements and research centred on small-scale farming.

6. *Increasing farm size:* Arresting a further decline in land size per small-scale farm and maintaining or even increasing farm plots would be beneficial for moderate mechanization and modernization, even in small-scale farming.

7. *Promoting sustainable land management:* Reversing further degradation of land on small-scale farms would ensure increased productivity and generate other ecosystem services from soil, water and biodiversity.

8. *Removing subsidies:* subsidies for agricultural products, particularly in developed countries and transition economies, should be removed, as they create price distortions and affect international commodity markets.

9. *Internalizing transaction costs:* incorporating transaction costs in food and feed prices, including global taxation on fossil fuels, would enable equal access to markets for large- and small-scale farming alike.

10. *Anticipating climate change:* there is need for a better understanding of the implications of climate change and appropriate measures to be taken against it through research, early warning and early action.

Implications of land conversions. Small-scale farming is the most vulnerable to food insecurity, and it is likely to be very strongly affected by land conversions, particularly from cropland to livestock production, as a result of changing consumption patterns. Any likely bans on the extension of cropland into pastures and forests will place increasing and additional pressure on farm sizes, although the number of farms might decrease in the coming decades. Biofuel production and changes in livestock production are additional factors that will have a potentially growing influence on small-scale farming, provided current policies are maintained or enhanced. However, this latter pressure also concerns other land use and cover types, as biofuel will affect not only cropland but biodiversity and natural resources in other land-use systems as well.

Commentary I. Land Grabbing and Future Conflicts

Nnimmo Bassey
Executive Director, Environmental Rights Action; Chair, Friends of the Earth International; and coordinator, Oilwatch International

Abstract

On the grounds of equity and ethics, it is necessary to halt the unsustainable plunder or use of resources to the extent that they are permanently lost to future generations. Land grabbing, a manifestation of greed, shows a trend of people living as if there were no tomorrow. It is clearly not simply a desire to respond to food deficits somewhere, but a ploy to control the food systems of the world and subject people to the vagaries of speculation.

The web of global crises currently confounding the world has had deep impacts on vulnerable communities in developing countries. As the world lurches from one crisis to another, bids to find solutions have been merely compounding, rather than resolving, the crises. For example, with regard to the fossil-fuel-driven climate crisis, some saw agrofuel production and use as a key solution. However, agrofuels cannot replace fossil fuels because there is simply not enough arable land to cultivate the amount of crops needed to meet the voracious appetite of combustion engines in cars and machinery. Moreover, agrofuels retain the fossil fuel production, transportation and utilization paradigm (e.g. refineries, pipelines) thus causing the world to imagine there is a change when in fact it is business as usual.

Moreover, the conversion of land from the cultivation of crops for food to crops for agrofuels has had an impact on food supply. Some argue that agrofuel production runs parallel to that of food production, and that one does not impact the other. Considering that the same workforce is engaged in both processes, it is evident that the two cannot be delinked and neither can land uptake – they are all interrelated. Some promoters of biofuels claim that they do not use food crops, and that their crops (such as jatropha) are grown on marginal lands. The jatropha plant and the claims around it have also raised new issues, including that lands considered marginal might appear so to persons who neither live in the locality nor understand the dynamics of local land-use systems. The marginal land argument is also seen as a ploy used by policymakers and speculators to mark out such lands for grabbing while marginalizing the people who own, understand and use those lands.

The United Nations estimates that Africa has at least 500 million hectares (ha) of marginal, unused and underused land and that the Democratic Republic of the Congo is believed to have around 150 million hectares (Dynes, 2008). However, the classification of land as being marginal or not can be contentious, especially if it fails to consider local knowledge and technologies.

The food crisis has also triggered the search for land by speculators and others who see lands in Africa as suitable and available for purchase for crop production aimed at export out of Africa. This seems like the colonial cash-cropping system returning in a different guise. Interestingly, not all cases have concerned land grabbers from outside Africa. There have been instances of Africans grabbing lands in other African countries and others playing the role of middleman to facilitate the land grabs, as revealed in a report by GRAIN (2009), for example. The case of the Libyan Arab Jamahiriya's incursion into Mali is worthy of note in this regard. A multimillion dollar national rice initiative announced by the Government of Mali was intended to help local farmers produce more so that the country would no longer be dependent on rice imports.

However, the Government handed over an enormous tract of prime rice land to a Libyan investment fund and some Chinese companies. In addition, in 2004, Mali's President, Amadou Toumani Touré, offered up to 100,000 ha to the Libyan Arab Jamahiriya as part of a larger infrastructure investment project for the area that included the enlargement of a canal and the improvement of a road. This was within the framework of the Libya Africa Investment Portfolio (LAP). The arrangement showed that the infrastructure provision was contracted to CGC, a Chinese company owned by China's big oil corporation, SINOPEC, while an unnamed Chinese firm was contracted to supply Chinese hybrid rice seeds. The GRAIN report revealed that, although the project claimed to produce rice for Mali, there was "plenty of reason to suspect that the real motivation is to export rice to Libya."

A. Paths to land grabs

A land grab deal that would have swallowed up half of the arable land in Madagascar was aborted. In that deal, Daewoo, a company from the Republic of Korea, was to lease 1.3 million ha of arable land on that island State for the cultivation of corn and oil palm for export back to its home country. The oil palm seeds as well as corn were to be imported from Latin America. The objective of the scheme was to boost the Republic of Korea's food security by providing it with up to 2.5 million tons of corn per year, representing half of its corn imports. Hong Jong-Wan, a manager at Daewoo, was quoted as saying, "We want to plant corn there to ensure our food security. Food can be a weapon in this world. We can either export the harvests to other countries or ship them back to Korea in case of a food crisis." The protests that ensued after the revelation of the deal led to its cancellation, and the political fallout saw the unseating of the president of the country.[3]

Actions elsewhere also have the potential to intensify land grabs in Africa. For example, the move by the Government of Indonesia to impose a two-year moratorium on new palm oil plantations in order to protect its remaining rainforests has prompted agribusiness giants such as Sime Darby to switch their expansion plans to Cameroon, Ghana and Liberia. This rush into Africa is set to cause massive deforestation and loss of farmland of the local communities (Levitt, 2011), which are sure conflict trigger points. The implication of this shift is instructive: while the Indonesian plan is well-intentioned, it is clear that regulations limited to one country will simply cause investors and speculators to shift their activities elsewhere where regulations may be lax or non-existent.

B. Food crisis, land grabs and the "new colonization"

The food crisis of 2007–2008 was characterized by some analysts as a silent tsunami (*Economist*, 2008) that hit the developing world. However, there was nothing silent about it: the upheaval had been building up over time and the rumbles were audible and the waves visible. As noted by a recent report (Cissokho et al., 2011), developing countries have suffered for some decades from swift changes in the prices of their commodity exports, on which most of them rely heavily for their export earnings, and this problem has been compounded by rising price volatility in food imports from the global markets. Their proposed solutions include shielding their vulnerable markets from price volatility by promoting the production and consumption of what they term "non-traded" crops.

The food crisis combined with the financial crisis have prompted speculators to focus on investing in land for the cultivation of crops for energy and/or for food. This rush for land in countries in Africa, South-East Asia and Latin America by other countries and corporations has led to atrocious land grabs. The scale and purpose of the land grabs amount to nothing short of a "new wave of colonization". The crops cultivated in the grabbed lands are not intended to feed local populations; instead, they are mainly produced for export back to the home countries of the "investors," as exemplified by the land-grab deal involving Daewoo, cited above.

Another example of an attempted land grab deal was in South Sudan where one "paramount chief" signed off 600,000 ha of community land, with a possibility of ceding a further 400,000 ha, to a Dallas-based firm in 2008. Through the deal, the firm was set to enjoy a 49-year lease of the land at a princely sum of $25,000. The terms of the lease offered the company full rights to exploit all natural resources in the leased land, including the right to:

- Develop, produce and exploit timber/forest resources, including, without limitation, the harvesting of current tree growth, the planting and harvesting of hardwood trees, and the development of wood-based industries;
- Trade and profit from any resulting carbon credits from timber on the leased land;
- Engage in agricultural activities, including the cultivation of biofuel crops (e.g. jatropha plants and palm oil trees);

- Explore, develop, mine, produce and/or exploit petroleum, natural gas and other hydrocarbon resources for both local and export markets, as well as other minerals, and also engage in power generation activities on the leased land;
- Sublease any portion or all of the leased land or sub-license any right to undertake activities on the leased land to third parties.

However, resistance to this deal by the people, supported by solidarity actions from groups such as the Oakland Institute, succeeded in defeating the deal (OI, 2011).

This example of a land-grab deal, though foiled, shows the main attractions for speculators. These include the possibility to exploit surface resources, such as timber, and subsoil resources such as oil, gas and solid minerals. The speculators aim to engage in comprehensive exploitation of their grabbed land in all ways possible. This is why, in this case, they even laid claim to the carbon stock in the trees on the land. With new types of carbon sinks being "commodified", it is conceivable that land grabbers will seek to obtain carbon credits from soil carbon sequestration. Arguably, this wave of land grabs is more objectionable than colonialism. Although this land-grab deal fell through, there are others just as obnoxious that have not been stopped.

Sometimes land grabs may pass unnoticed, as with the recent decision by a mining company, African Barrick Gold, in the United Republic of Tanzania to erect a 14-kilometre concrete fence around its mining concession, ostensibly to keep villagers from sneaking in to steal gold (*Reuters*, 2011). Completion of its so-called security fence in 2012 will suggest that its grabbing of the territory is in perpetuity, and with this stroke of genius the company is possibly depriving the citizens of access to parts of the land on which they could still eke a living without interfering with the mining activities of the company. Equally, the communities are deprived of access to the beauty of the natural landscape, although the relentless claws of mining machineries may have already scarred it.

C. Conflicts and resistance

Conflicts and resistance over land grabs are also increasing in the Ogoni land of Nigeria. The people of this region are known for their epic battles against degradation of their territory through the oil

extraction activities of Shell Petroleum Development Company (Shell) and the Nigerian National Petroleum Corporation (NNPC). Shell was expelled following mass peaceful uprisings in 1993. Since then there have been attempts to reopen the oil wells in Ogoni, but without success. Possibly as a step towards ensuring a return of the oil giant into the territory, the United Nations Environment Programme (UNEP) was commissioned to assess the environmental situation of Ogoniland.

The UNEP assessment (2011a) presented to President Goodluck Jonathan on 4 August 2011 showed hydrocarbon pollution in surface water throughout the creeks of Ogoniland and up to 8 cm in the groundwater that feeds drinking wells at 41 sites, including a serious case in Nisisioken Ogale in Eleme, Rivers State. Soils were found to have been polluted with hydrocarbons up to a depth of 5 metres in 49 observed sites, while, benzene, a known cancer-causing chemical was found to be present in drinking water at a level 900 times above the level deemed acceptable by the World Health Organization (WHO). The report also documented that fisheries have been destroyed and that wetlands around Ogoniland are highly degraded or facing degradation (Environmental Rights Action, 2011). These impacts combined, have led to an irreparable loss of livelihoods, and will take 30 years to remediate. Pollution appears to have made a permanent grab on Ogoni lands.

While the Government of Nigeria and Shell dither over what to do about the destroyed Ogoni environment, there are persistent efforts by both government and private entities to further grab massive tracts of what is left of land in the territory for banana and other plantations. One company is canvassing the idea of producing what it euphemistically calls "Ogoni oils" from jatropha. Because of the highly sensitized state of the Ogoni people, there is determined resistance, and this is clearly not a land grabbers' haven.

D. Conclusion

The push by transnational corporations for land to grow crops for export and biofuels in addition to supply their need for pulp and paper is compounded by the appetite of emerging economies such as Brazil, China and India for increasing amounts of other natural resources, including water and minerals. For example, it is said that the Government of Mozambique is allocating 60,000 square kilometres of land (7.6 per cent of the country) in four of its provinces – Nampula, Niassa, Zambezia and Cabo Delgado – to 40 Brazilian farmers for commercial soy cultivation to supply the ever-expanding Chinese market (Nhantumbo, 2011). The issues raised by land grabs are indeed diverse and severe.

Land grab is a real menace in a world ridden with crises. Watson, a leading figure in setting up the Intergovernmental Platform on Biodiversity and Ecosystem Services, suggests that global ecosystems face severe threats from five key drivers: land conversion (such as deforestation), overexploitation (such as overfishing), the introduction of exotic species, pollution and climate change (cited by McCarthy, 2011).

On the grounds of equity and ethics, it is necessary to halt the unsustainable plunder or use of resources to the extent that they are permanently lost to future generations. Land grabbing, a manifestation of greed, shows a trend of people living as if there were no tomorrow. It is clearly not simply a desire to respond to food deficits somewhere, but a ploy to control the food systems of the world and subject people to the vagaries of speculation.

Land grabbing is an unsustainable path and needs to be reigned in. Only a global examination and a global regulatory framework will be able to stem the flood. Apart from regulating this scourge, there is also the need to secure land rights and ensure that those rights are respected, especially in the more vulnerable regions and countries where such laws do not exist. The world cannot afford new forms of conflict arising from land grabbing. More and more people are being displaced by land grabs, livelihoods are being destroyed, and hunger is being imported while food products are exported.

Commentary II. Evaluation of Land Investment Deals in Africa: Preliminary Findings

Anuradha Mittal
Oakland Institute

Abstract

The Oakland Institute's analysis on land investment deals has identified three major lacunae, which point to the need for:

- better data on and a better understanding of the concept of "land availability",

- a better understanding of the land deals (i.e. their nature and their implications for developing countries and for food-insecure populations), and

- addressing the issue of land rights.

Instead of using marginal or infertile land as is often claimed, most deals identified are actually taking place in the vicinity of water resources that offer irrigation potential, or near other infrastructure (railways, roads) or on fertile soils. Major African rivers, such as the Nile, the Zambezi and the Niger, are tapped by these land grab deals, which give the investors control not only of the land, but also of water.

Despite widespread claims, the Oakland Institute's field research and analysis of the land deals in seven African countries has found that their promises of economic development through their investments in land and agriculture are often overstated. Large-scale land investment may improve some macroeconomic indicators of development, but it may also result in considerable environmental and social costs to the host country, and loss of livelihoods or lost economic opportunities for its citizens.

Land investments – the purchase or lease of vast tracts of land from mostly poor, developing countries by wealthier, food-insecure countries and private investors for the production and export of food and agrofuel crops – have grown into an international phenomenon. According to the World Bank, in 2009 alone nearly 60 million hectares of fertile land throughout the world (i.e. almost 4 per cent of global cropland) were acquired by investors, often at giveaway prices. Over 70 per cent of these land deals were in Africa.

International aid agencies and multilateral lending institutions have commonly supported foreign direct investment (FDI) as a way to eradicate hunger and poverty. Many of them suggest that FDI can help developing countries by generating income and employment and enabling the transfer of technology and know-how. In addition, it is believed to promote the development of processing and economic and social infrastructure in "host" countries. This implies that African countries are therefore beneficiaries in such deals. However, currently, little is understood of the legal, social and economic implications of the land deals involving FDI. The authors of a comprehensive research on land grabs (FAO/IFAD/IIED, 2009) recognized that their report had "only started to scratch the surface of a very complex set of issues." The Oakland Institute's own analysis has identified three major lacunae, which point to the need for: (i) better data on and a better understanding of the concept of "land availability", (ii) a better understanding of the land deals (i.e. their nature and their implications for developing countries and for food-insecure populations), and (iii) addressing the issue of land rights.

Given the paramount importance of addressing this knowledge gap, the scale and rate at which these land deals are happening, and the complete lack of transparency surrounding them, the Oakland Institute initiated a research project, entitled Understanding

Land Investment Deals in Africa in 2009, which studied seven countries: Ethiopia, Mali, Mozambique, Sierra Leone, South Sudan, the United Republic of Tanzania and Zambia. In June 2011, the Institute released a paper which highlights some of the main findings of its first phase of research on land investment deals in Africa.[4]

A. Who are the investors?

News coverage has tended to emphasize the role that countries such as China and the Gulf States have played in the acceleration of land acquisitions in Africa. However, the Oakland Institute's investigation, involving over 50 deals in the seven African countries covered, revealed a major role played also by Western firms, wealthy United States and European individuals, and investment funds with ties to major banks such as Goldman Sachs and JP Morgan. Other investors include alternative investment firms such as London-based Emergent Asset Management that seeks to attract speculators, including universities in the United States such as Harvard and Vanderbilt, with the promise of gaining access to agricultural land that will yield high financial returns for their endowments. Another example concerns several Texas-based interests that are associated with a major 600,000 ha deal in South Sudan which involves Kinyeti Development, LLC – an Austin, Texas-based "global business development partnership and holding company," managed by Howard Eugene Douglas, a former United States Ambassador at Large and Coordinator for Refugee Affairs.

A key player in the largest land deal in the United Republic of Tanzania is Iowa agribusiness entrepreneur, Bruce Rastetter, who concurrently serves as CEO of Pharos Ag, co-founder and Managing Director of AgriSol Energy and CEO of Summit Farms, and is an important donor to Iowa State University. Rastetter was recently appointed to the Iowa Board of Regents by Terry Branstad, Iowa's Governor. Iowa State University has provided "private" research services that benefit Rastetter's investments in the United Republic of Tanzania.

Many European companies are also involved in land deals in African countries, often with support provided by their governments and embassies in those countries. For instance, Swedish and German firms have strong interests in the production of biofuels in the United Republic of Tanzania. Major investors in Sierra Leone include Addax Bioenergy of Switzerland and Quifel International Holdings of Portugal. And Sierra Leone Agriculture is actually a subsidiary of Crad-l (CAPARO Renewable Agriculture Developments Ltd.) based in the United Kingdom.

B. Are investors buying unused available land?

The Oakland Institute's research found several cases where small farmers, viewed as "squatters", have been forcibly removed from their ancestral lands with no compensation in order to make room for the cultivation of export commodities, including biofuels and cut flowers. In Ethiopia, for example, the villagization process of nearly 700,000 indigenous people is taking place in the very same areas targeted for land investment by large-scale investors. People who are being forced off their ancestral lands are afraid to oppose displacement for fear of their lives and threats of imprisonment in a country where political violence and human rights violations are common.

In Samana Dugu in Mali in 2010, when bulldozers moved in to clear the land, men, women and youth from the community who protested the cutting of their trees were met by police force, and were beaten and arrested. And in the United Republic of Tanzania, the memorandum of understanding between AgriSol Energy from the United States and the local government stipulates in its first article that the two main locations – Katumba and Mishamo – for the company's project are refugee settlements that will have to be closed before the project can start. Yet the 162,000 refugees living there had fled Burundi in 1972 and have been farming this land for 40 years.

Overall, when farmers are not simply removed from their land, the land leased to investors in Africa is either fallow land or forests, generally used by the local population for a wide range of purposes (e.g. collection of timber, wild food, firewood, medicinal plants, conservation of watersheds and protection against erosion). Instead of using marginal or infertile land as is often claimed, most deals identified are actually taking place in the vicinity of water resources that offer irrigation potential, or near other infrastructure (railways, roads) or on fertile soils. Major African rivers, such as the Nile, the Zambezi and the Niger, are tapped by these land grab deals, which give the investors control not only of the land, but also of water.

C. Does foreign investment in land lead to economic development?

The belief that large-scale land investment in Africa will result in much-needed economic development is strongly promoted by foreign investors, government officials and international institutions. As a result, many African governments fervently encourage foreign investment in agricultural land, and offer what some have called "mouthwatering" incentives to investors.

Officials trust that land deals will spur growth with incoming capital, assist with infrastructure and create employment for local people. On their part, investors reinforce these ideas with bold promises of economic development, "modernization" and numerous jobs. Despite widespread claims, the Oakland Institute's field research and analysis of the land deals in the seven countries has found that their promises of economic development through their investments in land and agriculture are often overstated. Large-scale land investment may improve some macroeconomic indicators of development, but it may also result in considerable environmental and social costs to the host country, and loss of livelihoods or lost economic opportunities for its citizens. An analysis of various economic issues related to foreign investment in land demonstrates that the opportunities for economic development are in fact limited. There are several reasons for this as discussed below.

D. Investor incentives resulting in forgone public revenues

African governments are offering a wide range of incentives to attract foreign investment. These include fiscal incentives, such as duty exemptions, full or partial tax holidays, and/or reductions in the tax rate for specific types of activities, as well as non-fiscal incentives, including allowing expatriate employment and remittance of profits and other benefits for foreign personnel. The foregone public revenues as a result of investor incentives can severely undermine a country's tax base. Import duties, for example, represent approximately 15 per cent of total government revenue in Mozambique and 45 per cent in Sierra Leone. The 2009/10 tax exemptions in the United Republic of Tanzania amounted to 95 billion Tanzanian shillings ($425 million) – more than half the 1.3 trillion Tanzanian shillings ($795 million) the Government planned to borrow from commercial sources for infrastructure financing in 2010/11. Had it been collected, it would have provided 40 per cent more resources for education or 72 per cent more resources for health in 2009/2010.

E. Low land prices and rental fees

In Africa, land is readily offered in the form of huge tracts at extremely low prices or lease rates compared with those in other continents (tables 4 and 5).

Table 4: Sampling of farmland lease fees, by land deal

Location	Deal	Price ($/ha/yr)	Lease terms
Ethiopia	Saudi Star	Free land rent	10,000 ha; 60-year lease
Mali	Malibya	Free land rent	100,000 ha; 50-year lease
Ethiopia	Karuturi	6.75[a]	300,000 ha; 99-year lease
Sudan	Nile Trading and Development	0.04	600,000 ha at $25,000; 49-year lease
Sierra Leone	Sierra Leone Agriculture	2	43,000 ha; 45-year lease
Sierra Leone	Quifel Agribusiness SL Limited	5	126,000 ha; 49-year lease

Source: Based on Oakland Institute field research, October 2010-June 2011.
Notes:[a]Karuturi initially leased land for just $1.25/ha (20 birr/ha), but in subsequent negotiations with the federal Government, that price was raised to $6.75/ha (111 birr/ha).

Table 5: Sampling of average farmland prices, by selected countries, 2010	
Location	**Average price ($/ha/yr)**
New Zealand (dairy)	23,000
United Kingdom (average – all land types)	22,000
United States (dryland in corn belt)	16,000
Poland	4,550–8,125
Brazil (Mato Grosso dryland)	7,000
Argentina (Central provinces)	5,000–10,000

Source: The Knight Frank Farmland Index 2010.

Low prices are certainly attractive to foreign investors. According to Susan Payne, Chief Executive Officer (CEO) of Emergent Asset Management, "In South Africa and Sub Saharan Africa the cost of agriland, arable, good agriland that we're buying is one-seventh of the price of similar land in Argentina, Brazil and America. That alone is an arbitrage opportunity. We could be moronic and not grow anything and we think we will make money over the next decade." (see: http://www.oaklandinstitute.org/emergent-video).

The benefits from the investments for the host countries are undermined by these low prices. Payne alludes to the fact that, because of low land prices, it is perhaps in the investor's best interest to sit on the land and profit from arbitrage between low land acquisition prices compared with their sales values as the market improves. While such speculation often entails higher risk, returns on speculative investments in African farmland have been reported to reach 25 per cent. Indeed, many of the land deals investigated by the Oakland Institute are not yet operational, indicating that the investments may have been made solely for speculative rather than productive purposes.

F. Does foreign investment in agriculture lead to job creation?

The promise of job creation is often the argument presented by investors, governments and international institutions to convince local communities of the benefits of foreign investment in agriculture. Because of the large role agriculture plays in African economies,

the sector has great potential as a driver of their economic development and job creation. Activities such as storage to reduce post-harvest losses and to get the best from market opportunities, as well as investments in value-added production, such as processing, seem particularly relevant to make the most of the tremendous potential of African agriculture. Improving smallholder productivity and production is also essential for a sector largely dependent on family farms.

Yet the majority of land deals investigated by the Oakland Institute offer basic wage labour employment, mostly low-paying positions which present a number of disadvantages. Often, it is unclear how many jobs will be created, or whether those jobs will offer fair compensation for local farmers' lost lands and livelihoods. Furthermore, modern agricultural schemes are highly mechanized and provide relatively few, often short-term, seasonal jobs. There is no indication that investors are seeking to maximize local employment or that governments are giving priority to job creation. On the contrary, investors often find scalable, mechanized agriculture to be more manageable, and governments lure these investors by placing few or no limits on expatriate workers. It appears, therefore, that lofty employment claims made by investors generally are not substantiated by actual job creation, or by jobs that bring significant development benefits. Indeed, evidence shows that large-scale agricultural investments provide minimal benefits to local communities, and this should be taken into consideration by development practitioners and policymakers when evaluating the legitimacy of "responsible" agro-investment. To truly spur job creation, host governments would need to establish investment agreements that contribute to, rather than detract from, local livelihood options.

Oakland Institute's evidence is supported by other findings, including a study by the World Bank (2010) which found scant evidence that foreign land investment was creating many local jobs. The requirements for labour vary greatly among crops and production systems, such that crop choice and organization of production will have far-reaching impacts on the potential for agricultural investment to create employment. A 10,000-ha maize plantation in the Democratic Republic of the Congo, for example, created only 0.01 jobs per hectare, while a sugarcane plantation generated 0.351 jobs per hectare. The

World Bank report found job creation in Ethiopia to be similarly limited, with an average of 0.005 jobs/ha in cases where figures were provided. The report noted, "The patchy data that are available suggest that investments create far fewer jobs than expected." Comparing these figures with the labour intensity of family farms, smallholder soybean production, for example, creates 0.125 jobs/ha – nearly eight times more jobs than the 0.016 jobs/ha created by large-scale soybean production.

Also according to the World Bank, wage labour income is 2 to 10 times lower than the income of the average smallholder. Moreover, as mentioned earlier, most agricultural wage labour positions are seasonal. Thus the impressive number of positions Karuturi claims it will create – as many as 20,000 to 30,000 – in Ethiopia is misleading in terms of actual employment creation for local development.

A large body of research supports the notion that small farms are more productive, biodiverse and sustainable than large, industrial-style plantations. Furthermore, in terms of local peoples' well-being, small-scale agriculture offers a number of benefits. In the first place, the production of goods by small farms is relatively less capital-intensive (meaning that more labour is used to produce each unit of the good) than that by large farms. This implies that small farms employ relatively more labour, including rural unskilled labour, than do large farms, and thus provide more gainful livelihood options for locals. Secondly, small farms have higher output per land unit because they utilize their land more efficiently, growing multiple crops, and thereby improve local food security. Small farms also are more productive because of their relatively high concentration of labour per hectare compared with larger farms. Additionally, because the household provides most of the workforce, the costs of supervision are low, since household labour is generally self-supervising in effort and diligence.

Lastly, since small farms utilize relatively more labour per land unit, they distribute a relatively larger proportion of their profits, revenues and output to their labourers. The average farm size for crop-based farming in Mali is just 4.7 ha, and one third of the 805,000 farm households cultivate less than 1 ha. To put this in perspective, the area covered by the recent large land deals identified by Oakland Institute's

research in Mali could sustain, conservatively, 112,537 farm families – well over half a million people (686,478). Instead, that land is now concentrated in the hands of 22 investors, who are planning to employ only a few thousand plantation workers.

G. Does investment improve food security?

Most of the countries targeted by investors suffer from food insecurity. Though the food security argument is often put forward by governments and investors in support of large-scale agricultural investments, Oakland Institute's research finds little assurance that those investments have improved food security. In many cases local food farms are sold in order to make room for the cultivation of export commodities, including crops for biofuels and cut flowers. Many of the land leases identified are for the production of agrofuels. In Mali, half of the investors with large land holdings in the Office du Niger intend to grow crops for agrofuels, such as sugarcane, jatropha or other oleaginous crops. Similarly, in Mozambique most of the investments are in the timber industry and agrofuels rather than in food crops. Food crops represented only 32,000 ha of the 433,000 ha that were approved for agricultural investments between 2007 and 2009.

H. Are plantations more productive and profitable than small-scale farms?

Another argument put forward in favour of large farms is that they are supposedly more productive. However, here too, the Oakland Institute's investigations confirm the existence of a large body of previous research which shows that in many instances small farms are more productive than large plantations. In Mali, for example, where the system of rice intensification has been adopted along the Niger River near Timbuktu, farmers have been able to attain yields of 7 to 15 tons/ha/yr, (or an average of 9 tons/ha/yr), which is more than twice the conventional irrigated rice yield in the area, and more than the forecasts of the Moulin Moderne du Mali, one of the major investors in large-scale rice production. The small-scale, village-based irrigation schemes involve plots of just 35 ha of land, shared by as many as 100 farmers, thus each household has access to only one third of a hectare. Yet from that piece of land they are able to earn $1,879

– more than double the average annual per capita income of $676.

If the rice intensification scheme were to be replicated successfully in the Office du Niger, 10,000 ha of such small-scale irrigation schemes could provide livelihoods for 285,715 farmers and dramatically increase rice production and revenues.

I. Placing sustainable agricultural development in the proper context

Research conducted by the Oakland Institute demonstrates that a renewed focus on agriculture is crucial for overcoming the current crisis of world hunger in the context of climate change, and for providing livelihoods to farmers while enabling developing countries to meet the Millennium Development Goals. However, the Institute's research also shows that investment in agriculture does not necessarily translate into food security or livelihoods for smallholder farmers who form the bulk of the world's poor. As pointed out by Olivier De Schutter (2009), United Nations Special Rapporteur on the Right to Food, the issue is not one of merely increasing budget allocations to agriculture, but rather, "that of choosing from different models of agricultural development which may have different impacts and benefit various groups differently."

References

Angew W, Wily LA, Cotula L and Taylor M (2012). Findings of the global commercial pressures on land research project. Paper commissioned by IIED, CIRAD and International Land Coalition, Rome. Available at http://www.ciral.fr.

Anseeuw W, Boche M, Breu T, Giger M, Lay J, Messerli P, Nolte K (2012). Transnational Land Deals for Agriculture in the Global South. Report for the Land Matrix Partnership - CDE, (CIRAD, GIGA, GIZ, ILC), Bern, Montpellier, Hamburg. Available at: www.cirad.fr.

Arndt C, Benfica R, Tarp F, Thurlow J, Uaiene R. (2009). Biofuels, poverty, and growth: A computable general equilibrium analysis of Mozambique. 2009 IOP Conf. Ser.: Earth Environ. Sci. 6 102008. http://iopscience.iop.org/1755-1315/6/10/102008.

Bouwman AF, Van der Hoek KW, Eickhout B, Soenario I. (2005). Exploring changes in world ruminant production systems. *Agricultural Systems,* 84(2):121–153.

Bowyer C (2010). Anticipated indirect land use change associated with expanded use of biofuels and bioliquids in the EU – An Analysis of the National Renewable Energy Action Plans. Study by the Institute for European Environmental Policy, November. Available at: http://www.ieep.eu/news/2010/11/the-indirect-land-use-change-impact-of-biofuels-ieep-launches-analysis-of-eu-nations-projected.

Breu T, Portner B, Herweg K, Messerli P, Wolfgramm B, Hurni H (2011). Sustainable land management and global change: Factors affecting land users' efforts to sustain the productive use of natural resources. In: Wiesmann U, Hurni H, eds. *Research for Development – A Synthesis of NCCR North-South Research, 2001-2008* [working title]. Vol. 6. Perspectives of the Swiss National Centre of Competence in Research (NCCR) North-South, University of Bern, Bern, *Geographica Bernensia.*

Bruinsma JE (2003). *World Agriculture: Towards 2015/2030. An FAO Perspective.* London, Earthscan Publications Ltd.

Burgers P, Rizki Pandu Permana, Tran Nam Tu (2011). Fuelling conflicts: Overcoming asymmetry between global interests in Vietnam and Indonesia. *Development,* 54(1): 77–84.

CGIAR (2005). *Research & Impact: Areas of Research: Livestock.* Washington, DC. Available at: http://www.cgiar.org/impact/research/livestock.html.

Chalmers J, Kunen E, Ford S, Harris N, Kadyzewski (2011). Biofuels and indirect land use change. Winrock International.

Chomitz KM (2007). At loggerheads? Agricultural expansion, poverty reduction, and environment in the tropical forests. Washington, DC, World Bank.

Cissokho M, Lines T, Nissanke M and Smith A (2011). Food security, finance and international trade: How to protect developing countries from volatile global markets. Paris, Veblen Institute for Economic Reforms.

Cotula L (2011). Land deals in Africa: What is in the contracts? London, International Institute for Environment and Development.

Cotula L, Finnegan L and Macqueen D (2011). Biomass energy: Another driver of land acquisitions? The global land rush. IIED briefing. London, International Institute for Environment and Development.

De Fraiture Ch, Giordano M and Yongsong Liao (2008). Biofuels and implications for agricultural water use: Blue impacts of green energy. *Water Policy,* 10(1): 67–81.

De Schutter O (2009). Contribution of the Special Rapporteur on the Right to Food, 17th session of the UN Commission on Sustainable Development, New York, 4-15 May. Available at: www.un.org/esa/dsd/resources/res_pdfs/csd-17/submission_of_the_Special_Rapporteur.pdf.

DEFRA (2010). The 2007/08 agricultural price spikes: Causes and policy implications. Annex 5. In: DEFRA, *The Role of Demand for Biofuel in the Agricultural Commodity Price Spikes of 2007/08.* London. Available at: http://archive.defra.gov.uk/foodfarm/food/pdf/ag-price100105.pdf.

DeFries R and Rosenzweig C (2010). Toward a whole-landscape approach for sustainable land use in the tropics. *Proceedings of the National Academy of Sciences,* 107:19627–19632.

DeFries RS, Rudel T, Uriarte M, Hansen M (2010). Deforestation driven by urban population growth and agricultural trade in the twenty-first century. *Nature Geoscience Advance* (an online publication).

Delgado CL (2003). Rising consumption of meat and milk in developing countries has created a new food revolution. *The Journal of Nutrition,* 133(11): 3907S–3910S. Available at: http://jn.nutrition.org/content/133/11/3907S.full.pdf+html.

Delgado CL, Rosegrant M, Steinfeld H, Ehui S, Courbois C (1999). *Livestock to 2020: The Next Food Revolution.* Food, Agriculture and the Environment Discussion Paper 28. Washington DC, Rome, Nairobi, International Food Policy Research Institute, FAO and International Livestock Research Institute.

Dufey A (2007). International trade in biofuels: Good for development? And good for environment? IIED Briefing. London, International Institute for Environment and Development.

Dynes M (2008). Growing up. Available at: http://www.africainvestor.com/article.asp?id=2725.

Economist (2008). The silent tsunami. 19–25 April. Available at: www.economist.com/node/11050146.

Environmental Rights Action (2011). UNEP Report: ERA seeks $100 bn for Niger Delta. Available at: http://www.eraction.org/media/press-releases/321-unep-report-era-seeks-100-bn-for-niger-delta.

FAO (2006a). *Livestock's Long Shadow: Environmental Issues and Options.* Rome. Available at: ftp://ftp.fao.org/docrep/fao/010/a0701e/a0701e00.pdf.

FAO (2006b). *World Agriculture: Towards 2030/2050.* Interim Report. Rome.

FAO (2008). Climate change, biofuels and land. Information sheet. Rome.

FAO (2009a). *The State of Food and Agriculture: Livestock in the Balance.* Rome.

FAO (2009b). How to feed the world in 2050? Conference synthesis report. Rome, Italy.

FAO and OECD (2009). *Agricultural Outlook 2009-2018.* Highlights. Rome and Paris. Available at: www.fao.org/es/esc/en/highlight_599_p.html.

FAO and OECD (2011). *Greening the Economy with Agriculture* (GEA). Report of the FAO/OECD Expert Meeting, Paris, 5–7 September 2011. Available at: http://www.fao.org/rio20/fao-rio-20/gea/en/.

FAO, IFAD, IIED (2009). Land Grab or Development Opportunity? Agricultural investment and international land deals in Africa. Rome.

FAO Stat (2006). Resources - Land. Rome. Available at: http://faostat.fao.org/site/377/default.aspx.

FAOStat (2011). *Live Animals: Production.* Rome. Available at: http://faostat.fao.org/site/573/default.aspx#ancor (accessed 27 September 2011).

Fargione J, Hill J, Tilman D, Polasky S, Hawthorne P (2008). Land clearing and the biofuel carbon debt. *Science Vol 31: 1235-1238.* Available at: http://pdf.usaid.gov/pdf_docs/PNADP308.pdf.

Findlater KM and Kandlikar M (2011). Land use and second-generation biofuel feedstocks: The unconsidered impacts of Jatropha biodiesel in Rajasthan, India. *Energy Policy,* 39(6): 3404–3413.

Fischer G, Hyzsnyik E, Prieler S, Shah M, van Velthuizen H (2009). Biofuels and food security. Implications of an accelerated biofuels production. Vienna, The OPEC Fund for International Development.

Foley JA, DeFries R, Asner GP, Barford C, Bonan G, Carpenter SR, Chapin FS, Coe MT, Daily GC, Gibbs HK, Helkowski JH, Holloway T, Howard EA, Kucharik CJ, Monfreda C, Patz JA, Prentice IC, Ramankutty N, and Snyder PK (2005). Global consequences of land use. *Science,* 309: 570–574.

Franco J, Levidow L, Fig D, Goldfarb L, Hönicke M, Mendonça ML (2010). Assumptions in the European Union biofuels policy: Frictions with experiences in Germany, Brazil and Mozambique. *The Journal of Peasant Studies,* 37(4): 661–698.

Gao Y, Skutsch M, Drigo R, Pacheco P, Masera O (2011). Assessing deforestation from biofuels: Methodological challenges. *Applied Geography,* 31(2): 508–518.

Gawel E and Ludwig G (2011). The ILUC dilemma: How to deal with indirect land use changes when governing energy crops? *Land Use Policy,* 28(4): 846–856.

Geist HJ and Lambin EF (2002). Proximate causes and underlying driving forces of tropical deforestation. *Bioscience,* 52: 143–150.

German L, Schoneveld G, Skutch M, Andriani R, Obidzinski K, Pacheco P, with Komarudin H, Andrianto A, Lima M, Dayang Norwana AAB (2010). The social and environmental impacts of biofuel feedstock expansion. A synthesis of case studies from Asia, Africa and Latin America. *Infobrief* 34. Bogor Barat, Centre for International Forestry Research.

GLP (2005). Science Plan and Implementation Strategy. IGBP Report 53, IGBP Secretariat, Stockholm. Available at:

www.igbp.net/publications/reportsandscienceplans/reportsandscienceplans/reportno53.5.1b8ae20512db692f
2a680006692.html.

Gmünder S and Portner B (2010). Biofuels and developing countries. In: Zah R, Binder C, Bringezu S, Reinhard J,
Schmid A, Schütz H. *Future Perspectives of 2nd Generation Biofuels*. Bern, Centre for Technology Assessment.

Godfray HCJ, Beddington JR, Crute IR, Haddad L, Lawrence D, Muir JF, Pretty J, Robinson S, Thomas SM, Toulmin C
(2010). Food security: The challenge of feeding 9 billion people. *Science*, 327: 812–818..

GRAIN (2009). Rice land grabs undermine food sovereignty in Africa: Against the grain. Available at: www.grain.org/
atg/.

Havlik P, Schneider UA, Schmid E, Böttcher H, Fritz S, Skalský R, Aoki K, De Cara S, Kindermann G, Kraxner F, Leduc
S, McCallum I, Mosnier A, Sauer T, Obersteiner M (2010). Global land-use implications of first and second
generation biofuel targets. *Energy Policy*. Vol. 39, Issue 10: 5690-5702.

Hawkes C (2006). Uneven dietary development: linking the policies and processes of globalisation with the
nutrition transition, obesity and diet-related chronic diseases. *Global Health*, 2: 4. Available at: http://www.
globalizationandhealth.com/content/2/1/4.

Hazell P and Pachauri RK, eds (2007). Bioenergy and agriculture: Promise and challenges. Focus, 14. Washington
D.C. International Food Policy Research Institute.

HLPE (2011a). Price volatility and food security. Report 1 by the High Level Panel of Experts on Food Security and
Nutrition. Rome, Committee on World Food Security.

HLPE (2011b). Land tenure and international investments in agriculture. Report 2 by the High Level Panel of Experts on
Food Security and Nutrition. Rome, Committee on World Food Security.

Hurni, H. with an international group of contributors (1996). Precious earth: From soil and water conservation to
sustainable land management. Bern, International Soil Conservation Organisation and Centre for Development
and Environment. ISBN 3-906151-11-5. 89 pp.

IAASTD (2008). *Global Report.* International assessment of agricultural knowledge, science and technology for
development (IAASTD): Global report. Island Press. Available at: www.agassessement.org.

IEA (2006). *World Energy Outlook 2006*. Paris.

IEA (2009). *World Energy Outlook 2009*. Paris.

IEA (2010a). *World Energy Outlook 2010*. Paris.

IEA (2010b). *Energy Technology Perspectives: Scenarios and Strategies to 2050*. Executive Summary. Paris. Available
at: http://www.iea.org/techno/etp/etp10/English.pdf.

IFAD (2011). *Rural Poverty Report 2011*. Rome.

ILC (2011). Securing land access for the poor in times of intensified natural resources competition. Rome, International
Land Coalition.

IPCC (2007). *Climate Change 2007*. Synthesis Report. Geneva, International Panel on Climate Change.

Koh LP and Wilcove DS (2008). Is oil palm agriculture really destroying tropical biodiversity? *Conservation Letters*, 1:
60–64.

Koh LP, Miettinen J, Liew SC, Ghazoul J. (2011). Remotely sensed evidence of tropical peatland conversion to oil palm.
Proceedings of the National Academy of Sciences of the United States of America, 108(12): 5127-5132.

Lambin EF and Meyfroidt P (2011). Global land use change, economic globalization, and the looming land scarcity.
Proceedings of the National Academy of Sciences of the United States of America, 108(9): 3465–3472.

Lapola DM, Schaldach R, Alcamo J, Bondeau A, Koch J, Koelking C, Priess JA (2010). Indirect land-use changes can
overcome carbon savings from biofuels in Brazil. *Proceedings of the National Academy of Sciences of the United
States of America,* 107(8): 3388–3393.

Levitt T (2011). Palm oil giants target Africa in 'land grab' following Indonesia deforestation ban. *The Ecologist*, 25
March. Available at: http://www.theecologist.org/News/news_analysis/823928/palm_oil_giants_target_africa_in_
land_grab_following_indonesia_deforestation_ban.html.

Li TM (2011). Centering labor in the land grab debate. *The Journal of Peasant Studies,* 38(2): 281–299.

Liniger HP, Mekdaschi Studer R, Hauert C, Gurtner M (2010). *Sustainable Land Management in Practice: Guidelines and Best Practices for sub-Saharan Africa.* Bern and Rome, TerrAfrica, World Overview of Conservation Approaches and Technologies (WOCAT) and FAO.

Lininger K (2011). Small-scale farming and shifting cultivation. In: Union of Concerned Scientists, *The Root of the Problem: What is Driving Tropical Deforestation Today?* Cambridge, MA. Available at: www.ucsusa.org/ whatsdrivingdeforestation.

Malik US, Ahmed M, Sombilla MA, Cueno SL (2009). Biofuels production for smallholder producers in the Greater Mekong sub-region. *Applied Energy*, 86(1): 58–68.

McCarthy M (2011). Why protecting the world's wildlife is good for our wallets - New body aims to promote economic as well as ethical side of biodiversity. *The Observer,* 3 October. Available at: http://www.independent.co.uk/ environment/nature/why-protecting-the-worlds-wildlife-is-good-for-our-wallets-2364701.html.

Melillo JM, Reilly JM, Kicklighter DW, Gurgerl AC, Cronin TW, Paltsev S, Felzer BS, Xiaodong Wang, Sokolov AP, Schlosser CA (2009). Indirect emissions from biofuels: How important? *Science,* 326: 1397–1399. 10.1126/science.1180251.

Mertz O., S. Leisz, A. Heinimann, K. Rerkasem, W. Dressler, P. V. Cu, V. K. Chi, D. Schmidt-Vogt, C. J. Colfer, M. Epprecht, Padoch C (2009). Demography of swidden cultivators in Southeast Asia. *Human Ecology* 37:281–289.

Murphy R, Woods J, Black M, McManus M (2011). Global developments in the competition for land from biofuels. *Food Policy,* 36(1): 52–61.

Nardone A, Ronchi B, Lacetera N, Ranieri MS, Bernabucci U (2010). Effects of climate changes on animal production and sustainability of livestock systems. *Livestock Science,* 130(1–3) 57–69.

Nellemann C, MacDevette M, Manders T, Eickhout B, Svihus B, Prins AG, Kaltenborn BP (2009). *The Environmental Food Crisis: The Environment's Role in Averting Future Food Crises.* A United Nations Environment Programme (UNEP) Rapid Response Assessment. Nairobi, UNEP.

Nhantumbo I (2011). Climate conversations: REDD+ in Mozambique: A new opportunity for land grabbers? Available at: http://www.iied.org/blogs/redd-mozambique-new-opportunity-for-land-grabbers, 15 September.

Oakland Institute (2011). Understanding land investment deals in Africa: Nile Trading and Development Inc. in South Sudan. Land Deal Brief, Oakland, CA.

OECD and FAO (2011). *Agricultural Outlook 2011-2020.* Paris and Rome.

OECD-DAC (2010). Measuring aid to agriculture. Paris. Available at: http://www.oecd.org/dataoecd/54/38/44116307. pdf (accessed 4 October 2011).

OI (2011). (Mis)Investment in agriculture: The role of the International Finance Corporation in the global land grab. Oakland, CA, Oakland Institute.

Oldeman LR (1994). The global extent of soil degradation. In: Greenland DJ and Szabolcs I, eds. *Soil Resilience and Sustainable Land Use*. Wallingford, CT, Centre for Agricultural Bioscience International: 99–118.

Popkin BM (1998). The nutrition transition and its health implications in lower-income countries. *Public Health Nutrition*, 1: 5–21.

Randolph TF, Schelling E, Grace D, Nicholson CF, Leroy JL, Cole DC, Demment MW, Omore A, Zinsstag J, Ruel M (2007). Invited review: Role of livestock in human nutrition and health for poverty reduction in developing countries. *Journal Animal Science,* 85: 2788–2800.

REN21 (2011). *Renewables 2011: Global Status Report.* Paris, Renewable Energy Policy Network for the 21st Century Secretariat.

Reuters (2011). Barrick builds wall to prevent gold theft at Tanzania mine. Available at: http://www.mineweb.com/ mineweb/view/mineweb/en/page504?oid=136698&sn=Detail&pid=102055, 3 October.

Rist L, Feintrenie L and Levant P (2010). The livelihood impacts of oil palm: Smallholders in Indonesia. *Biodiversity and Conservation,* 19(4): 1009–1024.

Rosegrant M, Zhu T, Msangi S, Sulser T (2008). Global scenarios for biofuels: Impacts and implications. *Review of Agricultural Economics,* 30(3): 495–505.

RSB (2011). The Roundtable on Sustainable Biofuels. Available at: http://rsb.epfl.ch/.

Rudel TK, Flescher K, Bates D, Baptista S, Holmgren P (2000). Tropical deforestation literature: geographical and historical patterns. Unasylva 51:11-18.

Schoneveld G, German L, Andrade R, Chin M, Caroko W, Romero-Hernández O (2011). The role of national governance systems in biofuel development. A comparative analysis of lessons learned. *Infobrief*, 35. Bogor, Centre for International Forestry Research.

Seré C, van der Zijpp A, Persley G, Rege E (2008). Dynamics of livestock production systems, drivers of change and prospects for animal genetic resources. *Animal Genetic Resources Information,* 42: 3–27.

Smeets EMW, Faaij APC, Lewandowski IM, Turkenbur WC (2007). A bottom-up assessment and review of global bio-energy potentials to 2020. *Progress in Energy and Combustion Science,* 33: 56–106.

SOFA (2008). Biofuels: Prospects, risks and opportunities. The State of Food and Agriculture (SOFA). Rome, FAO. ftp://ftp.fao.org/docrep/fao/011/i0100e/i0290e.pdf.

Steenblik R (2007). Biofuels – At what cost? Government support for ethanol and biodiesel in selected OECD countries. A synthesis of reports addressing subsidies for biofuels in Australia, Canada, the European Union, Switzerland and the United States. Geneva, The Global Subsidies Initiative of the International Institute for Sustainable Development.

Steinfeld H, Mooney HA, Schneider F, Neville LE (2010). *Livestock in a Changing Landscape: Drivers, Consequences, and Responses.* Washington, DC, Island Press. Available at: http://www.fao.org/docrep/013/am074e/am074e00.pdf.

Sulle E and Nelson F (2009). Biofuels, land access and rural livelihoods in Tanzania. London, International Institute for Environment and Development.

Thornton PK (2010). Livestock production: Recent trends and future prospects. *Philosophical Transactions of the Royal Society,* 365: 2853–2867.

Thornton PK , van de Steeg J, Notenbaert A, Herrero M (2009). The impacts of climate change on livestock and livestock systems in developing countries: A review of what we know and what we need to know. *Agricultural Systems,* 101(3): 113–127.

UNEP (2007). Global environment outlook: environment for development, *GEO,* 4. UNEP/Earthprint.

UNEP (2011a). Environmental Assessment of Ogoniland. Available at: http://postconflict.unep.ch/publications/OEA/UNEP_OEA.pdf.

UNEP (2011b). *The Bioenergy and Water Nexus.* Paris, Freiburg, Darmstadt and Berlin, United Nations Environment Programme, Oeko-Institut and IEA Bioenergy Task 43.

Van Gelder JW and German L (2011). Biofuel finance. Global trends in biofuel finance in forest-rich countries of Asia, Africa and Latin America and implications for governance. *Infobrief,* 36. Bogor Barat, Centre for International Forestry Research.

Vermeulen S and Cotula L (2010). Over the heads of local people: Consultation, consent, and recompense in large-scale land deals for biofuels projects in Africa. *The Journal of Peasant Studies,* 37(4): 899–916.

Vermeulen S, Sulle E and Fauveaud S (2009). Biofuels in Africa: Growing small-scale opportunities. Briefing business models for sustainable development. London, International Institute for Environment and Development.

Von Braun J (2005). Small-scale farmers in liberalised trade environment. Proceedings of the seminar on small-scale farmers in liberalised trade environment, Haikko, organized by the University of Helsinki, October 2004: 21–52.

WHO and FAO (2003). Diet, nutrition and the prevention of chronic diseases. Report of the joint WHO/FAO expert consultation. *WHO Technical Report Series*, No. 916 (TRS 916), Geneva.

Wirsenius S, Azar C and Berndes G (2010). How much land is needed for global food production under scenarios of dietary changes and livestock productivity increases in 2030? *Agricultural Systems,* 103(9): 621–638.

Wood S, Sebastian K and Scherr SJ (2000). Pilot analysis of global ecosystems: Agroecosystems. Washington, DC, International Food Policy Research Institute and World Resources Institute.

World Bank (2010). Rising global interest in farmland: Can it yield sustainable and equitable benefits? Washington, DC.

World Bank (2011). Forest area (sq. km) data. Washington, DC. Available at: http://data.worldbank.org/indicator/AG.LND.FRST.K2/countries?display=default (accessed 27 September 2011).

Zah R, Böni H, Gauch M, Hischier R, Lehmann M, Wäger P (2007). Ökobilanz von Energieprodukten: Ökologische Bewertung von Biotreibstoffen. St. Gallen, Empa.

Zika M and Erb KH (2009). The global loss of net primary production resulting from human-induced soil degradation in drylands. *Ecological Economics,* 69: 310–318.

Notes

1   The authors gratefully acknowledge the support provided by the University of Bern, Centre for Development and Environment and the Department of Integrative Geography, through the Special Research Project of the National Centre of Competence in Research NCCR North-South in the preparation of this article.

2   Land-use changes are categorized as direct and indirect changes. Direct changes occur when biofuel feedstock, such as soybean for biodiesel, displaces an existing land use system, such as grazing land for cattle. This in turn may lead to a change in another area, for example from forest to grazing land, which is then known as an indirect change.

3   See: Hope for Madagascar, at: http://fanantenana.wordpress.com/2009/06/18/the-truth-about-land-grab/.

4   For more information about this research project, see: http://media.oaklandinstitute.org/special-investigation-understanding-land-investment-deals-africa.

Chapter **5**
The Importance of International Trade and Trade Rules for Transforming Global Agriculture

Lead Article: THE IMPORTANCE OF INTERNATIONAL TRADE,
                  TRADE RULES AND MARKET STRUCTURES

Lim Li Ching
Third World Network, and Martin Khor, South Centre

Abstract

Reforms of the international trade regime require a significant reduction or removal of harmful subsidies currently provided mainly by developed countries, while at the same time allowing special treatment and safeguard mechanisms for developing countries in order to promote their smallholder farmers' livelihoods. Such reforms, coupled with policies in support of sustainable small-scale agriculture in developing countries, would improve local production for enhancing food security.

There is also a need for regulatory measures aimed at reorganizing the prevailing market structure of the agricultural value chain, which is dominated by a few multinational corporations and marginalizes smallholder farmers and sustainable production systems. Policies that increase the choices of smallholders to sell their products on local or global markets at a decent price would complement efforts to rectify the imbalances.

In addition, a shift to more sustainable and ecological agricultural practices would benefit smallholder farmers by increasing productivity while strengthening their resilience to shocks, such as climate change, and reducing the adverse impacts of conventional agricultural practices on the environment and health. The trade policy framework should therefore support such a shift.

A. Introduction

The intersection of international trade and agriculture has become increasingly important as more and more countries and their farmers participate in global markets. National trade-related policies, such as subsidies and support measures, trade restrictions and tariffs, have a major impact not only on national agricultural and food systems, but also on agricultural performance in other countries. Due to the increasing importance and binding nature of multilateral, regional and bilateral trade agreements, the rules established therein have significant effects on national trade policies as well as on the structure and nature of the global system of agricultural trade and production patterns. National trade policies and international trade rules can therefore have a significant impact on food security.

The trade framework that has influenced the policies and practices of many developing countries comprises the following: loan conditionalities of the international financial institutions, rules of the World Trade Organization (WTO), rules in bilateral and regional trade agreements as well as unilateral policy measures (South Centre, 2011). Guided or obliged by the rules and conditionalities within this framework, many developing countries have significantly lowered their agricultural tariffs and their domestic support for farmers. At the same time, liberalization of markets has increased pressure on costs, prompting producers towards greater specialization, which often results in monocropping, increased mechanization and utilization of chemicals (leading to higher dependence on external inputs), and enhanced scales of production.

In contrast, developed countries have not been subject to the conditionalities of the international financial institutions. Moreover, WTO rules, by and large, have allowed them to maintain their traditional support for domestic agriculture through a combination of high subsidies, high tariff peaks and export promotion. And in the free trade agreements (FTAs) involving developed and developing countries, agricultural subsidies are generally omitted from the agenda. The trade framework governing global agriculture is thus an awkward combination of liberalization and protectionism. While developing countries are required to undertake greater liberalization, developed countries have been able to retain their protectionist policies.

Although increased agricultural trade can offer opportunities for the poor, the benefits have been unevenly distributed. Growing evidence indicates that, to date, small-scale farmers and rural communities in many countries have not benefited significantly from agricultural trade liberalization (IAASTD, 2009); instead it is the largest agricultural producers who have been able to benefit more easily from the opportunities resulting from improved market access. Thus, overall, the distributional effects of trade liberalization, among and within countries, have resulted in the poorest developing countries and farmers being net losers.

The most vulnerable groups who experience hunger are the smallholders, landless labourers, pastoralists, fisherfolk, forest dwellers and the urban poor. Any trade regime that fails to benefit these groups, or affects them negatively, is likely to lead to the denial or violation of the right to food (De Schutter, 2009a). Such a denial of an essential right underlines the importance of ensuring access of all people, especially the poor, to food, as well as the need for giving priority to food security in developing countries.

While many developing countries once sought food self-sufficiency, this objective was gradually tempered by a perception of economic efficiency that recognized the advantages of importing food at cheaper cost, so long as there was sufficient foreign exchange to pay for the imports. As a result, local food production was not given high priority in national policies. Cheaper food imports took an increasing share of the domestic market in many countries. However, while this gave consumers access to lower priced food, there were drawbacks, including a decline or stagnation in domestic food production and adverse effects on small farmers' livelihoods and rural development. In some cases, the foods imported from developed countries were heavily subsidized, while the poorer countries did not have the resources to match the subsidies.

This situation has been exacerbated by rising world prices of many food items in recent years, resulting in more expensive food imports and inflation of food prices in local markets, often leading to social instability. A further increase in world food prices in 2011 and 2012 has given rise to uncertainty and insecurity in the net food importing countries. As a result, some of these countries have shifted their focus back to achieving greater self-sufficiency and increasing local food production, and to adopting trade policies in support of this objective (IAASTD, 2009; Khor, 2009; South Centre, 2011).

It is now increasingly recognized that the immediate need is to ensure availability of food in countries currently dependent on imports. However, a long-term solution should include boosting local food production in developing countries where conditions are suitable. While there are many factors involved in increasing local production, an appropriate trade policy framework is a very important requirement. Trade policy reform aimed at creating a fairer global trading system could make a positive contribution to food security and poverty alleviation.

At the same time, there is a growing realization that agriculture cannot proceed on the energy- and input-intensive paths of the past, and that a paradigm shift towards sustainability is needed, where small-scale farmers and agroecological methods provide the way forward (e.g. De Schutter, 2010; Herren et al., 2011; IAASTD, 2009). Reducing dependence on fossil energy inputs and cutting down on greenhouse gas (GHG) emissions from agriculture will require increasing local food self-sufficiency and promoting less fuel- and petrochemical-intensive methods of production (see comment by Heinberg in this chapter).

To the extent that trade rules are fair and promote sustainable or ecological agriculture, they should be maintained and promoted. However, there are aspects of existing international and regional trade rules that run counter to the promotion of a trading system supportive of sustainable agriculture. In addition, the prevailing market structure, where the supply chain is dominated by a few multinational companies, has led to the marginalization of small farmers and the further entrenchment of unsustainable agricultural practices. This situation is exacerbated by pressure on countries to specialize in producing commodity cash crops and undertake large-scale farming.

This chapter thus addresses four key interrelated areas: structural adjustment and import liberalization, the imbalance in trade rules governing agriculture, the imbalance in market structure, and environmental sustainability. It raises issues that need to be addressed with a view to establishing a trade policy framework that is supportive of food security and sustainability.

B. Structural adjustment and import liberalization

An important factor in the decline of agriculture in many developing countries, especially in Africa, has

Table 1: Import surges of selected commodities, and their impact on local production volume, various years

Country/commodity	Extent of increase in imports	Percentage fall in local production	Time periods compared
Senegal: tomato paste	15 times	50 per cent	1990–1994; 1995–2000
Burkina Faso: tomato paste	4 times	50 per cent	1990–1994; 1995–2000
Jamaica: vegetable oils	2 times	68 per cent	1990–1994; 1995–2000
Chile: vegetable oils	3 times	50 per cent	1985–1989; 1995–2000
Haiti: rice	13 times	Small	1984–1989; 1995–2000
Haiti: chicken meat	30 times	Small	1985–1989; 1995–2000
Kenya: dairy products	52 times	Cut local milk sales	1980–1990; 1990-1998
Benin: chicken meat	17 times	Stunted	1985–1989; 1995–2000

Source: Based on FAO, 2003, and Action Aid, 2008.

been the structural adjustment policies prescribed by the international financial institutions. These polices affected rural producers directly, as they led to the dismantling of institutions and national policy measures that assisted farmers, including the reduction or removal of subsidies and credit, assistance in marketing and food processing, and a drastic reduction in agricultural tariffs (De Schutter, 2009a; Khor, 2009). The implementation of the WTO Agreement on Agriculture also led countries to liberalize their agricultural trade, thereby compounding the effect on agricultural producers in developing countries.

Studies by the Food and Agriculture Organization of the United Nations (FAO) have revealed that many developing countries significantly liberalized their agricultural imports by lowering tariffs as required by the conditionalities attached to loans extended by the international financial institutions. As observed by the FAO:

Structural adjustment programmes implemented over the past few decades have resulted in radical reform of the agricultural sectors of many developing countries, a period during which the majority of OECD agricultural sectors have continued to be heavily protected. The process adopted has, in many cases, severely damaged the capacity of developing countries to increase levels of agricultural production and/or productivity. These unilateral reforms tend to have been reinforced by multilateral agreements (FAO, 2003: 75, cited in South Centre, 2011).

At present, many of the poor countries that had originally lowered their applied tariffs under structural adjustment policies in the 1980s and 1990s are no longer so tightly bound by loan conditionalities.

However, several of these countries still maintain their low applied tariffs, which are far below their WTO bound rates (South Centre, 2011). For example, many African countries have applied agricultural tariffs of 10–20 per cent, compared with their bound rates of 80–100 per cent (WTO, 2010).

As a result, a number of countries that were net exporters or self-sufficient in many food crops have experienced a rise in imports – some of which are heavily subsidized – and a decline in local production. Table 1 highlights some cases of import surges, the extent of the surges and the impact on local production. The import surges (FAO, 2003 and 2006) have led to such low prices on domestic markets that they have tended to drive local producers out of business, threatening the ability of those producers to feed themselves and their families (De Schutter, 2009a and 2011c).

There have been many case studies of the incidence and damaging effects of import liberalization on local communities and rural producers in developing countries (see, for example, Action Aid, 2008; FAO, 2003; Raman, 2004). These studies show how farmers involved in the production of various food commodities (e.g. staple crops such as rice and wheat, as well as other produce such as milk and other dairy products, vegetables and fruit, poultry and sugar) experienced a fall in incomes and threats to their livelihoods as a result of an influx of imports which undermined otherwise viable, efficient domestic production (see box 1 for a case study of Ghana). As a result, the development of the agricultural sector in developing countries, and therefore agriculture's significant potential growth multiplier for the whole economy, was undermined. And the effects on human welfare, national food production and food security were severe.

The situation has been exacerbated by high agricultural subsidies in developed countries, which enable them to penetrate developing countries' markets with cheap exports, thereby disrupting local production in the importing countries, preventing access by those countries to developed-country markets and outcompeting developing countries' products in third markets (South Centre, 2011). Several studies have shown that the high subsidies have allowed many agricultural products to be sold below the cost of production (see also the comment in this chapter by Lilliston and Hansen-Kuhn regarding the extent of United States "dumping"). For example, a calculation of the dumping margins for United States commodity crops

from 1990 through 2003 showed that wheat, corn, soybeans, rice and cotton were consistently exported at well below the cost of production, ranging from 10 per cent for corn to more than 50 per cent for cotton.

According to the United Nations Special Rapporteur on the right to food, the opening up of the agricultural sector to competition by binding countries to low import tariff rates may therefore constitute a serious threat to the right to food, especially in the least developed countries (LDCs) where agriculture remains a fragile sector (De Schutter, 2009a). This is because the greatest threat to food security is in the rural areas, and a larger proportion of the populations in the countries that are the most vulnerable depend on agriculture for their livelihoods.

Box 1: The impact of trade liberalization in Ghana

The policies of food self-sufficiency and government encouragement of the agricultural sector in Ghana (through marketing, credit and subsidies for inputs) helped to increase food production (for example of rice, tomatoes and poultry). However, these policies were reversed starting from the mid-1980s, and especially in the 1990s. For example, the price of fertilizer increased following an elimination of the subsidy, and the marketing role of the State was phased out. In addition, the minimum guaranteed prices of rice and wheat were abolished, as were many State agricultural trading enterprises and the seed agency responsible for producing and distributing seeds to farmers. Subsidized credit was also discontinued. Applied tariffs for most agricultural imports were reduced significantly to the present 20 per cent, even though the bound rate committed to the WTO by Ghana was around 99 per cent. As a result, local farmers were no longer able to compete with imports, the prices of which were kept artificially low by high subsidies in exporting countries, especially for rice, tomatoes and poultry.

Rice output in the 1970s could meet all the local needs, but by 2002 imports constituted 64 per cent of domestic supply. Rice output fell from an annual average of 56,000 tons (in 1978–1980) in the northern region to only 27,000 tons for the whole country in 1983. In 2003, the United States, which provided subsidies to its farmers for rice amounting to $1.3 billion, exported 111,000 tons of rice to Ghana. A study by the United States Government found that 57 per cent of United States rice farms would not have covered their costs without subsidies. In 2000–2003 the average cost of production and milling of United States white rice was $415 per ton, but it was exported for just $274 per ton – a price 34 per cent below production cost.

Tomato production in Ghana, especially in the upper eastern region, had been thriving until a privatization programme resulted in the selling off or closure of tomato-canning factories, while import tariffs were reduced. This enabled the heavily subsidized EU tomato industry to penetrate Ghana, displacing the livelihoods of tomato farmers and industry employees. Tomato paste imported by Ghana rose from 3,200 tons in 1994 to 24,077 tons in 2002. Local tomato production has stagnated since 1995. Meanwhile, tomato-based products from Europe have made inroads into African markets. In 2004, EU aid for processed tomato products was €298 million, and there were many more millions in indirect aid.

Ghana's poultry sector began growing in the late 1950s, reached its prime in the late 1980s then declined steeply in the 1990s. The decline was due to the withdrawal of government support and the reduction of tariffs. Poultry imports rose by 144 per cent between 1993 and 2003, a significant share of which consisted of heavily subsidized poultry from Europe. In 2002, 15 European countries produced 9.010 million tons of poultry meat and 1.147 million tons were exported at a value of €928 million, or an average of €809 per ton. It is estimated that the total subsidy on exported poultry (e.g. export refunds, subsidies for cereals fed to the poultry) was €254 per ton. Between 1996 and 2002, EU frozen chicken exports to West Africa rose eightfold, mainly due to import liberalization. In Ghana, this adversely affected half a million chicken farmers. In 1992, domestic farmers supplied 95 per cent of Ghana's market, but this share fell to 11 per cent in 2001, as imported poultry became cheaper than local poultry.

Sources: Khor, 2008.

C. Imbalance in trade rules governing agriculture

The trade rules that underpin the global agricultural trade regime are also a source of concern. The WTO's Agreement on Agriculture contains rules in three areas – market access, domestic support and export subsidies – in which the developed countries were expected to reduce their protection. However, they have done very little in this regard.

There are many loopholes in the system, which allow the developed countries to continue to subsidize and protect their agriculture at the expense of the developing countries. The average support to agricultural producers in the major developed countries as a percentage of gross value of farm receipts was 30 per cent during the period 2003–2005, representing almost $1 billion per day. These policies cost developing countries about $17 billion per year, a cost equivalent to five times the recent levels of official development assistance (ODA) to agriculture (Anderson and Van der Mensbrugghe, 2006, cited in Hoffmann, 2011). It should be pointed out that these figures refer exclusively to agricultural subsidies, and do not include indirect subsidies for energy (fuel and electricity) used in agriculture.

The situation has improved only slightly in recent years: the Organisation for Economic Co-operation and Development (OECD, 2010) estimates that the subsidies given to farm producers in all OECD countries totalled $252 billion in 2009, which is 22 per cent of the total value of gross farm receipts that year. This is about the same level as in 2007 and 2008. The level of support is even higher than this average in some countries: in 2006–2008, it was 27 per cent in the EU, 49 per cent in Japan, 60 per cent in Switzerland and 62 per cent in Norway (OECD, 2009). The level of support is also very high for certain products. Specific support for rice amounted to 60 per cent of total producer rice receipts in 2006–2008 (OECD, 2009).

There are at least three adverse effects of developed countries' subsidies on farmers in developing countries:
(i) they are unable to export to the subsidizing developed countries' markets;
(ii) they are unable to compete in third markets because the developed countries' products are sold at artificially low prices; and
(ii) they have to compete in their own local markets with subsidized products coming from developed countries, which adversely affects their market share, incomes and livelihoods (South Centre, 2011). The elimination or substantial reduction of both subsidies and protectionism in industrialized countries is therefore important, particularly for small-scale farming around the world (IAASTD, 2009).

Under the WTO, there has been some apparent progress in trying to address export subsidies. The WTO Hong Kong Ministerial Conference in 2005 agreed that as part of the Doha Round of trade negotiations, export subsidies of the developed countries would be eliminated by the end of 2013. However, this may not be realized if the Doha negotiations are not concluded, and there has not been a binding agreement on these elements as yet.

On the issue of domestic subsidies, a major loophole in the WTO Agreement on Agriculture is that countries are obliged to reduce their bound levels of domestic support that are deemed "trade distorting", but there are no constraints on the amount of subsidies deemed to be non-distorting or minimally distorting, which are placed in the so-called Green Box. Recent studies have shown that many of the Green Box subsidies are also trade distorting as they have significant effects on the market and on trade. Therefore, the major subsidizing countries can reduce their "trade- distorting subsidies" while changing the types of domestic subsidies they give, effectively providing similar levels or even increasing the total amount of subsidies (Khor, 2009). Unfortunately, the Doha negotiations are unlikely to impose new effective disciplines on the Green Box items, as the developed countries have successfully insisted that there be no new rules that would place a cap on the Green Box subsidies (South Centre, 2011). The current negotiating text proposes some changes to the Green Box, but these do not alter the basic elements, especially as there is no cap on the Green Box subsidies. Thus they could increase without limit in the future.

The Doha negotiations are mandated to substantially reduce (other) domestic support in developed countries. However, to date, the offers of the United States and the EU indicate their overall trade-distorting support (OTDS) would be reduced at the bound level, but not at the applied level (Khor, 2009). At present, the level of the actual OTDS of these two economies is far below the level of their total allowed trade-distorting support. Therefore, they can afford to reduce the level of allowed trade-distorting support significantly before the cut reaches the level where the present actual trade-distorting support is affected (South Centre, 2011). In other words, they would only cut "water" (i.e. the difference between allowed and actual subsidies) and not their actual subsidies.

The figures in the agriculture negotiating group Chair's text would not reduce the actual present domestic support for the United States. The allowable OTDS for this country is to be cut by 70 per cent (i.e. from the present $48.3 billion allowable level to $14.5 billion). The proposed $14.5 billion level is in fact double the estimated 2007 actual OTDS of $7–8 billion, thus effectively allowing the United State considerable "water" to increase from this level. Meanwhile, the allowable OTDS for the EU is to be cut by 80 per cent, which would reduce the EU's present allowable OTDS of €110.3 billion to €22 billion. According to one estimate, however, the actual OTDS is expected to drop to €12 billion at the end of the Common Agricultural Policy reform in 2014. Thus the cut, though it appears to be large, would allow for "water" vis-à-vis what is planned.

While there has been a lowering of the applied OTDS of the United States and the EU in recent years, this has been accompanied by a rise in their support to Green Box items. As actual OTDS is cut, subsidies could be shifted to the Green Box and therefore total domestic support may not decline. Thus the cuts in their allowable OTDS may appear large, but in fact will not reduce applied or planned reductions in OTDS, and moreover, these will be offset by an increase (in the case of the EU) in Green Box subsidies (South Centre, 2011). An objective conclusion would be that the OTDS figures of 70 per cent cut for the United States and 80 percent cut for the EU are not adequate as they do not constitute effective and substantive, or real, cuts.

Meanwhile, the developing countries are being asked to reduce their agricultural tariffs further. The Chair's proposal at the Doha talks is for a maximum 36 per cent tariff cut by developing countries, while the LDCs are exempted from any tariff reduction, and small, vulnerable economies will be accorded more lenient treatment. However, the combination of high subsidies in developed countries and low applied tariffs in developing countries has caused highly frequent import surges, which have adversely affected farmers' livelihoods and incomes.

Due to increasing concern over this, a majority of developing-country members of the WTO (which include the G-33, the African Group and the LDC group) have proposed two new instruments – Special Products (SP), and a Special Safeguard Mechanism (SSM) – to be introduced into the rules of the WTO as part of the Doha negotiations. The objective of both instruments is to promote the livelihoods of small farmers, food security and rural development in developing countries. Such policy flexibility is critically important to advance development and sustainability goals (IAASTD, 2009), and would shield developing countries' producers from competition from industrialized countries' farmers (De Schutter, 2009a).

Under the SP concept, developing countries would be entitled to have no or lesser reductions of tariffs on a certain percentage of their agricultural tariff lines as part of the Doha Round's agriculture modalities. Under the SSM, developing countries would be allowed to impose an additional increase in tariffs, on top of bound rates, in situations of reduced import prices or increased import volumes, in order to protect local farmers from import surges and to avoid possible damage to domestic productive capacity.

Acceptance of these two instruments was formalized in the WTO's Hong Kong Ministerial Declaration of 2005, which stated:

> Members will have the flexibility to self-designate an appropriate number of tariff lines as Special Products guided by indicators based on the criteria of food security, livelihood security and rural development. Developing country Members will also have the right to have recourse to a Special Safeguard Mechanism based on import quantity and price triggers, with precise arrangements to be further defined.

The acceptance of these two concepts and instruments was a major step forward in recognition by the WTO of the right of developing-country governments to take trade measures in defence of their farmers' livelihoods.

However, there is considerable opposition from some agricultural commodity-exporting countries, including several large developing-country agricultural exporters,[1] which fear that the use of the SSM could result in losses of legitimate exports. However, the restrictions they have proposed would prevent this instrument from working in an effective and simple way. As such, the SSM, even if established, may have very limited use in enabling developing countries to protect their farmers from import surges. In any case, the Doha negotiations have hit an impasse, and it is unlikely that the SSM will be established any time soon.

Ironically, there is already an agricultural safeguard in the WTO (known as the special agricultural safeguard, SSG), but the eligibility criteria have disadvantaged most developing countries, resulting in only 20 developing countries being eligible to use the safeguard. Thus, most developing countries have no proper instrument to counter import surges. In order to rectify the imbalance and enable developing countries to safeguard their food security and farmers' livelihoods, more countries should be eligible to make use of the SSG.

In addition, regional and bilateral FTAs have prevented developing countries from using the flexibilities in the WTO agreements (De Schutter, 2009a). Moreover, many of these FTAs require developing countries to reduce or eliminate their tariffs even further (Khor, 2009; De Schutter, 2011b). For example, in the Economic Partnership Agreements between the African, Carribbean and Pacific (ACP) countries and the EU, the ACP countries are asked to eliminate their tariffs on 80 per cent of their tariff lines, including for agricultural products, over varying time periods. Yet the reduction of agricultural subsidies is not part of the FTA agenda. Thus developing countries are not able to gain from what may have been the most advantageous for them, while having to eliminate their agricultural tariffs to a larger extent than required of them by their obligations at the WTO (South Centre, 2011).

D. Imbalance in market structures

Increased trade in agricultural products implies that food production is redirected towards serving external instead of domestic markets. In addition, as larger farmers are more easily able to access foreign markets and benefit from such access, the increase in agricultural trade risks marginalizing small farmers. And since market power is rarely equally distributed along the value chain, this enables the more powerful actors to pass on costs and risks to the weaker actors – typically smallholder farmers (IFAD, 2010).

As such, the role of multinational corporations, particularly commodity traders, food processors and global retailers, becomes more important (De Schutter, 2009a; Herren, 2011). The world has witnessed a trend towards agribusiness consolidation, and this trend is seen all along the value chain, with a few multinational companies providing the majority of inputs such as pesticides, seeds and crop genetic technologies, or undertaking marketing, food processing and retailing. This has resulted in national, regional and global supply chains that bypass traditional markets where smallholders sell to local markets and traders (World Bank, 2008).

The world seed, agrochemical and biotechnology markets are dominated by a few mega companies (see the comment of Elenita Daño in this chapter). In 2004, the market share of the four largest agrochemical and seed companies reached 60 per cent for agrochemicals and 33 per cent for seeds, up from 47 per cent and 23 per cent in 2007 respectively (World Bank, 2008). Where new technologies and products (e.g. transgenic seeds) have been developed and protected by intellectual property rights (IPRs), industry consolidation has taken place rapidly (PANNA, 2010). The four leading companies in terms of ownership of biotechnology patents had a market share of 38 per cent in 2004, and one company had a 91 per cent share of the worldwide transgenic soybean market (World Bank, 2008).

These companies have a vested interest in maintaining a monoculture-focused, carbon-intensive industrial approach to agriculture, which is dependent on external inputs (Hoffmann, 2011). International supply chains, often dominated by major food processors and retailers, also tend to source from large-scale monocrop production, rather than from diverse multicropping and integrated livestock and crop farming systems. This trend reinforces the marginalization of small farmers and of sustainable production systems. In addition, to comply with the standards of global retailers, many farmers are encouraged to use improved varieties of seeds and external inputs, often supplied by oligopolistic companies, which further exacerbates dependence and reliance on conventional agriculture (De Schutter, 2009a).

Given their increased market power, commodity buyers and larger retailers which dominate global food chains impose their prices on producers (who are in an unfavourable bargaining position) and set standards that many small-scale farmers are unable to meet (De Schutter, 2009a; PANNA, 2010). Small-scale farmers are therefore unable to compete and are relegated to low-value, local markets, which strongly disadvantage them in the competition for land, water or other productive resources (De Schutter 2009b and 2011b). This risks perpetuating unsustainable agricultural practices, as small farmers are further marginalized. Furthermore, dependence on this increasingly concentrated global food supply chain intensifies vulnerability to shocks, whether from extreme weather events or excessive financial speculation in agricultural markets (see comment by Lilliston and Hansen-Kuhn in this chapter).

However, multinational corporations are neither subjected to much discipline, nor to obligations relating to their exercise of power on the market, which results in a critical governance gap (De Schutter, 2009a). Because of this and their market positions, most of the benefits from global food supply chains accrue to commodity buyers, food processors and retailers, rather than to developing-country producers (De Schutter, 2009b and 2011b).

Improving the rural poor's market participation is important, because if these markets work well and are inclusive of smallholder farmers, they can provide strong incentives for those farmers to make the necessary investments and take the requisite risks to enhance their ability to respond to market demand (IFAD, 2010), including investing in ecological agriculture for which there are valuable niche markets (e.g. for organic produce, as discussed in the next section). Moreover, if poor rural farmers were able to benefit from their participation in markets, they could gradually save and accumulate assets, increasing not only their own prosperity but also their capacity to deal with risks and shocks (IFAD, 2010). This would also enable them to deal better with some of the challenges associated with climate change, for example.

E. Environmental sustainability

Conventional and intensive agriculture is characterized by mechanization and the use of chemical fertilizers and pesticides, as well as a reliance on irrigation and fossil fuels. These have contributed to considerable environmental damage, including accelerated loss of biodiversity and ecosystem services such as those necessary for the production of food and water or for controlling disease, increased GHG emissions, as well as considerable health impacts (IAASTD, 2009; World Bank, 2008).

Moreover, climate change has the potential to undermine the resource base on which agriculture depends. Agriculture has to cope with increased climate variability and more extreme weather events. While local mean temperature increases of 1°–3°C would affect crop productivity differently depending on latitudes, with tropical and arid regions suffering more, warming above 3°C would have increasingly negative impacts in all regions (Easterling et al., 2007). In some African countries, yields from rain-fed agriculture, important for the poorest farmers, could be reduced by up to 50 per cent by 2020 (IPCC, 2007b), which would increase the number of people at risk of hunger.

However, the impacts of agriculture on the environment and human health, and the relationship between agriculture and climate change, are usually ignored in international trade discussions, despite the repercussions these could have on the right to adequate food (De Schutter, 2009a).

A progressive switch to more input- and energy-intensive forms of agricultural production cannot be attributed directly to the increase in global trade in agricultural commodities, but this trend has been encouraged by the specialization of countries in cash crops for export (De Schutter, 2009a). Intensive, large-scale industrial export-oriented agriculture has increased under the trade liberalization agenda (see comment by Lilliston and Hansen-Kuhn in this chapter), with adverse consequences such as the loss of soil nutrients and water from agricultural lands, and unsustainable soil and water management (IAASTD, 2009).

In addition, the failure of markets to value and internalize environmental and social costs in the prices of traded agricultural products, or to provide incentives for sustainability, has also played a part in entrenching unsustainable practices in agriculture (IAASTD, 2009). Inappropriate pricing and subsidy policies and the failure to manage externalities also hinder the widespread adoption of more sustainable agricultural practices (World Bank, 2008). The situation is compounded by price volatility, where extremely low agricultural commodity prices over the past two decades followed by the recent price hikes has discouraged long-term investments in more sustainable, ecological agriculture (see comment by Lilliston and Hansen-Kuhn in this chapter).

Given the growing concerns about climate change and the imperative for alleviating rural poverty, there is an urgent need to move towards more sustainable, environmentally friendly agricultural practices that are more resilient and less input- and energy-intensive (De Schutter, 2009a and 2010). This is especially pertinent in the current context of the scarcity and high prices of oil (see comment by Heinberg in this chapter). There is increasing evidence that sustainable or ecological agriculture can contribute to climate change adaptation and mitigation while also being productive (e.g. De Schutter, 2010; ITC and FiBL, 2007; Niggli et al., 2009; Scialabba and Müller-Lindenlauf, 2010; also comment by Heinberg).

According to the United Nations Special Rapporteur on the right to food, future regulation of international trade in agriculture should take into account the impact of various modes of agricultural production on climate change to allow countries to provide incentives in favour of forms of production, such as organic agriculture and agroecological practices, which respect the environment while at the same time contributing to food security. This supports the call by the International Assessment on Agricultural Knowledge, Science and Technology for Development (IAASTD) for a paradigm shift in agriculture towards agroecology.

A major task is to transform the uniform model of quick-fix industrial agriculture that is highly dependent on external inputs into flexible, "regenerative" agricultural systems that continuously recreate the resources they use and achieve higher productivity and profitability (of the systems, but not necessarily of individual products) with minimal external inputs, including energy (Hoffmann, 2011). A mosaic of regenerative systems may include biodynamic agriculture, organic agriculture, agroecology, integrated crop and livestock farming, and similar practices.

The trade policy framework should support such a transformation of agriculture, rather than encourage the prevailing unsustainable system. Moreover, if the impacts of structural adjustment and import liberalization and the imbalances in trade rules and market structure are not addressed, countries are unlikely to move towards more sustainable modes of production. It is unlikely, for example, that large farms that rely on significant subsidies to be profitable will make a significant shift to ecological agriculture practices, unless there is comprehensive reform of the system of subsidies, including lowering or removing some of the so-called "green" subsidies that fall in the Green Box (Hoffmann, 2011). At the same time, farmers should be given adequate support for ecological agriculture practices.

However, a supportive trade framework should avoid protectionism in the guise of environmental protection (South Centre, 2011). It should also support the "greening" of subsidies and in ways that will give greater policy space to developing countries. Environmental standards, labelling and other issues would also need to be dealt with from a "sustainable development" perspective. Developing countries should be provided with resources and technologies for upgrading their existing environmental technologies and standards. In addition, the full and effective participation of developing countries in setting international standards should be assured, as also the concomitant assistance, particularly to small-scale farmers, to comply with such standards.

Measures should also be taken to encourage organic farming, which is not only beneficial to the environment, but also provides trade opportunities for smallholder farmers in developing countries. Niche markets such as organic can provide price premiums and/or long-term contracts (IFAD, 2010). The total global organic market was worth $55 billion in 2009, having grown by 5 per cent from the previous year, despite the economic and financial crisis (Willer and Kilcher, 2011). Global revenues have increased more than threefold from $18 billion in 2000, and double-digit growth rates were observed each year, except in 2009. As there is a significant increase in consumer demand for organic foods worldwide, there is also an opportunity for small farmers to market their surplus organic products in national, regional and global markets. Thus a change in consumer tastes and demand towards organic foods, or more generally foods produced using ecological agriculture methods, can motivate changes in production systems. At the same time, it can increase the opportunities and markets for small farmers, thereby improving their livelihoods (South Centre, 2011).

Many governments in both developed and developing countries have announced plans to increase organic farming practices. However, while developed-country governments offer significant subsidies for organic farming, similar financing is scarce in developing countries. More proactive measures are required in developing countries to promote organic farming and to overcome obstacles to production, marketing and trade.

One issue that needs to be addressed is the difficulties faced by developing-country producers in adhering to organic standards. This is not so much an issue at the national level, but is a major problem for potential exporters who need to comply with many technical regulations, standards and certification systems. As UNCTAD (2004) points out, it is important to find a balance between the need for harmonization for trade and fair competition, and the need to take into account local and regional conditions and requirements. To overcome the challenge of third-party certification faced by smallholder farmers in developing countries, which is expensive, various schemes have been developed, such as participatory guarantee systems and group certification. These alternatives, which are more accessible to smallholder farmers and provide the quality assurance that consumers need, should be further promoted (also see the comment of Twarog in this chapter).

A supportive trade framework can thus assist in the transition to ecological agriculture and organic farming. Farmers using sustainable approaches should be supported by proactive State intervention (South Centre, 2011), including public sector financial and technical support, as well as extension services to introduce best practices in ecological agriculture. Other State-led services could include ecological rehabilitation, provision of organic seeds, credit and marketing support. Concurrently, the domestic tariff policy should enable small farmers to withstand competition from imports.

F. A trade framework supportive of food security and sustainability

A trade framework that is supportive of food security and sustainability will need to focus on smallholder farmers in developing countries, and encourage domestic production. This could be achieved by helping small-scale producers improve their productivity, particularly through ecological means, and strengthening their access to local markets while shielding them from the negative impacts of unduly subsidized imports of food commodities (De Schutter, 2009a). Support to sustainable small-scale agriculture, especially in terms of ensuring access to land, water, genetic resources and credit, and by investing in and improving access to rural infrastructure is critical, as is the need to untangle local food economies from the grip of supply chains dominated by multinational corporations (see also comment by Lilliston and Hansen-Kuhn in this chapter).

In other words, the plight of small-scale farmers in developing countries should be addressed through

a combination of policies that support ecological agriculture (through investments in R&D, extension services and rural infrastructure, subsidies and marketing support) along with an appropriate trade policy that protects farmers from cheap imports. At the same time, reform of the international trade regime should include requiring developed countries to sufficiently reduce or remove harmful subsidies, while providing developing countries with special treatment and safeguard mechanisms to promote their small farmers' livelihoods (Khor, 2011).

At the international level, this should include the elimination of subsidies for agricultural exports (as agreed in the WTO's Hong Kong Ministerial Declaration, 2005) and further discipline on domestic support, and the reduction of trade distortions caused by the large domestic subsidies provided by developed countries (as stated in the WTO's Doha Ministerial Declaration).

At the national level, developing countries should calibrate their degree of trade liberalization so that it is in line with their objectives and national realities. Countries that do not have the potential or intention to produce certain foodstuffs may have low or no import tariffs to enable their populations to obtain imported food at the lowest cost. Those countries that intend to increase food production can take advantage of the flexibilities allowed in the WTO by setting their tariffs at the appropriate levels in order to nurture a viable domestic food sector, as long as the applied tariffs do not exceed the bound rates (South Centre, 2011). Furthermore, those developing countries with an export interest should be given the opportunity to expand their export earnings through improved market access.

However, the flexibilities available in WTO agreements may be affected if countries enter into FTAs in which they commit to eliminate their tariffs for a large percentage of their products. Furthermore, although LDCs are exempted from reducing their bound tariffs in the Doha negotiations, they are not provided with similar exemptions on the basis of their LDC status in FTA negotiations. Thus bilateral FTAs should allow sufficient policy space for developing countries to promote their agricultural development.

Besides the establishment of an appropriate tariff policy, governments can provide various forms of encouragement to boost agricultural activities, including subsidies, credit, establishing security of land tenure and provision of inputs (South Centre, 2011). The WTO Agreement on Agriculture sets the rules on the extent of subsidies allowed. Since many developing countries previously provided only limited subsidies, if any (mainly because they lacked the financial resources), they are not allowed to provide the high levels of support given by developed countries. However, the Agreement on Agriculture allows developing-country governments to provide a certain level of *de minimis* support, equivalent to 10 per cent of total agricultural value, as well as to make use of the category of non-trade-distorting support known as the Green Box. The developing countries can avail themselves of these flexibilities to provide subsidies, as they deem appropriate, especially for ecological agriculture. However, many of them face budgetary constraints or simply lack the financial resources to do so.

The international trade regime needs to be reformed to bolster efforts to promote ecological agriculture systems, which would benefit smallholder farmers by increasing productivity, while also being more resilient to shocks such as climate change. Such systems would also reduce the impacts of agriculture on the environment and health, and are therefore urgently needed.

The options for action discussed below are based on the four themes of this lead article.

1. Review of structural adjustment recommendations and agricultural liberalization policies

In general, the need for special treatment for food products, allowing gradual and lenient liberalization, instead of steep tariff reductions, is important for developing countries. They should be allowed to provide adequate support to their agricultural sectors and to have realistic tariff policies to advance their agriculture, especially in view of the persistently high subsidies of developed countries (Khor, 2009). The developing countries should be allowed to calibrate their agricultural tariffs in such a way as to ensure that their local products can be competitive, farmers' livelihoods and incomes sustainable, and national food security assured.

(1) The policies of the international financial institutions and regional development banks should be reviewed and revised as soon as possible, so that they do not continue to serve as barriers to food security

and agricultural development in developing countries (Khor, 2009). An independent ongoing review of the trade aspects of the present and proposed conditionalities of loans is needed.

(2) Loan conditionalities should not oblige developing countries to undertake liberalization (in rate and scope) that is beyond their coping capacity, or which would be damaging to the livelihoods and incomes of their rural producers. The approach to liberalization in developing countries should be reoriented to be more realistic, especially since developed countries continue to maintain high subsidies (South Centre, 2011).

(3) At present, developing countries have flexibilities under WTO rules to adjust their applied tariffs upwards to their bound rates, and even beyond the bound rates in certain circumstances. Loan conditionalities should not prevent or hinder developing countries from making use of these flexibilities (South Centre, 2011).

(4) There is an urgent need to provide a special safeguard facility which could be used simply and effectively by developing countries so that the needed increase in tariffs can better protect their producers from the impacts of import surges (as discussed in the next section).

(5) Revenues from such tariffs could be used to finance rural development and infrastructure schemes aimed at benefiting farmers. Public investment in social protection for non-food-producing households living in poverty is also needed (De Schutter, 2011b). Complementary policies and programmes to facilitate transitions from conventional to sustainable agriculture, and to support the net trade losers through public investment to stimulate long-term growth in the agricultural sector are also important (World Bank, 2008).

2. Reforming trade rules governing agriculture

A major challenge at the international level is to modify a number of key market distortions that act as a disincentive to the transition to sustainable agricultural practices in developing countries (Hoffmann, 2011). Such distortions arise from the significant subsidization of agricultural production in developed countries and their export of this output to developing countries. As long as such subsidies are not significantly altered by the current WTO negotiations, it is difficult to imagine how developing-country producers could implement a paradigm shift towards ecological agriculture on the massive scale necessary to have an impact. Apart from real reduction of domestic support in developed countries, reforms should include improved market access for developing-country produce and policy space to support the agricultural sector, allow expansion of local food production, and the use of effective instruments to promote food security, farmers' livelihoods and rural development. This necessitates a reconsideration of trade rules in the WTO and in various FTAs (South Centre, 2011) as follows:

(1) Export subsidies in developed countries should be eliminated by 2013, as agreed in the WTO's Hong Kong Ministerial Declaration.

(2) There should be an effective deep reduction of domestic support (in actual levels, and not just the bound levels) in developed countries, with as few loopholes as possible and with no or minimal "box shifting" (i.e. shifting of subsidies towards those deemed to be non-distorting or minimally distorting, which are not subject to any disciplines, but which could also have significant effects on the market and on trade). This should include reductions in the actual OTDS as well as an objective review of the nature and effects of various subsidies now classified as Green Box subsidies, leading to stricter disciplines and reductions.

(3) Developing countries should be allowed adequate policy space to enable them to use domestic subsidies for supporting farmers' livelihoods and food security. These could include the provision of low-cost credit, assistance for the supply of inputs, storage facilities, road and transport infrastructure, strengthening of extension services, marketing facilities and networks, and support for value-added processing of agricultural products. Developing countries could examine the avenues available to them for making use of domestic subsidies, for example through the *de minimis* subsidies, and if this is not sufficient, to explore the possibility of using more subsidies, including those in the Green Box.

(4) Developing countries should have adequate policy space to make use of tariffs to protect the interests of their domestic farmers and promote food security and rural development. They should be able to use the flexibilities in the WTO rules to adjust their applied tariffs to the appropriate level as long as these do not exceed the bound level.

(5) The WTO rules should enable developing countries to promote food security, farmers' livelihoods and rural development through the effective use of the SP and SSM instruments. So far, only developed countries and a few developing countries are able to make use of a special agricultural safeguard (SSG); all developing countries should be allowed to make use of this facility to prevent import surges until a permanent SSM for developing countries is established.

(6) The developing countries' goals of food security and protection of farmers' livelihoods should be given priority by negotiators of FTAs. The percentage of goods identified for tariff elimination by developing countries should be adjusted, if necessary, to accommodate the need to exclude sensitive agricultural products. In the light of the food crisis, developing countries that have signed or are negotiating FTAs should ensure that such agreements will provide enough policy space to allow them to impose sufficiently high tariffs on agricultural imports so that they can rebuild and strengthen their agriculture sectors in order to achieve food security and promote farmers' livelihoods and rural development.

3. Addressing imbalances in market structure

Steps should be taken for the establishment of national and international rules for regulating the activities of commodity buyers, processors and retailers in the global food supply chain. Specific policies to support smallholder farmers, particularly women farmers, in gaining access to markets would also be important.

(1) The application of competition law to prevent the creation, maintenance and abuse of buyer power/domination positions in supply chains is necessary. Competition regimes sensitive to excessive buyer power in the agrifood sector, and competition mechanisms that allow affected suppliers to lodge complaints without fear of reprisal by dominant buyers are needed (De Schutter, 2009b).

(2) There is a need for antitrust measures to break up monopolies and global price-fixing cartels, an international review mechanism to investigate and monitor concentration in the agrifood sector, and investigations into the behaviour of international corporations engaged in agricultural trading and food retailing, and their impacts on farmers, farm workers, consumers and vulnerable populations (PANNA, 2010).

(3) States should proactively adopt public policies aimed at expanding the choices of smallholders

to sell their products on local or global markets at a decent price by strengthening local and national markets and supporting continued diversification of channels of trading and distribution; supporting the establishment of farmers' cooperatives and other producer organizations; establishing or defending flexible and efficient producer marketing boards under government authority but with the strong participation of producers in their governance; using the public procurement system to support small farmers; and promoting and scaling up fair trade systems, including by ensuring access to productive resources, infrastructure and technical assistance (De Schutter, 2009b; IFAD, 2010; PANNA 2010).

(4) Understanding gender-related opportunities and risks in agricultural value chains and markets, and promoting gender equality in accessing emerging opportunities, are important to support the emergence of pro-poor agricultural markets (IFAD, 2010).

(5) Agricultural research and aid have often served powerful commercial interests, including multinational seed and food retailing companies, at the expense of the values, needs, knowledge and concerns of the very people who provide the food. Farmers and other citizens need to play a central role in defining strategic priorities for agricultural research and food policies (Hoffmann, 2011; see also Herren in chapter three of this Review).

4. An agenda for environmental sustainability

The regulation of international trade in agricultural commodities should take into account the impact of various modes of agricultural production on the environment and climate change in order to allow countries to provide incentives in favour of sustainable production, such as organic farming or agroecological practices, both of which respect the environment and contribute to food security (De Schutter, 2009a).

(1) Perverse incentives and subsidies that promote or encourage the use of chemical pesticides and fertilizers, water and fuel, or encourage land degradation, should be avoided (IAASTD, 2009; World Bank, 2008). At the same time, regulations and their implementation are needed to protect the environment and address pollution, as input-intensive agriculture has adverse impacts on the environment and human health (IFAD, 2010).

(2) Agricultural subsidies need to be redirected to encourage diversified crop production for long-term

soil health and improved environmental impacts. A major shift in subsidies is needed so that governments can help reduce the initial costs and risks to farmers of transitioning towards more sustainable farming practices (Herren et al., 2011). Subsidies should be confined to those essential for facilitating the transition to sustainable production methods, such as support for extension services and research and development, rewarding environmental services, ensuring protection against volatile prices and providing specific support to smallholders (Hoffmann, 2011).

(3) Farmers should be given access to support for ecological agriculture practices. Developing countries could consider devoting a larger share of their agricultural budgets to promoting ecological agriculture, which can boost both small farmers' livelihoods and food production, while protecting the environment and conserving resources such as soil fertility and water. The support should include extension services to train farmers in the best options available for sustainable development techniques, and the development of ecological infrastructure, including improved water supply and soil fertility. Farmers should also have access to credit and marketing support.

(4) Both developing and developed countries should be encouraged to take measures to facilitate trade in organic foods originating from developing countries. Developing countries could consider the following measures: (i) increase awareness of the benefits of organic food production and trading opportunities; (ii) promote research and development and training; (iii) identify marketing strategies and partnerships, with government support; (iv) provide financial support to organic producers; and (v) promote farmers' associations and non-governmental organizations (NGOs) (UNCTAD, 2004).

(5) Importing countries could also implement measures to promote imports of organic foods from developing countries by providing information on organic standards, and on regulations and market opportunities for developing countries' exporters. They should also facilitate access to their organic food markets by simplifying requirements and procedures for importing products from developing countries and applying the concept of equivalence between national organic standards (UNCTAD, 2004).

(6) Bilateral and multilateral donor agencies could provide appropriate technical assistance for the

export of organic products from developing countries.

(7) More generally, developing countries could consider the following strategies to promote organic agriculture: (i) organic policy and action plans should be linked to the overarching objectives of the country's agriculture policies to make them mutually supportive, and to remove obstacles and biases against organic agriculture; (ii) the government should give recognition and encouragement to the organic sector, closely cooperate with the sector's organizations and farmers, and play an enabling and facilitating role; (iii) establish a participatory process, with action plans and projects based on overall policies and objectives (UNCTAD and UNEP, 2008a).

(8) Barriers to the participation of small farmers from developing countries in organic markets should be removed. Efforts to address issues such as difficulties of market access, lack of market infrastructure, prohibitive third-party certification, the lack of research, technical, policy and financial support are needed (UNCTAD and UNEP, 2008a). Growing domestic markets are also important, and urban markets could start to provide significant opportunities for smallholder farmers (IFAD, 2010).

(9) Efforts should be made to enable smallholder farmers, particularly women farmers, to access productive resources and participate in agricultural decision-making, so as to facilitate their investment in and adoption of ecological agriculture approaches.

Commentary I: Ensuring Food Security and Environmental Resilience – The Need for Supportive Agricultural Trade Rules

Nikolai Fuchs, Nexus Foundation, and Ulrich Hoffmann, UNCTAD secretariat[2]

Abstract

Despite some recent improvement the pressing – and to date unresolved – crisis of hunger and mal-nutrition as well as the looming dangers from the environmental crisis of agriculture call for a more fundamental change than is currently under way. Both crises are also closely linked to trade rules. Agriculture has always been a stumbling bloc in GATT and WTO rounds of trade liberalization, yet agriculture's specificity has never been sufficiently reflected. Rather, agriculture has increasingly been treated like any other industrial sector that should strive to enhance (mostly labour) productivity, based on specialization, economies of scale and industrialization of production methods. But this runs counter to the need for strengthening rural livelihoods, food security and such agricultural practices, which respect the planetary boundaries through enhancing the reproductive capacities, the latter being the essence of real sustainability. Based on a better understanding of the specificity of agriculture, more regionalized/localized food production networks should be encouraged by trade rules, without excluding the supplementary role trade will have to play. The key question is whether such transformation can be achieved through fully exploiting existing flexibilities in WTO rules, or whether this will require a more fundamental change in the trade tool-box.

A. Introduction

After twelve years in the third millennium it has become evident that several of the Millennium Development Goals (MDGs), chiefly among them the abatement of hunger, will be very difficult, if not impossible to achieve. Besides, humanity today is consuming an amount of resources equivalent to those of 1.5 earths[3], with a pronounced worsening tendency. Climate change has become a reality, and it is highly unlikely that the 2-degrees warming limit, which global governance seeks to meet, can be kept.[4] The planetary boundaries for nitrogen and bio-diversity have already been crossed mostly due to industrialized agriculture. Be it economic crises, be it systemic weaknesses, be it missing political will – the reasons for not yet being able to reverse this trend up to date might be multiple. But if we take ourselves and our own intents, like the pledges for fulfillment of human rights and the implementation of recent government summit declarations seriously, new efforts and new approaches to address the global challenges seem to be necessary.[5] This commentary, thinking out-of-the-box, attempts to analyze what type of trade rules is required to encourage and support a desirable, much-needed transformation of the food and agricultural sector, as outlined in chapters one to four of this Review.

B. What is at stake?

In today's world, 870 million people[6] still suffer from hunger and more than a billion from mal-nutrition. Despite recent resurgence of public and private sector attention in agriculture the hunger problem persists. Moreover, the worsening environmental crisis of agriculture is unlikely to be checked, even if today's concept of green economy (mostly based on the paradigm of "producing more with less"[7]) is being turned into practice.[8] There are many reasons for hunger, mal-nutrition and environmental degradation, but international trade, its rules and resulting incentives play an important role in the whole setting. It is questionable whether with the currently existing WTO tool-box the drastic problems analyzed in this Review can effectively be tackled. Despite some calls for completely excluding agriculture from the WTO, we search for a better pathway in a multilateral, but as well bilateral and regional trade framework.[9] But this then needs major adjustments in respect to agriculture.

C. The broader context

Driven by climate change and the associated melting of the glaciers in the water castles of the world, more extreme weather patterns will occur, with damaging effects to the already most vulnerable regions in the developing world, in particular sub-Saharan Africa and South Asia. The still rising world population (with highest rates in Africa and South Asia, where hunger and poverty problems are already the most acute), over-consumption, high food waste and changing consumption patterns to more meat-based diets with the associated spiraling expansion of concentrate feed production, as well as growing amounts of bio-fuel production add pressure on the already limited land resources. Volatile financial markets, scarcity of raw materials and the closer link between food and energy prices increase food price volatility through the financialization of commodity markets. Besides the loss of land for the already vulnerable through land-use changes and "landgrabs", land degradation and water shortages compound resource scarcities. Loss of biodiversity might further reduce the resilience of the agricultural systems. Against this very background, food security might turn from already being the "hidden driver of world politics" (Lester Brown, 2011) to the most pressing international development and security issue of the 21st century.

D. The hunger challenge

If present trends continue unabated, food riots and mass migration are likely to become more pronounced in the future. In 2008, some governments were already shaken - rising food prices were among the causes for the "Arab spring". This food crisis was an important catalyst for realizing the need for fundamental transformation and questioning some of the assumptions that had driven food and agricultural policy in recent decades. The crisis led to a reversal of the long-term neglect of agriculture as a vital economic sector. Also, the declining trend of public funding for agriculture was arrested and some new funding secured, as pledged at the L'Aquila G 8 summit in July 2009, which however is still much behind commitments and real requirements. Some of the additional funding has been going to important areas, such as smallholder support, role of women in agriculture, the environmental crisis of agriculture, including climate change, and addressing weaknesses of international markets through aid for trade targeting trade infrastructure, information, finance and facilitation. Yet,

these measures fill gaps, but are insufficient to lead to the much-needed turn-around.

Although, there is a better understanding of the circumstances and a growing political will for change, there is no consensus on how to bring about the U-turn and what direction needs to be taken in this regard. As things stand at the moment, priority remains focused on increasing production, which is still very much biased towards expansion of "somewhat-less-polluting", external-input-dependent industrial agriculture (a sort of 'ecology light' approach), with governments, large agro-food and agro-chemical enterprises tempted to follow this line in search for 'jobs and growth'. Rather the aim should be towards sustainable, site-specific and affordable (not external-input-intensive) production methods that provide multifunctional benefits and employment creation as part of a coherent and more holistic approach reflecting the specificity of agriculture.

E. Rural economies

About 70 per cent of the hungry live in rural areas (they are family farmers or agricultural laborers). Neo-liberal policies (i.e. the Washington Consensus), still prevailing massive subsidies for agriculture in developed countries and focus of the political elite on urban areas in the South have led to a discriminatory treatment of rural regions in developing countries. However, according to FAO, smallholder farmers provide up to 80 per cent of the food supply in Asia and sub-Saharan Africa (FAO, 2012). That is why small-scale agriculture needs special attention. Interestingly, small-scale agriculture is often more productive than large-scale industrial farming (see Carletto et al., 2011). For assuring food security, boosting total factor, rather than only labour productivity is a very necessary requirement.

There are different ways of intensification to boost productivity. Industrialization of agriculture, the development, for which the "green revolution" is the best known symbol, and the liberalization and globalization of markets have undoubtedly contributed to food security of a growing world population. Today five billion people have enough to eat, which is a great success. But, at the same time, the share of the hungry and malnourished in total world population has not significantly declined and their absolute numbers have even increased. The industrialization of agriculture and concomitant market liberalization have thus not succeeded in overcoming the hunger problem. That is mainly because hunger is not primarily a supply-related, but a poverty-linked issue of appropriate access to food (both items are therefore combined in MDG goal one). In this regard, the current system reaches its limits.

An alternative production-intensification strategy is the eco-functional-intensification approach (Bommarco et al. 2012) in agro-ecological systems (agro-ecological systems are more open, even to inputs than pure organic farming systems, thus having a higher yield potential)[10] (see Altieri et al., 2011 and Branca et al., 2013). The aim is to boost yields of the total production system (rather than only specific crops) relying on strengthening site-specific ecological production methods that harness the multi-functionality of agriculture and strengthen its resilience. These agro-ecological approaches, through the use of local resources, skills and inputs, fit well into strategies for strengthening rural economies and livelihoods. Although such forms of agriculture are knowledge-intensive, virtually all of these skills and technologies are readily available (a major difference to most other sectors, where many new technologies for enhancing energy/material/resource efficiency still have to be developed). What is rather lacking is adequate public support to efficient extension services for knowledge dissemination, public investment in adequate physical infra-structure, land reform for secure tenure rights (including for women) and access to financing. The agricultural industry is already, and in the future will even more support such approaches for specific products and processing methods.[11] Governments should follow this trend.

Increasing productivity must, on the one hand, be integrated into a broader social and environmental framework of providing sufficient rural livelihoods - with rural economies moving into the focus - and, on the other hand, guarantee the regenerative capacity and enhanced resilience of the natural resources and production factors, culminating in permanently high soil fertility.[12]

Even if it was in the market-logic of the past to concentrate on regions and areas where sufficient purchasing power prevailed, revitalizing rural economies and lifting people out of poverty creates new markets for the future. Besides, at times of ever higher public indebtedness, which makes social safety nets flimsy and thin, vitalized rural regions become essential for the viability of communities. From a political perspective, revitalized rural economies reduce the pressure on migration to urban areas and beyond borders, thus preventing national and international political tensions.

F. The high environmental costs of the current mode of agricultural industrialization

Besides the unresolved hunger problem, agricultural industrialization has come at high environmental costs. Today's conventional agriculture, being a very external-input-dependent production system with a negative, if not rarely 'catastrophic' energy balance (see the commentary of Rundgren in chapter 1), despite some improvements disproportionately contributes to climate change, pollution of water, land degradation and biodiversity loss. The already crossed planetary carrying capacity for nitrogen does not allow any uncritical future input intensification in agriculture. Agriculture and related land-use changes cause at least one third of global GHG emissions (if indirect emissions in plant and equipment, transport, as well as along the food processing and marketing chain are taken into account, agriculture's contribution to climate change is well over 40 per cent, see the commentary of GRAIN in chapter one). GHG emissions of agriculture are set to increase by 40-60 per cent till 2030, whereas a decline of the same order of magnitude would be required in order not to exceed the two degree global warming goal. Besides, a higher trade intensity may further contribute to climate change (see Schmitz et al., 2012) and raise health related costs.[12]

G. The countervailing effect of trade is limited

The damage to agriculture is not only costly, it is also a serious environmental, health and life threat for the future development of all of us. Climate change and the environmental crisis of agriculture, which is caused by the "mining" of the most critical resources for regenerative agriculture, like soil organic content, will drastically constrain supply, mainly in already vulnerable regions. In theory, trade can bridge some of the regionally arising supply gaps, but the higher the frequency and severity of droughts and floods, the more insecure the availability[14] and affordability[15] of imported food.

H. Questions

This takes us to a number of questions resulting from

the above-made analysis:

- How big is the chance of addressing these problems with today's trade tool boxes?
- Will it be possible and sufficient to tackle the huge challenges by fully exploiting the existing flexibility options and mechanisms in the current trade rules?
- Or is a more fundamental change needed in order to solve the 21st century issues of hunger, rural poverty, lingering mass migration and required strengthening of agricultural resilience?

We want to explore these questions by starting from the fundamental observation that agriculture is special.

I. Agriculture is special

Agriculture has been and still is in nearly any bilateral or regional negotiations a major obstacle to free trade agreements. Agriculture seems to be special; and indeed there are good reasons for agriculture's special role. Agriculture, being a management system for half of the terrestrial biomass producing areas, and being therefore critical in many environmental respects, is bound to the land, which means it cannot be moved to more favourable conditions. It has long investment intervals (whether to have milk cows or not is – including breeding – for example a very long-lasting decision, which is as well influenced by policies e.g. milk quotas). Agriculture is the item for food security, it is a strong component for rural development, it is closely linked to landscape and its care, to local climate, ecology and biodiversity, it is mainly organized in family and generational structures and it is strongly based on local or site-specific traditions and identification patterns (a farmer is not only a producer of goods, but also a manager of an agro-ecological system and a social fabric) (see Brodheur et al., 2010). This is true not only in Europe, but principally as well in key agricultural exporting countries like Australia and Brazil, or in the African countryside. Besides, agriculture employs billions of people in the developing world.[16]

Agriculture's role for development has for long been undervalued, and has only very recently been reinvigorated. It has the potential to lift people out of poverty (see World Bank, 2008), provide many ecological and amenity services and could be turned from a key source of global warming into a sector that can significantly mitigate it and adapt food production to the perils of climate change at very low costs relative to other sectors. To exploit this potential, agriculture

needs a shift to strengthen its regenerative potential. Trade rules need to support, not compromise this move.

Unfortunately, the externalities produced by industrial agriculture are not, and will not, at least in the foreseeable future[17], be integrated in product prices. In fact, enhanced external input use[18] and specialization have made it harder to internalize externalities, because agricultural input-price dynamics has outpaced the evolution of food prices (see figure 1) (the higher the input prices, the more unlikely that they are taxed, for example). Conversely, really sustainable forms of production, such as agro-ecological approaches, systemically embody large parts of external costs, because their preventive approach avoids or minimizes most externalities. Such production methods generate many public benefits and goods, such as strengthening biodiversity, avoiding ground water and river pollution or reducing GHG emissions, to name but a few. Yet, neither the avoided public costs nor the public benefits are recognized by the market, which encourages increased labour, but not total factor/system productivity. As if that where not enough, organic producers especially have to provide documentary evidence (in the form of inspection, auditing and certification) that their products are indeed meeting stringent standards. Market logic is thus put on its head; instead of rewarding the most efficient, clean and sustainable production system, prevailing market rules award the 'polluting' free riders.[19]

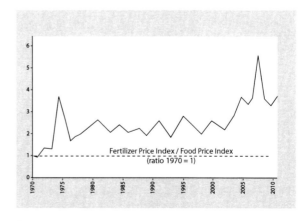

Figure 1: Development of food and fertilizer prices, 1970 to 2010

Fertilizer Price Index / Food Price Index
(ratio 1970 = 1)

Sources: Limes (2012: 10), referring to Kotschi (forthcoming).

Faced with this dilemma and as a result of enhanced liberalization, the increased competitive pressure in the prevailing distorted market conditions hits hard particularly the farms that produce the most common goods and services (whether in developed or developing countries). Given this dilemma, a new approach to address this issue is overdue.

Although GATT and WTO have treated agriculture in a specific agreement (here, because of the political sensitivity of food security and agriculture's close association with natural resources and the health and safety of people), even lately the sector profited only from some «end-of-pipe» flexibilities and special safe-guards, while subjecting agriculture to the across-the-board «industry» logic of liberalization (see below).

Green Box measures, besides being misused for at least indirectly supporting conventional forms of agricultural production (recently, of all domestic agricultural support, green-box subsidies accounted for between 75 and 85 per cent in the EU and the US, respectively, Lunenborg, 2013), have so far been only marginally effective in reducing problematic impacts.

As outlined above, this generic industry-biased approach to agriculture contributed to the prevailing problems of rural poverty, food insecurity, malnutrition and environmental degradation in agriculture we currently observe. Yet, to boost total factor and system productivity, resource, material and energy efficiency will require fundamental changes in how we grow and consume food - nothing less than a new vision is necessary of how we farm, take better care of the planet's biological resources and live equitably within our planetary means.[20] The key question is whether such far-reaching changes can be achieved through fully exploring existing flexibilities in the current trade tool-box, or if it will necessitate a different development and trade focus as part of a fundamental transformation of global agriculture.

Some fundamentals have to be taken into account when trying to answer this question.

J. Agriculture's diversity is key

Nature depends on interaction (plants with insects, soil fertility with soil microbes, etc.) and therefore on diversity. Diversity plays a pivotal role in agriculture (FAO, 2004). Specialization in agriculture is an issue, but at the same time it must be integrated in a strategy of diversification.[21] Tscharnke et al. (2012) point out, that integration strategies, combining crop and wildlife, are more suitable for food security than segregation, i.e. separating crop production from wildlife areas, which is mainly advocated by today's agricultural industry. This observation speaks for agro-ecological approaches, which follow an integrated diversity strategy, keeping also an eye on flourishing wildlife. On the latter, a recent EU estimate concludes that the Natura 2000 network in the EU alone produces eco-system services worth some 300 billion Euros.[22]

Snapp et al. (2010) in a large long-term and partly participative study in Malawi have found that crop diversification could secure yields with a stabilizing effect at half of the fertilizer rate.[23] Besides, diversity is a core item for resilience against natural shocks, but as well against market disruptions, ever more important in today's fragile world. Moreover, diverse nutrient availability is an essential objective of sustainable food security.

Soil fertility - the heart of truly sustainable (regenerative) and resource-efficient agriculture for food security - can best be assured by poly-culture, adequate nutrient recycling, the integration of crop and livestock production and the effective use of functional biodiversity. Future trade rules should mirror and support this interplay.

In the end, any agricultural management approach

Box 2: The treadmill of external-input intensive production: experience of a soy farmer in Argentina

Fabricio Castillos is a soy farmer in the small town of Laboulaye in Argentina. According to Mr. Castillos, he can no longer make a profit on his 130 ha farm, specialized in soy production for export (destined either for bio-diesel or concentrate animal feed). Somebody with a current farm size of 500 ha is still profitable, but if input price trends continue one might need 5,000 ha in the future to make a profit. According to Mr. Castillos, this will speed up the concentration of land ownership so that the land will increasingly be owned by a few institutional investors.

Source: Huismann (2012: 193).

would have to meet the four principles of sustainable agriculture as mapped out in the Report of the Royal Society (2009): to be long-lasting, resilient, autarkic and prosper, by not over-extracting resources.

K. The current approach of the WTO

In the Doha Round negotiations, the modalities of 2008 on agriculture in respect to food security are mainly met by proposals for special safeguard mechanisms (SSM)[25], special products (SP) and few other special and differentiated treatment (SDT) provisions. Single (staple) crops ("special products") for specific countries could therefore, at least for certain periods, be excluded from the liberalization process. The negotiations on these issues have become very complex; perhaps too complex to conclude the round. Besides, SDT as of today in the WTO rulebook with its focus on single crops does not systemically take into account the diversity imperative of agriculture. A more locally and regionally-oriented trade approach could help to strengthen rural economies with diverse production patterns, which will be supplemented by trade for selling surplus produce and enriching local supply. We argue that SDT, SSM and the special and sensitive product provisions of today as being concentrated on countries (not local regions) and single crops or products, moreover in a limited timeframe, will not be sufficient to meet long-term food security, environmental and livelihood needs, as they are not targeted, in the end, to strengthen rural economies (see as well Häberli, 2010: 304).

Trade, instead of being just a method of matching supply and demand – in its recent terms, pushing for open markets and liberalization – requires in the logic of seeking absolute or comparative advantage ever higher levels of specialization, industrialization and scale of production. The recently often highlighted global value chain concept pronounces this concept even further. It is not by chance that agriculture has been the biggest stumbling bloc in nearly all trade negotiations. It is not only tradition-based reluctance for change in the agricultural sector that creates difficulties for further trade liberalization, it is its diversity, livelihood and inherent non-industry and assurance of self-sufficiency logic, that causes this resistance.

While the preamble of the Agreement on Agriculture (AoA) recognizes food security as a legitimate concern, the actual provisions of the agreement treat food security as a deviation from the primary objective of agricultural trade liberalization (De Schutter, 2011c:7).

L. The required paradigm shift – beyond the dichotomy of liberalization and protection

We need to resist the temptation of resorting to shortcuts that cure symptoms, rather than dealing with root causes.

Recent reports like the Ecofair Trade Dialogue (2009), IAASTD (2009), SCAR (2011), FAO/GEA (2012), point at the importance of a renewed (rather than only reformed) trade architecture to play its proper role in

---

Box 3: Soil fertility and the importance of humus

Be it climate change with more extreme weather patterns, over-usage (degradation) of land, loss of biodiversity or oversimplification through specialization, agriculture needs a thorough regenerative potential, not least for efficiency reasons, as repair is always more costly.[24] To guarantee and strengthen the regenerative potential should be at the center of all future measures. One key element for the regenerative potential in many respects is humus. High humus content copes with many of the endangering issues, and strengthens the resilience capacity of almost all crops. Increasing the humus content leads to a "living" soil. Composting – and this is why we highlight it here explicitly as an example – and its use for enhancing the humus content of soils is also a very effective and cost-efficient method of carbon sequestration. According to IPCC (2007c: section 8.4.3), soil organic matter sequestration accounts for almost 90 per cent of the technical carbon sequestration potential of agriculture and is thus the pivotal climate mitigation measure (in contrast, more efficient application of fertilizers represents not more than some 2 per cent of the carbon sequestration potential). In this respect, agro-ecological production methods with - inter alia - various compost techniques have proven to serve the regenerative agricultural potential while mitigating potentially very significant amounts of CO_2 (see the commentary of Leu in chapter 1 and Gattinger et al., 2012, for a more elaborate analysis). Agro-ecological approaches are also more diverse approaches. Trade rules should facilitate and support such production methods and also respect local and regional diversity and preference requirements.

improving food security, farmers welfare and environ-mental issues.[26] This need for a new approach to the trade architecture, we mean, should go beyond the traditional dichotomy of liberalization and protection.

a) The problems with the current international rules relating to agricultural trade

The problems with the current international trade rules relating to agriculture are three-fold: (i) they still al-low unfair conditions (high subsidies, partly shifted to the green box in the North); (ii) a too early push for open markets in the South (although the North kept its borders closed till the sector was sufficiently com-petitive); and (iii) following the absolute and compara-tive advantage approach for industrial sectors, foster specialization, economies of scale and closely-related industrialization of agriculture, with all its negative im-pacts.

Whereas WTO disciplines for the first two issues (un-fair conditions) are currently just too weak and can be 'flexibilized' or bypassed by regional free trade agreements and bilaterals, the third issue – the inher-ent trend to specialization and industrialization – is more fundamental. The incentives on specialization, industrialization and economies of scale run the risk of jeopardizing long-term overall agricultural productivity growth and the resilience of agricultural production.

b) A basic pre-condition: Balance between the paradigms of food sovereignty and liberalization

It becomes more and more visible that *prosperity* (conventionally measured in GDP) is not the same as *welfare*, or well being. Welfare, especially in relation to food, also relates to health, trust and identification. People look for such items more strongly today. There is greater consumer attention to credence values like animal welfare, local origin of products and how food safety is assured.[27] People live up to values like self-determination and sovereignty, as well in raising their voice politically, but especially in respect to food.

Therefore "Food Sovereignty" came up as a term to express this attitude.

By having full respect for this attitude, food sover-eignty, unless integrated in an overall framework, might lead to too fragmented organizational patterns in terms of differing regulations, making (trade-) ex-change between regions, which will still be necessary and beneficial, too complicated and at last costly. Therefore a balanced approach between liberalization and food sovereignty is required.

Liberalization or food sovereignty against this back-ground is not an either-or question, but one of bet-ter synergizing the benefits of both approaches. We see this synergy in a greater emphasis on regional-ized/localized (see box 4 below) food production networks, aimed at strengthening site-specific eco-logical approaches that provide multi-functional and rural livelihood benefits while not excluding trade (we emphasize, that we don't advocate self sufficiency at household level; production should be market-oriented, by leaving not marketable goods for self-consumption). Such approach – locally-adapted mo-saic production patterns that integrate global market concerns – was termed by the Millennium Ecosystem Assessment (MEA) "glocalization", which we think should be given more attention today.[28]

Based on the above, we would see the following guid-ing principles for future agricultural trade.

c) Guiding principles for agricultural trade

i) *The pre-eminence of overall land-use*
    Given that agricultural land is scarce, to feed 9 billion people every patch of suitable land is needed for cultivation. Agricultural production cannot only concentrate on most favoured regions, as the common trade theory would suggest. *All* available land has to be used – so every region has to be productive and lesser favoured regions have to contribute their share. So sub-optimum use has to be integrated into the overall food supply strategy.

Box 4: Avoiding confusion on the terms "regional" and "local"

The emphasis on the promotion of regionalized or 'localized' food production does not suggest an anti-globalization, nor a pro self-sufficiency drive. Rather, we are convinced that producing for customers in regional/local markets (and using surplus produce for home consumption and trade) is a more sustainable mode of production from a reproductive angle. The terms 'regional' or 'local' denote an overseeable geographical region like a district, county or province that might extend across borders. In the following we use the term "regional/local" to clarify, that we don't mean the village-level, but rather a county or provincial level.

ii) The pre-eminence of diversity

As outlined above, diversity is a key component of agriculture. The specialization potential is therefore limited. Due to diversity requirements regions cannot concentrate solely on one crop. A minimum of diversity requires a mix of products (crop rotation), where not every crop can have a comparative advantage. Diverse production patterns buffer price hikes and guaranty a more stable profit. And diversity is a nutritional requirement, too. Last, but not least, diversity is imperative for improving the future resilience of agriculture to climate change. Thus it makes sense to primarily orient diverse production patterns towards local demand.[29]

iii) The pre-eminence of regional/local food production

Regional/local food production and consumption is being identified as a new mega trend.[30] Regional/local production has benefits on environmental and social grounds. On the social side, more regionally/locally-oriented market relations promise more decent jobs in rural areas not only in agriculture, but in rural support services as it creates a rural economy. The environmental benefits of a regional/local focus are primarily in diverse production patterns, which – through more mosaic-like structures – serve biodiversity issues better, increase close nutrient cycles, tend to reduce external input use and strengthen resilience of the production and the eco-system at large.[31]

Moreover, there is growing preference of people for regional/local production due to trust and identification. People want to have a close relationship with their food and food producers. Besides, freshness is of growing value. Such food is best produced regionally/locally and imports complement in terms of addition and supplementation, availability, seasonality and cultural diversity.[32] Traded goods should also be resorted to in cases where local products would have a distinct negative environmental or social impact, such as greenhouse production in winter, intensive irrigation or long-term cold storage. This is a fundamentally different approach to the comparative advantage/free trade model that concentrates specialized production in the most favourable production sites, leaving the distribution to (global) trade.

Moreover, food safety issues play an important part in this regard. The recent horse meat scandal in Europe has made visible, how vulnerable large cascaded value chains in food production are. Not the least against this background, food industries increasingly tend to source locally.[33] Politics should follow suit in adjusting concerned policies.

iv) The pre-eminence on specialties

Export in relation to food should be focused on specialties (where the value added is high) and surplus produce. Agricultural specialties mirror necessarily the origin – and originality – of the region as well as comparative physical and climatic advantages. The trade system needs to facilitate and supplement such approaches and structures, rather than wheeling the baton of mass-production and the "industrialization" logic.[34]

v) Trade as a complement

Trade is a driver for prosperity. Disregarding perverse subsidies, trade drives costs down, which makes food more affordable and accessible. Trade also contributes to cultural diversity of food. At the same time, (hyper-)liberalized trade concepts find their limits when it comes to too narrow specialization, mono-cropping, high market-power concentration, and erosion of local and regional identities and cultures. Trade in food should not, or not primarily, replace localized supply,[35] but rather complement it.

If these preconditions were met, food security and the environmental crisis of agriculture could be addressed in a pro-active and constructive manner.[36]

d) The new trade formula

As a guiding principle for future trade in agricultural goods we suggest the formula: "Regional is first choice", or, to read it differently: "as much regionalized/localized food production as possible; as much traded food as necessary".

For the time being, as externalities are mainly not internalized, carbon taxes are the rare exception rather than the rule and carbon-offset markets are largely dysfunctional – all of which factors that would prioritize regional/local production through 'logical' market mechanisms – regional/local preferences like "buy local" schemes should be respected by trade rules.

Systematic concentration on globalized food supply is partly undermining the endeavour of establishing regionally/locally appropriate and truly sustainable production and consumption patterns (if there is too much export orientation and therefore specialization, there are too many import surges, too much focus on just economic efficiency, and too little heed paid to the multi-functionality, reproductive and resilience capacity of agriculture) (Howse and Teitel, 2007: 11).

It makes a difference whether enhanced regionally/locally-focused production and consumption happen more by chance – through higher priced consumer preferences – despite a general export orientation, or whether the regional/local focus is part of a strategy, and any surplus is traded away in an organized manner. It would be a task for trade policies to shape adequate normative rules that create the right incentive structure in this regard.[37] Karapinar and Häberli (2010) advocate a "rainbow revolution" (instead of "just" a green revolution) in this respect, where tailor made approaches to each specific locality are tackled in a broad inclusive approach.

Against the background of these principles, what can be achieved with the current trade-rule tool box?

M. The current trade tool box in regard to regional/local food supply

Some of the applied WTO rules include a range of policy measures that are of some support to regional/local food production:

- The provisions on the "green box" in Annex II of the AoA.[38]
- The use of the *de minimis* provision on trade-distorting support (up to 10 per cent of the total value of agricultural production and 10 per cent of the value of any specific crop in a given year for most developing countries).
- regional content requirements; and
- geographical indications (to be extended to food items).

But these rules have an overall limited effect on fostering regional/local food production and consumption. The achievement of food security is basically treated by the existing WTO rules as grounds for exception for a very limited range of trade liberalization measures (De Schutter, 2011c:16).

As pointed out in the lead article of this chapter by Lim Li Ching and Martin Khor, there is still quite some room for improvement in fully exploiting existing flexibilities on SDT, SSM and SP as well as the green box to achieve a better level of food security. No doubt, this track should be followed. Yet, with the benefit of hindsight, it seems to be far more complex for interested governments to turn concept into action in this regard.

First, to be effective, such approach requires a clear willingness and strategy by concerned governments. Due to the neo-liberal policies of the last decades and the current financial crisis states have been weakened in their regulatory and financial capacity to devise such strategies. Second, proactively exploiting the flexibilities in the existing WTO tool-box also requires a level of co-operation and tolerance by other WTO member countries.

The 'jobs and growth' dependency of states and the interest of commercial pressure groups that profit from the status quo, who have contributed to shaping and building up current neo-liberal market structures, may stand against the required level of co-operation and tolerance. Third, in particular developing countries err on the side of caution not to violate WTO commitments. Their governments are thus not very likely to launch policies that fully exploit the flexibilities in the WTO agreements without strong assurance and confidence that these initiatives might not negatively affect third parties' commercial interests and leave them exposed to potential litigation (De Schutter, 2011c:3). Fourth, existing flexibilities can be limited or made difficult to exploit by regional or bilateral trade agreements that create WTO-plus disciplines.

All in all, the existing flexibilities in WTO rules are not sufficient and are unlikely to be fully exploited.

N. Already existing regional/local food approaches

In the light of the growing concern of citizens on where their food comes from[39], many retail businesses already offer growing numbers of regional products. Regarding a higher level of food sovereignty and the growing role of civil society in this respect, some contours of regional food policy councils[40] or localized/regional food networks are already visible.[41] These regionalized/localized food networks make decisions on their food, as it already happens today when regions call themselves "GMO free region", for example (others might opt for GMOs). The Brazilian city Belo Horizonte[42] is a good example on how a regional/local structured pattern has overcome the food security problem in a very short time (Belo Horizonte then became the blueprint for the "fome zero" programme which nearly eradicated hunger in Brazil).

Trade rules would have to tolerate and public and private procurement would have to accept such systems of preferences for regional/local produce. Where people decide consciously about their food and nutrition, this should not be overruled by any, particularly mercantilist doctrine.

O. Outlook

There are many reasons why the situation of food security and the environmental crisis of agriculture is unsatisfactory today. If we seriously want to achieve food security, practice equality and protect the planet, having already crossed some planetary boundaries, the current system needs adjustment. For the future, we have to think out of the box. To respect the principal regional/local nature of agriculture and adjust related policies could be one of the first steps. What is re-

quired is a strengthening of regional and site-specific holistic approaches that provide diverse benefits as part of more localized food production networks. It should however be emphasized in this regard that it is not our intention to create new protectionist measures. Rather, we want to advocate a more reasonable food-market approach, which harnesses the potential of really sustainable agricultural production to (i) enhance sustainable productivity of the whole production system (not only individual products); (ii) assure food security and rural livelihoods; (iii) reflect and capitalize on the diversity of agriculture to assure its re-productive capacity; (iv) strengthen functional bio-diversity, and (v) build up resilience to resource constraints and climate change as well as improve agriculture's climate mitigation potential.

Commentary II: From Dumping to Volatility: The Lessons of Trade Liberalization for Agriculture

Ben Lilliston and Karen Hansen-Kuhn, Institute for Agriculture and Trade Policy

Abstract

The weakening of agricultural, financial and trade rules has contributed significantly to increased volatility and corporate concentration in agricultural markets. This increased volatility is harmful to long-term investments to protect the environment and build climate resilience in agriculture. Public investment and regulation is needed to ensure stable food supplies and fair prices, and to facilitate a shift to sustainable agricultural practices.

Much of the international debate on trade and agriculture, from the founding of the World Trade Organization (WTO) to the recent rise of agricultural commodity prices, has focused on the damaging effects of agricultural dumping (i.e. exporting at below cost of production) by agribusiness corporations based in the EU and the United States. Since 2008, as a result of the global food price crisis, this focus has shifted to concerns about price volatility. But both dumping and volatility are symptoms of the same bad policy decisions: a weakening of government oversight in setting and implementing agricultural, financial and trade rules. While this approach has been a boon to agribusiness companies operating around the globe, it has been damaging to farmers and those struggling with food insecurity. Equally important, this era of volatility threatens to overwhelm efforts to transition to more resilient, ecologically friendly agricultural production that is essential in the present context of climate change. The international debate needs to shift once again to a focus on the right kinds of rules to rebuild resilient food systems. Substantive structural reforms of agricultural, financial and trade policies would be a major step forward.

A. Liberalizing trade and increasing food insecurity

The liberalization of trade rules greatly accelerated in 1994 with the passage of the North American Free Trade Agreement (NAFTA), which set the standard for subsequent bilateral and regional trade agreements involving the United States, such as the Central America-Dominican Republic-United States Free Trade Agreement (CAFTA), and those negotiated

between Mexico and other trading partners. It also influenced the nature of trade deals pursued by the EU. Shortly after the passage of NAFTA, the WTO came into being in 1995, and various WTO agreements (particularly the Agreement on Agriculture) induced the further opening up of markets in developing countries. These bilateral and multilateral agreements limited the policy options available to these countries to protect their farmers from dumped imports and to support their farmers in boosting food production. This wave of agreements to liberalize trade and deregulate capital movements opened developing economies to foreign corporate investment that focused on expanding large-scale industrial food production for export. As a result of these changes, many countries that had previously produced most of their own food became dependent on imports. A dramatic example is that of Haiti, which produced 80 per cent of its rice requirements in the 1980s, but now, following decades of deregulation and liberalization, imports 80 per cent of its rice (Guereña, 2010).

During the WTO's first decade of existence, dumping by multinational agribusiness companies was both widespread and highly destructive. The Institute for Agriculture and Trade Policy (IATP, 2005) calculated dumping margins for United States commodity crops during the period 1990–2003 and found that wheat, corn, soybeans, rice and cotton were consistently exported at well below the cost of production (ranging from 10 per cent for corn to more than 50 per cent for cotton). A subsequent study by Wise (2010) also found that dumping of United States commodity crops and meat on Mexico was commonplace during the period 1997–2005.

While trade liberalization, or free trade, was touted as a way to improve food security, it has unquestionably failed (Murphy, 2009). Floods of dumped imports, especially during the harvest, can be devastating for developing-country farmers, and they increase dependence on food imports. Additionally, trade rules have facilitated the further concentration of global food supply in large private firms, thereby disempowering not only farmers and consumers, but even governments. Dependence on this increasingly concentrated global food supply chain, dominated by private players, increases importing countries' vulnerability to shocks, whether from extreme weather events or excessive financial speculation in agricultural commodity markets. Moreover, the shift towards a greater role for the private sector in managing the global food supply has coincided with rising global rates of hunger – from 788 million worldwide in 1995–1997 to 925 million in 2010 (FAO, 2011).

B. United States agricultural policy: Freedom to fail

Working in tandem with efforts to further liberalize trade, United States farm policy has retreated from its traditional role in managing agricultural markets. Over the past half century, the country's agricultural policy has shifted from a system of supply management that helped moderate prices for both farmers and consumers, to a system more dependent on so-called free-market forces. This transition culminated in the 1996 Farm Bill (known as Freedom to Farm), which removed the last vestiges of supply and price management (except for sugar), ostensibly to allow farmers to respond to market prices and export to new markets overseas. But as farmers expanded production with no supply management, agricultural commodity prices collapsed. The following decade of low prices – often below the cost of production – not only led to increased dumping on export markets, but also spurred the United States Congress to attempt to compensate for its policy failure by approving a series of emergency subsidy payments, and ultimately making those payments permanent in the 2002 Farm Bill.

During this decade of low prices and increased dumping, United States farm subsidy payments soared, peaking in 2000 and 2001, and again in 2005. But since 2005, payments to domestic farmers have steadily dropped as commodity prices have risen.[43] Higher commodity prices have not necessarily meant higher profits for farmers. Costs of inputs, including seeds and fertilizer, have also dramatically increased, reducing the potential profits of small and medium-sized farmers in the United States (Wise, 2011; USDA, 2010). The cost/price squeeze accelerated the trend in United States agriculture away from small and medium-sized farms to very large farms that were able to spread costs over larger land areas. These large farms were also the beneficiaries of about 75 per cent of commodity programme subsidies. As a result, over the past 25 years, the number of small, commercially viable farms (with sales of between $10,000 and $250,000) has fallen by 40 per cent, and that of very large farms (with sales of more than $1 million) has increased by 243 per cent (Hoppe, MacDonald and Korb, 2010). Also during this period, the percentage of United States agricultural production controlled by the top four firms in a given sector has increased substantially. For example, in beef packing it rose from 72 per cent in 1990 to 83.5 per cent in 2005 (Hendrickson and Heffernan, 2007).

EU subsidies to agriculture under the Common Agricultural Policy (CAP) are now largely decoupled (unconnected to production or prices, making them "minimally trade-distorting" to the WTO). While the true extent of the decoupling depends on how the subsidies are measured, total EU subsidies have not varied as dramatically as those of the United States over the past few years (Berthelot, 2011).[44] While the CAP differs substantively from the United States Farm Bill, the underlying challenge is the same – how to redirect support away from large-scale production for export towards programmes that can provide greater food security, rural livelihoods and a transition to sustainable agriculture. The current complex system of support enables agribusinesses to exploit the system to the detriment of farmers in both developing and developed countries.

C. Financial market deregulation

How financial markets and commodity futures markets are regulated is another factor that strongly affects agricultural production. A series of laws passed by the United States Congress, beginning in the early 1990s and culminating in 2004, succeeded in opening up commodity futures markets to a flood of new speculative money. In 2004, Hank Paulson, Treasury Secretary in the George W. Bush Administration and then chief executive officer of Goldman Sachs, successfully lobbied for an exemption from the rule that investment banks maintain large enough currency reserves to cover their unsuccessful trades. The rule exemption freed billions of dollars that Goldman Sachs and four other banks used for high-risk investments, including commodity index fund bets (IATP, 2008). Commodity index funds (which deal in agriculture, energy and metals) exploited these new loopholes and flooded commodity markets with money, betting thereby to drive up prices, regardless of the market fundamentals of supply and demand. For example, in March 2008, the unregulated biggest players, Morgan Stanley and Goldman Sachs, owned 1.5 billion bushels of Chicago Board of Trade corn futures contracts, while all corn producers and processors had the means to hedge only 11 million bushels against price swings. These unregulated funds controlled 33 per cent of all United States agricultural futures contracts during the period 2006–2008 (Suppan, 2009). Most of this excessive speculative activity takes place in over-the-counter trading, which is traded off-exchange and is not subject to trade data reporting requirements, or to margin collateral and other requirements of regulated exchanges. When these Wall Street funds sold off their contracts in mid-2008, prices tumbled. Overleveraged financial firms, without reserves to cover losses, were insolvent counterparties to these risk bets until they were recapitalized by the United States Congress and taxpayers. Today, these same financial speculators continue to destabilize commodity markets in the United States and elsewhere (see also the comment of Müller in this chapter).

The role of excessive speculation on international agriculture markets has been well documented by a host of international agencies and research institutions, including, most recently, UNCTAD (2011). The UNCTAD report, through an analysis of data as well as extensive interviews with financial traders, describes the new forces of financialization in commodity markets, beginning in 2004, and their contribution to steadily rising prices and increasing volatility.

Finally, it is impossible to overstate the enormous costs of financial market deregulation to government budgets around the world. Agriculture has not been spared by the global financial collapse, as less and less money is now available for food aid, and for investments for increasing production in developing countries, for promoting sustainable agriculture and for agricultural adaptation to climate change, among many other needs.

D. Investments in ecological agriculture undermined by volatility

Extremely low agricultural commodity prices over the past two decades, followed by recent spikes in prices, discourage long-term investments in more sustainable, ecological agriculture that will benefit the environment, water quality and quantity, and the climate. When prices are low, farmers struggle to make a living, and focus almost exclusively on increasing production to make up for the low prices. When prices shoot up or are projected to increase, governments and academics often advise farmers to devote even more land to production, often in environmentally sensitive areas. This tension between the usually futile efforts to respond to prices and investments for long-term environmental sustainability is evident in recent challenges facing United States conservation programmes, specifically the Conservation Reserve Program (CRP) and the Conservation Stewardship Program (CSP).

The Conservation Reserve Program is part of the Farm Bill that pays farmers to set aside and protect marginal farmland from agricultural production. CRP land is critical to slowing down soil erosion, and protecting wildlife and waterways. Indeed, it has protected tens of millions of acres over the years. But this popular programme has seen a significant decline in participation as farmers have taken over more land for production in an attempt to benefit from rising commodity prices. From October 2008 to July 2010, 3.4 million acres of CRP land went back into farm production (Cowan, 2010).

The Conservation Stewardship Program is the country's largest conservation programme, covering 35 million acres nationwide, and it is accessible to all farmers regardless of size or type of crop production. It rewards farmers based on their conservation practices that protect the soil, water, air and natural resources. In past Farm Bills, the CSP was woefully underfunded. The 2008 Farm Bill took a major step forward by allowing an estimated 13 million acres to be eligible for CSP's multi-year contracts each year. Despite this funding increase, only 57 per cent of eligible farmers could participate in the programme in 2009 and 2010 because of a lack of funds, according to the United States Department of Agriculture (USDA). And the programme is likely to face cutbacks under current efforts to reduce government debt. A 2012 budget bill passed by the House of Representatives in June 2011 would cut over $1 billion in conservation spending, including $210 million directly from the CSP (currently funded at $1.2 billion a year), and potentially force the USDA to break contracts with farmers that were signed earlier this year.[45] It is unclear exactly how much funding for conservation programmes will be cut as part of the recent debt ceiling bill passed in August 2011. Although some conservation programmes in the United States Farm Bill support practices that will both reduce carbon emissions and increase adaptation to climate change, the bill does not explicitly address climate change. Despite the lack of comprehensive climate change legislation, the Obama Administration and the USDA have strongly supported treating agriculture largely as a source of carbon emission offset credits for polluters participating in a carbon market. This perspective on agriculture's place within climate policy is reflected in a June 2011 USDA announcement of grants for projects geared almost entirely to measuring GHG emission reductions, and how those reductions could be converted into offset credits for a carbon market (USDA, 2011). There are no government plans or significant resources focused on helping agriculture in the United States to transition towards more climate-resilient practices and production.

The expected cuts in conservation programmes in the United States, and the denial by Congress of climate change as a major destabilizing factor in agricultural production are in contrast with Europe's climate change orientation within its Common Agricultural Policy. That climate change is happening and must be addressed in agriculture policy is understood within the CAP. In May 2011 the European Parliament's Agriculture Committee agreed to maintain funding for agriculture and to increase its emphasis on producing enough food while improving environmental practices. In addition to increasing incentives for sustainable production, the EU will more directly link payments to "greening measures" that reduce GHG emissions (EurActiv, 2011).

E. From volatility to sustainability

The seeds of current price and supply volatility in agricultural markets were planted several decades ago through a series of policy decisions that have gradually strengthened the hold of large agribusinesses over markets and disempowered both farmers and countries struggling with food insecurity. To help address the enormous challenges related to food insecurity and environmental and climate degradation in the coming years, market reforms are needed to make agriculture more economically and environmentally sustainable. The issue is not only related to trade; it also involves disentangling local food economies from the grips of vulnerable supply chains dominated by transnational corporations. It is not only about whether subsidies are right or wrong, but rather how best to invest public money and establish regulatory oversight to create the right food system. A new set of values must be injected into policy-making that gives priority to food security, farmers' livelihoods, environmental sustainability and resilience, and democratic decision-making.

The following are some initial steps that should be taken:

- A reassessment of trade rules to enable developing countries to protect and support sectors vital to their food security and rural livelihoods.
- Support for the establishment of food reserves as a tool to mitigate price and supply volatility and strengthen food security when domestic production fails.
- Prevention of excessive speculation in commodity markets through the establishment of commodity-specific position limits and increased transparency in over-the-counter trading.
- Greater investment in agroecological farming practices, as outlined in the reports of the International Assessment of Agricultural Knowledge Science and Technology for Development (IAASTD, 2008), to strengthen both food security and resilience to climate change, with an emphasis on supporting small-scale farmers, particularly women.
- Reform of national farm policies, particularly the United States Farm Bill and the EU's Common Agricultural Policy, to eliminate dumping, encourage environmental sustainability and prevent oligopolistic control of market prices and practices.

Commentary III: Rethinking Food Security Strategies in Times of Climate Change: The Case for Regionalization of Agricultural Trade and Local Markets

Christine Chemnitz, Heinrich Böll Foundation, and
Tilman Santarius, Germanwatch

Abstract

A sustainable transformation of small farm systems in developing countries will only succeed if it is integrated into overall agricultural and food development strategies. Issues concerning the agricultural trading system, as one of the major drivers of the existing food production system, need to be linked to the debate on agriculture's contribution to adaptation and climate change mitigation. Since trade liberalization and export orientation tend to undermine adaptive strategies and encourage input-intensive, "climate-unfriendly" farming, the sustainable transformation of the agricultural sector requires a fundamental rethinking of current trade policies.

The principle of "economic subsidiarity" offers guidance for this transformation (Sachs and Santarius, 2007). It implies that economic exchanges in the food system should be carried out preferably at the local and national levels, while exchanges at the continental or global level should have only a complementary function.

In many developing countries, agriculture is the main source of rural livelihoods and the foremost provider of employment. More than one third of the world's population derive their livelihoods from land, growing food for their families and for local markets – primarily staples grown mainly on small land holdings. Thus, small farm systems de facto remain the backbone of food security in developing countries even today.

However, rural poverty and rural hunger are widespread, and the majority of all poor and hungry people worldwide live in rural areas (IFAD, 2010). To address this situation, governments need to rethink current food security strategies. Since the 1980s, policies concerning food security have been increasingly trade-oriented. Due to low world market prices, cheap imports of food products have been favoured over national production for achieving food security. Moreover, it has been a common belief that overall economic growth would automatically lead to the alleviation of hunger (FAO, 2008), and that the integration of small and medium farmers into export-oriented, global value chains would help reduce poverty and hunger in developing countries.

Yet, looking at small producers and the food security situation in various developing countries today, overall, this strategy has not delivered. On the contrary, food insecurity and poverty in rural areas have increased in recent years (FAO, 2008). Small producers have faced multiple crises, among them high price volatility, the economic downturn due to the global financial and economic crisis, and weather extremes due to climate change – all of which have exacerbated each other (Fan and Heady, 2010). Since small producers often have limited adaptive capacity and resilience to adequately react to external shocks, the level of uncertainty, in particular, threatens their economic situation. All signs point to this level of uncertainty increasing as a result of a worsening of anthropogenic climate change in the coming years and decades.

Therefore, it is necessary to rethink current food security strategies, including the role and system of agricultural trade in the light of global warming. Food security strategies now have to cope with three challenges:

(i) agricultural production is becoming increasingly affected by changing climatic conditions;

(ii) in parallel, agriculture markets are being destabilized by climatic impacts; and

(iii) at the same time, agriculture has to contribute to mitigating climate change and must augment its carbon sink capacities, rather than remaining a major source of greenhouse gas emissions. Given these challenges, food security strategies that rely on trade and that push for the further integration of developing countries' food production systems in the global market are not appropriate.

In this paper, we first analyse how the present system of globalized agricultural production and marketing exacerbates anthropogenic climate change, and why small producers that are integrated into global value chains are particularly at risk due to climate change. We then discuss how the current pattern of agricultural trade and production should be modified in order to stop the vicious circle of increased trade-orientation exacerbating climate change, and increased climate change endangering small farmers' food security. Finally, we present policies for a regionalization of agricultural trade flows and the integration of smallholders in local and regional markets.

A. The global agricultural trading system is contributing to climate change...

Humans have exchanged agricultural products ever since they started farming. The main purpose of those trade flows was to supplement the diet with products that could only be grown in other climatic zones and geographical settings. With trade liberalization, trade in agriculture started to serve an additional purpose: to advance economic efficiency through increased competition among producers worldwide. Agricultural production can respond to increased competition in a number of ways, two of which, in particular, can have negative impacts on climate, namely an expansion of the area under cultivation, and specialization and intensification of production processes.

The expansion of agriculture is the main reason for the clearing of primary forests, and for the conversion of natural prairies to land for growing crops or for livestock grazing. It is also responsible for the draining of wetlands for irrigation and cultivation (CBD, 2003). Today, changes in land use in agriculture and forestry, as well as emissions from farming and livestock, contribute over 30 per cent to global anthropogenic GHG emissions, releasing in particular methane, nitrous oxide, and, to a lesser extent, carbon dioxide (IPCC, 2007a; see also the comment of GRAIN in chapter 1 of this Review). The conversion of tropical forests and savannahs into agricultural land is particularly emission-intensive, primarily due to the burning of the biomass originally existing on the land, and to the release of organic carbon stored in soils (Steffen et al., 2004).

Besides the conversion of land for agriculture, increased specialization and intensification of production, which enables farmers to participate in global markets, generally entails the greater use of pesticides, fertilizers, water and fuel. Huge amounts of GHGs are emitted through the production and use of external inputs, such as agrochemicals, farm machinery and pumped irrigation. In the United States, for example, farm inputs account for more than 90 per cent of the total direct and indirect energy used in agriculture (Saunders, 2004). Likewise, downstream emissions increase as the processing, packaging and retailing of food items that are exported become more energy-intensive.

At the same time, growing competition is likely to undercut less intensive farming practices that sustain a broad variety of crops, hedges, trees and cultural landscapes, and thus threatens small-scale, site-oriented, integrated farming systems, particularly in developing countries (CBD, 2003). For instance, with animals moving from pastures to intensive feed-lot production, and the number of cattle, pigs and poultry steadily increasing to meet growing meat-based diets, more methane is released from enteric fermentation and animal waste; in contrast, grass-fed animals emit less methane than livestock that is fed on a high protein diet (Saunders, 2004; Kotschi and Müller-Sämann, 2004; see also the lead article of Idel and Reichert in chapter 2 of this Review).

In addition to the impacts of climate change from the intensification and expansion of agricultural production for export, the overall volume of transport increases as trade grows. Average distances of food shipments are set to increase even more, as fresh fruit reach Europe from India, for instance, and soybean shipments from Brazil to China rise. However, the explosion of food miles is the Achilles' heel of global value chains in agriculture, making them vulnerable to steep rises in oil price and the impacts of climate change.

B. ...while climate change is endangering small producers

Notwithstanding these environmental challenges, and a growing awareness of climate-change-related issues, efforts to integrate small and medium producers into global value chains continue unabated. Marketing chains are being improved and small producers are being encouraged and assisted in complying with international private and public food quality and safety standards (see, for example, Humphrey, 2005; and Pingali, Khwaja and Meijer, 2005). Small producers in global value chains have always faced certain risks because usually they are the least powerful and most vulnerable players in the chain, and because they are price takers for both their production inputs and their output. Moreover, they are often confronted with a fragile balance between (a) production for the market, and thus income generation, (b) production for their own consumption, and (c) household expenditure for food. However, these three aspects are increasingly affected by changing temperatures, more frequent weather extremes such as droughts or heavy rains, and growing instability of ecosystem services. Thus climate change has become an important factor in destabilizing the fragile food security situation of small producers in global value chains.

Looking at smallholders' production for the market, participation in global value chains often demands specialization in a few cash crops and an intensification of production. As a consequence, many farmers have given up more diversified production systems, such as mixed cropping. However, mixed cropping is much better suited to coping with the impacts of climate change. In contrast, if weather extremes or newly introduced parasites hit the few cash crops grown in specialized farms, producers risk a total loss of their harvest. Furthermore, as specialization is at odds with sustainable land and water management, it decreases rather than builds up soil fertility. And a poor soil structure risks erosion and reduces the soil's ability to capture water and store carbon. This too weakens the ability of the production system to cope with extreme droughts or heavy rains. Thus sustainable soil and water management are undisputedly among the most important elements for agricultural adaptation and for the resilience of small producers.

As specialized smallholders must rely on buying their own food from the market, they risk being hit twice by the impacts of climate change. An increasingly volatile and fragile global food production system due to climate change means that small producers face a higher risk not only of production losses, but also of sharply increasing food prices. The volatility of food prices has increased tremendously over the past few years, in part due to harvest losses resulting from climate change. Yet several studies show that high prices on world markets are seldom passed on to benefit small producers; rather, they are often transferred directly to consumer prices (see, for example, Jha, 2007; and Höffler and Ochieng, 2009). Thus small producers face the prospect of having to spend more money to buy their food while their incomes either fall or remain stagnant.

C. Rethinking the economics of developing countries' food systems

Over the course of the past few decades, various concepts and strategies have been developed that both reconcile agriculture with ecological cycles and at the same time give small producers greater economic stability and resilience. Examples of such strategies include resource-conserving agriculture, agroecology and organic agriculture (see, for example, Altieri and von der Weid, 2000; Pretty, 1995; and Pretty et al., 2006). The FAO has recently called for a significant transformation of the agricultural sector in order to meet climate change and food security challenges. The FAO's concept of "climate smart" agriculture aims to sustainably increase productivity, enhance resilience (adaptive capacity) and reduce GHGs (mitigation), and thus contribute to the achievement of national food security and development goals (FAO, 2010).

However, these strategies mark only the beginning of a sustainable reform of the food system. As they neglect to take trade and economic conditions into account, they risk succumbing to high price volatility, import surges and unregulated competition, as well as to the overwhelming power of food companies (e.g. processors, retailers and distributors) in the global trade arena. Increasingly, this is occurring even in the newly globalized market for organic produce. As long as market incentives remain unchanged, investments in business-as-usual practices will continue.

A sustainable transformation of small farm systems in developing countries will only succeed if it is integrated into overall agricultural and food development strategies. Issues concerning the agricultural trading system, as one of the major drivers of the existing food production system, need to be linked to the debate on agriculture's contribution to adaptation and climate change mitigation. Since trade liberalization and export orientation tend to undermine adaptive strategies and encourage input-intensive, "climate-unfriendly" farming, the sustainable transformation of the agricultural sector requires a fundamental rethinking of current trade policies.

The principle of "economic subsidiarity" offers guidance for this transformation (Sachs and Santarius, 2007). It implies that economic exchanges in the food system should be carried out preferably at the local and national levels, while exchanges at the continental or global level should have only a complementary function. Economic subsidiarity aims at localizing economic activities whenever possible and reasonable, and is committed to shorter rather than longer commodity chains. Instead of endangering small producers through volatile world market prices and making them the hubs for the extraction of capital, goods and resources, the regionalization of trade flows could serve as a catalyst to spur sustainable development at the local level. It will be successful particularly if production involves forward and backward linkages with other sectors of the local economy, such as with local input providers, processors and traditional retail outlets. If smallholder agriculture is well integrated into the local economy, and rural non-farm employment in the production of off-farm goods and services is stimulated, the regionalization of trade flows will contribute significantly to poverty alleviation and to overall economic development (see also, FAO, 2005).

D. Policies to promote sustainable local food systems

In order to launch a transition towards a (re-)regionalization of trade flows, and to foster short production chains, policy changes are required at subnational, national and international levels. At the national level, first and foremost governments need to ensure that they are allowed sufficient policy space vis-à-vis existing bilateral and multilateral trade obligations. This includes allowing governments adequate space to stabilize domestic food prices and protect small farmers from excessive price volatility. Countries also need to be able to implement policies and measures that chart their own defined paths to sustainable agriculture and food systems (see this chapter's lead article by Li and Khor). Policy space not only implies having more flexibility in the use of tariffs, quotas and other border control measures; it also, implies freedom from constraints imposed by bilateral and multilateral agreements on domestic regulatory competence or on investments which influence the agricultural sector's production structure.

The main task at the subnational level is to enable small farmers to regain long-term access to their domestic and local markets. First and foremost, this includes policies that go beyond trade, which protect the land rights of communities and their access to basic natural resources, and especially those that strengthen women's rights and land entitlements. Policies should promote a decentralized rural infrastructure to foster local marketing and ensure that rural and urban areas are sufficiently connected so that the hinterlands become the main suppliers of food for towns and cities. Most importantly, small farmers should be supported in achieving a "critical economic mass" through associative forms of economic activity, such as cooperative forms of production, storing and marketing. Developing-country governments as well as international donors should provide institutional and financial support, including public finances for microcredit and loan programmes, to foster such associations.

Furthermore, a range of policies that have proved viable in the past could accelerate the transition from conventional to more sustainable farming practices. For instance, penalizing polluters with taxes and levies will induce them to reduce their emissions. Subsidies for fertilizers and pesticides should be abolished, and taxes on fertilizers and other industrial farm inputs imposed or increased so as to accelerate the transition towards farming practices that cultivate on-farm nutrient cycles. In addition, governments could foster the development of sustainable agricultural process and production standards, including standard monitoring and verification schemes. The implementation of such schemes could be supported by low-interest loans for investing in sustainable farming practices. Those loans could be offered by communities, national governments and international donors. If farmers' training and field schools for sustainable farming practices are supported, and if the capacities of local NGOs are scaled up, this will catalyse further activities in the farming communities and generate local ownership in the process. Last but not least, communication strategies that provide better information to the public could promote a shift in consumption patterns towards more sustainable and locally produced food items.

The transition towards more sustainable food systems can be further advanced through a set of policies at various multilateral forums. In particular, policies that make long-distance transportation more expensive could contribute significantly to the (re-)regionalization of production chains. Since agricultural trade is very transport-intensive, the expansion of global markets and value chains would not have been profitable if freight costs had been high. In particular, foreign products can compete in domestic markets (e.g. Brazilian chicken legs competing with local poultry in West Africa) only if transport costs are low; otherwise, the lower marginal production costs abroad would soon be negated by higher transport costs. Over and above the rising oil prices that can be expected

in the face of the global peak oil scenario, measures to internalize environmental costs in transport prices should be pursued. For instance, the inclusion of air traffic in the European Emissions Trading Scheme is a first step in this direction. Additional measures could be advanced through negotiations at the United Nations Framework Convention on Climate Change, the International Civil Aviation Organization, and the World Maritime Organization.

Commentary IV: Getting Farmers off the Treadmill: Addressing Concentration in Agricultural Inputs, Processing and Retail Markets

Elenita C. Daño,
Action Group on Erosion, Technology and Concentration

Abstract

As corporations become bigger and fewer at both ends of the agricultural value chain, farmers are sandwiched between the spiralling costs of agricultural inputs dictated by the seed and agrochemical companies and the ever-increasing pressures on the prices of their produce imposed by mega-processors and mega-retailers that gobble up available supply in the market. This has grave adverse impacts on the local economies and on the livelihoods of farmers, on local food security and community resilience, and on biodiversity and the environment.

The dominant market structure and policy approach of the prevailing model of industrial agriculture have resulted in concentration and control by a handful of giant corporations over agricultural inputs, processing and retail markets. This allows them to dictate the prices of both inputs and produce. Oligopolies upstream and downstream of the agricultural market pose serious threats to world food security, aggravate climate change, imperil the livelihoods of millions of people and communities that depend on agriculture and greatly reduce their resilience to environmental and human-induced shocks. The paradigm of accumulation underlying this agricultural model breeds income disparity and highly skewed power relations. The resulting social inequity and environmental degradation effectively cancels out the supposed benefits from higher productivity and more efficient production systems.

A. Corporate concentration in agricultural inputs, processing and retailing

About 73 per cent of the total global commercial market for seeds, estimated at $27.4 billion, was controlled by the top 10 companies in 2009 (ETC Group, 2011b). Just three companies controlled 53 per cent of that

Table 2: World's top 10 seed companies, 2009

Companies by ranking	Seed sales ($ million)	Market share (per cent)
1. Monsanto (United States)	7 297	27
2. DuPont (Pioneer) (United States)	4 641	17
3. Syngenta (Switzerland)	2 564	9
4. Groupe Limagrain (France)	1 252	5
5. Land O' Lakes/Winfield Solutions (United States)	1 100	4
6. KWS AG (Germany)	997	4
7. Bayer CropScience (Germany)	700	3
8. Dow AgroSciences (United States)	635	2
9. Sakata (Japan)	491	2
10. DLF-Trifolium A/S (Denmark)	385	1
Total sales and market shares of the top 10	20 062	73

Source: ETC Group (companies' reporting, currencies have been converted to US dollars using historical average exchange rates).

Table 3: World's top 10 agrochemical companies, 2009

Companies by ranking	Agrochemical sales ($ million)	Market share (per cent)
1. Syngenta (Switzerland)	8 491	19
2. Bayer CropScience (Germany)	7 544	17
3. BASF (Germany)	5 007	11
4. Monsanto (United States)	4 427	10
5. Dow AgroSciences (United States)	3 902	9
6. DuPont (United States)	2 403	5
7. Sumitomo Chemical (Japan)	2 374	5
8. Nufarm (Australia)	2 082	5
9. Makhteshim-Agan Industries (Israel)	2 042	5
10. Arysta LifeScience (Japan)	1 196	3
Total sales and market shares of top 10	39 468	89

Source: ETC Group (companies' reporting, currencies have been converted to US dollars using historical average exchange rates).

total market, with Monsanto – the world's largest seed company and fourth largest pesticide company – accounting for 27 per cent of the world's commercial seed market (table 2).

The commercial seed sector, which supplies an estimated 20 per cent of the total seed requirements globally, is inextricably linked to the agrochemical market. Of the top six agrochemical companies, five are among the world's largest seed companies. Nearly 90 per cent of the world market for agricultural chemicals in 2009, estimated at $44 billion, was controlled by the top 10 pesticide companies (UK Food Group, 2010; ETC Group, 2011b). The top six companies, which sell proprietary formulas, accounted for over 72 per cent of the global agrochemical market (table 3).

Intellectual property rights (IPRs) such as patents, trade secrets and plant variety protection are key to protecting the business interests of giant corporations by allowing them monopoly control over their proprietary products and processes (Heinemann, 2009; IAASTD, 2009). Companies use patents to edge out competitors and impede further innovation on proprietary products and processes which could otherwise be adopted or improved on by others. Anticipating the devastating effects of climate change on agriculture, giant companies have started to position their commercial interests in the development of so-called "climate-

ready" or "climate-smart" crops. Between June 2008 and June 2010, the world's six largest seed and agrochemical companies filed patent applications on traits and genes that developed crop resistance to abiotic stresses such as drought, pests and salinity (ETC Group, 2011a). The "patent grab" corresponds to 261 patent families involving 1,663 patent documents worldwide. Even in the face of the climate crisis, the profit motive reigns supreme among corporate players in the seed and agrochemical industries.

Oligopolistic trends also reverberate down the agricultural value chain, particularly in the processing and retailing sectors. In 2009, the 10 largest food and beverage companies accounted for more than 37 per cent of the total revenue of this sector (Leatherhead Food, cited in ETC Group, 2011b). The three largest companies – Nestlé, PepsiCo and Kraft – together control 45 per cent of the revenues generated by the world's top 10 firms and 17 per cent of the revenues generated by the top 100 firms in the food processing sector (ibid.) (table 4).

In the retail market, the world's 10 biggest retail companies had combined sales of $753 billion in 2009, accounting for 41 per cent of the total revenues earned by the top 100 grocery retail firms valued at $1.84 trillion (Planet Retail, cited in ETC Group, 2011b). The combined share of the top three supermarket

Table 4: World's top 10 food and beverage companies, 2009

Companies by ranking	Food and beverage sales ($ million)	Total sales ($ million)	Market share (per cent)(as percentage of share of top 10)
1. Nestlé (Switzerland)	91 560	98 735	23.6
2. PepsiCo (United States)	43 232	43 232	11.2
3. Kraft (United States)	40 386	40 386	10.4
4. ABInBev (Belgium)	36 758	36 758	9.5
5. ADM (United States)	32 241	69 207	8.3
6. Coca-Cola (United States)	30 990	30 990	8.0
7. Mars Inc. (United States)	30 000	30 000	7.7
8. Unilever (The Netherlands)	29 180	55 310	7.5
9. Tyson Foods (United States)	26 704	26 704	6.9
10. Cargill (United States)	26 500	116 579	6.8
Total sales and market shares of the top 10	387 551	547 901	100

Source: Leatherhead Food Research, cited in ETC Group, 2011b

Table 5: World's top 10 food retailers, 2009

Companies by ranking	Grocery sales ($ million)	Market share (as percentage of share of top 10)	No. of countries of operation
1. Walmart (United States)	191 711	25.5	15
2. Carrefour (France)	104 290	13.9	34
3. Schwarz Group (Germany)	65 012	8.6	23
4. Tesco (United Kingdom)	63 288	8.4	14
5. Aldi (Germany)	62 268	8.3	15
6. Kroger (United States)	61 772	8.2	1
7. AEON (Japan)	52 874	7.0	9
8. Edeka (Germany)	51 625	6.9	2
9. Rewe Group (Germany)	51 435	6.8	14
10. Ahold (United Kingdom)	48 553	6.4	10
Total Top 10	752 829	100	

Source: Planet Retail at: http://www.planetretail.net.

chains – Walmart, Carrefour and Schwarz Group[46] – accounted for 48 per cent of the total revenues of the top 10 companies in that sector in 2009 (table 5).

As the purchasing power of consumers in emerging economies gains strength and the markets in many developed countries stagnate, the world's largest processors and retailers are rapidly moving into those economies. In particular, in Brazil, China, India and the Russian Federation, where demand is expanding and even outpacing that in industrialized countries. Giant supermarkets are scrambling to establish operations, forging joint ventures with major local retailers and swapping assets among them to ensure market dominance. In 2009, mergers and acquisitions in the food and beverage sector were valued at $43 billion (IMAP, 2010).

1. Farmers and oligopolies in the agricultural value chain

As corporations become bigger and fewer at both ends of the agricultural value chain, farmers are sandwiched between the spiralling costs of agricultural inputs dictated by the seed and agrochemical giants and the ever-increasing pressures on the prices of their produce imposed by mega-processors and mega-retailers that gobble up available supply in the market. This has grave adverse impacts on the local economies and on the livelihoods of farmers, on local food security and community resilience, and on biodiversity and the environment.

2. High input costs and low product prices

While the commercial seed sector may represent only about 20 per cent of the total seed requirements of farmers worldwide, the oligopoly enjoyed by the large seed and agrochemical companies enables them to wield immense control over agricultural inputs in general. This is because commercial seeds are often developed by the same companies that sell pesticides, and are marketed in tandem with agricultural chemicals that are promoted to protect crops from pests and diseases and to yield higher and better quality produce. Furthermore, as a result of massive promotion and government support of agrochemicals for "crop protection", even farmers who depend on traditional sharing and exchange of seeds have become consumers of pesticides, herbicides and fungicides. The agrochemical market is dominated by giant pesticide companies that have the power to dictate the prices and supply of their products globally, at least

so long as the lifespan of the patents granted to them (usually 20 years).

In the processing and retailing sectors, companies claim to procure their products and raw materials locally through such schemes as contract growing and local partnerships. Nestlé, for example, boasts of innovative partnerships with local milk producers in Pakistan to supply its expanded operations in the country (Farming First, 2010). Walmart's 2009 annual report projects that its stores will buy from over one million Chinese farmers in 2011, which would further boost the mega-retailer's standing as China's sixth largest export market (Elliot, 2005 cited in ETC Group, 2011b). Such practices claim to increase farmers' incomes, but processing and retailing companies such as Walmart exert "never-ending downward pressure on its suppliers to provide it with increasingly lower prices that simply aren't sustainable" (Donnelly, 2011 cited in ETC Group, 2011b).

3. Disempowering farmers

Contract farming or commercial growing arrangements by processing and retailing companies in many developing countries often require farmers to use a package of commercial seeds, synthetic fertilizers and agrochemicals, and to adopt specific farming practices to comply with strict market requirements for uniformity, which are guaranteed by complying with strict processes and production standards such as GlobalGAP, at prices largely dictated by the often exclusive buyer. While documented cases show that contract farming generally increases income and improves technical capabilities of middle-income farmers, small-scale farmers face a power imbalance, social differentiation, risks of contract violations and an unsustainable environment resulting from the use of agrochemicals and uniform varieties in their small landholdings (Minot, 2007).

Some policies of governments and private banking institutions also explicitly or implicitly promote and support the use of commercial seeds and chemical inputs, such as providing crop insurance and production loans only to users of packages of agricultural inputs (IAASTD, 2009; Greenpeace, 2009). Such policies deter farmers from adopting eco-functional farming systems, thus effectively limiting the possibilities for them to exercise their rights to make decisions on their farms.

4. Monocropping and uniformity

In developing countries, the vast majority of farmers are still sourcing their seeds through traditional saving, reusing, sharing and exchange practices. However, giant seed companies are steadily expanding to these potentially lucrative markets to sell commercial seeds, often aided by governments in their efforts to increase commodity exports. Indeed, some governments are actively promoting and even supporting the use of commercial seeds touted by the corporations for increasing productivity. Massive promotion of commercial seeds breeds monocropping and uniformity, thereby pushing out traditional food crops and local varieties (Barker, 2007).

The highly mechanized bulk processing of food and feed products by processors also requires uniformity in terms of features and qualities of raw materials sourced from farmers. Retailers likewise impose on farmer-suppliers uniform quality requirements on standard varieties to cater to consumer demands and to facilitate bulk handling, packaging, storage and retail display.

5. Threats to local food security and livelihoods

Such pressure to produce for the market can have adverse impacts on local food security (Barker, 2007; Utviklingsfondet, 2010). Small-scale farmers caught up in contract farming and commercial growing arrangements often end up with no land to cultivate their households' food requirements and many lose their lands in cases of crop failures (Minot, 2007). Even those who grow food crops sometimes end up selling all their products and buying cheaper and lower quality food for their own consumption in the local market.

The expansion of mega-retail companies in many developing countries where the retail industry (including the so-called underground economy led mainly by women entrepreneurs) constitutes a major sector in the national economy poses a serious threat to local livelihoods. In India, for example, retail is the second-largest employer after the agricultural sector, employing some 33 million people (Arnoldy, 2010 and Nair-Ghaswalla, 2010, cited in ETC Group, 2011b) whose jobs and livelihoods are threatened by the entry of transnational mega-retail chains on the domestic scene.

Prevailing practices in the agricultural input, processing and retail industries also raise serious ethical questions about global food security. Decades of breeding for higher yields and industrial farming practices have resulted in the decline of essential nutrients and minerals in the food supply (Jones, 2004, cited in ETC Group, 2009). Consumers and retailers in developed countries waste almost as much food annually (222 million tons) as the entire net food production of sub-Saharan Africa (230 million tons) (ETC Group, 2011).

6. Reducing farmers' resilience and capacity to adapt to the adverse impacts of climate change

Monocropping and uniformity adversely affect farmers' capacity to respond to environmental and human-induced stresses, since crop and varietal diversity in farms are the farmers' best insurance against the adverse effects of climatic change. IPRs on seeds impede farmers' rights to save, reuse, share and exchange seeds, and they reduce the capacity of communities for on-farm innovations and development of locally adapted varieties that respond to new environmental challenges (Heinemann, 2009).

7. Agriculture for equity and well-being

Agriculture for development has been so tragically narrowed down to increasing productivity in order to boost economic development by raising GDP, that it has not really translated into benefits for the majority of farmers who are still mired in poverty. The current industrial agriculture model breeds oligopolies across the agricultural value chain and is incompatible with an eco-functional agricultural system. The current system accumulates profits for a few at immeasurable costs to the environment and society. A shift to environmentally sustainable, socially equitable and economically viable agriculture will require a fundamental transformation of the dominant agricultural system and development model to one that promotes equity and the well-being of people and the planet as explicit goals.

8. Enabling sustainable economies

Agriculture as the backbone of the economy in most developing countries should support and promote rural livelihoods. Through strategic public investments as well as policies and support programmes that have an inherent bias to uplift smallholders and support eco-functional farming practices, productive activities on- and off-farm have the potential to create jobs and livelihoods in rural areas. This could effectively arrest the continuing tide of migration to cities and its associated negative social, economic and political consequences (IAASTD, 2009; Greenpeace, 2009;

Utviklingsfondet, 2010).

As a complement to interventions at the local and national levels, trade practices that breed oligopolies and inhibit competition need to be curbed at the global level. This requires stricter regulation of corporate practices, anti-trust actions and a moratorium on mergers and acquisitions (Barker, 2007; UK Food Group, 2010). IPRs and technological "advances" (e.g. hybridization, genetic engineering and terminator technology which inherently prohibits sharing, reuse and saving of seeds among farmers) that promote monopoly control over products and impede innovations by smaller players should be reviewed and corrected. Subsidies that benefit only the big players in the agricultural sector should be phased out, and policies that exert pressure on farmers to adopt commercial agricultural inputs reversed.

9. Conserving diversity

Long-term sustainability in agriculture can only be realized when supported by healthy ecological and biologically diverse ecosystems. Crop and varietal diversity are the smallholder farmers' best insurance against crop failures, agro-ecological stresses and climate change (Ho, 2008; IAASTD, 2009; UK Food Group, 2010). Diversity nurtured on-farm by farmers provides a wealth of healthy and sustainable products that can cater to the demands of consumers who are becoming increasingly aware of environmental, health and food issues. On-farm and *in-situ* conservation of agricultural biodiversity should be promoted and supported by providing appropriate incentives and recognition to farmers and communities. In addition, the rights and access of communities to these resources need to be protected from misappropriation and biopiracy.

10. Empowering smallholders

Governments can play a key role in increasing the quality and quantity of public investment in agriculture, and making product markets work better for smallholders (World Bank, 2008). The performance of small-scale producer organizations and smallholders practicing agroecological farming can be enhanced by building their capabilities, facilitating their access to financial services, improving price incentives and reducing their exposure to uninsured risks (IAASTD, 2009; World Bank, 2008).

Beyond economic empowerment, some fundamental steps towards empowering smallholders include protecting their tenure rights over land, improving

their access to productive resources, increasing their political voice and enabling their active participation in decision-making (World Bank, 2008; IAASTD, 2009; UK Food Group, 2010). Providing access to basic services and social protection, such as education, health, nutrition, social welfare and infrastructure, are also essential for farmer empowerment (WFP and FAO, 2009).

11. Promoting food sovereignty and the right to food

Global and national food security can be sustained only if local food security is assured, both in communities that produce food and in urban areas that depend on the former for their food supply. Food sovereignty – the right of sovereign States and communities to democratically determine their own agricultural and food policies – should begin at the local level with communities taking centre stage (IAASTD, 2009; Greenpeace, 2009; Utviklingsfondet, 2010; UK Food Group, 2010). Food sovereignty goes beyond food self-sufficiency; it incorporates agrarian reforms, local markets, biodiversity, autonomy from external pressures, cooperation and all aspects of local food production (IAASTD, 2009).

Governments and the international community need to respect and ensure the right of every person to adequate food as a fundamental component of sustainable solutions to food challenges (WFP and FAO, 2009; Utviklingsfondet, 2010). Respecting farmers' rights to agricultural genetic resources is an essential component of promoting the right to food.

12. Supporting agro-ecological farming

The viability and benefits of agro-ecological farming systems have been well established in numerous studies. There is now a need to redirect research and investments at the national and international levels in order to increase productivity in an environmentally sustainable and socially equitable manner (Ho, 2008; Greenpeace, 2009; UK Food Group, 2010; Utviklingsfondet, 2010). National support programmes and agricultural education curricula need to be reshaped, and decision-makers, implementers and extension service providers reoriented towards respecting and supporting the central role of smallholder farmers and peasants in agricultural development through agro-ecological farming (IAASTD, 2009).

Commentary V: Soaring Oil and Food Prices Threaten Affordable Food Supply

Richard Heinberg,
Post Carbon Institute

Abstract

The current global food system is highly fuel- and transport-dependent. Fuels will almost certainly become less affordable in the near and medium term, making the current, highly fuel-dependent agricultural production system less secure and food less affordable. It is therefore necessary to promote food self-sufficiency and reduce the need for fuel inputs to the food system at all levels.

The connection between food and oil is systemic, and the prices of both food and fuel have risen and fallen more or less in tandem in recent years (figure 1). Modern agriculture uses oil products to fuel farm machinery, to transport other inputs to the farm, and to transport farm output to the ultimate consumer. Oil is often also used as input in agricultural chemicals. Oil price increases therefore put pressure on all these aspects of commercial food systems.

Thus there is concern that high and volatile prices of crude oil may cause food prices to continue to increase (Bloomberg, 2011).

Moreover, as oil prices rise, so does demand for biofuels, which are the only non-fossil liquid fuels able to replace petroleum products in existing combustion engines and motor vehicles. But biofuels are often made from corn and other agricultural products. As

demand for these alternative fuels increases, crop prices are forced upwards, making food even less affordable.

Export-led agricultural strategies also increase the world's vulnerability to high oil prices. Most donor agencies have encouraged the less industrialized countries to focus on the production of cash crops at the expense of staples for local consumption. As a result, people in these countries are forced to rely increasingly on imports of often subsidized cereals or those funded by food aid programmes. However, rising transport costs contribute to rising prices of food imports, making them ever less affordable. Fuel costs represent as much as 50 to 60 per cent of total ship operating costs.[49] From early 2007 to mid-2008, as fuel prices soared, the cost of shipping food aid climbed by about $50 per ton – a nearly 30 per cent increase, according to the United States Agency for International Development (Garber, 2008).

Meanwhile, many poor farmers who cannot afford machinery, fuels and commercial farm inputs find themselves at a disadvantage in the global food economy. Compounding this are agricultural policies in industrialized food-exporting countries that subsidize domestic producers and dump surpluses onto developing countries, thus adding to the economic disadvantages of the smallholder farmers in those countries. As a result, millions of those farmers are being driven out of business annually. At the same time, developing countries are giving increasing priority to production for export, despite a burgeoning landless, poor urban class (whose immediate ancestors were subsistence farmers) that is chronically malnourished and hungry.

Soaring food and fuel prices have a disproportionate

Figure 2: Evolution of food and fuel prices, 2000 to 2009

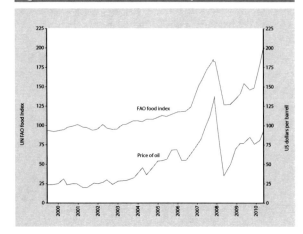

Sources: US Energy Information Administration and FAOstat.

impact on developing countries and on poor people in developed countries. Americans, who, on average, spend less than one tenth of their income on food, are able to absorb the higher food prices more easily than the world's poorest 2 billion people, who spend 50 to 70 per cent of their income on food.

Why are oil prices so high? Speculative investment in commodities plays a role, though there is a persuasive case to be made that oil prices would be rising even if oil futures speculation were entirely curtailed. The oil industry is changing, and rapidly. As Jeremy Gilbert, former chief petroleum engineer for BP, has put it, "The current fields we are chasing we've known about for a long time in many cases, but they were too complex, too fractured, too difficult to chase. Now our technology and understanding [are] better, which is a good thing, because these difficult fields are all that we have left" (Gilbert, 2011).

The trends in the oil industry are clear and undisputed: exploration and production are becoming more costly, and are giving rise to greater environmental risks, while competition for access to new prospective regions is generating increasing geopolitical tensions. According to the International Energy Agency (IEA, 2010a), the rate of world crude oil production reached its peak in 2006. The IMF has joined a chorus of energy industry analysts in concluding that scarcity and high prices are here to stay (IMF 2010 and 2011).

A collapse in demand for oil resulting from sharply declining global economic activity could cause oil prices to fall, as happened in late 2008. Indeed, this is fairly probable. But while it would make oil *cheaper*, it would not make fuel more *affordable* to most people. It is theoretically possible for the world to curb oil demand through policies that limit consumption, and it is also conceivable that some unexpected technological breakthrough could rapidly result in a cheap, effective alternative to petroleum. However, these latter two developments are rather improbable. Thus there is no likely scenario in which the services provided by oil will become more affordable within the context of a stable global economy at any time in the foreseeable future.

While wealthy consumers are able to absorb incremental increases in food prices, a sudden interruption in the availability of fuel (due to geopolitical events) or a significant gradual curtailment of fossil fuel production (due to the continuing depletion of world hydrocarbon reserves) could lead to a breakdown of the food system at every level, from farmer to processor to distributor to retailer, and finally to consumer.

To summarize, high oil prices contribute to soaring food prices. Our modern global food system is highly oil-dependent, but petroleum is becoming less and less affordable. Extreme weather events also contribute to high food prices, and, to the extent that such events result from anthropogenic global warming, they are also ultimately fuel-related. Thus there is no solution to the world's worsening food crisis within current energy and agricultural systems.

What is needed is a major redesigning of both food and energy systems. The goal of managers of the global food system should be to reduce its dependence on fossil energy inputs while also reducing GHG emissions from land-use activities. Achieving this goal will require increasing local food self-sufficiency and promoting less fuel- and petrochemical-intensive methods of production.

Given the degree to which the modern food system has become dependent on fossil fuels, many proposals for delinking food and fossil fuels may seem radical. However, efforts to this end must be judged not by the degree to which they support the existing imperatives of the global food system, but by their ability to solve the fundamental challenge that faces us: the need to feed a global population of seven billion (and counting) with a diminishing supply of fuels available to fertilize, plough and irrigate fields, and to harvest and transport crops. Farmers need to reduce their dependence on fossil fuels in order to build resilience against future resource scarcity and price volatility.

In general, farmers can no longer assume that products derived from petroleum and natural gas (chiefly diesel, gasoline, synthetic fertilizers and synthetic pesticides) will remain affordable in the future, and they should therefore change their business plans accordingly. While many approaches could be explored, which in any case would depend on specific geographic locations, the necessary outlines of a general transition strategy are already clear, as discussed below.

- Farmers should move towards regenerative fertility systems that build humus and sequester carbon in soils, thus contributing to solving climate change rather than exacerbating it.
- Farmers should reduce their use of pesticides in favour of integrated pest management systems that

rely primarily on biological, cultural and physical controls.

- More of the renewable energy that will power farming activities can and must be generated on farms. Wind and biomass production, in particular, can provide farmers with added income while also powering farm operations.

- Countries and regions should take proactive steps to reduce the energy needed to transport food by reorganizing their food production systems. This will entail support for local producers and for local networks that bring producers and consumers closer together. More efficient modes of transportation, such as ships and trains, must replace less efficient modes, such as trucks and planes.

- The end of the fossil fuel era should also be reflected in changes in dietary and consumption patterns among the general population, with a preference for foods that are grown locally, that are in season and that undergo less processing. Also, a shift away from energy- and meat-intensive diets should be encouraged.

- With less fuel available to power agricultural machinery, the world will need many more farmers. But for farmers to succeed, current agricultural policies that favour larger-scale production and production for export will need to change in favour of support to small-scale subsistence farming, gardening and agricultural cooperatives. Such policies should be formulated and put in place both by international institutions, such as the FAO and the World Bank, and also by national and regional governments.

If such a transition is undertaken proactively and intelligently, there could be many additional benefits, with more employment in farming, more environmental protection, less soil erosion, a revitalization of rural culture and significant improvements in public health. Some of this transformation will inevitably be driven by market forces, led by the rising price of fossil fuels. However, without planning, the transition may prove destructive, since market forces acting alone could bankrupt farmers while leaving consumers with few, if any, options for securing food supplies. Removing fossil fuels from the food system too quickly, before alternative systems are in place, would be catastrophic. Thus the transition process requires careful consideration and planning.

There are reasons for hope. A recent report on African agriculture by UNCTAD and UNEP (2008b) suggests that organic, small-scale farming can deliver the amount of increased yields thought to be possible only through industrial farming, and without the environmental and social damages caused by the latter. Recent research by Badgley et al. (2007) also concludes that organic and low-input methods can increase yields in developing countries while maintaining yields in industrialized countries.

Generally, smaller farms have greater biodiversity (Hole et al., 2005), place greater emphasis on soil-building (D'Souza and Ikerd, 1996) and display greater land-use efficiency than large farms (Rosset, 1999).

Nevertheless, despite these promising trends and findings, it is axiomatic that no food system tied to the earth's finite soil and water resources can support an ever-expanding and ever more resource-demanding population. The prudent path towards reforming the global food system must therefore coordinate agricultural policy with appropriate population, education, economic, transport and energy policies. The transition to a post-petroleum food system will need to be comprehensive. In its scale and required speed it promises to be one of the greatest challenges in human history. But the challenge will only grow the longer it is postponed.

Commentary VI: A Critical Analysis of Commodity and Food Price Speculation

Dirk Müller
Finance Ethics Ltd.

Abstract

There is an urgent need for policymakers to find ways of keeping financial investors out of commodity markets. Investment funds should be mobilized and encouraged to invest in production and research and development, rather than virtually or physically hoarding commodity stocks for merely speculative purposes, thus keeping them away from real economic activity. There is no economic justification for such siphoning away of production factors.

A. The extent of speculation

Until the turn of the century, there was very little speculation and financial investment in food; at best, very few specialized traders and financial analysts were active in this area. However, this has dramatically changed in recent years. During the period 2003–2008 alone, investment in the two biggest global commodity index funds shot up from $13 to $317 billion – a spectacular growth of 2,300 per cent.[48]

Originally, commodity exchanges, at which for instance wheat futures contracts are traded, played a constructive role for "real" agriculture. Farmers were able to sell their production to the miller at the "future" price quoted on the commodity exchange well in advance of the harvesting date. In this way, both sides could better plan their business, because they knew at what price the product would be sold, and the farmers were no longer exposed to further price fluctuations. Thus commodity exchanges provided risk management, or rather risk reduction, services. Since about 1999, the international finance lobby persuaded regulators to relax or lift restrictions on commodity futures trading, which banks and investment fund managers viewed as a lucrative business. However, this eventually led to a perverse market situation. The fact that speculators at commodity exchanges only need to have a fraction of their contracts backed by proper (real) funds (the so-called margin) results in an artificial increase in investments through credit.

The Chicago Board of Trade (CBOT) Exchange Volume Report of May 2011, reported trading of some 2.6 million futures and options contracts in that month. With a single contract, about 136 tons of wheat (5,000 bushels at 27 kg) were traded, resulting in a total trading volume of 358 million tons of wheat (at a value of about $90 billion), and that at just one commodity exchange in Chicago.[49] By way of comparison, this trading volume is equivalent to some 52 per cent of the total global wheat production of 2009.

Besides "formal" trading operations at commodity exchanges, many deals are made directly between financial market participants outside the official exchanges via telephone or via so-called "dark pools" (as over-the-counter (OTC) transactions). The supervisory authorities get very little information on the nature and volume of such deals. This is symptomatic and a contributory cause of the current financial crisis: since policymakers and regulators are not aware of the risk exposure and what consequences and domino effects the default of one market participant may have on the stability or fragility of the financial system, they do not have solid information on the basis of which to make informed and reasonable decisions. This also applies to the commodity trading market.

According to the Bank for International Settlements (BIS), the total volume of OTC transactions in 2010 amounted to $601 trillion. This amount is equivalent to 10 times the size of the world's GDP, estimated at around $60 trillion that year. The largest share of OTC transactions concerned interest-related deals, but commodity transactions were estimated to amount to about $3 trillion – almost the equivalent of Germany's GDP.

B. Impact on commodity prices

Price volatility in certain commodity markets, including for some grains, has significantly increased, though it is very difficult to determine to what extent this is

Figure 3: Correlation between the number of OTC contracts and commodity price development, 2006–2009

Source: Ghosh, 2010.

due to the effect of escalating speculation on specific commodity prices. Whereas in the distant past prices varied only marginally, today a doubling of prices or a drop of 50 per cent or more is no longer a rare occurrence. This level of extreme volatility can hardly be explained by market fundamentals alone. A recent study by Lagi, Bar-Yam and Bertrand (2011) attributes food price volatility largely to speculation and, to a lesser extent, to the expansion of biofuel production.[50]

An illustrative example of speculative activities can be seen in the history of oil prices, specifically of West Texas Intermediate (WTI), over the past five years (figure 4). From the level of $60 per barrel at the end of 2006, the price shot up to over $140 per barrel (i.e. by some 140 per cent), only to fall sharply shortly thereafter by over 70 per cent, to some $40 per barrel. Without doubt, the economic crisis of 2008–2009 dampened oil demand, but unlikely by as much as 70 per cent. Likewise, it is highly unlikely that demand in the two preceding years rose by 140 per cent. And there was no shortage of supply that might have justified such an aberration.

During the long phase of rising commodity prices, mostly from 2003 onwards, many arguments were advanced to explain the increase, including rising demand in rapidly industrializing countries and the political insecurity in several producing regions such as Iraq. Although the global economic crisis in 2008–2009 dampened oil demand, the fundamental factors persisted, so that it is unlikely that those factors caused oil prices to ease by as much as 70 per cent. Rather,

it was the considerable speculation in the market that drove those prices; this applied both to their upward and downward movements.

In the course of the second half of 2008, numerous speculators were hard hit by the dramatic developments in the world's financial markets and the resulting loss in the face value of bonds and shares. Speculators were obliged to liquidate loans for which they no longer had sufficient cover. As a result, any positions on the major players' books that still had any value and could be sold easily to generate liquidity in a crashing environment, including a significant volume of forward contracts on commodities, were sold, which led to a considerable easing of commodity prices. Other actors who also had small collateral on forward contracts got into trouble because falling

Figure 4: Development of the price of oil (WTI), 2007–2011

Source: http://www.finanzen.net.

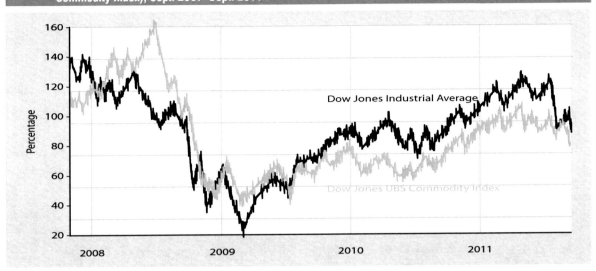

Figure 5: Correlation between share and commodity prices (Dow Jones Industrial Average versus Dow Jones UBS Commodity Index), Sept. 2007–Sept. 2011

Source: http://www.tradesignalonline.de.

cornprices had eaten into their collateral. They too had to sell their positions in order to meet their payment obligations. This avalanche of selling continued and caused a massive price decline, dropping below the level of departure before the price rise even though all "market fundamentals" that should have driven prices up still persisted. Neither producers nor consumers of commodities can adjust their level of production and consumption to such extreme and quick price movements. The erratic price behaviour therefore becomes a serious problem.

Apart from higher price volatility, an unusually high correlation (see figure 5) has also recently been observed in the price movements of apparently economically separate markets, such as for shares and commodities. In theory, that should make little sense, as their rationales and fundamentals are very different. Indeed, high commodity prices should dampen profit expectations of companies. The reason for this correlation is that, until a few years ago, commodity market developments were chiefly a function of physical supply and demand, and had little to do with developments in the financial markets. However, the increasing standardization and simplification of commodity exchange trading led to financial investors becoming increasingly attracted to alternative forms of investment that did not follow the trend of conventional financial markets, so as to spread their risk. Paradoxically, this run on commodity exchange contracts ultimately led to a neutralization of the very benefit they offered. At the

same time, developments on commodity markets have converged with those on international financial markets, contrary to what should occur, given that it is market fundaments, such as harvest volume or extreme weather events, that normally should have the major impact on commodity prices.

C. The role of speculators

The above analysis shows that supply and demand between producers and consumers are no longer the exclusive determinants of commodity prices; the driving forces and interests of financial markets are also increasingly influencing those prices. This makes commodity prices dependent on international monetary policy and the capital stock situation of large banks. Such a development is highly problematic, because every local financial crisis can easily trigger a global economic one, as witnessed over the past three years.

For the majority of financial actors, whether they are banks or investment funds, the overriding interest is to make money from commodity price volatility, and not the acquisition of real goods. They buy forward contracts on the delivery of commodities in the future at an already predetermined price. Shortly before such contracts become due, they conclude other contracts to even out their financial positions without having ever moved a kilogram of metal or a bushel of grain. If their bet turns out to be successful, they make some money; otherwise they incur a loss. It is estimated that

Figure 6: Evolution of production and consumption of wheat (1,000 tons)

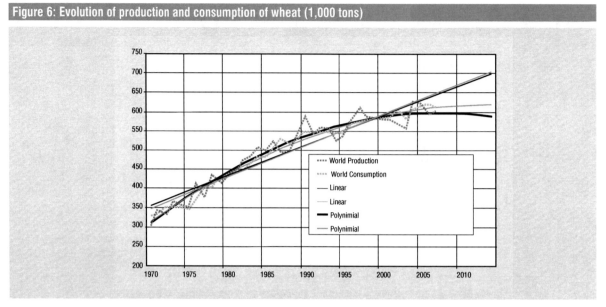

Source: United States Department of Agriculture, *Production, Supply and Distribution database*, 2008 (http://www.fas.usda.gov/psdonline/).

currently only about 2 per cent of futures contracts lead to a real physical delivery of commodities; the rest are liquidated before delivery. Yet, contrary to what would be assumed, this liquidation does not trigger a price decline, because the resulting freed investment capital is immediately reinvested in new contracts – the so-called "rollover" of contracts.

Capital invested in this way tends to stay in commodity futures markets in the medium term, which leads to price bubbles that in turn attract more speculative investment. This is what happened in the period 2003–2008 and again in the subsequent two years. If the market thus attracts more and more money via commodity index funds or similar vehicles, this accelerates price developments. Thus the increasing participation of financial investors in commodity markets for speculative purposes drives up futures prices and index funds, just as with shares on the stock exchange, because for each buyer there exists a seller.

The investment funds manager also sells commodity investments if the price persistently declines (or if investors pull their money out of the funds), and thus reinforces the declining price trend. No investor, speculator or fund manager buys an agricultural commodity at times of bumper harvests or low demand; rather, they are attracted by harvest failures and extreme demand situations. This is why both speculators and financial investors reinforce erratic price fluctuations. Their role in price formation for

food must therefore be viewed with considerable scepticism and concern.

In the case of wheat, the economic data provide a rather solid picture – production has always kept pace with demand (figure 6). It is therefore paradoxical that in recent years the price of wheat has been very volatile.

Since early 2009, large financial investors have invested in commodities by acquiring the stocks of entire warehouses, and since these are acquired directly from the producers, they do not feature in the real economy. This provokes production shortages and price booms with the simple objective of profit maximization by the international financial sector, which is detrimental to the real economy and to society at large.

There is no real need for the agro-food industry or the economy to give financial investors virtual or physical bags of wheat or other scarce commodities for diversifying their financial portfolio and thus creating artificial demand. The world market for food and other commodities is already under heavy demand pressure, which the food and commodity sector has managed to keep in check by expanding production. However, if there is additional and unnecessary demand pressure from financial investors, this fragile market equilibrium will be jeopardized.

Commentary VII: Let the Good Products Grow and Flow

Sophia Twarog
UNCTAD secretariat

Abstract

Reducing technical barriers to trade in organic agricultural products through harmonization and equivalency of organic standards and conformity assessment systems is of major importance for increasing organic markets, boosting trade in organic products and reducing transaction costs. This would promote the much-needed global shift towards sustainable and ecological food and agricultural systems.

The drive for high productivity and profitability through agro-industrial models has created serious environmental and social problems. Thus business as usual is not an option. The world needs to undergo a fundamental shift towards sustainable and ecological agricultural and food systems. This has been highlighted by an increasing number of United Nations studies, including a report by the International Assessment of Agricultural Knowledge, Science and Technology for Development (IAASTD, 2008), many UNCTAD reports (including its *Trade and Environment Review 2006*[51] *and 2010*), UNEP's *Green Economy Report (*UNEP, 2011*)*, and reports by the High Level Panel of Experts on Food Security and Nutrition (HLPE, 2011), and the United Nations Special Rapporteur on the Right to Food (Human Rights Council, 2010).

Within the broad scope of environmentally friendly agriculture, organic agriculture plays a very important role,[52] being, in many ways, the gold standard leading the way. It is also clearly defined and therefore verifiable. There are standards for organic production and processing which can be used both to guide operators and to assess if a system is organic or not. Such clarity enables producers to claim with sufficient backing that their products are organic, and to be economically rewarded for their sustainable production practices, since organic products can generally be sold at higher prices and are in high demand.

Organic guarantee systems (OGSs) are set up to guarantee to consumers that products have been produced in accordance with organic principles and practices. The main components of an OGS are:
- A production and processing standard, and
- A conformity assessment system to ensure that the standard is being followed.

There are different options for conformity assessment. Self-claim, relationships based on personal trust, participatory guarantee systems[53] and third-party certification can all work well at local and national levels. For exchanges across distances (including regional or international trade), usually third-party certification is needed. In countries that regulate their markets and certification systems, there is generally an additional layer, that of accreditation, supervision or approval of certification bodies. The organic private sector system also offers this additional layer of global organic guarantee through the International Organic Accreditation Service.

In recent decades, there has been a proliferation of public and private OGSs worldwide. Often these systems are islands: products sold as organic must comply 100 per cent with all the details of any particular system, and each OGS has usually been set up with local or national circumstances in mind. Little thought has been given to the benefits of the flow of products across systems, particularly inward flows. Small details or differences in OGS – at the levels of standards, certification or accreditation/approval – can become big barriers to trade. This lack of harmonization and equivalency across systems is a major hindrance to the development of the organic sector.

This comes at a high price. Farmers struggle to demonstrate that they meet all the rules and requirements in all the different markets where they wish to sell, which could even be two different stores on the same street. Similarly, processors and traders struggle to source acceptably certified final products and ingredients for processed products. And certification bodies pay high costs for multiple accreditations. Moreover, dealing with OGS diverts resources from more core activities such as production. At the same time, consumers pay higher prices and have fewer organic products to choose from. Finally, as growth in organic agriculture is hindered in these ways, the environment becomes more degraded due to the spread of non-organic, environmentally damaging forms of agriculture.

A. Importance of organic trade

The world needs strong, vibrant local food systems with local markets and local relationships. These should be actively supported by local consumers, retailers and governments alike. There is a whole array of actions that need to be undertaken, including development of local and regional infrastructure such as roads and markets, provision of missing services such as credit to smallholder farmers, support for the conservation and exchange of local seeds, breeds and related traditional knowledge, participatory research in partnership with local operators and in response to local needs, extension services to support organic production, and support to smallholder farmers to organize into groups (UNCTAD-UNEP, 2008a).

Trade in organic products can also play an important complementary role. Organic products currently account for a very small share of overall sales of food and agricultural products. There is great potential for this share to increase. Over the past few decades, the biggest constraint on growth in organic sales has been the shortage of a consistent supply.

Most operators and governments readily welcome opportunities to export organic produce as it provides sources of income and ways to stimulate domestic production. However, what is often overlooked is the important role that imports (e.g. of fresh produce, processed products or ingredients for processing) can play in expanding domestic organic markets. The larger the range of organic products on offer, the greater is consumer interest. As the markets grow, the high transaction costs and logistical inefficiencies are reduced as quantities increase, knowledge and experience are gained, short and long supply chains are developed and maintained, and trust is built along the supply chain through stable relationships. In general, the overall benefits from increasing the size of the organic market by attracting new organic consumers will outweigh the possible disadvantages some domestic producers fear in terms of competition in their home markets.[54] Since consumers of organic

products will still generally prefer local products, domestic organic operators can benefit from this by marketing their products as
• national, through a national label such as the national flag, and/or
• local, through direct sales or by signs on local products at point of final sale.

These local or national labels may even attract new consumers of organic, who are interested in buying local products. In addition, ingredients for processed products often have to be sourced from many different countries, which means that imports are necessary for developing the organic processed products industry, which is one of the most rapidly growing segments of the organic market.

Openness to trade in organic products also shows solidarity with the rest of the organic world, especially with organic producers from developing countries. In most of these countries, the domestic organic markets are particularly small. Therefore, organic exports can be an important pull factor for the development of sustainable agricultural practices and improved livelihoods for the world's poor. On smallholder farms in developing countries, often one or two products are exported, but dozens of other products are being produced in an organic manner and sold locally. This improves food security (UNCTAD-UNEP, 2008b) and the health of local populations.

In general, organic trade acts as an important stimulus to organic production and sales. However, its potential is limited by technical barriers to trade due to differences in OGSs. Consequently, it produces the odd situation that conventional products can cross borders more easily than organic products. This only serves to exacerbate another more fundamental tilt against organic products in the market's playing field. At present, apart from fair-trade products, organic products are the only goods that have internalized some environmental costs in their prices. In contrast, the considerable damage to the environment, health and other economic sectors caused by agro-industrial agriculture is not at all reflected in the prices of conventional food and agricultural products. These costs to society and to the planet are very high, but are paid by society in terms of higher health costs, environmental clean-up, and job losses in fisheries that are affected by agrochemical run-off, to cite a few costs. For example, the first ever pan-European Nitrogen Assessment performed a cost–benefit analysis of nitrogen fertilizer use in Europe, which revealed that the overall environmental costs "(estimated at €70–€320 billion per year at current rates) outweigh the direct economic benefits of reactive nitrogen in agriculture. The highest societal costs are associated with loss of air quality and water quality, linked to impacts on ecosystems and especially on human health" (Sutton et al., 2011). However, these costs are not reflected in the prices of the food and agricultural products produced with heavy inputs of the synthetic nitrogen fertilizers. The long-term solution to this problem clearly should be to change the underlying incentive structures so that negative externalities are duly reflected in the prices of all agricultural products. At the very least, governments should stop subsidizing these harmful inputs. This could ultimately result in organic production becoming the norm, with OGSs no longer needed. In the meantime, however, it is important to reduce the technical barriers to trade caused by differences in OGSs so that the organic agriculture sector can grow. The main tools for this are harmonization and equivalence.

B. Facilitating organic trade through harmonization and equivalence

Equivalency should be the basis for international trade in organic products, supplemented by harmonization where desired and applicable. National organic standards and regulations should be in line with international organic standards and also, very importantly, take into account national agroecological, socio-economic and cultural perspectives. International trade should be based on mutual respect for this policy space.

Countries and private sector standard setters should not force the rest of the world to comply in a prescriptive manner with every single detailed specification in their OGSs, which might not fit well in the others' contexts. Rather, the way forward is to expect the best while at the same time embracing diversity. Countries and private OGSs should allow imports of organic products that are produced and guaranteed in a manner equivalent (not identical) to their own.

For over a decade, UNCTAD, FAO and the International Federation of Organic Agriculture Movements (IFOAM), through their joint International Task Force on Harmonization and Equivalence in Organic Agriculture (2002–2008), have worked together, along with a host of key public and private sector actors, to

develop the following tools to foster trade based on equivalency:
- For conformity assessment, the International Requirements for Conformity Assessment Bodies (IROCB) are performance requirements for organic certifiers adapted from ISO 65, which facilitate recognition across systems.
- For production and processing standards, the Equitool is a guide to assessing differing standards in a structured and transparent manner.

Under a successor joint initiative, the Global Organic Market Access (GOMA) project, the Equitool has been enhanced through the development of the Common Objectives and Requirements for Organic Systems (COROS). COROS helps governments and other organic standard setters to identify the underlying objectives their organic production and processing systems aim to achieve, and then to evaluate other standards to see if, on the whole, they achieve those objectives (in a similar or different but equally valid manner). IFOAM, the international private sector standard setting body, is using COROS to develop the IFOAM family of standards – those which have been assessed and found to be overall equivalent to COROS.

The public and private sectors should make full use of these tools. Specifically, for the purpose of trade in organic products, and particularly as regards imports of organic products from other systems, public and private sector actors involved in regulating organic guarantee systems should:

1. For production and processing standards,
- Use COROS and the Equitool to evaluate other production and processing standards to determine if compliance with those standards would, as a whole, achieve the most important underlying objectives of organic production systems.

2. For conformity assessment systems,
- Build trust among accreditors and supervising bodies (including governments) to mutually recognize accreditation/approval systems of certification bodies and other means of conformity assessment.
- Use IROCB to evaluate the performance requirements for certification bodies.

The landscape of international trade in organic products is currently changing. Many regions are undergoing regional harmonization of parts or all of their OGSs. For many years, the EU had the only harmonized system, although the development of the National Organic Program in the United States could also be considered a sort of internal harmonization of a web of private and State OGSs. Since 2005, with the support of IFOAM, FAO, UNCTAD and UNEP, various developing-country regions have also engaged in regional cooperation and harmonization.

- In East Africa, the East African Organic Products Standard (EAOPS) was developed through a regional public-private sector consultative process in 2005–2007, and adopted as the East African Community standard in 2007.
- The Pacific Islands followed this model to develop their own regional standard, which they adopted in 2008.
- The Central American countries plus the Dominican Republic are currently finalizing full harmonization of their organic regulations relating to standards plus conformity assessment aspects.
- Public and private sector actors from South, East and South-East Asian countries have been cooperating since 2010 to develop the Asian Regional Organic Standard (AROS), the draft of which was finalized in February 2012.

These efforts at harmonization can both expand the regional markets and develop a sense of common regional identity, with positive spillover effects in terms of South-South cooperation in a number of areas.

Regulations concerning organic imports need to be updated to reflect this shifting landscape and allow for recognition of regional organic standards. This would involve separating equivalency determinations of standards and of conformity assessment systems. Currently this is not the case. For example, under the EU import approval system there is no avenue for the East African Community to submit the EAOPS for approval because a common organic conformity assessment system comprising accreditors and supervision of certification has not yet been developed. Thus the region does not fit into the category of a third-country list.

For regulations that maintain lists of approved certification bodies (such as in the EU and the United States), certification bodies should be allowed to certify to different standards in different regions. For example, a European certification body operating in Europe and in East Africa should be able to use the EU standard for operators in Europe and the East African Organic Products Standard for operators in East Africa.

C. A landmark in facilitating organic trade

In 2008, Canada and the United States signed an equivalency agreement with full system recognition, including for imports. Certification bodies around the world need only obtain one accreditation and operators only one certification to access both markets. This equivalency agreement thus promotes organic trade creation without trade diversion, which may occur under more exclusionary agreements. It thus shares the benefits with the rest of the world. It is a best practice to be emulated, and hopefully also replicated multilaterally worldwide.

Commentary VIII: Community-Supported Organic Production: The Case of the Regional Value-added Citizen Shareholder Corporation in Southern Germany

Christian Hiss
Regional Value-added Citizen Shareholder Corporation

Abstract

The Regional Value-added Citizen Shareholder Corporation supports:

• The creation and sustainable operation of small and medium-sized enterprises in the local production, processing and marketing of organic food through a dedicated investment strategy that assures the economic independence of enterprises through shareholder participation of interested citizens and consumers of the region and collaboration in existing clusters.

• The gathering and evaluation of data on non-monetary benefits or services generated by supported farmers and enterprises on the basis of 64 social, economic and ecological indicators.

The Regional Value-added Citizen Shareholder Corporation (RVACSC) in the region of Freiburg in southern Germany is an innovative enterprise in the area of social-ecological investment. It aims at acquiring agricultural enterprises in the region of Freiburg with cash investments from local consumers and citizens, who take an active interest in the sustainable development of organic agriculture and the provision of safe and good quality food from the region. The funds raised are used by RVACSC to acquire or participate in production facilities that are then leased to interested RVACSC member farmers or entrepreneurs according to criteria set by the RVACSC.

Acquisitions concern the production, processing and distribution of organic produce, including seeds, farms, energy generation, fertilizer production, restaurants and hotels, as well as retail outlets. As a citizen corporation, it aims to attract private and institutional investors, who provide small and medium-sized enterprises with a solid capital base aimed at building and consolidating sound, regionally-focused economic structures.

A. Assuring sustainable management and appropriate return on investment

The pressure of securing sufficient capital returns has a major bearing on agricultural production, and therefore on the lives of farmers and agricultural producers. Specialization, mechanization and economies of scale tend to become the lynchpin, even for organic production at enterprise level.

However, the orientation of agriculture based only on return-driven criteria implies losses on the socio-ecological side, because manpower is replaced by technology or low-income, seasonal labour. This changes the cultural landscape. A further consequence of this development is that technically disadvantaged regions become more marginalized over time. The same applies to sectors that are less lucrative, such as dairy farming, small-scale agriculture in general, or breeding of new, regionally cultivated plant varieties. From an agricultural point of view, it makes more sense to have an interconnected and multifunctional management approach.

Yet in order to survive competitive market pressure, a significant share of the costs of conventional agricultural producers becomes externalized. Against this background, the prevailing capital return concept needs to be called into question. One therefore wonders whether the creation of specific socio-ecological values does not also represent a kind of "net yield".

RVACSC shareholders obtain two types of returns on the capital they invest: a monetary and a qualitative one. The organization's annual business report, in addition to providing information on the net monetary yield of its investments, also takes into account the

Table 6: Key sustainable management criteria

Staffing	Ecological criteria	Economic variables
Structure of employment	Soil fertility	Distribution of value creation
Level of wages	Biodiversity	Value creation for the region
Fluctuation	Development of organic cultivation area	Regional engagement
Quality of job functions	Resource consumption	Dialogue within the value-creation chain
	Implementation of EU Directive on Organic Agriculture	

social and ecological effects of RVACSC activities by providing information on the creation of value other than only material value. The fact that every economic process has a positive and negative impact on value creation for the economy is beyond doubt. Therefore, for each RVACSC share, both the micro- and macro-economic revenues are reported. The categories of sustainable management include the variables in Table 6.

B. New opportunities through regional networks

Through the engagement of the RVACSC in areas beyond only agricultural production, less lucrative operations and entities can be supported or strengthened. Likewise, cross-linking enables the RVACSC to channel capital from urban centres into rural areas.

C. Farm succession

For years, the number of people taking over their family farms has been constantly declining. On the other hand, there are many well-trained farmers and gardeners who cannot acquire their own farms due to the high capital requirements. With the instruments and intermediation provided by the RVACSC, a farm can be acquired by an interested farmer if there is

no family successor interested in running it, thus facilitating continuity of production and the robustness of the regional network.

D. Community and consumer participation and dialogue

The term "citizen shareholder corporation" was intentionally used for RVACSC. It denotes that, with the acquisition of shares, interested citizens and consumers from the region around the city of Freiburg become partial owners of the land and assets of RVACSC. They take an active interest in the sustainable management of the network, the management of the soil and conservation of the environment as well as in improving rural livelihoods. The principles of the RVACSC envisage a permanent dialogue between the shareholders and the operators/tenants of the individual entities on the most desirable direction of their activities and related production methods.

E. Regional versus global market orientation

The business model of RVACSC has a clear regional focus. Value creation remains within the region, and capital is sought from citizens within the region who take an active interest in sustainable agriculture, its

Figure 7: The conceptual structure of RVACSC

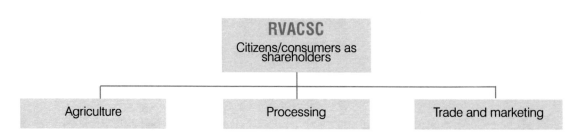

multi-functionality – including the conservation of local biodiversity and the environment – and the creation of rural livelihoods. This model offers a number of economic, environmental and social benefits.

1. Economic benefits:

- No one-sided specialization of production: the networking and consultative approach as well as the principals of organic agriculture prevent lopsided specialization;
- Less pressure to reduce costs and increase the scale of production;
- Priority given to quality over economies of scale through active support to smallholder farmers and small-scale processing and marketing companies;
- Mutual support within the network through counselling and support of partner companies;
- No dependence on specific marketing systems

and marketing partners;
- Maintaining managerial sovereignty through shareholder involvement, as there is no dependence on external financial agencies;
- Contribution to rural development and sustainable livelihoods through the creation of new companies and farms; and
- Mobilization of capital from within the region.

2. Environmental benefits:

- Short transport distances;
- Small producing units that respect the multi-functionality of agriculture;
- Promotion of organic agriculture and sustainable processing and marketing methods (with resulting improvements in soil fertility and biodiversity, and contribution to climate change mitigation); and
- Direct contribution of consumers to transforming

Table 7: Overview of key investments of RVACSC

Project	Nature of investment	Invested capital (€)
Dairy farm, Groos	Purchase and lease	297,628
Market garden, Feldmann	Purchase and lease	106,294
Real estate investments	Purchase and lease	116,449
Crop area: 7,94 ha	Purchase and lease	228,500
Natural food wholesale company, Bodan Ltd.	Silent partner	20,000
Food retail outlet, Rieselfeld Ltd.H	Shareholder	10,000
Organic-Catering, Mocellin	Silent partner	15,000
Fruit garden, Joel Siegel	Silent partner	45,000
RVACSC Delivery Service Ltd., Biohöfe Frischekiste	Shareholder	15,000
RVACSC Delivery Service Ltd., Biohöfe Frischekiste	Loan	25,000
RVACSC Real Estate	Shareholder	76,000
RVACSC organic market outlet, BioMarkt GmbH Breisach	Shareholder	35,000
RVACSC Real Estate	Loan	70,000
Invested capital		**1,059,871**
Approved investment projects		
Agricultural machinery	Purchase	35,000
Construction of farm house	Loan	270,000
RVACSC Delivery Service Ltd., Biohöfe Frischekiste	Increase of shares	15,000
RVACSC Delivery Service Ltd., Biohöfe Frischekiste	Loan	20,000
Total:		**340,000**
Planned projects		
Processing facility for dried fruit and vegetables	Purchase of suitable building	180,000
Market garden in Donaueschingen (new enterprise)	Partial ownership	60,000
Increasing the number of outlets for RVACSC organic market outlet Biomarket in the city of Freiburg and in adjacent areas	Increase of shareholding	280,000
Fruit garden (creation of new enterprise)	Partial ownership	50,000
Organic chicken farm (creation of new enterprise)	Partial ownership	80,000
Vegetable processing facility (creation of new enterprise)	Partial ownership	35,000
Cash reserve for land acquisition		100,000
Required capital		**785,000**

agricultural practices to more environmentally friendly ones.

3. Social benefits:
- Better working and social conditions;
- Greater recognition of the farming profession;
- Increased attractiveness of agriculture for young people and the local community; and
- Assistance to young people for creating agribusinesses.

F. RVACSC governance bodies and current capital

An RVACSC share currently costs €500, and takes the form of a registered share with restricted transferability, so that it cannot be sold without the explicit consent of the other shareholders. Currently, the RVACSC has 470 shareholders and a capital stock of €1.7 million. The current capital is invested in the farms and enterprises as shown in Table 7.

Commentary IX: The SEKEM Initiative: A Corner Pillar for the Community

Helmy Abouleish and
Matthias Keitel, SEKEM

Abstract

The great challenges confronting our world today – food insecurity, climate change and poverty – are long-term problems, mainly caused by unsustainable economic practices. These common economic practices have to be transformed into sustainable ones, preferably in a holistic way. The SEKEM[55] Initiative has adopted this approach since its inception in 1977. Its holistic business model not only follows economic principles, but also attempts to integrate ecological, societal and cultural dimensions. It thereby meets market demands and complies with standard economic procedures, protects the environment and promotes climate change adaptation and mitigation, guarantees ethical standards and human rights, and promotes the human development of its employees, suppliers and the surrounding communities.

31 October 2011 – this date will go down in history as the day when the world population exceeded 7 billion people. One major concern revolving around this landmark is how to provide enough food for the world's growing population when already around one billion people worldwide are suffering from hunger. In addition, climate change threatens hundreds of thousands of farmers with unpredictable weather events and shifts in seasons, which in turn exacerbate food insecurity.

Egypt reflects this global picture: its population is growing by around 2 per cent annually, while the Nile Delta, the most fertile and therefore the most important land strip for Egypt's domestic agricultural production, is threatened by rising sea levels. Already today, salinization of groundwater constitutes a problem that will most likely worsen in the future.

Business-as-usual approaches struggle to deliver solutions, while climate change is worsening and a billion people still suffer from hunger. At the same time, big agribusiness corporations increase their profits through questionable approaches, such as the use of genetically modified seeds or vast monoculture fields.[56] The success of SEKEM shows that ecological farming can adapt better to climate change and has the potential to feed the world if it is adopted widely over the next years.[57]

Despite their shortcomings, businesses are crucial to tackling the issues related to food insecurity and

climate change. However, to be effective, those businesses need to ensure that the surrounding communities, which are usually their suppliers, participate in tackling the challenges and benefit from the businesses. Only if these people are included in the process and benefit from the businesses can sustainable solutions for food security and climate change be found.

The SEKEM Initiative follows such a community-based approach. SEKEM was founded with the idea of promoting sustainable development benefiting the local community and the environment in the surrounding villages.

A. Vision and mission of SEKEM

The SEKEM Initiative was established by Dr. Ibrahim Abouleish over 34 years ago about 60 km north-east of Cairo in rural Egypt. On returning to Egypt after 21 years of study and work in Austria, he noticed how Egypt's socio-economic fabric had deteriorated. His response to this was to develop the following vision for his country:

"Sustainable development towards a future where every human being can unfold his or her individual potential; where mankind is living together in social forms reflecting human dignity; and where all economic activity is conducted in accordance with ecological and ethical principles."

Figure 8: SEKEM's activities based on its vision for Egypt

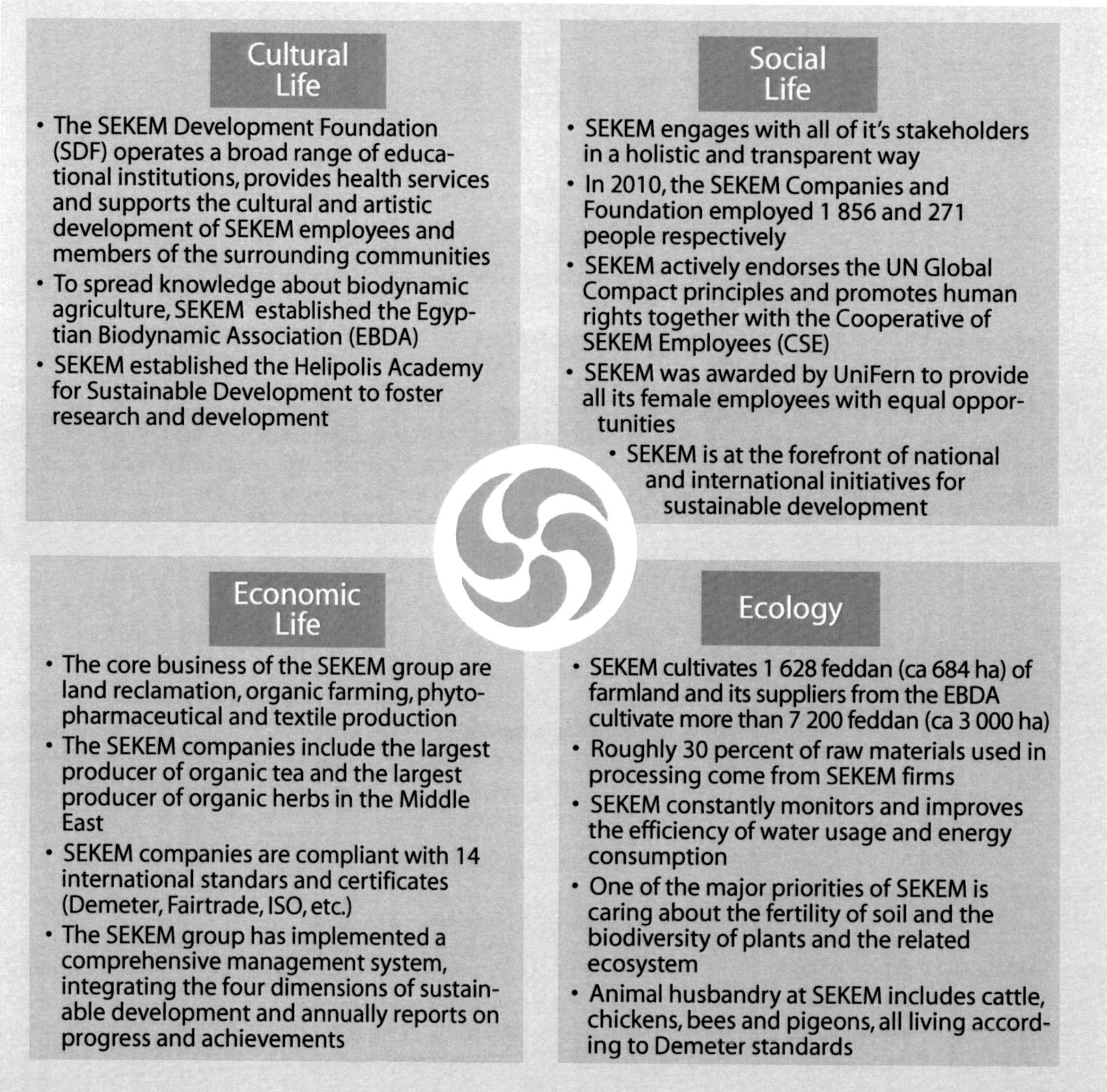

Cultural Life

- The SEKEM Development Foundation (SDF) operates a broad range of educational institutions, provides health services and supports the cultural and artistic development of SEKEM employees and members of the surrounding communities
- To spread knowledge about biodynamic agriculture, SEKEM established the Egyptian Biodynamic Association (EBDA)
- SEKEM established the Heliopolis Academy for Sustainable Development to foster research and development

Social Life

- SEKEM engages with all of it's stakeholders in a holistic and transparent way
- In 2010, the SEKEM Companies and Foundation employed 1 856 and 271 people respectively
- SEKEM actively endorses the UN Global Compact principles and promotes human rights together with the Cooperative of SEKEM Employees (CSE)
- SEKEM was awarded by UniFern to provide all its female employees with equal opportunities
  - SEKEM is at the forefront of national and international initiatives for sustainable development

Economic Life

- The core business of the SEKEM group are land reclamation, organic farming, phyto-pharmaceutical and textile production
- The SEKEM companies include the largest producer of organic tea and the largest producer of organic herbs in the Middle East
- SEKEM companies are compliant with 14 international standars and certificates (Demeter, Fairtrade, ISO, etc.)
- The SEKEM group has implemented a comprehensive management system, integrating the four dimensions of sustainable development and annually reports on progress and achievements

Ecology

- SEKEM cultivates 1 628 feddan (ca 684 ha) of farmland and its suppliers from the EBDA cultivate more than 7 200 feddan (ca 3 000 ha)
- Roughly 30 percent of raw materials used in processing come from SEKEM firms
- SEKEM constantly monitors and improves the efficiency of water usage and energy consumption
- One of the major priorities of SEKEM is caring about the fertility of soil and the biodiversity of plants and the related ecosystem
- Animal husbandry at SEKEM includes cattle, chickens, bees and pigeons, all living according to Demeter standards

Source: Reproduced from SEKEM (2010).

This vision integrates ecology with economic, societal and cultural life and is the guiding principle of all SEKEM activities as shown in figure 8.

B. Implementing SEKEM's vision

1. Establishing biodynamic agriculture as a competitive solution to the environmental, social and food security challenges of the twenty-first century

SEKEM's business model is based on the concept of "biodynamic agriculture", a specific form of organic agriculture that views the farm as "a self-contained, self-sustaining ecosystem responsible for creating and maintaining its individual health and vitality without any external or unnatural additions. [...] Soil, plants, animals and humans together create this image of a holistic living organism".[58]

With this form of agriculture, yields in traditional farming systems in developing countries and in regions where soils are degraded can be increased by up to 180 per cent (Scialabba, 2007). In Egypt, where desert land on which SEKEM started its operations is the most degraded form of soil possible, SEKEM has significantly contributed to the availability of healthy and affordable food through this form of organic agriculture. Indeed, it is a pioneer in biodynamic agriculture in the MENA (Middle East and North Africa) region, and in establishing the organic market in Egypt.

Today, the organization and its biodynamic suppliers own over 20,000 acres of farmland of which 9,000 acres are cultivated. To spread knowledge about biodynamic agriculture, SEKEM actively supports the Egyptian Biodynamic Association (EBDA) which offers training on the application of biodynamic methods. Currently there are about 200 farms under the EBDA. About 1 per cent of the overall agricultural land in Egypt has been converted to organic agriculture.

2. Supporting individual development through holistic education and medical care

To promote human development, the SEKEM Development Foundation (SDF) was founded in 1983 under its previous name, Association for Cultural Development in Egypt. It supports and operates a broad range of educational, social and cultural institutions. There is a kindergarten, various programmes for socially disadvantaged children, schools and a vocational training centre, which together educate about 600 children and students. The SDF provides health services through a medical centre which serves 30,000 people in surrounding villages. It also supports cultural and artistic development. All of these programmes create jobs, provide better learning opportunities and health care for the people in the surrounding villages, and enable the societal inclusion of children with special needs, thus contributing to the alleviation of poverty, fighting social exclusion and improving literacy. It also ensures the integration of SEKEM within the wider social community of the region, and thereby contributes to cultural understanding between the local population and the SEKEM staff who might have a different background.

3. Creating workplaces that respect human dignity and support employee development

The SEKEM Group consists of eight companies: two of them process the raw materials grown on its fields (Libra and SEKEM for Land Reclamation), while Lotus processes herbs and spices, ISIS produces high-quality organic foodstuffs, NatureTEX manufactures textiles and ATOS Pharma manufactures phyto-

pharmaceuticals. These products are distributed and sold on the domestic (70 per cent) and international markets (30 per cent). The eighth company is El Mizan which offers grafting and plant cultivation services for fruit and vegetable growers.

The SEKEM Group of companies therefore forms an integrated value chain as all companies are closely interlinked. In 2010, these companies employed over 1,800 people, mostly hired from among the surrounding local communities. They offer health insurance and pension schemes – which promote social security – and equal opportunities through training, particularly to advance the professional equality of women in the workplace, promoted through the project "One Business Community… equal opportunity", which was started in 2009. The Code of Conduct of SEKEM is based on its vision for sustainable development, which is depicted through the Sustainability Flower (figure 8) and further refined using the principles of the United Nations Global Compact (UNGC) and the relevant conventions of the United Nations and the International Labour Organization.

4. Building business models in accordance with ecological and ethical principles

Ecological and ethical principles should go beyond labour rights and organic agriculture. They should run through the entire business model starting with resource efficiency, awareness raising within and beyond the company and educating and exchanging views with others about them. Through its education, training and consultancy, SEKEM seeks to create capacity in order to scale up successful and sustainable business models. These are provided by the Sustainable Development Center of the Heliopolis Academy, the SEKEM schools and through the policy work of SEKEM's management. Additionally, SEKEM has developed close ties with different businesses throughout the world which follow the same ecological and ethical principles. These ties go beyond normal business relationships. In 1996, the International Association for Partnership in Ecology and Trade (IAP) was formed, which developed the Sustainability Flower (figure 9) that serves as the conceptual framework for performance monitoring and evaluation. The SEKEM Group has implemented this comprehensive management system, integrating the four dimensions of sustainable development (ecology, economy, society, culture), and provides annual reports on progress and achievements relating

Figure 9: The Sustainability Flower

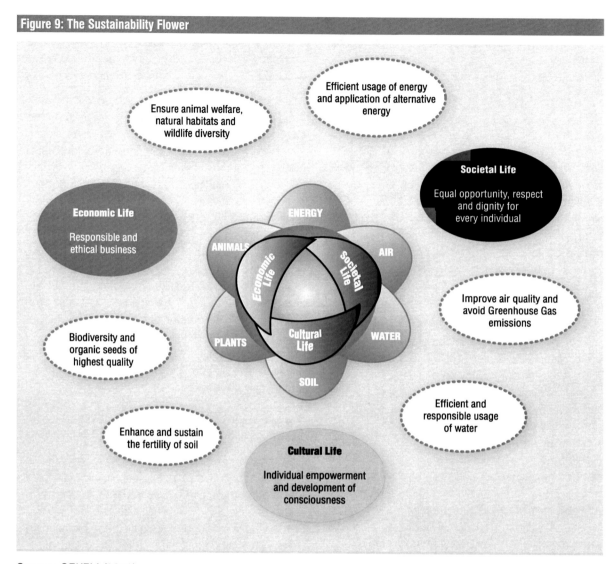

Source: SEKEM (2010).

to the Flower.

5. Innovating for sustainable development through research in natural and social sciences

Sustainable businesses need to be innovative in order to remain sustainable and competitive. The Heliopolis Academy for Sustainable Development, established by the SDF, aims at improving the capacity to conduct, publish and disseminate relevant social and scientific research in the areas of medicine, pharmaceuticals, renewable energy, biodynamic agriculture, arts and social sciences. One among many such scientific services is the breeding of predators that serve as a form of biological pest control.

Incorporated within the Heliopolis Academy are several laboratories and the Sustainable Development Center, which is the focal point for all issues revolving around sustainable development, while El Mizan provides healthy, profitable indoor and outdoor grafted seedlings to Egypt's vegetable producers and to SEKEM for Land Reclamation.

6. Advocacy for a holistic approach to sustainable development

It requires more than just a few sustainable businesses to contribute to food security and to climate change mitigation and adaptation. The policy engagement of the SEKEM management focuses on this aspect. In addition, SEKEM is seeking to institutionalize its efforts through the Heliopolis University for Sustainable Development – the first non-profit university in the region. The university seeks to educate the youth, both in Egypt and those coming from abroad, on the concept of sustainability and its further applications in all the different sectors of the economy. Responding to the challenges of the twenty-first century such as climate change, resource scarcity, a growing population and extreme poverty, Heliopolis University was established to drive research and deliver innovative findings that could provide sustainable solutions for some of the major problems confronting Egyptian society.

C. Concrete sustainability effects and gains in terms of economic, social and environmental impacts

The activities of SEKEM have had substantial positive impacts on the community, nature and businesses. The community has profited significantly from the cultural activities of the SEKEM Development Foundation, which is mainly funded through the SEKEM Group. Over 600 students in its school and the vocational training centre profit every year from the education they receive. The schools are open to everyone and are accredited by the Government. The dual system of the vocational training centre (offering practical experience in the workshops as well as theoretical courses) is a huge success, and its graduates are in great demand. Additionally, the medical centre provides health-care services to over 30,000 people in the surrounding villages and to employees of the SEKEM companies. Other facilities, such as concerts and art courses, promote the individual development of the participants.

With regard to the environment, SEKEM has created a new biotope by turning desert land into fertile and living soils through compost and biodynamic agricultural methods. The soil's water holding capacity has been increased, and thereby water consumption reduced. New technologies, such as subsurface irrigation, have further contributed to cutting down on water consumption. SEKEM's main farm site serves as a habitat for more than 60 species of birds – both migrating and local – more than 90 varieties of trees and shrubs, and a broad range of small animals such as hedgehogs, lizards, snakes and foxes. Furthermore, over the years, over one million tons of CO2-equivalents have been sequestered in the

soil, which shows the great potential of agriculture to mitigate climate change. The positive effects of the introduction of organic agriculture into the region are manifold and invaluable for the environment. For example, SEKEM has succeeded not only in refraining from pesticide use in its own operations, but, more broadly, cutting chemical use by more than 90 per cent on Egyptian cotton farms. To replace chemicals, SEKEM uses pheromone traps and cultivates microorganisms that serve as natural forms of pest control. As a result, the average yield of raw cotton has increased by almost 30 per cent, while the cotton's elasticity and overall quality is superior to that of conventionally grown cotton. While SEKEM is not growing cotton on its farms any more, it still benefits from its former engagement through the increased cotton quality from its suppliers.

In terms of economics, the SEKEM Group has achieved an annual growth rate of about 15 per cent over the past few years. Its holistic approach and its social and cultural activities have strengthened social cohesion within SEKEM, which was evident in the aftermath of the Egyptian uprising when some SEKEM employees even volunteered to protect the SEKEM premises at night.

D. Lessons to be learned

SEKEM sees itself as part of a cultural society in which its economic activities – meaning business revenues – play an important part, but not the major role. Rather, the financial aspect is considered to be only one of many other aspects such as promoting education and the arts, cultivating land and providing health care. Over 30 years of experience have proved that human development is crucial for sustainable farming. People have to be at the centre of such efforts: the more an institution cares for the people (e.g. through better employment conditions, equal treatment, education, medical care, insurance and pension schemes), the more the people will care for the organization and everything vital for its business.

However, organic farming is not enough; organic farms do not necessarily employ, for example, sustainable energy management systems. Some organic farmers might even cultivate their land with monocultures, thereby neglecting biodiversity and the benefits of agricultural methods such as agroforestry. Well aware of this, SEKEM applies biodynamic agriculture approaches, or agroecological farming, which goes beyond the usual organic standards. This should be a guiding principle for management in order to effectively embed these ecological and ethical principles within the corporate culture. SEKEM is currently seeking to develop and standardize generic guidelines for the Sustainability Flower, as well as to integrate the guidelines and performance indicators into an assessment software. Through this new platform, agricultural producers, traders, brand owners and other stakeholders will be able to assess, continuously improve and jointly communicate their sustainability performance. The Sustainability Flower guidelines are based on the sustainability reporting standards of the Global Reporting Initiative (GRI), but are adjusted to the needs of the agricultural sector.

References

Action Aid (2008). Impact of import surges on developing countries. Johannesburg, Action Aid International.

Altieri A and von der Weid J (2000). Prospects for agroecologically based natural-resource management for low-income farmers in the 21st century. Available at: http://agroeco.org/fatalharvest/articles/agroeco_resource_mgmt.html.

Altieri MA, Funes-Monzote, FR and Petersen, P (2011). Agroecologically efficient agricultural systems for small holder farmers: contributions to food sovereignty. In: Agronomy for Sustainable Development, Institut National de la Recherche Agronomique (INRA). Available at: www.agroeco.org/socla/pdfs/Altieri-Funes-Petersen-Palencia.pdf.

Azeez G (2009). Soil carbon and organic farming. Soil Association, London.

Badgley C, Moghtader J, Quintero E, Zakem E, Chappell MJ, Avilés-Vázquez K, Samulon A and Perfecto I (2007). Organic agriculture and the global food supply. *Renewable Agriculture and Food Systems*, 22, 86–108.

Barker D (2007). The rise and predictable fall of globalized industrial agriculture. San Francisco, International Forum on Globalization.

Berthelot J (2011). The lessons to draw for the CAP from the huge predominance of contra-cyclical aids in the U.S. Solidarité. Available at: http://solidarite.asso.fr/Papers-2011.

Bloomberg (2011). Food Prices may extend gains on volatile oil costs, FAO says. Available at: www.bloomberg.com/apps/news?pid=20601012%20&sid=adOeoL6mibks, 12 May.

Bommarco R, Kleijn D and Potts S (2012) Ecological intensification: harnessing ecosystem services for food security. Trends in Ecology and Evolution. Available at: www.cell.com/trends/ecology-evolution/abstract/S0169-5347%2812%2900273-X.

Branca G, Lipper L, McCarthy N and Jolejole MC (2013). Food security, climate change, and sustainable land management: A review. Agronomy for Sustainable Development, February. Available at: http://link.springer.com/content/pdf/10.1007%2Fs13593-013-0133-1.

Brodeur J, Colas B, Del Cont C, Doumbia S, Jacquot M, Parent G, Régimbald G, Roux D, Victor M and Wilson D (2010). Legal analysis: Improving the coherence of international standards: Recognizing agriculture and food specifity to respect human rights. Thomson Reuters Canada.

Brown L (2011). The new geopolitics of food. Foreign Policy, 8 June. Available at: www.foreignpolicy.com/articles/2011/04/25/the_new_geopolitics_of_food?page=0,0.

Brüntrup M, Brandi C, Fuchs N (2011). Agriculture is Special: Conclusions Drawn from the Death Throes of the Doha Round for a Development-friendly Agricultural Trade Policy. DIE Briefing Paper 14/2011, Bonn.

Carletto C, Savastano S and Zezza A (2011). Fact or Artefact? The Impact of Measurement Errors on the Farms Size-Productivity Relationship. Policy Research Working Paper 5908, The World Bank, Washington D.C. Available at: http://elibrary.worldbank.org/docserver/download/5908.pdf?expires=1357561151&id=id&accname=guest&checksum=7A36497FDCD9D8BCA94B2C2616C7492F.

CBD (2003). Domestic support measures and their effects on agricultural biological diversity. Note by the Executive Secretary, COP 7, 9–20 February 2004.

Chen Rui (2009). Analysis on "new fundaments" and range of oil price trend. London, World Energy Council.

Cowan T (2010). Conservation Reserve Program: Status and current issues. Washington, DC, Congressional Research Service. Available at: http://www.cnie.org/nle/crsreports/10Oct/RS21613.pdf, 14 September.

D'Souza G and Ikerd J (1996). Small farms and sustainable development: Is small more sustainable? *Journal of Agricultural and Applied Economics*, 28: 73–83.

De Schutter O (2009a). Report of the Special Rapporteur on the right to food: Addendum, Mission to the World Trade Organization (25 June 2008). A/HRC/10/5/Add.2. Human Rights Council, Geneva.

De Schutter O (2009b). Report of the Special Rapporteur on the right to food: Agribusiness and the right to food. A/HRC/13/33. Human Rights Council, Geneva.

De Schutter O (2010). Report submitted by the Special Rapporteur on the right to food. A/HRD/16/49. Human Rights Council, Geneva.

De Schutter O (2011a). Agroecology and the Right to Food. Report by the Special Rapporteur on the right to food to the United Nations.

De Schutter O (2011b). The Common Agricultural Policy towards 2020: The role of the European Union in supporting the realization of the right to food. Comments and recommendations by the United Nations Special Rapporteur on the right to food (17 June 2011).

De Schutter O (2011c). The World Trade Organization and the Post-Global Food Crisis Agenda: Putting food security first in the international trade system. Briefing Note 04 by the UN Special Rapporteur on the Right to Food. Geneva. November. Available at: www.ohchr.org/Documents/Issues/Food/20111116_briefing_note_05_en.PDF.

Easterling WE, Aggarwal PK, Batima P, Brander KM, Erda L, Howden SM, Kirilenko A, Morton J, Soussana J-F, Schmidhuber J and Tubiello FN (2007). Food, fibre and forest products. In: Parry ML, Canziani OF, Palutikof JP, van der Linden PJ and Hanson CE, eds. *Climate Change 2007: Impacts, Adaptation and Vulnerability.* Contribution of Working Group II to the Fourth Assessment Report of the Intergovernmental Panel on Climate Change. Cambridge, Cambridge University Press: 273–313.

ETC Group (2009). Who will feed us? Questions for the food and climate crises. Communique No. 102, November.

ETC Group (2011a). Capturing climate genes. April 2011.

ETC Group (2011b). Who will control the green economy? Communique, October.

EurActiv (2011). EU lawmakers back CAP budget status quo. Available at: www.euractiv.com/en/cap/eu-lawmakers-back-cap-budget-status-quo-news-505153, 30 May.

European Commission (2013): The economic benefits of the Natura 2000 Networks. Available at: http://ec.europa.eu/environment/nature/natura2000/financing/docs/ENV-12-018_LR_Final1.pdf.

European Environment Agency (2013): Road user charges for heavy goods vehicles. Available at: www.eea.europa.eu/publications/road-user-charges-for-vehicles.

Fan S and Headey D (2010). Reflections on the global food crisis. How did it happen? How has it hurt? And how can we prevent the next one? IFPRI Research Monograph 165, IFPRI, Washington, DC.

FAO (2003). Some trade policy issues relating to trends in agriculture imports in the context of food security. Committee on Commodity Problems, CCP 03/10, Rome.

FAO (2004). Biological diversity is fundamental to agriculture and food production. Rome. Available at: www.fao.org/docrep/006/y5418e00.htm.

FAO (2005). Towards appropriate agricultural trade policy for low-income developing countries. FAO Trade Policy Technical Notes No. 14. Rome.

FAO (2006). Import surges: What is their frequency and which are the countries and commodities most affected? FAO Briefs on Import Surges – Issues No. 2, Rome.

FAO (2008). Hunger on the rise. Briefing paper, 17 September. Rome.

FAO (2009). The State of Agricultural Commodity Markets in 2009: High food prices and the food crisis – experiences and lessons learned. Rome. Available at: www.fao.org/docrep/012/i0854e/i0854e00.htm.

FAO (2010). *"Climate Smart" Agriculture – Policies, Practices and Financing for Food Security, Adaptation and Mitigation.* Rome.

FAO (2011). The State of Food Insecurity in the World 2011. Rome. Available at: http://www.fao.org/hunger/en/.

FAO (2012). Smallholders and Family Farmers. Factsheet of FAO for the Rio+20 Conference. Rome. Available at: www.fao.org/fileadmin/templates/nr/sustainability_pathways/docs/Factsheet_SMALLHOLDERS.pdf.

Farming First (2010). Partnership to train female dairy farmers in Pakistan. Available at: http://www.farmingfirst.org/2010/06/partnership-to-train-female-dairy-farmers-in-pakistan/, 28 June.

Garber K. (2008). Fuel costs cut deeply into food aid. US News and World Reports, 7 July. Available at: www.usnews.com/news/articles/2008/07/07/fuel-costs-cut-deeply-into-food-aid.

Gattinger A, Müller A, Haenia M, Skinnera C, Fliessbach A, Buchmann N, Mäder P, Stolze M, Smith P, El-Hage Scialabba N and Niggli U (2012). Enhanced top soil carbon stocks under organic farming. Proceedings of the National Academy of Science of the United States of America, Vol. 109, No. 44: 18226–18231. Available at: www.pnas.org/content/early/2012/10/10/1209429109.full.pdf+html.

Ghosh, J (2010). Commodity speculation and the food crisis. New Delhi. Paper prepared for the World Development Movement, October. Available at: www.wdm.org.uk/food-speculation/commodity-speculation-and-food-crisis-prof-jayati-ghosh.

Gilbert J (2011). No we can't: Uncertainty, technology and risk. Lecture at the ASPO-USA Conference, Washington, DC, 9 October 2010 (cited in Richard Heinberg R, 2011, *The End of Growth*. Gabriola Island, BC, New Society Publishers).

Greenpeace International (2009). Agriculture at a crossroads: Food for survival. Amsterdam.

Guereña A (2010). Having Hunger: Still Possible? Oxfam Briefing paper 139, Oxfam International, September.

Halberg N (2007). *Global Development of Organic Agriculture: Challenges and Prospects.* London, CABI Publishing.

Häberli C (2010). Food Security and WTO Rules. In: Karapinar, B., Häberli, C. (Ed): Food Crises and the WTO. Cambridge University Press.

Heinemann JA (2009). Hope not hype: The future of agriculture guided by the IAASTD. Penang, Third World Network.

Hendrickson M and Heffernan W (2007). Concentration in agricultural markets. Factsheet. Saint Louis, Missouri, Department of Rural Sociology, University of Missouri, April.

Heinrich Böll Foundation, MISEREOR (2009). Slow Trade, Sound Farming. Ecofair Trade Dialogue.

Herren HR et al. (2011). Agriculture: Investing in natural capital. In: UNEP, *Towards a Green Economy: Pathways to Sustainable Development and Poverty Eradication*. Geneva: 31–77.

Hine R (2008). Organic Agriculture and Food Security in Africa. UNEP-UNCTAD Capacity Building Task Force on Trade, Environment and Development. Geneva, UNCTAD.

HLPE (2011). Price volatility and food security. A report by the High Level Panel of Experts on Food Security and Nutrition of the Committee on World Food Security, Rome.

Ho, Mae-Wan et al. (2008). Food futures now. London and Penang, Institute of Science and Society and Third World Network.

Höffler H and Ochieng B (2009). High commodity prices – Who gets the money? A case study on the impact of high food and factor prices on Kenyan farmers. Berlin, Heinrich Boell Foundation.

Hoffmann U (2011). Assuring food security in developing countries under the challenges of climate change: Key trade and development issues of a fundamental transformation of agriculture. UNCTAD Discussion Paper No. 201, UNCTAD, Geneva. Available at: http://unctad.org/en/Docs/osgdp20111_en.pdf.

Hole D, Perkins A, Wilson J, Alexander I, Grice P, and Evans A (2005). *Does organic farming benefit biodiversity?* Biological Conservation, 122: 113–130.

Hoppe RA, MacDonald JM and Korb P (2010). Small farms in the United States: Persistence under pressure. Washington, DC, USDA Economic Research Service, February.

Howse R and Teitel ZG (2007). Beyond the Divide – The Covenant on Economic, Social and Cultural Rights and the World Trade Organization. Friedrich Ebert Foundatin, Geneva.

Huismann W (2012). Schwarzbuch WWF: Dunkle Geschäfte im Zeichen des Panda (Shaming the WWF: dubious deals in the name of the panda). Gütersloher Verlagshaus, Random House Publishing Group, Munich.

Human Rights Council (2010). Agroecology and the right to food. Report submitted by the Special Rapporteur on the right to food, Olivier de Schutter, at the 16th session of the United Nations Human Rights Council, March 2011. (A/HRC/16/49). Available at: www.srfood.org.

Humphrey J (2005). Shaping value chains for development, global value chains in agribusiness. Eschborn, GTZ.

IAASTD (2008). International Assessment of Agricultural Knowledge, Science and Technology for Development. Global Report. Johannesburg, Available at www.agassessment.org.

IAASTD (2009). *Agriculture at a Crossroads.* Washington, DC, Island Press.

IATP (Institute for Agriculture and Trade Policy) (2005). WTO Agreement on Agriculture: A decade of dumping, United States dumping on agricultural markets. Available at: http://www.iatp.org/files/451_2_48532.pdf.

IATP (2008). Commodities market speculation. Available at: http://www.iatp.org/files/451_2_104414.pdf, November.

IEA (2010a). Executive summary. In: *World Energy Outlook 2010*. Paris, OECD/IEA.

IEA (2010b). Key graphs: World oil production by type in the new policies scenario. In: World Energy Outlook 2010. Available at: www.worldenergyoutlook.org/docs/weo2010/key_graphs.pdf.

IFAD (2010). *Rural Poverty Report 2011 – New realities, New Challenges: New Opportunities for Tomorrow's Generation.* Rome.

IFOAM (2008a). Definition of organic agriculture. Ratified by the IFOAM General Assembly in June 2008. Available at: www.ifoam.org/growing_organic/definitions/doa/index.html.

IFOAM (2008b). Definition of Participatory Guarantee Systems. Established by PGS Task Force in June 2008. Available at: www.ifoam.org/about_ifoam/standards/pgs.html.

IMAP (2010). *Food & Beverage Industry Global Report 2010*. Available at: www.imap.com/imap/media/resources/IMAP_Food__Beverage_Report_WEB_AD6498A02CAF4.pdf.

IMF (2010). IMF Sees Oil Prices Staying High. Washington, DC. Available at: http://www.imf.org/external/pubs/ft/survey/so/2011/RES040711A.htm, April 7.

IMF (2011). Impact of High Food and Fuel Prices on Developing Countries —Frequently Asked Questions. Available at: http://www.imf.org/external/np/exr/faq/ffpfaqs.htm.

INRA (2012). L'INSTITUT NATIONAL DE LA RECHERCHE AGRONOMIQUE, Sustainable Food Systems: Challenges, State of the Art and Questions for Research. Presentation at the European Commission hearing/workshop on sustainable food, entitled Feeding the planet sustainably: from foresight to better integrated policies, Brussels, 19-20 November. Available at: http://ec.europa.eu/agriculture/events/2012/food-sustainabilty/esnouf_en.pdf.

Inter-Academy Council (2004). Realizing the promise of African agriculture. Amsterdam. Available at: www.interacademycouncil.net/CMS/Reports/AfricanAgriculture.aspx.

Interagency Report to the Mexican G20 Presidency (2012). Sustainable agricultural productivity growth and bridging the gap for small-family farms. Report prepared for the G20 by Biodiversity International, CGIAR, FAO, IFAD, IFPRI, IICA, OECD, UNCTAD, UN-HLTF on Global Food Security, WFP, World Bank and WTO. Available at: www.fao.org/fileadmin/templates/esa/Papers_and_documents/G20_agricultural_productivity_draft_report_Publication.pdf.

IPCC (2007a). *Climate Change 2007: The Physical Science Basis* (Solomon S, Qin D, Manning M, Marquis M, Averyt KB, Tignor M and Miller HL, eds.). Contribution of Working Group I to the Fourth Assessment Report of the Intergovernmental Panel on Climate Change, 2007. Cambridge and New York, Cambridge University Press.

IPCC (2007b). Summary for policymakers. In: Parry ML, Canziani OF, Palutikof JP, van der Linden PJ and Hanson CE, eds. *Climate Change 2007: Impacts, Adaptation and Vulnerability*. Contribution of Working Group II to the Fourth Assessment Report of the Intergovernmental Panel on Climate Change. Cambridge, Cambridge University Press: 7–22.

IPCC (2007c). Intergovernmental Panel on Climate Change, Climate Change 2007: Mitigation of Climate Change. Working Group III Report of the Fourth Assessment Report of IPCC. Available at: www.ipcc.ch/publications_and_data/ar4/wg3/en/contents.html.

Ismail F A K (2009). Reforming the World Trade Organization. World Economics, Vol. 10, No. 4. Available at: www.gtdforum.org/download/World%20Economics%20Faizel%20Ismail%20reforming%20the%20WTO.pdf.

Ismail F A K (2012). Towards an alternative narrative for the multilateral trading system. South Views, No. 40. Geneva. Available at: www.southcentre.org/index.php?option=com_content&view=article&id=1873%3Atowards-an-alternative-narrative-for-the-multilateral-trading-system-7-november-2012&catid=150%3Asouthviews&Itemid=358&lang=es.

ITC and FiBL (Research Institute of Organic Agriculture) (2007). Organic farming and climate change. Geneva, ITC.

Jha B (2007). India's dairy sector in the emerging trade order. Delhi, Institute of Economic Growth, Delhi University.

Johnston I (2011). Sustainability under Scrutiny: Real values and their role in promoting the new economics of growth. The Club of Rome, Discussion Paper No. 1/11. Available at: www.clubofrome.org/cms/wp-content/uploads/2011/11/CoR-Discussion-Paper-Series-01-2011-Ian-Johnson.pdf.

Jordan R (2009). *Organic Agriculture – A Guide to Climate Change and Food Security*. Bonn, IFOAM.

Karapinar B, Häberli C (2010). Conclusion and policy recommendations. In: Karapinar, B., Häberli, C. (Ed): Food Crises and the WTO. Cambridge University Press.

Khor M (2008). The impact of trade liberalization on agriculture in developing countries: The experience of Ghana. Penang, Third World Network.

Khor M (2009). The food crisis, climate change and the importance of sustainable agriculture. *Environment & Development Series 8*. Penang, Third World Network. Paper presented at the High-Level Conference on World Food Security: The Challenges of Climate Change and Bioenergy, Rome, 3–5 June 2008.

Khor M (2011). Challenges of the green economy concept and policies in the context of sustainable development, poverty and equity. In: United Nations, Division for Sustainable Development, UN-DESA, UNEP and UNCTAD, *The Transition to a Green Economy: Benefits, Challenges and Risks from a Sustainable Development Perspective.* Report by a Panel of Experts to the Second Preparatory Committee Meeting for the United Nations Conference on Sustainable Development. New York and Geneva.

Kotschi J (forthcoming). Mineral fertilizers and the perspective of tropical smallholdings. Paper for the Heinrich Boell Foundation and WWF-Germany, Berlin.

Kotschi J and Müller-Sämann K (2004). The role of organic agriculture in mitigating climate change: A scoping study. Bonn, International Federation of Organic Agriculture Movements.

Lagi M, Bar-Yam Y and Bertrand KZ (2011). The food crises: A quantitative model of food prices including speculators and ethanol conversion. Cambridge, MA, New England Complex Systems Institute. Available at: http://arxiv.org/PS_cache/arxiv/pdf/1109/1109.4859v1.pdf.

Limes T (2012). Primary commodity prices and global food security: Why farmers still struggle when food prices rise. Green House. Dorset, United Kingdom. Available at: www.greenhousethinktank.org/files/greenhouse/home/Food_smaller.pdf.

Lotter DW (2003). The performance of organic and conventional cropping systems in an extreme climate year. *American Journal of Alternative Agriculture*,18(2). Available at: http://donlotter.net/lotter_ajaa_article.pdf.

Lunenborg P (2013). Small-scale farming and rural livelihoods. Presentation at the UNCTAD seminar on the importance of small-scale and family farming for food security. Geneva, 26 February.

Mayet M (2007). The new green revolution in Africa: Trojan horse for GMOs? In: Norstad A, ed. *Africa Can Feed Itself.* Oslo, The Development Fund.

Minot N (2007). Contract farming in developing countries: Patterns, impact, and policy implications. Ithaca, NY, Cornell University.

Murphy S (2009). Free trade in agriculture: A bad idea whose time is done. *Monthly Review*, July/August 2009. Available at: http://monthlyreview.org/2009/07/01/free-trade-in-agriculture-a-bad-idea-whose-time-is-done.

Nassar A, Rondriguez-Alcala M L, Costa C and Nogueira S (2009). Agricultural subsidies in the WTO green box: Opportunities and challenges for developing countries. In: Meléndez-Ortiz R, Bellmann C and Hepburn J (eds.), Agricultural Subsidies in the WTO Green Box: Ensuring Coherence with Sustainable Development Goals, pp. 320-368. Cambridge University Press. Cambridge.

Netherlands Environmental Research Agency and Stockholm Resilience Center (2009). Getting into the Right Lane for 2050. A Primer for EU Debate. Netherlands Environmental Assessment Agency, Bilthoven/Den Haag and Stockholm.

Niggli U, Fließbach A, Hepperly P and Scialabba N (2009). Low greenhouse gas agriculture: Mitigation and adaptation potential of sustainable farming systems, Rev. 2. Rome, FAO, April.

OECD (2009). Agricultural policies in OECD counties: Monitoring and evaluation. Paris.

OECD (2010). Agricultural policies in OECD countries: At a glance. Paris.

PANNA (Pesticide Action Network North America) (2010). Scientists support farmers regaining control of agriculture. Findings from the UN-led International Assessment of Agricultural Knowledge, Science and Technology for Development. San Francisco.

Pingali P, Khwaja Y and Meijer M (2005). Commercializing small farms: Reducing transaction costs. In: IFPRI and ODI: *The Future of Small Farms.* Proceedings of a Research Workshop in Wye, 26–29 June 2005.

Pretty J and Hine R (2001). Reducing Food Poverty with Sustainable Agriculture: A Summary of New Evidence. SAFE-World, The Potential of Sustainable Agriculture to Feed the World, Research Project. University of Essex. Available at: www.essex.ac.uk/ces/occasionalpapers/SAFE%20FINAL%20-%20Pages1-22.pdf.

Pretty JN (1995). Regenerating Agriculture: Policies and Practice for Sustainability and Self-Reliance. London, Joseph Henry Press.

Pretty JN, Noble AD, Bossio D, Dixon J, Hine RE, Penning de Vries FWT and Morson JIL (2006). Resource-conserving agriculture increases yields in developing countries. *Environmental Science and Technology*, 40(4): 1114–1119.

Raman M (2004). Effects of agricultural liberalisation: Experiences of rural producers in developing countries. TWN Trade and Development Series 23. Penang, Third World Network.

Rosset PM (1999). The multiple functions and benefits of small farm agriculture. Paper presented at the FAO/ Netherlands conference on Cultivating Our Futures, Maastricht, 12–17 September.

Rundgren G (2012). Garden Earth: From hunter and gatherer to global capitalism and thereafter. Regeneration, Uppsala, Sweden. Available at: http://gardenearth.blogspot.ch.

Sachs W and Santarius T (2007). Slow Trade – *Sound Farming: A Multilateral Framework for Sustainable Markets in Agriculture*. Berlin/Aachen, Heinrich-Böll-Stiftung/ Misereor.

Saunders P (2004). Industrial agriculture and global warming. European Parliament Briefing, 20 October. Available at: http://www.indsp.org/IAGW.php.

SCAR – European Commission, Standing Committee on Agricultural Research (2011). Sustainable food consumption and production in a resource-constrained world. The 3rd SCAR Foreseight Exercise. Available at: http://ec.europa.eu/research/agriculture/scar/pdf/scar_feg3_final_report_01_02_2011.pdf.

Schmitz C, Biewalda A, Lotze-Campena H, Poppa A, Dietricha J P, Bodirskya B, Krause M and Weindl I, (2012). Trading more food: Implications for land use, greenhouse gas emissions, and the food system. Global Environmental Change, Vol. 22, Issue 1, Pages 189–209. Available at: www.sciencedirect.com/science/article/pii/S0959378011001488.

Schweizer Bauer (2013). Issue of 7 January. Available at http://schweizerbauer.ch/artikel_8670.

Scialabba N El-Hage (2007). Organic agriculture and food security. Rome, FAO, 5 May.

Scialabba NE and Müller-Lindenlauf M (2010). Organic agriculture and climate change. *Renewable Agriculture and Food Systems*, 25(2): 158–169.

SEKEM (2010). Report on Sustainable Development 2010. Available at: www.sekem.com/sites/default/files/files/SEKEM%20%20Report%20on%20Sustainable%20Development%202010_en.pdf.

Seufert V, Ramankutty N and Foley J.A. (2012). Comparing the yields of organic and conventional agriculture. Nature. Available at: www.nature.com/nature/journal/v485/n7397/abs/nature11069.html.

Shiva V (2007). Not so green revolution: Lessons from India. In: Norstad A, ed. *Africa Can Feed Itself*. Oslo, The Development Fund.

Snapp S S, Blackieb M J, Gilbertc R A, Bezner-Kerrd R and Kanyama-Phirie G Y(2010). Biodiversity can support a greener revolution in Africa. Proceedings of the National Academy of Sciences of the United States of America (PNAS) 107/48, 20840-20845. Available at: www.pnas.org/content/107/48/20840.full.

South Centre (2011). Papers prepared for the FAO initiative, Greening the Economy with Agriculture (draft). Geneva.

Steffen W, Sanderson A, Tyson PD, Jäger J, Matson PA, Moore B III, Oldfield F, Rich¬ardson K, Schellnhuber HJ, Turner BL and Wasson RJ (2004). *Global Change and the Earth System: A Planet under Pressure*. Berlin, Heidelberg and New York, Springer-Verlag.

Suppan S (2009). A better future for food and energy: Reforming commodity futures markets. London, IATP. Available at: http://www.iatp.org/files/451_2_106284.pdf, June.

Sutton MA, Howard CM, Erisman JW, Billen G, Bleeker A, Grennfelt P, van Grinsren H and Grizetti B (2011). The European Nitrogen Assessment. Cambridge University Press, Cambridge, UK. Available at: www.nine-esf.org/ENA-Book.

Swanson T (2007). *The Economics of Environmental Degradation—Tragedy for the Commons?* Cheltenham, Edward Elgar and UNEP.

The Royal Society (2009). Reaping the Benefits: Science and the sustainable intensification of global agriculture. London. Available at: http://royalsociety.org/uploadedFiles/Royal_Society_Content/policy/publications/2009/4294967719.pdf.

Thompson CB (2007). Africa: Green revolution or rainbow evolution? Foreign Policy in Focus, July. Available at: http://www.fpif.org/fpiftxt/4398.

Tscharnke T, Clough Y, Wanger T C, Jackson L, Motzke I, Perfecto I, Vandermeer J and Whitbread A (2012). Global Food Security, Biodiversity Conservation and the Future of Agricultural Intensification. Biological Conservation 151 (2012) 53 – 59. Available at: http://xa.yimg.com/kq/groups/399598/933395563/name/2012_Tscharntke_Global+food+security,+biodiversity+conservation+and+the+future_BiolCons.pdf.

Twarog S (2006). Organic agriculture: A trade and sustainable development opportunity for developing countries. In: UNCTAD, Trade and Environment Review 2006. New York and Geneva, United Nations.

UK Food Group (2010). Securing future food: Towards ecological food provision. UK Food Group briefing, London.

UNCTAD (2004). *Trading Opportunities for Organic Food Products from Developing Countries: Strengthening Research and Policy-Making Capacity on Trade and Environment in Developing Countries*. New York and Geneva.

UNCTAD (2006). *Trade and Environment Review 2006*. New York and Geneva, United Nations. Available at: www.unctad.org/en/docs/ditcted200512_en.pdf.

UNCTAD (2010). *Trade and Environment Review 2009/2010: Promoting Poles of Clean Growth to Foster the Transition to a More Sustainable Economy.* (UNCTAD/DITC/TED/2009/2). New York and Geneva, United Nations.

UNCTAD (2011). *Price Formation in Financialized Commodity Markets.* Geneva. Available at: http://www.unctad.org/en/docs//gds20111_en.pdf, June.

UNCTAD/UNEP (2008a). Best practices for organic policy: What developing-country governments can do to promote the organic agriculture sector. UNEP-UNCTAD Capacity Building Task Force on Trade, Environment and Development, New York and Geneva. Available at: www.unctad.org/trade_env.

UNCTAD/UNEP (2008b). Organic Agriculture and Food Security in Africa. Report of the UNEP-UNCTAD Capacity Building Task Force on Trade, Environment and Development (CBTF). Geneva. Available at: http://archive.unctad.org/trade_env/documentsPUBLI.asp.

UNEP (2011). *Towards a Green Economy: Pathways to Sustainable Development and Poverty Eradication*. Available at: www.unep.org/greeneconomy.

UNRISD (1974).The social and economic implications of large-scale introduction of new varieties of food grain: Summary of conclusion of a global research project, Report No. 74.1 Geneva.

USDA (2010). Farm income and costs, 2010: Farm sector income forecast, 30 November. Economic Research Service Online Briefing Room. Available at: http://www.ers.usda.gov/Briefing/FarmIncome/nationalestimates.htm.

USDA (2011). USDA funds projects to reduce greenhouse gas emissions in 24 states. Available at: http://www.nrcs.usda.gov/news/releases/2011/cig_ghg_6.8.11.html, 8 June.

Utviklingsfondet (2010). *A Viable Food Future* (Parts I and II). Oslo, The Development Fund/Utviklingsfondet.

WFP (World Food Programme) and FAO (2009). *The State of Food Insecurity in the World*. Rome.

Willer H and Kilcher L, eds. (2011). *The World of Organic Agriculture: Statistics and Emerging Trends 2011*. Bonn, IFOAM, and Frick, FiBL.

Wise T (2010). Agriculture dumping under NAFTA. Boston, MA, Global Development and Environment Institute,Tufts University. Available at: http://www.ase.tufts.edu/gdae/policy_research/AgNAFTA.html.

Wise T (2011). Boom for whom? Boston, MA, Global Development and Environment Institute, Tufts University. Available at: http://www.ase.tufts.edu/gdae/policy_research/FarmIncome.html, March.

World Bank (2008). *World Development Report 2008: Agriculture for Development.* Washington, DC. Available at: http://web.worldbank.org/WBSITE/EXTERNAL/EXTDEC/EXTRESEARCH/EXTWDRS/0,,contentMDK:23062293~pagePK:478093~piPK:477627~theSitePK:477624,00.html.

World Bank (2012). 4° Turn Down the Heat: Why a 4° warmer world must be avoided. A Report for the World Bank by the Potsdam Institute for Climate Impact Research and Climate Analytics. Washington. November. Available at: http://climatechange.worldbank.org/sites/default/files/Turn_Down_the_heat_Why_a_4_degree_centrigrade_warmer_world_must_be_avoided.pdf.

WTO (2010). *World Tariff Profiles 2010.* Geneva.

Notes

1   Many developing countries have adopted a defensive stance in relation to the liberalization of trade in agriculture. However, the developing countries with more efficient agricultural sectors, which would benefit from higher earnings from their exports if there were fewer restrictions on their market access, especially to developed countries, have now been at the forefront of attempts to liberalize global agricultural trade through the Doha negotiations. There is tension between these countries and the majority of developed countries that have tried to retain their sizeable agricultural support and relatively high tariffs, as well as between them and those developing countries that are seeking to defend their small farmers' livelihoods from import surges. The agriculturally efficient countries have been advocating restrictions on the use of the SSM for developing countries to avoid import surges, on the grounds that their own farmers would be affected by import restrictions (South Centre, 2011).

2   The authors would like to thank the following peer reviewers for their comments on earlier versions of this commentary: Klemens van de Sand, Olivier de Schutter, Gunnar Rundgren, Hans Herren, Mark Halle, Nadia El-Hage Scialabba, Peter Lunenborg, Stephan Albrecht, Sophia Murphy, Lim Li Ching, Franz-Theo Gottwald and Thomas Braunschweig.

3   For more information, see: http://awsassets.panda.org/downloads/lpr_2012_summary_booklet_final.pdf.

4   The World Bank has just published a first study (prepared by the Potsdam Institute for Climate Impact Research and Climate Analytics) examining the specific implications of a global warming of 4 degrees by the end of this century (World Bank, 2012).

5   For more information, see the Club of Rome discussion paper by Johnston (2011).

6   See: http://www.fao.org/news/story/en/item/161819/, using a new estimation methodology. In previous years, based on the previous methodology of estimation, close to one billion hungry were reported. The new report emphasizes that concentration on export crops does often not work in respect to food security.

7   For more information, see Interagency Report to the Mexican G20 Presidency (2012).

8   For a more elaborate critique, see Hoffmann (2011).

9   Brüntrup et al. (2011).

10 Today the average yields of *organic* systems are estimated to be about 75 per cent of those of conventional systems (Seufert et al. 2012). Agro-ecological systems are more open to inputs and can therefore be more productive, see Snapp 2011, footnote 22.

11 See for example Bayer producing biological remedies http://www.presse.bayer.de/baynews/baynews.nsf/id/Bayer-Crop_science-acquires_Germany-based-biocontrol-company-Prophyta_GmbH?open.

12 The preservation of the "regenerative capacity of agriculture" was at the very root of the concept of "sustainability", which was first coined as a principle in German forestry by Carl von Carlowitz more than 300 years ago.

13 A recent EU survey estimates the health costs of road transport alone to be 100 billion Euro annually in Europe (European Environment Agency, 2013). The transport of agricultural goods and foodstuffs accounts for about 20 per cent of total transport (INRA, 2012).

14 In autumn 2012, the Ukraine, for instance, announced new export restrictions for wheat.

15 In Egypt, for example, where most food is imported, due to currency exchange rates food has recently become more and more costly (Schweizer Bauer, 2013).

16 Of the developing world's 5.5 billion people, some 3 billion live in rural areas - more than 40 per cent of humanity. Of these rural inhabitants, an estimated 2.5 billion are in households involved in agriculture, and 1.5 billion are in smallholder households. Agriculture provides the livelihood for approximately 2.6 billion people (World Bank, 2008 and UNEP, 2011).

17 The attempt of the European Commission to skip value-added tax reduction for unsustainable production is at least a promising step in the right direction (see Agrar-Info 183, July/August 2012, Hamburg, Germany).

18 Since the 1960s, global per capita cereal production increased by roughly a third. Conversely, global use of nitrogen and phosphorus fertilizers soared by 8 and 2.5 times; global pesticides use expanded by 8 times and water consumption for irrigation doubled (IAASTD, 2009: 7).

19 As aptly put by Rundgren (2012), "how we define 'efficiency, productivity and related technology' will determine the objectivity of our discourse on what we understand by 'modern agriculture'. Paradoxically, we currently consider

production methods as 'modern' that are among the most pollutant, most resource-squandering, most energy-intensive and most dependent on subsidies".

20 The 3rd EU SCAR Foresight Exercise talks about a "radical change in food production and consumption", which is necessary (SCAR, 2011:129).

21 See also Netherlands Environmental Research Agency and Stockholm Resilience Center (2009).

22 European Commission (2013).
Natura 2000 is the centrepiece of EU nature and biodiversity policy. It is an EU-wide network of nature protection areas established under the 1992 Habitats Directive. The aim of the network is to assure the long-term survival of Europe's most valuable and threatened species and habitats. It is comprised of Special Areas of Conservation designated by Member States under the Habitats Directive, and also incorporates Special Protection Areas, which they designate under the 1979 Birds Directive. Natura 2000 is not a system of strict nature reserves, where all human activities are excluded. Whereas the network will certainly include nature reserves most of the land is likely to continue to be privately owned and the emphasis is on ensuring that future management is sustainable, both ecologically and economically. The establishment of this network of protected areas also fulfils a Community obligation under the UN Convention on Biological Diversity. Natura 2000 protects around 18 per cent of land in the EU countries. For more information, see http://ec.europa.eu/environment/nature/natura2000/.

23 This ten-year partly participative study in Malawi (a country that temporarily used a 90 per cent subsidy for fertilizers and better seeds to boost maize yields) compared monoculture maize with legume-diversified maize that included annual and semiperennial (SP) growth habits in temporal and spatial combinations, including rotation, SP rotation, intercrop, and SP intercrop systems. Modest fertilizer intensification doubled grain yield compared with monoculture maize. Biodiversity improved ecosystem function further: SP rotation systems at half-fertilizer rates produced equivalent quantities of grain, on a more stable basis (yield variability reduced from 22% to 13%) compared with monoculture. Across sites, profitability and farmer preference matched: SP rotations provided twofold superior returns, whereas diversification of maize with annual legumes provided more modest returns. The study thus provides evidence that, in Africa, crop diversification can be effective at a countrywide scale, and that shrubby, grain legumes can enhance environmental and food security.

24 A recent European Nitrogen Assessment, prepared in the context of the 6th EU Research Framework Programme, found that the costs of nitrogen use in agriculture in EU countries might be significantly higher than its benefits (Sutton et al., 2011).

25 The objective of the SSM is to address situations of a serious decline in national prices because of surges of cheap imports. Therefore, the SSM does not target upward swings in prices, which is the current challenge for most countries.

26 For example: "The governance and regulation of trade, the resilience of food exchange patterns, will therefore be at the heart of future food systems and food security, even in a scenario where maximum regional food self sufficiency is sought. Innovation in regulation systems of global agricultural trade is therefore crucial, but at the same time is at the heart of very important controversies in the field of economics." (The SCAR report, 3rd edition, 2011).

27   See the different food safety approaches in the US and the EU. In the US, for instance, cleaning of beef carcasses before distribution as an end-of-the-pipe-approach with lactic acid, or broilers with chlorine is practiced, whereas the EU is having a strict hygiene regime 'from farm to fork', looking for harmful microbes like salmonella not to appear in any product at any step of the value chain. These are different cultures, which could – the European model being more costly – strongly be affected if free trade agreements come into force. These cultural differences cannot only be matched by scientific justification, as it is the case under current WTO rules.

28 When in 2005 the Millennium Ecosystems Assessment (with some 1300 experts involved the largest ever global assessment) was concluded, four scenarios/development paths were presented: the global orchestration, the order through strength, the adapting mosaic and the techno garden scenario. The mood of the conclusion was that the authors would, if asked, opt for the global orchestration scenario. Now, seven years and many summits and the economic crisis of 2008 later, at least for agriculture and food security we would more opt for the adapting mosaic scenario. It looks for regional solutions, by having the global issues in mind. In the MEA assessment this approach was called "Glocalization" (for more information, see www.maweb.org/en/index.aspx).

29   Experience of organic production systems in East Africa, for instance, show that of the diverse basket of produced items at farm level, only few are destined for marketing beyond the local/regional level, including for export. This concerns items such as spices, vegetables, flowers, nuts, roots or fruits. For more information, see UNEP-UNCTAD, 2008b.

30	See *inter alia* www.lebensmittelpraxis.de/handel/entscheider/1638-megatrend-regionalitaet.html.

31	At the World Economic Forum 2012, Graciano da Silva, Director-General of FAO said in respect to food security: "To stimulate local markets is a key issue" (www.weforum.org/videos/ensuring-food-security-annual-meeting-2012).

32	Dacian Ciolos, EU Commissioner for Agriculture and Rural Development highlighted in a speech on Local Farming and Short Supply Chains: Enhancing the Local Dimension of the Common Agricultural Policy" on 20 April 2012 the importance of short supply chains and the related consumer preferences, which the European Commission wants to support (http://europa.eu/rapid/press-release_SPEECH-12-283_en.htm).

33	See Nestlés approach to source locally whenever possible and to strengthen rural development (www.nestle.com/csv/ruraldevelopment).

34	Interestingly specialties are often the non-industrial, more artisanal products like Swiss cheese, based on grass and hay- (not silage) feed. With 64.000 tons, Switzerland exports one third of its cheese production.

35	Not "food must travel", as Pascal Lamy claimed in February 2012 in Geneva at the conference of the "Economist" on Feeding the World – the 9 billion dollar question.

36	It should not go without comment at this juncture that agriculture is not the only sector that requires a more local/regional focus faced with new environmental and economic challenges than practices in the last few decades. The much-required drastic changes in the energy mix towards renewable sources are bound to go in tandem with a much higher focus on local/regional production, which matches local/regional consumption and thus avoids transmission and conversion losses. 'Distant' sources of energy supply will still be required to match local/regional production-consumption gaps.

37	See also the discussion and suggestions in De Schutter (2011c).

38	Estimates suggest that some 60 per cent of total support developing countries have provided to their agricultural sector in recent years is linked to green-box measures (Nassar et al., 2009). As the AoA does not set any spending limits on the green box, developing countries' flexibility in pro-actively using it is then a function of budgetary capacity or constraints. The existing set of green-box measures largely reflects the policies of developed countries in place during the Uruguay Round negotiations. The box thus needs to better reflect interests in protecting food security, rural livelihoods and resilience.

39	In many restaurants in Western Europe, the origin of the meat has to be or is being announced these days to build consumer confidence.

40	See www.farmandfoodproject.org.

41	See www.terramadre.org/pagine/rete/comunita.lasso.

42	See www.worldfuturecouncil.org/future_policy_award_shortlist.html.

43	See USDA briefing, at: http://www.ers.usda.gov/Briefing/FarmPolicy/gov-pay.htm.

44	However, Berthelot argues that the United States VEETC tax credits for ethanol production should be counted as subsidies to agriculture, which would raise the total support to agriculture provided by the United States. It should be noted, though, that the VEETC tax credits are scheduled to end in 2012.

45	House Agriculture Appropriations Bill, amended June 13, 2011. See: http://republicans.appropriations.house.gov/UploadedFiles/6.13.11_FY_12_Agriculture_Conference_Summary.pdf.

46	Schwarz Group owns the Lidl and Kaufland supermarket chains.

47	World Shipping Council, Record fuel prices place stress on ocean shipping, at: www.worldshipping.org/pdf/WSC_fuel_statement_final.pdf, 2 May 2008.

48	For more information, see: http://news.orf.at/stories/2082522/.

49	According to FAOstat and the CBOT Exchange Volume Report of May 2011; see: (www.cmegroup.com/wrappedpages/web_monthly_report/Web_Volume_Report_CBOT.pdf).

50	Lagi et al. have also reviewed the importance of key market fundaments as explanatory factors for food price hikes, in particular: (a) weather, particularly droughts in Australia, (b) increasing demand for meat in the developing world, especially in China and India, (c) currency exchange rates, and (d) linkage between oil and food prices through higher production and transportation costs. The authors found no significant correlation in this regard.

51	In that volume, see particularly Twarog for an overview of organic agriculture as a trade and sustainable development opportunity.

52 According to the definition by IFOAM (2008a), "organic agriculture is a production system that sustains the health of soils, ecosystems and people. It relies on ecological processes, biodiversity and cycles adapted to local conditions, rather than the use of inputs with adverse effects. Organic agriculture combines tradition, innovation and science to benefit the shared environment and promote fair relationships and a good quality of life for all involved." Note that organic agriculture does not by definition have to be certified; certification is simply one way to guarantee the organic integrity of a product for consumers.

53 These are locally based quality assurance systems that certify producers based on the active participation of stakeholders and built on a foundation of trust, social networks and knowledge exchange (IFOAM, 2008b).

54 This is not to argue for complete liberalization of agricultural markets. Particularly in poorer developing countries where agricultural support structures have been dismantled (e.g. in many African countries), it is difficult for local producers to compete with imports, especially when those imported products have been subsidized or otherwise publicly supported in their countries of origin. Even in developed economies, some individual farmers may struggle to compete.

55 SEKEM in ancient Egyptian means "vitality from the sun".

56 This issue is discussed extensively in the literature. See, for example, UNRISD, 1974; Swanson, 2007; Inter-Academy Council, 2004; Thompson, 2007; Shiva, 2007 and Mayet, 2007.

57 This contention is supported by numerous studies, such as those by Pretty and Hine, 2001; Lotter, 2003; Badgley et al., 2007; Halberg, 2007; Scialabba, 2007; Hine, 2008; Jordan, 2009; Azeez, 2009; IAASTD, 2009; and De Schutter, 2011a. UNCTAD/UNEP, 2008b.

58 See: Demeter USA, Biodynamic Agriculture – At a Glance, 2009, at: http://demeter-usa.org/downloads/Demeter-At-A-Glance.pdf.

DATE DUE